DYNASTY OF THE HOLY GRAIL

Dynasty of the Holy Grail

MORMONISM'S SACRED BLOODLINE

VERN GROSVENOR SWANSON

CEDAR FORT, INC.
SPRINGVILLE, UTAH

ISBN 13: 978-1-55517-823-5
ISBN 10: 1-55517-823-5

Published by CFI, an imprint of Cedar Fort, Inc., 925 N. Main, Springville, UT, 84663
Distributed by Cedar Fort, Inc. www.cedarfort.com

LIBRARY OF CONGRESS CATALOGING-IN-PUBLICATION DATA

Swanson, Vern G.
  Dynasty of the Holy Grail / by Vern Grosvenor Swanson.
      p. cm.
  Includes bibliographical references and index.
  ISBN 1-55517-823-5 (hardbound : alk. paper)
  1. Church of Jesus Christ of Latter-day Saints--Miscellanea. 2. Mormon Church--Miscellanea. I. Title.

  BX8638.S92 2006
  289.3--dc22

                          2006013690

Cover and book design by Nicole Williams
Cover design © 2006 by Lyle Mortimer
Cover Painting by James Christensen
Printed in the United States of America

10   9   8   7   6   5   4   3   2   1

Printed on acid-free paper

TO MY LOVING DAUGHTERS,

AMBER CHRISTIE SWANSON AND

ANGELA RENEE SWANSON JONES,

MY MUSES

CONTENTS

LIST OF ILLUSTRATIONS

Frontispiece: James C. Christensen (1944–), Orem, Utah, *Jesus and Mary Magdalene* (2005, acrylic on board, 12" x 11"), in possession of the artist. Between the arches at Rosslyn Chapel can be seen Jesus and Mary Magdalene. The lion represents the kingly scepter of Judah, while the unicorn represents the birthright of Ephraim.

Plate 1: Sir Lawrence Alma-Tadema (1836–1912), *Joseph, Overseer of Pharaoh's Granaries* (Opus CXXIV, 1874, oil on board, 13" x 17"). Collection Dahesh Museum of Art, New York City. Joseph of Egypt held great authority as a vizier to Pharoah.

Plate 2: Steven Adam (?–1910), British, *The Marriage of the Lamb and His Bride* (c. 1906–1910, stained-glass window). Located at St. Mary's Kilmore Church in Dervaig, Isle of Mull, Scotland. The window was probably meant to represent Christ and the Church, but its verisimilitude gives the impression that it is an actual marriage between Mary of Bethany and Jesus Christ. An inscription quotes Luke 10:42, mentioning Bethany.

Plate 3: John Melhuish Strudwick (1849–1937), British, *The Ten Virgins* (1883, oil on canvas, 29"x 60"). Courtesy of John Schaeffer, Melbourne, Australia.

Plate 4: Unknown artist, Spanish colonial, *Joseph of Arimathea with a Child of Jesus* (seventeenth-century, oil on tin, 10 1/8" x 8 ½"). Painting in the possession of Brian Kershisneck of Kanab, Utah. The work possibly represents Joseph of Arimathea with the son of Jesus and holding a budding or flowering staff, or perhaps Jesus Himself with His son.

Plate 5: Nicolàs Rodriguez Juarez (1667–1734) ,Mexico City, *The Holy Family* (1690, oil on panel, 13" x 17½"). Courtesy of Christie's New York Old Masters. The painting is meant by the artist to portray the Virgin Mary and Joseph with the Christ child. However, it is used here to represent Mary Magdalene and Jesus with their firstborn son in their hands.

Plate 6: Simon Dewey, *For She Loved Much* (2001, acrylic on canvas). Courtesy of the artist. Here is Mary Magdalene washing and anointing Christ's feet at the House of Simon the Pharisee in Galilee.

Plate 7: Gustave Moreau (1826–1898), French, *La Licorne* (1884–85, oil on canvas, 19⅞" x 13⅜"). Christie's London, 24 November 2004 (23). We are not sure of the woman's identification, but for our purposes she perfectly fits the image of Mary Magdalene, crowned and robed, with the symbol of her tribe, the white unicorn. Her nudity represents the bride as chastity and the Christian church.

Plate 8: Michel Sytal, *Mary, Mother of Jesus* (sixteenth-century, oil on panel) from a reproduction in Bruce E. Dana book written in Chinese (ZITO, 2003), page 90. It originally depicts the Virgin Mary, but could just as easily be Mary Magdalene kneeling in a garden before the throne of God, receiving her crown and benediction of exaltation from the Father and the Son.

Plate 9: William Blake (1757–1827), British, *Christ the Mediator: Christ Pleading Before the Father for St. Mary Magdalene* (c. 1799, pen and grey ink and tempera on canvas, 10 ¾" x 15 ¼"). From the collection of the late George Goyder, C.B.E., his sale at Christie's London, 14 June 2005 (10). There is no biblical text for the subject, but in general it is derived from 1 Timothy 2:5, "For there is one God, and one scripture." 1 John 2:1 notes, "My little children, these things write I to you, that ye sin not. And if any man sin, we have an advocate with the Father, Jesus Christ the righteous." In this picture Mary Magdalene may represent all mankind as a whole.

Plate 10: Raphael (1483–1520), Italian, *Portrait of a Lady with a Unicorn* (c. 1505–06, oil on wood transferred to canvas, 67.8 x 53 cm) From the collection of the Museo e Galleria de Villa Borghese, Rome (inv. 371). It was once titled *Portrait of Maddelena Doni.*

Plate 11: Side of Church of St. Sarah, Les-Saints-Maries-de-la-Mer in the Camargue delta of the Rhône River, France. Embedded into the south wall of this eleventh-century fortress church are two carved animals, a lion and possibly a unicorn, in a much older marble, set into an indented arch. To the left is a she lion and cub, and to the right is possibly a unicorn or a male lion.

Plate 12: Unknown artist, Northern France, *The Stuttgart Psalter: Crucifixion of Christ* (820–830, painted miniature). From Württemburgische Landesbibliothek, Stuttgart, Germany. (Bibl. fol. 23, fol. 27r) The Grail chalice can be seen between the unicorn of Ephraim and the lion of Judah. The Psalter probably illustrates Psalm 22:21.

Plate 13: Unknown artist, *The High Priestess* (fifteenth-century, tempera on paper). Supposedly this card is from a tarot pack. See Knight and Lomas, *The Second Messiah*, 1997, 90. The columns represent Boaz and Jachin, the families of Judah and Ephraim.

Plate 14: Unknown artist, France, *Utrecht Psalter: Catching the Blood at Calvary* (Universiteitsbibliotheek der Rijksuniversiteit, Utrecht MS 32, f. 67). A miniature ink drawing illustrating Psalm 115 from Reims in the mid-ninth century (c. 830). Illustrated in Richard Barber, *The Holy Grail: Imagination and Belief,* 2004, 121. See K. Van der Horst (editor), *Utrecht Psalter in Medieval Art* (1996).

Plate 15: Unknown artist, *The Deposition* (twelfth century, miniature). From the collection of Abbey of Weingarten, Landesbibliothek Fulda, South Germany. (MS Aa35, fol 81: Bildarchiv Foto Marburg). This miniature from a gospel book depicts the Deposition with Joseph of Arimathea collecting Christ's blood. This is, according to Richard Barber, 2004, page 124 (illustration), the first evidence of this tradition, nearly a hundred years before Robert de Boron.

Plate 16: Principato di Seborga, an independent principality near Bordighera. In the distance can be seen the French Riveria. This was the supposed hiding place for the Sadducees after their escape from Jerusalem. The Church of St. Barnard can be seen to the lower right.

Plate 17: General view of Les-Saintes-Maries-de-la-Mer in southern France. The Church of St. Sarah can be seen in the middle of the town.

Plate 18: John William Waterhouse (1849–1917), British, *Tristan and Isolde* (1916, oil on canvas, 42"x 32"). Courtesy of Frederick C. and Sherry L. Ross, New Jersey. The Celtic legend was retold by Sir Thomas Malory of the couple who accidentally drank a love potion from a Grail. His name means "sadness." He was killed by the jealous King Mark, husband of Isolde. She died of grief and was buried beside Tristan; a vine grew entwining their graves.

Plate 19: Gloria Montgomery, Utah, *"Joseph of Arimathea's Budding Rod of Glastonbury"* (2004, pencil drawing).

Plate 20: Brian Kershisknek (1960–   ), Kanab, Utah, *The "Children" of Joseph of Arimathea* (2003, oil on board). Courtesy Diane and Sam Stewart collection. The painting depicts Joseph of Arimathea with a blossoming staff and the children of Christ, who were called the "children of Joseph of Arimathea" for their own protection.

Plate 21: William Blake (1757–1827), *Joseph of Arimathea Preaching to the Inhabitants of Britain* (nd, tempera painting). Blake's portrayal of the Arimathean was one of a number he painted of Joseph of Arimathea. Courtesy of Sir Geoffrey Keynes Coll., Cambridgeshire, UK, and Bridgeman Art Library International.

Plate 22: The eleventh-century Cistercian Valle Cruses Abbey on the Plain of Maelor in Valley Eglywsey, very near Llangolan, is on the sacred Dee River in North Wales. It was here that the Virgin Mary was supposedly taken for safety. Reproduction courtesy of Tony and Traci Fieldsted, Springville.

Plate 23: Unknown artist's rendering of twelve huts in a circle, around the "old wattle church" depicts the settlement at Glastonbury sometime after Joseph of Arimathea's arrival in A.D. 37.

Plate 24: Sidney Harold Meteyard (1868–1947), *The Passing of Arthur* (nd, watercolor), sold Christie's London auction-house (June 1999). In a painting of the dying King Arthur we see him passing the sword, Excalibur, on to Galahad to be cast back into the lake (ocean?). Perhaps Excalibur represents the Sword of Judah in the same fashion as the Sword of Laban represents the Sword of Joseph/Ephraim? It might have been taken by St. Brendan to the promised land in A.D. 570.

Plate 25: The Lady Chapel at the Abbey Ruins in Glastonbury, Somerset.

Plate 26: Don Thorpe's photograph of the Hill Cumorah in upstate New York. This may possibly be the location of the records of the Celtic Church as well as the Nephite peoples. Used with permission.

Plates 27a and 27b: Never before illustrated and little remarked upon, center "Shiloh" or "Salaam" column at Rosslyn Chapel in Roslin, Scotland, with detail of its capital. Its position between the Apprentice and Master columns is fraught with meaning regarding the Grail dynasty. Note the upper right of column's capital, where it has been chipped away. Perhaps this was the severed head of Brân the Blessed.

Plate 28: Photograph of the Tower of Magdale at Rennes-le-Château, France. The entire hoax of Rennes has badly damaged Grail studies. Courtesy of Tony and Traci Fieldsted of Springville, Utah.

Plate 29: Jan Van Scorel (1494–1562), Dutch, *Mary Magdalene* (1530, oil on canvas, 26" x 30"), Rijksmuseum, Amsterdam. Mary Magdalene in center, and to the right can be seen the root-stump of promise.

Plate 30: Sir Frank Dicksee (1853–1928) England, *Chivalry* (1885, oil on canvas, 72" x 53¾"). Courtesy of John Schaeffer, Sydney Australia.

Mark Girouard's book *The Return to Camelot* (1981) shows the ideal of chivalry preoccupied the Victorians. The author has imputed this meaning into this painting. The grail knight, Joseph Smith Jr., has clain the adversary and is about to free (restore) the church (the woman in the wilderness) from bondage. Also see John Everett Millais (1829–1896), British, *Knight Errant* (1870, oil on canvas) in the Tate Gallery, London. Here the woman is depicted nude as a representation of purity and innocence in the primitive Christian church. In both pictures the knight frees the Church (woman) from the bondage of the apostasy and "restores" her to her rightful place.

Plate 31: John Henri Moser (1876–1951), Logan, Utah, *Portrait of Joseph Smith* (1930, oil on canvas, 32" x 26"). Courtesy Springville Museum of Art, Springville, Utah.

Plate 32: David Wilson (1980–), Provo, Utah, *Joseph Smith, Proclaimed King of All Israel by Hosannahs* (2005, oil on canvas, 24" x 18"). Courtesy of the artist.

Plate 33: Charles Z. Landelle (1812–1908), France, *Angel of the Holy Grail* (1812, oil on canvas). Courtesy collection of Frederick C. and Sherry Ross, New Jersey.

Plate 34: James C. Christensen (1944–), Orem, Utah, *The Shiloh-Dynasty of the Holy Grail* (2005, acrylic on board, 12" x 11"), in possession of the artist. Between the arches of Rosslyn Chapel can be seen Jesus and Mary Magdalene. The lion represents the kingly scepter of Judah while the unicorn represents the birthright of Ephraim. Courtesy of the artist.

PREFACE

When the pupil is ready, the Master will appear.
—CELTIC WISDOM

his book to me is a rough-cut study into the connection between the Lord's gospel and the Holy Grail. None of the theories contained in this book are necessarily true, and certainly they are not Mormon doctrine. They are merely plausible musings inferred from scholarly investigation that might offer insights into God's reason for appearing to Joseph Smith Jr. in the spring of 1820.

There was no special revelation in writing this publication, just speculation built upon voluminous research but a modicum of solid facts. The ideas in this book are not official LDS teachings but merely reflect the opinions of the author and others. They are given with reservation because, as Dr. William E. Phipps once noted, "Few have ventured to blaze a trail into this obscure area because it is overgrown with cultic taboos."[1]

Allow me to start at the beginning and reveal how I came to write this book and those who are responsible for its progress. When I was a fourteen-year-old convert of one week to The Church of Jesus Christ of Latter-day Saints (LDS Church/Mormon Church), my distraught mother made me meet with a Church of Christ minister, the Rev. Everett Cade, of Medford, Oregon. Mother hoped that this anti-Mormon "deprogrammer" would dissuade me from continuing as a member of the "satanic" LDS cult. Throughout the later part of July until school started in the fall of 1959, I met each Saturday morning with Rev. Cade.

In the most kindly manner, he negatively cited every controversial LDS practice, historical point, and theological concept. Adam-God, Blood Atonement, Church succession, the Danites, a married Jesus, Mountain Meadow massacre, polygamy, polytheism, and Satan as the brother of Christ were just a few of the more heretical topics. But being a totally ignorant recent convert, these intellectual syllogisms had little effect on my intense but clueless testimony. Like Parzival, my brain simply didn't know enough to appreciate his sophisticated and scholarly diatribes. However, unlike Rev. Cade, I would rather be ignorant than misinformed.

In retrospect, most of my gospel research and apologetics since that time have centered on the critical protestations of Rev. Cade. His research focused on a common motif of the eighteenth to twentieth centuries in the northeastern United States. Rev. Cade had discovered nearly forty people who had gone into groves, woodsheds, attics, or bedrooms and received some kind of sacred epiphany.

These individuals then organized religious movements.[2] Religious leaders, such as Jemima Wilkinson, Mary Baker Eddy, and Ellen G. White, he claimed, had spiritual visions and then founded religious organizations.[3] "How could we be sure that God really visited Joe Smith," he quizzed, "when so many have claimed the same thing?" My answer, "He just did!" seemed anemic even at that time of my young life.

Yet Rev. Cade's questions crowded my mind, "Why Joe Smith from upstate New York? Why not some other sincere seeker? What was so special about Joe Smith that God should visit him and not another?" Again my answer to the minister—"He was a nice guy"—seemed lame. This all stuck in my craw from that time onward and was ultimately responsible for my writing this book. My quest stemmed from these questions.

For years the distinguishing factor that set Joseph Smith Jr. apart from the other claimants eluded me. I understood that anciently God had selected his prophets, such as Moses and Samuel, from among the tribes of Israel. But here was a "gentile" from Vermont claiming the prerogatives of God's "chosen" people. How could this be? Ultimately came the discovery that another Joseph—Joseph of Egypt—was the key to everything (D&C 107:40).

While working on my Ph.D. in London between 1978 and 1980, I became intellectually interested in the British-Israelite movement. At the LDS Hyde Park Ward in South Kensington, I met Michael Danvers-Walker. He claimed that his heritage came through Joseph of Arimathea, and he introduced me to a number of books sold by the British-Israel World Federation, then housed at No. 10 Buckingham Gate in London.[4]

Their idea that Christ visited Somerset and Cornwall (the Cassiterides area) as a youth intrigued me. Also mesmerizing were the concepts that a Christian Church in Britain was founded by Joseph of Arimathea and that the Virgin Mary and Mary Magdalene visited this area. Ever since my first visit to Glastonbury in Somerset with Utah artists Dennis V. Smith and Trevor J. T. Southey in 1979, I have experienced a special tug to understand more about this fascinating topic.

By 1979 I had read most of the LDS books on the subject, including those by James H. Anderson, E. L. Whitehead, LeGrand Richards, and Ogden Kraut.[5] But it was while reading the book *Words of Joseph Smith* (1980), edited by Andrew Ehat and Lyndon Cook, that my interest became fixated on the heritage of Joseph Smith Jr., the man "nobody knew." Soon I began to realize that Joseph Smith was of the lineage of Jesus Christ, which legitimized his authority to organize the Lord's Church in the latter days. By the autumn of 1981 the first draft of what eventually became this book was written.

I have had many mentors in writing and researching this tome on the Holy Grail. My wife, Judy Nielson, has supported me in this extensive project, even accompanying me to Rosslyn Chapel with our friend Jerald H. Jacobs in June 1997. With the help of my publishers, Lyle Mortimer and Lee Nelson, I visited the Holy Land in 2004, which solidified my research of two and a half decades. Without the help and traveling companionship of Tony and Traci Fieldsted, searching for the Holy Grail would not have been as rewarding or successful.

My friend Robyn Bird Lamm, the Arthurian scholar, has been a font of wisdom and knowledge, as has my brother Robert D. Hill, BYU religion professor Dr. Eric D. Huntsman, genealogist Michael Kennedy, genetic scientist Ugo Perego, esotericist John Michell of London, educator Dr. Chase Petersen, Grail enthusiast Ellie Sonntag, and *New York Times* best-selling author Al Switzler. However, they are not to be blamed for this publication's many shortcomings, but it would have been worse without them. James C. Christensen's marvelous cover painting for the book will undoubtedly win more awards than the book itself.

This book is dedicated to broaching a wide array of fact and theory regarding the bloodline of Jesus Christ down to Joseph Smith Jr. By publishing it now, I hope that public interest will lead to a more unblemished and complete future publication. This topic is serious business, and we all want to eventually get it right. Therefore I enlist all readers' assistance in helping to perfect this volume's second revised edition. In this I concur with Dr. William E. Phipps, who asked for similar help:

> In order that a verified hypothesis regarding Jesus' marital status may emerge, a mutual exchange of insight is needed. I share Charles Peirce's position that scientific truth on any issue is that eventual position that emerges as unchallenged after competent investigators have reviewed the evidence, contributed their individual half-truths, and corrected one another. For this reason the candid criticism of readers from various religious traditions is solicited. All responses will be cordially received and carefully considered. I would be especially interested to learn of errors of fact or of judgement contained in this volume and suggestions of other ramifications and new sources of information.[6]

My daughters, Amber and Angela, have been my inspiration for this book. Amber has always taken a keen interest in genealogy, especially the Joseph Smith Jr. bloodline. She was the first to persuade me to publish this volume. Angela has been my chief editor and critic. She helped shape the book and round it to completion. I am eternally thankful for their inspiring testimonies of the gospel of Jesus Christ and their encouragement to seek the Holy Grail.

NOTES

1. Phipps, *Was Jesus Married?* 4.
2. See also Vogel, *Religious Seekers and the Advent of Mormonism.*
3. In *Celsus on the True Doctrine,* Hoffman observed, "One cannot but be impressed by the number of women-founded sects known to Celsus," the anti-Christian polemicist who lived about A.D. 170.
4. Michael Danvers-Walker's mother and father were officers in the British-Israel World Federation. The three books affecting me most immediately were J. H. Allen's *Judah's Sceptre and Joseph's Birthright,* John W. Taylor's *The Coming of the Saints,* and George F. Jowett's *Drama of the Lost Disciples.*
5. See Anderson, *God's Covenant Race;* Whitehead, *House of Israel;* Richards, *Israel, Did You Know?* and Kraut, *Jesus Was Married,* respectively. Then in 1984 I read *Mormon Enigma: Emma Hale Smith,* by Newell and Avery.
6. Phipps, *Was Jesus Married?* 233–34.

INTRODUCTION

The things of God are of deep import; and careful and ponderous and solemn thoughts can find them out.

—JOSEPH SMITH, 1839[1]

Nothing written here should be construed as Mormon doctrine, for the early Latter-day Saint literature regarding the marriage of Jesus was never elevated to that status. I fully endorse The Church of Jesus Christ of Latter-day Saints's statement of 16 May 2006 in response to *The Da Vinci Code* book and movie:

> The belief that Christ was married has never been official Church doctrine. It is neither sanctioned nor taught by the Church. While it is true that a few Church leaders in the mid-1800s expressed their opinions on the matter, it was not then, and is not now, Church doctrine.

I do not teach of Christ's possible marriage as Church doctrine but only as a probable postulate.

What is written are perspectives of an active Mormon examining the question of the Holy Grail (bloodline) legends in relationship to The Church of Jesus Christ of Latter-day Saints. The two have much to say to each other. In the end, I conclude that Jesus was married and this marriage healed the breach between the tribes of Judah and Ephraim. Then His children (the Shiloh Dynasty) in two lines representing these tribes again converge in the person of Joseph Smith Jr. From this lineal heirship, Joseph derived much of his right to open the last dispensation.

The quest for the Holy Grail is a crusade of righteous endeavor for the divine within us all.[2] Because of the formidable cultural, historical, and sectarian obstacles that must be overcome, the truth of the Grail, while offered to all, is understood by a relative few. The words *quarens fides intellectum* ("To believe in order to know") places our knowledge first on faith and then on fact. This "leap of faith" into the Lord's gospel will bring knowledge and happiness to all sincere seekers of the Holy Grail (D&C 103:17).

Only the restored Church of Jesus Christ of Latter-day Saints has the moral core and theological vision to challenge the world's view dramatically for the better. By clear-minded, valiant, humble, and righteous wholeheartedness, we can win this most exquisite prize. We bask in the exploits of the knight Don Quixote, for he was such a quester on a fool's errand.[3]

And the world would be better for this,
that *one man*, torn and covered with scars,
still fought with his last ounce of courage,
to reach the unreachable stars.

There was "one man" who most resembles the aspirations of this remarkable ballad. This Galahad-like knight was "the best blood of the nineteenth century" (D&C 135:6). He was Joseph Smith Jr., a farm boy from upstate New York. This young prophet's life and mission have caught the imagination of sincere seekers everywhere. His quest led to all manner of evil being spoken of him, to relentless persecution, and, eventually, to his death by a ruthless mob.

This martyr discovered in himself the Holy Grail, the vessel of the *sang real*, meaning "blood royal." The Grail was therefore not just a goblet or chalice but a human "earthen" receptacle that carried the holy blood through certain lineages of promise. As the medieval writer Robert de Boron proclaimed, "This vessel should indeed be called the Grail."[4]

The old Pentecostal hymn "There's Power in the Blood" powerfully announces that it is through the wellspring blood (real, not metaphorical) of Jesus Christ that all mankind is saved. All true Christians believe in the atoning blood shed on the cross; Mormons have added the blood that was shed in Gethsemane as having equal or perhaps superior redemptive value. However, there is a third place in which the blood of Jesus Christ may have atoning worth for the salvation of souls. It is not just in the blood Jesus shed but also in the blood Jesus shared. It is through His living bloodline, perpetuated through His seed, that a wasted world will be saved.

It was a crimson bloodline flowing down through the centuries. Of it Joseph might have said, *"Flumen sacrum bene cognosco"* ("I recognize this sacred stream"). After about seventy generations, the Grail was more than just a bloodline; it was the very *power* of Jesus Christ unto salvation (Mosiah 18:2). Joseph used it to divinely restore the wasteland, making it verdant in the latter time.

Patriarch John Smith said of Joseph, "I have thought when the Prophet Joseph began to trace his genealogy I should learn some things."[5] What he learned was that Brother Joseph was descended through the earthly family of Jesus Christ and Mary Magdalene. Then, through revelation, Joseph revealed to the world the lost secret of an even greater Holy Grail. It was a heavenly birthright, or spirit-line, descending from celestial parents.[6] This book, however, shall deal only with the earthly Grail vessel of the rosy bloodline from Adam to Jesus, then to Joseph Smith Jr., and beyond.

Once, the established Christian churches were only interested in criticizing the Mormon idea of the marriage of Jesus. Then they wisely refused to engage radical feminist and gnostic polemicists regarding the sacred marriage. Since the 1970s the field has been entirely given up to left-wing liberal writers and their fantasies of a Priory de Sion, Merovingian, Cathar, Knights Templar, and Rennes-La-Château connection to Christ's bloodline. This all changed in 2003 when Dan Brown's best-selling novel *The Da Vinci Code* burst upon the scene as a means of airing corrosive anti-Christian ideology. Since then, a spate of at least eighteen Christian books and a host of Web sites give cross-examinations to the question of Christ's and the Magdalene's relationship.

Now we have the opportunity to read rebuttals and hear counterarguments as to Jesus' marital and familial status, esoteric secret societies, and dangerous conspiracies. Scholars from both sides of the equation are thoroughly engaged in these questions. The topic has now become one of central concern to Latter-day Saints, Protestant, and Catholic members who were concerned over the "factual" information found in the fictional *The Da Vinci Code*. A Hollywood movie version of Dan Brown's novel will soon undercut the book's already marginal factual base.[7] We have also learned that Dan Brown's next novel will negatively center on the Mormons and the Freemasons.[8]

Forewarned is forearmed. The purpose of this publication is to provide honest research and sound methodology on the topic because many people do not have sufficient gospel framework to interpret Grail findings. Too often when they receive contrary data or hear false propaganda, they often scuttle the little framework they have. Through this apologetic, I want to fortify LDS members' resolve with a faithful text and meaningful context, hopefully with no pretext. Still I worry about those who might not be ready for this publication (Matthew 7:6). Yet to do nothing would be a regrettably missed opportunity to be prepared for imminent assaults in this area.

For some time now, the leaders of The Church of Jesus Christ of Latter-day Saints have understandably been "reverentially silent" on the concept of a married Jesus Christ. Because of historic persecution and possible harm to missionary work, I cautiously enter into a discussion on the topic. Of course anti-Mormons already have all the ammunition they need on our views of the marriage of Christ to attack the LDS Church and its members.[9] On the other hand, the growing popularity of the idea of a married Jesus might not hurt our proselytizing efforts.

This book needs to be published because almost all the gentile literature on the topic since 1982 has been ideologically corrosive to faith in Jesus Christ.

I broach the topic humbly and with a belief that the truth will prevail only when it is presented. We should not give up the field to our antagonists, but we should stand up for the truth as far as revelation, logic, and historical evidence will allow us. In the Lord's due time we shall all know the truth and errors as set forth in this volume.

There is always the possible danger of writing a historical and theological treatise "after one's own image" of the truth. But if fear of error prevented inquiry into the above proposition, then we would be unworthy seekers. As the cynic demands "proof" of this unique thesis, one can say, "But will you accept my evidence as proof?" Mr. F. M. Cornford realized the difficulty in attempting to prove a postulate:

> Many literary critics seem to think that an hypothesis about obscure and remote questions of history can be refuted by a simple demand for the production of more evidence than in fact exists. The demand is as easy to make as it is impossible to satisfy. But the true test of an hypothesis, if it cannot be shown to conflict with known truths, is the number of facts that it correlates and explains.[10]

This is reminiscent of the take on the question by Orson Hyde, President of the Quorum of the Twelve: "'Well,' you say, 'that appears rather plausible, but I want a little more evidence, I want you to find where it says the Savior was actually married.'"[11] There is never enough empirical evidence or hard facts. Of course plausibility does not equal actuality. Certainly this volume does not represent official LDS doctrine or present the LDS Church's theological positions. Neither is it a complete analysis of the topic.

Risking being called "unnuanced" and ridiculed for being a "literalist" archaic Christian, I commence this study of blended history and myth. "History," writes Malcolm Godwin, "is doggedly linear by nature while myth is cyclic."[12] The oil and water of history and myth do not naturally fuse, so I cleverly attribute all problems with this book to this quandary. Fortunately I had the richest of all Western myths and history to work with.

The following suppositions and research have explained much to the author, but I fear it will not sway the critic or the cynic. Brigham Young often said about such conundrums, "and when we go through the veil we shall know much more about these matters than we now do."[13] I have faith that, with your help and assistance, a better volume will eventually come because of this initial publication.

NOTES

1. Smith, *Teachings of the Prophet Joseph Smith*, 137; see also Smith, *History of the Church*, 3:295.
2. The quest for the Holy Grail has taken on other meanings in modern times. For instance, in physics the search for a unified theory is so described. In mathematics the solution of the Riemann hypothesis, which would explain the apparently random pattern of prime numbers, is also described as a quest for the Holy Grail. See Haag and Haag, *Rough Guide to The Da Vinci Code*, 108.
3. Miguel de Cervantes Saavedra, the author of *Don Quixote: The Man from La Mancha*, which was the first modern novel of deconstruction, fought in the Reconquista of Spain at the Battle of Lepanto, the great Christian victory of the Holy League against Islam. He was scarred from many wounds and enslaved by the Moors for five years. Quixote spoke of the truth of the quest for the Holy Grail, which he called Grail, and the love of Guinevere and Lancelot. See Sinclair, *Discovery of the Grail*, 157, 159.
4. Robert de Boron, *Merlin and the Grail*, 22; *Joseph d'Arimathie*, 254–63; as quoted in Barber, *Holy Grail*, 42.
5. John Smith, in "A Family Meeting in Nauvoo: Minutes of a Meeting of the Richards and Young Families Held in Nauvoo, Ill., 8 January, 1845," *Utah Genealogical and Historical Magazine* 11 (July 1920): 115.
6. The heavenly birthline is perhaps Joseph Smith's greatest revelation and is found in the King Follett discourse in Nauvoo. See *Journal of Discourses* (6 April 1844), 6:1–9.
7. Sony Pictures came out with the movie in June 2006, directed by Ron Howard and starring Tom Hanks, Audrey Tautou, Sir Ian McKellen, and Alfred Molina.
8. David A. Shugarts, as quoted in Burstein, *Secrets of the Da Vinci Code*, 254–55: "It is said that Smith not only used lots of Masonic symbology, but also wore a talisman containing mysterious symbols. Further, that there are Mormon-identified locations in the United States that lie due west of the Temple of Solomon (by no coincidence, of course). . . . We're just guessing, but we believe the new Dan Brown book will not be called *Widow's Son*, but something like it, and will be a Mormon-Mason treasure hunt throughout America." In *Truth behind the Da Vinci Code*, 12, Abanes notes: "His next novel, too, will be based on a conspiracy theory-its subject will be Freemasonry, which has long engendered fear and paranoia." The book, *The Solomon Key*, will probably cast the LDS Church in the place of the Catholic Church and the Danites in place of the Opus Dei.
9. This book reveals no secrets that anti-Mormon agitators do not already have. There are numerous Web sites detailing in harshest terms the LDS idea of the sacred marriage.
10. Cornford, *Origin of Attic Comedy*, 220.
11. Orson Hyde, in *Journal of Discourses* (6 October 1854), 2:81.
12. Godwin, *Holy Grail*, 184.
13. Brigham Young, in *Journal of Discourses* (3 June 1860), 8:279–80. See John Taylor, *Times and Seasons* (1844), 5:662.

PART ONE

THE GRAIL COVENANT OF THE OLD TESTAMENT

As it was with Noah, so shall it be with thee [Abraham]; but through thy ministry my name shall be known in the earth forever.

—ABRAHAM 1:19

In considering the subject of the Holy Grail, several questions present themselves. Where does the root of the story begin? Celtic scholar R. S. Loomis believed that the tradition began in Ireland.[1] Others believe that the Grail romances originated in Wales with Irish influence.[2] But the further we look into the past, the more we find convergences that relate to our account. We might even find it as broadly as the enduring fairy tales of *Sleeping Beauty, Snow White, Cinderella,* or Mozart's *Magic Flute*.[3] But where does it really begin? Unquestionably the legend of the Holy Grail originates, on this earth at least, with Adam and Eve. Therefore we must start at the beginning and trace God's dealings with mankind through the ages.

Often when the prophets expound upon the sacred things, they rehearse the history of the gospel from the days of the great patriarchs to the last generation. Any discussion of the Grail promises of God to man needs to be prefaced by a recitation of these covenants from the time of the Ancient of Days (Michael-Adam) to the last days. From the far reaches of time through the intricate paths of the biblical chronicle, the descendants of Adam and Eve have been under special covenants unto the Lord. These covenants have often been received or renewed through "the cup to the lips," or, to drink to it, as in the Last Supper (Matthew 26:27). Thus the cup represents the promises from the Father to the sons.

From Heavenly Father, the archangel Michael was ordained to be the Father of the human race. Modern scripture states that Michael is the selfsame person as Adam from the Garden of Eden (see D&C 27:11). Therefore, he shall be called Michael-Adam throughout most of the text. His position as head of the human family came with the keys of priesthood and bloodline authority.

This authority "to act in the name of God" comes in two ways: by covenant with a people and by covenant with a person. The first way is by being "born under a covenant" and the second is having authority given by blessing through "the laying on of hands." Both the patriarchal and the Melchizedek orders should be present in order to have a fully living and true gospel.[4]

The Holy Grail is here associated with the descent of Heavenly Father's family on earth, passed genetically down through the ages by the Patriarchs to this day. As a vehicle for passing down the authority of God, it is something more than a bloodline, as it is much more than just a cup. On earth this authority passed from Adam to Enoch, and then to Noah, Abraham, Isaac, Jacob, Joseph in Egypt, and on to its greatest holder, Jesus Christ. The dynasty then, according to our theory, passed directly onward to Joseph Smith Jr. in the nineteenth century.

This study seeks to answer fundamental questions about origins, lineage descent, line of authority, and the legend of a hidden king. These are the ideas we shall probe. It is not just the Grail vessel we are concerned with, but as well the hollow of the Grail vessel and its precious contents.

Notes

1. Loomis, *The Grail*, 272–73.
2. Goetinck, *Peredur*, 275.
3. In Sleeping Beauty, the Princess Aurora was known as Rose or Briar Rose, which often symbolizes the Divine womb and its descendants.
4. Smith, *Teachings of the Prophet Joseph Smith* (5 January 1841), 180. Joseph taught that "all priesthood is Melchizedek, but there are different portions or degrees of it." He also said that there were three orders of the priesthood: Melchizedek, Patriarchal, and Aaronic (see ibid., 244, 322).

CHAPTER ONE
THE BIRTHRIGHT AND THE LINEAGE

*It was conferred upon me from the fathers; it came
down from the fathers, from the beginning of time,
yea, even from the beginning, or before the foundation of the earth, down to the present time, even the
right of the firstborn, or the first man, who is Adam,
or first father, through the fathers unto me.*

—ABRAHAM 1:3[1]

PREMORTAL BIRTHRIGHT

Joseph Smith restored what he called "the Ancient Order," the "patriarchal priesthood . . . this 'holy order' of parents and children back to Adam."[2] Along these lines, Brigham Young established a trajectory of thought. He pronounced that the "Seed of Abraham" would continue until the latter days and through it would come the keys of religious authority: "Hence the calling out of Abraham and the re-establishing of a Government of God, *to be perpetuated in his lineage forever, which lineage is elected, to reign and rule and hold the Keys of Religion, Priesthood, Power and Government, while the earth endures, and in worlds without end. . . . Behold the result descending the stream of time, and tracing the fortunes of the chosen or Royal Lineage.*"[3]

The historical sacred record of the covenants and the genealogy of God's "chosen race," whom we consider as the living vessel of the Holy Grail, has not always been clear or complete.[4] Ezra 2:59 describes the problems that some had in ancient days, "but they could not shew their father's house, and their seed, whether they were of Israel." Then a few verses later we learn, "These sought after their register among those that were reckoned by genealogy, but they were not found: therefore were they, as polluted, put from the priesthood" (Ezra 2:62–63).

Although lost to the understanding of contemporary society, birthright and lineage combine to form a foundation structure for Judeo-Christianity. The idea of binding a literal and adopted "Covenant People" between those whom He has chosen and those who have chosen Him is the basis upon which the greater gospel rests. This vanguard people, or race, were given special responsibilities to bless the world for the betterment of all its peoples. They were to be servants, not masters.

It is a well-known principle that a "few people do most of the work." It is also well known that the Hebrew (Jewish) people, the "apple of God's eye," have vastly out-contributed their fellow beings in terms of the arts, politics, commerce, science, and philosophy. That the world has been blessed through the Jewish people is undeniable, except for the opinions of the most recalcitrant anti-Semite. After all, it is from this lineage that the Savior Jesus Christ was born. And we shall later learn that this might apply to those born from the Lord's seed, "[For] blessed is he through whose seed Messiah shall come" (Moses 7:53). "For it shall be the seed of the woman, not the offspring of the man" (Genesis 3:15). "Either literal seed or adopted through faith, it is the same" (D&C 104:33).

Yet most people do not understand what the Lord says about the children of Abraham and Joseph and how through their "seed shall the kindred of the earth be blessed" (D&C 124:58). Even they, the birthright lineage themselves, do not fully understand the inner workings of the kingdom of God on this earth. These are temporal things tied directly to celestial councils. But the world does not understand, as Jesus rightly pointed out, "If I have told you of earthly things, and ye believe not, how shall ye believe, if I tell you of heavenly things?" (John 3:12).

Many earthly blessings were predicated upon premortal calling and ordinations. Everybody who has lived upon this earth had a life as a spirit before being born as a mortal being. Whatever degree of attainment achieved during the First Estate (premortality) had its effect on our mortal lives.[5] Many noble spirits were accorded the privilege of choosing their birthright lineage. Parley P. Pratt takes note of this principle: "As in the case of Abraham, Isaac, and Jacob, it is with a view of the noble spirits in the eternal world coming through their lineage, and being taught in the commandments of God. Hence the Prophets, Kings, Priests, Patriarchs, Apostles, and even Jesus Christ, were included in the election of Abraham, and of his seed, as manifested to him in an eternal covenant.[6]

The principles of superiority of intellect, nobleness

of action, and capacity to act were all duly noted before we left our heavenly home for this Second Estate (mortality) on earth. Were there certain advantages for those who served or contributed more in the preexistence? Were those spirits interested in coming through special lineages on this earth? Pratt answers: "Yes, they would; for they could say—'Now there is an opportunity for us to take bodies in the lineage of a noble race, and to be educated in the true science of life, and in the commandments of God'"[7] (Abraham 1:18).

Thus we see that the priesthood of God is the birthright of the people of God, and then only as they are worthy of possessing it. As only an innocent and righteous Sir Galahad (Hebrew name: Gilead) could possess the Holy Grail, so also is the priesthood birthright covenant (the Holy Grail) only secured by those faithfully committed to the gospel of Jesus Christ. Only through righteousness can one be inducted into the lineage of the priesthood and drink from the cup that Jesus promised to drink with us at the Last Supper—the cup of the Holy Grail.

THE VESSEL OF THE HOLY GRAIL

The Holy Vessel—be it a literal cup, chalice, cruet, or cauldron—is the symbol of the Holy Grail and not the Holy Grail itself.[8] It is used as a point of reference with non-Mormon literature to help us understand that the religious history of the world is a Grail history. Numerous cups have been mentioned in ancient scripture that have played many important roles. It is enticing to think that the cup of the Holy Grail had more ancient roots than just the Last Supper. Perhaps the Pythagorean *Cup of Lethe,* which souls drink to forget premortal life, was this self-same vessel?[9] Possibly it was Adam and Eve's cup with which they drank from the Fountain of Youth at the Tree of Life in the Garden of Eden?[10]

What about the divining silver "cup in Benjamin's sack" that was owned by Joseph of Egypt? (Genesis

40:11; 44:2). Perhaps this glorious cup was inherited by Joseph's son Ephraim. Then the Bethany family possibly inherited this heirloom through direct lineal descent. Or, what if this same cup was part of Mary Magdalene's dowry at her marriage in Cana?[11] If this hypothesis is true, then the cup of the Last Supper could have been this exquisite silver cup of Joseph. As we dream of these things, little documented fact gives way to much speculative hypothesis.

Perhaps the most important sip of all was taken from the bitter cup of Gethsemane, full with fury and dregs. (It might have been from this sacred cup [Isaiah 51:17, 22].) For it is said, "I will take the cup of salvation and call upon the name of the Lord" (Psalm 116:13). Is this the cup that the Father gave Jesus? (John 18:11). Then there is the mysterious pagan "cup of power" associated with the magical sword and lance[12] (1 Corinthians 10:21).

And then there is "the portion of their cup" (Psalm 11:6) that all men must drink in the Last Day. For it has been decreed, "The Lord is the portion of mine inheritance and my cup" (Psalm 16:5). Whether this inheritance is a fulness (Psalm 23:5; Matthew 20:23) or a cup of astonishment and desolation (Ezekiel 23:31–33; Revelation 14:10) depends upon the individual's personal worthiness.

If not silver, then what is the "cup of the Lord's right hand" (Habakkuk 2:16) made of? Perhaps it is the "golden cup in the Lord's hand" spoken of in Jeremiah 51:7, or fired clay as in "the sherds thereof" in Ezekiel 23:34. One of the most famous was the cup of blue glass with a green surround, decorated with tiny crosses, found in 1906 in Glastonbury's "Bride's Well." Originally the cup came from Bordighera, near Seborga, Italy, in the 1890s and was hidden in the well in 1898, only to be "discovered" eight years later.[13]

Another glass bowl described as a Holy Grail is the Antioch cup, which resides in the Cloisters at the Metropolitan Museum in New York. Discovered in 1910, it came to the Cloisters in 1950, and while magnificent in its silver-gilt framework, the museum notes that it is no earlier than the sixth century A.D. That the Grail must positively be a glass chalice first occurs in a lecture given in 1927 in Manchester, England.[14] However, such certainty is difficult to muster in the early twenty-first century.

Where is the great and mysterious Grail itself? The Italian cathedral of Genoa claims to be in possession of the authentic vessel.[15] The Spanish cathedral of Valencia has now joined the squabble, claiming that they house the sacred chalice.[16] However, the quest for the Holy Grail transcends any search for a sacred artifact and becomes the very quest for the truth of our own and mankind's origin and destiny. Another cup in Trent, Italy, also purports to be the Grail.

Instead of gold, silver, lead, pottery, enamel, emerald, onyx, amethyst, enamel, stone, glass, or crystal, perhaps the cup was a simple lathed cup of olive wood made from the trees of Gethsemane.[17] England professes to hold the true Grail, the Nanteos Cup owned by the monks of Glastonbury Abbey when they fled to Wales after the dissolution of the Roman Catholic Church in England by Henry VIII.[18] This cup was supposedly made by the young Jesus himself in his father's workshop. It is considered exceedingly precious not only because Christ used it but also because he made it. What could be more appropriate than to have the cup made of olive wood and used in Gethsemane, except that all experts understand this mazer (bowl) hails from medieval times and is made of wych-elm?[19]

Grail author Graham Phillips notes that in 1920 a small onyx scent jar was found in Hawkstone Park dating from the first century. He believes it was used at the tomb by Mary Magdalene to collect blood from Jesus.[24] How this could happen when Jesus was already resurrected when she got to the tomb is unexplained.

On the other hand, the paper or plastic cup of the weekly Sunday LDS sacrament cannot be ignored in light of the above-mentioned prominent cups. For certainly it is a cup of remembrance (Luke 22:19–20) and a cup of consolation (Jeremiah 16:7). Ultimately the cup equates with a vessel, and the vessel with a human, and the human with a dynasty (chosen race), and the dynasty with the very power of God. The Holy Grail was more than just a cup container; it was a living vessel. The only Christian church that gives such a prominent place to genealogical authority is The Church of Jesus Christ of Latter-day Saints.

THE TWO FAMILIES

You only have I known of all the families of the earth.

—Amos 3:2

Considerest thou not the two families which the Lord hath chosen?

—Jeremiah 33:24[21]

An interesting episode occurred to the Lord's Chosen People at the time of Jacob-Israel's twelve sons. Reuben was Jacob's eldest son by his first wife, Leah, and was heir to the full patriarchal birthright. But he was guilty of gross misconduct in defiling his father's bed when he lay with Bilhah, his father's concubine (Genesis 35:22). Thus, Reuben and his posterity lost all rights of the firstborn when he was found to be unstable (Genesis 49:3–4; 1 Chronicles 5:1–3). It would have been impossible to have given the corrupted Reuben the birthright (the Messianic covenant of the royal line) and then say, "I had planted thee a noble vine, wholly a right seed" (Jeremiah 2:21). Often this is symbolized by a rose or grapevine weaving its way through the annals of time.[22]

Jacob's wife Leah was Laban's eldest daughter. She had been palmed off on Jacob after he worked seven years for the hand of Rachel, the younger sister and

fourth matriarch of the Israelites. When Leah's child Reuben lost his birthright, it did not go to her second or third sons, Simeon or Levi, who had overzealously defended their sister Dinah's honor by murdering the perpetrator and his entire family (Genesis 34:5).

Instead the birthright went to the firstborn of Rachel, Jacob's second and favored wife. In the blessing for brides (Ruth 4:11), Rachel is named first above her older sister Leah. This child, Joseph, was the eleventh of Jacob's twelve sons and became the anointed one.[23] His name meant "fruitful." Perhaps this was the true reason why he was sold into Egypt by his elder brothers, especially the ringleaders Simeon and Levi, who were supposedly "in line" to receive the birthright.

But since Rachel was originally scheduled to be the first wife and Joseph was already born by the time of Reuben's sin (1 Chronicles 5:1–2; Jeremiah 31:9), Joseph became the holder of the birthright.

The covenant blessing of the royal scepter went to Judah, the fourth son of Jacob and Leah. Since Judah was the first righteous son of Jacob and much older than Joseph, the birthright was divided so that the scepter was given to the elder son, but the blessings of the firstborn otherwise went with Joseph. With the division of birthright power between Joseph and Judah and the later conferral of priesthood authority to the sons of Levi through Aaron, we see an important but dangerous pattern emerging.

When the priesthood mantle fell on Jacob, he was a patriarch holding all the keys pertaining to the birthright. But when his young grandson Ephraim took his place, it was the end of the old patriarchal system and the beginning of a "power sharing" era. Although Moses and later David would hold great authority in their hands, the birthright blessings were divided: A line of kingly issue would come from Judah through the House of David, and the birthright bloodline would be traced from Joseph through the tribe of Ephraim.

THE BOOK OF JOSEPH

Joseph is a fruitful bough, even a fruitful bough by a well (water); whose branches run over the wall. The archers have sorely grieved him, and shot at him, and hated him: But his bow abode in strength, and the arms of his hands were made strong by the hands of the mighty God of Jacob; (from thence is the shepherd, the stone of Israel): . . . . The blessings of thy father have prevailed above the blessings of my progenitors unto the utmost bound of the everlasting hills: they shall be on the head of Joseph, and on the crown of the head of him that was separated from his brethren.

—GENESIS 49:22–26

The history of the covenant lineage through Joseph of Egypt is very important in understanding the concept of God's "Chosen People" (see Plate 1). [24] In Genesis 48:19, "Thy seed shall become a *multitude of nations,*" the italicized part may be translated as the "fulness of the gentiles." [25] For Joseph was a "fruitful bough" from which came a throng of nations, now considered by Jewry as "gentiles." Yet, through his seed the entire world was blessed, including the gentiles through whom they were scattered.

Nearly a fourth of the book of Genesis, which spans over 2,000 years of history, is devoted to the life of Joseph of Egypt (ca. 1661–1551 B.C.). [26] As scripture scholar Robert J. Matthews points out, "That proportion ought to give us an idea of how Moses, the inspired author of Genesis, felt about the importance of Joseph's story." [27] Although Joseph was the chosen birthright son of Jacob-Israel, there is hardly a more ignored patriarch than this seer. Yet most Christian authors have looked upon the life of Joseph as a type and shadow of the life of Jesus

Christ. [28] We read from Genesis 37:3–4: "Now, Israel loved Joseph more than all his children, because he was the son of his old age: and he made him a coat of many colours [lengths]. And when his brethren saw that their father loved him more than all his brethren they hated him, and could not speak peaceable unto him." [29]

Jacob's great love motivated a prophetic birthright blessing upon his favored son that is very evocative. Jacob's reference to the "Everlasting Hills" in the blessing might be interpreted as the Western Hemisphere—namely North and South America (Genesis 49:25–26). The declaration that he would be "separated from his brethren" was partially fulfilled during Book of Mormon times when Lehi left Jerusalem for the Americas (Ether 13:2–11; 3 Nephi 20–21), and later during the northern European colonization of the New World. Joseph Fielding Smith explained: "Because of his faithfulness and integrity, Joseph received greater blessings than the progenitors of Jacob and was rewarded with the land of Zion." [30]

Zion was not only in Jerusalem but also in the Americas. Just how important Joseph of Egypt is can be seen in Lehi's statement that "I am a descendant of Joseph who was carried captive into Egypt. And great were the covenants of the Lord which he made unto Joseph. Wherefore, Joseph truly saw our day" (2 Nephi 3:4–5). Then his son Nephi revealed that "He [Joseph] truly prophesied concerning all his seed. And the prophecies which he wrote, there are not many greater" (2 Nephi 4:2; see also 3:4).

Many of these prophecies were written in a scripture we title the book of Joseph. Joseph Smith noted that he wanted to translate the scroll of the book of Joseph that was found, like the book of Abraham, among the Michael Chandler Egyptian papyri in 1835. Sadly he never accomplished this task, which might have been the proof text to the author's present efforts. Though it was never translated, we gather from a letter written by Oliver Cowdery to a Mr. Frye that it included vital information on the Godhead, the fall of Adam, and other important facts regarding this earth.[31] Perhaps this ancient text would have revealed the importance of Joseph Smith's birthright lineage.

Because of his brilliance as a seer, Joseph was given the Egyptian name Zaphnath-paaneah by the Pharaoh, which means "he who reveals that which is hidden" (Genesis 41:4, 5; see also 2 Nephi 3:7, 15). In the Samaritan tongue, the name for Joseph is Taheb, or "The Restorer." Certainly these names reference the restoration of light and knowledge that would become the mission of Joseph and his posterity.

Like all who hold positions of authority in God's ministry, Joseph was chosen and ordained in the Grand Council of Heaven during his First Estate.[32] Among his blessings was the greatness of his offspring. The secret of Joseph's progeny would, as Melvin J. Ballard surmises, unlock the mystery of God's chosen people: "If we could find in the earth somewhere today the descendants of Joseph, we would find the chosen people of God."[33] This is confirmed by Joseph of Egypt's prophecy that a choice seer would appear from his seed (2 Nephi 3:6, 11; JST Genesis 50:27–28).

Many of the prophecies of Joseph were recorded on the Plates of Brass, some were recorded in 1 and 2 Nephi 3, 5, and in JST Genesis 48, 50. Joseph's ancestry and posterity were supposedly written in a book of remembrance for his family. These records were kept up to date right to the time of Zedekiah, approximately 600 B.C., and were in the custody of "Laban [who] also was a descendant of Joseph, wherefore he and his father had kept the records" (1 Nephi 5:16).

In this same year, these records were wrested from the hands of the wicked Laban by Nephi, one of Joseph's descendants, who held the right to possess them (1 Nephi 3, 4).[34] Ultimately the history of Joseph's progeny is the history of the Holy Grail, for it is half the stock from which The Seed descends.

EPHRAIM BECOMES THE BIRTHRIGHT HEIR

For I am a father to Israel, and Ephraim is my firstborn. Hear the word of the Lord, O ye nations, and declare it in the isles afar off, and say, He that scattered Israel will gather him, as a shepherd doth his flock.

—JEREMIAH 31:9

Manasseh was the first son of Joseph and his wife, Asenath.[35] Joseph's wife had another son, Ephraim, which means, "For God hath caused me to be fruitful in the land of my affliction" (Genesis 41:45–52; 46:20). Jacob-Israel gave precedence to the younger Ephraim, "even though he linked Ephraim and Manasseh together as paradigms for future generations."[36] Ephraim's ascendancy over his elder brother was first indicated by his grandfather Jacob's blessing as recorded in Genesis 48. Ephraim was, at that time, about twenty-one years old, for he was born while Joseph was Vizier of Egypt, before the beginning of the seven-year famine. Like the preceding three generations, there was an interesting subterfuge regarding the birthright and the blessing.

Joseph brought his two sons with him when all the twelve sons of Jacob were to receive their blessings at Jacob's sickbed. While the other sons of Jacob received their individual blessings, Joseph was given two blessings, one for each of his two sons born in Egypt. Though only grandchildren, Ephraim and Manasseh were adopted by Jacob as if they were his own children, and, consequently, their descendants were regarded as two tribes instead of one.[37] All the posterity of Joseph, both from a historical and a prophetic standpoint, are of these two young men: "And now thy two sons, Ephraim and Manasseh, which were born unto thee in the land of Egypt before I came unto thee into Egypt, *are mine*; as Reuben and Simeon, they shall be mine" (Genesis 48:5).

Even though Manasseh was the firstborn, Jacob intentionally placed his right hand upon Ephraim's head and his left upon Manasseh's. Jacob might have known that the sign of the cross above their heads had an additional meaning; he gave this blessing: "The Angel which redeemed me from all evil, bless the lads; and let my name be named on them, and the name of my fathers Abraham and Isaac; and let them grow into a multitude in the midst of the earth" (Genesis 48:16).

What Angel could have redeemed Jacob except Jesus Christ himself? For there is "none other name under heaven given among men, whereby we must be saved" (Acts 4:12). When Joseph protested the order of the hands' placement, Jacob refused his remonstration to change the sequence, explaining: "I know it, my son, I know it; he [Manasseh] also shall become a people, and he also shall be great; but truly his younger brother shall be greater than he, and his seed shall become a multitude of nations. And he blessed them that day saying, In thee shall Israel bless, saying God make thee, as Ephraim and as Manasseh: and he set Ephraim before Manasseh" (Genesis 48:19–20).

With this blessing, Joseph received a double portion of the blessing of Jacob upon all his sons. It is a testimony to the power and worth of faith, for it was written, "By faith Jacob when he was dying, blessed both the sons of Joseph" (Hebrews 11:21). Thus both Ephraim and Manasseh took their place among the twelve tribes of Israel, replacing the sons of Levi as a separate tribe.[38]

In a vision, Joseph saw Ephraim's children of the third generation (Genesis 50:23). He had the opportunity to see Jacob's blessing upon Ephraim begin to come to pass. The import of this blessing is just now beginning to be understood. We may understand that the later unique blessings as stated by Moses upon Ephraim and his elder brother Manasseh extend to the very last days: "His glory is like the firstling of his bullock and his horns are like the horns of unicorns: with them he shall push the people together to the ends of the earth: and they are the ten thousands of Ephraim, and they are the thousands of Manasseh" (Deuteronomy 33:17).

The "firstling of his bullock" alludes to the birthright coming through Joseph to his child Ephraim.[39] The mythical unicorn likely makes reference to a wild ox. This is seen in Joseph Smith's Inspired Version of the Bible (JST), where he has changed the word from unicorn in Isaiah 34:7 to wild ox or to a large antelope (orrock) living in Israel in that day but which are now extinct. All these symbols or allegories are an important part of this Ephraimite lineage that shall become part of the new *Shiloh-dynasty* of the Holy Grail.

After this time, little is known about the life of Ephraim a minor personality himself, or his posterity, even though his name becomes the primary focus for the genealogy of this sacred birthright. According to scripture, he was fruitful, though his two sons were slain while raiding the cattle of the Philistines. At the first census, Ephraim's tribe of 40,500 men was the smallest of all, excepting his brother Manasseh's and his uncle Benjamin's (Numbers 1:33). Undoubtedly this was because the other tribes were somewhat older. However, taken together, Joseph's sons formed the largest group. In fact, the tribe of Ephraim would dominate the later history of this earth in a very real way, both in terms of population and authority. Wilford Woodruff and Orson Pratt pointed this out: "The salvation of both Jew and Gentile, this people hold in their hands the salvation of the twelve tribes of Israel. It was not the oldest son, but to Ephraim, the son of Joseph, that these promises were made. Joseph was the youngest but one of the Twelve Patriarchs [*sic*], and through his son Ephraim God has raised you up and has put this power into your hands, and you hold the keys for the salvation of Israel."[40]

Then later, Apostle Erastus Snow, speaking in the Salt Lake Tabernacle in October 1882, reasserted the latter-day promises in Genesis: "He [God] has declared that in the last days Ephraim shall be his first-born; them he would gather together, and upon them he would place his holy priesthood, and them he would use as his servants and as his instruments to push the people together from the ends of the earth.[41]

These quotations demonstrate that God has not forgotten the Ephraimitic tribe as the leader in the Dispensation of the Fulness of Time. Ultimately Ephraim's and Judah's lot will be grafted together during the Meridian of Time into a new Grail dynasty.

JOSHUA THE EPHRAIMITE

And Joshua the son of Nun was full of the spirit of wisdom; for Moses had laid his hands upon him: and the children of Israel harkened unto him, and did as the Lord commanded Moses.

—DEUTERONOMY 34:9

Only when Joshua the Ephraimite[42] comes into the narrative at the time of the Exodus does the tribe of Ephraim regain its reputation, even though it numbered only 32,500 men (Numbers 26:37). Because of his military exploits, Joshua became more famous than anyone in his clan, more so than Ephraim, the *pater familias* of the tribe (Joshua 19:50; 24:30). One would assume that Joshua was, in fact, the birthright heir, not only of his tribe but also of all Israel.[43]

Joshua was the captain of the armies of Israel. At the end of the forty-year sojourn in the wilderness by divine direction, Moses placed Joshua before the high priest and the congregation in Shittim and publicly ordained him to be his successor[44] (Numbers 27:18–23; Deuteronomy 1:38). Then just before his death, Moses took Joshua to the Tabernacle to receive this charge from the Lord (Deuteronomy 31:14, 23).

With this high authority Joshua conquered the land of the Canaanites and even commanded that the sun stand still. We are told that he had help from an angel with drawn sword, who explained that he was the commander of God's heavenly armies and helped Joshua to victory over Jericho[45] (Joshua 5:14).

After the conquest, Joshua, as birthright heir, then divided the land of Israel amongst the twelve tribes. He gave his own tribe the land in the central hill country of Palestine, north of the tribe of Benjamin. Ephraim's eastern border was the Jordan River and to the west was the country of the Philistines on the Mediterranean coast; on the north was the territory assigned to Manasseh (1 Chronicles 7:28).

The major sacred cities of the area were Bethel, Shechem, and Shiloh. Bethel was technically in the lands of Benjamin (Joshua 18:13, 20) but was located closer to the children of Ephraim. Shechem was also in the land of Manasseh. After moving the tabernacle and priesthood to the Ephraimite city of Shiloh, Joshua named refuge cities and the Levitical towns.

Before he died, Joshua convoked an assembly at Shechem, the place of Abraham's first altar when entering Canaan.[46] In a powerful address, he covenanted with the people to remember the Lord (Joshua 24:25). Soon afterward, at the age of 110, the same age as Joseph when he died, Joshua was buried at Mount Ephraim in the town of Timnath-serah.[47] From the death of Joshua until Samson, judges ruled the land, which has been called Israel's iron age.[48]

The twelve judges were often warrior-heroes who saved the country and were accorded the privilege of judging it in political and judicial matters. Due to the lack of leadership, Israel often lapsed into idolatry and bickering. No longer was there a single powerful patriarchal figure like Abraham, who by right of birth or worthiness was given great priesthood power. Perhaps this was because the Ephraimites, after being given authority, again lapsed into prideful apostasy (2 Nephi 19:9).

While there was a certain lack of cohesion between the tribes, there were some bonds of national feeling and a single tabernacle, "the house of God," at Shiloh that joined them together. Little wonder that eventually the tribes wished to have a king rule over them who could assert leadership and unity. However, it did not fall upon the tribe of Ephraim to possess the prerogative of the birthright at this time. Neither did it fall upon them to possess the mantle of the priest.

It is not known who the Ephraimite posterity of Joshua was, except to say that they possessed their inheritance and prospered in the land. It is enticing to believe that Mary Magdalene, "Our First Lady of the Quest," was his and his wife's direct heir. She may have been nobility of his house, in line to inherit the Silver Cup of Joseph. It is the author's contention that this was, in fact, the Grail Cup of later legend.

THE SCEPTER OF JUDAH

Moreover he refused the tabernacle of Joseph, and chose not the tribe of Ephraim: But chose the tribe of Judah, the mount Zion which he loved.

—PSALM 78:67–68[49]

Through the centuries the two most powerful tribes and the heirs of the two strongest blessings from Jacob became bitter enemies. The northern Ephraimite kingdom fell into idolatry, went into bondage, and were eventually dispersed across the face of the earth. But Judea remained for a time: "Ephraim compasseth me about with lies, and the house of Israel with deceit: but Judah yet ruleth with God, and is faithful with the saints" (Hosea 11:12).[50]

After Judah's children Er and Onan died without children, Shelah, the third son of Judah, would normally have held the right of firstborn. But since he was a Canaanite woman's offspring, he could not

hold this birthright. Upon the death of Er, his wife, Tamar, mated with his father, Judah, and had twin sons, Perez and Zerah. Perez was given the status of firstborn after a confusing birth sequence (Genesis 38:29–30); Perez's family would become celebrated, while the significance of Zerah's lineage would remain a mystery.[51]

At about 1000 B.C., the nation of Israel wanted a king instead of the judges, for to their thinking, they were a step down from a Patriarch, the ultimate theological king. After the troubled kingship of Saul the Benjaminite, the right to rule fell to the tribe of Judah, from Boaz and Ruth, through Jesse. But, why did the Ephraimite prophet Samuel choose a son of Jesse for the kingly line in the first place?[52] Was he the purest of the lineage of Judah's line?

Because of the disobedience of King Saul, the Lord commanded the prophet Samuel to fill his horn with oil and seek out one of the sons of Jesse to be king. Jesse's first son, Eliab, was impressive in appearance, but Samuel felt inspired not to choose him. One after another Jesse brought seven of his sons to be examined by Samuel, but none were chosen.

Disheartened, Samuel begged Jesse, "Are here all thy children?" He learned that the youngest child, David, was left to tend the sheep. When he arrived "the Lord said, Arise, anoint him: for this is he," and David was anointed in the midst of his brethren.[53] Samuel's calling and anointing of David to be the first Jewish king of Israel was in similitude of Jesus Christ. As Joseph F. McConkie notes, "Consider how perfectly it [the calling of David] foretells both the setting and the events that would surround the coming of Christ"[54] (see 1 Samuel 16).

While David was "chosen" of God, he was not perfect. In fact, except for Jesus Christ, none of God's servants through the history of the world seems to have been very perfect. "It is not widely appreciated," writes Knight and Lomas, "that when David was on the run from Saul he served in the armies of the

Philistines against the Israelites; a strange qualification for the founder of the greatest line in Israel's history."[55] Yes, but it was one that later allowed him to understand these armies and defeat them.

David's kingly line was the chosen channel for the scepter.[56] In fact a scripture notes that there shall never be a time when there is not a king from this lineage, "David shall never want a man to sit upon the throne of the house of Israel" (Jeremiah 33:17). We can imagine this to mean that there always was a bloodline heir to the throne, even if there was no throne to sit upon.

NOTES

1. The Lord spoke to Abraham, giving him this unconditional promise: "And I will establish my covenant between me and thee and thy seed after thee in their generations for an everlasting covenant, to be a God unto thee, and to thy seed after thee" (Genesis 17:7–8). Also, "for thou art an holy people unto the Lord thy God; the Lord thy God hath chosen thee to be a special people unto himself, above all people that are upon the face of the earth" (Deuteronomy 7:6).

2. Andrew F. Ehat, "Joseph Smith's Introduction of the Temple Ordinance and the 1844 Mormon Succession Question," 142, as quoted in Nibley, *Temple and Cosmos*, 424.

3. Brigham Young (15 December 1852), in Collier, *Teachings of President Brigham Young*, 160–61.

4. To some this may seem a bestowal of "superior race" rights upon those who claim or prove Israelite blood, but the promises had to do with service, not rule, and they quickly evaporate at the first sign of tyranny, sin, or apostasy (see D&C 121:36–37). Remember that they were a special and holy people unto the God of the Israelites only. Unto the rest of the world, these promises meant little in a direct sense.

5. This is similar to Doctrine and Covenants 130:18–21, only one step backward to the premortal, not forward to the postmortal, world.

6. Parley P. Pratt, in *Journal of Discourses* (10 April 1853), 1:258a.

7. Ibid., 1:259a.

8. The size or shape of this vessel is unknown. The author thinks it has a holding stem and a wide mouth and is somewhat deep. This is exactly the state of the Qalal goblet, a vessel that held the ashes of the red heifer sacrifice as depicted on a silver coin minted in the third year of the Jewish revolt (ca. A.D. 67). The Celtic Ardagh Chalice (Irish, eighth century) is only seven inches high but reminiscent of the author's idea of what the cup may have appeared to be, only without the jewels (see Godwin, *Holy Grail*, 52–53). Originally the idea of a platter or dish was in vogue. Other kinds of Grails—such as the legendary Irish Cauldron of the Dagda (plenty), or the Cauldron of Diwrnach (curative), the Cauldron of Cormac (truth), and the Cauldron of Ceridwen (knowledge)—all had their purposes.

9. Nibley, *Message of the Joseph Smith Papyri*, 110–11. It is said that when a soul comes down to earth, the "Archon who is at the head of the place gives that preexistent soul a cup of forgetfulness . . . mixes the cup of forgetting . . . who hands the cup of forgetting to souls, bringing a cup filled with the water of Forgetfulness, and giving it to the soul, which drinks and forthwith forgets every place and every realm in which it has ever been" (ibid., 276).

10. The Leonard John Nuttall Journal (1834–?), BYU Library Special Collections (entry dated 1877). He was an aide to Brigham Young and worked on his estate after Brigham's death in 1877; he was also secretary to President John Taylor for three years. Nuttall suggests that President Young taught that Adam and Eve ate or drank from the Tree of Life after 930 years of age to purify their bodies and return to their previous resurrected immortal state.

11. Baigent, Leigh, and Lincoln, *Holy Blood, Holy Grail*, 108. They say, without documentation, that it was the wedding cup of Jesus and Mary Magdalene, bearing the later inscription (translated): "He who drinks well will see God. He who quaffs at a single draught will see God and the Magdalene."

12. Fanthorpe and Fanthorpe, *World's Greatest Unsolved Mysteries*, 105.

13. Barber, *Holy Grail*, 298–99. Wellesley Tudor Pole, an eccentric character who suffered from religious mania, had a vision to find it, which he did, of course. Mark Twain saw the cup/bowl and wrote, "No Sir Galahad, no Sir Bors de Ganis, no Sir Lancelot of the Lake—nothing but a mere Mr. Pole." How interesting that it comes from Bordighera, within two miles of Seborga, which has strong Grail connections.

14. J. Rendel Harris, "Glass Chalices of the First Century," *Bulletin of the John Rylands Library Manchester* 11 (1927): 286–95, as noted in Barber, *Holy Grail*, 301.

15. The Grail of Italy, the Sacra Catino, came to Genoa in

1102 from Jerusalem. Supposedly this chalice was carved from a huge green emerald. Napoleon took it to Paris for analysis and discovered it to be Roman glass from the time of Christ. See Sinclair, *Discovery of the Grail,* 172.

16. Phillips, *Marian Conspiracy,* 2. The onyx and gold chalice at Valencia Cathedral, which purports to be the Grail (san calis), is the only one declared to be authentic by the Vatican (see Ralls-MacLeod and Robertson, *Quest for the Celtic Key,* 251). Sinclair notes that the archives of the Crown of Aragon confirmed this legend of the gift of the Grail by the Pope to Saint Lawrence, which is now in San Juan de la Peña for safekeeping (*Discovery of the Grail,* 150).

17. Among René d'Anjou's treasures was a magnificent Egyptian cup of red crystal.

18. The Nanteos Cup measures about five inches in diameter. It was taken for safekeeping to Strata Florida, a remote part of Wales. When this site became unsafe, it was taken to the Powell family in nearby Nanteos. It has since moved about and is now hidden in Wales in a secret guardianship (see Fanthorpe and Fanthorpe, *World's Greatest Unsolved Mysteries,* 103–6).

19. Barber, *Holy Grail,* 300. "But the myth of the Nanteos Grail is alive and flourishing, as a search on the Internet will show."

20. Phillips, *Chalice of Magdalene.*

21. The text seems to indicate that the Levites and House of David (Judah) were the two families referred to by Jeremiah; however, Dr. J. H. Allen feels that it refers to Judah and Ephraim (*Judah's Sceptre and Joseph's Birthright,* 49–50).

22. Harpocrates is the Greek god of silence and was sometimes represented with a crown of roses. Consequently, the rose began to symbolize silence or secrecy. Thus the phrase *sub rosa* meant "something secret." In this case, the rose vine is a symbol of the secret Grail lineage, while the grapevine is symbolic of the bloodline of the Grail.

23. The ancient Egyptian pharaohs were anointed with the fat of the holy crocodile (the Messeh), thereby attaining the fortitude of the Messeh, from which stems the Hebrew term Messiah (anointed one).

24. Sir Lawrence Alma-Tadema (1836–1912), *Joseph, Overseer of Pharaoh's Granaries* (Opus CXXIV, 1874, oil on board, 13" x 17"). Collection Dahesh Museum of Art, New York City.

25. Grant and Rowley, *Dictionary of the Bible,* 689–90.

26. McConkie, *His Name Shall Be Joseph,* 3.

27. Matthews, "Our Heritage from Joseph of Israel," 1–2.

28. McConkie, *His Name Shall Be Joseph,* 78. Both Joseph and Jesus were cast into a pit: Christ into the world of spirits, Joseph into an empty cistern where he remained for three days and three nights, according to Jewish tradition. See Ginsberg, *Legends of the Jews,* 2:14; Genesis 37:24; Isaiah 24:22.

29. Edersheim, *Bible History Old Testament,* 1:144.

30. Smith, *Doctrines of Salvation,* 3:68.

31. Cowdery, "To the Elders of the Church of the Latter Day Saints," 236–37.

32. Smith, *Teachings of the Prophet Joseph Smith* (2 May 1844), 365.

33. Melvin J. Ballard, Conference Report, October 1924, 28. Elder Ballard is quoting an article, in an unidentified national magazine, titled "Are the Jews the Chosen People of God?"

34. Because these records were lost to the Jewish people, the record of Joseph was not included in the Old Testament; therefore, Joseph plays a lesser role in Hebrew scripture.

35. Asenath means "belonging to Neith," a very ancient Egyptian goddess of hunting whose worship at Sais in the western Delta dated to pre-dynastic times. Neith acquired the titles of "Great Goddess," "mother of the Gods," "Mother and daughter of Ra," and "protector of women." The priest of On (her father) probably dedicated her to Neith, though Asenath was a Semite like Joseph. See McConkie, *His Name Shall Be Joseph,* 189, 205ff.; see also Smith, *Answers to Gospel Questions,* 1:169–71, who says that Asenath was a direct matrilineal descendant of Shem's wife. She probably possessed the pure lineage of Eve in her mtDNA.

36. Wigoder, *Illustrated Dictionary and Concordance of the Bible,* 324.

37. Davis, *Dictionary of the Bible,* 225.

38. They were spread throughout Israel in "refuge" cities.

39. Shute, Nyman, and Bott, *Ephraim,* 24.

40. Wilford Woodruff, in *Journal of Discourses* (8 October 1875), 18:127.

41. Erastus Snow, in *Journal of Discourses* (7 October 1882), 23:298b.

42. It is known that the word *Ephrathite* means "Ephraimite."

43. As quoted in Freke and Gandy, *Jesus and the Goddess,* 14. See Philo, De Sept 3:4, as quoted in Kingsland, *Gnosis or Ancient Wisdom,* 106. His importance is realized when we understand that the Hebrew name Joshua/Jesus was written with the letters YHSVH (Yod Heh Shin Vah Heh). This is close to the sacred and unpronounceable name of God, YHVH (Yod Heh Vah Heh), usually rendered as Jehovah or Yahweh with the added vowels. "As Philo explains, when the middle letter Shin (S), known as the Holy Letter, is added, the name means 'Saviour of the Lord.'"

44. Davis, *Dictionary of the Bible*, 438.
45. Perhaps this angel was Michael-Adam, the commander of the Lord's army (see Revelation 12:7).
46. This was the same city to which the children of Israel carried the bones of Joseph from Egypt, where they buried them as they had promised (Genesis 50:24–25; Joshua 24:32).
47. The suburbs of Shechem were in Mount Ephraim, which was the saddle between Mount Gerizim and Mount Ebal, the two highest mountains in the area.
48. Davis, *Dictionary of the Bible*, 447.
49. "There shall come a Star out of Jacob, and a Sceptre shall rise out of Israel" (Numbers 24:17).
50. "Once have I sworn, by my holiness, that I will not lie unto David. His seed shall endure forever, and his throne as the sun before me. It shall be established forever as the moon and as faithful witness in the heaven" (Psalm 89:35–37).
51. A spurious publication by John Arthur Goodchild entitled *The Book of Tephi* is said to be possibly based on the Book of Mormon.
52. Then again why did Samuel call Saul, a Benjaminite, to be the king in the first place? Perhaps Saul the great warrior was needed at the time and was really just a regent king for the youthful David. Because of Saul's not being of the right lineage, perhaps it was hoped he would not mind giving up the throne when David came of age.
53. The word *David* means "beloved son."
54. McConkie, *Gospel Symbolism*, 6.
55. Knight and Lomas, *Hiram Key*, 164–65.
56. In Leviticus 2:13 and Numbers 18:9, the covenant of salt was an eternal covenant. Abijah spoke as recorded in 2 Chronicles 13:5: "Hear me, thou Jeroboam, and all Israel; ought ye not to know that the Lord God of Israel gave the kingdom over Israel to David forever, even to him and to his sons, by a covenant of salt?"

CHAPTER TWO
ISRAEL SIFTED AMONG ALL THE NATIONS

I will sift the house of Israel among all nations, like
as corn is sifted in a sieve, yet shall not the least
grain fall upon the earth.

—AMOS 9:9

Israel shall blossom and bud, and fill the face of the
world with fruit.

—ISAIAH 27:6[1]

he tearing down, rooting out, and plucking up of the house of Israel and the house of David are integral to our understanding of the Holy Bloodline of Christ or the Holy Grail. The reason for Israel (Ephraim) to be sifted or scattered is revealed in Jeremiah 3:11, which states that "backsliding Israel hath justified herself more than treacherous Judah." The Northern Kingdom of Israel became apostate earlier than the Southern Kingdom of Judea. It reaped the consequences and was—for the time being—lost throughout the world. However, the bloodline was not utterly lost, as we shall see.

DIVISION OF ISRAEL AND JUDAH

And the man Jeroboam was a mighty
man of valor: and Solomon seeing the
young man that he was industrious, he
made him ruler over all the charge of
the house of Joseph.

—I KINGS 11:28

At the death of Solomon, the royal successor was his son Rehoboam, who gathered all Israel to Shechem. There he heard grievances regarding the enormous tax for building the temple and royal palaces. These projects were now completed and yet the tax continued. Only the tribe of Judah had any reprieve. The people were rebuffed, so they stoned the tax collector and incited a civil war.

Jeroboam, the son of Nebat the Ephrathite (meaning Ephraimite), was a servant of Solomon. God had told Solomon that he would give his kingdom to his servant, but not all. Ahijah the prophet caught the garment of Jeroboam, tearing it into twelve pieces, giving Jeroboam ten. Because of the wickedness of the house of David, the kingdom was divided in 925 B.C. into the Southern Kingdom of Judah and the Northern Kingdom of Israel (Ephraim).

When Rehoboam gathered an army to go against Jeroboam, the word of the Lord came to him through Shemaniah, saying, "Thus saith the Lord, Ye shall not go up, nor fight against your brethren the children of Israel: return every man to his house; for this thing is from me" (1 Kings 12:19–24).

Rehoboam's arrogance had led to rebellion and division between the two major tribes of Israel—Ephraim and Judah (1 Kings 11:26). This led directly to another major breach paradigm in God's kingdom on earth. "Manasseh, Ephraim; and Ephraim, Manasseh: they together shall be against Judah" (2 Nephi 19:21; Isaiah 9:21).

Now the birthright of Ephraim in the person of Jeroboam ruled the house of Israel, while the scepter of the House of Judah in the hands of Rehoboam ruled in Jerusalem. Jeroboam prospered for a while, building his capital at Shechem in Mount Ephraim. But he worried that if the people made pilgrimages to Jerusalem they would soon return to the fold of Rehoboam, so he set up two calves of gold for the purpose of worship, one in Bethel and one in Dan. This was, of course, a great sin (1 Kings 14:15–16).

The Kingdom of Judah was then composed of three and two-thirds full tribes, plus "those scattered families out of all the rest of the tribes who would not forsake the worship of the God of Israel."[2] These included Judah, Benjamin, the absorbed tribe of Simeon, and most of the Levites. Israel was, in contrast, composed of a little more than nine tribes: Ephraim, Dan, Reuben, Gad, Manasseh, Issachar, Zebulun, Naphtali, Asher, and a third of the Levites.

The Lord speaks of both commonwealths: "For the children of Israel and the children of Judah have only done evil before me from their youth" (Jeremiah 32:30; 3:8; 3:11; Hosea 4:15). In Hosea 5:5, God says of His people, "Israel and Ephraim stumble in their iniquity; Judah also stumbles with them." Hosea 5:7 says that they have begotten *"pagan children,"* or "strange children," as the marginal reading suggests.

Yet even during their evil works the Lord had not forgotten the two houses entirely. In fact he promises a blessing to come when He states, "Behold the days come, saith the Lord, that I will perform that *good thing* which I have promised unto the house of Israel and to the house of Judah" (Jeremiah 33:14). The reunion of the division of these two divided kingdoms of the seed of Jacob was certainly the Lord's desire (Jeremiah 3:18). However, this was not immediately possible as He Himself explains: "For as a girdle cleaveth to the loins of a man, so have I caused to cleave unto me the whole house of Israel and the whole house of Judah, saith the Lord; that they might be unto me for a people, and for a name, and for a praise, and for a glory; *but they would not hear*" (Jeremiah 13:11).

After a number of conspiring kings, King Omri built the city of Samaria (Shomron), which became the permanent capital of Israel (ca. 876 B.C.). Israel nevertheless continued their wicked ways despite the Lord's desire to "heal" them, as contemporary scripture points out in Hosea 7:1. And in Hosea 6:4, "O Ephraim, what shall I do unto thee? O Judah, what shall I do unto thee? For your goodness is as a morning cloud, and as the early dew it goeth away" (see also Hosea 5:12–15).

What did happen then? More than two hundred years after the revolt of the tribes, Israel formed an alliance with Syria to march against Ahaz, king of Judah, who similarly formed an alliance with the king of Assyria to defeat Israel. Thus for the first time in scripture the word "Jews" is used in contradistinction to the enemy the Israelites (2 Kings 16:1, 2, 5–7). The breaking of this brotherhood between Judah and Israel is exemplified in Zechariah 11:7–14: "I took unto me two staves [sticks]; the one I called Beauty [Israel] and the other I called Bands [Judah]. . . . And I took my staff, even Beauty, and cut it asunder, that I might break my covenant which I had made with all the people. And it was broken in that day: and so the poor of the flock that waited upon me knew that it was the Word of the Lord. . . . Then I cut asunder mine other staff, even Bands, that I might break the brotherhood between Israel and Judah."

We shall later see why this shifting of the seed of Abraham was important to the world. Also, one can read of the reversal of this broken contract in Zechariah 11 and in Ezekiel 37:16–17, 22. Ultimately, a sacred marriage contract with the two major Houses of the Lord would reunite the bond and heal the wasteland between them. Nothing less than a Grail marriage between noble scions of the two tribes would suffice.

SCATTERED ISRAEL AND JUDAH AMONG THE HEATHEN

Son of man, when the house of Israel dwelt in their own land, they defiled it by their own way and by their doings: their way before me as the uncleanness of a removed woman. . . . And I scattered them among the heathen, and they were dispersed through the countries: according to their way and according to their doings I judged them. . . . For I will [eventually] take you from among the heathen, and gather you out of all countries, and will bring you into your own land.

—Ezekiel 36:17, 19, 24

The hostility between the two major tribes of Israel is well noted in 2 Nephi 19:21, where it is written before Christ, "and Ephraim, Manasseh; they together shall be against Judah." Thus we shall later see that the Lord "will remove Judah also out of my sight as I have removed Israel" (2 Kings 23:27). The Northern Kingdom of Israel was conquered by the Assyrians in 722–721 B.C. Because of worshiping other gods, Judah

was not immune to the same fate that won Israel its condemnation. Jeremiah 7:12–15 warns the men of Judah: "But go ye now unto *my place, which is Shilo*, where I set my name at first, and see what I did to it for the wickedness of my people Israel. . . . And I will cast you out of my sight, as I have cast out all your brethren, even the whole seed of Ephraim."

The Southern Kingdom of Judah was first conquered by the Babylonians in 598 B.C., and then again under King Nebuchadnezzar in 587–586 B.C. This casting out came to pass during the Babylonian deportation in 598–582 B.C.. The exile, or captivity, lasted until 538 B.C. when the Jews were allowed to return. These conquests scattered Israel and the Jews broadly as did the Diaspora after A.D. 70.

The dispersion of the house of Israel was done to save that house and to work as a leaven to benefit the whole world. Paul reaffirms this point when he said, "Know ye not that a little leaven leaveneth the whole lump?" (1 Corinthians 5:6; Matthew 13:33). Like the promise to Abraham that through him and his posterity the whole world would be blessed, the scattering of Israel not only preserved that House from total corruption but also blessed the entire planet. The Lord spoke through the prophet Amos in prophesying this dispersion: "For, lo, I will command, and I will sift the house of Israel among all nations, like as corn is sifted in a sieve, yet shall not the least grain fall upon the earth" (Amos 9:9; 7:3, 6).

There had been much dissemination of the people of God throughout history. This occurred first with the expulsion of Adam and Eve from the Garden of Eden, then with the scattering as a result of the Tower of Babel, and later with Joseph's bondage in Egypt. All nations have been beneficiaries of the chosen ones, "where I had driven them" (see Jeremiah 23:8; 2 Nephi 10:8). The "where" is important to our study, for apparently there are certain sanctuaries of refuge.

The dispersions that most concern this study

begin with the dispersion of the lost ten tribes at the time of Shalmaneser's deportation of Israel in 723 B.C.[3] At this time the Kingdom of Israel (or Ephraim) had sunken into apostasy due to its worship of the calves of Jeroboam. The Ephraimitic prophet Hosea declared the withdrawal of God's spirit when he stated, "Ephraim shall be desolate in the day of rebuke" (Hosea 5:9, 13–14; 2 Nephi 17:8; Isaiah 7:8).

Judah received a similar warning when Jeremiah said, "And I will cast you [Judah] out of my sight, as I have cast out all your brethren, even the whole seed of Ephraim" (Jeremiah 7:15). Then, as it was foretold, came the Babylonian captivity of the Kingdom of Judea about 586 B.C. Jeremiah noted these two singular scattering: "Israel is a scattered sheep; the lions have driven him away: first the king of Assyria hath devoured him; and last this Nebuchadnezzar king of Babylon hath broken his bones" (Jeremiah 50:17).

Thus we see how they became "a hiss and a byword" with "their name for a curse," and they would "cry for sorrow of heart and shall howl for vexation of spirit" (Isaiah 65:14). Just how close did Ephraim come to losing all the promises made unto her is seen in Hosea 9:16: "Ephraim is smitten, their root is dried up, they shall bear no fruit: yea, though they bring forth, yet will I slay even the beloved fruit of their womb."

This is an ominous warning for Ephraim, yet we will see that God will not forget them and will reaffirm His promise with them as His covenant people. The scattered remnants of Israel leavened the meal of the earth and especially the earlier colonizers of the Isles of the Sea. The Lord does not forget them, however, as 2 Nephi 10:22 states, but uses them for his purposes: "For behold, the Lord God has led away from time to time from the house of Israel, according to his will and pleasure. And now behold, the Lord remembereth all them who have been broken off, wherefore he remembereth us also."

Though lost for a season, they will play an important role in the life of Jesus Christ and the reestablishment of the gospel in the latter days. It will happen as the house of Israel is refashioned in the British Isles, but far beyond the understanding of present day British-Israelite devotees. This makes them an essential part of the history of the Holy Grail.

NOTES

1. In Isaiah 30:28 we read that in the future the Lord will "sift the nations with the sieve of vanity." Then in Luke 22:31 we read, "Satan hath desired to have you, that he may sift you as wheat." The idea of God and Satan separating out "their own" is a well-rehearsed biblical concept.

2. Allen, *Judah's Sceptre and Joseph's Birthright,* 63. These people were undoubtedly assimilated into one of the tribes of this kingdom, namely Judah, Benjamin, Simeon, and the Levites.

3. The Assyrian invasion lasted between 740 and 721 B.C.

PART TWO

THE LEGITIMATE DAVIDIC LINEAGE

he notion of a royal bloodline from Adam to Christ is well accepted by all Christians. However, the idea of a *double* Judaic sceptered lineage for Christ is not well understood. The significance of the Virgin Mary's bloodline may seem to pale beside that of Heavenly Father's spiritline, but it is not insignificant. Her two-fold Judaic lineage is a topic rife with scriptural implications and with the power to excite our imagination.

CHAPTER THREE

OUT-OF-BRITAIN THEORY

The hidden royal lineage of Judah's twin son Zerah (Zarah) was first harbored in Galilee and then, according to the Irish Chronicles, planted in the British Isles, lost to the worthies in Jerusalem until the meridian of time, at which point a son of the House of David (Perez) and the House of the Scarlet Thread (Zerah) appeared to the world in the person of Jesus Christ. [1] The following chapters illustrate the descent of the House of Judah through his two sons and then to Jesus Christ himself.

Thus we see that Jesus is pure Judah from both sons of that patriarch. That it was protected in a far-flung "garden" of the British Isles may seem unusual (see Jacob 5). Yet it would have been much more difficult to preserve such a lineage in the environment of apostate Israel. We see how the sifting of Israel through the world established Diaspora colonies among the Isles of the Sea, from which God would eventually graft his chosen Grail seed.

THE SCARLET THREAD OF TARA

And it came to pass, in the time of [Tamar's] travail, that, behold, twins were in her womb.

And it came to pass, when she travailed, that the one put out his hand: and the midwife took and bound upon his hand a scarlet thread, saying, This came out first.

And it came to pass, as he drew back his hand, that, behold, his brother came out: and she said, How hast thou broken forth? this breach be upon thee: therefore his name was called Pharez [Perez].

And afterward came out his brother, that had the scarlet thread upon his hand: and his name was called Zarah [Zerah].

—GENESIS 38:27–30

This is a most curious account of the birth of the twin sons of Judah and Tamar. The very name Perez means "a breach," while the name Zerah denotes "the seed," or "to shine or come forth." Medically, during the birth of twins the first baby comes out head first while the second is born breech (feet first). Any observer of the remarkable episode might have proclaimed Perez the second born because he was born breech. Yet he was pronounced the firstborn, precisely because he was born first.

Zerah, who was the first to begin the birth process, received the scarlet thread on his right wrist, only to withdraw back into the womb, and was born second. Miraculously he was born head first, the way a firstborn was normally born, with the scarlet thread of primogeniture around his wrist. This confusing circumstance undoubtedly created dissension within the tribe of Judah, which would take more than a millennium to repair.

The "scarlet line," or lineage, is of great importance to our narrative. In Hebrew the word for "line" is *tiqvah*. It is always translated in our Bible as "hope" or "expectation" (see Hebrews 11.1). Thus we could say that the "scarlet line" is a lineage of hope that points us toward Jesus Christ. The Israelites brushed blood on their doorways with hyssop branches, with the expectation that the Angel of Death would "pass over" the household. Likewise, a red line was marked around the altar of the temple to delineate between the blood sacrifices above the line to be eaten and those below the line to be consumed by fire.[3]

The parallel tale of Rahab of Jericho (who hid the two spies of Israel) tells how she and her family were saved when the scarlet line was placed in her window prior to that city being utterly destroyed. The scarlet line, or mark, is thus a recurring motif in Old Testament scripture. "In addition,"

writes Higgenbotham, "the scarlet line is a picture of a bloodline because Rahab is an ancestor of Christ Himself" (see Matthew 1:5).[4] Karen Boren notes, "Whether one speaks of the bloodlines of Christ [Rahab], the scarlet thread used to determine birthright [the twin sons of Judah and Tamar in Genesis 38:28], or the scarlet line on the Temple altar, the Hope of Israel is in the blood of Jesus Christ."[5]

These statements are very provocative for our understanding of the Holy Grail, or lineage of Christ. The story of the "scarlet thread of Tara Hills" as a "new Jerusalem" begins just after the cleaving of the House of Judah into two parts.[6] Like the story of the House of Joseph, it too was split between two sons, although with Joseph's sons, Manasseh and Ephraim, we see a cooperative spirit. However, the struggle for dominance within the tribe of Judah is reflected in the story of twin sons, Perez (Pharez) and Zerah. In Judah's case, competitive leadership arose between the sons from Judah and Tamar.

How like the story of Jacob and Esau, who tumbled in the womb and wrestled during Rebekah's travail. As there was a breach between Isaac and Ishmael, Jacob and Esau, Ephraim and Judah, so there was a breach between Perez and Zerah. Since Judah held the scepter, the law of primogeniture prevailed so that his eldest son would ascend to the throne.

The unhealthy fissure between Perez and Zerah was only symptomatic of the much greater breach created between a wounded Judah and Ephraim. Throughout the history of the world many such breaches and healings would transpire. In the latter days we have seen the breach between the children of Hyrum Smith (Joseph F. Smith) and the children of his brother Joseph Smith Jr. (Joseph Smith III).

The Perez or "breach" line became, with some question, the kingly line. Of the Zerah line, his firstborn son, Zimri (Zabdi), carried on the feud (1 Chronicles 2:6; Joshua 7:1). This eventually led to his family line being forced out of the Holy Land.[7]

The Zerah line, however, was very important because it possessed the "scarlet thread," the symbol of primogeniture.

According to legend, part of the Zerah lineage began to colonize Ireland as early as 900 B.C. The medieval Celtic text Lebor Gabåla Érenn (Book of Invasions of Ireland) states that the Irish were descended through Míl of Spain from the "Phoenicians."[8] This Zerah migration pattern would be retraced about three hundred years later with a Judaic king's daughter.

After Jerusalem was destroyed by the Babylonians, the famous prophet Jeremiah and his scribe Simon Baruch (Brec) escaped to Egypt with the daughters of King Zedekiah, including the Princess Tephi-Tea (Tamar, Tarah) and Mirabel.[9] Mulek, King Zedekiah's son, had already escaped to the New World in the Western Hemisphere, while the rest of the extended family were murdered (see Helaman 6:10).[10]

Jeremiah and his charges supposedly fled to Egypt and dwelt in the Milesian garrison at Taphanhes (Daphnae) in Egypt, called "The Palace of the Jew's Daughter," according to later Arabs.[11] Irish historians called her Tamar, "The Daughter of Pharaoh," in memory of her stay in Egypt. The fact that she fled Palestine is preserved in her name Tarah, meaning "one banished" or "flight."[12] Or as it was said, "And I will make thee to pass with thine enemies into a land which thou knowest not" (Jeremiah 15:14; see also Jeremiah 40:4; 41:10; 43:6–8). LDS Apostle Anthony W. Ivins relates their departure to Egypt:

> Zedekiah, at the time, had two daughters . . . These two beautiful Girls were protected against the Babylonians by being placed in the caves of Jeremiah, the prophet. He became the guardian, the custodian of [their] welfare . . . Jeremiah took them down into Egypt, it is said, to the same place where Joseph and Mary went with Christ, our Lord, at the time of the execution of the decree by Herod. . . . They abode there, at a place called Taphanes.[13]

Legend states that, upon hearing the threatening news of Nebuchadnezzar's planned invasion of Egypt, the group fled Egypt and took to the sea.[14] Ivins also describes the band's subsequent journeys after Egypt:

> Just at that time a ship landed upon the coast of Spain, from which an old man [Jeremiah] and his secretary [Baruch] and two young women disembarked. They remained for a short period in that country, where one of the girls married into the reigning house of Spain, but the old man, who is referred to in Ireland as *Ollamh Fødhla* [the old prophet, wise one], in the traditions and the songs which they still sing of him, passed across the channel and landed on the coast of Ireland, taking with him the elder of the two girls, whose name is Tamar [Tea] Tephi, which translated from Hebrew to English means the beautiful palm, or the beautiful wanderer.[15]

From there with Gathelus at the helm, the ship's precious and sacred cargo of relics, with Jeremiah as guide, Baruch as scribe, Tamar, and the now-married Mirabel, sailed onward toward the Hill Tara in the Boyne Valley of Ireland about 584–582 B.C. Undoubtedly they had taken whatever relics they could before Jerusalem was destroyed.[16]

The *Múr Ollaman* in Tara was considered by British-Israelites to be a type of "School of the Prophets" founded by Jeremiah. Supposedly, Jeremiah attempted to establish a "New Jerusalem" at Tara, restore the monarchy of Judah, and found a new kingdom. His choice of Tara was no accident, for his plans centered on curing the breach between the two branches of the House of Judah. He assertively bridged this breach by arranging a marriage for Tephi-Tea, a "Princess of the Line of David."[17]

At the time that Heremon (*Eire-amhon*) Eochaidh, a Prince of Judah-Zerah, was awaiting his coronation, he met the Princess Tamar Tephi-Tea, the "slight and tender twig." They fell in love and soon married, thus uniting the prophetic lineages of Perez and Zerah, and became the direct ancestors of the Virgin Mary. Mairéad Carew explains, "According to Irish legend, Tea came from Thebes. She married Érimon [Heremon], a son of Míl of Spain."[18] She was of the royal House of David and her marriage to Eochaid, the second Milesian (Spanish) monarch of Ireland, had dynastic import.

King Heremon was of the Scarlet Thread, or the Zerah Branch of the House of Judah.[19] It is doubtful that E. L. Whitehead's and Vaughn E. Hansen's shared belief that King Heremon was from the Northern Kingdom of Israel and an Ephraimite is true.[20] *O'Hart's Irish Pedigrees* indicates that he sprang from a Phoenician trader, clearly noting that he was descended from Japheth, the son of Noah.[21] Shem, the son of Noah, is the line from which all the Israelites sprang, so any Japhethite would be outside the loop for marriage consideration. Although most of the later Phoenicians were considered to be of the tribe of Asher, an Israelitish tribe, they were still of the wrong tribe for the promised blessings.[22] Heremon, in order to be eligible, needed to be a scion of the tribe of Judah through Zerah.

As oral legends were not altogether in an orderly fashion or laid out in perfect sequence, we can only surmise the full significance of this important marriage. In Jewish tradition, according to Rabbi Kleiman, tribal bloodline comes through the father but the national inheritance follows the mother's side.[23] This is however a faulty indicator of tribal origin since the mother's mtDNA is passed to both male and female lines, while the Y chromosome is only passed through the male. Thus, this unified dynasty would be of the House of David (Perez), which would be dominant over Zerah, because the mother/wife was of the lineage of David and their posterity was focused on the Virgin Mary.

However, the inheritance rights of the line are not passed through the mother except for a little-known exception to the rule. Numbers 27:8 says if there is no male heir, a female may pass on the inheritance if she marries within her own tribe (Numbers 36:6).[24] In this case, both husband and wife were of the tribe of Judah though from different branches, but Jesus would receive the promise through his mother, who will be a direct descendant of Tamar.

Their union mended the Breach, and tied together the *Scarlet Thread*. There in the "Diaspora" they met and married. The new "healed" dynasty began in about 580 B.C., when King Eochaid and Queen Tephi-Tea united Judah's two major bloodlines, Zerah and Perez, thus forming a new and better line of Judah than just the House of David alone. Professor C. A. L. Totten has given a genealogy of the Zerah royal house, and according to his research there were twenty-four generations between Judah and this sacred marriage in Tara.[25]

British-Israelites believe that the marriage bridged the rift between the two royal houses of Israel after four hundred years of separation.[26] Although this may all be true, it cannot be proven by any genealogy at hand. Supposedly they had but a son, Irial Faidh, and even legend makes no reference to an all-important daughter.[27] Shortly after the birth of their son,

Tamar died and was buried in the great "Mergech" (a mound or tomb).[28]

Allen claims that Christ came through the family line of Judah, David, Josiah, and Jeconiah (Jehoiachin, Coniah). But, this is Joseph the Carpenter's line from which Jesus did not biologically descend. Furthermore, Jeconiah's offspring were cursed never to sit upon the throne of David (Jeremiah 22:24–30). Jesus came through the Josiah line and not the Jeconiah line. These lines diverge at the great king Josiah, and it is through Jeconiah's uncle Zedekiah that both Joseph of Arimathea and the Virgin Mary were descended.[29] Eventually, according to Allen, it will be given to a son of the Judeo-David house:

> When he [Christ] comes, as Shiloh, God will give it to him, for unto him shall the gathering of the people be. At that time the breaches will be healed and he shall be called "The Restorer of the BREACH.[30]

The dispersions of the family of King Zedekiah and other such dispersions nourished the nations of the world. They especially leavened the British Isles with the blood of Israel to such a degree that the later arrival of the seed of Jesus and Mary Magdalene found a fertile place to root.

It is very probable that the Virgin Mary was related directly to this united "full Judah" dynasty. With this line of reasoning, could the Virgin Mary have been a native British woman? And did her uncle, Joseph of Arimathea, return her to England, the land of her birth, after the crucifixion? If true, then the Virgin Mary's bloodline was vastly more important to the birth of Christ than previously supposed. The author contends that the "Son of David" (Jesus Christ) was indeed of these two preferred lineages of Judah.[31]

Then will a new Grail dynasty begin, and from Jesus Christ arise, centuries later, a son who shall be an Ephraim-Judah scion, the preserved seed, their descendant Joseph Smith Jr.[32] Like Christ, Joseph Smith was high by birth but low in the sense of non-ruling and un-esteemed by the world.

MORMON MARIOLOGY

A virgin, most beautiful and fair above all other virgins.

—1 NEPHI 11:15

The idea that the Virgin Mary was uniquely fitted to be the mortal mother of the Messiah has led to the idea that she was not tainted in the womb by the "original sin of Adam." She was, according to the Catholic Church, born through the miraculous event of the Immaculate Conception and was the only perfectly pure and sinless woman.[33]

Bruce R. McConkie has written emphatically against this position, "the immaculate conception has reference to the birth of Mary and is a false doctrine."[34] This may be true of her conception, but Edward Tullidge and Eliza R. Snow leave the door open on the idea that the Virgin Mary lived a sinless life, "God's nature in Christ needed no regeneration. Nor did the woman's nature need regeneration, when thus found pure, as in [the Virgin] Mary."[35]

The Catholic notion of an immaculate conception might be replaced by a more Mormon concept of "chosen lineages." We seek to demonstrate that Mary's lineage was directly through the full "scepter" tribe of Judah (combined Zerah and Perez), not just through the royal House of David. Mary was ascribed the position of "Mother of God" on the earth (1 Nephi 11:18, 1st ed.),[36] thus proving her *bona fides* as the legitimate Mother of the Only Begotten.

Upon the Virgin Mary was bestowed the favored commission to give birth to the Messiah. This, not only because of her premortal and mortal righteousness, but also because she held within herself the true Grail lineage. Mary, being both of the Scarlet Thread and the House of David is of preeminent importance. Otherwise, Jesus biologically could not claim descendance from the House of Jesse-David or full Judah. He would have been adopted by His stepfather Joseph and thus his claim to the scepter was weakened in the eyes of many.

If Matthew pursues the lineage through Joseph the Carpenter, this would be agreeable to Jewish law. Joseph's act of naming the child in the temple, which is the prerogative of the father, is also an act of adoption. There are no assertions in the gospels that Joseph was the foster father or legal guardian of Jesus, only that he was the father of Jesus Christ. Of course, Mormons know that Joseph actually adopted Jesus as his own for time and God, the Father of the Only Begotten, allowed him to do so.[37]

There are at least two reasons to infer that Joseph the Carpenter was not the father of Jesus. These stem from the cases of Solomon and Jechonias. If the lineage was traced through David's son, King Solomon, there is a problem because Solomon's line was cursed through Uriah's wife (Jeremiah 36:30). Matthew's genealogy pursued Joseph's line through Jeconiah (Coniah) and, as mentioned above, this line was also cursed by God who vowed that no one from this line should sit on the throne (Jeremiah 22:24–30).

This would be further proof that Joseph was not the biological father and that the Lord God Almighty was the father of the Christ child himself. Therefore Jesus would not partake of the curse by being literally related to Coniah. Since he was legally adopted by Joseph, in a certain sense Jesus did partake of the curse, because during his mortality Jesus never did sit upon the throne of David.[38] In the marriage of Mary and Joseph, both the legal and royal rights to the throne are united with its attendant blessings and cursings.[39]

The authentic tribe of Judah and royal House of David bloodline was something sorely missing in the Holy Land during that period. Bernheim states that "according to some sources this royal line was extinct some centuries before the birth of Jesus."[40]

In fact, the Hasmonean princes who occupied the throne of David were actually of the tribe of Levi.[41]

Later, King Herod the Great was not a Jew at all, being an Edomite, a descendant of Esau (an Idumaean).[42] He married the beautiful Mariamne, a granddaughter of the last Hasmonean ruler, Hyrcanus II, in an attempt to legitimize his claim to the throne. It was difficult, if not impossible to find a pure royal descendant of Judah in the Levant (Holy Land).[43]

By Christ's time it was a much-decayed royal lineage, except in a certain spot of Galilee where there remained a small remnant. In this area was a rustic little village of "disrepute" called Nazareth, where it was asked if "any good thing" could come from such a "terrible place."[44] Why would the Savior come out of such an exposed and provincial location just north of Samaria?[45]

It is likely, although not mentioned by other scholars, that Nazareth—and also Capernaum— was in "disrepute" because both were located where a branch of the Zerhites (Scarlet Thread) lived in the northern edge of Palestine. Because the lineage of Zerah claimed the scepter of Judah and was exiled, it suggests that the Perez line of Judah demeaned Nazareth.

The constant references to Christ being a son of David probably stems from the desire of local Jewish disciples to dissociate him with the primary branch of Judah. The secret mystery about Jesus Christ was that he was the paladin of the whole House of Judah, not just one branch of the House of Judah.[46]

It could be said that the kingdom of God on earth is a "family affair." Every significant player seems to be related to one another in some way. For example, according to many writers, Salome, the mother of James and John (the Sons of Thunder), was the Virgin Mary's sister (see John 19:25).[47] While this is a possibility, it has raised some intriguing discussions. When he learned of this conjecture, Graham Phillips wrote: "It was beginning to look as if [the Virgin] Mary might have been far more important in the scheme of things than I had thought—and it had something to do with her bloodline."[48]

The relevance of the tribal origin of Virgin Mary is now becoming recognized. The genealogy of Christ, as found in the Books of Matthew 1:1–17 and Luke 3:23–38, illustrates the difficulty of ascertaining Mary's lineage. James E. Talmage offered this opinion:

> Luke's record is regarded by many, however, as the pedigree of Mary, while Matthew's is accepted as that of Joseph. . . . A personal genealogy of Joseph was essentially that of Mary also, for they were cousins. Joseph is named as son of Jacob by Matthew, and as son of Heli by Luke; but Jacob and Heli were brothers, and it appears that one of the two was the father of Joseph and the other the father of Mary and therefore father-in-law to Joseph.[49]

Most LDS scholars side with Talmage's view of Joseph and Mary's kinship. So if Christ is of the prophesied lineage only through adoption to Joseph, a legalistic non-natural condition, then Jesus' connection with the sceptered pedigree is attenuated at best. If the claim to the Throne of David comes through His adoption to Joseph the carpenter, then He would have no claim at all since this was a cursed lineage. He would have adopted the cursing as well as blessings. However, if He were of the true line of David by birth through His mother's line, then his

claim would have validity outside of any adoptive process and judiciary means. But if God's bloodline DNA signature was the same as Judah's, then the seal is affixed. The more the blessings of Judah can be ascertained in Christ's ancestry the more the promises of the sceptered line may be invoked.

Scripturally there is justification that Mary is of the royal lineage of David, as Romans 1:3 states, "Concerning his Son, Jesus Christ our Lord, which was made of the seed of David according to the flesh" (see Psalm 132:11). The archaic phrase "according to the flesh" may sensibly be translated as "biologically."[50] This boldly states that he was a "literal," not just an "adopted," Son of David. Pierre-Antoine Bernheim states, "But at that time legal paternity, which had priority over biological paternity, conferred all the hereditary rights."[51] Thus Jesus had both biological and legal right to the Throne of David.

Let us first look at a lineage chart of the Virgin Mary, for in her we have a blessed lineage protected by "God's own hand" (see Figure 1). As is typical in the scriptures, there seems to be more to the story than the sacred texts delineate. As broached in the discussion of the Scarlet Thread, this treatise proposes that the Virgin Mary was directly related to the unified "All-Judah" dynasty.[52]

With the healing of the fissure between the Perez "breach" and the Zerah "seed," through marriage, great possibilities existed.[53]At Tara Plantation (Ireland), Argyle (Scotland/Alba), Wales, Devonshire, and Somerset and Cornwall in the West Country, colonies of pure Judah were planted. It was not in the Hellenist Holy Land (except perhaps the Nazareth area), but only in this isolated Isle of the Sea, that a community of the chosen race could be hidden.

If this sacred marriage at Tara was historical, it would have led to a singular lineage with a special purpose. The Virgin Mary, although a descendant of this line, in theory, would have been disqualified to transfer the rights of her lineage to her son Jesus,

FIGURE I
HOLY GRAIL LINEAGE

[Mary] a precious and chosen vessel.
—ALMA 7:10

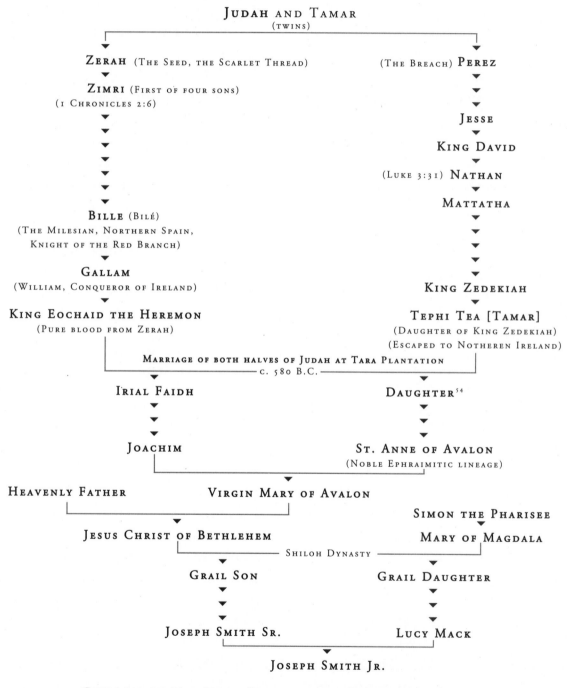

JUDAH AND **TAMAR**
(TWINS)

ZERAH (THE SEED, THE SCARLET THREAD)

(THE BREACH) **PEREZ**

ZIMRI (FIRST OF FOUR SONS)
(1 CHRONICLES 2:6)

JESSE

KING DAVID

(LUKE 3:31) **NATHAN**

MATTATHA

BILLE (BILÉ)
(THE MILESIAN, NORTHERN SPAIN,
KNIGHT OF THE RED BRANCH)

KING ZEDEKIAH

GALLAM
(WILLIAM, CONQUEROR OF IRELAND)

KING EOCHAID THE HEREMON
(PURE BLOOD FROM ZERAH)

TEPHI TEA [TAMAR]
(DAUGHTER OF KING ZEDEKIAH)
(ESCAPED TO NOTHEREN IRELAND)

MARRIAGE OF BOTH HALVES OF JUDAH AT TARA PLANTATION
— C. 580 B.C. —

IRIAL FAIDH

DAUGHTER[54]

JOACHIM

ST. ANNE OF AVALON
(NOBLE EPHRAIMITIC LINEAGE)

HEAVENLY FATHER   **VIRGIN MARY OF AVALON**

SIMON THE PHARISEE

JESUS CHRIST OF BETHLEHEM   **MARY OF MAGDALA**

— SHILOH DYNASTY —

GRAIL SON   **GRAIL DAUGHTER**

JOSEPH SMITH SR.   **LUCY MACK**

JOSEPH SMITH JR.

CHURCH OF THE FIRST BORN OF THE BLOOD OF THE LAMB
(THE CHURCH OF JESUS CHRIST OF LATTER-DAY SAINTS)

except for a little known exception to the rule.[55] This explanation is possibly traceable to Justin Martyr (ca. 100 – ca. 165) in the second century, though Annius Viterbo (ca. 1490) popularized it during the Reformation.

Usually lineal descent passes through the man, but in the case of Judith (8:1) and the heiresses in Numbers and Chronicles, it could also pass matrilineally. Such exceptions allow for the existence of the genealogy of the Virgin Mary, in spite of Talmudic injunctions against matrilineal genealogies. The Virgin Mary supposedly had no brothers (*The Catholic Encyclopedia*) and thus she was able to pass on the inheritance of the full house of Judah to Christ.

Mary came to her "most favored among women" status by birthright, not happenstance. Her family was from that special unified lineage, whose tribal purity was protected to her by God Himself. Brigham Young's statement that God had watched over and protected Joseph Smith's ancestry, appears equally relevant to both the Virgin Mary, Mary Magdalene, and the Bethany sisters:

> The Lord had his eye upon him [Joseph Smith], and upon his father, and upon his father's father, and upon their progenitors clear back to Abraham and from Abraham to the flood, from the flood to Enoch, and from Enoch to Adam. He [God] has watched that family and that blood as it has circulated from its fountain to the birth of that man.[56]

If this is so, its significance would be beyond the possibility of quibbling. Although this theory cannot be proven in the genealogy of Luke, nor by the historical record, it has legendary support and possesses a certain logical symmetry to it. If legend is sound and with this new paradigmatic thinking, expansive vistas open before us and a path has been found to bring to pass the purposes of the Lord.

Roman Catholics and Greek/Russian Orthodox churches pay special attention to the Virgin Mary. They have her being born of the solely legendary Joachim and St. Anne (Anna) of Bethlehem. "Spotless Anna! Juda's glory!" as she was praised.[57] St. Anne had long been barren, like other elderly women mentioned in scripture: Sarah, Hannah (Samuel I), and Elizabeth. The elderly Joachim was even barred from offering sacrifice because he had no offspring. They prayed for a child, which Anne vowed would be dedicated to the service of God in the temple.[58] According to Catholic legend, an angel appeared to Anne and announced that she should have a daughter.[59]

There is an amazing legend that answers the question about St. Anne's historical background. Celtic legend has it that Anne herself was born not in Bethlehem but rather in Britain![60] And why not? For Saint Jerome once said, "Heaven is as near to us in Britain as in Palestine."[61] Nicholas R. Mann reports: "The folk traditions of the Southwest [Britain] support the tradition of Christ's coming to Avalon. Some say he came to see the homeland of his mother's mother, St. Anne. This Cornish Queen had immaculately conceived a child and her husband had cast her out from her home. Joseph of Arimathea on one of his trips to trade for British tin—took her [Anne] with him back to the Holy Land [*sic*]."[62]

While logical trajectory had already decreed that the Virgin Mary was born in Britain, this bit of information gives further confidence to the postulate that the Virgin Mary herself was not born in the Holy Land, but was also a native of the Isles of the Sea. According to the legend, Mary's parents took her to serve in the Temple in Jerusalem at the age of three.[63] Jewish newborns and young orphans did serve in the temple.[64] However, it was possible that Joseph of Arimathea, after her parents' deaths, took her to the Jerusalem Temple and eventually, after the crucifixion, returned her to the land of her birth![65]

If this is true, then the Virgin Mary's bloodline is even more important as a contributing factor to the birth of Christ than heretofore supposed. The genealogy through "only the House of David" scenario may now be overturned for the more restorative combination of the Scarlet Thread and Davidic line combination. It was from this chosen branch of righteousness (Zerah/Perez line), hidden in the British Isles, that the Savior was born. Otherwise, His claim to the throne of David would always have an asterisk beside it, placed there by his detractors on both sides of the family of Judah. Being from this proper branch, through the pure genealogy of mother Mary, Jesus in turn was eligible to do the "good thing" promised Ephraim (Israel) and Judah. "Behold, the days come, saith the Lord, that I will perform that good thing which I have promised unto the house of Israel (Ephraim) and to the house of Judah. In those days, and at that time, will I cause the Branch of righteousness to grow up unto David; and he shall execute judgment and righteousness in the land" (Jeremiah 33:14–15).[66]

The Grail lineage now begins to poignantly gather in the person of the Virgin Mary. Thus we see when and why the young Jesus went to England. Amazingly everything dovetails together. Salient answers to new questions appear when this new paradigm is evoked. All things lead to the "good thing" that Jesus will perform in Cana.

NOTES

1. The tribe in Judah had a family within it called Zarhites (Numbers 26:20) and also called the "children of Zerah" who dwelt in Jerusalem after the return from the Babylonian Exile (1 Chronicles 9:6; Nehemiah 11:24). It is not known if they were of Judah's son Zerah or from a descendant of Perez named Zerah.

2. Judah married a Canaanite woman, Shuah, from an Adullamite town (Arab), and together they had three sons: Er, Onan, and Shelah. Tamar was the wife of Er, and when he died, she married the next son, Onan, who also died (Genesis 38:6–10). These deaths may have occurred so that the lineage did not go through a Canaanite mixed marriage. Tamar was then promised to the youngest son, Shelah, but he reached maturity without marrying her. This story illustrates the Hebrew Levirate law (Latin, *levir,* meaning "husband's brother"). When a married man died without children, then the brother would marry and "raise up" children that were counted as the first husband's children. When Onan married his brother's wife, however, he refused to have children by her because they would not be his own. Onan was afraid that the inheritance promised his brother would not go to his own children but to the children through him and Tamar, assigned to Er. Onan was therefore punished by death (Deuteronomy 25:5–10 gives the option of a brother refusing). But Tamar was now in a quandary, unable to produce children for her deceased husband. So after Onan's death, in order to fulfill her obligations, Tamar masqueraded as a prostitute, seduced her father-in-law, Judah (who did not recognize her), and produced children for an inheritance. Onan's father, Judah, thus became the father of twin sons, Perez and Zerah, by Tamar.

3. Edersheim, *The Temple,* 55.

4. Higginbotham, *Color in Scripture,* 10.

5. Boren and Boren, *Following the Ark of the Covenant,* 40.

6. Tara Hills is about two miles from Kilmessan, County Meath, Ireland.

7. However, a small Judaean clan of Zerahites remained (see Numbers 26:20).

8. Carew, *Tara and the Ark of the Covenant,* 24. Often the word *Phoenician* simply meant anyone from the eastern Mediterranean Sea.

9. Allen, *Judah's Sceptre and Joseph's Birthright,* 197. Some scholars say there may have been two or even three daughters (princesses). In a sense, Jeremiah is playing the role of Joseph of Arimathea with the Grail ancestors instead of the Grail seed.

10. Most interesting is the Book of Mormon city that the Mulekites founded, Zarahemla, because of its prefix "Zarah." Mulek's sister, Tamar Tephi-Tea, seems to have married a descendant of Zarah, and here in the New World, the Mulekites are founding a city in the "seed" line that had always been at odds with Mulek's own Pharez bloodline. The connection is obscure, but could it be that a separate bloodline of Zarah from an

independent migration centuries earlier had made it to the New World and eventually united with Mulek?

11. The Greek (Ptolemaic) fortress of Daphnae is now modern Tel Defneh, located on the caravan route known as Qast Bint el Yehudi (The Palace of the Jew's Daughters). See Boren and Boren, *Following the Ark of the Covenant*, 35.

12. Allen, *Judah's Sceptre and Joseph's Birthright*, 249.

13. Anthony W. Ivins, "Israel in History and Genealogy," *Utah Genealogical and Historical Magazine* 23 (January 1932). Ivins was a member of British-Israel World Federation in London before World War II, and his writings were certainly influenced by their teachings.

14. Ralls-MacLeod and Robertson, *Quest for the Celtic Key*, 27.

15. Anthony W. Ivins, "Israel in History and Genealogy," *Utah Genealogical and Historical Magazine* 23 (January 1932).

16. This coincided with the Jerusalem Temple guard's instruction to remove sacred treasures from the grasp of the invading king of Babylon (see Ralls-MacLeod and Robertson, *Quest for the Celtic Key*, 25). These relics may have included the Bethel Stone, which the Irish called Lia Fail—the "Stone of Destiny," "Jacob's Pillow," or "Coronation Stone." Mentioned in Genesis 28:10–22, the stone would become the symbol of a British-Israel connection for the next 2,500 years. The stone was kept in the Teamhair Breagh Palace for fifty-six high kings, or Ard-Righ (sometimes Ardath). Laidler, *Head of God*, 58, says the stone was kept in Teamhair for 1,040 years, but this number is probably closer to 1,072. Eventually the relic was taken to Scotland in about A.D. 487. Other relics may have included the ark of the covenant, the Sword of Methuselah, and David's Harp, which adorns the modern flag of the Republic of Ireland.

17. Glover, *England, the Remnant of Judah and the Israel of Ephraim*, 70. This is typical British-Israel thought.

18. Carew, *Tara and the Ark of the Covenant*, 24–25.

19. Albany, *Forgotten Monarch of Scotland*, 69, as quoted in Ralls-MacLeod and Robertson, *Quest for the Celtic Key*, 24–25: "It was Eirhe Ahmon's son Eochaid, High King of Ireland, who married Tamar Tephi, the daughter of King Zedekiah of Judah, in about 586 BC. With her father a captive in Babylon, and her brothers murdered by Nebuchadnezzar, Tamar had escaped to Ireland with the prophet Jeremiah, and with them came the Stone of Destiny."

20. Whitehead, *House of Israel*, 131–32, and Hansen, *Whence Came They?* 85. Laidler, *Head of God*, believes him to be aligned with the tribe of Dan.

21. "Lineal Descent of the Royal Family of England," *O'Hart's Irish Pedigrees*, 41.

22. In his "Race Origins," Bruce Hanny states, "The Phoenicians were Israelites" (Elder, *Joseph of Arimathea*, 7). It should be remembered that the Hamite former Phoenicians were Canaanites; they were driven out by Joshua, and their land was allotted to the tribe of Asher.

23. Kleiman, *DNA and Tradition*, 41. The author thinks that tribal identification comes through the father (Y chromosome) and the mother (mtDNA).

24. In the book of Numbers 26 and 27, Zelophehad had no sons, only daughters. After his death the daughters came before Moses and argued their plight. Because their father had died with no sons, all their rights of inheritance were to be lost and they felt this was unfair. So Moses inquired of the Lord, who gave an exception to the rule. The Lord told Moses that the inheritance could flow through a female if two requirements were fulfilled: first, there could be no male offspring in the family (Numbers 27:8) and, second, the female must marry within her tribe (see Numbers 36:6). In Tephi-Tea's case, her brother Mulek may or may not have been an "heir" son of King Zedekiah because of his location or personal righteousness. Later the Virgin Mary supposedly had no brothers (*HarperCollins Catholic Encyclopedia*, 832–38). Thus she was able to pass on the inheritance of the full House of Judah to Christ. See endnote 54.

25. Totten, *Our Race*, diagram 5.

26. Anderson, *God's Covenant Race*, 18–19.

27. The mtDNA could only pass from Tamar to a daughter and eventually to the Virgin Mary. Otherwise the Judah-Perez line would be extinguished matrilineally, and the Blessed Mary would have been unable to pass the tribal heritage of the house of David to Jesus Christ.

28. Boren and Boren, *Following the Ark of the Covenant*, 37. *Mergech* meant "repository" and denotes a place of buried treasure. These treasures supposedly included the Title Deeds to Palestine and Evidences (believed to be deeds to the Temple mount for the eventual rebuilding and restoration of the Temple). These were probably later in the hands of St. Brendan.

29. Joseph of Arimathea supposedly was a pious, rich, and powerful Israelite leader whose influence upon the inner circle of the Holy Family is impossible to ignore. Joseph was probably from the same fertile Gennesaret (meaning "Gardens of the Princes") plain as Mary Magdalene. Joseph was probably born in the town of "Arimathea" (Arimeth, Ramath, Rameth, Ramathaim Zophin, and afterward Ramula) near Sophim on Mount Ephraim, overlooking the Sea of Galilee (see Davis, *Dictionary of*

the Bible). Formerly it was allotted to the Levites (see anonymous, *The History of the Holy Disciple Joseph of Arimathea* [University of Rochester, Great Britain, ca. 1770]). The Arimeth, Ramah, or Ramath in Ephraimitic lands (Samaria in the time of Jesus) was also the home of the prophet Samuel (1 Samuel 1:1, 19). This was one of the areas that the remnants of the House of Zerah supposedly settled after abandoning hopes of ascension to the scepter of Israel. Thus it was called "a city of the Jews" (Luke 23:50).

30. Allen, *Judah's Sceptre and Joseph's Birthright,* 215.

31. Is it possible that this Y chromosome was perfect (unmutated) from Father Adam and was then the main line of the Patriarchs down to Joseph and Judah, then to David and eventually down to Joseph Smith?

32. Humpherys, *You and I, Who Are We?* 158. She boldly states, "It has been said that the lineage of Jesus Christ came down through the Welsh to Joseph Smith, the Prophet and his line."

33. Birch, *Veritas and the Virgin,* ix, has spoken against this position by asserting that Mary made a "sin offering" (Luke 2:22–24) in the temple: a pair of turtledoves or two young pigeons, as proscribed for mothers in Leviticus 12:8. Yet this does not prove that Mary was a sinner because of this rite. For example, John baptized Christ for "sin," when in fact He had none.

34. McConkie, *Mormon Doctrine,* 375–76. The LDS Church is opposed to mariolatry (excessive veneration of the Virgin Mary), not mariology (the study and doctrine of the Virgin Mary). See Smith, *Answers to Gospel Questions,* 3:182.

35. Tullidge, *Women of Mormondom,* 539. The idea that Mary was pure has nearly universal acceptance; that she was perfectly sinless is another matter.

36. At the Council of Ephesus in A.D. 431, the Virgin Mary was proclaimed "The Mother of God." This possibly vouchsafed her future role as a Mother of God in heaven.

37. This is assumed by the trajectory of the logic established by the following. President Brigham Young in August 1866 gave added credence to this idea: "The man Joseph, the husband of Mary, did not, that we know of, have more than one wife, but Mary the wife of Joseph had another husband" (in *Journal of Discourses,* 19 August 1866, 11:268). Later, the prophet Joseph F. Smith in 1914 confirmed this as an LDS belief: "Now, my little friends, I will repeat again in words as simple as I can and you talk to your parents about it, that God, the Eternal Father is literally the Father of Jesus Christ. Mary was married to Joseph for time. No man could take her

for eternity because she belonged to the Father of her Divine Son" (conference address, 22 September 1914; published in *Box Elder News,* 28 January 1915; also in Clark, *Messages of the First Presidency,* 4:330).

38. That is, at least until after His resurrection.

39. Orr, *50 Most Frequently Asked Bible Questions,* 7.

40. Bernheim, *James, the Brother of Jesus,* 40.

41. They were descendants of the family of Judas Maccabbeus.

42. Allen, *Judah's Sceptre and Joseph's Birthright,* 369. To establish his authority King Herod beheaded the last of the House of Hamon and the entire Sanhedrin. He reigned for thirty-three years, dying just after Christ's birth.

43. Wigoder, *Illustrated Dictionary and Concordance of the Bible,* 775. It is stated in Nehemiah 11:6 that 468 descendants of Perez were mentioned in the list of inhabitants to Jerusalem at the time of Nehemiah. Of course, not all (or any) may have come down from Perez through Jesse and David.

44. One is reminded of the statement, "This is a terrible place," used to describe Rennes-le-Chateau in southern France. See Picknett and Prince, *Templar Revelation,* 181–83. The Latin "Terribilus est locus iste," taken from Genesis 28:17, actually means "Venerable is this place."

45. The settlement of Nazareth was not mentioned by Flavius Josephus when he commanded troops in Galilee. The term is derived from the sect name Nazoreans or Nazorites, of which Samson is said to have been a member.

46. The word *Nazarene* comes from the Hebrew word *nēzer,* meaning "branch, shoot, or sprout of Jesse" (Barnum, *Comprehensive Dictionary of the Bible,* 694). Barnum continues, "Whenever men spoke of Jesus as the Nazarene, they either consciously or unconsciously pronounced one of the names of the predicted Messiah, a name indicative both of His royal descent and His humble condition."

47. Bernheim, *James, the Brother of Jesus,* 13. Mention is also made of another sister, Miriam. See Wieseler, Lange, Meyer, and Alan Alford (Vatican Librarian).

48. Phillips, *Search for the Grail,* 166–67.

49. Talmage, *Jesus the Christ,* 83–90.

50. Schonfield, *Radical Translation and Reinterpretation,* 343. Schonfield's translation of Romans 1:3 is even more compelling: "concerning his Son, Jesus Christ our Master, born in the physical sense of the line of David." Thayer, *New Thayer's Greek-English Lexicon of the New Testament,* 570, notes that this passage means "born by natural generation" and not "by supernatural

power of God, operating in the promise."

51. Bernheim, *James, the Brother of Jesus,* 39.

52. See Erastus Snow, in *Journal of Discourses* (20 January 1878), 19:323b, saying that Luke traces the lineage through the mother. Then Erastus Snow, in *Journal of Discourses* (3 March 1878), 19:271b, misspoke, saying that Luke traces the lineage through the father.

53. Allen, *Judah's Sceptre and Joseph's Birthright,* 206.

54. This daughter's existence is speculated upon by the author. Her place is to add DNA symmetry to the paradigm presented here and later.

55. See Numbers 26–27. See also notes 23 and 24 of this chapter.

56. Brigham Young, in *Journal of Discourses* (9 October 1859), 7:289–90; also Widtsoe, *Discourses of Brigham Young,* 108. See also 2 Nephi 3:6–15.

57. *Basic Catechism* (Boston: By the Daughters of St. Paul, St. Paul Editions, 1984), 36, 48: "Who was Jesus' Mother? Jesus' Mother was the Blessed Virgin Mary, a Jewish girl from Nazareth. Tradition tells us that her parents were Saints Joachim and Ann." Also see Fr. Robert Fox, *The Marian Catechism* (Washington, N.J.: AMI Press, 1985), 17. The *Protevangelium of James* states that Joachim, Mary's father, was a very rich man.

58. This is according to the second-century Protevangelium of James and the gospel of Pseudo-Matthew in the eighth century. Her feast day is July 26. In Talmudic literature, children were born and placed in the temple.

59. Normally, having a daughter rather than a son would have been seen as a curse, except in this remarkable case. The date for this appearance was December 8, the Feast of the Immaculate Conception. Church tradition has Mary's birthday celebrated on September 8, exactly nine months later.

60. It may be that her ancestry came out of Bethlehem because she was a pure daughter of David, whose city was Bethlehem.

61. As noted in Sinclair, *Discovery of the Grail,* 102.

62. Mann, *Isle of Avalon,* 59. Mann says that Mary was born in the Holy Land, but she may have been born in the British West Country and taken to Israel at about the age of three years, where Joseph of Arimathea placed her in temple service.

63. James of Ephesus is attributed to have written the Proto-Evangelium of James, a second-century book known by later copies. This details Mary's life. Instead of the Jerusalem temple, where girls and women could only serve in the Court of the Women and outward, she was taken to the Temple of Diana, according to the Proto-Evangelium. There, young girls worked as temple maidens to serve the goddess until puberty.

64. Rabbi Chaim Richman, "The Red Heifer: The Order of Burning the Red Heifer," (2005), www.templeinstitute.org/red_heifer/burning_red_heifer.htm. The Catholic legend of Joseph of Arimathea placing the orphaned Mary in the temple at age three is wholly unsubstantiated; however, Rabbi Richman reveals that the sprinkling of the priest in the course of the Week of Separation with a solution of the Water of Separation and ashes was done by prepubescent children (usually under the age of eight). The children were born in the temple or orphans placed within the courtyard for the purpose of service. Their children would gather waters from the Shiloach spring or pool. Riding on boards between two oxen, they would gather these waters to purify the priests and the altar.

65. Professor Hugh Nibley notes: "The main theme is Mary's service in the temple, 'behind the veil of the altar,'" where she offered up sacrifices—a strange thing for a woman to do. "Her tunic came down over her seal, and her head-cloth came down over her eyes; she wore a girdle round her tunic, and her tunic was never soiled or torn," as quoted from Budge, *Miscellaneous Coptic Texts in the Dialect of Upper Egypt,* 655; see also Nibley, *Temple and Cosmos,* 316–17.

66. Through His marriage at Cana to Mary Magdalene.

CHAPTER FOUR

THE ORIGIN, BIRTH, AND YOUTH OF CHRIST

*As God the Father begat the fleshy body of Jesus,
so He, before the world began, begat his spirit. As
the body required an earthly Mother, so his spirit
required a heavenly Mother.*

—ORSON PRATT[1]

As in many theological areas Mormonism operates on a different paradigm. Joseph Smith knew that having an accurate conception of who God is was the essential first step: "It is the first principle of the gospel to know for a certainty the [true] character of God."[2] Latter-day Saints see Heavenly Father as a fully human, exalted, and resurrected man.[3]

"The Prophet Joseph feeds our soul: 'God himself was once as we are now. . . .' That is the great secret. If the veil were rent today, and the great God who holds this world in its orbit and who upholds all worlds and all things by His power, was to make himself visible,—I say, if you were to see him today, you would see him like a man."[4]

So who was this Jesus Christ, whose bloodline had been so well protected and nourished? He was the firstborn spirit child of Heavenly Father and Mother for this Round of Eternity or royal generation. However, it was His perfection that vouchsafed for Him the honor of being the Savior of mankind.

His obedience to the will of Heavenly Father led to His being chosen at the Grand Council of Heaven to be the Mortal Messiah on Earth (Abraham 3:22–28). Lucifer challenged Christ's role and waged a war in heaven. With Satan's defeat He and one-third of the "Host of Heaven" were cast to this earth to carry on the evil battle on this earthly frontier.

According to the Grail romances and particularly Wolfram von Eschenbach's *Parzival*, we hear that a middle third of the host of heaven were neutral in the war-in-heaven.[5] The upper third were valiant on the Lord's side. These two-thirds of the spirits were to be born on earth with mortal bodies. Many it is supposed came through certain lineages according to their faithfulness in the first estate or to meet certain purposes of God.

From Adam to Noah, then from Abraham and Jacob, the Grail seed, "the sons of God," though sometimes hidden among "the daughters of men," were traced through the bloodline and priesthood-line of the patriarchs (Genesis 6:2, 4). But after Jacob the chosen bloodline was split in two, between Joseph (Ephraim) and Judah. After this, Israel was never so stable again. Justin Martyr wrote that "Joshua was a figure of Christ," thus relating the Old Testament hero of the tribe of Ephraim to the later Davidian son of the Virgin Mary.[6] Jesus' life was foretold through a living stream of heroes and prophets. The penultimate Grail child, though, was Jesus Christ Himself. That the Grail is a child is explained in the *High Book of the Grail*:

> And there in the centre of the Grail he [Gawain] thought he could see the shape of a child.[7]

Jesus came at the Meridian of Time, as the promised Only Begotten Son of God, the Messiah. This was the mortal coming of the Savior to the World. Jesus Christ's earthly mission was to atone for mankind, heal the curse of the wilderness, and bring forth the kingdom of God. It partially depended upon promised blessings bestowed upon certain tribes of Israel. As with every king of "All Israel" he needed to be of the sceptered lineage.

Jesus' father, Heavenly Father (God), was not a Middle-Eastern Palestinian Jew in the ethnic or racial sense. Remember that the Virgin Mary was probably from the northern climes of the British West Country. It is altogether possible that Jesus probably looked more like the representations of him in Pre-Raphaelite paintings, green eyes and red hair, than what the sculptors and researchers on TV's Discovery Channel created.[8]

The Nordic Christ of official Mormon art, a la "The Christus" of Berthe Thorvaldsen or paintings by Heinrich Hofmann and Carl Bloch, could be more accurate than the well-known Semitic-looking image of Jesus in "Crucifixion of Christ" (1999, oil on canvas), painted by Steve Gjertsen of Minneapolis.

Who was this Jesus of Nazareth? As Bernheim notes, he has been variously portrayed as a Zealot revolutionary, a Nazarite ascetic, an exorcist and magician, a pious and charismatic *hasid*, a Pharisaic disciple of Shammai, an Essene, a Galilean proto-rabbi, a peasant Cynic sage with a social program, a social prophet, an eschatological prophet, a messianic prophet, a subversive wise man, a rustic itinerant, a Davidic Messiah, and a son of God.[9] We now delve deeper into the mystery of Christ's origin, birth, and youth.

JESUS AS THE LEGAL HEIR OF KINGSHIP

And there shall come a Star out of Jacob [Bethlehem, where Jacob set up a pillar] and a Sceptre [a king] shall rise out of Israel.

—NUMBERS 24:17

Weep not: behold the Lion of the tribe of Judah, the root of David . . .

—REVELATION 5:5

I Am the root and the offspring of David, and the bright and morning star.

—REVELATION 22:16

Our story begins in ancient Palestine where the Virgin Mary has just given birth to the Christ child, the promised Messiah. Great care was given to validate his pedigree, for there were many other pretenders to the Messiahship at this time. While it was well known that the Savior would come from the House of David, through exactly which Davidic lineage the Christ would come was unknown. Because of early anti-Christian writers, the authors of the gospels felt compelled to establish Christ's genealogical *bona fides* from Adam to Abraham and finally from Jesse the Bethlehamite to the Messiah himself.

It was common practice in antiquity to compile genealogies, especially amongst the Hebrews, Egyptians, and Chinese. Tribal and priesthood leadership often depended upon lineage. Israel was able to trace Jesus' genealogy to Adam and Eve, our first parents (Numbers 1:2, 18; I Chronicles 5:7, 17). Some biblical genealogies were not exclusively concerned with purely biological descent. Generation was only one means of acquiring a son; adoption was also acceptable, as in the case of Melchizedek and Abraham, Jacob and the sons of Joseph, and more poignantly Jesus. But limitations were placed on the uses of such genealogies:

> *Neither give heed to fables and endless genealogies, which minister questions, rather than godly edifying which is in faith: so do.*
>
> —I TIMOTHY 1:4

> *But avoid foolish questions, and genealogies, and contentions, and strivings about the law; for they are unprofitable and vain.*
>
> —TITUS 3:9

Mormons have been strongly criticized by other Christians for placing such great emphasis on genealogy. Timothy's and Titus's injunction against genealogies prove, in their minds, that Mormonism is not a New Testament church. Of course, LDS Church members counter with the two genealogies of Christ in the New Testament. True genealogies were significant in the Old Testament because of the patriarchal lineages of the house of Israel, particularly the House of David and Levi (see 1 Chronicles 5:1; 9:1; 31:9; Ezra 2:62; 8:1; Nehemiah 7:5, 64). The Matthew and Luke genealogies, proving Christ's descent, are the last and most needful genealogy mentioned in scripture.

Both Timothy and Titus were refuting the "false Jewish tradition that salvation was for the chosen seed as such was known by genealogical recitations."[10] We know that the accurate keeping of genealogies or "generations" was the basis of inheritance, histories, and the census.[11] The Lord specifically commanded that the house of Israel should maintain them, "after their families, by the house of their fathers" (Numbers 1:2) because it was a given that one should choose a wife from the house (tribe) of his father.

Anciently genealogies were patriarchal, "by the house of their fathers," but also matriarchal by the "blood of their mothers." In other words, the male lines of inheritance were listed by genealogy, but the tribe was ascribed through the mother's tribe. Thus a man's genealogy said he was a Benjaminite, but the next generation might have his child listed as an Ephraimite, if the mother of that generation was an Ephraimite, etc. (see Deuteronomy 7:3).[12]

Since the later noncanonical Talmud did not countenance female genealogies, only the male would be traced. Yet mitochondrial DNA (mtDNA), unlike nucleic DNA, is inherited exclusively from the mother and is transferred to the child basically intact from generation to generation. Therefore, in Jesus' case there was no scientific need of a genealogy for Mary, because through her mtDNA, not Joseph's Y chromosome, his *bona fides* would be established. Furthermore, Jesus' Y-chromosome would be transferred intact to his male children.

How could the genealogy of Christ's father be traced, except to simply say "Heavenly Father"? Thus the generations of His earthly adopted father were given instead. The New Testament gives two genealogies of one person—Jesus Christ.[13]

How it was reckoned is a mystery but is of paramount importance. Ultimately the question, "Why a Carpenter's son from Nazareth?" is the ultimate question.

A similar refrain would later be asked, "Why Joe Smith from upstate New York?" It can be shown through study of most great men's biographies that they usually come from out of the way places. Orthodox Christianity finds the genealogies in Matthew and Luke as proof-texts suggesting Jesus' right to be "King of the Jews." Yet they see this ancestral line stopping with Christ. What would prevent it from continuing right on to the present time? What if Joseph Smith Jr. was "King of All Israel" by genealogical descent in the latter days?

If the lineage meant something before Christ, why wouldn't it mean something after him? While many exegetes believe that everything ended with Jesus, there are those who believe it just got started with Him. Of course, if it did continue, it would require that Jesus be married and have children—to which orthodox Christianity would never consent. However, Jewish tradition believed that the Messiah would have children: "The Messiah will die, and his son will become king in his stead."[14] Ultimately this is what happened.

"AND DID THOSE FEET IN ANCIENT TIME"

And did those feet in ancient time,
Walk upon England's mountains
green?
And was the holy Lamb of God,
On England's pleasant pastures seen?

And did the Countenance Divine,
Shine forth upon our clouded hills?
And was Jerusalem builded here,
Among these dark Satanic Mills?

—WILLIAM BLAKE'S
"*JERUSALEM*"[15]

From this English anthem, we are left to wonder, "Did the young Jesus walk in verdant Britain" as unverifiable legends lead us to believe? Furthermore, what significance would this have had upon his genealogy? Though the entire Glastonbury mystique begins with Joseph of Arimathea taking the juvenile Jesus 3,300 miles from Jerusalem to Britain, can we rest our faith upon this assertion?[16] While these were the cloaked silent years of Jesus' life, can we fill them with tales of adventures in the mists of Avalon?

These "infancy" years have been filled by apocryphal tales recounting Christ's exploits in the mysterious lands of the Baltic Sea, Persia, India, Tibet, Egypt, etc.[17] Yet it is still a fascinating prospect to ponder that Jesus may have visited Britain, possibly the birthplace of his mother and uncle, sometime between A.D. 13 and A.D. 20. It was probably at age seventeen that Jesus came, because in Celtic custom a boy becomes a man at this age.[18] As we have seen from previous chapters, such a possibility might be a likelihood, when contemplated deeply. A number of writers could see the possibilities: "In Somerset the story was that Christ and Joseph came by ship to Tarshish and stayed in Summerland, another name for the country, and in a place called Paradise."[19] "The [tradition] says that Jesus and Joseph of Arimathea stayed in the mining village of Priddy, north of Glastonbury, in the Mendip Hills of Somerset County."[20]

Yet the fact that the earliest monks of Glastonbury "never so much as hint" that Christ came to Avalon is, in the minds of many, evidence of the falsehood of the claim.[21]

The flaw in this assumption is that the monks could even speak their own mind for there was an aura of obfuscation about. Celtic monks, when the Roman Church predominated with the Anglo-Saxons, from the seventh and eighth centuries, were painfully obliged not to make mention of a distinctive British Christian church before Catholicism. This would have threatened the primacy of the Roman Church and put monk or laity at risk.

When Abbott Thurstan confronted the Saxon monks at Glastonbury in the eighth century, many lost their lives, thus influencing thought and commentary within the monastery. Throughout the centuries more expunging of the record occurred. The suppression of a rich Celtic oral tradition subsided for a few hundred years, only to reemerge after the Reformation. These legends exist only because they could not be entirely stamped out and have again come to the surface in residual form.

They are now being dealt with by exegetes willing to understand that oral tradition, or *pericopes*, is not always un-factual, and legend often contains hidden knowledge. Unfortunately, "no lost manuscript has been dug up in Glastonbury, St. Just or Looe," writes Celtic scholar Gordon Strachan. "Neither has anyone added to the scraps of oral tradition gathered by eccentric Anglican vicars earlier this century."[22] Modern archaeology and recent analysis of existing materials has brought us a little closer to the truth regarding Joseph of Arimathea and Jesus as found in primeval Britain tales. Literary inferences and circumstantial evidence have brought us from plausibility to possibility when dealing with these exciting "monkish fables."

There are numerous British traditions, collected by nineteenth-century Anglican clergyman, of Jesus traveling to Britain as a youth with his great-uncle, Joseph.[23] The Rev. H. A. Lewis claims that Joseph came by boat to St. Just-in-Roseland, Falmouth, or St. George's Island off Looe. Rev. C. C. Dobson suggests that he came to Glastonbury up the River Brue from Burnham or Uphill on the Somerset coast.[24]

Then the fine harbor at the mouth of the Camel River in Cornwall is still called "Jesus' Well." Archaeologist and Reverend Nicholas R. Mann provides interesting comment on this trip:

> Christ stopped in several places when he returned with his uncle to the home of his grandmother [Anna]. He was said to have cured a leper colony at Culbone near Porlock in north

Devon, to have founded the ancient churches at Godney and Christon in Somerset, and to have visited the centre of the lead and silver trade at Priddy on the Mendips overlooking Avalon. Whenever local folk wished to be adamant about something, they would say, "As sure as Christ was at Priddy![25]

Even the generally skeptical Geoffrey Ashe in his monumental work, *Mythology of the British Isles,* continues along the same lines:

> Some say that Jesus himself visited Britain during the hidden years before his public ministry. He was in Somerset, perhaps for an appreciable time. The Druids were prepared for him because they had a god Esus or Yesu. On the future site of Glastonbury Abbey, he put up a small building which was his home for a while. He walked over the Mendip Hills to the north where Priddy now is. He may also have been in Cornwall, where the Jesus Well near the mouth of the Camel is said to commemorate him, and there are scraps of folklore about his visit in other places, such as St. Just-in-Roseland.[26]

Somerset tradition asserts that they "came to Summerland in a ship of Tarshish and sojourned at the place called Paradise" for at least two trips.[27] Old ordinance survey maps from the district around Burnham show that this area in Somerset was called Paradise. The Isle of Tarshish is Britain in general, and more specifically to the Isle of Avalon. Another name for this area is Glastonbury, known to the Celts

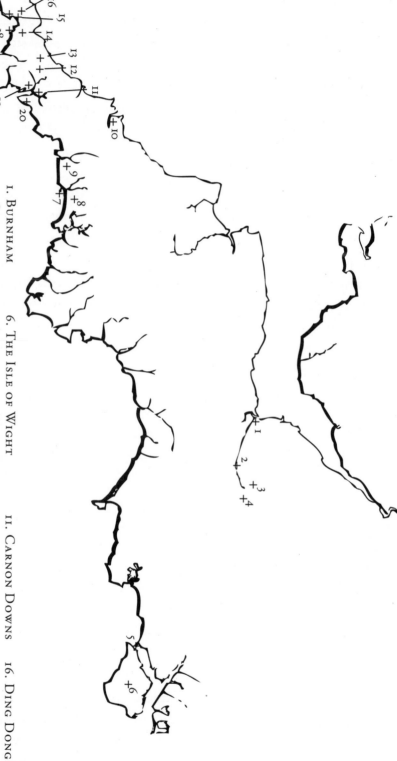

FIGURE 2
JESUS IN ENGLAND

1. Burnham
2. Glastonbury
3. Priddy
4. Pilton Hills
5. Hurst Castle
6. The Isle of Wight
7. Lammana or Looe Island
8. Looe
9. Portruan by Fowey
10. Jesus Well
11. Carnon Downs
12. St. Day
13. Redruth
14. Nancledra
15. Penzance
16. Ding Dong
17. Mousehole
18. St. Michael's Mount
19. Falmouth
20. St. Just-in-Rowland

as the Happy Island of the Blest, cut off from the turmoil of the world by its girdle of marsh and mere.

Christ's long absence from His Palestinian homeland may explain why John the Baptist, although a relative of Jesus, seems not to recognize him when they meet in the river Jordan.[28] Moreover, when the Elders ask, "Is not this the carpenter's son?" (Matthew 35:56), their question signals that they hardly knew anything about him, as if he had dropped out of sight for a long period. This somewhat long period of absence may be the time when he was "traveling."

THE YOUNG JESUS IN BRITAIN

But why and to what purpose would Jesus have come to this backward bywater? In the face of such criticisms the answer to "Why?" becomes the story itself. If, indeed, the young Savior actually visited Britain, it would portend a significant role for this land as a designated Holy Grail territory. There seem to be five concurrent ideas for Joseph of Arimathea to bring the youthful Christ with him to Western Britain, the land of the Druids.[29]

- *For travel and work experience in his great-uncle's tin mines.*

The main reason given by the Anglican reverends for Christ's sojourn to Britain was to work in the tin mines. However, this was inadequate to explain any real motive for traveling to such a remote wilderness. That he would wander to faraway Britain for on-the-job training smelting tin seems rather unconvincing. Of course, it might be said that if the family had no idea of his true mission, then the possibility of inheriting his uncle's tin mines might seem a compelling enough reason. However, his mother Mary had understood from the annunciation of the Archangel Gabriel (Noah) that Jesus had a special mission far beyond any commercial prospects.

Unfortunately, all early writers on the subject are able to say only that he went to work at the tin mines in the family business overseas in Britain. Perhaps this was ostensibly the stated reason he went, but its very inconsequentiality begs further justification. Was he just biding his time until his Messianic mission began or was this valuable time used wisely?

Sabine Baring-Gould, however, could find no other reason:

> Another Cornish story is to the effect that Joseph of Arimathea came in a boat to Cornwall, and brought the child Jesus with him, and the latter taught him how to extract the tin and purge it of its wolfram[ite, ore]. This story possibly grew out of the fact that the Jews under the Angevin kings farmed the tin of Cornwall.[30]

- *Visit His extended family and do genealogy*

A less trivial motive for the youthful Jesus to come to this area was to visit His relatives and to study His genealogy. If His grandmother Anna was born in Glastonbury, then He certainly would have extended family to meet, enjoy, and learn from. Rev. Nicholas R. Mann recounts:

> The folk traditions of the Southwest [Britain] support the tradition of Christ's coming to Avalon. Some say he came to see the homeland of his mother's mother, St. Anne.[31]

Most of Jesus' family in Galilee was from Joseph the Carpenter, His stepfather's side. Not being blood kin, it is altogether possible that Jesus desired to travel with His great-uncle to His mother's family's ancestral homeland. And what would have precluded the now widowed Virgin Mary from accompanying her son and Joseph of Arimathea to her homeland?

This explanation makes sense for a couple of reasons. Jesus was obligated to prepare this area to receive the gospel and to search after His own "kindred dead."

Like others of the human race, He too was accountable for the salvation of His ancestors. Perhaps He went throughout Cornwall and Somerset gathering genealogy of His family tree.[32] If there existed ancient Jewish colonies in Britain possessing the full-Judah lineage, then Jesus would have had a fruitful expedition to this arcadia. The book of His pedigree would unlock knowledge of His own family heritage and the history of Israel and Britain as well. This may well be the famous Grail book of Jesus Christ: "The Book of the Holy Vessel" treated in a later chapter.

The anonymous eighth-century Scottish text *The Chronicle of Helinandus* was later rewritten by a French monk of Froidmont in 1204. In this book Froidmont states that the Grail was the *escuele* or dish/cup (Latin, *gradales*: "by degrees") that Jesus used at the Last Supper.[33] Froidmont's French translation of *Grand Saint-Graal* also notes that there was a book with a pedigree or genealogy of Jesus Christ. The story says that on the eve of Good Friday in A.D. 717, Christ appeared to the hermit Waleran and said:

> This is the book of thy descent,
> *Here is the Book of the Holy Grail,*
> *Here begin the terrors,*
> Here begin the marvels.[34]

Norma L. Goodrich assumes that it was Christ's genealogy back to Solomon. She states, "To think that there may once have been a book of the Bible actually written by Jesus Christ, in His own handwriting, and that it contained his genealogy, brings shivers to the reader."[35] But perhaps the book was Christ's genealogy forward to at least the author of *The Chronicle of Helinandus* in the eighth century.

Lest we think that Jesus was involved in "vain genealogies" let us consider that "baptism for the dead" was a known practice of the primitive Church after its establishment by Christ. Such vicarious work was noted by the Apostle Paul, who wrote, "Else what shall they do which are baptized for the dead, if the dead rise not at all? Why are they then baptized for the dead?" (1 Corinthians 15:29). It is probable that the ordinance of baptism for the dead and other temple rituals were later performed for the family of Jesus from the genealogy collected by Him at this early date.[36]

- *Be an Elias figure to His family*

At least as important as genealogy was the preparing of His family's land for the receipt of the gospel. This would be greatly aided by a visit from the Savior Himself. This was not His "official" mission per se, but rather a personal mission to those of His own family tree, not to greater Britain at large. The beneficial effects of his presence would have been immeasurable, and the later work of Joseph of Arimathea and the Holy Family would have been enhanced by Jesus' personal visit.

In a true sense, he was acting as an Elias or forerunner for the reception of the gospel light in this small part of the Lord's vineyard. This was asserted by the early chronicler Gildas III (A.D. 516–570), when he wrote the immortal line, "Christ, the True Sun" afforded His light to Britain (D&C 93:2).[37] This message was reiterated in the words attributed to the Celtic bard Taliesin, about A.D. 550, who explained: "Christ, the word from the beginning, was from the beginning our Teacher, and we never lost his teachings."[38]

- *To build a wattle church (booth)*

Another possible purpose for the young Jesus' journey to Glastonbury was to build a small wattle church, which he dedicated to his mother, the Virgin Mary, wattle being a plating or interweaving of reeds, twigs, or green boughs to form a lattice framework or wall to help build a structure. Over this network is often pushed in daub, a mud or clay that completes the hut or humble dwelling. It was the simplest and most unpretentious structure, a shanty for peasants.[39] While it was unassuming to the world, its importance to the Grail story is immeasurable.

Although the account of Jesus' building a little wattle church is captured in several legendary sources, its significance has never been explained until now.[40] This little structure might relate to the Festival of Tabernacles, or *Sukkoth* (Succoth meaning tabernacles, booths or huts), where a wattle-and-daub booth was made from "the boughs of green trees." It would have been set up during the Autumnal Equinox during the month of Tishri.[41] Erecting such a "little church" could actually have been a little "booth" built by Jesus in accordance with an ancient Hebrew *mitzvah* (law or performance) for a son. At a certain age, a Jewish son was to build a booth and dedicate it to his parents, usually at their birthplace.[42]

Christ building such a booth in England further suggests it was the location of Mary's own birthplace. It also magnifies the significance of the site as where the "mother of God" took flesh in a mortal tabernacle.[43] It would also be symbolically significant because Jesus, "God Incarnate," actually sat in this booth. This would make sense, because in the Festival of Tabernacles, a wattle booth (church) symbolized, according to the Rabbis, "Where God comes to dwell on earth in the flesh."[44]

Most believe that the booth relates to the Israelites in the wilderness exodus, but they dwelt in tents, not booths.[45] Perhaps a better idea rests with a place east of the Jordan where Jacob, on his return from Mesopotamia after crossing the Jabbok (Genesis 32:22, 33:17), built himself a house, with booths (*succoth*) for his cattle. It may symbolically represent the manger, a hut for animals, perhaps similar to the one Jesus was

born in. Thus the statement, "Where God comes to dwell on earth in the flesh" has added resonance.[46]

We first know about this area of Glastonbury from St. Augustine of Canterbury, who went to Britain at the behest of Pope Gregory the Great about A.D. 596–597.[47] A Roman monk, he became the first Archbishop of Canterbury and with forty missionaries converted the Anglo-Saxons. He was, however, unable to come to an understanding with the British Christians, who were somewhat tinctured with Druidism. It was Augustine's letter to the Pope that provides us with an source document regarding this unique wattle building's divine foundation:

> In the Western confines of Britain, there is a certain royal island, called in the ancient speech Glastonia . . . dedicated to the most sacred of deities. In it the earliest neophytes of the Catholic rule, God guiding them, found [discovered] a church, not built by art of man they say, but prepared by God himself for the salvation of mankind, which church, the heavenly Builder himself declared—by many miracles and many mysteries of healing—he had consecrated to himself and to the holy Mary, Mother of God.[48]

These "neophytes of the Catholic rule" were probably Sts. Fagan (Faganus) and Dyfan (Deruvianus), who visited the Vetusta Ecclesia ("Old Church" of Glastonbury) in A.D. 166–167.[49] They were supposedly requested by Good King Lucius from Pope Eleutherius in Rome, who at this early date maintained good relations with their northern brethren.[50]

A record of Fagan's and Dyfan's journey might have been the source of St. Augustine's information when he visited the Old Church in Glastonbury with his companion Paulinus. In his earlier book, *The Acts of the Kings of England*, historian William of Malmesbury notes that about A.D. 597, Augustine left his assistant Paulinus behind to cover the Old Church with protective boards in order to preserve it.[51]

In another version or translation of this letter, St. Augustine claimed that the Old Church, was "constructed by no human art, but by the hands of Christ himself, for the salvation of his people."[52] The Archbishop's testimony vouchsafes the existence of an early tradition of Christ himself building a structure. This tradition is strengthened by another story of St. David, the patron saint of Wales. He had come to rededicate the Old Church in Glastonbury, not many years before St. Augustine of Canterbury arrived.[53] St. David had a night vision in which Christ sternly warned him not to do so because he had already dedicated it to his mother.[54]

This little building may have employed elements of sacred architecture and esoteric wisdom. We know that later versions of the structure incorporated principles of sacred geometry and divine symmetry. Was Jesus "the heavenly Builder," as claimed by St. Augustine? Certainly in the *Domesday Book* of 1086 it is recorded that "the Domus Dei [Home of God], in the great monastery of Glastonbury, is called the Secret of the Lord."[55] What esoteric secret is found therein?

Is it possible that the little wattle structure built by Christ was more than just a church or booth? We may cite William of Malmesbury, who describes the Old Church (*vetusta ecclesia*), a later version of this same building, in his book The Acts of the Kings of England: "We may note in the pavement on either side, stones carefully placed, either in triangles or squares, and sealed with lead; beneath which, if I believe some holy secret to be held, I am doing no harm to religion."[56]

Again we quote Malmesbury: "The church of which we are speaking—from its antiquity called by the Angles, by way of distinction '*Ealde Chiche*,' that is the "Old Church" of wattle work at first, savoured

somewhat of heavenly sanctity even from its very foundation, and exhaled it over the whole country, claiming superior reverence, though the structure was mean."[57]

- *To study at the Druidic learning centers.*[58]

> *"Jesus is my Druid."*
>
> —WORDS OF ST. COLUMBIA[59]

It is said that Jesus as a youth went to study in India and Nepal in the Himalayas. Then afterward, he went to "Britashtan, the seat of religious learning."[60] Could Britashtan be Britain, a place of higher spiritual learning? What secret was held in this far-flung hermitage? Could it be that Glastonbury, like Chartres Cathedral in France, was one of the so-called colleges of Druidic philosophy with thousands of students mentioned by Gildas?[61] Julius Caesar wrote of the Druids: "Many come, in their own right, to entrust their education in their [the Druids'] hands, but many are sent by their parents and relatives; it is said that they learn a very great number of verses there by heart; thus some remain in school for as long as twenty years."[62]

Often a full score of years was required to master the full Druidic curriculum of astronomy, arithmetic, geometry, medicine, poetry, law, judging, natural philosophy, and public speaking.[63] Ammianius quoted first-century BC philosopher Timagenes, who says the Druids investigated "problems of things secret and sublime."[64] Diodorus Siculus said they were "philosophers [lovers of Sophia] and men learned in religious affairs."[65]

Caesar continues: "They have also much knowledge of the stars and their motion, of the size of the world and of the earth, of natural philosophy, and of the powers and spheres of action of the immortal gods, which they discuss and hand down to their young students.[66]

Dio Chrystostom in the first century A.D. equated Druids with the Persian magi, Egyptian priests, and Indian Brahmins.[67] Caesar also wrote that their learning was mainly through oral tradition and memorization, rather than from books. However, the Druids did have libraries, for the medieval manuscript the *Yellow Book of Lecan* describes how St. Patrick burned 180 books of the Druids.[68]

But like Joseph Smith Jr., who reached the 33rd degree in Freemasonry very quickly, perhaps Jesus learned the Druidic curriculum in far less than twenty years. Public speaking in story and parable was very important to the Druids. More than other societies or cultures, they used this method to instruct and inspire. The scriptures, generally, do not use parables as much as Jesus did. He may have learned and practiced this system while with the Druids.[69]

There was something simpatico with Jesus and this verdant land. For example, we know that the Druids taught a form of the doctrine of the atonement and the need of a Savior. They even possessed this messiah's name, "Yesu," which was the same as the young Jesus' name.[70] "It is a remarkable fact," writes Rev. C. C. Dobson, "that Druidism never opposed Christianity, and eventually became voluntarily merged with it."[71] History professor at Oxford University Karen Ralls-MacLeod and co-author Ian Robertson make similar observations: "St. Augustine declared that their philosophy almost exactly approached that of Christian monotheism, as the Druids believed in one divine spirit. . . . The Druids held a particular reverence for the number three."[72]

An article written in 1985 entitled, "Did Jesus Go to High School in Britain?" proposes in its very title that the Son of God actually studied in the West Country.[73]

He supposedly received an education in Britain and it served Him well, for later John 7:15 notes that "the Jews marvelled, saying, How knoweth this man letters, having never learned?" In fact, Rev. Dobson concludes that Christ studied Mosaic law in combination with Druidic oral secrets at Glastonbury: "In Britain He would be free from the tyranny of Roman oppression, the superstition of Rabbinical misrepresentation, and the grossness of pagan idolatry, and its bestial, immoral, customs. In Druid Britain He would live among people dominated by the highest and purest ideals, the very ideals He had come to proclaim.[74]

Dobson had studied the antiquarian R. W. Morgan ("Iolo Morganwg"), who had been influenced by Edward Williams (1747–1826). In speculative British-Israelite fashion, they believed that Druidic theology was quite similar to the patriarchal religion of the Old Testament. This present author speculates that the Druids were an apostate body of priests from the combined tribes of Judah, of both the House of Zerah and Perez. They believed in an elevated level of secret teachings, though not of the typical gnostic sort through Pythagoras. Of one thing we are certain, the Druids were not idol worshippers, for few have been found in Scotland and Britain.

Cassell's *History of England* suggests that "the Druidical rites and ceremonies in Britain were almost identical with the Mosaic ritual." To this, Gordon Strachan aptly announces, "The question was rhetorical. Jesus had come to Britain in order to return to the source of his distant forbearers' religion."[75] Some contend that the Druids were highly influenced by the Greeks, but Julius Caesar noted that the Druidic discipline "developed first in Britain, and thence was introduced to Gaul; and to this day those who wish to pursue their studies of it more deeply, usually go to Britain for the purpose."[76]

Here we have it, the *raison d'etre* for Jesus coming to Glastonbury. He wished to pursue megalithic cultural wisdom, from the days of Enoch, at its very source. He desired to inquire deeper into the sacred architecture of geometry, proportion, measure, number, weight, and symmetry. However, Jesus did not come unprepared to this university of high learning.

There is a distinct possibility that Jesus' adopted father, Joseph the carpenter, was a master builder or *tekton*, or a wise teacher.[77] Joseph might have been a designer or architect in Sephoris, the gentile Galilean capital, which was being massively rebuilt by the Jews during the time of Jesus.[78] It was only six kilometers or a one-hour walk to the northwest of Nazareth, putting it in reach of the Holy Family. Joseph the carpenter, therefore, would have been a "wise-man." The word meant something well beyond a mere carpenter, but a designer, construction engineer or architect, who could build or design a temple, like Hyrum Abif.

Far from being a poor peasant, Joseph was probably of some means. The sacrifice of two turtledoves (Luke 2:22–24) after the birth of Christ did not denote that Joseph and Mary were poor, but as Nazirites they had taken a vow of poverty.[79] Perhaps one of the reasons that Jesus would later express solidarity with the *anawin* (the "little poor") was because of this upbringing. Alfred Edersheim elaborates: "We remember that the mother of Jesus availed herself of that provision for the poor, when at the same time she presented in the Temple the Royal Babe, her first son. On bringing her offering, she would enter the Temple through 'the gate of the first-born,' and stand in waiting at the Gate of Nicanor, from the time that the incense was kindled on the golden altar."[80]

Mary's firstborn was then redeemed by the Temple priests for five shekels of silver, two benedictions, and hymns. "The Rabbis lay it down that redemption-money," notes Edersheim, "was only paid for a son who was the firstborn of his mother and who was 'suitable for the priesthood,' that is, had no disqualifying bodily blemishes."[81]

Of course, Jesus was highly qualified for the priesthood.

We can easily believe that Joseph the carpenter was an observant Jew, learned in the Law and a scrupulous observer of all the instructions (*halakhah*). As such, he would have certainly taught his sons well. Jesus' surprisingly sophisticated teachings in the Temple at the age of twelve could have possibly come by the tutelage of His elder stepbrother James the Just. James was also highly educated, as established by his book in the New Testament, which was considered advanced in the principles of Greek rhetoric. James' education certainly would have predated Jesus' possible visit to Glastonbury.

It was by no accident that pious, learned, and charismatic men of antiquity such as Honi the "Circle-Drawer" and geometrist Hanina ben Dosa, came from Galilee.[82] Jesus certainly knew about the mysterious number for Phi (1.618), which is the Golden Section or the ultimate Divine Proportion. The southeast entrance to Chartres Cathedral, "Door of the Knights," is presided over by Jesus Christ. Some scholars believe that Christ in this tympanum, "Holds a closed book containing 'the exact proportions of the Golden Number.' "[83]

It was also no accident that the pre-Druids and Druid "astronomer-priests" were among the elite class of scholars from Christ's own ancestral homeland—Britain. There seems to be a connection between Galilee and Britain through the united Zerah-Perez line. There is something in the line that promotes true intellectualism and interest in proportion, number, geometry, sacred architecture, and order. There seems to be a deep-seated connection of Christ with the British Isles.

Unlike the "transmitter" Pythagoras, we may see that in finding the roots of Neolithic-megalithic wisdom, Christ was also an originator and a transmitter of insight based on number.[84] Britain is one of the "chosen lands"—a hotspot of intellectual inquiry and talent, a perfect place for His line or posterity to find root. Gordon Strachan records:

If this were the case, then it would have been very important for him [Jesus] to come to Hyperborea-Britain, for to do so would have been to tap into the fount of Pythagorean-Apollonion wisdom. It would have been to return to the source of this mighty river that had flowed south over the millennia spreading its life-giving waters over all the known world. It would have been to acknowledge the origin of the truth he had come to embody. It would have been, humanly speaking, to return home.[85]

He might be termed *Hyperborean Apollo* because of his association with the land of the Hyperboreans (upper north; such as Britain) and the Sun (Son) God, who is Jesus Christ himself.[86] It is possible that Jesus traveled widely in the British Isles, going to Tara Hills and Newgrange in Ireland, the temple in mid-Wales, Stonehenge or Avebury in Wiltshire, the Orkney islands, the Druid strongholds on the islands of Anglesey and Iona (*Inis Druineach*), and Callanish on the Isle of Lewis in Scotland. He studied and understood.

Now that He was educated in all facets of archaic learning He needed to ascend into the bridal chamber of even higher wisdom. This brings us back to the *Hieros Gamos* (sacred marriage) and the Grail lineage, which would eventually grow where it was planted—in Britain.

Notes

1. Orson Pratt, *The Seer* 1 (October 1853): 158–59.
2. Joseph Smith, as quoted by Hinckley, *Faith, the Essence of True Religion,* 20. See Ehat and Cook, *Words of Joseph Smith,* 340, where the Prophet says, "If men do not comprehend the character of God they do not comprehend themselves, what kind of being is God?"
3. Brigham Young said, "God is a man in form like unto ourselves, and I expect His society, or the society of His children, the Prophets, Kings, Lords, Princes, Queens, Goddesses, just the same as in this world." See Brigham Young, in "A Family Meeting in Nauvoo: Minutes of a Meeting of the Richards and Young Families Held in Nauvoo, Ill., 8 January, 1845," *Utah Genealogical and Historical Magazine* 11 (July 1920): 114.
4. Joseph Smith Jr., King Follett Discourse (7 April 1844). See Ehat and Cook, *Words of Joseph Smith,* 344, 357.
5. Barber, *Holy Grail,* 81. "Those who stood on neither side when Lucifer and the Trinity began to contend." See also Godwin, *Holy Grail,* 53, 141. The possibility of neutrality of the Blacks in heaven and thus their being denied the priesthood was once espoused by some in the LDS Church. Since 1978 it is quite unpopular and politically incorrect to say that premortal valiance had any bloodline or lineage implications or that there were neutral spirits in the war in heaven. The lower third followed Lucifer and were cast out of heaven to this earth without the right to gain a physical body. The position of the neutral third during their mortal probation has yet to be determined.
6. Justin Martyr, *Dialogue with Trypho,* chapter 113, as quoted in Freke and Gandy, *Jesus and the Goddess,* 215 ff40.
7. *High Book of the Holy Grail* 79; Perlesvaus, I, 118–20, as quoted in Barber, *Holy Grail,* 49.
8. Discovery Channel, "How Did Jesus Look?" September 2004.
9. Bernheim, *James, the Brother of Jesus,* 104. This would also include a number of different combinations of these descriptions.
10. McConkie, *Doctrinal New Testament Commentary,* 3:127. In the latter days, genealogical research is for the salvation of the dead, not arrogant certifications of salvation for the living.
11. The false and foolish genealogies mock true and meaningful ones. For instance, LDS families that claim lineage from Charlemagne, Thor, Odin, and King David are pretentious. These vain and fruitless genealogies are a mockery and should be avoided. Those that unite and help redeem the dead are most useful.
12. Kleiman, *DNA and Tradition,* 41. I believe that Kleiman has it exactly backwards.
13. Small genealogies were often given in the New Testament, which state parentage or offspring with one generation, such as "John and James the sons of Zebedee." However, except for Matthew and Luke, lengthy genealogies were

never given because these scriptures dealt with but one or two generations.

14. Greenstone, *Messiah Idea in Jewish History,* 147.

15. William Blake (1757–1827) was an English artist, poet, and visionary of the late eighteenth and early nineteenth centuries. His poem "Jerusalem" enunciated Blake's desire to see a new Jerusalem built on the ashes of the Industrial age, being vouchsafed by Christ's own visit. The rest of the poem goes:

Bring me my bow of burning gold!
Bring me my arrows of desire!
Bring me my spear! O clouds unfold!
Bring my Chariot of Fire!

I will not cease from mental fight,
Nor shall my sword sleep in my hand
Till we have built Jerusalem
In England's green and pleasant land.

The Mormon Tabernacle Choir sang Blake's "Jerusalem" in London in June 1998. Craig Jessop, the Choir leader, had served a mission in Britain and chose this song, an anthem in Britain. It was also sung as an encore.

16. Archibald F. Bennett, "Did Joseph of Arimathea Come to Britain?" *Deseret News,* 24 September 1932, 3.

17. One of these tales, Jesus in India, is an English version of Masih Hindustan Mein, an Urdu treatise written by the "Holy Founder" of the Ahmadi in Islam, Hazrat Mirza Ghulam Ahmad(as) (1835–1908).

18. Ralls-MacLeod and Robertson, *Quest for the Celtic Key,* 48. The number 17 plays an important part throughout Irish and Vedic mythology. Jewish custom has 18 being adulthood.

19. Sinclair, *Discovery of the Grail,* 17.

20. Prophet, *Mysteries of the Holy Grail,* xliv-xlv.

21. Castleden, *King Arthur,* 196. See William of Malmesbury, who visited Glastonbury in 1129–39 and wrote *De Antiquitate.* Unfortunately, nothing from this year survived, only an annotated version from 1247. It followed the late twelfth-century Glastonbury promotional campaign. According to Castleden, *King Arthur,* 196, "William of Malmesbury provides us with good evidence that Glastonbury's past was being deliberately manipulated, glamorized and falsified in the late twelfth century."

22. Strachan, *Jesus the Master Builder,* 40.

23. These are recorded by the Anglican clergymen of Celtic sympathies: Rev. R. W. Morgan's *St. Paul in Britain;* Rev. Lionel Smithett Lewis's *St. Joseph of Arimathea at* *Glastonbury;* Rev. C. C. Dobson's booklet, *Did Our Lord Visit Britain As They Say in Cornwall and Somerset?* Rev. Sabine Baring-Gould's *Book of Cornwall;* George F. Jowett's *Drama of the Lost Disciples;* and E. Raymond, *The Traditions of Glastonbury.* However, Daniel C. Scavone's *Joseph of Arimathea* states that Joseph of Arimathea never went to Britain but that the royal palace complex in Edessa (today Urfa, Turkey) in Asia Minor was called "Britio Edessenorium."

24. Strachan, *Jesus the Master Builder,* 43.

25. Mann, *Isle of Avalon,* 59.

26. Also quoted in Ashe, *Avalonian Quest,* 145.

27. Anonymous, "The Introduction of Christianity into Britain" (April-June 2002), typescript copy of MS in the author's possession. Perhaps the first trip he went as a young boy and then as a young man and resident of Glastonbury? The question may be asked, "Did Christ visit Britain after His Resurrection?" Perhaps the British Isles were a part of the "other sheep" Nephi predicted would inhabit the isles of the sea at the time of the Crucifixion (see 2 Nephi 16:4, 17:4, 19:10).

28. See Taylor, *Coming of the Saints,* 20: "John the Baptist was Jesus' second cousin, James and John the sons of Zebedee, were second cousins also, their mother Salome, or Mary Salome, being (like Elizabeth) first cousin to the Blessed Virgin, while, according to Hegesippus, Cleopas, who married any Mary (Mary the wife of Cleopas) was the brother of St. Joseph."

29. The Druids were the priests of the early Celts of Britain, Gaul, and Germany. They supposedly possessed advanced knowledge of geometry, natural philosophy, and theology. They may have arrived in Britain between 1200 and 600 B.C. and remained until they merged with Christianity. The author thinks that they are a culturally advanced remnant of the ancient Hebrews, perhaps of the Full-Judah line mentioned above.

30. Baring-Gould, *Book of Cornwall,* 57; see also Prophet, *Mysteries of the Holy Grail,* xliv. The quotation continues: "When the tin is flashed [in smelting], then the tinner shouts 'Joseph was in the tin trade!' which is possibly a corruption of 'St. Joseph to the tinner's aid.'"

31. Mann, *Isle of Avalon,* 59. He says that Mary was born in the Holy Land, but she was probably born in the West Country and then taken to Israel.

32. Cornwall and parts of Somerset originally spoke Welsh, according to Blake and Lloyd, *Keys to Avalon,* 48.

33. Sinclair, *Discovery of the Grail,* 56. The dish or plate was brought to the table during various stages (Latin, *gradus*) or courses of a meal.

34. Godwin, *Holy Grail,* 10. The monk was undoubtedly of

the direct bloodline of Christ; otherwise why would the Savior say, "thy descent?" The author of *The History of the Grail* was this anonymous hermit who had a mystic vision. He was given a small book from a man identified as the Fountain of Wisdom and the Perfect Master. The copied book became *The History of the Grail*. The Grail was called the literal Word of God (Jesus Christ?).

35. Goodrich, *Holy Grail*, 5.

36. These ordinances were probably not performed in a temple, given that they did not have much access to the Jerusalem temple of Herod (D&C 124:30). But perhaps they were performed in an ancient equivalent to the Endowment House.

37. Taylor, *Coming of the Saints*, 141.

38. As quoted in Strachan, *Jesus the Master Builder*, 47.

39. Jowett, *Drama of the Lost Disciples*, 135, "In the Glastonbury tradition of 'Our Lady's Dowry,' bequeathed to her by Jesus Himself, the 'Dowry' being the little wattle temple Jesus built with His own hands at Avalon."

40. The church in one form or another lasted until after the Norman invasion when it was accidentally burned in the year A.D. 1184. Glastonbury Abbey was built over the site.

41. The Festival of Tabernacles was one of the three main annual pilgrim festivals. The booths were, according to the Mishna, to stand alone, not leaning against any building or under a tree. They were not to be covered with skins or cloth, but rather green willow boughs, sticks and reeds. There was to be no roof, but open sky, for man looks to the heaven for protection. The Festival of the Tabernacles was a harvest festival of thanksgiving and a time when the Israelites dwelt in tents in the wilderness. It was observed between the 15 and 22 of Tishri in the autumn, this would be about 23 September to 1 October, or the Equinox.

42. Robert Paxton (June 1999) has consulted several Rabbis who say that it was either age 18 or 20 for a young man to build a booth for Sucoth.

43. Two observances relating to the Feast of Tabernacles not found in the Old Testament but found in the New Testament are: the ceremony of pouring out some water of the pool of Shiloam (Shelah, Shiloah, John 9:7, 11) and the display of some great lights in the Court of the Women. This last observance probably started with Christ, honoring his mother's service in the Court of the Women when she was a young girl. Two of the four lamp stands in the Court were lighted and many in the assembly carried flambeaux. See Barnum, *Comprehensive Dictionary of the Bible*, 1082.

44. This is according to a number of Rabbis consulting over the Internet with Robert Paxman of Springville (June 1999).

45. See Wigoder, *Illustrated Dictionary and Concordance of the Bible*, 965.

46. Another idea expands the significance of the succoth, booth or hut. It is the marital connotations it carried that relate to our discussion. Nibley, *Message of the Joseph Smith Papyri*, 175, explains: "Throughout the ancient world the ritual marriage at the Solstice or Equinox takes place in a ritual booth of green boughs, a fixture never missing from the 'great assembly.'" The seven-day Festival of Tabernacles culminated with a "Solemn Assembly" on the eighth day. See Wigoder, *Illustrated Dictionary and Concordance of the Bible*, 965. Could the number 7 associated with the marriage nuptials have to do with this same wattle booth?

47. St. Augustine of Canterbury died about A.D. 605. He should not be confused with the more famous, St. Augustine of Hippo who lived between A.D. 354 and 430.

48. Augustine's letter to Pope Gregory is recorded by Henrici Spelman in his report, Lecreta, Leges, Constitutiones, In Re Ecclesiarium Orbis Britannici (London, 1639). The word "found" may have two meanings; they "discovered" it or they "made" it. I tend to concur with the former. This has been widely quoted in nearly every British-Israel publication. The present location of this letter, supposedly in the Vatican Library, has never been found. Without the ability to examine it or a later copy of it we are unable to ascertain its validity.

49. Mann, *Isle of Avalon*, 41. However, Strachan and Blake and Lloyd, *Keys to Avalon*, 212, note that the date should be closer to between A.D. 174 and 180, because Pope Eleutherius reigned from A.D. 174 to 192.

50. This letter from King Lucius to Pope Eleutherius first appears in an extract from the Liber Pontificalis (also known as Catalogus Felicianus), recorded between A.D. 483 and 492. See Baring-Gould and Fisher, *Lives of the British Saints*, 3:353. It was also reported in Bede's *Ecclesiastical History* of 731. Unlike the letter mentioned above, there is strong documentation.

51. Dobson, *Did Our Lord Visit Britain*, 26. Eventually a church of stone was constructed, and it is said by Taylor, *Coming of the Saints*, 155, that the Patriarch of Jerusalem presented a sapphire for its altar. Interestingly, Ralls-MacLeod and Robertson, *Quest for the Celtic Key*, 161, say that William of Malmesbury notes that Augustine left his assistant Paulinus behind at the church on Anglesey to help with its repairs. They are the only ones to quote Malmesbury as saying Anglesey rather than Glastonbury.

52. Henrici Spelman, *Concila, Decreta, Leges, Constitutiones, in re Ecclesiarum orbis Britannici* (1639), 5. The letter from St. Augustine to Gregory I about A.D. 600 notes in full: "In the western confines of Britain there is a certain royal island of large extent, surrounded by water, abounding in all the beauties of nature. In it the first neophytes of Catholic law, God beforehand acquainted them, found a Church constructed by no human art, but by the hands of Christ Himself for the salvation of His people. The almighty has made it manifest by many miracles and mysterious visitations that He continues to watch over it as sacred to Himself, and to Mary, the Mother of God."

53. St. David, or Dewi, was a sixth-century abbot and bishop of Menevia, Wales. Little is known of this patron saint of Wales, but he seems to have had a monastery in Pembrokeshire.

54. This is narrated in the later edition of William of Malmesbury's *De Antiquitate*. Malmesbury's chapter on King Ine (ca. A.D. 700) gives further reference to Christ as quoted in Dobson, *Did Our Lord Visit Britain*, 28: "To the ancient Church, situated in the place called Glastonbury (which Church the Great High Priest and Chiefest Minister formerly through His own ministry, and that of angels, sanctified by many an unheard-of miracle to Himself and the ever-virgin Mary, as was formerly revealed to St. David) do grant . . . etc."

55. Dobson, *Did Our Lord Visit Britain*, 27.

56. Lewis, *Christ in Cornwall and Glastonbury*, 17.

57. Lewis, *St. Joseph of Arimathea at Glastonbury*, 68. In the British sense *mean* is defined as "humble," not "miserly" or "cruel."

58. Certainly there is a case to be made of an antediluvian wisdom, with continuity from the Stone Age to Druidic times. Pliny the Elder believed the word *Druid* was a cognate with the Greek word *drus*, meaning "an oak." Combined with *wid* (means "to know" or "to see," as in the Sanskrit *vid*), therefore they might mean, "oak knowledge" or "oak wisdom. Or from the Indian Vedic *Dru-vid* means "knower of the wood." Scholar Rudolf Thurneysen believed that the word *Druid* was from the Old Irish *dru* prefix meaning "thorough," and *vid*, meaning "to know"; thus, a Druid was a person of great knowledge and wisdom (see Ralls-MacLeod and Robertson, *Quest for the Celtic Key*, 40).

59. Hopkins, Simmans, and Wallace-Murphy, *Rex Deus*, 290.

60. Prophet, *Mysteries of the Holy Grail*, xlviii.

61. Dark Ages historian Gildas II wrote this (see Frawley, *Gods, Sages and Kings*, 102). Gildas mentions sixty colleges with sixty thousand students.

62. Markale, *Druids*, 32.

63. Prophet, *Mysteries of the Holy Grail*, xlix.

64. Ralls-MacLeod and Robertson, *Quest for the Celtic Key*, 58.

65. Diodorus Siculus, *Library of History*, 31:1. Lucan notes that the Druids claim to understand astrology as well as the secrets of divinity. See Ralls-MacLeod and Robertson, *Quest for the Celtic Key*, 59.

66. Julius Caesar, *Gallic War*, VI.13–14, as quoted in Ralls-MacLeod and Robertson, *Quest for the Celtic Key*, 75.

67. Piggott, *Druids*, 102, as noted by Ralls-MacLeod and Robertson, *Quest for the Celtic Key*, 44.

68. Ralls-MacLeod and Robertson, *Quest for the Celtic Key*, 41.

69. My thanks to Tony Fieldsted of Springville for this insight.

70. Strachan, *Jesus the Master Builder*, 51.

71. Dobson, *Did Our Lord Visit Britain*, 37.

72. Ralls-MacLeod and Robertson, *Quest for the Celtic Key*, 59. The Druids also believed that every person had a soul and an afterlife. They seemed not to be determinists who believed in fate, but in "the process by which we can co-create our lives with the sacred" (ibid., 60). They had a veneration for the cube, which symbolized truth, the planet Mercury, and the God "Hu" (see ibid., 41, 66).

73. Anonymous, "Did Jesus Go to High School in Britain?" *Heart: For the Coming Revolution* (Winter 1985), 112–15.

74. Dobson, *Did Our Lord Visit Britain*, 37.

75. Strachan, *Jesus the Master Builder*, 57. He quotes Cassels, *Real Jesus*.

76. Caesar, *De Bello Gallico* VI, 14. See also Mackie, *Science and Society in Prehistoric Britain*, 228.

77. See Strachan, *Jesus the Master Builder*, which has this as its main thesis. See also Justin Martyr, *Dialogue with Trypho*, who says that Jesus was specifically a maker of yokes and ploughs. Geza Vermes and David Fluser believe that "carpenter" was used metaphorically, as in the case of rabbinic literature, to denote a wise or knowledgeable man. See Bernheim, *James, the Brother of Jesus*, 41.

78. Phillips, *Marian Conspiracy*, 56. Also see Shanks and Witherington, *Brother of Jesus*, 101. Other research shows that the city was rebuilt by the Romans (Kittin).

79. George Wesley Buchanan believes that Joseph's family belonged to the Palestinian upper class. See Bernheim, *James, the Brother of Jesus*, 42.

80. Edersheim, *The Temple*, 344.

81. Ibid., 345.

82. Bernheim, *James, the Brother of Jesus*, 74. Also one can think of the Wandering Jew and the Seven Sleepers; see

Joseph Gaer, *The Legend of the Wandering Jew* (New York: NAL/Mentor, 1961), 88–94.

83. Louis Charpentier, *The Mysteries of Chartres Cathedral* (1966), 192–193. The book also contains the exacting dimensional properties found in every natural thing—from plant and animal, including human life, to the very spirals of the galaxies, symbolic of creation and God's ordered universe.

84. Knight and Lomas, *Uriel's Machine.*

85. Strachan, *Jesus the Master Builder,* 246. However, Pythagoras only gnosticized Druidic thought.

86. The word *hyperborean* means "far north" or "beyond the north wind." It was symbolized by the aurora borealis, or northern lights.

PART THREE

THE HIEROS GAMOS

Is it not yet time to resurrect the hieros gamos of the eternal bride and bridegroom that images God as intimate partners—the joyful partnership that could at least restore the mythology of 'sacred union' at the heart of the original Christian community?

—MARGARET STARBIRD[1]

he now popular theme of *hieros gamos* (sacred marriage) is a controversy for both orthodox and Mormon Christianity for quite the opposite reasons. Mainstream Mormonism does not want to be out in front on controversial issues, while other Christian churches are troubled by their practitioners' interest in the question of Jesus and Mary Magdalene's marriage. Being nonbiblical, untraditional, and making Jesus all-too-human, they are scandalized by the idea of *hieros gamos* (sacred marriage). Yet many popularizing writers believe that "quite simply there is no reason why Jesus could not have married and fathered children while still retaining his divinity."[2]

Deeper levels of meaning require broader perspectives. The Christian world is already willing to accept the general concept of the blood of Israel being dispersed throughout the world or even spiritual adoption into the seed of Abraham. This concept is underscored by Mosiah 15:12 in the Book of Mormon, "And now, are these [the faithful] not his seed?" This "seed of Christ" is symbolized by the ordinance of adoption (see Mark 3:33–35). Yet, Christianity as a whole has not been willing to accept a biological posterity or literal seed for the Messiah. However, things are changing rapidly in receptiveness regarding this sensitive issue.

Early LDS documents that cite an earthly marriage for the Savior are an authentic part of our literary heritage. They make all the logical sense in the world, given the intellectual trajectory of gospel doctrine. Several Mormon authors, such as Joseph Fielding Smith, Bruce R. McConkie, and Dr. Victor C. Ludlow, establish a foundation for such a philosophy. However, other LDS writers on the subject, such as James Anderson, E. L. Whitehead, LeGrand Richards, Joseph Fielding McConkie, Vaughn Hansen, and Doris F. Charriere, fail to respond to this prospect. The present author believes the reason the *hieros gamos* is not taught in the LDS Church today is precisely because "the world" does not accept it.

Being members of a missionary Church, Latter-day Saints have been loath to trumpet this ontologically divisive issue. While Mormonism has the most to gain or lose and certainly the strongest "Grail" case, Church authorities have rightly not tried to step out in leading this study. However, through personal research by lay members of the LDS Church, it now seems to be the right time for a full investigative foray into this supposition.

For Latter-day Saints, the family—not the Church *per se*—is the basic unit of the gospel and kingdom of Jesus Christ. Mother, father, and children living in a loving home is the eternal principle upon which everything else is based. Like all the commandments of God, not everyone can righteously live this principle, for example practicing homosexuals and adulterers. But the Lord wisely announced, "Neither is the man without the woman nor the woman without the man in the *Lord*" (1 Corinthians 11:11; emphasis added).

The second veil covered the secret inner sanctum of the "interior of interiors."[3] It represented the bridal chamber, as the Coptic *Gospel of Philip* explains: "The bridal chamber is hidden. It is the Holy of Holies." The veil at the Holy of Holies conceals how God arranged things to be, but when the veil is rent, the things inside are revealed.[4]

CHAPTER FIVE
GNOSTIC AND PAGAN SEXUAL BALANCE

Gnosis: knowledge, but not primarily rational knowledge. The word is best translated as "insight" or "intuition" of oneself and the cosmos.[5]

In contemporary Gnosticism, "salvation" is not something that comes *to* the world, but rather is *from* the world through understanding the mysteries.[6] The serpent in the Garden of Eden was, according to gnostic-feminist mysticism, inspired and guided by the divine Sophia (wisdom) that Eve's "eyes might be opened." This gnostic Grail allegory of John's poison chalice is a mythical schema that asserts a higher knowledge (*gnosis*) and technique (magic) in order to gain salvation. In Gnosticism, "salvation" does not come through proper faith as in orthodox Christianity but through proper understanding[7]—not in believing in Christ's passion, but by interpreting his sayings.[8]

The ethic of Gnosticism was based upon cooperation with the world process; therefore it was both ascetic and libertine.[9] The practitioner could be a strict vegetarian (ascetic) and sexually licentious at the same time (libertine), all in the name of purification and enlightenment. Sexual balance could be found through experimentation into alternative lifestyles, even those that society called taboo. A liberalizing force, Gnosticism sought to expand accepted human behavior while eschewing religious codes or commandments.

However, contemporary Gnosticism has become increasingly uncoupled from serious erudition and scientific scrutiny. The dialectic method of choice in feminist scholarship and ideology is rhetorical criticism rather than empirical and analytical reasoning.[10] This kind of approach is called "iconoclastic scholarship," in which the tools of academia are used evangelically to support a personal agenda or ideology. Philip Jenkins uses the phrase "inverted fundamentalism" to describe this condition.[11]

THE DIVINE FEMININE AND THE GODDESS MOVEMENT

In short, the new Mary Magdalene is an old gnostic . . . even the figure of

Mary Magdalene can be prostituted for polemical purposes.

—KENNETH WOODWARD[12]

The Jesus-Mary myth in Gnosticism "represents Consciousness objectifying itself as psyche."

—FREKE AND GANDY[13]

The basic concept of the "divine feminine" is universal and eternal, for there is something female in the divine and there is something divine in the female.[14] The gnostic god was a negative philosophical abstraction, while the gnostic goddess was of a more personal nourishing nature. The rise of the Goddess Movement in the twentieth century is philosophically based upon the idea of the divine feminine.

Gnostic belief emphasizes the elitist notion that the spark of the divine within "some" people is in fact a part of the feminine deity Sophia, who has come to be trapped in the world of gross matter. The idea of the body as a "bag of excrement" is typical of almost all gnostic literature.[15] Although anti-materialism is a different issue from the divine feminine, both share a distrust of the objective world. Alchemy, on the other hand, rejected gnostic teachings that matter was inherently fallen or evil.[16]

As is typical of Gnosticism, little is consistent. For example, the Coptic *Gospel of Thomas* (Logion 114) does not celebrate the feminine but rather the masculine, saying that only men can enter the kingdom.[17] The lack of tolerance for women in Gnosticism can be seen in a number of its factions. For instance, the gnostic semi-Islamic sect Alawis of Syria does not allow women to be initiates and does not credit them with having souls.[18]

However, the "sacred feminine" changed through the nineteenth century when neopagan ideas of the mother-sister goddess entered romantic poetry. Then in the early twentieth century, Jane Harrison forwarded the idea of a woman-centered idyllic prehistoric world.[19] This notion was later expanded by English poet Robert Graves in his book *The White Goddess* (1948). His book, filled with willful ignorance or purposeful malice, became the centerpiece of feminist ideology about how atavistic (throwback) patriarchy destroyed peaceful matriarchy.[20]

The mother-sister-daughter goddess of radical feminist worship entails the dethroning of the patriarchal father god. But Jesus never worshiped anyone but His "Father." Within the New Testament, "Father" is the Savior's common epithet for God, occurring forty-five times in the Gospel of Matthew alone. Never in the gospels does it mention a divine "mother" or "sister" or any other feminine sobriquet.[21] Yet evidence is syncretistically spun into the tapestry of pagan mythology to allow "worship" of diverse goddesses.

This philosophy is opposed to Mormon theology that points toward family, especially fatherhood and motherhood, as the fullest means to enlightenment and the only way to emulate our Father and Mother in Heaven. Contemporary feminists invite women to eclectically make up their own soup of deities. Radical feminism, wiccans, and neopagans are intent upon "recovering the goddess." Yet, how many of them really do believe in an actual "nonmetaphorical" goddess?[22]

As critics of LDS culture, many members of the Mormon Women's Forum have a fuzzy gnostic, leftwing, liberal, and adamantly feminist bias. Essentially committed to the *Divine Feminine*, the forum is not certain what it means, offering a welter of definitions while opinions proliferate.[23] At risk of sounding overly polemical, little is absolutely sure for them, except perhaps the wanting nature of the literalist Church of Jesus Christ of Latter-day Saints and conservative Christianity as a whole.

Christians are held to a "different standard" than other religions are, perhaps using the criteria,

"Unto whom much is given much is expected" (or "much will be required"). If a Christian spits on the sidewalk, it equals a pagan murder. How strong this is we can see in the pernicious rantings of Malcolm Godwin: "But no religion, even today, is so tyrannical and unjust to women as the Christian church, Roman or Reformed."[24] Just because women's rights are stronger in traditional Christian countries and Western societies does not mean that in their minds they are as good for women as Islam or Hinduism.[25]

Ironically, according to some feminists, Mary Magdalene comes by her divine status through association with Jesus, who is, in gnostic parlance, "only a man." Or as Francis Cardinal George, Catholic archbishop of Chicago, exclaimed, "What! Jesus isn't a God, but Mary Magdalene is a goddess? . . . If he's not God, why is he married to a goddess?"[26] The illogicality of this position is numbing. For gnostics the Nag Hammadi documents are most precious, but one of them, the Coptic Apocalypse of Peter, is a thorn in their side. "As it turns out, though," writes Ehrman, "rather than opposing (orthodox Christianity) for thinking that Jesus was divine, it opposes them for thinking that Jesus was *human*."[27]

Radical feminists do not criticize the Magdalene for sinning as much as they do for her repenting. A growing number of neognostics prefer the Magdalene not to be morally straight (inhibited) or repentant (compliant). They see in terms of "illusion and enlightenment, not of sin and repentance as did the Jesus of the New Testament."[28] Sin, they believe, is not a moral category but a cosmological one. While most are willing to forgive her for crying when Peter pounced upon her in the Gospel of Mary, they don't like it.[29] But like it or not, in the gospels Mary Magdalene is always described as crying: at the anointing, at the cross, and at the tomb.

Recently, Mary Magdalene was rehabilitated from her prostitute role, only to have a second generation of feminists put her back into the role of whore, not as Jesus' wife but as His trollop. She again plays the role of the consort Ennoia ("First Thought") to Simon Magus the Sorcerer. Nikos Kazantzakis's novel *Last Temptation of Christ* alludes to the idea that Jesus and the Magdalene were carnal lovers. Lynn Picknett and Clive Prince, Freke and Gandy, and others subscribe to the consort-not-spouse paradigm.[30]

The Goddess Movement of today is similarly dominated by left-wing militant feminism. Such feminism, in turn, is instructed by ideological mythology and pseudo-scientific archeology, anthropology, and archetypal psychology. The starting premise and central hypothesis is that in the distant past, sometime before 3500 B.C., cultures were peacefully Goddess-centered. Once upon a time, "people worshipped Nature's divine order, which involved a balance between the male and female spiritual principles."[31]

No reputable scholar outside the Goddess Movement actually believes that there was such a "golden age" of women, although numerous cultic objects, such as the Venus of Willendorf, seem to emphasize this claim. More likely such objects support a fertility cult among women as the animal paintings of Lascaux and Altimira support hunting cults among men. Where great claims are made, great scholarship should accompany them, but in this case the facts are exaggerated or nonexistent. LDS academic Zina N. Petersen comes to this conclusion:

> Though scholarship has been slower to verify many of these claims, the political, spiritual, and cultural appeal of the idea was too hot to wait; it was simply consumed—inhaled and swallowed whole during the last decades of the 20th century. Dan

Brown's sources, whether acknowledged or not, are all from the popularizing arm of the movement, and none of the sources he used are at all critical or even questioning of the assumptions made about 'the Goddess' by the movement's adherents.[32]

With men as the antagonists and women as the protagonists, the Goddess Movement offers harsh matriarchy instead of harsh patriarchy.[33] This has proven so alluring to millions of feminists that no scientific proof of a matriarchal society is needed, only faith that it once existed. For this reason they have received Mary Magdalene as a counterfeit of the true Goddess or divine female in the pagan pantheon. Because belief in this ideology is so fervent, we might call it left-wing fundamentalism or radical evangelicalism.[34]

Not knowing the gospel of Jesus Christ and holding animosity toward Christianity, many ill-advisedly go after strange and "uppity" goddesses. While not really having faith in their literal existence, feminists often pray to and worship the "attributes" or archetypal story of these goddesses. "So they turn to Kali or Astarte or Diana or Asher or Lilith for their Mother Goddess needs," writes Petersen. "They do so because in the post-Christian, New Age thinking of the goddess movement, these goddesses are not under the control of the patriarchy."[35]

In most scholarly circles, sexual language of the divine feminine suggests a mystical union, not a literal one, except in Mormon theology. The barrenness of a gnostic androgynous afterlife, haunted by the memory of sexual profundity in the evil world, is repugnant to LDS sensitivities. The allure of this kind of pseudognosticism can damage the wholeness of the Mormon woman. It releases her from the rigors of obedience to God's law to the shifting sands of personal interpretations of God's spirit. This

movement misinterprets almost everything about the divine feminine and builds its foundation on victimization and anger, rather than love (*agape*) and service.

Mormon doctrine stands in stark contrast to Gnosticism's sexually confused notions. It preaches the eternal nature of gender and the union of the sexes through "eternal marriage," not a melding of the feminine and masculine elements into one androgynous or hermaphrodite whole.[36] So it is that some gnostics believe in a nonsexual "other world," or a transsexual existence.

In fact, LDS descriptions of Adam and Eve in heaven depict them as parents. While Joseph Smith prayed with Zebedee Coltrin and Oliver Cowdery on 19 April 1834, they experienced that the blue sky and heavens opened and they saw a man and a woman sitting upon thrones: "Joseph asked us if we knew who they were. We answered 'No.' Joseph said, 'That is father Adam and mother Eve.' Their heads were white as snow, and their faces shone with immortal youth."[37]

Many gnostics believe in some transsexual amalgam called "masculofeminine." But Latter-day Saints believe in a heavenly realm where the highest attainment has distinctive masculine men and feminine women. The form of Christianity radical feminism gravitates toward is not the orthodox Judeo-Christian view of neutered angels. The LDS view of the relationship of Jesus and His wife would be one of wholesomeness and health. They were, in fact, acting in their respective manly and feminine roles. They are the models of true saints to emulate.[38]

Even the pseudepigraphal *Gospel of James*, far from being a love story between Jesus and Mary Magdalene as is generally assumed, has at its core the teaching of celibacy. Why it would have the two main characters in the text being literally married is beyond comprehension. Zina Petersen believes that neoplatonic celibacy was inherited by the Church early on: "And thus Satan used the Catholic church's sad misunderstanding of sexuality to weed the best and the brightest right out of the gene pool; for though they took the titles of fathers and mothers, brothers and sisters, the religious of the middle ages were by definition, by a twisted ideal, barren, and family-less."[39]

Against a background of celibacy in the *Gospel of Philip,* BYU professor Stephen E. Robinson, mis-understands Gnosticism's general play for celibacy. While he is correct about a "married Christ," he is in error about the gnostics believing it: "Gnosticism knows a married Christ, or at least a Christ with a sexual nature, as opposed to the asexual Christ of orthodoxy. The apostles also are married, and in the *Second Book of Jeu* the resurrected Jesus has them form a circle around an altar with their wives at their left in order to teach them the true mysteries."[40]

Most gnostics not only believed that Jesus had no sexual relations with women but also that he had no corporeal substance. This Docetism even reached the point of having Jesus not leaving footprints when He walked about![41] The historical Christ disappears in a welter of fanciful contentions. That Jesus was an otherworldly celibate is ill-founded and based on phi-losophy rather than fact. In almost every aspect of its appropriation of Christianity, Gnosticism perverted every doctrine it touched. This would be impossible, except that behind the beautiful facade loomed a darker aspect. Gnosticism's source was, in fact, black.

THE GNOSTIC DOCUMENTS

As there is no concrete evidence of either a marriage or child, I would give no credence to this hypothesis. . . . I person-ally do not think Jesus and Mary Mag-dalene were married. . . . We have no evidence of a child, and the Merovin-gian link is very unlikely.

—SUSAN HASKINS[42]

The early gnostic and Coptic documents and their interpretations by feminist authors have played a decisive role in formulating the idea that Christ was married. Except in Mormonism in the 1850s, this concept simply did not exist in society until af-ter their discovery and publication in the 1950s. But does creating the idea really establish that the idea is true? The above quotation is the opinion of femi-nist author Dr. Susan Haskins, the leading scholar on Mary Magdalene. From her examination of the forty-six different works in the *Nag Hammadi* codices and elsewhere, she remains skeptical of the "Sacred Marriage" between Jesus and Mary.

In fact, these documents, as highly touted as they are, offer few illuminating details about the life of Christ or events in the early Church.[43] This is also the view of most female scholars on the subject, such as Elaine Pagels, Karen L. King, and Esther de Boer.[44] These and other apocryphal and pseudepig-raphal documents do not amount to convincing evi-dence that Jesus and Mary Magdalene were married or had sexual relations.

But most feminists are dealing with the "herme-neutics of suspicion" of biblical texts and scholarship. These orthodox texts are so distrusted by New Age and militant liberal sophists that they have sought other esoteric sources. The incorrect notion of the Bible being a concoction, constructed by 312 male bishops and the emperor Constantine (ca. 325–337), has forced feminist scholars to "retrieve" gnostic apocrypha as their primary source material. Their legitimacy comes from wistful down-dating of these *Nag Hammadi* and other gnostic codices and tracts to as close to the four biblical gospels as possible.[45]

Furthermore, members of the feminist side of the continuum are inclined to interpret all sacred writings symbolically and metaphysically, in typical Joseph Campbell fashion. They are misled in believ-ing that the gnostic writings are consistently pro-woman, while the Bible is antiwoman. Elaine Pagels notes that this position is incorrect, and many of the gnostic texts clearly refer to the feminine with contempt.[46] The most misogynous statements came not from antiquity or the Middle Ages but from the "enlightened" nineteenth and twentieth centuries. Liberal iconoclasts such as Kant, Schopenhauer, Virchow, Nietzsche, and Ester Vilar were, according to Manfred Hauke, expressly antifemale.[47]

How credible are the gnostic gospels when their accounts are at such odds with each other? While the biblical gospels may vary in some few details, gnostic writings hardly agree at all. So which gnostic scripture do we leave out and which do we include—none, some, or all? Is it all true in its own truth? One might think so because contradiction, ambiguity, and enigma are the essence of the gnostic stew. They tend to fuse Christianity with Greek philosophy, and Egyptian mysticism with Eastern elements.

Gnostic teachings of the first- to fourth-centuries were really the "conservative orthodoxy" of the Platonic and pagan "background noise" to the new Christian revolution.[48] As James the Just was in some respects a Judaizer away from extreme Christianity, so the gnostics were the Hellenizers away from that same radical Christian impulse. Christian gnostic texts tend to accommodate Hellenistic and Neoplatonic mysteries into a "more acceptable" and compromised form of nuanced Jesus occultism.

Today these desert codices or gnostic gospels seem "outsider," whereas in their day they preached accommodation to the prevailing philosophies. The leading gnostic contemporary popularizers are Henry Lincoln, Michael Baigent, Richard Leigh, Lynn Picknett and Clive Prince, Timothy Freke and Margaret Starbird. They attempt to use gnostic, Valentinian apocrypha folios, such as *Gospel of Philip* (A.D. 180–250) to prove that Jesus and Mary Magdalene were married or were lovers.[49] None of these "experts" is a scholar or historian.[50]

More rigorous scholars on gnostic studies, such as Elaine Pagels and Esther de Boer, have strongly stated that the *Gospel of Philip* and other documents prove no such thing.[51] In fact, they may contain another interpretation completely foreign to the more obvious one that sexual relations are defiling. Wesley Isenberg, a translator of the *Gospel of Philip*, explains, "'defiled women' are all women who participate in sexual intercourse, as in 'marriage of defilement,' which is fleshly and lustful."[52]

Most writers who say, "Jesus made the Magdalene the head of his church," tend to use the *Gospel of Philip* as their proof-text.[53] After all, it does positively proclaim, "The companion of the [gap in manuscript] Mary Magdalene [gap] more than [gap] the disciples [gap] kiss her [gap] on her [gap]."[54] But this worn and "holey" gnostic tractate says nothing about a literal marriage or Jesus ordaining Mary Magdalene to take over the Church for him.[55] In fact the earliest documents, the books of the Bible, say that Christ ordained only men, not women, to be His chief officials in the Church. Furthermore, no gnostic document contradicts this New Testament canonical list of leaders, but rather affirms it.

In another more fulsome translation of the same verse from the *Gospel of Philip*, Jesus' love for the Magdalene is pronounced to his followers' exasperation: "And the companion of the Savior is Mary Magdalene. But Christ loved her more than all the disciples and used to kiss her often on her mouth. The rest of the disciples were offended by it and expressed disapproval. They said to him, 'Why do you love her more than all of us?' The Savior answered and said to them, 'Why do I not love you like her?'"[56]

Did Mary Magdalene receive kisses from Jesus on the mouth in a sexual sense as in the opening line of the Song of Songs 1:2, "Let him kiss me with the kisses of his mouth: for thy love is better than wine"? According to a number of scholars the answer is "No." Rather, they kiss in a spiritual sense, as to receive special guidance. Esther de Boer notes that the *grace* which those who kiss exchange makes them born again.[57] This is clearly shown earlier in the same tractate of Philip:

> If the children of Adam are numerous, although they die, how much more the children of the perfect man who do not die but are continually born anew. They receive nourishment from the promise, to enter into the place above. The promise comes from the mouth, for the Word has come from there and has been nourished from the mouth, and become perfect. The perfect conceive through a kiss and give birth. Because of this we also kiss one another. We receive conception from the grace which we have among us.[58]

This was probably not too far from the "salute one another with an holy kiss" mentioned in the New Testament that each member is to give to another (Romans 16:16; 1 Corinthians 16:20 and 2 Corinthians 13:12; 1 Thessalonians 5:26) Such kisses on the mouth need not have sexual connotations. For instance, the *Second Apocalypse of James* has Jesus calling James the Greater "my beloved" and bestowing deeper understanding upon him than others had received with a kiss on the mouth.[59] In fact both the *Second* and *Third Apocalypse of James* have Jesus and James kiss and embrace each other as an indication of their particular spiritual relationship.[60] Professor James M. Robinson claims that "If one reads the entire *Gospel of Philip* it becomes clear that the writer disdains physical sex as beastly, literally comparing it to animals. In the early Church, a kiss was known as a metaphor for giving birth. And too much has been made out of this kiss."[61]

The third-century gnostic text, *Pistis Sophia* notes

that Philip, John, James, Matthew, and Mariamne (Mary) were all spoken of as beloved of Jesus.[62] In the *Didcot* and *Vulgate* scriptural editions, James the Just, Lazarus, Peter, and Joseph of Arimathea are given distinctive treatment with "the secret words of Jesus."[63] We are not talking about hetero- or homosexual relationships but those with special capacity for spiritual insight. In one *Gospel of Thomas* Logion we read about imparting "drink" from Jesus' mouth: Jesus said, "Because you have drunk, you have become drunk from the bubbling stream which I have measured out. . . . He who will drink from my mouth will become as I am: I myself shall become he, and the things that are hidden will be revealed to him."[64]

The *Gospel of Philip* further says, "There were three who always walked with the Lord: Mary his mother, his sister and Magdalene, who is called his *companion*. His sister, his mother, and his *companion* were all called Mary. And the companion of the Savior is Mary Magdalene."[65] The Greek word *koinonos* (literally "a partaker with you") has a wide range of meanings, but applied to Mary in certain texts usually is translated "companion."[66]

Liberal feminists insist that it means wife or sexual partner. According to Susan Haskins, it is more correctly translated as "partner" or "consort," a woman with whom a man has had sexual intercourse.[67] However, professor Craig Blomberg of Denver Seminary notes, "No Aramaic or Hebrew words for 'companion' normally mean spouse!"[68]

Margaret Mitchell, a professor of Early Church history at the University of Chicago Divinity School takes a position that the word *koinonos* "is usually translated as friend or companion."[69] Neither is she an actual spouse, for Dr. Haskins sees it symbolically, with the bridegroom as the Savior, the bride is Sophia (Greek for Wisdom) or *Chokmah* (Hebrew for Wisdom) in the bridal chamber. The *Pleroma* (fulness) is the archetypal bridal chamber.[70]

Haskins sees in the tractate of Philip two levels,

one symbolic of the love of Christ for the Church, and the other in the person of Mary Magdalene. The second one represents a historical situation in which she symbolizes the feminine element in the Church.[71] In other words, their real-life relationship was Platonic. The *Gospel of Philip* does not prove any marriage or sexual relationship, and neither does any other ancient documentary evidence. While there was a sacred Holy Grail marriage, careful research shows that none of the gnostic documents confirms it.

The major theme of the *Gospel of Philip*, though rambling and disjointed, is androgynous and nullifying of sexual differentiation, claiming that sexual relations are intrinsically debasing. But for Haskins, this is sexual imagery, a metaphor of the bridal chamber and the reunion between the polarities of male and female, where gender becomes abolished into androgyny. The significance of the relationship between Jesus and Mary Magdalene rested on its symbolizing that perfect spiritual union.[72]

In the Coptic *Nag Hammadi* text, *Dialogue of the Savior*, Mary Magdalene is a conversation partner in doctrinal discussions, without any protestations of the apostles.[73] Yet Peter (Logion 114) of the apocryphal *Gospel of Thomas* needed correction from Jesus as to a woman's right to the sacred and inclusion in the circle of the disciples: "Simon Peter said to them, 'Let Mary [Magdalene] leave us, for women are not worthy of life [the mysteries].' Jesus said, 'I myself shall lead her in order to make her male so that she too may become a living spirit resembling you males. For every woman who will make herself male will enter the Kingdom of Heaven.'"[74]

Peter was not suggesting that women should be killed when he said they "are not worthy of life" but rather that women should leave the room when the highest order of sacred and secret endowments were being discussed. The words of life had traditionally been withheld from Jewish women, only being discussed among men who were counted as worthy.

Jesus says that he would teach (endow) her himself, thus making her "male" or rather like the other males in this respect.[75]

In 1896, a third- or fourth-century Coptic papyrus was discovered in Upper Egypt and came onto the Cairo antiquities market.[76] It was purchased by a German scholar who took it to Berlin, but it was not published until 1955. This was the famous apocryphal "Redeemer Text," the *Gospel of Mary* (Magdalene).[77] It has Peter exclaiming that Jesus and Mary Magdalene were intimate, "Sister, we know that the Savior loved you more than other women."[78]

Then there arises a conflict between Peter and Mary Magdalene when she goes a bit further than his understanding would (traditionally) allow. Andrew (Levi) intervenes and says to Peter, "But if the Savior made her worthy [see *Gospel of Thomas*, Logion 55], who are you indeed to reject her? Surely the Savior knows her very well. That is why he loved her more than us."[79] While personally concluding that they were married, these documents do not automatically return a "married" verdict.

The secret and controversial *Gospel of Thomas* was discovered in the 1890s in fragment form, but eventually the entire text was found at Nag Hammadi. It implied that Jesus had a twin brother named Judas Didymus Thomas. The text was written in Coptic from the original Greek and dates to about A.D. 350–390, but may be as early as A.D. 140–200. Irenaeus, the orthodox Bishop of Lyon, France, writing about A.D. 180 asserts that heretics "boast that they possess more gospels than there really are" and complains that they have wide circulation.[80]

Certainly the Great Apostasy began from the earliest dates of Christianity, and these texts may be evidence of this falling away. Mark 9:38 and Luke 9:49 speak of the apostles forbidding (berating) those that used Jesus' name, because these people were not actually followers of Jesus Himself. Similarly, it is amazing that even during the lifetime of Joseph Smith other churches and schisms broke off.[81] Certainly the primitive Jesus Movement exploded in terms of size and territory covered, with claims from many sources of visions and gnosis. This rapid expansion must have been problematic to the Church, which had to respond with, "Which are the right ones [writings] and which are the wrong ones?"

The ancient gnostic movement produced a rapid-fire avalanche of documents coming from every direction, with a veneer of Christianity often adhered to gnostic paganism. Even contemporary gnostics believe in mounds of documents, which they can't quite lay their hands on. The following inaccuracies are typical of their mentality: "Purportedly a genealogy of the early descendants of Jesus has been preserved, along with the Q-document, which may be an account of Jesus's life and ministry written in his own hand, as well as Mary Magdalene's own diaries. Among these papers, too, are thought to be the Purist Documents, tens of thousands more pages of information written by the early followers of Jesus."[82]

Somehow standards of authenticity and orthodoxy needed to be established. Not every contradictory writing by an ecstatic ancient mystic could be squared with the older writings of those who knew Christ or the original apostles. From this perceived need and to refute Marcion's heretical compilation of books, an initial canon of the scriptures was compiled as early as A.D. 150.[83] However, it would take another two hundred years of sorting before a definitive canon was produced.

What then should Latter-day Saints believe about the gnostic gospels? The far right would have us believe that they are so heretical that there is nothing of value to be gleaned from them. The far left are excited about these texts that tell of alternate Christianities, which they can plunder tidbit by tidbit, as to their liking.[84] A middle ground between these polar positions is more akin to the

LDS preference. These Christian-like gnostic writings could be read for the truth they have to offer, realizing that they also contain much falsehood. This is much closer to the position the Lord gave in Doctrine and Covenants 91:1: "Verily, thus saith the *Lord* unto you concerning the Apocrypha—There are many things contained therein that are true, and it is mostly translated correctly; There are many things contained therein that are not true, which are interpolations by the hands of men. . . . Therefore, whoso readeth it, let him understand, for the Spirit manifesteth truth; and whoso is enlightened by the Spirit shall obtain benefit therefrom; And whoso receiveth not by the Spirit, cannot be benefited."[85]

If a list of all the Mormon-like doctrines is made, and of all the grotesque doctrines found in these same writings, the latter would be slightly longer.[86] It is probably true that some items were preserved in these writings, or elucidated more thoroughly than in the standard canon, but as a whole this is not the Christianity we understand to be true. Yes, one can read them and profit from them, but remember that they result in a consortium of conflicting ideas. Most teach of celibacy; of the evil of this material earth and our own corporeal bodies; or praise androgyny or a final outcome of Nirvanaesque oblivion. True Christian Mormonism exalts the family, gender, and eternal bliss in literal, resurrected bodies. These are the true Holy Grail Quests.

NOTES

1. Starbird, *Magdalene's Lost Legacy*, 133–34. While Starbird does not understand exactly what early Christian teachings really were—she substitutes gnostic blather instead—she knows that something incredible was taught.
2. Baigent, Leigh, and Lincoln, *Holy Blood, Holy Grail*, 408.
3. Edersheim, *The Temple*, 62.
4. As quoted in Freke and Gandy, *Jesus and the Goddess*,

160. According to Dr. Eric D. Huntsman, the *Gospel of Philip* is dated anywhere between the 150s and as late as the late 300s.

5. Elaine Pagels in Burstein, *Secrets of the Da Vinci Code,* 93.

6. This relates to twentieth-century Gnosticism, but might not be exactly the same as second- and third-century Gnosticism. Postmodernism and deconstructionism are based upon the premise that meaning comes from one's social group and culture, and that absolute knowledge and meaning does not really exist. They undermine "facts" or "objectivity" and are inherently antirational. Transcendent truth is suspect, as are the claims of science, received or inherited ideas, established norms, and patriarchal authority. There is a natural skepticism, even cynicism, to their philosophies. The empirical gives way to the experiential, and group individualism is exalted. Everything is relativistic except the statement "Nothing is true," and perhaps "my truth." Ultimately the movement is self-absorbed, self-conscious, and self-serving.

7. Gnostics saw humans as being of three groups: hylics, psychics, and pneumatics, with the psychics redeemed by faith and the pneumatics by gnosis, the latter being of a higher order.

8. Ehrman, *Truth behind the Da Vinci Code,* 63. In LDS theology, both faith and knowledge must come into play in order to gain salvation. But this comes through obedience to the divine truth and the commandments of God (see *Gospel of Thomas,* Logion 2). Ehrman notes that "knowledge is to be sought after, and when you realize that everything you thought you knew about this world is wrong, you become troubled. But then you realize the truth about this world, and you become amazed. And when that happens, you return, ultimately, to the divine realm from which you came, and rule with the other divine beings over all there is."

9. See Moehlman, *Encyclopedia of Religion,* 301. Dr. Eric D. Huntsman, "Mary Magdalene: Biblical Enigma," BYU Museum of Art presentation, 25 February 2004 (revised 26 May 2004) notes that "as a result different gnostics went to two extremes in regard to moral behavior. Some were Libertines, meaning they did whatever they wanted because this physical body and what we did with it did not matter—one is saved by knowledge anyway, so one could indulge in all kinds of conduct. Others went to the other extreme—since the body was bad, these gnostics did not want anything to do with it, so they became extremely ascetic. Some of these gnostic texts describe our bodies as living corpses."

10. Perhaps the best two studies on Mary Magdalene using this rhetorical method are Jane Schaberg's recent *Resurrection of Mary Magdalene* and Fiorenza's classic *In Memory of Her.*

11. Jenkins, *Hidden Gospels.*

12. Kenneth Woodward in Burstein, *Secrets of the Da Vinci Code,* 54, 55. This is not Woodward's belief but rather his analysis of feminist thinking.

13. Freke and Gandy in Burstein, *Secrets of the Da Vinci Code,* 81. "In the Christian parable, Jesus (consciousness) shows Mary (fallen psyche) the magical woman (higher psyche), who is Mary's original nature. Jesus then makes love with the woman, representing the consummation of the mystical marriage in which Consciousness and psyche commune in the realization of their essential Oneness." This is gibberish of the first order.

14. Petersen, "Divine Feminine and the Goddess Movement," 5.

15. Haag and Haag, *Rough Guide to The Da Vinci Code,* 76. They note that gnosticism is elitist, esoteric, pessimistic, and even antisocial: "It was not a creed that any society could adopt, and by the time of Constantine its vogue was over."

16. Godwin, *Holy Grail,* 205.

17. The *Gospel of Thomas* was found in Nag Hammadi with a manuscript dating to about A.D. 400, although the text upon which it is based probably originated in Syria in the Greek language around A.D. 150. See Ehrman, *Truth behind the Da Vinci Code,* 69. The quotation says that Jesus "will make Mary male." The logic of "Thomas" is summarized thusly: Women are less perfect than men; men are less perfect than the gods. It is required therefore that all divine spirits return to their place of origin. But for women to achieve this salvation, they obviously must first become male. Thus it seems that woman must transcend the feminine and become more male. Also see Logion 22 to say that ultimately both female and male must eventually be transcended into androgyne.

18. Haag and Haag, *Rough Guide to the Da Vinci Code,* 101.

19. Greer, *New Encyclopedia of the Occult,* 200. Jane Harrison argued, as quoted in Greer: "That prehistoric southeast Europe had been the site of an idyllic, peaceful, woman-centered civilization worshipping a three-fold goddess of nature. Patriarchal invaders, she claimed, had destroyed this civilization, before the dawn of history. These ideas were based on very little concrete evidence, and were fiercely contested by other scholars. Despite this, they had an enormous impact on the popular imagination."

20. Olson and Miesel, *Da Vinci Hoax,* 37.

21. Ehrman, *Truth behind the Da Vinci Code*, 180.

22. Davis, *Goddess Unmasked*, x.

23. See "Real Goddesses Have Curves," session at 2004 Salt Lake City Sunstone Symposium (August 2004).

24. Godwin, *Holy Grail*, 212. One wonders if the learned Godwin has ever heard of Islam.

25. See ibid., 242. Godwin says, "The Eastern religions of Buddhism, Jainism, or Hinduism are more inclined to the female way, and are noticeably nonviolent compared with the Western male oriented religions." However, women and children are often treated as slaves in these religions, and in Hinduism women were sometimes murdered to join their dead husbands. Moreover, how many radical feminists would trade Christian society for Islamic Shiara law?

26. Cathleen Falsani, "Cardinal Takes a Crack at The Da Vinci Code," *Chicago Sun-Times*, 9 January 2004.

27. Ehrman, *Truth behind the Da Vinci Code*, 56.

28. Elaine Pagels in Burstein, *Secrets of the Da Vinci Code*, 93. The author believes that Mary Magdalene was always a virtuous woman.

29. This gnostic gospel was probably written between A.D. 180 and 250. In it we find, in typical gnostic fashion, the exploration of the soul and its journey through spiritual realms. According to Dr. Eric Huntsman, it shows how the soul migrates through planetary spheres and has conversations with hostile powers as well as with friendly guardians.

30. Picknett, *Mary Magdalene*, 67–68, 220–22.

31. Haag and Haag, *Rough Guide to the Da Vinci Code*, 12.

32. Petersen, "Divine Feminine and the Goddess Movement."

33. We should mention Margaret Toscano's "Beyond Matriarchy, Beyond Patriarchy," while feminists attempt to conciliate the differences of both positions.

34. This is a position held by Philip Jenkins.

35. Petersen, "Divine Feminine and the Goddess Movement," 8.

36. The First Presidency of the LDS Church, "The Family: A Proclamation to the World," 23 September 1995, asserts the true and healthy marriage relationship.

37. Calvin Robert Stephens, "The Life and Contributions of Zebedee Coltrin" (master's thesis, Brigham Young University, Provo, Utah, August 1974, 46–47). He was quoted from the minutes of the Spanish Fork high priests meeting of February 5, 1878. These minutes are located in the Church Historical Department, Salt Lake City. See also Salt Lake School of the Prophets minutes (3 and 11 of October 1883), 70; Oliver B. Huntington Diary 1847–1900 (typed copy, II) Special Collections at Brigham Young University. This seems to be a different incident from the one where four elders offered the prayer, because in that vision Sidney Rigdon was present and Adam and Eve are not mentioned. Coltrin mentions this event on the 11th of October 1883 and was recorded in *Wilford Woodruff Journal*, 8:200–201: "He (Coltrin) said He was with Joseph and another Man in the woods praying and Heavens was opened and they saw a Man sitting upon a throne whose hair was white as wool and a woman sitting beside of him, both dressed in white. Joseph said it was Adam and Eve."

38. The scriptures are not explicit in depicting them as our model. The reason may lay in the revisionism of those celibates that did not "translate" them correctly. (See Article of Faith 8.)

39. Petersen, "Divine Feminine and the Goddess Movement," 9.

40. Robinson, "The Apocalypse of Adam," *BYU Studies* 17, 2 (Winter 1977): 133. Scholarship since 1977 has shown more fully that the second- to fourth-century gnostics did not believe in a married Christ.

41. "Adrian II," *New Catholic Encyclopedia*, 2002 ed.

42. Susan Haskins in Burstein, *Secrets of the Da Vinci Code*, 24.

43. Olson and Miesel, *Da Vinci Hoax*, 63. This is because they were written so late and have a gnostic anti-historical bias. The gnostic gospels, unlike the biblical gospels, tell us little of contemporary society, religious, political or historical life. Rather they are more ideologically then theologically based, in some timeless never-never land. Christ is a phantom, who talks in ways that few people can understand.

44. Elaine Pagels has a Ph.D. from Harvard University. She is the Harrington Spear Paine Professor of Religion at Princeton University. Her books *Gnostic Gospels* and *Beyond Belief: Secret Gospel of Thomas* helped bring attention of the New Testament apocryphal texts to a wider audience. Karen L. King is a Wynn Professor of Ecclesiastical History at Harvard University. Her *Gospel of Mary Magdala*, while very good, is fraught with agendas and bias.

45. Karen L. King has been guilty of this; see her books *Images of the Feminine in Gnosticism, What is Gnosticism?* and *Gospel of Mary of Magdala: Jesus and the First Woman Apostle*.

46. Pagels, *Gnostic Gospels*, 66.

47. See Hauke, *Women in the Priesthood?* 470. See also Olson and Miesel, *Da Vinci Hoax*, 60.

48. While we have little in the way of first-century gnostic texts, according to Moehlman, *Encyclopedia of Religion*,

300, it had pre-Christian oriental mystic origins. From Plato and a·philosophical base it moved toward mysticism and primitive religious elements. Moehlman notes, "Gnosticism has become a syncretistic whirlpool with one eddy the orientalization of the Graeco-Roman civilization and the other the hellenization of the Orient."

49. According to James M. Robinson, professor of religion emeritus, Claremont Graduate University, and general editor of *The Nag Hammadi Library*, this codex and other Nag Hammadi documents are really a collection of excerpts from scattered materials of various sources. They are not "gospels" but "tracts" and have no resemblance to the gospels in the New Testament. "They were attempting to influence what we might call left-wing Christianity—somewhat similar to the New Age phenomenon in our time"; as quoted in Burstein, *Secrets of the Da Vinci Code*, 99.

50. Margaret Starbird holds an M.A. in comparative literature and German. Lincoln is a BBC television personality and scriptwriter. Picknett and Prince are conspiracy theorists with interest in the occult, paranormal, and UFOs. Baigent has an undergraduate degree in psychology and is pursuing an M.A. in mysticism and religious experience.

51. This does not mean that these feminist writers do not have deconstructive agendas. It should also be noted that Valentine was not opposed to marriage, but rather espoused it. Therefore Phipps, *Was Jesus Married?* 138, believes that the *Gospel of Philip* bolsters the "Jesus was married" argument and promotes the Valentinian origin of the document. He notes the scholarship of Johannes Leipoldt and H. M. Schenke, *Koptisch-Gnostische Schriften aus den Papyrus-Codices von Nag-Hamadi* (Hamburg, 1960), 34–38. But more recent research questions this analysis.

52. Isenberg, "The Gospel of Philip," in Robinson, *Nag Hammadi Library in English*, 139.

53. One of the first was Phipps, *Was Jesus Married?* in 1970; but after Baigent, Leigh, and Lincoln's *Holy Blood, Holy Grail* in 1982, almost every author heavily relied upon the Coptic *Gospel of Philip* as their primary source material for this teaching.

54. Ehrman, *Truth behind The Da Vinci Code*, 178, translation of the *Gospel of Philip* saying no. 55 (63.34–35). Also see Wellnitz, *Christ and the Patriarchs*, 194.

55. Mary Magdalene is named only thirteen times in the gospels of the New Testament, while Peter's name in conjunction to leadership occurs over ninety times.

56. "Gospel of Philip," in Robinson, *Nag Hammadi Library in English*, 138. The word *companion* may mean "consort," "partner," "wife" or "spouse," or just "friend or associate."

57. Esther de Boer in Burstein, *Secrets of the Da Vinci Code*, 43.

58. *Gospel of Philip* 58:20 to 59:6. In another translation we read: "For it is by a kiss that the perfect conceive and give birth. For this reason we also kiss one another. We receive conception from the grace which is in one another." See Isenberg, trans., "The Gospel of Philip," in Robinson, *Nag Hammadi Library*, 148.

59. *The (Second) Apocalypse of James*, accessed at http://www.gnosis.org, (June 2005). In brief it says, "And he [Jesus] kissed my mouth. He took hold of me, saying, 'My beloved! Behold, I shall reveal to you those things that (neither) the heavens nor the archons have known.'" Such kissing was the transmittal of revealed knowledge or gnosis.

60. Deirdre Good in Burstein, *Secrets of the Da Vinci Code*, 48.

61. Robinson, as quoted in Burstein, *Secrets of the Da Vinci Code*, 99.

62. This gnostic Christian Coptic text was published by Schmidt, *Pistis Sophia*.

63. Phillips, *Search for the Grail*, in Knight and Lomas, *Second Messiah*, 112.

64. Ehrman, *Truth behind The Da Vinci Code*, 67, Gospel of Thomas, Logion 108.

65. Blake and Blezard, *Arcadian Cipher*, 135.

66. See Danker and Bauer, *Greek-English Lexicon of the New Testament* (2000). The word in Matthew 2:14 means marriage partner, in Philemon 17 a companion in faith, in 2 Corinthians 8:23 a co-worker proclaiming the gospel, and in Luke 5:10 a business associate. See Marjanen, *The Woman Jesus Loved*, 151. In biblical Greek, the usual word for *marry* is *gameo*. The words for *bride* are *numphe* and *nymphios*. *Virgin* is *parthenos* and *wife* is *gyne*. See also Olson and Miesel, *Da Vinci Hoax*, 94.

67. Haskins, *Mary Magdalen*, 37, 40. For this she quotes R. McLellan Wilson, *Gospel of Philip* (1962), 35, where the word *koinonos* is rendered as "consort."

68. Craig Blomberg, "The Da Vinci Code," *Denver Seminary Journal* 7 (2004)

69. Margaret Mitchell, as cited by Linda Kulman and Jay Tolson in "Jesus in America" *U.S. News and World Report*, 22 December 2003; see also Abanes, *Truth behind the Da Vinci Code*, 39.

70. *Pleroma* means fulness or completeness or perfection. *Kenoma* means deficiency or incompleteness. See Galatians 4:4; Romans 11:36; 13:10; Colossians 1:19; 2:9; 3:11.

71. Haskins, *Mary Magdalen,* 41.

72. There were some gnostics who were not strict dualists, who put erotic concepts into practice that were profane reenactments of Christian ritual. According to Epiphanius they had a book called *The Great Questions of Mary [Magdalene?]* where Christ revealed to Mary Magdalene obscene sexual ceremonies which the members of the sect had to perform for their salvation.

73. Esther de Boer in Burstein, *Secrets of the Da Vinci Code,* 44.

74. *Gospel of Thomas,* Logion 114. The phrase "to make her male" might mean that Jesus would marry her and share in the priesthood through marriage.

75. The concept of a woman becoming male in order to enter the kingdom of heaven stems from the gnostic belief that the spirit, the divine spark trapped inside a person's soul, was originally male, even if the outer shell is now female (see Collins, *Twenty-First Century Grail,* 125). Other gnostic belief has it that Sophia (female principle) split into a million pieces to form the divine sparks in people (see Ehrman, taped Lecture 9, "Thomas's Gnostic Teachings," in *Lost Christianities* [2002], The Teaching Co., Chantilly, Virginia.) Joseph Smith Jr. would later restore Jesus' authentic teachings in this matter that there are both male and female spirits.

76. The composition of the original text is given at about A.D. 125–175 in Holzapfel, et al., *What Da Vinci Didn't Know.*

77. Karen L. King, professor of ecclesiastical history at Harvard University and leading feminist interpreter of Christian literature notes, "For example, the Gospel of Mary's rejection of the body as one's true self is highly problematic for contemporary feminism which affirms the dignity of the human body," as quoted in Haag and Haag, *Rough Guide to The Da Vinci Code,* 76.

78. *Gospel of Mary* (Magdalene) (Papyrus Berolinensis 10), as quoted in Seaich, *Ancient Texts and Mormonism,* 41.

79. Robinson, *Nag Hammadi Library in English,* 525–27.

80. Burstein, *Secrets of the Da Vinci Code,* 91.

81. Shields, *Divergent Paths,* 19–29, 249, 300. Most interesting was a church founded in 1840 by George M. Hinckle and provocatively called The Church of Jesus Christ, the Bride of the Lamb's Wife. It included William E. McLellin, an apostate from the Quorum of the Twelve. The title of the church is quite poignant, but we don't know about its teachings as to the "Bride of the Lamb's Wife." Like other Mormon-based faiths, they used the Book of Mormon, Joseph Smith, and his revelations.

82. Haag and Haag, *Rough Guide to The Da Vinci Code,* 19. The Q comes from the German word *Quelle,* meaning source. Q is a saying gospel, not a narrative one, and no scholar that Dr. Eric Huntsman knows believes it might have been from Jesus' own hand. See Eric D. Huntsman e-mail to Vern G. Swanson, 24 August 2005. Modern (liberal) biblical scholars believe that the gospels draw from some other source(s) that existed in oral tradition or in written documents that are now lost. But a reconstruction of sorts, they believe, can be made through careful "straining" of the existing gospels. The secret Sangraal Documents handed down by the Priory de Sion, are as elusive as the Q-Document—neither exists.

83. Morton Scott Enslin, *The Encyclopedia of Religion* (1945), 468. Marcion was born about A.D. 100 and lived in Rome by the middle of the century. He sought to cleanse Christianity of all contact with Judaism. He accepted the gnostic idea of the two gods (the demiurge or creator) and the good god. But he was not given to gnostic mystical speculation. He considered Christianity in apostasy, and he was a reformer. He rejected the Old Testament and replaced it with his own list of accepted New Christian scriptures. He accepted ten letters of Paul, Luke (but not Acts) as genuine. His was the first Christian canon, which forced the issue of canonization. See A. Harnack, *Marcion: das Evangelium vom fremden Gott* (1924).

84. See Holzapfel, et al., *What Da Vinci Didn't Know.*

85. This is referring to the Old Testament apocrypha appearing in some Bibles.

86. Dr. Eric H. Huntsman e-mail to Vern G. Swanson, 24 August 2005.

CHAPTER SIX

THE SACRED MARRIAGE OF JESUS CHRIST

Let us be glad and rejoice, and give honour to him:
for the marriage of the Lamb is come, and his wife
hath made herself ready.

—REVELATION 19:7

f course, someday Jesus will be married," writes senior pastor Erwin W. Lutzer. "We all anticipate his future wedding. Jesus is now engaged to us, the church—his bride."[1] The marriage of Jesus Christ to the Church is well accepted, as Robert Graves attests, "the mystic marriage of the Lamb to a White Princess identified with the Church remains orthodox doctrine in every Christian profession."[2] Speculation beyond this biblical analogy, however, is considered indiscreet in many quarters.

Any hints and nudges that Jesus and Mary Magdalene had more than a celibate platonic relationship evokes a strong negative response from most conservative Christians. Beginning in 2003 an avalanche of "Jesus was NOT Married" rebuttal books began to appear in response to *The Da Vinci Code*.[3] William E. Phipps exclaims: "It is difficult for Christians even today to weigh judiciously the telling shreds of evidence about Jesus' marital status. The virus of pagan sexual asceticism has eaten like a cancer into the body of Christ, causing sick attitudes and practices."[4]

For mainstream Christians, to conceive of the Holy Sinless One—God Incarnate—having carnal sexual relations with a supposedly wanton prostitute would fly in the face of 1,900 years of Christian tradition. While Latter-day Saints have an extremely high opinion of Mary Magdalene and women in general, others do not. Earlier in 1914, the Protestant church historian Philip Schaff wrote, "The Son of God and Savior of the world was too far above all the daughters of Eve to find an equal companion among them."[5]

"If he had married," writes Lutzer, "presumably it would have been to someone as holy as he—which severely limited his options!"[6] Thus, in Lutzer's opinion, nobody was worthy of His marriage band. Christian churches have strongly protested against an earthly marriage for Christ, as both unscriptural and demeaning to His deity.[7] It smacked too much of rapacious paganism or perhaps Arianism to them.[8]

The Roman Catholic Church has been the most concerted enemy of a married Savior. Pope Paul VI rehearsed this traditional position in a 1967 encyclical: "Christ remained throughout his whole life in the state of celibacy, which signified his total dedication to the service of God and men."[9] While this is an adamantly held position, it was nibbled at through ideas such as the nuptials of St. Agnes, the "Mystic Marriage of St. Catherine," and celibate nuns being espoused to Jesus Christ.[10] Patristic fathers, such as Tertullian, Origen, and Cyprian, were among the first to refer to celibates as spouses of Christ.[11]

Metaphorically the mystic marriage expresses the highest union with God, as when the Lord took Israel as bride (Hosea 2:19) or Jesus as the allegorical bridegroom (Matthew 9:15). Origen, Gregory of Nyssa, and Bernard of Clairvaux were key articulators of this nuptial symbolism. Later, Teresa of Avila in Ecstasy and St. Mary Alacoque were the classical brides of Christ in faith.

And still, the only church in Christendom that gives a place, though not officially, for a married Heavenly Father and Jesus Christ is The Church of Jesus Christ of Latter-day Saints. Mormons were also the first people or religious organization to historically record that Jesus was married and had children. Theirs is also the only sensible explanation of the sacred Grail marriage, which has full theological construction in the broadest perspective and deepest sense. LDS president Joseph F. Smith spoke that the "patriarchal order of marriage" was "the same law that Our Heavenly Father" has kept. "The word of the Lord to us was that if we did not obey we could not go where our Heavenly Father dwells. A man obeying a lower law is not qualified to preside over those who keep a higher law."[12]

This was not exactly a secret teaching, but rather a quiet or reverential one. Only later did other non-Mormon individuals catch on to this possibility. In 1977, non–Latter-day Saint scholar on *Nag Hammadi*

Wesley Isenberg writes along these lines: "Just as husband and wife unite in the bridal chamber, so also the reunion effected by Christ takes place in a bridal chamber, the sacramental, spiritual one, where a person receives a foretaste and assurance of ultimate union with an angelic heavenly counterpart.[13]

Lest we think that the above quote refers only to some heavenly "bridal chamber" or *Pleroma*, Isenberg also mentions that the earthly ordinance of marriage was but a "foretaste" of the heavenly or eternal nuptial bliss to follow in the next life for exalted couples. Another non-LDS scholar, R. McLain Wilson, notes a sacred marriage took place on earth and it had eternal marital consequences. Not only this, but other men and women partake of the same principle shown by Christ. For this reason, "to see the Bridegroom and the Bride one must become a bridegroom or a bride [oneself]."[14]

In other words, we must all become "sons [and daughters] of the bridal chamber" or have a marriage partner, in order to inherit exaltation, the highest degree of the celestial kingdom (D&C 131:1–3). In 1839, Joseph Smith Jr. related to Parley P. Pratt the principles of eternal marriage: "The highest dignity of womanhood was to stand as a queen and priestess to her husband and to reign for ever and ever as the queen mother of her numerous and still increasing offspring."[15]

This quotation establishes marriage as a central doctrine since the LDS Church's beginning. The following figure lays out the eternal plan of marriage and family as an integral part of Latter-day Saint theology:

The figure on the opposite page outlines the various relationships of marriage between the LDS temple, priesthood, celestial kingdom, the Trinity, and eternal progression. At its core, everything The Church of Jesus Christ of Latter-day Saints teaches directs all people to marry in the temple and point their lives toward being an exalted family. The

FIGURE 3
HIEROS GAMOS

Marriage—Bridal Chamber—Family

TEMPLE JERUSALEM	MELCHIZEDEK PRIESTHOOD [16]	CELESTIAL DEGREE [17]	GODHEAD	PROGRESSION (MOSES 6:60)
HOLY OF HOLIES (BRIDAL CHAMBER)	HOLY OR PATRIARCHAL ORDER (FAMILY)	EXALTATION [18] (MARRIAGE)	FATHER (PATRIARCH) [BLOODLINE]	BLOOD (SANCTIFIED)
HOLY PLACE PRIESTS	MELCHIZEDEK ORDER (CHURCH)	ADMINISTERING ANGELS	SON (HIGH PRIEST) [19]	SPIRIT [OIL] (JUSTIFIED)
THE PORCH (MINISTERING)	AARONIC ORDER [20] (PREPATORY)	MINISTERING ANGELS	HOLY GHOST (MINISTER)	WATER (OBEDIENCE)

Church has set a lofty goal based upon these foundational principles of truth, love, service, progression, and obedience. With these in mind we now examine the possibilities of the sacred marriage.

THE JUDAIC MARRIAGE—IMPERATIVE

A man with no wife becomes a homeless wanderer. . . . So who will trust a man who has no home, and lodges wherever night finds him?[21]

In the Garden of Eden the unmarried state was "not good," and man (*adham*) was required to use the sexual impulse to "multiply and replenish the earth," (Genesis 1:28; 9:1). For God said, "It is not good that the man should be alone; I will make him an helpmeet for him"[22] (Genesis 2:18). According to Rabbinical decree the first positive law and commandment was to propagate the human race.[23] However, we must use caution in using later Mishnah (as late as A.D. 200), Talmudic (as late as A.D. 500), and Rabbinical standards as perfectly representing Second Temple marriage practices. In most cases they are a fair reflection of Jewish traditional practice.

In Judaism, marriage was the established norm. The vernacular Hebrew word for marriage, *kiddushin*, comes from a root meaning holy, as in holy matrimony. "Since holiness is related to wholeness in Jewish theology," writes Phipps, "the union of husband and wife sanctifies life."[24] Rabbi Eliezar Ben-Asai emphasizes the seriousness of the marriage imperative: "Whoever renounces marriage violates the commandment to increase and multiply; he is to be looked upon as a murderer who lessens the number of beings created in the image of God."[25]

Although this is a late quotation, as an observant Jew, Christ might have been under the same (Hebrew) obligation to marry. Thus it is now profitable to understand the Jewish nuptial chain of events. In Jesus' day almost all Jewish marriages were arranged. "In essence, marriage was a property transaction meant to secure the future of one family through an alliance with another."[26]

So sacred was marriage that the primary obligation of every Jewish father was to find a suitable wife for his son before his twentieth birthday.[27] According to later Jewish sources, "Marriage is vitally important in Judaism. Refraining from marriage is not considered holy, as it is in some other religions. On the contrary, it is considered unnatural. The Talmud says that an unmarried man is constantly thinking of sin."

The Talmud tells of a rabbi who was introduced to a young unmarried rabbi. The older rabbi told the younger one not to come into his presence again until he was married. The Talmud recommends that a man marry at age eighteen, or somewhere between sixteen and twenty-four.[28]

As noted above, the Jewish Elders looked for every opportunity of accusing Jesus of breaking tradition or committing sin (Luke 11:54). As W. John Walsh notes, "Why didn't the Jewish Elders just abruptly dismiss him for this [unmarried] oversight?"[29] The Jewish laws and customs regarding marriage were deeply rooted at the time of Christ. We can only suspect that they continued past the Second Temple period and were accurately maintained. In the Diasporic traditional Hebraic ceremony, the potential bridegroom went to the house of his hoped-for bride. He carried three things: his best financial offering, a betrothal contract, and a skin of wine. These were presented to the patriarch of the house, who judged the offerings' merit. If acceptable he called his daughter to hear her response. If everything was agreeable, the bride-to-be drank the wine and a trumpet was sounded to announce their betrothal.[30]

During the year following their betrothal, the couple could not see one another alone, and a chaperone would always accompany them wherever they went. During this period the bridegroom would go to his father's house to prepare a place, a *chupah* or honeymoon bed and all other preparations for a house and a financial position. When asked about the wedding date, the future groom could make no reply except, "No one knows except my father."[31] This was because he could not go and get his bride until the father approved of his son's preparations.

The bride, therefore, had to be in a constant state of readiness, so that the marriage would not catch her by surprise. Thus the betrothal could take up to a year and during that time the bride-to-be would often put an oil lamp in the window, with an extra jar of oil on hand, to beckon her groom. When the man's father decided that everything was in place and his son could go and fetch his bride, a second trumpet was blown. John Hagee explains further:

> This trumpet, to announce the groom's coming, was called the 'last trump.' Thus announced, the bridegroom took the marriage contract to present to the father of his intended bride. He claimed her as his bride and took her from her father's house to his father's house. His father would be waiting to receive the couple, and then the groom's father would take the hand of the bride and place it in the hand of his son. At that moment she became his wife. That act was called the *presentation*.[32]

Upon hearing the second and last trump, the friends and family of the couple would come for the marriage feast. This all relates to the marriage of Jesus Christ to the Church (Matthew 9:15; Mark 2:19) as well as to a marriage to an individual maiden. "Come, I will show you the Bride, the wife of the Lamb," writes John in Revelation 19:7, which may have multiple meanings.

While Christ was visiting the Bethany sisters, Mary sat at Jesus' feet and listened, while Martha labored in the kitchen. The exasperated sister Martha makes demands that Christ have Mary assist her in the kitchen. But Jesus sides with Mary, allowing her to continue. "What was the relationship between Jesus a guest," Spong asks, "and Mary, Martha's sister, that would cause Martha to assume that Jesus had the authority to command and that Mary should obey? That authority did exist in Jewish society in the first century in the marriage relationship."[33] Dr. Eric Huntsman explains that this authority existed in the teacher-disciple relationship as well.[34]

In acceptance of a marriage proposal, a maid would drink from the skin of wine and make her vows. Then as a wise virgin bride, she would keep her lamps burning, but well trimmed. She waited in eager readiness for the time when her bridegroom (Christ) would appear with the *shofar* trump. She accepted the summons to come to the marriage feast of the bridegroom. Then after a conjugal tryst, this hypothetical couple would truly be married.[35]

"The woman is the glory of the man," writes Paul (1 Corinthians 11:7). This exaltation could have eternal consequences. While "some rabbis in Jesus' day assumed that marriage and propagation would continue unchanged in the life after death," the Sadducees did not.[36] Mormon theology does not allow for married angels in heaven, for only married people will be exalted[37] (see D&C 132). Living the angelic life on earth is a lower lifestyle. Latter-day Saints are encouraged to live as the gods, in marital harmony.[38] It is incongruous to desire to be equal to the angels, while at the same time to seek exaltation in the celestial kingdom.

The combination of the ▼ and ▲ into a hexagon during the twentieth century has been used to represent the Hieros Gamos, or Sacred Marriage paradigm in the cosmic temple.[39] The hexagon may have been a pentangle (pentacle), Solomon's knot of love, which is endless and without any joining parts. This Seal of Solomon or Star of David might be used to represent the balance between the sexes, but it is not traditionally used in this manner. The womb of Mary Magdalene, in neognostic circles, later became known as the sacred Chalice of the Womb.[40]

Flavius Josephus explains that the "married" cherubim on the ark of the covenant were called "bridegroom" and "bride" in Temple parlance.[41] As Eugene Seaich points out, this is another reason why Jesus was accused of equating himself with God because he called himself the bridegroom (Matthew 9:15; John 3:29; Mark 2:19–20). It was very provocative for Him to take upon Himself an epithet wholly reserved for Yahweh or God in the Holy of Holies.[42] The idea that only the married were allowed access to the Inner Sanctum reveals that exaltation within the celestial kingdom is reserved for the eternally married, not for single high priests.[43]

Some have argued that while marriage was the custom of most Jews at the time of Christ, it was not a requirement.[44] First-century Jewish apocalypticists, those with dire expectations, eschewed sexual relations. First-century philosopher Philo noted that "no Essene takes a wife," while historian Josephus also indicates that the Essenes shunned marriage. The Roman polymath, Pliny the Elder, indicated that the Essenes renounced sex and lived "without any woman."[45] Bart Ehrman agrees and notes that "scholars today do not think that Jesus himself was an Essene. But that he held a similar apocalyptic world-view."[46]

Some sects during the Second Temple period, including Essenes, practiced celibacy by separating themselves from their wives after fulfilling the command to procreate. "While, according to many scholars," writes Achtemeier, "members of the Dead Sea sect appear to have been celibate, they also seem to have been married, and a marriage ritual is presented in their scrolls."[47] They seemed to have copulated only for procreation.

According to his research, William E. Phipps found that "there is no definite indication of violators [of the command to marry] in any of the sects of ancient Judaism."[48] Phipps argues, point-by-point, that not only was it a custom for Jewish men to be married, but it was essential for a rabbi to be so. Phipps' scholarly tome fully examines early Jewish and Christian marriage culture to the effect that he pronounces them not in contradiction to a married Jesus.

According to later rabbinical tradition, he who is unmarried lives "without joy, without blessing, without goodness."[49] Jewish scholar Hirschel Revel asserts, "The voluntary renunciation of marriage is a conception utterly foreign to Judaism."[50] In the *Mishnah* a concession was given to a man preoccupied with religious matters, and then only with his wife's consent, to abstain from sex for up to a fortnight.[51] Dr. Eric Huntsman cautions: "If the Mishnah's later requirements for a rabbi happen to reflect the situation in the first century A.D., then this would suggest that Jesus would have been expected to have been married."[52]

The Hebrew word for "knowledge" is *daath*, which also means "sexual union."[53] Intuitively, the old Mormon saying, "You can be saved only as fast as you gain knowledge" may mean something more expansive than our parochial thoughts.[54] The mysteries of the Bridal Chamber can only be known through the good and proper relations of a married husband and wife. Its implications are summarized in a famous Jewish saying, "A man will have to give account on the judgment day of every good thing which he refused to enjoy when he might have done so."[55]

While symbolically rich, Hebraic marriage customs weakly conceive of the next life. They do, however, point to a direction encapsulating the Holy Grail archetype and the validity of Christ's marriage. Next we examine the New Testament and the early Christian conception of marriage and see that it had a deeper eternal perspective. This exploration is followed by the Mormon vista that stretches far beyond ancient normative Judaism and Christianity.

NEW TESTAMENT AND EARLY CHRISTIAN MARRIAGE—IMPERATIVE

For we do not have a high priest who is not able to enter experientially into a fellow-feeling with our infirmities, but one who has been tempted and tested in all points like as we are, without sin.[56]

—HEBREWS 4:15

All major Christian denominations strongly deny that Jesus Christ was married.[57] It is true that none of the early Christian sources, be they canonical, patristic, or apocryphal, has any reference to a marriage or wife for Jesus. Why would His wife never be mentioned? Perhaps it was for their protection. A second was editing of the scriptures once the Platonic idea of perfect virtue resting in celibacy became pronounced in the primitive Church.[58] However, as Rudolf Bultmann suggests, "The ideal of virginity . . . is entirely foreign to Jesus; he required only purity and the sanctity of marriage."[59]

Another reason may have been the immediate Tribulation and second coming expectation. This notion of an imminent crisis before the great and terrible day of the Lord led directly to a "putting off" of marriage and family until that settled time (1 Corinthians 7:26; Matthew 24:19). Thus devoting oneself completely to the kingdom rather than to nuptial bliss only made sense. Ehrman accepts this view of early Christianity: "Jesus believed that the ideals of the kingdom should be realized in the present. And He believed that in the kingdom there would be no marriage and no sexual relations. (Mark 12:25) Evidently this was believed by the Essenes as well as by their fellow apocalypticists. They implemented this vision by remaining celibate and unmarried. And it is entirely plausible—indeed likely—that Jesus did the same."[60]

The scriptures and post-Apostolic fathers are deafeningly silent on Jesus' marital status. If He were celibate it would have conspicuously marked Jesus as very different from his first-century colleagues.[61] This glaring situation would have needed some explaining. It is therefore more significant that the scriptures do not mention His marriage as it allows us to assume that He either was or wasn't, according to one's own presuppositions. While the numbers who believe Jesus was married have vastly increased, most do not think so.[62]

For instance, Neoplatonic distrust of the material world had so invested certain branches of gnosticized Christianity with the doctrine of an immaterial and transcendent God that the fact of Jesus being truly human and married became untenable.[63] These Docetist believers denied that Jesus neither got sick, was ever injured, nor ever cried. Only later when He cried for the sins of the world did he shed tears, and injury came only with the nail holes in His hands and the spear in His side.[64] The Docetist view was that Christ laughed at those who thought He was on the Cross. Of course they had Him so extrahuman as not to have had excretory functions. Evidently they deduced all this from the scriptures and the argument from silence.

Docetic doctrines deny the genuine flesh-and-blood humanity of Jesus, only to emphasize His spiritual nature and divinity. This was the classic battle between the gnostics, who believed that He was *either* divine or human, and the Christian literalists, who believed He was *both* divine and human. The First Epistle of John explicitly warns against this Docetist view, insisting that Jesus came "in the flesh" (1 John 4:2).

Christians traditionally believe that Jesus was 100 percent divine and 100 percent human.[65] Elder Bruce R. McConkie also sees Christ as both: "Jesus was no recluse, no hermit, no ascetic. He came eating and drinking, enjoying the natural, normal, and wholesome social intercourse of the day."[66] However, to the gnostics and ascetic dualists of a number of ascetic sects, copulation was inherently evil and its practice a sin; thus to their way of thinking, Christ's holiness precluded him from indulging in such activities.

This led to a monastical form of worship and celibacy inherited by the apostate Church. Even contemplating Christ as a married man and the father of children was abhorrent to them. That is another reason why we find Christ's bride and offspring were shunted aside, lost, and finally denied by the churches of Christendom. The Church became the virgin, not the wife. Notwithstanding this view, it still became the virgin bride "whom Christ loved so much he gave his life for her" (Ephesians 5:25).

The question of Christ's humanity and Jesus' divinity first came from the Savior's own mouth, "But, whom say ye that I am?" (Matthew 16:15; Mark 8:27; Luke 9:18–20) The idea that He is or was mortal and also God is nonsense to the unbeliever but the very basis of Christian faith in Jesus Christ. His condescension seems real enough in that most of Jesus' actions were fairly normal for mortals. Religiously, he was circumcised, presented in the Temple, and baptized. Did He not say, "for thus is it fitting for us to fulfill all righteousness" (Matthew 3:15). According to Phipps, "Jesus was reared in the tradition of Palestinian Judaism that survived the destruction of the Jewish state in A.D. 70 and was preserved in the Mishnah and in the Talmud."[67]

In these ordinances we understand that it is in the Law that a man, Jesus not excepted, was righteous. (Romans 2:26) Thus Jesus, like other good Jews, was also required to "raise up seed unto Abraham" like the "sand on the seashore" (as in Genesis 32:12). Yet, most Christian churches' teachings deviate from this principle, saying that Christ was "above all this."

Certainly we cannot say that Christ's life on earth was the same as ours because He performed the infinite atonement, but on the other hand it was related to ours in broad outline. For example, like Christ, we all must suffer our Gethsemanes, we all must die on our crosses, we will all be resurrected, and we will all ascend into heaven. (Mosiah 18:2) Christ's special body and the importance of His mission preclude us from saying that He operated under the exact same conditions as we do, but archetypally He did. Why? Because He was working out His and our salvation, as we work out ours and our families'. We suspect that marriage and propagation would have loomed large in His mortality, as they do for us. To know the subtle balance between the dual purposes of His life is to begin to understand the man Jesus and the enormity of His destiny.[68]

A careful reading of the New Testament will demonstrate that there was time and place enough for Christ to have had a full and fruitful marriage. For example, there was the decade between age eighteen to twenty, the time of marriage for orthodox Jews, and the beginning of His ministry at the age of thirty.[69] Was this just too normative for the radical teacher? Were these "silent years" filled with the stuff of life in Christ's two-fold path of first working out His own salvation, so that he could then work out ours?

Certainly Jesus demonstrated no prejudice against women or marriage. In the New Testament, Jesus asserted his approval of the conception of matrimony in Matthew 19. Then in Ephesians 5:32 the Apostle Paul reiterated the Genesis "one flesh" view of marriage. Paul, in the midst of defending his apostleship asserts, "Do we not have the right to be accompanied by a wife, as the other apostles and the brothers of the Lord and Cephas [Peter]?" (1 Corinthians 9:5). This is a recognized pattern, that wives may accompany their apostolic husbands. We know that a number of women followed Jesus and accompanied His devotees, the Galileans. The radical liberal Episcopal bishop, John Selby Spong, writes: "I mean nothing suggestive in these comments, but I must note that given the rules governing women in the first-century Jewish society, a group of women who followed a male band of disciples had to be wives, mothers or prostitutes."[70]

In Mark 15:41 we read, "Who also, when he was in Galilee, followed him, and *ministered unto him*; and many other women which came up with him unto Jerusalem" (see Matthew 27:55–56; Luke 8:2–3). Now if Mary Magdalene was a prostitute, and she was not, how is it that she financially supported Jesus?[71] However, if she was a righteous "traveling companion," she may have been Jesus' accompanying missionary wife ministering to Him, along the lines Paul mentioned in 1 Corinthians 9:5. Orson Hyde perceptively noted: "I will venture to say that if Jesus Christ were now to pass through the most pious countries in Christendom with a train of women, such as used to follow him, fondling about him, combing his hair, anointing him with precious ointment, washing his feet with tears and wiping them with the hair of their heads and unmarried, or even married, he would be mobbed, tarred, and feathered, and rode [out] not on an ass, but on a rail."[72]

While slaves and other servants were accustomed to washing their masters' and guests' feet, the anointing of one's feet was a wife's prerogative in Hebraic custom, according to some.[73] Close examination of the New Testament reveals that no other woman, other than Christ's mother, is mentioned more prominently than the Magdalene.[74] Her very prominence seems to conform to the first-century custom of affording status to a woman in direct relationship with the status of her husband.

She was no mere camp follower but seems to be an intimate of Jesus of Nazareth himself, not as a whore, but as a virginal bride and sacred wife. Generally speaking, only with the marriage union to a noble wife, does the king achieve the royal status of "Anointed One," or "Messiah" in ancient Egyptian and possibly Hebrew lore.[75]

The "lost bride" and "dark bride" (Lamentations 4:4–8) motif is explained in Song of (Songs) Solomon 1:6; and 3:2–4. Much later the Apostle Paul wrote to the Church, "For I am jealous over you with godly jealousy; for I have espoused you to one husband, that I may present you as a chaste virgin to Christ." (2 Corinthians 11:2) Thus we see how the Church also was a bride under conditions similar to the actual Jewish nuptial ceremony. Previous references explained the Hebrew marriage customs, which can be seen in direct language: "In my Father's house are many mansions: if it were not so, I would have told you. I go to prepare a place for you. And if I go and prepare a place for you, I will come again and receive you unto myself; that where I am, there ye may be also" (John 14:2–3).

Here the proverbial betrothed leaves his promised to "go to prepare a place [mansion] for you" that the couple may be together. It is here proposed that the groom's bride is not just the Church as a whole, but also specifically a personal bride. And in this case it could be Mary Magdalene, who is so beautifully portrayed in countless stories, paintings, and sculpture.

As mentioned previously, Judaism considered marriage as a consummation of the commandment to "be fruitful and multiply." The Pharisees would certainly have heaped the reproach of bachelorhood upon Christ if He had been a single man, over thirty, and a Rabbi who had studied the Torah. The *Talmud* records this custom, "A man shall first take unto himself a wife and then study Torah."[76] Then after three decades he is "at thirty for authority."[77]

Ludwig Köhler explains that the Old Testament has no word for bachelor, so unusual was the practice.[78] Non-LDS British author Charles Davis concluded that "any practice or advocacy of voluntary celibacy would . . . have been so unusual as to have attracted much attention and comment."[79]

The Johannine text has the disciple Nathaniel calling Jesus "Rabbi."[80] (John 1:49) The Jewish requirement, within a hundred and seventy year radius of the time of Jesus, would have called for a rabbi to be married, since Mishnaic Law commands, "An unmarried man may not be a teacher of children."[81] As we know Jesus often taught children. (Mark 10:14) They were literally commanded to wed, "He who does not marry thereby diminishes the image of God."[82] In the controversial novel *The Da Vinci Code*, Dan Brown correctly points out:

> "Because Jesus was a Jew," Langdon said, taking over while Teabing searched for his book, "and the social decorum during that time virtually forbade a Jewish man to be unmarried. According to Jewish custom, celibacy was condemned, and the obligation for a Jewish father was to find a suitable wife for his son. If Jesus were not married, at least one of the Bible's gospels would have mentioned it and offered some explanation for His unnatural state of bachelorhood.[83]

Other events at the tomb establish the Savior's relationship with Mary Magdalene. (John 20:11) Weeping, she stoops to see angels, who inquire as to the cause of her tears—"Because they have taken away my *Lord*, and I do not know where they have laid him," she cries. The phrase "my Lord" in this case would not be a doctrinal enunciation but rather a first-century Jewish woman painfully inquiring after her husband.[84]

Orson Hyde paraphrases it thus: She said unto them, "Because they have taken away my *Lord*," *or husband*, "and I know not where they have laid him."[85] The words spoken to Mary Magdalene on resurrection morning may confirm Christ's relationship with her. She is called by her name "Mary" thus fulfilling the scripture that says, "I have called thee by thy name: thou art mine." (Isaiah 43:1, 45:4) When she realizes that the gardener is really Jesus she calls "Raboni" the familial term of both rabbi (teacher) and husband.[86] (John 20:16) These words imply that they would share intimate relations through marriage.

At the tomb the Magdalene sees one whom she assumes to be the gardener. This figure repeats the above angelic question: "Woman, why are you weeping? Whom do you seek?" Mary replies, "Sir, if you have carried him away, tell me where you have laid him, and I will take him away." (John 20:15) She seems to be claiming the body of the deceased, a custom in that day assigned only to the nearest of kin. If this were so, it would have been highly inappropriate unless she claimed the position of wife, sister, mother, or daughter to the deceased Christ.

In fact, Paul writes that marriage was a qualification for those who held church offices (1 Timothy 3:1–2; Titus 1:6). Many later gnostics rejected "church office" (hierarchy) because of the marriage requirement and accepted the supposed "higher virtue" of celibacy over marriage. Thus both gnostic and orthodox Christian celibates lacked the psychosomatic wholeness that marital bliss could offer. Platonic Hellenistic pagan ascetics were often known for their celibacy. However, it can be argued that Christian celibacy was a reaction against the widespread promiscuous customs of the pagans and heathens.[87] All these conspired in a welter of voices directing antagonism toward sexual intimacy.

One reason why celibacy crept into the early Christian church was most likely the keen persecution of the Saints by the Romans. By accepting this pagan practice of celibacy, their religious beliefs were less open to the scrutiny of the world. Eventually perpetual virginity with martyrdom was seen as the supreme virtue. The rise of monasticism codified the sacred vocation of virginity and celibacy. With Christ seen as the exemplar, sexual indulgence was incompatible with total consecration to the heavenly ideal. Phipps notes that St. Augustine in the fifth century denounced as heretical Bishop Julian, "who held that sexual desire was not necessarily defiling and that it was intrinsic to human nature. Julian concluded that Jesus had sexual desire and that Christians who marry are not second-class citizens in the kingdom of God."[88]

While this data is not conclusive, its cumulative effect argues that Jesus, the "shepherd," was married and that the "shepherdess," Mary Magdalene, was His virgin bride. Further ideas suggest their relationship. The theologian William E. Phipps hypothesized that Jesus did not believe in celibacy and that Mary Magdalene may have been His wife.[89] Ultimately the notion that Jesus was married rests upon the most fundamental question, "Why would Jesus be denied a wife on earth?" If he came to fulfill all righteousness, then the commandment to marry and replenish the earth could or would equally apply to him.

THE MORMON MARRIAGE—IMPERATIVE

Yet, while our theology allows the possibility of a married Christ, our scriptures and official doctrine do not teach this.

—DR. ERIC D. HUNTSMAN[90]

Marriage and children in the eternal scheme of things are of paramount importance.[91] Being fruitful and obeying the scripture, "multiply and replenish the earth" (Genesis 1:28; 9:1) were primary commands of God in the Garden of Eden. Sacred marriage on earth is reflective of the pattern established in heaven, in the spirit of "As Above, So Below." This wisdom requires all of our Latter-day Saint leaders to marry.

Marriage and family are the most consequential

sacraments in The Church of Jesus Christ of Latter-day Saints. President David O. McKay firmly taught, "No other success can compensate for failure in the home."[92] Matrimony was a divinely commanded condition in Mormon theology. The sexual act within marriage is seen to be a gift of God like the rest of created order.[93] Just how important the Mormon marriage imperative is, Apostle Joseph F. Smith has unequivocally declared:

> Marriage constitutes the most sacred relationship existing between man and woman. It is of heavenly origin, and is founded upon eternal principles. As a part and portion of the great plan of salvation . . . it is destined to continue not only while time shall last but throughout all eternity. Indeed it is an exigency upon which man's happiness, the perpetuity of his earthly existence, and his future dominion, glory and exaltation depend, and which, in the wisdom of God, must of necessity continue as the seal of the natural, legitimate, and inevitable domestic union of the sexes forever.[94]

The highest order of living the gospel is the sacred marriage, sometimes called the Holy Order, Order of Enoch, United Order, patriarchal/matriarchal order, or Law of Consecration and Stewardship. A woman shall not hold the lower orders of the priesthood, but these are subsumed in the Holy Order, as she becomes a "Queen and Priestess." Joseph Smith administered the first ordinances of the Holy Order on 28 May 1843.[95]

The married couple, in the prescribed *hieros gamos* sealing, could claim their Temple marriage blessings for Eternity (see D&C 132). The Holy Order of the Fathers and Mothers is always held in conjunction with a worthy spouse. In the celestial kingdom it equates to exaltation and in the Temple it conforms to the Holy of Holies. It is the priesthood of the family and has to do with procreation, especially "eternal lives," worlds without end.

With such an exalted view of marriage, it is an unspoken understanding by most Latter-day Saints that Jesus was married. It is a core principle within the Church that we have a Heavenly Mother, who is an exalted companion to Heavenly Father. Eliza R. Snow's hymn "O My Father" inquires, "In the heavens are parents single?" and then exclaims, "No the thought makes reason stare."[96] For if we think that Heavenly Father is married, should we not also think that the Heavenly Son should be married as well? Thus we are led to the conclusion, "If Jesus married, shouldn't we follow Him in matrimony?" It is the root and flower of Mormon doctrine.

It would seem that Mormon piety requires all who are exalted to be celestially married, including Christ during His own Second Estate. (D&C 132:19) It is generally understood by Latter-day Saints that Christ too was going through a probationary period during his own mortality. In this sense, He would be obliged to receive the eternal ordinance of marriage, the same as everyone else. This trail of thinking leads us to suppose that the Son of God, in order to achieve exaltation in the highest level of the celestial kingdom, needed to have the earthly conducted ordinance of Eternal Marriage. (D&C 131:1–4)

This implies that He *is* married, not just that He will eventually have to be married, for only married spouses reside in exaltation.[97] This is the law, which even Heavenly Father obeys. Yet, one should not assume that Jesus passed up marriage on earth, only to be sealed vicariously by proxy later in the Temple.

Ultimately such a marriage makes all the logical sense in the world, given the intellectual trajectory of gospel doctrine. This order of the priesthood, meaning the new and everlasting covenant of marriage, is an ordinance that must be performed in mortality. Since marrying is an earthly ordinance with eternal duration, there is no marrying or giving in marriage in heaven (Matthew 22:30; Mark 12:25; Luke 20:35; also see D&C 132:15–19, 22–23).[98]

"If anyone does not receive it while he is in this world," writes LDS scholar Hugh Nibley, "he will not receive it in the other place."[99] Joseph Smith taught that a couple can only have the ordinance of being married for eternity performed "while in this probation."[100] Smith further taught in *History of the Church* that "a man and his wife must enter into the covenant in the world, or he will have no claim on her in the next world."[101]

For reasons of propriety, a few Latter-day Saints believe that Jesus was not married while in mortality but will be at a later date in heaven. If one does not have the opportunity for marriage while in mortality, that person's marriage will be performed by proxy in a temple before the end of the Millennium. Of course this is not the preferred way. Since Christ is our pattern in all things, even He is no exception to the law. He would not wait, for the Son will do the things that the Father has done. He is Our Exemplar, as Heavenly Father is His Exemplar.[102]

The Apostle and future Prophet Joseph F. Smith believed that Jesus would have accepted this covenant of marriage while in mortality. He articulated as much at the Sabbath School Conference in July 1883: "[Joseph F. Smith] did not think that Jesus who descended through polygamous families from Abraham down and who fulfilled all the Law even baptism by immersion would have lived and died without being married."[103]

Now, in Doctrine and Covenants 132:24 Jesus Christ told the Prophet Joseph Smith, "I am he. Receive ye, therefore, my law." "My law" refers to celestial marriage and is used twenty-nine times in this section alone. Christ was inviting the Prophet

to enter into this highest form of marriage covenant. Likewise, we can imagine that Jesus during His mortality was temple married according to "His law" and it was sealed by the Holy Spirit of Promise (see D&C 132:9, 19, 26). Joseph Smith taught, "and you have got to learn how to be Gods yourselves, and to be kings and priests to God, the same as all Gods have done before you."[104] It happens here as it happens in other worlds.

Christ did not declare, "Do as I say, not as I do," or "Go ahead, I'll catch up with you later." Instead He said, "Come, follow me." In essence He is saying in Doctrine and Covenants 132:24, "Receive the celestial law of marriage, which I live." Would Jesus command the Saints to live a law that He Himself did not live? It may only be asked, "Would our Exemplar command us to be married after this order of the priesthood and not have been so Himself?

Reason requires that Jesus Christ himself obeyed the same commandments He gave mankind.[105] Doctrine & Covenants 132:21–24 tells that the way to "exaltation and continuation of lives" is narrow, and straight is the gate. In other words no eternal law or divine commandment was "too carnal" for Jesus Christ to obey Himself because He wished it to be "on earth as it is in heaven" (Matthew 6:10). Jesus is called "The Way" for good reason. Joseph F. Smith wrote in the Millennial Star: "Jesus Christ never omitted the fulfilling of a single law that God has made known for the salvation of the children of men. It would not have done for him to have obeyed one law and neglected or rejected another. He could not consistently do that and then say to mankind 'follow me."[106]

Celestial marriage is essential to exaltation. The Prophet, Joseph Smith Jr., proclaimed, "If a man gets a fulness of the priesthood of God he has to get it the same way that Jesus Christ obtained it, and that was by keeping all the commandments and obeying all the ordinances of the house of the Lord."[107] Nearly fourteen years later, in March 1857, Orson Hyde continued this train of thought:

> Did Jesus consider it necessary to fulfil every righteous command or requirement of his Father? He most certainly did. This he witnessed by submitting to baptism under the hands of John. Thus it becometh us to fulfil all righteousness, said he. Was it God's commandment to man, in the beginning, 'to multiply and replenish the earth?' None can deny this, neither that it was a righteous command; for upon an obedience to this, depended the perpetuity of our race.
>
> Did Christ come to destroy the law or the prophets, or to fulfill them? He came to fulfill. Did he multiply, and did he see his seed? Did he honor his father's law by complying with it, or did he not? Others may do as they like but I will not charge our Savior with neglect or transgression in this or any other duty.[108]

Eternal marriage is one of these ordinances. The old Mormon adage, "Exaltation is theirs in pairs" applies to everyone, including Jesus. If the scriptures establish the broad concept of a married Christ, then the words of the latter-day prophets fill in the details. Let us now examine a small sampling of that body of writings by early Church leaders.

Perhaps the earliest LDS reference to Christ having descendants comes from Joseph Smith's brother-in-law Oliver B. Huntington sometime before 1843. His journal records an account of how Joseph Smith sealed a Sister Repshire to Judge James Adams of Springfield, Illinois. The entry explains that "the Prophet stated to her (Repshire) that *Judge Adams*

was a literal descendant of Jesus Christ."[109] In a similar vein, Apostle Abraham H. Cannon recorded at a First Presidency and Quorum of the Twelve meeting in 1894, that his father, George Q. Cannon said, "Heber C. Kimball once told me that I was a descendant of the Savior of the world."[110]

In October conference of 1854, Church leadership began to publicly assert that Jesus Christ was married and had children. Orson Hyde quoted verses from John 20 of Mary at the sepulcher and concluded that we were listening to a married couple:

> Is there not here manifested the affections of a wife? These words speak the kindred ties and sympathies that are common to that relation of husband and wife. Where will you find a family so nearly allied by the ties of common religion? "Well," you say, "that appears rather plausible, but I want a little more evidence, I want you to find where it says the Savior was actually married. . . . When does it say the Savior was married? I believe I will read it for your accommodation, or you might not believe my words were I to say that there is indeed such a scripture.[111]

Though no scripture or General Authority ever actually used the phrase "Holy Grail," or *hieros gamos,* itself, they do allude to a sacred marriage, bloodline, and the lineage of Christ. Brigham Young made a commentary on Orson Hyde's sermon, calling it a "splendid address from brother Hyde, for which I am grateful." Brigham continued, "I say to the congregation, treasure up in your hearts what you have heard tonight, and at other times. You will hear more with regard to the doctrine, that is, our "Marriage Relations." Elder Hyde says he has only just dipped into it, but, if it will not be displeasing to him, I will say he has not dipped into it yet; he has only run round the edge of the field. He has done so beautifully, and it will have its desired effect.[112]

Although Brigham Young's statement shows his approval for the teaching of Christ's marriage, the time was not quite right for an official pronouncement. It took another two and a half years before public mention was again made of the matter. Then, in March 1857, Hyde spoke of the strong reaction against Mormon acceptance of a married Jesus Christ at that time "Object not, therefore, too strongly against the marriage of Christ, but remember that in the last days, secret and hidden things must come to light, and that your life also (which is the blood) is hid with Christ in God."[113]

That is a powerful statement filled with deep meaning. The great secret of the bloodline of the Holy Grail is that it comes down to us this very day, and through it we have the privilege of the priesthood and saving ordinances of the gospel (D&C 107:40). The old Pentecostal hymn "There's Power in the Blood" is literally true. Not just in the atonal blood from Gethsemane and Calvary, but also the stream of a bloodline through the ages, in the "Y" Chromosome and Mitochondrial DNA (mtDNA) of this chosen lineage.

Mormon temple sealings form the connecting point of the bride and the bridegroom. This is the balance between the Sacred Feminine and the Sacred Masculine that militant feminists refuse to accept. Feminists are routinely dismissive of marriage because they view it as controlling, suppressing, and dominating a woman's full sexuality and independence.

Where once the world was not ready but was very critical and unwilling to countenance this romantic tale, it now begs to be hear and understand more. Once Latter-day Saints were ahead of the curve in teaching what the bloodline of the Holy Grail

actually meant. Now, self-censorship has placed them just slightly behind the curve of international interest, though still well ahead in terms of knowledge and understanding. After being persecuted for this unique peculiarity, the wise leaders of the Church have become "reverentially quiet" on the topic.[114] For 107 years, the topic has basically been "dropped."

The LDS Church came out with the news that Jesus Christ was married to Mary and had children nearly one hundred years before gentile writers became aware of it.[115] This occurred because gospel lenses brought the idea into perspective and sharper focus than these writers could achieve. In 1972, Non-Mormon scholar William E. Phipps was the first to recognize the Church's contribution: "Appreciation is overdue for a Mormon (Orson Hyde) who had the insight and courage to revive a Hebraic viewpoint toward Jesus' relationship with women. . . . Hyde's striking belief in Jesus' marriage gained wide acceptance in the pioneer Mormon community. . . . Joseph Fielding Smith may provide a clue when he points out that Hyde was sent to Palestine to do missionary work among Jews because he was "of the house of Judah."[116]

Of course, Latter-day Saints realized this wasn't just a pipe dream of Orson Hyde's but was first taught in this dispensation by Joseph Smith Jr. and was promulgated by most of the leading Mormon brethren of the nineteenth century. Christ's marriage was not a thin veneer overlaid upon Mormonism but was a central part of the foundation of the early Church's belief in the priesthood, eternal marriage, exaltation in the celestial kingdom, and blood lineages. Ontologically speaking it was akin to the tender "Mother in Heaven" teaching and central to what makes distinctive Mormonism unique. If the Holy Grail was the lineage of the Lord's leaders, then Jesus Christ's marriage became the quintessential bloodline of God.

THE MARRIAGE OF CANA

Gentlemen, that is as plain as the translators, or different councils over this scripture, dare allow it to go to the world, but the thing is there; it is told, Jesus was the bridegroom at the marriage of Cana of Galilee, and he told them what to do.

Now there was actually a marriage [of Cana]; and if Jesus was not the bridegroom on that occasion, please tell who was. If any man can show this, and prove that it was not the Savior of the world, then I will acknowledge I am in error. [117]

—ORSON HYDE (1854)

Mormon Apostle and President of the Quorum of the Twelve Orson Hyde seems to be the spokesman for the LDS Church for this matter, in much the same way as John was designated spokesman in the New Testament. However, John only tells the fragmentary story of the wedding feast in Cana of Galilee. (John 2:1–11) Before the beginning of his ministry, Christ has only four Galilean disciples, Andrew and his brother Peter, Philip and his friend Nathanael (possibly Bartholomew). John, a Judean disciple, probably heard of the event from Jesus' mother. On *the third day of the week*, they go to the wedding about eighteen miles north of the village of Nazareth (Inspired Version/JST, John 2:1).

Bruce R. McConkie believes Christ's mother was the hostess, the one in charge, and responsible for the entertainment of the guests. "Considering the customs of the day," writes McConkie, "it is a virtual certainty that one of Mary's children was being married."[118] Certainly it was a family affair. Feminist and Episcopalian bishop John S. Spong explains his understanding of Cana: "I have never attended a wedding with my mother except when it was the wedding of a relative. The only time my mother and my closest friends were at a wedding together with me was my own wedding!"[119]

More to the point, religious scholar A. N. Wilson suggests, "the story of the wedding feast at Cana contains a hazy memory of Jesus' own wedding."[120] In 1857, Apostle Orson Hyde flatly states that Jesus was married at Cana: "It will be borne in mind that once [up]on a time, there was a marriage in Cana of Galilee; and on a careful reading of that transaction, it will be discovered that no less a person than Jesus Christ was married on that occasion."[121]

John relates how anxious Jesus' mother was because of the paltry supply of refreshments. Why would she be upset unless she was the mother of the bridegroom, hosting the wedding reception? Furthermore, Jewish wedding feast tradition required the groom's family to be responsible for the wine.[122] Her behavior, seen in this light, would be appropriate under the circumstances.

Prophet Brigham Young believed that Jesus was married at Cana. He stated, "Also, the bridal feast at Cana of Galilee, where Jesus turned the water into wine, was on the occasion of one of his own marriages."[123] The ubiquitous Orson Hyde offers some information in this regard. He quotes John chapter two, about the Marriage of Cana and the miracle of the conversion of water into wine: "When the ruler of the feast had tasted the water that was made wine, and knew not whence it was: (but the servants which drew the water knew,) the governor of the feast called the bridegroom, and said unto him—that is, the ruler of the feast said unto the bridegroom, 'Every man at the beginning does set forth good wine; and when men have well drunk, then that which is worse: but thou has kept the good wine until now.'"[124]

Jesus was "called" to the wedding of Cana. (John 2:2) Jewish tradition "calls" the bridegroom to the wedding. Certainly the Christian era began as the sacred vessels from Cana changed from water to wine by the greatest alchemist of all time. Supposedly, but not probably, the heirloom of the Magdalene, the Grail cup had engraved upon it:

> Whoso drinks me, God shall see.
> *Whoso at one good breath drains me,*
> Shall God and the Magdalen see![125]

Who was the "governor of the feast?" Perhaps the Master of Ceremonies for the feast was the marriage sealer as well? It could have been the family's guardian, Joseph of Arimathea, instead of the rightful father, Joseph the Carpenter, who was probably deceased by that time. As a rich man, Joseph of Arimathea may have known the subtle difference in the quality of wine. Perhaps the parable of the story is that Jesus saved the best until last, meaning in that the marriage that is finally exalted is best. Or, maybe it is an allegory of how the water of Judaism has turned into the wine of Christianity.[126]

But turning to the wedding itself, the Apostle and future Prophet Joseph F. Smith also believed that Jesus was married in Cana. He articulated this sentiment at the Sabbath School Conference in July, 1883, where it was recorded, "Joseph F. Smith spoke one hour & 25 minutes. He spoke upon the marriage in Cana at Galilee. He thought Jesus was the bridegroom and Mary & Martha the brides. . . . [He] spoke upon these passages to show that Mary & Martha manifested much closer relationship than merely a believer which looks consistent."[127]

There is a lovely stained glass window at St. Mary's Church in Dervaig, Isle of Mull, in Scotland from about 1906 to 1910 titled, *"The Marriage of the Lamb and His Bride"* (see Plate 2).[128] It depicts Jesus with a beautiful woman, who supposedly symbolizes the Church. They are too realistically described by the artist to be only allegorical emblems. Quite

pointedly, Christ would be the sacred Bridegroom and King of Israel with Mary of Magdala, Mary and Martha of Bethany being His Brides.

Marriage is a pure bond between two sympathetic souls. Jesus was married at Cana and the eternal consequences of this act will have eternal and infinite consequences for good. Why was the Grail marriage performed in Cana? Possibly because there was a temple in Cana, or maybe it had something to do with His friend Nathanael being from Cana. We are not certain.

There is one more question we must confront before we move on from Christ's marriage at Cana. What was his age at this important event? As mentioned above, in first-century Palestine, the normal age for Jewish men to marry was sixteen to twenty years of age.[129] However, most commentators believe he was about thirty years old at the time of his marriage at Cana![130] This would have been considered very late to marry by Jewish standards of the first century. Even in contemporary Mormon culture this would be late. Brigham Young was supposed to have said, "Any man who is not married by the time [he is] twenty-five is a menace to society."[131]

In John 2:13–21 an event took place during the last week of Jesus' life: the overturning of the money changers in the temple and noting that Jesus would rebuild the temple in three days. Alfred E. Garvie notes that "it is held by many scholars that the evangelist for his own didactic aims displaced the incident."[132] This event set within the same chapter as the marriage of Cana verses 1–11 describes supposedly the beginning and end of the Savior's ministry.

These two events are conflated, leading to the idea that John was not concerned with strict chronology. Christ saying to His mother, for "mine hour had not yet come" (John 2:4), may relate to heralding abroad His miraculous powers was yet future.[133] In fact the baptism of Jesus and relationship with certain disciples may also prefigure His ministry by a number of years.

Thus it is possible that the marriage in Cana occurred earlier in His life than when he was thirty years of age, the beginning of His official ministry. Orson Pratt accepts Cana, but notes, "We are not informed at what time Jesus was to be married to this King's daughter or any of the rest of His wives"[134] (see Psalm 45:13–14). We are certain that Christ's ministry began at the age of thirty, but that was the age at which a rabbi may teach in the temple. We might reasonably assume that Christ was probably first married at the age of twenty, as was typical in the first century.

CHRIST AND POLYGAMY

Indeed, the Psalmist, David, prophesies in particular concerning the Wives of the Son of God. We quote from the English version of the Bible, translated about three hundred and fifty years ago: "All thy garments smell of myrrh, and aloes, and cassia: when thou comest out of the ivory palaces, where they have made thee glad, Kings' daughters were among thine honorable wives: upon thy right hand did stand the Queen in a vesture of gold of Ophir."[135]

—ORSON PRATT,
PSALM 45:8–9

That Christ was married is hard enough to swallow for Mormonism's fellow Christian colleagues, but that He was a polygamist is unacceptable even to "alternative lifestyle" groups. Although today homosexual marriage is broadly accepted, adultery with multiple sex partners is mainstreamed, and underage sexual activity is encouraged by Planned Parenthood, polygamy is resolutely denounced, except by diehard

fundamentalists. Nevertheless it is currently practiced or praised by about one-fourth of the world's population.[136]

That Christ too may have participated in polygamy is an idea worthy of exploration. The early LDS Church had something to say regarding this topic. Mormon Seventy and later Apostle Jedediah M. Grant made a provocative declaration in August 1853. It was one of the earliest statements given by the Church on Christ's marital status:

> He [Celsus] says, "The grand reason why the Gentiles and philosophers of his school persecuted Jesus Christ, was because he had so many wives; there were Elizabeth, and Mary, and a host of others that followed him." . . . The grand reason of the burst of public sentiment in anathemas upon Christ and his disciples, causing his crucifixion, was evidently based upon polygamy, according to the testimony of the philosophers who rose in that age. A belief in the doctrine of a plurality of wives caused the persecution of Jesus and his followers. We might almost think they were "Mormons."[137]

This quotation from the Platonist Celsus is the oldest extant pagan polemic against Christianity.[138] It is the only place before Mormonism where Jesus is called a polygamist. Just two months after Grant's sermon, in a rather lengthy article in *The Seer* (October 1853), Apostle Orson Pratt wrote that Jesus had a number of wives:

> Next let us enquire whether there are any intimations in Scripture concerning the wives of Jesus. We have

already, in the 9th no. of this volume, spoken of the endless increase of Christ's government. Now, we have no reason to suppose that this increase would continue, unless through the laws of generation, whereby Jesus, like His Father, should become the Father of spirits; and, in order to become the Father of spirits, or, as Isaiah says, 'The Everlasting Father,' it is necessary that He should have one or more wives by whom He could multiply His seed, not for any limited period of time, but forever and ever: thus He truly would be a Father Everlastingly, according to the name which was to be given Him.

The Evangelists do not particularly speak of the marriage of Jesus; but this is not to be wondered at, for St. John says:

There are also many other things which Jesus did, the which, if they should be written every one, I suppose that even the world itself could not contain the books that should be written. (John 21:25)

One thing is certain, that there were several holy women that greatly loved Jesus—such as Mary, and Martha her sister, and Mary Magdalene; and Jesus greatly loved them, and associated with them much; and when He arose from the dead, instead of first showing Himself to His chosen witnesses, the Apostles, He appeared first to these women, or at least to one of them—namely, Mary Magdalene. Now, it would be very natural for a husband in the resurrection to appear first to his own dear wives, and afterwards show himself to his other friends. If all the acts of Jesus were written, we no doubt should learn that these beloved women were his wives.[139]

Interestingly, this is now as galling to the modern secular mind as it is to traditional orthodox Christian sensitivities. Together with slavery, they consider plural marriage as one of the "Twin Relics of Barbarism." In an 1867 sermon, Brigham Young said that this "relic," or polygamous practice, had an old pedigree: "Here is one of the 'relics of barbarism!' Yes, one of the relics of Adam, of Enoch, of Noah, of Abraham, of Isaac, of Jacob, of Moses, David, and Solomon, the Prophets, *of Jesus and his Apostles.*"[140]

Early LDS teaching to this effect came from the top echelons of the Church. In his famous October 1854 sermon, Orson Hyde responds to the detractors who question this practice:

Then you really mean to hold to the doctrine that the *Savior of the world was married*; do you mean to be understood so? And if so, do you mean to be understood that *he had more than one wife?*"[141] . . . For I tell you it is the chosen of God, the seed of the blessed, that shall be gathered. I do not despise to be called a son of Abraham, if he had a dozen wives; or to be called a brother, a son, a child of the Savior, if he had Mary, and Martha, and several others as wives: and though he did cast seven devils out of one of them, it is all the same to me.[142]

This was precisely Elder Hyde's contention, that Jesus was indeed married to more than one woman, the implication of this statement being that Jesus not only believed but also practiced this principle of plural marriage. Dr. William E. Phipps noted that the belief that "Jesus married and married often!" was used to encourage and promote the doctrine of plural marriage amongst timid Latter-day Saints.[143] Brigham Young was recorded to have straightforwardly taught this belief: "The scripture says that He, the Lord, came walking in the temple, with His train; I do not know who they were unless His wives and children."[144]

Brigham Young's nineteenth wife wrote, "Jesus Christ was a practical polygamist; Mary and Martha, the sisters of Lazarus, were his plural wives, and Mary Magdalene was another."[145]

According to brethren of the early LDS Church, the Savior had a plurality of wives.[146] During the October 1854 General Conference of the Church, Apostle Orson Hyde gave a rather lengthy address on the subject.

> How was it with Mary and Martha, and other women that followed him [Christ]? In old times, and it is common in this day, the women, even as Sarah, called their husbands Lord; the word Lord is tantamount to husband in some languages, master, lord, husband, are about synonymous. In England we frequently hear the wife say, 'Where is my master?' She does not mean a tyrant, but as Sarah called her husband Lord, she designates hers by the word master.[147]

In March 1855, Orson Hyde pronounced that the Savior indeed had wives and children. This caused a great stir throughout the United States with newspaper editors publicizing it to humiliate the fledgling Utah church. Hyde, in commenting further, said, "I discover that some of the Eastern papers represent me as a great blasphemer, because I said, in my lecture on marriage, at our last Conference [October 1854], that Jesus Christ was married at Cana of Galilee, that Mary, Martha and others were his wives and that He beget children . . . if Jesus begat children he only 'did that which he had seen his father do.' "[148]

Although Christ as a polygamist is a provocative principle, polygamy itself is not an essential ordinance for exaltation. Most apostate LDS fundamentalists, however, insist that celestial marriage and plural marriage were synonymous. This may have been true in a classical sense during Joseph's and Brigham's days. However, in broader terms, celestial marriage now means eternal marriage sealed by the priesthood in an LDS temple, not specifically plural marriage. In a letter to the Church, the First Presidency in 1914 made this definition clear.[149]

One of the chief reasons why Christ is associated with the supposedly celibate Essene community was that Jesus was thought to be against the plurality of wives and even marriage itself. But according to Gordon Strachan, while He may have been a student of an Essene cult of Pythagoreans, He certainly was not an Essene.[150] Generally speaking, Pythagoreans were strict vegetarians and practiced celibacy, which Jesus did not. Opposed to the celibacy and monogamy of the Dead Sea sect (Essenes) was the Damascus Document of the sect of the Karaites, which gives a more rabbinical view on polygamy.

According to Israeli scholar Yigael Yadin, Christ was not an Essene because their strict legalistic and rigid reliance on the law of Moses was at odds with Christ's "the Sabbath was made for man" type of teachings.[151] Christ was probably closer to normative Judaism, based on traditional rabbinical interpretation of teachings on plural marriage.

Arguments against a married Jesus sometimes hinge on the injunction in Deuteronomy 17:17 that

"Neither shall he multiply wives to himself, that his heart turn not away." In the early post-Second-Temple Jewish document the *Mishnah,* it is written of the King: "Nor shall he multiply wives to himself—eighteen only. Rabbi Judah the prince says: 'He may multiply them to himself provided that they do not turn away his heart.'"[152]

This would not include Christ himself, because as the true Messiah his heart could never turn away. Furthermore, we only know of his having a few (three or four) wives, which is not many. These wives likely included Mary Magdalene, Mary and Martha of Bethany, and the mysterious Elizabeth mentioned by Celsus.[153] Should the King then have two, three, four, five, seven, or eighteen wives? We can only speculate. The exact number of Christ's wives is unknown; the important thing is that He was married, and if He had "wives" so be it.

As early Judaic-Christianity became ever more gentile and Hellenized, Greco-Roman monogamist aversion to polygamy replaced the "old style" Hebraic custom. Eventually the Church outlawed polygamy as it moved toward apostasy, and it was only practiced on the fringes of Christianity and Judaism. Yet it still was a theologically viable part of life in the early first century.[154]

Some see arguments against polygamy in the Genesis quotations of "male and female he created them" and "two by two" going into the ark.[155] But it should be remembered that seven clean animals, not just two of each animal went into the Ark. (Genesis 7:2) This number reflects the number of wives mentioned by Isaiah 4:1, "And in that day seven women shall take hold of one man."

In Christ's parable of the wise and foolish virgins, five prudent virgins come to the wedding of the bridegroom. (Matthew 25:1–13) Ostensibly this parable has reference to the kingdom, but it might also apply to the King as well. The English Pre-Raphaelite artist John M. Strudwick in 1883 painted this beautiful representation of *The Ten Virgins,* which illustrates the allegory (see Plate 3). [156]

Non-Mormon Christians insist that the New Testament verse that a bishop must be "the husband of one wife" is proof of monogamy. (Titus 1:6) Of course this is a *non sequitur* because requiring that a bishop be the husband of at least one wife does not prevent him from being the husband of more than one. The word "only" does not appear, thus leaving ample room for more wives, if need be.[157]

Some detractors also quote the Hillel Pharisees questioning Jesus, who said, "For this cause shall a man leave father and mother and shall cleave to his wife, and the twain shall be one flesh." (Matthew 19:5–6) Again there is no prohibition against multiple wives in this verse. Nowhere in the Bible is there an actual injunction against polygamy; in fact there are several verses in which God allowed it. (Genesis 31:17; 32:22; Deuteronomy 21:15; Judges 8:30; and so on.) The Book of Mormon, however, forbids "wives and concubines" (Jacob 2:27, 3:5) unless God commands it (Jacob 2:30).

By the mid-1850s the idea that more than one woman was married to Jesus was widely accepted in Mormon circles. Anti-Mormon minister J. R. Church notes that "according to the guardians of the Grail, Jesus was supposed to have married both Mary [of Bethany] (who eventually became associated with the title, Magdalene) and her sister Martha."[158] The illusive non-LDS writer M. Zvi Udley somewhere found a source identifying Martha as a plural wife: "In all probability Simeon was a son of Jesus and Martha, and was that child who appeared at the crucifixion."[159]

Beyond this one source, nothing before 1945 in any gentile literature the author has read has mentioned plural wives for Jesus. Only Latter-day Saints do that. Mormon Apostle Orson Pratt, in November 1853, goes so far as to establish that even among plural wives one wife was preeminent, "Inasmuch as the

Messiah was to have a 'plurality of wives' will they not all be Queens? Yes; but there will be an order among them. One seems to be chosen to stand at his right hand; perhaps she may have merited that high station by her righteous acts, *or by the position she had previously occupied.* It seems that she was one of the daughters of a king."[160]

We think this has reference to Mary Magdalene, but what exactly Orson Pratt meant by "or by the position she previously occupied" we do not know for sure. Perhaps he had reference to a premortal position relating to her claim on Christ. This Queen at "the right hand" would have been chosen in the Councils in Heaven, rather than being left to the vagaries of this chaotic second estate.

In the above quotation Pratt relies upon Psalm 45:7–16 to state that the bride of the king would be a king's or queen's daughter—in other words, of a royal or noble lineage.[161] It might be a non-Judah noble family of Ephraimite origin. "In subsequent legends," note Baigent, Leigh, and Lincoln, "she [the bride] is said to have been of royal lineage."[162] Paul denied the over-spiritualizing of Christ's nature, when he noted that Jesus, "took not on him the nature of angels; but he took on him the seed of Abraham." (Hebrews 2:16) Orson Pratt underscored this assessment when he wrote:

> From the passage in the forty-fifth Psalm, it will be seen that the great Messiah who was the founder of the Christian religion, was a polygamist, as well as the Patriarch Jacob and the prophet David from whom He descended according to the flesh. Paul says concerning Jesus, 'Verily he took not on him the nature of angels; but he took on him the seed of Abraham.' Abraham the polygamist, being a friend of God, the Messiah chose to take upon himself his seed; and by marrying many honorable wives himself, show to all future generations that he approbated the plurality of wives under the Christian dispensation, as well as under the dispensations in which His polygamist ancestors lived.[163]

That Christ was married and had children would not have been bothersome in itself, except that He proclaimed Himself to be the Son of God. For some reason there are those who believe He was either a man or a God. The overly pious mind or incredulous personality could not meld the idea that He was fully both.[164] Eventually, the Nicean fathers in A.D. 325 correctly wrote that Jesus Christ was fully man and fully God.[165] Samuel W. Richards saw that such news would be disconcerting, even to the Latter-day Saints: "If these things have power to disturb the pure mind, we apprehend that even greater troubles than these may arise before mankind learn[s] all the particulars of Christ's incarnation—how and by whom he was begotten; the character of the relationships formed by that act; the number of wives and children he had, and all other circumstances with which he was connected, by which he was tried and tempted in all things like unto man."[166]

As if the concept of Christ's polygamy was not unsettling enough, Mormonism even taught in the nineteenth century that God the Father had a plurality of wives as well. Orson Pratt reports:

> We have now clearly shown that God the Father had a plurality of wives, one or more being in eternity, by whom He begat our spirits as well as the spirit of Jesus His First Born, and another being upon the earth by whom He begat the tabernacle of Jesus. . . . We have also proved that

both God the Father and our Lord Jesus Christ inherit their wives in eternity as well as in time; and that God the Father has already begotten many thousand millions of sons and daughters. . . . it being expressly declared that the children of one of His Queens should be made Princes in all the earth.[167]

Ultimately the marriage of the Lamb of God with several wise virgins had a leavening consequence upon the entire planet. Through them and their seed, the promises to Abraham reverberate, that "the whole world would be blessed." Their shared marriage and offspring preserved the hope of spring in an otherwise wintry world. Through these Grail spouses, "The wilderness and the solitary place shall be glad for them; the desert will rejoice and blossom as a rose." (Isaiah 35:1; see also Revelation 4) All righteous mankind, their literal and their adopted children, shall one day rise up and call them blessed.

NOTES

1. Lutzer, *Da Vinci Deception,* 56. Lutzer is senior pastor at the Moody Church in Chicago.
2. Graves, *White Goddess,* 425.
3. These books were published in the wake of the success of Dan Brown's novel. They include at least seventeen books debunking the content and accuracy of *The Da Vinci Code.* The best among them is Olson and Miesel, *Da Vinci Hoax.*
4. Phipps, *Was Jesus Married?* 187. Refers to celibacy being one of the "sick practices."
5. Schaff, *History of the Christian Church,* 2:397.
6. Lutzer, *Da Vinci Deception,* 56. Of course His mother Mary was mortal and righteous, so why not His wife, Mary Magdalene, being equally righteous and therefore worthy?
7. The Unitarian Church, not surprisingly, has not protested that Jesus Christ was married; neither has the Presbyterian Church.

8. Arius (ca. A.D. 250–336), a Libyan theologian, preached that Jesus' Father alone was the "One True God," inaccessible and unique. Christ, the Logos, was neither co-eternal nor uncreated because he had received life and being from the Eternal Father. According to Arius, his father was Joseph the Carpenter, but He was Son of God because of His spirituality and perfection.
9. Sacerdotalis Caelibatus, 21, as quoted in Phipps, *Was Jesus Married?* 1.
10. St. Catherine of Alexandria's feast day (25 November) was dropped from the liturgical calendar in 1969. St. Catherine of Alexandria (died about A.D. 310) is the patron saint of philosophers (lovers of wisdom, Sophia) and young unmarried women.
11. See Tertullian, *On the Veiling of Virgins* 16, and Origin, *Song of Songs* Homilies 1, 2 and *Romans* Homilies 7, 8. See also Cyprian, *Letters,* 61, 3. Richard Tinto, "Dick Tinto at Rome, 14 March 1855," *New York Daily Times,* 4 May 1855, 2. Just how far this mystic marriage is taken can be seen in the following statement from "Tinto": "A place is shown which was once inhabited by St. Dominic the founder of the Inquisition, who received letters from Heaven, written by the Holy Trinity. However, this is of a lower order of blasphemy than that indulged in at a little old house at Sienna, which produces the love correspondence of the Savior and St. Catherine. I hardly expect to be believed when I say that letters are actually shown which profess to have been written to her by our Lord. Those written by her to her husband Jesus Christ, and to her mother-in-law the Virgin Mary, may be seen by anybody. The exact spot is also pointed out where the Savior and St. Catherine stood when they were married, and where the wedding ring was put upon her finger."
12. *Wilford Woodruff Journal* (14 October 1882), 8:126. See Staker, *Waiting for the World's End,* 358.
13. Isenberg, as quoted by Robinson, *Nag Hammadi Library in English,* 131.
14. Wilson, *Gnosis and the New Testament,* 184; see also 121.
15. Pratt, *Autobiography,* 259–60. The quotation continues, "at that time, my dearly beloved brother, Joseph Smith, had barely touched a single key; had merely lifted a corner of the veil and given me a single glance into eternity."
16. Smith, *Teachings of the Prophet Joseph Smith,* 322; see Ehat and Cook, *Words of Joseph Smith* (27 August 1843), discourse by Joseph Smith as recorded by Willard Richards, 244. "Three grand orders of priesthood referred to here." (Hebrews 7:1–12) The Orders are listed in different arrangement here.
17. See Doctrine and Covenants 131:1–3. In a sense the

entire celestial kingdom is a holy temple. Bruce R. McConkie wrote, "Actually there is no temple in heaven, for heaven [celestial] itself is a temple, and "'the Lord God Almighty and the Lamb are the temple of it' (Revelation 21:22)" (*Doctrinal New Testament Commentary,* 3:514; see also 2:73–77).

18. McConkie, *Doctrinal New Testament Commentary,* 3:589: "The holy of holies in the Lord's earthly houses are symbols and types of the Eternal Holy of Holies which is the highest heaven of the celestial world." This is where the exalted live as married couples.

19. He was a High Priest after the Order of Melchizedek (Hebrews 7:1, 10–11, 15; 9:11).

20. The root of the Greek word *diakonein,* or *deacon,* means "to minister."

21. Sirach 36:24–26 (second century after Christ), as quoted in Phipps, *Was Jesus Married?* 102.

22. The word *helpmeet* is often translated "helper" but the Hebrew word *azar* is best given as "partner."

23. Moses Maimonides, *Minyan ha-Mitznet,* 212. This is a twelfth-century source and may not precisely reflect Second Temple marriage practices.

24. Phipps, *Was Jesus Married?* 16.

25. Talmudic commentary on scripture (Genesis 9:6–7), Yebamoth, 64a. See also, "Magdalene the Bride of Christ" (www.spiritbride. com; November 2004). In the century before the Christian era, the leading schools of Hillel and Shammai agreed upon at least one point, "No one may abstain from keeping the law, 'Be fruitful and multiply.'" See Yebamoth 6,6, as quoted in Phipps, *Was Jesus Married?* 16.

26. Shanks and Witherington, *Brother of Jesus,* 102.

27. Talmud, Kiddushin 29a. This is a late second- to third-century source. "He must circumcise him, redeem him, teach him Torah, teach him a trade, and find a wife for him." The sixteenth through twentieth year of the son was preferable for marriage. There are 613 requirements in Judaism; many have to do with the sanctity of the marriage. This is supposedly the number of seeds in a pomegranate, itself a symbol of marriage. The pomegranate is a symbol that graced the Mercy Seat on the ark of the covenant.

28. Judaism 101 (http://www.jewfac.org/index.htm)

29. W. John Walsh, "Why was Jesus never married?" (June 2005) (http://www.lightplanet.com/mormons/response/qa/marriage_jesus.htm). If Jesus were unmarried, would not the priests have simply been able to say: "Jesus, you are many years past the age of marriage. As an unmarried man, you are always thinking of sin. Leave and do not assume to teach the truths of God until you have obtained proper marriage."

30. This is similar to the return of Jesus Christ to the earth during the Second Coming (see D&C 88:92, 98).

31. Hagee, *Final Dawn over Jerusalem,* 183–85. This is similar to the scripture where Christ says, "But of that day and that hour knoweth no man, no, not the angels which are in heaven, neither the Son, but the Father" (Mark 13:32).

32. Hagee, *Final Dawn over Jerusalem,* 184.

33. Spong, *Born of Woman,* 195–96.

34. Dr. Eric D. Huntsman e-mail to Swanson, 24 August 2005. It would not be difficult to build a case for Mary Magdalene as a prize student and disciple of Jesus.

35. Phipps, *Was Jesus Married?* 21, notes: "Marriage was a covenant initiated by the heads of two families and consummated conjugally by the bride and groom. It was not a cultic rite solemnized by a priest at a shrine."

36. Phipps, *Was Jesus Married?* 94. Phipps relies on later Rabbinical sources to support his argument: Sanhedrin 92b; Shabbath 30b; "egeiro," TWNT; Berakoth 17a. Granted, this is a necessity because of the dearth of primary sources from the early first century. Tradition is a Jewish "tradition," so one might expect in the face of no contradictory evidence that these later sources reflected earlier mores.

37. Resurrected angels are men and women who are servants and messengers in an unmarried state in the celestial kingdom, while gods live as resurrected in the upper third of the celestial kingdom, called exaltation, as married couples.

38. Non-LDS sources have hinted at this relationship. Maurice Wiles, "Studies in Texts: Luke 20:34–36," *Theology* 60 (1957): 501–2, notes: "Is it not more reasonable that the life of heaven should involve a going on from, rather than a drawing back from, the highest kind of personal relationship known to us?" Emanuel Swedenborg believed that the animal body would be resurrected after death, with sexual desires and conjugal relations continuing in heaven. See his *Marriage and the Sexes in Both Worlds,* 14, 23, 28, 31, 38. See Phipps, *Was Jesus Married?* 94.

39. The blade and chalice symbols are quite modern, despite what *The Da Vinci Code* says (237). Abanes, *Truth behind The Da Vinci Code,* 47, carefully analyzes different symbols for man and woman through the centuries and comes to other conclusions. Interestingly in today's modern restroom we often see the symbols reversed for man and woman. When a head and feet are attached to the ⚦ and ⚧ symbols, they become women and men

symbols respectively! Olson and Miesel, *Da Vinci Hoax*, 181, state that in a pagan-friendly book by Gimbutas, *Goddesses and Gods of Old Europe*, there are no sexual symbols involving the chalice or blade.

40. Godwin, *Holy Grail*, 27.

41. Josephus, *Jewish Wars* 6:301, as quoted in Seaich, *Mormonism, the Dead Sea Scrolls, and the Nag Hammadi Texts*, 33.

42. Seaich, *Mormonism, the Dead Sea Scrolls, and the Nag Hammadi Texts*, 33.

43. This may be one reason why Christ was allowed entry into the heavenly Holy of Holies on Yom Kippur (Day of Atonement), because he was married (see Hebrews 9:11–13).

44. Ehrman, *Lost Christianities*, 155–56. This would be no different from today, whereas in Christ's time we might imagine it being more conservative.

45. John Collins, "Essenes," *Anchor Bible Dictionary*, 2:619–26. But there were two groups of Essenes: the larger group was much older and did not take wives but did not condemn it on principle; the smaller group did take wives.

46. Ehrman, *Lost Christianities*, 156. Where Ehrman got the idea that he followed their world view is difficult to understand.

47. Achtemeier, *Romans*, 609.

48. Phipps, *Sexuality of Jesus*, 44. The syncretistic sect of Therapeutae in Alexandria Egypt practiced celibacy, but they were more pagan than Jewish.

49. Mishnah, Yebamoth, 62b.

50. Revel, "Celibacy," *Universal Jewish Encyclopedia*. cf.Ford, op.cit, 59.

51. Mishnah, Ketuboth 5, 6. The Mishnah was completed about A.D. 200.

52. Dr. Eric D. Huntsman e-mail to Swanson, 24 August 2005. Dr. Huntsman wisely argues against reading too much into later texts and then reading them backwards to the time of Jesus.

53. See Freke and Gandy, *Jesus and the Goddess*, 160, 284ff45. The word *Daath*, from *yada*, means "to know." For its sexual connotations, see Genesis 4:1, where Adam "knew" his wife, Eve. Also see Armstrong, *History of God*, 59.   54.   Smith, *Teachings of the Prophet Joseph Smith*, 301, 357; Ehat and Cook, *Words of Joseph Smith*, 205–7, 342.

55. Mace, *Hebrew Marriage*, 144, as quoted in Phipps, *Was Jesus Married?* 16.

56. Wuest, *New Testament*, 519. The King James Version of Hebrews 4:15 reads: "For we have not a high priest which cannot be touched with the feelings of our infirmities; but

was in all points tempted like as we are, yet without sin."

57. Even the Unitarian Church is, as usual, uncertain. They "generally" say that "possibly" he was. Except for LDS offshoots, the author knows of no denomination that actually teaches that Jesus was married. Even the LDS Church is not assertive in this respect.

58. The Joseph Smith Translation does not restore any knowledge of the sacred marriage, but the Doctrine and Covenants does establish the raison d'etre for it (see D&C 131:1–4; 132:19–24).

59. Bultmann, *Jesus and the Word*, 99. See Phipps, *Was Jesus Married?* 54.

60. Ehrman, *Lost Christianities*, 157.

61. In A.D. 1015 the Catholic Church forbade clergy to marry. This was upheld in the Council of Trent in 1545. That council, however, said that it was a law of the Church, not of God.

62. Wilson, *Jesus: The Evidence*, throughout his book.

63. Tatian, *Address to the Greeks* (21), like Plato casts vitriol on those who "wallow in matter and mud."

64. Even then, most Docetists believe that "Christ" was above all, while "Jesus" was just a man. Jesus had foibles; Christ did not.

65. Abanes, *Truth behind The Da Vinci Code*, 26. To envision Jesus as a celibate and childless God does not make sense, in fact, it makes a mockery of His full humanity.

66. McConkie, *Doctrinal New Testament Commentary*, 1:136.

67. Phipps, *Was Jesus Married?* 13. The Talmud contains Jewish civil and religious law, folklore, history and cultural tradition. More than 2,000 scholars contributed to it between 450 B.C. and A.D. 500. The Mishnah (Hebrew for "repetition" and "instruction.") is the first part of the Talmud and sets down Jewish laws, traditions, and customs passed on orally for centuries. Jewish scholars about A.D. 200 completed the Mishnah.

68. Kahlil Gibran, *Thoughts and Meditations*, 50. Kahlil Gibran once wrote about such nuance:

To know the differences
between those things
which are seemingly similar,
and
To know the similarities
between those things
which are seemingly different—
Is to know the secret of the Cosmos.

69. Talmud, Kiddushin 29b-30a. "When a bachelor attains the age of twenty and is unmarried, the Holy One says,

'Let him rot!'"More liberal rabbis allowed the age to be twenty-four for the upper at limit of bachelorhood. Also see Aboth 5:21; Sanhedrin 76b; Kiddushin 76 b.

70. Spong, *Born of Woman*, 191.

71. She may have inherited her wealth, or shared in her family's wealth, or it was business income, but not from prostitution, which Jesus would not have countenanced.

72. Apostle Orson Hyde, in *Journal of Discourses* (March 1857), 4:259–60. Also quoted in William E. Phipps, "The Case for a Married Jesus," *Dialogue* 7, 4 (Winter 1972): 46.

73. While obviously no expert on Second Temple Jewish customs, George Reynolds of the First Council of the Seventy gives this as one of the reasons he believed Jesus was married. See First Presidency Letterpress Copybooks (1877–1949, 286–288) (CR/1/20/#19, 10 June 1890). Jesus' washing of his disciples' feet was related in the "servant" role, not as an anointing of the feet ceremony. In a later chapter this rite in early Mormon history will be discussed.

74. While there is no biblical evidence that Mary Magdalene was the "sinful" woman who washed Jesus' feet, this author believes that there are two instances in which this happened, one by the Magdalene and the other by Mary of Bethany.

75. See Nibley, *Message of the Joseph Smith Papyri*, 175. Most gnostic writers would put it "ritual" rather than marriage union to a "priestess" rather than noble wife. See Freke and Gandy, *Jesus and the Goddess*, 17–19.

76. Talmud: Kiddushin 29b. Dr. Eric Huntsman of BYU warns that this may not necessarily apply to the first-century and Second Temple period of Judaism. Farrar, *Life and Work of St. Paul*, 44–46, notes that Paul could not have attained leadership as a Jewish rabbi in his pre-Christian years had he not been married (see Acts 9:1–2, 22:3, 26:10; Galations 1:14).

77. Hertz, *Sayings of the Fathers*.

78. Kåhler, *Hebrew Man*, 89. See Phipps, *Was Jesus Married?* 26.

79. Charles Davis, as quoted in *The Observer*, London, 28 March 1971, 25.

80. Brown, Fitzmyer, and Murphy, *New Jerome Biblical Commentary*, 1319, notes that the term *rabbi* (literally meaning "my great one") was used honorifically, "but the title in pre-A.D. 70 Judaism was more loosely used than later on." Thus this line of reasoning, while valid, has its limitations.

81. Talmud, Kiddushin 4, 13. Phipps, *Sexuality of Jesus*, 4. See also Blake and Blezard, *Arcadian Cipher*, 145.

"Mishnaic Law states very clearly that unmarried men may not take on the role of teacher/rabbi."

82. Tosefta, Yebamoth, 8:4. See Seaich, *Mormonism, the Dead Sea Scrolls, and the Nag Hammadi Texts*, 33.

83. Brown, *Da Vinci Code*, 245.

84. Yet we may argue that a male disciple might say "my Lord" (Kyrias) and be correct in doing so. But would a close female disciple say the same thing?

85. Orson Hyde, in *Journal of Discourses* (6 October 1854), 2:81.

86. See Robinson, *Indexes to all Editions of Brown-Driver-Briggs, Hebrew-English Lexicon*. See also part three, chapter 5, footnote 59.

87. Devine, *Holy Virginity*, 82.

88. William E. Phipps, "The Case for a Married Jesus," *Dialogue* 4 (Winter 1972), 48. Phipps continues, "But the Bishop of Hippo [Augustine] argued that it was impossible for Jesus the perfect man to have sexual desire which is tainted with evil. Julian, who was condemned as a heretic, was closer than Augustine to the authentic biblical ethic pertaining to sex and marriage."

89. Phipps, *Was Jesus Married?* 39–40. See also Goodrich, *Holy Grail*, 47.

90. Eric D. Huntsman, "Mary Magdalene: Biblical Enigma," presentation at BYU Museum of Art, 25 February 2004 (revised 26 May 2004), KBYU Studios.

91. Joseph F. Smith, *Millennial Star* (19 May 1874): 312.

92. David O. McKay, Conference Report, April 1964, 5.

93. It is written in Genesis 26:8 that "Isaac was sporting with Rebekah his wife." Such pleasures were considered wholesome and condoned, as seen in Proverbs 5:18–19 (Anchor Bible) and Deuteronomy 24:5.

94. Joseph F. Smith, *Millennial Star* (19 May 1874): 312.

95. Ehat and Cook, *Words of Joseph Smith*, 303 fn 21.

96. Eliza R. Snow, "O My Father," in *Hymns*, no. 292. The hymn continues, "Truth is reason, truth eternal, tells me I've a mother there." Joseph F. Smith, John R. Winder, and Anthon H. Lund of the First Presidency, confirmed this doctrine officially in "The Origin of Man" (November 1909). They stated: "Man, as a spirit, was begotten and born of heavenly parents, and reared to maturity in the eternal mansions of the Father, prior to coming upon the earth in a temporal body to undergo an experience in mortality. . . . [Man is the] offspring of celestial parentage . . . [and] all men and women are in the similitude of the universal Father and Mother, and are literally the sons and daughters of Deity." In Clark, *Messages of the First Presidency*, 4:203, 205, 206.

97. Smith, *Teachings of the Prophet Joseph Smith*, 368;

Smith, *History of the Church,* 6:366.

98. The chief apostle, Peter, was a married man (Matthew 8:14; Mark 1:30; Luke 4:38).

99. Nibley, *Temple and Cosmos,* 203. Nibley is quoting the *Gospel of Philip* 86:307.

100. Smith, *Teachings of the Prophet Joseph Smith,* 300.

101. Smith, *History of the Church* (16 July 1843), 5:510.

102. See Smith, *Teachings of the Prophet Joseph Smith* (April 1844), 348. Here Joseph notes that Jesus did what he saw the Father do. "Jesus treads in the tracks of his Father, and inherits what God did before; and God is thus glorified and exalted in the salvation and exaltation of all his children. . . . When you climb up a ladder, you must begin at the bottom, and ascend step by step, until you arrive at the top; and so it is with the principles of the gospel—you must begin with the first, and go on until you learn all the principles of exaltation."

103. Quoting Joseph F. Smith in *Wilford Woodruff Journal,* 8:187 (22 July 1883)

104. Smith, *Teachings of the Prophet Joseph Smith* (April 1844), 346; Smith, *History of the Church,* 6:306.

105. In the Seventh Lecture on Faith 9, 16 at the School of the Prophets we learn that Jesus is, "the prototype or standard of salvation" just as the Father is "the great prototype of all saved beings." To be "assimilated into their likeness is to be saved; and to be unlike them is to be destroyed; and on this hinge turns the door of salvation."

106. Joseph F. Smith, *Millennial Star* 62 (1900): 97.

107. Smith, *Teachings of the Prophet Joseph Smith* (11 June 1843), 308. See also Ehat and Cook, *Words of Joseph Smith,* 307, where it is slightly abbreviated; emphasis added.

108. Orson Hyde, in *Journal of Discourses* (March[?] 1857), 4:260. See Orson Hyde, in ibid. (18 March 1855), 4:210, where he said: "All that I have to say in reply to that charge is this—they worship a Savior that is too pure and holy to fulfil the commands of his Father. I worship one that is just pure and holy enough 'to full all righteousness;' not only the righteous law of baptism, but the still more righteous and important law 'to multiply and replenish the earth.'"

109. Oliver Boardman Huntington Journal 2:259, 265. Judge Adams died in 1843. Huntington recorded this in his journal on Wednesday, 29 December 1886, which made it a late reference to an earlier event. Adams was one of the original nine men to receive the endowment when it was first given on 4 May 1842. Before his death, Joseph said he anointed him to the patriarchal power.

110. Abraham Hoagland Cannon Journal 17 (5 April 1894): 69–70.

111. Orson Hyde, in *Journal of Discourses* (6 October 1854), 2:81–82. The paragraph above this says: "When Mary [Magdalene] of old came to the sepulchre on the first day of the week, instead of finding Jesus she saw two angels in white, 'And they say unto her, Woman, why weepest thou? She said unto them, Because they have taken away my Lord,' or husband, 'and I know not where they have laid him. And when she had thus said, then turned herself back, and saw Jesus standing, and knew not that it was Jesus. Jesus said unto her, Woman, why weepest thou? Whom seekest thou? She, supposing him to be the gardener, saith unto him, Sir, if thou have borne him hence, tell me where thou has laid him, and I will take him away. Jesus saith unto her, Mary. She turned herself, and said unto him, Rabboni; which is to say, Master.'"

112. Brigham Young, in *Journal of Discourses* (6 October 1854), 2:90.

113. Orson Hyde, in *Journal of Discourses* (March 1857), 4:260a.

114. The persecution involved strong criticism for doctrinal differences from the orthodox norm of Christianity. This was occasionally manifested in violence, but more often in shunning, namecalling, and anti-Mormon campaigns from other churches.

115. Tom F. Driver, "Sexuality and Jesus," *Union Seminary Quarterly Review* (1945): 243, is the first person known to persuasively come out with this fascinating argument and then only obliquely.

116. William E. Phipps, "The Case for a Married Jesus," *Dialogue* 7, 4 (Winter 1972): 44. He quotes Smith, *Essentials in Church History,* 313.

117. Orson Hyde, in *Journal of Discourses* (6 October 1854), 2:81–82. See also Smith, *Teachings of the Prophet Joseph Smith* (15 October 1843), 327: "I believe the Bible as it read when it came from the pen of the original writers. Ignorant translators, careless transcribers, or designing and corrupt priests have committed many errors."

118. McConkie, *Doctrinal New Testament Commentary,* 1:135. McConkie says in *Mortal Messiah,* 1:448–49: "Scholars generally feel that some member of the Holy Family was being married, and that Mary was supervising and guiding what went on."

119. Spong, *Born of Woman,* 192.

120. Hopkins, Simmans, and Wallace-Murphy, *Rex Deus,* 73. It quotes A. N. Wilson, *Jesus.*

121. Orson Hyde, in *Journal of Discourses* (probably March 1857), 4:259. J. Carrigan, a Baptist minister, says that this sermon was given on the 21st of December 1856, but does not cite his source.

122. Phipps, *Was Jesus Married?* 20–26.

123. Young (Denning), *Wife No. 19,* 307. She is quoting her former husband, Brigham Young.

124. Orson Hyde, in *Journal of Discourses* (6 October 1854), 2:81–82.

125. Staley, *Heroines of Genoa and the Riviera,* 29. Certainly this was a nineteenth-century concoction.

126. Garvie, "John," in *Abingdon Bible Commentary,* 1068–69.

127. Quoting Joseph F. Smith, in *Wilford Woodruff Journal,* 8:187–88 (22 July 1883). See also Staker, *Waiting for the World's End,* 360–61. Joseph F. Smith referred to Luke 10:38–42; see also John 11:2, 5; 12:3; 10:8–18.

128. Steven Adam (?–1910), British, *The Marriage of the Lamb and His Bride* (ca. 1906–1910, stained-glass window). Located at St. Mary's Kilmore Church in Dervaig, Isle of Mull, Scotland. The window was probably meant to represent Christ and the Church, but its verisimilitude gives the impression that it is an actual marriage between Mary of Bethany and Jesus Christ. An inscription quotes Luke 10:42, mentioning Bethany.

129. Bruce R. McConkie noted: "Men married at sixteen or seventeen years of age, almost never later than twenty: and women at a somewhat younger age, often when not older than fourteen" (*Mortal Messiah,* 1:223).

130. See Phipps, *Was Jesus Married?* 76. The fourth decade of Christ's life would have made him "middle aged" by the society of the day. Phipps notes, "In light of such marital customs, it is possible that Jesus' first wife died and that afterward he married Mary during his intinerant years as a teacher." This view was taken up by Starbird in *Mary Magdalene.*

131. Unlocated, probably a folktale ascribed to Brigham Young.

132. Garvie, *Abingdon Bible Commentary,* 1069.

133. McConkie, *Doctrinal New Testament Commentary,* 1:136. If we are to believe that turning the water into wine was Christ's first miracle, then the miracle of "seeing" Nathanael under the fig tree from John 1 must have happened later.

134. Orson Pratt, *The Seer* 1, 11 (November 1853): 170.

135. Ibid., 1 (October 1853): 160.

136. Anne Wilde, 2004 Salt Lake City Sunstone Symposium (August 2004). These would include the 1.3 billion Muslims, millions of Africans, and numerous other peoples.

137. Jedediah M. Grant, in *Journal of Discourses* (7 August 1853), 1:345–46a. We have no idea who the above-mentioned Elizabeth is; she is only alluded to by Celsus. Who the "host of others" might be, we do not know.

See also Brigham Young, *Deseret News* (Salt Lake City, 10 February 1867)z; "Polygamist . . . and Jesus and his apostles."

138. Celsus, *True Doctrine* (ca. A.D. 178). It survives only as citations in Origen's *Against Celsus* (A.D. 248). Celsus ridicules Christianity as novel, parochial, irrational, quarrelsome, and a subversive movement founded by a sorcerer and proselytizing the uneducated. See *Encyclopedia of Catholicism* (HarperSanFrancisco, 1995), 291.

139. Orson Pratt, *The Seer* 1 (October 1853): 159–60; see also 169–72.

140. Brigham Young, in *Journal of Discourses* (10 February 1867), 11:328. This was one of the war cries against Mormonism before the Civil War.

141. Orson Hyde, in *Journal of Discourses* (6 October 1854), 2:80a.

142. Ibid., 2:82–83.

143. Phipps, *Was Jesus Married?* 10. Phipps believed that Brigham Young and others were using this idea only to spread LDS polygamy: "The same projection of cultural values was displayed in the early Mormon efforts to make Jesus the model man in the pioneer Utah community. In all of this there is an attempt to read history backward." Then after the 1890 Manifesto, which stopped the practice of polygamy, the teaching that Christ was "married and married often!" no longer was of any earthly use and thus was abandoned as a pronounced teaching within a decade of the Manifesto of 1890.

144. Brigham Young, in *Journal of Discourses* (13 November 1870), 13:309.

145. Young (Denning), *Wife No. 19,* 307. Although this wayward former wife wrote a vitriolic book on President Young, this quotation is in harmony with Young's other official recitations. It separates Mary Magdalene and the Bethany sisters as different people. See Kimball, *Heber C. Kimball,* 274. He is citing the Mary Ellen Kimball Journal, 54. In his biography on Heber C. Kimball, Kimball quoted the Apostle as saying "that Christ was married—indeed that Christ was married to both Mary and Martha and that the famous wedding of Cana was in reality Christ's own wedding."

146. Kraut, *Jesus Was Married,* though flawed in its scholarship, was the best single source for references on this topic. The LDS brethren who talked most on the subject were Brigham Young, Orson Hyde, Heber C. Kimball, Jedediah M. Grant, Lorenzo Snow, Orson Pratt, and Joseph F. Smith.

147. Orson Hyde, in *Journal of Discourses* (6 October 1854), 2:81–82.

148. Ibid. (18 March 1855), 2:210a; see Isaiah 53:10; Orson Hyde, in *Journal of Discourses,* 2:82–83; 4:260; Brigham Young, in ibid., 13:309. It should be noted or conjectured that Christ might also have had children from Martha or other unmentioned wives. Exactly which Eastern newspapers mentioned this issue is not known at present.

149. Letter of Joseph F. Smith, Anthon H. Lund, and Charles W. Penrose, in Clark, *Messages of the First Presidency,* 5:329. "Celestial marriage—that is, marriage for time and eternity—and polygamous or plural marriage are not synonymous terms. Monogamous marriages for time and eternity, solemnized in our temples in accordance with the word of the Lord and the laws of the Church, are celestial marriages."

150. Strachan, *Jesus the Master Builder,* 245.

151. Yadin, *Temple Scroll,* 240–41. Yadin writes: "Nevertheless, despite these parallels, I am convinced that Jesus was anti-Essene—as I hinted in our discussion of the Days of Ordination and the Herodians. Indeed, his whole approach was anathema to the Essenes, with their rigid legalism." In fact, an example of Christ teaching beliefs opposed to Essene theology is found in the Sermon on the Mount. Here Christ said, "You have heard that it has been said, 'You shall love your neighbor and hate your enemy.' But I say unto you, Love your enemies." Nowhere in Jewish tradition or the Bible does it say to hate your enemies. Yet in the Qumran sect it is written, "[It is the duty of members of the sect] to love everyone, whom he [God] has elected, and to hate everyone, whom he has rejected" (241).

152. Mishnah Tractate Sanhedrin 2.4 (written between A.D. 130 and 200) as quoted by Yadin, *Temple Scroll,* 201.

153. Collins, *Twenty-First Century Grail,* plate 32. Heraldic shield on the pulpit, Binsey's St. Margaret Church, about two miles from Oxford, England. It shows three crowned female heads above an ox crossing a ford (the symbol of Oxford). While not of particularly ancient age, the woodcarving may symbolically represent Christ's three Ephraimitic wives.

154. Rabbi Dr. Joseph H. Hertz, chief Rabbi for the British Empire, in Seder Nasltim 1:xvii, attempted to minimize Jewish practice of polygamy in antiquity, saying, "Polygamy seems to have well-nigh disappeared in Israel after the Babylonian exile." Yet the Misnah/Babylonian Talmud, Tractate Kethu Both, 91 a and 93 a and b, allows at least four wives. See Soncino, (1961 edition), 582, 590, 595.

155. Another symbolism after the pattern of the temple, is that the ark of the covenant was both the ship that Noah built and the sacred box in the Holy of Holies. Both were portable, both were entered by married people, two by two, both were God's foothold in the chaos of the earth and the cosmos.

156. John Melhuish Strudwick (1849–1937), British, *The Ten Virgins* (1883, oil on canvas, 29" x 60"). Courtesy of John Schaeffer, Melbourne Australia.

157. It is possible that eternal marriage in the celestial kingdom will also involve polygamy because of the number of unmarried woman worthy of that principle. See "Jesus Loves Polygamy, This I Know," *Las Vegas Weekly,* 11 February 2001, 22.

158. Church, *Guardians of the Grail,* 73. Church is a fundamentalist Christian minister who attempts to deny the marriage. "I have concluded that Mary Magdalene had nothing to do with the legendary bit of blasphemy that she became one of the wives of Jesus" (75). Rev. Church does not footnote the source or reason for "concluding" this. He also confuses the two Marys.

159. M. Zvi Udley, Ph.D., quoted in Kraut, *Jesus Was Married,* 92. Although he is quoted often, it is difficult to know exactly who Dr. Udley was. He is writing about the discovery in Jerusalem during the 1870s of a tomb and ossuary of a certain Simeon linked to a Jesus.

160. Orson Pratt, *The Seer* 1, 11 (November 1853): 169.

161. Orson Pratt may have also used Jeremiah 41, but perhaps not meaning Tamar, the daughter of King Zedekiah, the last of the Davidic kings of Israel. She was sister of Mulek who came to America (see Omni 1:13–18, in the Book of Mormon). See LDS scholar Anderson, *God's Covenant Race,* 219.

162. Baigent, Leigh, and Lincoln, *Holy Blood, Holy Grail,* 347.

163. Orson Pratt, *The Seer* 1, 11 (November 1853): 172.

164. Mormonism teaches that "As man is God once was; As God is, man may be" (Lorenzo Snow, LDS prophet). See Romney, *Life of Lorenzo Snow,* 46. It is taught that God the Father is an exalted resurrected Man and His bride is an exalted resurrected Woman. This is probably the single most edifying teaching of the restored Church of Jesus Christ of Latter-day Saints to a world that had completely abstracted and neutered God into a cosmic "force field" rather than an Eternal loving Heavenly Father.

165. Abanes, *Truth behind The Da Vinci Code,* 26. While almost every church teaches against Docetism, all teach that Jesus was NOT fully a man. The Council of Nicea was convened not to decide if Christ was merely human or divine, even Arius the heretic acknowledged that, but rather how it was to be understood.

166. Samuel W. Richards, *Millennial Star* 15 (1853): 825. Richards, the editor of the *Millennial Star*, noted that the "character of the relationship formed by that act" could very well refer to God the Father's marriage to the Virgin Mary.

167. Orson Pratt, *The Seer* 1 (1853): 172.

CHAPTER SEVEN
THE GRAIL SEED: THE SANGRAAL

Thy seed will I establish for ever, and build up thy throne to all generations.

—PSALM 89:4

As a married man, Christ would have lawfully continued his seed through the fathering of children.[1] *Anawim* is a Hebrew word denoting the "little ones of God," and such were the Savior's children. There seem to be at least three strategies used to protect these young and inexperienced offspring of the Savior. First was to have them as numerous as possible. Second was to give them a new identity, and third was to disperse them broadly. The Messianic bloodline was kept perfectly discreet and hidden by the Lord, without resorting to any secret society of mortal Grail guardians. Some of the children were undoubtedly placed in humble circumstances, without knowledge of who they really were.

Interestingly, the operative phrase for their new identity may have been "Children of Joseph of Arimathea." There are numerous references in Celtic literature to a Grail dynasty or family, most claimed descendance, for safety's sake, from the lineage of the Arimathean.[2] They were called this, to deflect attention away from their true parentage. After a short time, everybody believed this "cover story." However, they were in reality Jesus' own hidden offspring. Just how many children there were is impossible to tell, though to create two distinctive genetic fountains, both a brother and a sister sibling needed to be born.

There is a Spanish colonial painting on tin from the eighteenth century that may relate to the above expressed idea (see Plate 4).[3] It depicts a holy man with a beard and a halo, wearing a crown and holding a blooming staff of roses. He holds a sacred baby, who also has a halo. This unusual painting may be interpreted in several ways. Does it depict Jesus holding His son in one hand and a blooming staff represents His bloodline in the other? Could it be God the Father with baby Jesus, or even perhaps Joseph of Arimathea with the Grail heir?[4] The picture lends itself to this manner of explication.

The terms *Sangrael*, *Desposyni*, and *Rex Deus* all deal with the direct descendants of the "Chosen Seed." The *Sangrael* is the sacred bloodline of the two promised tribes of Israel, while the *Desposyni* are the children of the Virgin Mary, and the true *Rex Deus* is the hidden bloodline of Jesus Christ and His Ephraimatic wives.

The marriage of Christ would be meaningless without posterity. As children of the Savior, His seed would have a major role to play in the history of the world. It is a story largely untold and unheralded. We now turn our attention to these Grail descendants of Jesus Christ.

THE UNIQUE CHILDREN OF THE SAVIOR

And thine house and thy kingdom shall be established forever before thee: thy throne shall be established for ever.

—2 SAMUEL 7:16

Latter-day Saints have no problem accepting the idea that Jesus was married, piloted as they are by continuing revelation. If Heavenly Father is married, then why not Heavenly Son? Given our theology, it all makes logical sense, even if it might not have congealed into official doctrine.

The concept of the Savior having sexual coitus with his wife is difficult for Latter-day Saints and impossible for other Christians to accept.[5] Christian philosopher Justin Martyr in the mid-second century promoted an abstinent and continent Savior. He reckoned that since Jesus was even holier than the Virgin Mary, who did not have sexual relations, then certainly He did not either.[6] This Neoplatonic ethic of a virgin Jesus, as the paradigm of virtue, became the axiomatic position of the primitive Church as it descended into apostasy.

Because of this "tradition of the fathers," some Latter-day Saints think that Jesus had a *celibate marriage*, as a number of prominent early Christian fathers practiced.[7] About 15 percent of the LDS people

interviewed by the author on the subject objected to Christ having progeny. Whatever kind of marriage He had, in their minds, it neither did nor could produce children. Still, the notion that Jesus and his wives had progeny, who would be of His royal lineage, is intriguing to the Mormon mind.[8]

A number of Mormons struggle with the concept of Christ's immortality passing on to the next generation. Because Christ is half-immortal, the skeptics conclude, his children would either remain half or a quarter divine, with "special powers." One former BYU religion professor, Dr. Richard Lloyd Anderson, sees this as "all wrong," for it "couldn't or wouldn't happen."[9] Dr. Anderson believes it beneath the dignity of Christ to sexually beget children. He objects to Jesus as semi-immortal mating with a mortal. The famous biological scientist, Dr. James Jensen of Brigham Young University, sees it theologically, if not genetically, impossible that Christ had children.[10] Non-LDS professor Paul L. Maier sees only problems with the idea: "But one of the principal purposes of marriage is to have children and an enormous—even cosmic—problem would have arisen if Jesus and the Magdalene *had* produced offspring. Theologians would have argued for centuries as to whether such children did or did not participate in Jesus' divinity. And what of their children and grandchildren in turn? It would have caused no less than theological bedlam. That Christ remained celibate was very wise indeed!"[11]

Since a celibate Christ was easier for the theologians, the historical fact of a sacred marriage was scuttled. Following this line of reasoning, one might then also question that Heavenly Father as a fully immortal being could not conceive through a mortal, the Virgin Mary, a half-immortal child. Of course, contrary to the Jews' objection, Mary of Nazareth did conceive a child from Heavenly Father. Is it to the very uniqueness of these children that people object? Did it make them too much like the Savior or the Savior too much like them?

Was there a physiological purpose behind the distinctive genetic inheritance of these children? Just as Christ had to live in order to complete His mission on earth, so did His children have to live long enough to fulfill theirs, that is, pass on their lineage. Any special powers they might have possessed ensured their health and well being long enough to rear future generations. They were not sickly but rather robust to resist disease and exposure in an age when the mortality rate for children was extremely high.[12] Christ's offspring, then, had the physical wherewithall to live and be fruitful.

This theory might be true, for Doctrine and Covenants 113:4 says that upon "them" (a descendant of Jesse and Joseph) "there is laid much power." This "much power" was not of a magical but of a genetic kind. Like Christ's own power, it enabled His children to live under adverse conditions. This may have been the special purpose in the powers bestowed on these Grail children, especially in the first three generations—three because legend has it that Joseph of Arimathea had three successors or generations to hide the Grail children.[13] Of course this also allowed the bloodline to spread out broadly enough and to sink deep enough to ensure the sacred bloodline's continued existence.

As the posterity of the Holy Grail reached critical mass, the outstanding nuclear DNA genes inherited from the Savior would be diluted by half nearly every generation. Thus by three generations they would be indistinguishable from other people. On the other hand, the non-recombining Y-chromosome and mitochondrial DNA, while bestowing no traits (except maleness for the Y), would remain unmutated as an identifying marker through the centuries. Thus it was necessary for the Savior to have at least one male and one female child, to perpetuate the two distinct lineages of promise, coming from Judah and Ephraim respectively.

There is an engaging account of Jesus approaching the house of the deceased Lazarus, whom He will soon raise from the dead. In John 11 we read of Martha running off to greet him while he was away off (John 11:21, 28–29). At the same time, Mary her sister sat still in the house and waited for Jesus' visit. This seems opposite of the way it is normally scripted between the two sisters. Why didn't Mary also rush to greet the Savior, leaving Martha to tidy up the house? Perhaps Mary couldn't; perhaps she was "heavy with child" and unable to run, being a "sitting *shivah*" mourning her brother, Lazarus.[14]

Two ideas center upon this occasion. One was that she was not permitted to leave her duty unless her husband requested her presence. Thus Martha, instead of Mary, rushed to meet Jesus. It therefore follows in John 11:28 when Martha says, "The master is here and called thee,' As soon as she [Mary] heard this, she rose quickly and came to him." She could not leave her *shivah* post until her husband or master summoned her. Another idea is suggested when Mary sat at Jesus' feet instead of helping Martha with the meal. Was Mary pregnant with Christ's child, the "Holy Grail *in utero*?"

On earth, according to Orson Hyde, the Savior was fruitful. Hyde questioned, "Has He indeed passed by the nature of angels [celibacy], and taken upon Himself the seed of Abraham, *to die without leaving seed to bear His name on the earth? No!*" he answered.[15] In October 1854, Orson Hyde spoke strongly in favor of Christ begetting children:

> And if the Savior found it his duty to be baptized to fulfill all righteousness, a command of far less importance than that of multiplying his race, (if indeed there is any difference in the commandments of Jehovah, for they are all important and all essential) would he not find

it his duty to join in with the rest of the faithful ones in replenishing the earth?

"Mr. Hyde, do you really wish to imply that the immaculate Savior begat children? It is a blasphemous assertion against the purity of the Savior's life, to say the least of it. The holy aspirations that ever ascended from him to his Father would never allow him to have any such fleshly and carnal connexions, never, no never." This is the general idea; but the Savior never thought it beneath him to obey the mandate of his Father; he never thought this stooping beneath his dignity.[16]

Elder Hyde in March 1857 again speaks of the strong reaction against Mormon acceptance of a married-with-children Christ at that time:

At this doctrine the long-faced hypocrite and the sanctimonious bigot will probably cry, blasphemy! Horrid perversion of God's word! Wicked wretch! He is not fit to live! etc., etc. But the wise and reflecting will consider, read and pray. If God be not our Father, grandfather, or great grandfather, or some kind of a father in reality, in deed and in truth, why are we taught to say, "Our Father who art in heaven?

How much soever of holy horror this doctrine may excite in persons not impregnated with the blood of Christ, and whose minds are consequently dark and benighted, it may excite still more when they are told

that if none of the natural blood of Christ flows in their veins, they are not the chosen or elect of God.[17]

The concept of tribal bloodlines explains that there are particular channels or receptacles for awaiting premortal spirits to be born on earth through certain pedigrees. Many special spirits were assigned to come through to the Savior's seed. Christ's direct posterity may properly be called the true *Rex Deus*, "King of God," lineage to this day.

Maybe some of these unique children married sturdy peasant stock, while others went on to the aristocracy, becoming the foundation of many royal dynasties. From certain well-placed children this robust *Sangraal* (bloodline) may possibly have leavened the noble houses of Britain and Europe.[18] It is the author's opinion that their true identity was withheld even from them. It is possible that millions of people now partake of the Grail lineage.

There was, however, among the several children of Christ a singular child whom we might call the Patriarch, *Shiloh ben Jesus*. Perhaps it was to this child that the scriptures refer—"It is a servant in the hands of Christ, who is partly a descendant of Jesse as well as of Ephraim, or of the house of Joseph, on whom there is laid much power" (D&C 113:4). Our story centers around all the children of Christ, but most particularly two children, one blessed with the patriarchal and another with the matriarchal bloodlines.

The *Sangraal* (Holy Grail) has been defined as a cup or chalice that held the sacred blood of Jesus shed at the crucifixion. The word *graal* is from the *langue d'Oc* and with *grasal, grazal, grezal, gresal,* means a vessel in which is put liquid.[19] However, if the word is pronounced *sang raal* (réal) we have the Old French for "blood royal."[20] It was not a gold, silver, onyx, amethyst, glass, enamel or stone, or even an olive wood cup but rather a mortal earthen vessel—and that vessel being the uterine chalice or womb of Mary Magdalene and the Bethany sisters. The children, themselves became vessels of this bloodline, which still exists to this very day.

Through Christ's royal, and his wives' noble, lineage, the world was destined to be blessed (see 2 Corinthians 4:7). Starbird affirms that "through her [Mary Magdalene], dominion would one day be restored to Sion."[21] These chosen lineages in themselves do not bestow personal privilege, righteousness, and certainly no racial superiority.[22] As Malcolm Godwin noted, "Enlightenment has yet to be proved to be carried in the genes."[23]

Rather, these bloodlines helped prepare premortally chosen candidates for special earthly missions to serve mankind, not to rule them. All are God's children, for as the Apostle Paul noted, "And hath made of one blood all nations of men for to dwell on all the face of the earth" (Acts 17:26). Nevertheless, Erastus Snow gave the following insight: "For he has had his eye upon the chosen spirits that have come upon the earth in the various ages from the beginning of the world up to this time."[24]

Loving service was the epitome of the Grail code and chivalry. It would be through a destined divine channel that God would route spiritual blessings to an unhealed world. The house of Israel was uncommon in the promises given to its seed: "For thou art an holy people unto the Lord thy God: the Lord thy God hath chosen thee to be a special people unto himself, above all people that are upon the face of the earth" (Deuteronomy 7:6).

The Savior could have had several children from several wives. These infants, of both sexes, would form a distinct tribal ancestry. Mary Magdalene, Mary and Martha, and perhaps others may have been "Grail Mothers." By right of primogeniture, Mary Magdalene's first male child might have been given the name-titles of *Shiloh ben Jesus* or *Joseph bar Jesus*.[25]

And what of these children? Isaiah wrote of prophecies possibly relating to the posterity of Jesus Christ, "I saw also the Lord sitting upon a throne, high and lifted up, and his train filled the temple"[26] (Isaiah 6:1). The Lord's train or cortege could mean a number of retainers, or even His family. The latter view is clearly expressed by President Brigham Young: "The scripture says that He, the Lord, came walking [or sitting] in the temple, with His train; I do not know who they were unless His wives and children."[27]

There is another bit of information that favors Jesus Christ having children. After His resurrection, the Savior commanded Mary Magdalene not to touch him (John 20:17). This command may have been due to Mary Magdalene's condition. If she were in late-term pregnancy and followed the precepts for dynastic brides, "she was allowed no physical contact with her husband at that time."[28] However, it was the author Keith Laidler, who has found the most persuasive quotation to date:

> Until now, there has seemed to be no documentary evidence of any offspring of Jesus, and the argument has had to be supported by logical deductions, historical correspondences and later legendary accounts, and by noting intriguing gaps in the story of Christ. It seems to have passed the notice of every other researcher that, astonishingly, a reference to the children of Jesus actually exists in the literature.
>
> I found it in the Jewish writings, in the *Toldoth*. Here, we find a passage that confirms the gospel account that, just before the feast of Passover, Jesus entered the city of Jerusalem riding on an ass. But there is one telling addition to the story: "Now in that

year Passover fell on a Sabbath, and he *and his sons* came to Jerusalem, on the rest day of Passover, that is on a Friday, he riding on an ass and saying to his disciples: 'Of me it was said: Rejoice greatly, Daughters of Zion.'"[29]

The source is not quite as definitive as Laidler supposes for, the "he" is conjectured. However, the identification of the passage is fraught with Grail implications. For instance, "and his sons" could literally refer to His biological sons. His sireship of Grail children must have happened. For in him and in his seed "the whole world" would be blessed. Without children the ancient curse would remain.

"HE SHALL SEE HIS SEED"

We say it was Jesus Christ who was married, to be brought into the relation whereby he could see his seed, before he was crucified.

—ORSON HYDE[30]

The prophet Isaiah noted that the Messiah would see his posterity: "When thou shalt make his soul an offering for sin, He shall see His seed" (Isaiah 53:10). When Christ looked down from the oak Cross and "saw his seed," did he see his son, the rod (scepter), His daughter (the reed or tender twig), and other children? Perhaps the greatest treatise on the Savior being married and begetting children was Orson Hyde's lengthy address at October General Conference of the LDS Church in 1854. There he spoke of the seed of Christ having great influence in the latter days:

Has [Jesus Christ] indeed passed by the nature of angels, and taken upon himself the seed of Abraham, to die without leaving a seed to bear his name on the Earth?" No. But when the secret is fully out, the seed of the blessed shall be gathered in, in the last days. . . .

Well, then, he shall see his seed, and who shall declare his generation, for he was cut off from the earth? [Mosiah 14:8] I shall say here, that before the Savior died, he looked upon his own natural children, as we look upon ours; he saw his seed, and immediately afterwards he was cut off from the earth; but who shall declare his generation?[31]

This controversial quotation fairly bristles with information regarding the entire Holy Grail scenario. Most books dealing with the children of Christ, such as *The Da Vinci Code*, have Christ surviving the crucifixion so that He could have children. This, of course, is a *non sequitur*. With Hyde we precisely learn that He had children before Calvary—not after. We know that the Seed of Christ "passed into the shades of obscurity, never to be exposed to mortal eye as the Seed of the Blessed One" so they would not be killed.[32] And finally, we learn that they would be made known in the latter days. The Isaiah 53:8 question of "Who shall declare His generation?" has been answered.[33]

Hyde could hardly have been unaware of Abinadi's sermon on Isaiah 52:10 found in Mosiah 15:10–12. The Book of Mormon prophet states that the seed of Christ were those who hearken to the word of God and believed in the redemption of the people. "I say unto you," said Abinadi, "that these are his seed, or they are the heirs of the kingdom of God." Perhaps Hyde is seeing another level of understanding in that Christ's righteous posterity and the true believers of the Atonement together are His seed. "And now, are they not his seed?"

asks Abinadi (Mosiah 15:12, 5:7).

An anonymous French Grail romance entitled *Perlesvaus*, written between 1191 and 1212, claims to be based upon a Latin book written by a monk of Glastonbury. It offers a view of Christ on the wooden cross as he sees the Grail child below. In it we read how Sir Gawain, one of the five major knights of the quest, observed the treasured Grail: "In the midst of the Graal . . . the figure of a child. . . . He looketh up and it seemeth [to] him to be the Graal all in flesh, and he seeth above, as he thinketh, a King crowned, nailed upon a rood [cross]."[34]

The idea of Christ seeing His seed thus passes from theology to literature. How sad to think of Christ being torn from his tender children. Jesus' life has parallels with those of the prophets. Joseph Smith's incarceration in Liberty Jail elicited a revelation in March 1839, implying that Christ too similarly suffered:

If they tear thee from the society of thy father and mother and brethren and sisters; and if with a drawn sword thine enemies tear thee from the bosom of thy wife, and of thine offspring, and thine elder son, although but six years of age, shall cling to thy garments, and shall say, My father, my father, why can't you stay with us? O, my father, what are the men going to do with you? And if then he shall be thrust from thee by the sword, and thou be dragged to prison, and thine enemies prowl around thee like wolves for the blood of the lamb. . . know thou my son, that all these things shall give thee experience, and shall be for thy good. The Son of Man hath descended below them all. Art thou greater than He?

—D&C 122:6–8

Just as Joseph Smith was taken from his offspring seed, so was Jesus taken from His offspring as well. This reflects the scripture about Jesus that "yet learned he obedience [character] by the things which he suffered" (Hebrews 5:8). To have your offspring rent from you is amongst the most agonizing experiences any parent could have and was certainly a part of the suffering Christ had to endure during His Atonement. Eventually in "the Times of Restitution" things will again be put aright for the offspring of the House of Christ.

In summary, Joseph Smith quotes scripture of Jesus speaking in parables, relating to this proposition: "He answered and said unto them, 'He that soweth the *good seed* is the Son of Man; the field is the world; the *good seed* are the children of the kingdom.'"[35] The seed of Christ are not always literal blood descendants, but also those who are faithful to Christ. Sometimes those that are literal seeds are cast out because of unbelief. But when the literal and good seed are one and the same, we find the true family of Jesus.

THE ROD OF JESSE, "THE WIDOW'S SON"

What is the rod spoken of in the first verse of the 11th chapter of Isaiah, that should come of the stem of Jesse?

Behold, thus saith the Lord: [1] It is a servant in the hands of Christ, [2] who is partly a descendant of Jesse as well as of Ephraim, or the house of Joseph, [3] on whom there is laid much power.

—D&C 113:3–4

Isaiah foretold that the promise to restore the House of David would be fulfilled by "a rod out of the stem of Jesse, and a Branch shall grow out of his roots" (Isaiah 11:1; see 2 Nephi 21).[36] Doctrine and

Covenants 113:1–2 clearly explains that the "Stem of Jesse" is Jesus Christ himself. But who is the Rod out of the Stem and who is the Branch out of his Roots? Who is the Root? Elder Bruce R. McConkie in June 1967 thought we could figure out the answer to this question:

> Well, I know some others who are [descended from Christ's bloodline] and the fact of the matter is, if you want to have a real interesting period of scriptural analysis, just take what Isaiah said about the stem of Jesse and those related things, and then you take the revelation in Section 113 that the Lord gave interpreting the root of Jesse and the stem of Jesse and you figure out who it means. Now if you're just about as smart as you ought to be, you'll come up with the right answer. If you know who these things are talking about, and who the ancestor is of the person that it's talking about, it's talking about the things such as that we're talking about here. But it isn't in the revelation in plainness. Of course it isn't, and the reason is the same reason that the New Testament doesn't contain accounts of Jesus' intimate personal affairs.[37]

Elder McConkie had been talking about "the people who are the descendants of Christ" in his lecture. Yet a number of Mormon authors have concluded that the Rod and the root of Jesse, mentioned in verses 3 to 6 of section 113 are in fact, the same person—Joseph Smith Jr.[38] Sidney B. Sperry writes,

"I identify the individual of Doctrine and Covenants 113:4 with the one in Doctrine and Covenants 113:6."[39] Joseph F. McConkie also notes, "It has always been our understanding in the Church that the passage [D&C 113:4] applies to Joseph Smith, this being one of the reasons it was quoted to him by Moroni in September 1823."[40] Monte S. Nyman agrees, declaring: "This descendant of Jesse (Judah) and Joseph (the rod) is undoubtedly Joseph Smith himself. . . . The life of Joseph Smith also sustains himself as the root of Jesse spoken of by Isaiah."[41]

Interestingly, a twist by Hyrum Andrus places the "rod of Jesse" (verse 4) as Joseph Smith Jr. but not the "root of Jesse" [42] (verse 6)! But all these interpretations do not seem conclusive from the text itself. Just what the text has in mind is difficult to tell. It is likely that the "root of Jesse" refers specifically to the Prophet Joseph but not the "Rod of Jesse." In fact, other LDS scholars, such as Matthew Brown, Martin Tanner, and W. Cleon Skousen proffer the idea that while the "Root" is Joseph Smith Jr., the "Rod" might be another, as yet unknown, person. "The Rod which comes out of the Stem of Jesse. . . . One is almost tempted to assume that this refers to Joseph Smith, but his [Joseph's] calling is more clearly identified with "the root," which we will discuss in a moment. The Lord's description of the rod is not sufficient for us to positively identify the person he had in mind as yet, but we will no doubt be able to recognize him when he fulfills this assignment."[43]

Perhaps, contrary to Skousen's belief, the assignment of the Rod has already been fulfilled, long before Joseph Smith Jr. In Doctrine and Covenants 113:3–4 we read that the rod "comes out of the Stem of Jesse" (this stem is Jesus Christ according to verses 1–2). Therefore he comes directly out of Jesus, in much the same manner as "a Branch [shoot] shall grow out of his [Joseph Smith's] roots" (see Isaiah 11:1; D&C 113:5–6). That is, the Rod is an immediate descendant of Jesus Christ (Stem of Jesse) and the Branch is their descendant; in this particular case, it is Joseph Smith (root of Jesse and Ephraim).

We are told in Doctrine and Covenants 113:3–4 that the "rod of Jesse" is a "servant" in the hands of Christ and then in verses 5–6 that the "root of Jesse" is in the last days. Are they the same person? Who is this servant in the hands of Christ? There are three immediate answers:

- The first thought is that this "Rod" is a Christian, a person holding offices in the Church (disciple) of the Lord. He would of necessity be a high authority in the gospel kingdom because the verse says that upon this Grail servant-child was "laid much power." Some have postulated that if Christ having had a son were true, then the child would be a quarter divine and have "special powers." However, this is not important, for what is extraordinary is that this child had laid upon him special patriarchal authority by reason of both the Birthright and the Sceptre.

- Another idea from verse 4 contrasts with verse 6, which denotes the time frame of the existence of the character. Therefore he seems to have lived at the time of Christ, not in the latter day.

- If Christ actually held this rod "in his hands," then that rod might be a child being cradled by the Savior. This "Rod from the Stem" might be "a child from the loins" of Christ, or in other words, His son (see Plate 5).[44]

It is possible that the "Rod" was Mary Magdalene's firstborn child from her husband, Jesus Christ[45] (see Plate 6).[46] LDS scholar Matthew Brown affirms this conclusion when he states that "the Rod is a child of the Savior and the root is Joseph Smith.[47] This returns us to the original thesis of this book, that the promises of the scepter-kingship of Judah (Genesis 49:10) and the birthright of Joseph (1 Chronicles 5:2) were given to this child and his direct heirs or *Desposyni* [ancient Greek for "of the master"]."[48] In this respect the child would be a true "rod from the stem of Jesse."

From this we learn that the scepter was an Abrahamic inheritance of Leah, while the birthright was from Rachel. Most important and surprising, even to Latter-day Saints, is that Jesus had a son who inherited both. In the *Gospel of Philip* there is a passage placing the concept of a royal patrilineal heir sharply into focus: "There is the Son of man and there is *the son of the Son of Man*. The Lord [Jesus] is the Son of man, and *the son of the Son of Man* is he who is created through the Son of Man."[49]

Upon this dynastic head was bestowed the foundation of the most consequential house the world has known. One day we hope to read of the glorious exploits of this noble family. Through His posterity the entire earth is blessed in a perfectly Abrahamic way (D&C 110:11–16).

The following figure traces this one-servant lineage:

FIGURE 4

THE ROD AND THE ROOT OF JESSE

D&C 113:3–4   D&C 113:5–6

THE ROD OF JESSE THE WIDOW'S SON JOSEPH BAR JESUS (SHILOH BEN JESUS)	THE ROOT OF JESSE JOSEPH SMITH JR. MESSIAH BEN JOSEPH
SERVANT IN THE HANDS OF CHRIST (AT THE TIME OF CHRIST)	ENSIGN AND GATHERING IN LAST DAYS
DESCENDANT OF JESSE AND EPHRAIM	DESCENDANT OF JESSE AND JOSEPH
UPON WHOM IS LAID MUCH POWER	PRIESTHOOD AND KEYS OF THE KINGDOM

Thus we see a literal genetic trajectory is created from the Stem, to the Rod, to the root of Jesse, i.e., from Christ, to his son, the first of the new Grail dynasty. Then onward through time to Joseph Smith Jr., the great prophet and Fisher King of the last days. Once this novel premise is understood, that Christ had an heir/son, then Doctrine and Covenants 113:1–6 makes perfect sense with the above interpretation.[51] Joseph Smith was the root and flower of the latter days.

NOTES

1. Orson Hyde, in *Journal of Discourses* (March [?] 1857), 4:260. "Object not, therefore too strongly against the marriage of Christ, but remember that in the last days, secret and hidden things must come to light, and that your life also (which is the blood) is hid with Christ in God. . . . Abraham was chosen of God for the purpose of raising up a chosen seed, and a peculiar people unto His name. Jesus Christ was sent into the world for a similar purpose, but upon a more extended scale. Christ was the seed of Abraham."

2. Godwin, *Holy Grail,* 74, 106, 117. Others who claimed lineage through Joseph of Arimathea include Pelagius, King Arthur, Gawain, and Galahad.

3. Unknown artist, Spanish colonial, *Joseph of Arimathea with a Child of Jesus* (seventeenth century, oil on tin, 10 1/8" x 8 ½"). Painting in the possession of Brian Kershisneck of Kanab, Utah. The work possibly represents Joseph of Arimathea with the son of Jesus, or perhaps Jesus Himself with His son.

4. Or, it might even be interpreted as Joseph the Carpenter with the baby Jesus.

5. Seaich, *Mormonism, the Dead Sea Scrolls, and the Nag Hammadi Texts,* 42. Seaich makes reference to the third century "Bridal Chamber" scene in *Questions of Mary,* recorded by Epiphanius in the Panarion. There, Jesus is shown having carnal intercourse with Mary Magdalene, saying, "We must so do in order to have eternal life."

6. Justin, Dialogue with Trypho, 66–84. As quoted in Phipps, *Was Jesus Married?* 132.

7. Phipps, *Was Jesus Married?* 127. Tertullian advised Christians to share married life with their spouses in all aspects except the sexual.

8. Images of the many paintings by LDS artists, Simon Dewey and Greg Olson, and so on, depicting "Christ with the Children" come to mind. An interesting corollary is found in Soviet Socialist Realist art, where the murderous V. I. Lenin, who had no children, is often shown in propaganda paintings titled *Lenin with the Children.* While Lenin was sterile, we can't image that the Savior was. We must be left to think of Jesus being the example to all men of what true fatherhood was all about.

9. Swanson, personal interview with Richard L. Anderson at Springville Museum of Art, Saturday, 13 March 2003.

10. This was learned through the author's personal conversation with this eminent scientist and friend, Provo, Utah, 2000,

11. Maier and Hanegraaf, *Da Vinci Code: Fact or Fiction?* 21. Maier is a professor of ancient history at Western Michigan University.

12. Phipps, *Was Jesus Married?* 68, notes: "Also, the children could have died before Jesus became an itinerant teacher." Margaret Starbird suggested that Christ had a female child, who perhaps died before marrying (in answer to a question asked by author during workshop at the August 2004 Sunstone Symposium, Salt Lake City).

13. Godwin, *Holy Grail*, 88: "Christ appears to Joseph in prison with the vessel and tells him that he will have the guardianship of it. In token of the Trinity, there will only be three successors."

14. A "sitting shivah" is a woman performing official mourning or an ancient engagement custom.

15. Orson Hyde, in *Journal of Discourses* (6 October 1854), 2:82. Hyde furthered the idea that the "nature of angels," as opposed to exalted beings in heaven, are without "continuation of seed" and that it even extends to the lower portions of the celestial kingdom.

16. Ibid., 2:79–80. Then again six months later Orson Hyde spoke to this issue, ibid. (18 March 1855), 2:210a.

17. Ibid. (March 1857), 4:260a.

18. Knight and Lomas, *Second Messiah*, 80. Occult writers Knight and Lomas falsely believed that "[they] no doubt saw themselves as 'super-Christians,' descendants of the very first Church, and privy to the greatest secret this side of heaven. They were the silent elite—'the kings of God.'"

19. Another idea is the dish or plate that was brought to the table during various courses (Latin, gradus "stages") of a meal. The Grail was the escuele or dish/cup (Latin, *gradales,* "by degrees") Our English word *gradual* comes from this root word.

20. Baigent, Leigh, and Lincoln, *Holy Blood, Holy Grail,* 306.

21. Starbird, *Woman with the Alabaster Jar,* 5.

22. They must be accompanied by the spirits of "the noble and great ones" from the premortal world (Abraham 3:18–19, 22–23). After just three generations, no superman or mythic hero with magical powers would accrue from the children of Jesus Christ.

23. Godwin, *Holy Grail,* 193.

24. Erastus Snow, in *Journal of Discourses* (6 May 1892), 23:184.

25. Interestingly, the unreliable Gardner, *Bloodline of the Holy Grail,* 110, 115, 139–41, named a "Joseph" (Josephes) as Jesus' second son.

26. RV Isaiah 6:1, "I saw the Lord seated on a high and lofty throne with the train of his garment filling the temple."

27. Brigham Young, in *Journal of Discourses* (13 November 1870), 13:309.

28. Gardner, *Bloodline of the Holy Grail,* 94.

29. Laidler, *Head of God,* 137–38, quotes the Toldoth recession of the Strasburg MS, the same tract that contained the Ben Pandira information. (This could also be the Tosefta or the Tosafoth.)

30. Orson Hyde, in *Journal of Discourses* (6 October 1854), 2:81–82.

31. Ibid., 2:82–83.

32. Ibid.

33. Mosiah 15:10–11 reads: "Who shall declare his generation? Behold, I say unto you, that when his soul has been made an offering for sin he shall see his seed. . . . And who shall be his seed? . . . I say unto you, that all those who have hearkened unto their words, and believed that the Lord would redeem his people, and have looked forward to that day for a remission of their sins, I say unto you, that these are his seed, or they are the heirs of the kingdom of God."

34. As quoted in Prophet, *Mysteries of the Holy Grail,* xii.

35. Smith, *Teachings of the Prophet Joseph Smith* (*Messenger and Advocate,* December 1835), 100. This relates to Matthew 13:24–27.

36. Keil and Delitzsch, *Commentary on the Old Testament,* 7:281, translate this verse, "And there cometh forth a twig out of the stump of Jesse, and a shoot from its roots bringeth forth fruit." They relate it to the cedar forests of Lebanon, as the House of David, and the stump to apostasy of a felled tree, like a root without stem. It is the tree of Davidic royalty that has its roots in Jesse, the chosen royal family (see Matthew 2:23, Ezekial 17:22–23). The twig will become a tree and will have a crown laden with fruit.

37. Bruce R. McConkie, from the third lecture in a class series sponsored for the faculty of the Church Education System, conducted during first term of summer school June 1967 at Brigham Young University. Excerpt from a taped lecture on file in the Recording Library of the Church Education System in Salt Lake City.

38. Apostate fundamentalist Ogden Kraut incorrectly equates the Prophet Joseph with the Rod when he notes, "The 'Rod' has been identified as the Prophet Joseph Smith" (*Jesus Was Married,* 93).

39. Sidney B. Sperry, *Journal of Book of Mormon Studies* 4, 1 (Fall 1995): 203, 278.

40. Found in Joseph Smith 1 (now designated Joseph Smith–Matthew), Pearl of Great Price. Joseph F. McConkie,

"Joseph Smith as Found in Ancient Manuscripts," in Nyman and Tate, *Isaiah and the Prophets,* 10:17.

41. Nyman, "Second Gathering of the Literal Seed," in *Doctrines for Exaltation,* 186; Jackson, *Lost Tribes, Last Days.* These authors believe that both rod and root refer to Joseph Smith Jr.

42. Andrus, *Doctrinal Commentary on the Pearl of Great Price,* 463–64.

43. Skousen, *Isaiah Speaks to Modern Times,* 241–42. Skousen thinks that the person is yet a future personage, whereas this author thinks it is a historical figure. Martin Tanner is a Salt Lake attorney who has a Sunday radio program in Salt Lake City called "Religion on the Line." He thinks, as does the author, that the Rod and the root are different people and both have come already.

44. Unknown artist, Spanish colonial, *Untitled* (seventeenth century, painting on tin). Courtesy of Brian Kershisnek, Kanab, Utah.

45. Whitehead, *House of Israel,* 538, 540, says without the slightest footnoting: "Of recent date there has come to light a remarkable pedigree which establishes the fact that Joseph Smith did have the blood of Judah, of the course of Jesse flowing in his veins. One line of his pedigree shows him descended through sixty generations from Anna, called in ancient extant pedigrees, "Cousin of the Virgin Mary, and daughter of Joseph of Arimathea." Whitehead's "remarkable pedigree" must have been some passing apocryphal scrap of paper shoved under his nose.

46. Nicolôs Rodriguez Juarez (1667–1734), Mexico City, *The Holy Family* (1690, oil on panel, 13" x 17 ½"). Courtesy of Christie's New York Old Masters. The painting is meant by the artist to portray the Virgin Mary and Joseph with the Christ child; however, it is used here to represent Mary Magdalene and Jesus with their firstborn son in their hands.

47. Author's conversations with Matthew Brown (mid-1995 in Springville, Utah) We compared notes on this topic; both of us had independently come to this same conclusion.

48. See Eusebius of Caesarea, *Ecclesiastical History* (trans. Cruse), 3:11. According to Gardner, *Genesis of the Grail Kings,* 1, the *Desposyni* was "a hallowed style reserved exclusively for those in the same family descent as Jesus." See also Martin, *Decline and Fall of the Roman Church,* 43.

49. Robinson, "Gospel of Philip," in *Nag Hammadi Library in English,* 148. Also quoted in Baigent, Leigh, and Lincoln, *Holy Blood, Holy Grail,* 382. The gist of this publication is that Jesus had children and that those children's descendants still exist and a few somewhat understand who they are.

50. Book of Mormon, pages 236, 259, original 1830 edition (see Alma 5:48, 13:9). This passage could also refer to Jesus Christ being the Only Begotten Son of an Only Begotten Father. But this concept does not come into play in Mormonism until the King Follett Discourse in 1844. See Revelation 1:5–6.

51. There is an equally needed dynastic daughter, whose mtDNA would mark the matriarchal lineage descending from Mary Magdalene and/or the Bethany sisters to Joseph Smith Jr. through Lucy Mack Smith, his mother.

PART FOUR

MARY OF MAGDALA AND BETHANY

There of virgins none
Is fairer seen,
Save one,
Than Mary Magdalene.[1]

The two Marys are both historical and literary figures, living in time and space, while also serving as metaphors and object lessons. Mary (*Miriam* in Hebrew) was probably the most common name for Jewish girls in the first century. Typically, then, Marys abound in the New Testament to the point of confusion. One of the most problematic questions is the melding and separating of Mary Magdalene and Mary of Bethany. For example, most biblical scholars equate the "other Mary" with Mary the mother of James and Joses (Matthew 27:56). Certainly this is the most direct reading of the text. Perhaps, though, the "other Mary" mentioned in Matthew 27:61 and 28:1 and the "other women" noted in Luke 24:10, may overlap. It certainly opens the door for Mary of Bethany being at the tomb with Mary Magdalene.

Interestingly, Orson Hyde used the phrase "other Mary" in another context. He dealt with the "other Mary" as bride of the Savior. Here he makes her into Mary Magdalene, while Mary and Martha of Bethany are named outright: "If he [Jesus] was never married, his intimacy with Mary and Martha and the *other Mary* [Magdalene] also whom Jesus loved, must have been highly unbecoming and improper to say the best of it."[2]

At present it is best to keep the "other Mary" as the mother of James. Yet, we can speculate that perhaps Mary and Martha of Bethany were among the "other women" mentioned in Luke 24:10 at the tomb. Let us examine how they are different individuals.

CHAPTER EIGHT
WHO IS MARY MAGDALENE?

Mary Magdalene has been tacitly relegated to president of Jesus' "ladies' auxiliary."[3]

Could the Magdalene, like Emma Smith, have been appointed to the presidency of the ancient Relief Society, or something more? Depending upon one's ideological bent, other roles come to mind. Though Mary Magdalene's origins are enigmatic, her bloodline and her eminent spirit have combined to make her the heir of many promises. She appears to play a crucial, perhaps irreplaceable, role in early Christianity's defining moments.[4]

There are, at present, three different interpretations of the word *h Magdalhnh* [Magdalene], which appeal to orthodox, feminist, and then to gnostic evangelists:

1. *Magdala:* This is a toponym identifying that she was from a town in Galilee. This is the most ideologically neutral of the monikers and has been in place since St. Helen from about A.D. 300.

2. *Magdal-eder:* This is a title and means "watchtower of the flock" or "elevated"

one. This is preferred by militant feminists, who see Mary Magdalene exalted as the wife and successor to Jesus Christ, holding the keys of the Church instead of Peter.[5]

3. *M'gaddla:* This adjective means "dresser [curler] of women's hair" and signifies that the woman is a consort, sexual partner, or harlot. This is preferred by many neognostics who see sexual mysteries rather than home and family as the basis of deeper gnosis.[6]

Her identity and mission are of utmost importance. As if the name were not trouble enough, there seem to be at least nine ideas about her identity:

1. She was a woman from Magdala in Galilee who married Jesus Christ.

2. She was Mary of Bethany, the sister of Martha and Lazarus. This is the standard neognostic view.[7]

3. She was actually John the Beloved, author of the fourth gospel.[8]

4. She was the sister of John the Beloved, who is sometimes identified as Lazarus.[9]

5. She was the wife of John the Beloved.[10]

6. She was the ward of the translated being John the Beloved, who protects the entire family.

7. She and the Virgin Mary traveled with John the Beloved to Ephesus and lived out their lives there.

8. She and the Holy Family traveled with Joseph of Arimathea and Lazarus to southern France and perhaps Britain.

9. She and John the Beloved were androgynous figures together.[11]

We have already dealt with a number of these issues, especially item number one, which is a basis of this book. Idea number two is, however, the most perplexing. The Magdalene and Mary of Bethany are certainly among the most enigmatic women of the New Testament, the Middle Ages, and modern times. Who are these women?

Regarding Mary Magdalene, Bishop Hippolytus of Rome in the early third century held that the Bride in the *Song of Songs* (Canticle of Canticles) was not the Shulamite but rather Mary Magdalene, and the Bridegroom was not Solomon but Jesus Christ, "so that she might anoint His wounds in the garden and at the Tomb."[12] In ancient Near Eastern Sumerian prototypical rites, "it is the bride who, accompanied by her women, returns to the tomb (usually on the third day) and encounters her beloved resurrected in the garden."[13]

Hopkins believes that they were married: "It is significant that traditionally the Catholic Church, when celebrating her [Magdalene's] feast day, reads from Canticles of the bride searching for her bridegroom or beloved from whom she has become separated."[14] On 22 July, her feast day, a most curious biblical passage is read aloud in Catholic churches:

> By night on my bed I sought him whom my soul loveth;
> I sought him, but I found him not.
> I will arise now and go about the city in the streets and in the broad ways I will seek him whom my soul loveth;
> I sought him, but I found him not.
> The watchmen that go about the city found me: to whom I said, Saw ye him whom my soul loveth?
> It was but a little that I passed from them, but I found him whom my soul loveth; I held him, and would not let him go, until I had brought him into my mother's house, and into the chamber of her that conceived me. (Song of Solomon 3:1–4)

It is obvious that we have an enigmatic connection between Mary Magdalene and "the one my soul loveth" in these verses. Who is the one her soul loveth? The answer is explosive to the orthodoxy of the age. Now, in the last days the news of this secret has become front-page provocation. When Joseph Smith said that "the Songs of Solomon are not inspired writings," what did he mean?[15] So reliance upon this ancient book in the Bible should be used with caution (something like D&C 91:1–3). Not that it was entirely false or profane, for in places it was profound. It heralded the concept of a *Hieros Gamos* (sacred marriage).

There are twenty direct references to the Magdalene in the gospels. She is described as a woman who had seven demons expelled from her (Mark 16:9). In several others, she and other women are mentioned as accompanying Jesus in his mission and "ministered unto him of their substance" (Luke 8:1–3). She and Mother Mary were close witnesses of the crucifixion, proving that indeed the Savior had died (Matthew 27:56; Mark 15:40; John 19:25). She and other women saw where the body of Jesus was buried (Matthew 27:61; Mark 15:47). This provided crucial evidence later that the tomb was empty on Easter morning[16] (Matthew 28:1–10; Mark 16:1–8; Luke 24:10). Then after Jesus' resurrection, the Lord appeared first to Mary Magdalene (Mark 16:9; John 20:1–18). With the Virgin Mary, Mary Magdalene and Mary of Bethany are the most pronounced feminine names in the New Testament. We will now examine more closely these mysterious women of the gospels.

THE TWO MARYS: MAGDALENE AND BETHANY

The contemplative life of the most blessed Mary Magdalene, named with the highest reverence as the sweetest chosen of Christ, and by Christ greatly beloved, and the active life of her glorious sister, the minister of Christ, St. Martha, and the friendship and resurrection with which our Lord honoured their venerable brother Lazarus.

— RABANUS[17]

Was Mary Magdalene the star of the Bethany family, as noted in the Archbishop Rabanus' *Prologus*? What was the relationship between Mary Magdalene and Mary of Bethany? Were they the same or different persons? The ramifications of these questions are immense, for knowing the answer gives us better insight into the marital status of Jesus Christ.

The Eastern Orthodox Church has always considered Mary Magdalene and Mary of Bethany to be separate women.[18] They never conflated the two, nor identified either with the unnamed sinner of Luke 7:37–50. The profound Hebrew scholar Alfred Edersheim does not believe that the Marys of Bethany and of Magdala are the same characters.[19] Identifying the Marys as two people are the early Church Fathers, Irenaeus (ca. 125–189), Clement of Alexandria (ca. 155–220), and Origen (184–ca. 254)

The Greek and Russian Orthodox churches and to some degree the Protestants were always negative toward this conflated identification, while the Roman Catholic church until lately has supported the idea of one identity.[20] Since the Reformation, opinion has weighed both for and against identifying the Magdalene with Mary of Bethany. Most scholars have conflated these individuals because that simplified the scriptures and made the narrative read more smoothly.

However, Latter-day Saints have generally sided with the separate identification of the two Marys.[21] While we have no record of Joseph Smith Jr. on this topic, Brigham Young, Orson Hyde, Orson Pratt, B. H. Roberts, James E. Talmage, and Bruce R. McConkie conclude separate identities for Mary of Magdala and Mary of Bethany.[22] Brigham Young was quoted by his wayward nineteenth wife as saying: "Mary and Martha, the sisters of Lazarus, were his plural wives, and Mary Magdalene was another."[23]

Orson Pratt noted: "The Evangelists do not particularly speak of the marriage of Jesus. . . . One thing is certain, that there were several holy women that greatly loved Jesus . . . such as Mary and Martha her sister, and Mary Magdalene."[24] Elder James E. Talmage in his official account of the life of the Savior notes regarding the woman in Luke 7:

The name of the woman who thus came to Christ, and whose repentance was so sincere as to bring to her grateful and contrite soul the assurance of remission, is not recorded. There is no evidence that she figures in any other incident recorded in scripture. By certain writers she has been represented as the Mary of Bethany who, shortly before Christ's betrayal, anointed the head of Jesus with spikenard; but the assumption of identity is wholly unfounded, and constitutes an unjustifiable reflection upon the earlier life of Mary, the devoted and loving sister of Martha and Lazarus. Equally wrong is the attempt made by others to identify this repentant and forgiven sinner with Mary Magdalene, no period of whose life was marked by the sin of unchastity so far as the scriptures aver.[25]

Talmage's separate accounts of the two Marys imply that he viewed them as two different persons. While the earlier statements may or may not have been scholarly or doctrinal expositions, those by Talmage do have some official force. We might assume that these anointed leaders of the Lord's Church were speaking from some deep place. We might therefore conjecture that the best LDS understanding today states that Mary Magdalene and Mary of Bethany are two distinct and separate people.

There is, however, a strong tradition in Western Christian sources that Mary of Bethany and Mary Magdalene were the same person.[26] Ambrose (A.D. ca. 337–397) preferred to leave the question undecided. However, by A.D. 591, Pope Gregory I (A.D. 540–604) had officially collapsed the two into one identity, undoubtedly because it filled a deep-seated theological need.

Then again in A.D. 595 Pope Gregory conflated the "sinner" in the house of the Pharisee with Mary Magdalene and Mary of Bethany.[27] Thus, officially from the end of the sixth century we had a "composite" Mary. Much later, in the medieval version of the *Lives of the Saints*, *The Golden Legend*, the Magdalene is identified with Mary of Bethany.[28]

Furthermore, the scriptural accounts of the Marys demonstrate striking similarities. There is something about Mary of Bethany sitting, listening intently to the Savior, to hear the message of the gospel. This is so reminiscent of Mary Magdalene. She also chose the better part and eagerly sought to be a part of the divine teacher's ideas and plan. Yet their identities should not be subsumed into each other.

Tenuous and construed evidence mounts for a unified Mary. Along this same line we read in the Gospel of Luke (7:38) how Mary Magdalene or Mary of Bethany wipes Jesus' feet with her hair. According to Hopkins, Simmans and Wallace-Murphy, "The wife was also the only woman allowed to sit at a man's feet."[29] Furthermore, "according to Jewish Law," write Freke and Gandy, "only a husband was allowed to see a woman's hair unbound."[30] If a woman let down her hair for other men, it was a sign of impropriety and was grounds for mandatory divorce. They continue, "This incident, then, can be seen as portraying Jesus and Mary either as man and wife or as libertine lovers with scant regard for moral niceties."[31]

Nowhere in the scriptures are Mary of Magdala and of Bethany mentioned together, thus the speculation that they are the same person. Where were Martha, Lazarus, and Mary of Bethany whom "Jesus loved" (John 11:5) during the Crucifixion, the time He needed them most? Nothing is mentioned in scripture. Mary of Bethany would have been remiss in not being there, unless she was present under the name of Mary Magdalene. All four gospels mention Mary Magdalene at the Crucifixion, but none mention the Bethany family, even though they were together shortly before the Passover. It would seem improbable that these three highly important people in Jesus' life would simply not be mentioned in the account or that they were, in fact, missing.

At this point we cannot say for sure which way historical fact on this issue of identification will fall. Indeed, it really does not change much one way or another. Unless new information comes forth, we must await the definitive answer to this question. However, the question of Mary's identity does have some important ramifications for the Grail, such as, Who was the first wife through whom the inheritance proceeds?

This book takes the LDS standard position that they are separate beings. We shall now look deeper into this question.

THE "SINNER" AND SEVEN DEVILS

Now when Jesus was risen early the first day of the week, he appeared first to Mary Magdalene out of whom he had cast seven devils.

—MARK 16:9

The story that gets all the press, which is told and retold, is the sinful woman in Luke 7. This occurred in the house of Simon the Pharisee some time during Christ's second Galilean ministry, preceding the miracles of the loaves. It raises the question: Is the woman in Matthew, Mark, and John who anoints Christ's feet the same as the woman in Luke? This study leans toward the negative for numerous reasons.

It would be instructive to our examination to consider that Mary Magdalene might in fact be the woman of Luke 7:36–50. Not because the scholars "know" anything about it, but for technical and theological reasons it would be best to keep this option

open. Amongst other reasons, it would greatly simplify this study if the "sinner" and Mary Magdalene were, in fact, the same person. More importantly, it would prove that there was more than one anointing sequence, demonstrating that Jesus had at least two intimate companions. Of course, feminists will not countenance this.

Matthew, Mark, and John are probably dealing with the same event, whereas Luke deals with a similar but separate occasion. While we cannot be sure that Luke 7 and 8 are dealing with the same woman, this is the hypothesis presented here.[32] However, Bruce R. McConkie adamantly separates Mary Magdalene of Luke 8 from the sinner in Luke 7.[33]

The woman in Luke was called a "sinner" three times (Luke 7:37, 39, 47). Yet verse 47 notes that "Her sins, which are many, are forgiven; for she loved much" (see Plate 6).[34] Luke's choice of word for sin, *harmartolos*, is interesting because it means one who has committed a crime against Jewish law. The human condition being what it is, we assume that it was a sexual transgression, but the word *pornin* would have best described a promiscuous condition: *porneia*, unlawful sexual intercourse. But *harmartolos* relates to "uncleanliness," not "unholiness"; thus the word could be rendered "filthy."[35]

The key to its meaning may already have been embedded in Luke 7:21: "And in that same hour [Jesus] cured many of their infirmities and plagues, and of evil spirits; and unto many that were blind he gave sight." Then in Luke 8:2 we read: "And a certain woman, which had been healed of evil spirits and infirmities, Mary called Magdalene, out of whom went seven devils."

In both verses we read about people, especially women, whom Jesus "cured" and "healed." In each, infirmities and evil spirits are mentioned together, implying that sickness of some sort was at the heart of the matter. Dr. Eric D. Huntsman favors the idea that the sin was a malady suffered by the Magalene.[36]

As Luke 7:21 says, "many that were blind he gave sight." Interestingly, this may relate to the man who "was born blind" in John 9:1–2: "And as Jesus passed by, he saw a man which was blind from his birth. And his disciples asked him saying, Master, *who did sin, this man, or his parents, that he was born blind?*"

Thus we see that during the Second Temple period Jews believed that people were blind because of sin. In the very next verse, Luke 7:22 mentions specific problems, the blind to see, the lame to walk, and the lepers to be cleansed, deaf to hear, and the nonbeliever to hear the gospel. Perhaps "the devils" in Jewish parlance were the sickness of leprosy.[37] Leprosy was the standing symbol of sin in the Levant during the first century.[38] These suggest that Mary Magdalene may have perhaps been smitten with seven maladies, including blindness, lameness, leprosy, deafness, and so forth.

The degree of this illness must have been extreme, for Christ to "cast out seven devils," or afflictions, is radical therapy, to say the least.[39] During this time, and in the parlance of the day, the healing process for the sick and "infirm" required the dispersing of "devils" or illnesses. During that day, anyone who was ill was thought to be possessed. James M. Robinson, professor of religion emeritus at Claremont Graduate University and general editor of *The Nag Hammadi Library,* gives a reasonable but not necessarily true answer: "I think the seven demons that Jesus cast out of her may have referred to some sort of nervous problem or mental illness, like epilepsy. She was challenged, he helped her, and she became a disciple, loyal to the bitter end."[40]

Some theologians suggest that the "seven devils" cast out of Mary Magdalene, mentioned in Mark 16:9, had reference to mental illnesses or insanity.[41] What was this possession and did Jesus perform an exorcism? Mark 16:9 says, "Mary Magdalene, out of whom [Jesus] had cast seven devils." This verse is actually missing from the very ancient *Codex Sinaiticus*

recovered from St. Catherine's monastery and is thus believed to be a later addition. Even if it was a later insertion, it may contain a nugget of truth. We learn that the devils were "cast" or thrown out by Jesus. Eric Huntsman posits, "If Mary's possession is seen as a sign of being in a state of sin, the emphasis in the exorcism is not on the sin as much as it is on her being freed from it."[42]

Both Jesus Christ and Simon the Pharisee agree that the woman in Luke 7 has many sins, but what kind of sins and how grievous are not mentioned. She may have been sinful ritualistically in the eyes of the Pharisees and in Christ's eyes only to the degree that all mortals sin. The seven demons cast from Mary Magdalene might imply that she was deemed unclean by the Pharisaical law but not necessarily by God's law. In fact, in Luke 7:33–34, both John the Baptist and the Son of Man are considered spectacular sinners by the ever-accusing Hillel Pharisees. Christ was considered a sinner in the eyes of the Pharisees.[43] Seeing the woman's love, Jesus said: "Wherefore I say unto thee, Her sins, which are many, are forgiven; for she loved much: but to whom little is forgiven, the same loveth little. And he said unto her, Thy sins are forgiven. . . . And he said to the woman, Thy faith hath saved thee; go in peace" (Luke 7:47–48, 50).

Many have thought that because she was the carrier of a nonapostolic line of succession in the Church, the Catholics (and other sects) felt obliged to belittle her. This is not so. Such words as "hijacked," "smear campaign," "cover-up," or "conspiracy" are not useful in trying to understand the historical persona of Mary Magdalene in the Church. Pope Gregory the First, who brought Christianity to Britain a second time after the Saxon conquests, was the culprit to some degree.

There is no need to consider Pope Gregory's stance as a gross misrepresentation of history or a malicious act. True, the Church did profit from calling Mary Magdalene a "penitent" in order to focus on the papal power of granting repentance and emphasize Christianity's forgiving nature.[44]

She became a homily for the truly humane teaching: "Though your sins be as scarlet, so shall they be as white as snow" (Isaiah 1:18). Through repentance and the forgiveness of Jesus Christ (see 1 Timothy 1:15), Mary thus became a symbol of repentance and forgiveness.

Historically, radical feminists believe the apostate Israelite worship of the sacred prostitute Asherah (Ashtoreth, Anat Jahu) foreshadows Christ's union with Mary Magdalene (Deuteronomy 16:21; Judges 6:25; 1 Kings 21:7) This is a feeble, misguided, and salacious attempt to show how God redeems his people, through marrying fallen women. Yahweh's union with adulterous Israel, as symbolized in Hosea's marriage to the prostitute Gomer, was intended to demonstrate a groom's redeeming love to a weaker vessel, His bride (Hosea 1:2; see also Ephesians 5:25–27). This should not be viewed as a representation of Mary Magdalene.

It is more likely that Christ's marriage to virtuous Mary Magdalene was the reclaiming of Ephraim's debased birthright—"O Ephraim, thou has committed whoredom. Israel is defiled" (Hosea 5:3). Thus the taint on the tribe of Ephraim was removed, because Ephraim's noble representative, Mary Magdalene, was claimed in marriage to the Redeemer. By the same token, Judah was also reclaimed by Christ's marriage to the Magdalene. It was a symbiotic relationship, as we see in Hosea 4:15, "Though thou, Israel [Ephraim] play the harlot, yet let not Judah offend" (see also Hosea 5:5).

By calling her after His name, He took away her (Ephraim's) reproach (barrenness or childlessness). The same applies to all women who seek a righteous marriage: "Let us be called by thy *name* to take away our reproach" (Isaiah 4:1). For it is only through Christ's name that all humanity is saved (Acts 4:12; Philippians 2:9).

However, Christ did not arrogantly condescend to marry the Magdalene, He did so gladly because of her heavenly attributes, and he benefited greatly by the marriage. In the book of Proverbs 12:4, we learn that "a virtuous woman is a crown to her husband." And Paul writes, "The woman is the glory of the man" (1 Corinthians 11:7). In this union the sought-for balance was achieved for: "Nevertheless, neither is the man without the woman, neither the woman without the man, in the Lord" (1 Corinthians 11:11).

The scriptures are replete with the righteous number seven. One reads in Revelation 1:4 of "the seven Spirits before his throne." And Revelation 1:12–15 refers to the seven golden candlesticks holding seven stars in His hand. These scriptural phrases correspond to the seven lamps of the golden candelabrum of the temple and stand opposed to the seven deadly sins. Seven is also associated with the seven churches.

Or it could be that the casting out of seven devils referred to Mary Magdalene's conversion to the gospel? The number seven's connection with Mary suggests that she has worked out her salvation and exaltation: "Wisdom [Sophia] hath builded her house, she hath hewn out her seven pillars" (Proverbs 9:1). Quite possibly this text could refer to Mary Magdalene passing through veils to ever-higher heavens (seventh heaven?) toward exaltation in the celestial kingdom.[45] Could this be a plausible reading of the seven devils, as they relate to Mary Magdalene?

Or, as the author is convinced, the preponderance of evidence leads to the idea that Mark 16:9 and Luke 8:2 simply refer to the Magdalene's initiation and marriage to Christ or to her being chronically sick. Perhaps, as Gardner believes, the earlier or original text of the scriptures, "describes the unmarried Magdalene as a sinner (which actually meant that she was a celibate *almah* [virgin] undergoing assessment in betrothal)"[46]

The seven devils would not have been a cult initiation at all, but rather a sacred temple ordinance reserved for her marriage in Cana to Jesus. In Mormon temples one receives certain initiatory rites, one of which is the anointing with oil. Seven parts of the body are anointed to reverse the curse placed upon Adam and Eve in the Garden. Could the casting out of seven devils simply be Christ conducting Mary Magdalene through the initiatory rites of the temple endowment prior to her marriage? As her betrothed, it would be His responsibility to do just this.

Given Mormonism's understanding of ancient Hebrew theology, which included the basis for such a belief, far from being a pagan cult member, she may have been initiated into this mystery, ceremony, or ordinance by Jesus Himself. Nothing should obfuscate Mary Magdalene's sacred role in the life of Christ, though many have tried. "Thou shalt no more be termed Forsaken; neither shall thy land any more be termed Desolate; but thou shall be called Delightful [espoused], and thy land Union; for the *Lord* delighteth in thee, and thy land shall be married" (JST Inspired Version, Isaiah 62:4).

MARY OF BETHANY, "IN MEMORY OF HER"

Why trouble ye the woman? For she hath wrought a good work upon me. . . . Verily I say unto you, Wheresoever this gospel shall be preached in the whole world, there shall also be this, that this woman had done, be told for a memorial to her.

—MATTHEW 26:10, 13

Mary of Bethany, the lady of Matthew's and Mark's gospels, received the glorious encomium, "She hath wrought a good work upon me" (Matthew 26:6–13). Christ said of the woman with the jar of precious nard (unguent, perfumed ointment), "Wheresoever this gospel shall be preached throughout the whole world, this also that she hath done shall be spoken of for a memorial of her"[47] (Mark 14:9). Yet few Christians have heard a single "memorial" about this woman by name. Who is she? Without doubt, she is Mary of Bethany.

While Mary Magdalene's anointing was more famous, this other anointing seems to be even more significant. In John's account (12:1–9) this consecration took place in Bethany six days before the Passover.[48] Although both Matthew and Mark state that about "two days before Passover," they were likely referring to the meeting of the High Priests, instead of the actual anointing. So it is entirely possible that anointings mentioned by all three authors happened six days before the Passover and were in fact the same anointing.[49]

We now need to examine the scriptures side-by-side to ferret out any meaning we can. There are a number of differences, some significant, but all within range of each other to believe that we are looking at four accounts of two incidents. We should allow the scriptures to speak for themselves and leave our interpretation with a comfortable margin for error.

FIGURE 5
THE ANOINTINGS OF CHRIST

	MATTHEW 26: 6–13	MARK 14: 1–9	LUKE 7: 36–50	JOHN 11:2, 12:1–9
LOCATION	Home of Simon the leper, Bethany	Home of Simon the leper, Bethany	Home of Simon the Pharisee, Galilee?	Unnamed home, Unnamed man, Bethany
TIME	Two days before Passover	Two days before Passover	Not stated, but apparently during his second Galilean ministry. Precedes the miracle of the feeding of the five thousand and the third Passover	Six days before Passover went to the house. Probably the same as Matthew and Mark
NAME OF WOMAN	Unnamed	Unnamed	Unnamed	Mary of Bethany
TYPE OF OINTMENT	"Very precious Ointment"	"Spikenard very precious"	"Ointment"	"Spikenard, very costly"
ALABASTER BOX/ CRUSE MENTIONED?	Yes, but did not break it	Yes, did break it	Yes, but did not break it	Not mentioned
HOW JESUS WAS ANOINTED	Poured on his head	Poured on his head	She washed his feet with her tears, wiped them with her hair, kissed his feet, and anointed them with ointment	Anointed his feet and wiped them with her hair
PROTESTS REGARDING ANOINTING	By Judas: the ointment might have been sold "for much" and given to the poor	By "some": the ointment might have been sold for 300 pence and given to the poor	By Simon, who thought within himself that Jesus should have known "what manner of woman this is that toucheth him: for she is a sinner"	By Judas: the ointment might have been sold for 300 pence and given to the poor

	MATTHEW 26: 6–13	MARK 14: 1–9	LUKE 7: 36–50	JOHN 11:2; 12:1–9
JESUS' STATEMENT REGARDING THE WOMAN	"Why trouble ye the woman? For she hath wrought a good work upon me. For ye have the poor always with you; but me ye have not always. For in that she hath poured this ointment on my body, she did it for my burial"	"Let her alone; why trouble ye her? She hath wrought a good work on me. For ye have the poor with you always, and whensoever ye will ye may do them good: but me ye have not always. She hath done what she could"	"Her sins, which are many, are forgiven; for she loved much. . . . Thy sins are forgiven. . . . Thy faith hath saved thee; go in peace"	"Let her alone: against the day of my burying hath she kept this. [JST: for she hath preserved this ointment until now, that she might anoint me in token of my burial] For the poor ye always ye have with you; but me ye have not always"
A MEMORIAL	"Verily I say unto you, Wheresoever this gospel shall be preached in the whole world, there shall also this, that this woman has done, be told for a memorial of her"	[JST: "and this which she has done unto me, shall be had in remembrance in generations to come, wheresoever my gospel be preached; for verily] she is come aforehand to anoint my body to the burying. Verily I say unto you, Wheresoever this gospel be preached throughout the whole world, this also that she hath done shall be spoken of for a memorial of her."		

It is most interesting to note that Talmage supposes that Simon the Leper was the father of Mary, Martha, and Lazarus.[50] It might be that Simon the Leper and Simon the Pharisee are called by two different names because they are in fact two separate people,[51] and the descriptive names of Leper and Pharisee are used to separate the two Simons, the fathers of Mary of Bethany and Mary Magdalene respectively.

Whoever the woman in Luke was, she was married to Jesus Christ, for the ordinance of anointing and washing the feet was one that a wife does for her husband. Likewise, LDS Apostle Orson Hyde suggested that it was Jesus' wife who washed his feet and wiped them with her hair.[52] Mary of Bethany's anointing of Christ with the pungent ointment at the feast of Bethany may have been, in a sense, an ordinance similar to the washing of the feet in the second anointing ceremony (see John 11:2; 12:3). The washing also has to do with one's "calling and election made sure," a ceremony within Mormon temples. Here the husband's wife washes and anoints her spouse's feet after they have received the fulness of the priesthood.[53]

The washing of his feet and anointing of His head was an ordinance that is normally administered by a wife on her husband.[54] The JST (Inspired Version) notes, "Then said Jesus, let her alone; for she hath preserved this ointment until now, that she might anoint me in token of my burial" (JST, John 12:7). This was an anointing for His death and resurrection (see Matthew 26:7–12).

Like the ritual anointing with the sacred olive oil that occurred at Gethsemane, Mary's precious ointment "marked" the one appointed unto torture, sacrifice, and death. Interestingly, it too was also administered on the Mount of Olives, since Bethany is on a southern spur of that incredibly significant hill. This was performed by a woman—his wife anointing him to be sacrificed and buried. In the allegorical Songs of Solomon 1:12, it appears that the wife handled the king's perfume: "While the king sitteth at his table, my spikenard sendeth forth the smell thereof."

Heber C. Kimball wrote about this ordinance that he and his wife received in February 1844: "Myself and wife Vilate [were] anointed Priest and Priestess unto our God under the hands of Brigham Young and by the voice of the Holy Order."[55] Later Heber wrote:

> I Heber C. Kimball received the washing of my feet, and was anointed by my wife Vilate for my burial, that is my feet, head, stomach. Even as Mary did Jesus, that she might have a claim on Him in the Resurrection.
>
> In 1845 I received the washing of my feet by [the rest in Vilate's handwriting] I Vilate Kimball do hereby certify that on the first day of April 1844, I attended to washing and anointed the head, / stomach / and feet of my dear companion Heber C. Kimball, that I may have claim upon him in the morning of the first Resurrection. Vilate Kimball.[56]

This ordinance is reserved specifically for spouses and was based on Mary's anointing of Christ. It suggests that all the above scriptural accounts refer to those women who have claim on Christ in the resurrection. Thus we can see how Jesus' wife(s) anoints Him as a sacrifice (Mount of Olives), observes the Crucifixion, notes where He was buried, and witnesses his resurrection. The essential elements of the Atonement are all observed as a memorial to her.

This is but one of the proofs that Jesus was married, for this is a wife's ordinance on her husband as a token of his burial[57] (JST, John 12:7). It now becomes apparent why Mary Magdalene and other women, probably including Mary and Martha of Bethany, saw Him first after His resurrection. In fact, the ordinance is the great "memorial" wherever the fulness of the true gospel is preached and temples erected. It is one of the signs of the true Church, and it is only practiced by Latter-day Saints.

THE SAINTED MAGDALENE

Mary Ellen A. Kimball's journal recorded her husband, Heber C., saying, "He then spoke of our Savior and his wives but more particularly of Mary [and her] faithfulness to her Lord."[58]

The name *Mary* means "exalted" and, according to Robert Millet, it was the "looked for" name of the mother of the forthcoming Messiah.[59] Many of the early patristic fathers saw the Marys of Nazareth and Magdala as the "new Eve" in the message of redemption as they saw Jesus Christ as the "new Adam."[60] However, as the years passed, the intentional transmogrification of the Magdalene and the worship of Mother Mary began to appear. This "whore and the virgin" myth has produced sinister effects on our understanding of gospel history. While the mother was elevated, the wife was denigrated, in much the same way that Eve was impugned. Bruce R. McConkie taught this: "[Mary Magdalene was] one of the most virtuous and righteous women ever to follow Jesus. So great was her faith and so extensive her good works that she was singled out to stand as the first mortal person to see our Lord after his resurrection."[61]

In Roman Catholicism, sacred attributes and protective responsibilities fall to those who are sainted. St. Mary Magdalene was sacred to people for a myriad of reasons. She was a powerful, independent, intelligent, righteous, and loyal role model. The hagiology (literature of veneration) of Mary Magdalene is deep and diverse, especially during the Middle Ages when she was especially venerated. Since the Magdalene was at the Garden Tomb, she was sacred to gardeners. Because she had a vase of unguents she

received petitions of apothecaries. And because of the aromatic oils she poured on the Savior's feet, perfumers gave her special countenance.[62]

To the gnostics she is Sancta Sophia, goddess of Wisdom. Because her garments were soiled with sin but then were washed clean, she is the patron saint of laundresses. The Talmud even calls her a *m'gaddla* "dresser of woman's hair."[63] Her "supposed" high life of luxury, before her repentance, was celebrated by makers of gloves and shoes and by the drapers of Bologna. Her reputation as a reformed prostitute made her sacred to repentant ladies of the street and all hopeless women. Such rescued females often lived in houses called Magdalinas. Andrew Sinclair continues: "The people of Bolzano prayed to her to help their vintages, while the water-sellers of Chartres also sought her benediction. Her healing by Christ, who had also cured her brother, made her an apostle to the sick *and to lepers*, while her penitence endeared her to prisoners, who dedicated their chains to her at Vézelay. She was the most charismatic woman saint of the Middle Ages."[64]

Yet, ultimately, it was not what society thought of Mary Magdalene, but what God perceived that really counted. Just how elect she was in the sight of God is shown in St. Andrew's reminder to an irritated brother Peter, "For the Savior has known her thoroughly enough and loved her more than us."[65] The very name *Magdala* literally means "tower" or "elevated, great, magnificent." One could almost call her, "Mary the Magnificent!" She was a queen, and perhaps even the marital cosmic counterpart of the King, Jesus Christ, Himself.

There is a picture by French painter and symbolist artist Gustave Moreau (1826–1898) entitled *La Licorne* (unicorn) that may be a representation of a crowned (exalted) Mary Magdalene. In the Middle Ages a nude representation of a woman was often a symbol of chastity, purity, and the Christian Church, as in the "bride of Jesus." In Moreau's painting we see a nude woman with a unicorn who, being pure, is drawn to virginal women (see Plate 7).[66] Though essentially nude, she wears a royal red cloak and hat, with a crown on her head. She touches the unicorn, an emblem of Ephraim, with one hand. With her other hand she holds a palm frond, the symbol of the House of David and Christ's kingship (Mark 11:8; Luke 19:35). Perhaps Moreau has painted Mary Magdalene as the queen of the King?

In the minds of many, her exalted status is vouchsafed by being the witness of the Resurrection. This is remarkable because the testimony of women had little authority during first-century Jewish culture. Some believe that Jesus' injunction "go to my brethren [the apostles], and say unto them, I ascend unto my Father" (John 20:17) made her the *Apostola Apostolorum*.[67] Those with the agenda of making her the highest disciple, according to Eric Huntsman, play off the word *apostolos* (meaning, one who was sent), making it "the apostle [sent one] to the apostles." However, as she points out, the word used in John is *poreuou*, an imperative verb, which is completely different from the infinitive *apostello*, meaning "to send."[68] All this did not equate to ecclesiastical power but rather to a personal command. While radical writers assert that she was chosen by Christ to head the Church, she is merely being "used" for their ideological purposes. Pheme Perkins and Robert M. Price believe "Mary Magdalene is merely a literary mouthpiece in these texts."[69]

Ironically, gnostic and feminist writers claim Mary Magdalene's ascendence through her witnessing the resurrected Christ and his command to her to go and tell the apostles that he had risen. They assert that Jesus transmitted the true revelations of esoteric secrets and authority to Mary Magdalene at the tomb. However, they deny that a literal physical resurrection ever occurred. So, if logic prevails, her authority supposedly received at the resurrection site must stand suspect.

Though blessed to be the first to commune with the resurrected Jesus, Mary Magdalene was not the only woman privileged to see the empty tomb and the two angels, for perhaps as many as fourteen did[70] (Mark 16:9). The Magdalene was not even the only woman to speak with the newly resurrected Christ (Matthew 28:9), nor the only one who told the apostles of the risen Christ (Luke 24:10–11).

The Magdalene's most significant title could be "faithful companion." She was depicted as kneeling at the heavenly throne receiving the benediction of Jesus Christ (see Plate 8).[71] Unlike the androgynous being worshiped by most gnostics, she is shown with a very feminine celestial body beside Christ in the hereafter. One can imagine her saying, "I am the rose of Sharon, the lily of the valleys" (Song of Songs 2:1). She is a true woman with body, parts, and passions.

A plethora of gnostic and apocryphal texts assign a great deal of knowledge and power to Mary Magdalene, strengthening our opinion that she was a woman of status. "Mary," Jesus praised in apocryphal *Pistis Sophia*, "you blessed one, who shall be inducted into all the ordinances from on high. Speak openly, whose heart is more directed toward the kingdom of heaven than that of your brethren."[72] Peter later said: "Sister, we know that the Savior loved you more than other women. Tell us all that you can remember of what the Saviour said to you alone—everything that you know of him but we do not."[73]

The discernment of Mary Magdalene likens her with the name Sophia, which literally means wisdom (see Proverbs 9:1). The fourth-century gnostic apocryphal text *Dialogue of the Savior* esteems Mary after the resurrection as "a woman who completely understands."[74] In another translation of this text, Mary Magdalene was said to speak "as a woman who knew the All."[75] Then, in the *Gospel according to Mary*, the resurrected Christ divulges the inner mysteries (*gnosis*) of Christianity to Mary, who then communicates them to the other disciples.[76]

How esteemed Mary was compared to other women is also seen in another passage from the Coptic *Pistis Sophia* of A.D. 250. She is one of the seven women and twelve men gathered to hear the Lord just after the resurrection. It reads, "And it happened when Mary [Magdalene] had ended her words, He said, 'Excellent, Mary, for you are blessed above all women on the earth, because you will be the fulness of all fulness, and completion of all completion.'"[77]

At the end of the discourse in the *Pistis Sophia* Jesus tells this little group, "I have given you [not just Mary] authority over all things as children of light."[78] Thus Mary Magdalene is included, undoubtedly because of her faith, understanding, and spiritual perfection. It is possible that Acts 1:13–14 is being referred to in the *Pistis Sophia*. After the Ascension of the risen Lord from the Mount of Olives, the apostles retired to the upper room. There "these all continued with one accord in prayer and supplication, with the women, and Mary the mother of Jesus, and with his brethren." The phrase "with the women" is a translation of *syn gynaixin*, and since *gyne* also means "wife," it could, according to Eric Huntsman, refer to the wives of the apostles or of the brothers of the Lord. "If so, Mary Magdalene again is portrayed as an intimate associate, even a family member."[79]

The *Gospel of Philip* has Mary Magdalene as one of the three Marys "who always walked with the Lord" and as his companion.[80] Again the *Pistis Sophia* places things into perspective when it notes: "But Mary Magdalene and John [the Beloved], the virgin disciple, shall surpass all my disciples and all men who will receive the ordinances [mysteries] of the unspeakable. They will be on my right hand and on my left, and I am they and they are I."[81]

In this quotation we see that they are closely tied in Heaven, on thrones to the left and the right of the Savior. Perhaps we see the Savior's bride, Mary Magdalene, "on my right hand" and hear the words of the Lord, "Excellent, Mary, you blessed one,

[you] will inherit the kingdom of light."[82]

In Psalm 45:9 we read, "Upon thy right hand did stand the Queen in a vesture of gold of Ophir." Apostle Orson Pratt proceeds along similar lines: "One seems to be chosen to stand at his right hand; perhaps she may have merited that high station by her righteous acts, *or by the position she had previously occupied*. It seems that she was one of the daughters of a king."[83]

In some gnostic texts the Great Mother is called "She of the Left Hand," perhaps indicating that she sits on the throne at the left hand of God, instead of His right, where one day we might be invited to sit.[84] This does not mean that others will not sit on the Lord's right hand.[85] We can 'expect that Mary will on occasion. William Blake's mystical picture entitled *Christ Pleading before the Father for St. Mary Magdalene* depicts Jesus presenting the humble Mary Magdalene before Heavenly Father. There she will be invited to sit on the right hand (see Plate 8).[86]

NOTES

1. Patmore, *Deliciae Sapientiae De Amore* (19th century).
2. Orson Hyde, *Journal of Discourses,* 4:259 (probably 1857).
3. Price, *Da Vinci Fraud,* 211.
4. Van Biema and McLaughlin, "Mary Magdalene: Saint or Sinner?" *Time,* 11 August 2003, 53.
5. Starbird, *Mary Magdalene,* 52–67. Starbird gives the most detailed analysis, but it is definitely skewed toward the feminist position.
6. See Price, *Da Vinci Fraud,* 235. This is from the Toldoth Recession of the Strasburg MS, the same tract that contained the Ben Pandira information. (This could be the same as Tosefta or the Tosafoth). The fourth-century Babylonian Talmud Gemara has a reference to m'gaddela nashaya "dresser of women's hair" listing it as the profession of the Virgin Mary. See Starbird, *Mary Magdalene,* 56.
7. This was also the Roman Catholic view until 1969 when the two identities were separated. Starbird, *Mary Magdalene,* 60, believes this was a misguided position

for the Catholic church to take, though she welcomes that ecumenical council's reversal that Mary Magdalene was a prostitute.

8. A Roman Catholic scholar, Jusino, *Mary Magdalene*, promotes this idea. He strongly bases much of his work on Brown's research in *Community of the Beloved Disciple*, a man who really does not believe they were the same person.

9. This would also make her the sister of James, the brother of John, and the daughter of Zebedee—a most difficult arrangement at best.

10. This is a story invented in the sixth and seventh centuries by Gregory of Tours and Modestus the patriarch of Jerusalem. It was created to purify the Magdalene's and John's traveling and living arrangements together in Ephesus. Certainly earlier there were equally strong statements saying the John the Evangelist was celibate. Then according to Jacobus de Voragine's fifteenth-century work, *The Golden Legend*, the Magdalene was betrothed to John. Assuming this to be John the Beloved/Revelator, it only muddies the water of our understanding.

11. Collins, *Twenty-First Century Grail*, 131. The couple he says might well have become "one" to form the perfect androgyne. While John is often shown in feminine terms, Mary Magdala is never shown in masculine.

12. Sinclair, *Secret Scroll*, 57. Actually Hippolytus does not believe the two were actually married, but wedded in a spiritual sense.

13. Starbird, *Magdalen's Lost Legacy*, 132.

14. Hopkins, Simmans, and Wallace-Murphy, *Rex Deus*, 77.

15. Elder B. F. Cummings, "The Prophet's Last Letters," *Improvement Era*, February 1915, 388. Cummings notes that he saw the original pages of the inspired revision of the Bible in 1909 saying, "As I was turning its leaves I came to a page on which was written in a bold hand and large letters, bolder and larger than the rest of the writing on that page, this sentence, which, unless memory is at fault, I here reproduce verbatim: "The song of Solomon is not inspired writing," As quoted in Matthews, *"A Plainer Translation,"* 87, 215. Cummings got the quote slightly incorrect (it should read "The Songs of Solomon are not inspired writings") and the letters are not larger or bolder, but rather smaller.

16. Eric D. Huntsman, "Mary Magdalene: Biblical Enigma," BYU Museum of Art presentation, 25 February 2004 (revised 26 May 2004), in author's possession.

17. Rabanus, as quoted in Taylor, *Coming of the Saints*, 82; emphasis added. Collins, *Twenty-First Century Grail*, 148, believes that this publication is of the mid-twelfth century.

18. The Greek Church maintains that Mary Magdalene retired to Ephesus with the Blessed Virgin and there died and that her relics were transferred to Constantinople in 886.

19. Edersheim, *Life and Times of Jesus the Messiah*, 2:358. Those, if any, who identify this Mary of John 12:1–9 with the Magdalene, and regard the anointing of St. Luke, 7:36, &c, as identical with that of Bethany.

20. According to Dr. Eric D. Huntsman, Jerome, the translator of the Bible from Greek to Latin, may have been the first to begin to associate Mary Magdalene with the sinful woman of Luke 7 and the adulterous woman of John 8. See Olson and Miesel, *Da Vinci Hoax*, 77. There is no separate Catholic feast day for Mary of Bethany, although the Eastern Church has it on the 18th of March close to the feast day on March 21 of "the unnamed sinner." Interestingly, the feast day for Mary Magdalene was celebrated on July 22nd, one week before the Catholic feast day of Martha of Bethany.

21. Brooke Foss Westcott speaking on John 11:1 stated "that the identity of Mary [of Bethany] with Mary Magdalene is a mere conjecture supported by no direct evidence and opposed to the general tenor of the gospels." Mormons generally follow this reasoning. See "Mary Magdalene," in *Catholic Encyclopedia*.

22. Roberts, *Defense of the Faith*, Roberts quotes Brother Hyde's remarks identifying the two Marys and Martha as Jesus' wives.

23. Young (Denning), *Wife No. 19*, (1876), 307.

24. Orson Pratt, *The Seer* (October 1853), 159; see also160, 169–72. See Orson Hyde, in *Journal of Discourses*, 4:259 (probably 1857), where he mentions all three as wives of Jesus.

25. Talmage, *Jesus the Christ*, 263–64. Later, in pages 432, 511, 522–23, Talmage does not specifically say one way or the other. He does not, however, say they were the same person. Thus he surely felt that they were two separate Marys.

26. Taylor, *Coming of the Saints*, 36. This proposition was accepted by certain early patristic fathers and scholastics, including Tertullian, Jerome, Augustine, Venerable Bede, Rabanus Maurus, St. Odo of Cluny, Bernard of Clairvaux, and Thomas Aquinas.

27. Susan Haskins interview in Burstein, *Secrets of the Da Vinci Code*, 24.

28. Sinclair, *Secret Scroll*, 59. These imaginative tales by Bishop Jacobus de Voragine date from about 1260. There are an incredible one thousand manuscripts of *Legenda Aurea (The Golden Legend)* in existence, attesting to its popularity in the Middle Ages.

29. Hopkins, Simmans, and Wallace-Murphy, *Rex Deus,* 74. In Luke 10 we read,"And she had a sister called Mary, which also sat at Jesus' feet, and heard his word."

30. Freke and Gandy, *Jesus and the Goddess,* 95. "It was the greatest disgrace for a woman to unbind her hair in the presence of men." See Haskins, *Mary Magdalen,* 18. This is still the case in much of the Middle East. It is a symbol of sexuality.

31. Freke and Gandy, *Jesus and the Goddess,* 95.

32. While saying that the woman in Luke 7 was Mary Magdalene, I do not cast the Magdalene as the nameless woman "brought in adultery" to Christ mentioned in John 8:7. They were entirely separate individuals.

33. McConkie, *Doctrinal New Testament Commentary,* 1:266. "She is not to be confused with the unnamed though repentant sinner who anointed Jesus' feet in the home of Simon. It is one of the basest slanders of all history to suppose that Mary of Magdala was a fallen woman and therefore to use the term Magdalene as an appellation descriptive of reformed prostitutes." McConkie assumes that the "sinner" of Luke 7 has committed grievous sins. This is not necessarily the case.

34. Simon Dewey, *For She Loved Much* (2001, acrylic on canvas). Courtesy of the artist. Here is Mary Magdalene washing and anointing Christ's feet at the House of Simon the Pharisee in Galilee.

35. It is possible that this most despicable disease which renders its victims "untouchable" was the physician Luke's "sinful woman."

36. Eric D. Huntsman, "Mary Magdalene: Biblical Enigma," BYU Museum of Art presentation, 25 February 2004 (revised 26 May 2004).

37. Talmage, *Jesus the Christ,* 555. It was broached by James E. Talmage that Simon the Leper was the father of Mary of Bethany; we might also say that Simon the Pharisee was the father of Mary Magdalene. If she was the daughter of Simon the Leper, as several scholars have hypothesized, this may well have been the case, but it would put the story backward.

38. Barnum, *Comprehensive Dictionary of the Bible,* 545.

39. That this is all mentioned less than a week before the death of Christ is to rehash the previous problem. Simon's critique in Luke is not so much that she *is* a sinner (sick), but that she *was* one. He does not understand the eternal nature of healing or forgiveness.

40. As quoted in Burstein, *Secrets of the Da Vinci Code,* 99.

41. Myriam Marquez, *Provo Daily Herald,* 16 April 1995.

42. Eric D. Huntsman, "Mary Magdalene: Biblical Enigma," BYU Museum of Art presentation, 25 February 2004 (revised 26 May 2004).

43. Christ is criticized for healing on the Sabbath, being a wine bibber, and blasphemously forgiving sin, etc.

44. One theory postulates that it was an attempt to reduce the number of people named Mary. Others blame misogyny, the hatred of women.

45. Doresse, *Secret Books of the Egyptian Gnostics,* 88. See Fred Collier's paper "The Decline of the Hebrew Goddess," at Sunstone Symposium in Salt Lake City, 25 August 1989.

46. Gardner, *Bloodline of the Holy Grail,* 119; *Illustrated Bloodline of the Holy Grail,* 87.

47. Nard is a very costly essence extracted from the root of an Indian plant of the family of Valerianae, which grows exclusively in the Himalayas (see Collins, *Twenty-First Century Grail,* 118).

48. Edersheim, *Life and Times of Jesus the Messiah,* 2:359. Usually the high priest, bridegroom, and king are ordained six days before the Passover. Historically, the anointing of the sacrifice occurred six days before Yom Kippur (Gethsemane) and the Passover (Crucifixion). Thus it might be that the Magdalene anointing happened six months earlier.

49. But then again, it may be that the anointing by Mary mentioned in John did not take place upon His arrival, but rather two days before Jesus' third Passover in conjunction with Matthew and Mark. I like the six days because that is the traditional date for the anointing of sacrifices in Israel. Although Mary of Bethany is mentioned in John, the Gospels of Matthew and Mark leave the identity of the woman unstated. Thus it left some room for Martha assisting Mary at the anointing of Jesus. Mary could have prepared the ordinance while Martha prepared dinner. Then they could have come together for the ordinance with Mary of Bethany being the sealer and mouth.

50. Talmage, *Jesus the Christ,* 511. Talmage does not say for sure if this is the case, "but of such relationship we have no proof." But he at least countenanced the idea.

51. Of course one could argue that Simon "the leper" and Simon "the Pharisee" are not mutually exclusive names but just happen to be two descriptive names of the same person. See Collins, *Twenty-First Century Grail,* who believes that they were the same person. But it could be argued just as effectively, or perhaps more so, the other way.

52. Orson Hyde, in *Journal of Discourses* (6 October 1854), 2:80; see also *Journal of Discourses,* 4:259.

53. This is the Holy Order of the Melchizedek Priesthood.

54. There is an LDS ordinance, similar in most respects to this washing and anointing, that usually occurred late

in life (as it does in Jesus' case) by the wife, in order to claim her husband at the resurrection. In the restored gospel the washing of the feet is an ordinance patterned after John 13, which would admit one into the School of the Prophets. It represents the recipient's being made clean from the blood and sin of this generation and to unite our hearts against the adversary (D&C 88:131, 138–41).

55. Heber C. Kimball diary, "Strange Events" (February 1, 1944).

56. Kimball, *On the Potter's Wheel*, 56–57. The ordinance is usually one received by the man from his wife, and through it she lays claim on him during the resurrection. He is a savior in the sense that it entitles her to be resurrected by him through the Holy Priesthood. From the "Record of Lewis Dunbar Sr. and Nancy Ann Wilson (20 July 1851) of events about 20 January 1846: 'At the temple at Nauvoo she received her washings and anointings even to become a queen and priestess, after which time she attended to one other ordinance which was to wash the feet of her husband and anoint him to be her king and priest and Savior, that she might have claim on him at the resurrection.'" From the Samuel Hollister Rogers Journal (22 September 1879, BYU Special Collections, Mss/1134/vol. II, p. 78: "I dedicated the house and room also blest the oil after which my Ruth anointed my feet and wiped them with the hair of her head, then kissed them after the pattern as written in the Testament of the Lord Jesus Christ." From *Wilford Woodruff Journal* (5 May 1844), 2:393: "Phebe [Woodruff's wife] washed my feet that I might be clean every whit."

57. The two anointings may have been somewhat different and for somewhat different purposes.

58. Mary Ellen A. Kimball, Journal (18 February 1857), CHO.

59. BYU religion professor Robert Millet notes that this was the reason why so many parents called their daughters Mary (Miriam).

60. Ester de Boer in Burstein, *Secrets of the Da Vinci Code*, 44.

61. McConkie, *Doctrinal New Testament Commentary*, 1:266.

62. Durrant, *Age of Faith*, 743.

63. Toldoth recession of the Strasburg MS, the same tract that contained the Ben Pandira information. (This could be the same as Tosefta or the Tosafoth). See Price, *Da Vinci Fraud*, 235. This was also the profession listed for the Virgin Mary.

64. Sinclair, *Secret Scroll*, 62. Again the leper idea crops up, perhaps signifying that she was a leper herself, particularly Mary of Bethany.

65. Evangelium Mariae, 18. It is also called Gospel of Mary Magdalene (Papyrus Berlinensis 8502.) as quoted in Wellnitz, *Christ and the Patriarchs*, 192. This fourth-century Berlin Codex is a fragment of the gnostic "Gospel of Mary" in which Jesus held her in special esteem. In the 2005 Salt Lake City Sunstone Symposium (29 July 2005), Margaret Starbird notes that Andrew, not Peter, was the head of the Church of Light.

66. Gustave Moreau (1826–1898), French, *La Licorne* (1884–1885, oil on canvas, 19 7/8" x 13 3/8"). Christie's London, 24 November 2004 (23). We are not sure of the woman's identification, but for our purposes she perfectly fits the image of Mary Magdalene, crowned and robed, with the symbol of her tribe, the white unicorn. Her nudity represents the bride as chastity and the Christian church.

67. Godwin, *Holy Grail*, 205. Mary Magdalene was first noted as "the apostle to the apostles" by the antipope Hippolytus (ca. 170–ca. 236) in his commentary on the Song of Songs.

68. See Eric D. Huntsman, "Mary Magdalene: Biblical Enigma," BYU Museum of Art presentation (25 February 2004; revised 26 May 2004).

69. Price, *Da Vinci Fraud*, 218. See also Perkins, *Gnostic Dialogue*, 136. Price believes, "It seems to me that Mary Magdalene is another like Joseph of Arimathea. Her apostleship is a later propaganda argument on behalf of one side in a theological dispute between Catholic and other types of Christianity" (219).

70. John 20:12 and Luke 24:1–10. Among these were the Virgin Mary, the Magdalene, Mary the mother of James, Joanna the wife of Chuza, etc. I think that Mary and Martha of Bethany and perhaps the elusive Elizabeth were also among the fourteen.

71. Michel Sytal, *Mary, Mother of Jesus* (sixteenth century, oil on panel), from a reproduction in Bruce E. Dana book written in Chinese (ZITO, 2003), 90. It originally depicts the Virgin Mary, but could just as easily be Mary Magdalene kneeling in a garden before the throne of God, receiving her crown and benediction of exaltation from the Father and the Son.

72. Pistis Sophia 17. This apocryphal gnostic book deals extensively with Mary Magdalene, as quoted in Wellnitz, *Christ and the Patriarchs*, 194.

73. Nag Hammadi Codex BG 8502, 1, as quoted in Gardner, *Bloodline of the Holy Grail*, 98. In the Golden Legend, Voragine says that Mary Magdalene was told to preach by Saint Peter. One of the male converts is so doubtful about this that he goes to Rome to ask Peter if it is true. See Voragine, *Legenda Aurea (The Golden*

Legend), 1:377–79, as noted in Newman, *Real History behind The Da Vinci Code,* 157.

74. The Dialogue of the Savior NHC, 3.5.139, as quoted in Freke and Gandy, *Jesus and the Goddess,* 98. In The Dialogue of the Savior, Mary Magdalene participates, along with Matthew and Thomas-Judas in an extended discussion with Jesus. Mary asks several questions as a prominent member of the disciple group, and she is the only woman mentioned. In response to her insightful questions the Lord says, "You make clear the abundance of the revealer!" (140:17–19). Then at another moment when Mary has spoken, the narrator exclaims, "She uttered this as a woman who had understood completely" (139:11–13). Mary is counted among those of the disciples who fully comprehended the Lord's teachings (142:11–13). This is similar wording to the Pistis Sophia.

75. As quoted by Sinclair, *Secret Scroll,* 37; Knight and Lomas, *Second Messiah,* 91.

76. Freke and Gandy, *Jesus and the Goddess,* 116. Here, the supposedly misogynistic (showing a distrust of women) Peter, annoyed that the resurrected Jesus has given secret teachings to Mary and not to him, is somewhat indignant. In other places Christ also gives the gnosis to Peter, James the Just, and Joseph of Arimathea.

77. Pistis Sophia (ch. 19), as quoted in Wellnitz, *Christ and the Patriarchs,* 194.

78. Pistis Sophia (ch. 19), as quoted in Wellnitz, *Christ and the Patriarchs,* 195.

79. Eric D. Huntsman, "Mary Magdalene: Biblical Enigma," BYU Museum of Art presentation, 25 February 2004 (revised 26 May 2004).

80. The Coptic *Gospel of Philip* 58:6–11. This included the Virgin Mary, Mary Magdalene, and Mary Salome.

81. Pistis Sophia 96. Again this relates the Magdalene and John together, as one theory of this paper has them as brother and sister (Mary of Bethany and Lazarus) or companions. Haskins, *Mary Magdalen,* 158, notes that a sixth-century legend has John the Evangelist as the bridegroom at the wedding of Cana. This is ascribed to St. Augustine who does not name the bride. But Collins, *Twenty-First Century Grail,* 126, argues against this position.

82. Pistis Sophia 61, as quoted in Wellnitz, *Christ and the Patriarchs,* 194.

83. Orson Pratt, *The Seer* 1, 11 (November 1853): 169. Perhaps a reference to her premortal valiance.

84. Mead, *Gnosis of the Mind,* 334, as quoted in Freke and Gandy, *Jesus and the Goddess,* 263. George Robert Stowe Mead was Madame Blavatsky's personal secretary.

85. Also Salome once asks the Savior if her sons James the Greater and John the Beloved may be on His two hands when He comes into His kingdom (Mark 16:1).

86. William Blake (1757–1827), British, *Christ the Mediator: Christ Pleading Before the Father for St. Mary Magdalene* (ca. 1799, pen and grey ink and tempera on canvas, 10 ¾" x 15 ¼"). From the collection of the late George Goyder, C.B.E., sale at Christie's London, 14 June 2005 (10). There is no biblical text for the subject, but in general it is derived from 1 Timothy 2:5: "For there is one God, and one scripture." 1 John 2:1 notes: "My little children, these things write I to you, that ye sin not. And if any man sin, we have an advocate with the Father, Jesus Christ the righteous." In this picture Mary Magdalene may represent all mankind as a whole.

CHAPTER NINE
THE NEED FOR AN EPHRAIMITE

In order to demonstrate the prophetic connections between tribal Judah and Joseph, it is necessary to establish that Mary Magdalene and the Bethany sisters were, in fact, of the House of Ephraim. If there was a Grail marriage and children, as possibly referred to in Doctrine and Covenants 113:3–6, we may conclude that they were of the Houses of Jesse and Joseph/Ephraim. Although there are no proponents for an Ephraimitic Magdalene or Bethany sisters, this position can be argued from existing evidence. But evidence is not necessarily proof. Therefore we shall assert the need and the logic of reconciliation between Judah (Kingdom of the Jews) and Ephraim (Kingdom of Israel). It is from this premise we proceed with the Grail story.

EPHRAIMITE WIVES

For Judah prevailed above his brethren,

and of him came the chief ruler; but the birthright was Joseph's.

—1 CHRONICLES 5:2

For I am a father to Israel, and Ephraim is my firstborn.

—JEREMIAH 31:9

At this point it is important to argue the lineage of Christ's wives and to understand its portent. Their marriage to Jesus Christ was not only a romantic or domestic affair but also held strategic value of the utmost political and theological consequence. It must have had similar potential, like Romeo and Juliet's star-crossed relationship, to heal the rift between families. It did, in fact, heal the bitter breach between two noble tribes. Thus the royal House of Judah marrying into the birthright House of Ephraim made great political sense and good prophecy.

No known scholars or churchmen have stated in

writing that Mary Magdalene or the Bethany sisters were literal Ephraimites. Usually they claim a Benjaminite or Judaic lineage for them. However, it is the contention of this book that they originally descended from the city of Shiloh in Mount Ephraim. Interestingly, Jesus, just before His last Passover, resorted to a "City of Ephraim," which was probably in the wilderness of Shiloh where "the house of *God*" once stood[1] (John 11:54; Judges 18:31). After Gilgal, Shiloh was the center place of Israel in the days of Joshua.

Perhaps Christ and his disciples went up "to worship and to sacrifice unto the Lord of hosts in Shiloh" (1 Samuel 1:3). The preaching and miracles performed by Christ, as with the prophet Samuel in Shiloh, made "the ears of every one that heareth it . . . *tingle*" (1 Samuel 3:11). Perhaps it was this time in Christ's life that he mysteriously fulfilled the messianic prophecy "until Shiloh come" (Genesis 49:10). We read that the Lord had revealed Himself in Shiloh unto Samuel (Samuel 3:21). Perhaps He now revealed Himself once more in Shiloh, only this time in the mortal flesh. Around A.D. 33 Shiloh was "in the wilderness," so perhaps Jesus was giving one more teaching moment to his disciples like that prophesied in Jeremiah:

> *But go ye now unto my place, which was in Shiloh, where I set my name at the first, and see what I did to it for the wickedness of my people Israel.*
>
> *Therefore will I do unto this house, which is called by my name, wherein ye trust, and unto the place, which I gave to you and to your fathers, as I have done to Shiloh.*
>
> *And I will cast you out of my sight, as I have cast out all your brethren, even the whole seed of Ephraim.*
>
> —JEREMIAH 7:12, 14–15
> (SEE 26:6, 9)

If Mary Magdalene's and the Bethany sisters' ancestral home was at Shiloh, Jesus' going there before the final curtain would have made sense. Discerning their hereditary home and establishing them as "daughters of Shiloh" is of paramount consequence (Judges 21:21). Upon it rests the reconciliation of Israel and, by extension, all the world. In the past, wicked Ephraim was cast out of the Holy Land, but after the crucifixion, the righteous "seed of Ephraim" was cast out of wicked Palestine.

The two head tribes, Judah and Ephraim, had become alienated into two separate political and religious entities. They needed to make amends, to bridge the breach and heal the wasteland caused by their continual warfare, idolatry, and arrogance. Representatives from these two tribes should, according to theory, marry in a strategic marriage uniting all of Israel together.

Internal theological logic requires that the wife of Jesus Christ would be an Ephraimite woman of noble blood. Her being an Ephraimite would make the sacred symmetry of the gospel story work out. Given the thrust of many scriptures, this spouse could not be of any other tribe of Israel but Ephraim. The reasons are numerous, and the most compelling are listed below:

1. Since Jesus is of the tribe of Judah, the wive(s) needed to be of another tribe to bring unification to Israel.

2. The wife(s) needed to somehow be related to the City of Ephraim, called Shiloh (Genesis 49:10).

3. In marrying, Jesus needed to have added strategic healing value. Thus, Christ marrying an Ephraimite woman would mend the breach between Judah and Ephraim.

Although no other tribal relationship had as many factors in its favor as the Judah/Ephraim alliance, no contemporary scholar has ventured to postulate this union. However, Medieval hagiographers were not deterred from hypothesizing Mary's lineage. In the eleventh century, Humbert of the Romans sermonized that the Magdalene was "descended from *stirpe regia*," or royal stock.[2]

John W. Taylor states that the Magdalene was of the royal house of Israel. Without any evidence he proclaims that she was distantly related to St. Joseph and the Virgin.[3] Taylor mistakenly believes that a Jewess of the House of David and a maiden of the house of Israel are the same. She was not royal, but she certainly was noble.

There were also numerous attempts to identify Mary Magdalene and the Bethany sisters' parents. A twelfth-century Cistercian text notes that their "mother Eucharia came from the royal house of Israel, while her father Theophilus descended from noble satraps and was governor of Syria."[4] Supposedly Rabanus Maurus (Maar) (776–856), the bishop of Mayence (Mainz) and Abbé of Fuld, and certainly, Jacobus de Voragine, Archbishop of Genoa (b. 1228), believed that Mary Magdalene's father was Syrian and that her mother was a Jewess named Eucharia of the House of David.[5] They further specify that the mother was related to the Levitical Hasmonaean royal house of Israel.[6] Thus Mary and Martha are Jews of the house of David and Levi.

The identity of Mary Magdalene's father is more confusing. Laurence Gardner claims that her father's name was Syro (Syrus or Cyrus) from Syria.[7] Others have postulated that her father was named, according to the Cistercian document mentioned above, Theophilus ("Lover of God").[8] He was supposedly a Syrian prince and governor of a maritime country.[9] He may have been related to those of the Kingdom of Israel that had been taken into Assyrian captivity in 721 B.C. Despite these theories, there is little true documentation regarding Mary Magdalene's parentage.[10]

While this is great legend, it is not really history. Others have claimed for Mary Magdalene and Bethany a Syrian, Philistine, Egyptian, or Sumerian heritage. For the most part, these lines of thinking are founded upon her supposed triple goddess titles of Mari-Anna-Ishtar. Lynn Picknett depicts her as a black Jewish-Ethiopian, goddess-worshiping, priestess of Johannite Christianity.[11] Her *persona* is malleable in the hands of mythmakers.

Likewise, Mary Magdalene and Bethany have variously been ascribed to the Israelite tribes of Benjamin, Judah, Levi, Reuben, Dan, and Asher.[12] Some latter-day gnostics have wrongly concluded that Mary Magdalene was the daughter of Jairus, the chief of the synagogue at Capernaum.[13] But, for the most part, she was considered to be a Benjaminite because of her Bethany roots. Sophie Neveu in *The Da Vinci Code* questions, "She was of the House of Benjamin?" "Indeed," Teabing said, "Mary Magdalene was of royal descent."[14] However, this myth was not the case.

Then who is she? First of all we should divide the identities of Mary of Magdala and Mary of Bethany and her sister Martha. We suggest that they are separate people with different parents but the same Ephraimitic background. Mary Magdalene's father we submit is Simon the Pharisee (Luke 7:36), and the Bethany sisters' father is Simon the Leper (Matthew 26:6; Mark 14:1).

"A CUP IN BENJAMIN'S SACK"

And put my cup, the silver cup, in the sack's mouth of the youngest [brother].

—GENESIS 44:2)

Since Magdalene's marriage to Christ was a source of healing to a divided nation, one would have to disagree with a number of esoteric and feminist writers about which tribe the Magdalene belonged to. Henry Lincoln, Lynn Picknett, and Margaret Starbird strongly claim that Mary Magdalene was of the tribe of Benjamin.[15] Keith Laidler bases his entire book *The Head of God* upon the premise that Mary Magdalene was a Benjaminite.[16] He wrongly supposes that a dynastic marriage between representatives of the tribes of Benjamin and Judah would have remedied divisions in Israel.

Laidler believes that some of the Sons of Belial (Beliel) were actually Benjaminites of Gibeah (Judges 20:13) who escaped from the war mentioned in Judges 21 and worshipped Isis.[17] King Saul was also from Gibeah. Seeing this as more than a coincidence, Laidler broaches that the Magdalene was one of these Isis-worshiping Benjaminites. However, Laidler's argument is ill-founded for a number of reasons.

The Hebrew word *Belial* refers to wicked persons and wickedness in general.[18] In 2 Corinthians 6:15, it is a name for Satan, or he who is utterly opposed to Jesus. These "sons" have no place in an examination of Mary. Like many neognostic writers who insist that Mary is a Benjaminite, Laidler rushes off in so many directions, it is difficult to keep track.

The claim of Mary's Benjaminite descent is made because almost all popularizing writers believe that Mary Magdalene and Mary of Bethany are the same person. Thus, they reason, since she held property at Bethany located in Benjaminite land, she must be of this tribe. Furthermore, they speculate she would be of royal descent from the Benjaminite Saul, the first king of Israel. However, this analysis is shallow, for in weighing the evidence, logical momentum sides with her being an Ephraimite. Robert Eisenman notes that at the time of Christ, "Benjamin" was a terminology applied to all "overseas persons or Diaspora Jews."[19] Thus it may have been applied to Mary Magdalene in a general sense without any obfuscation of her true Ephraimitic tribal roots.

Margaret Starbird quotes Genesis 44:2, 12, to prove that Mary Magdalene was a Benjaminite. Verse 2 has Joseph say, "And put my cup, the silver cup, in the sack's mouth." Verse 12 says, "and the cup was found in Benjamin's sack." Starbird is misleading in telling her version of the story: "Now he must choose his bride from the tribe of Benjamin, for it was written in the first book of the Torah that the silver chalice was hidden in the sack of Benjamin. According to their inspired teachers, this meant that a woman from Benjamin's tribe would be the instrument for the reconciliation and healing of Israel."[20]

Did this chalice actually indicate which tribe should unite with Christ? Yes. Was this cup the symbol of the Holy Grail? Yes, one of them. But it should be remembered that Joseph of Egypt put his own silver cup or grail into Benjamin's sack in order to snare Judah and the son's repentance (Genesis 42–45). It was prophetic bait to bring all the family of Israel together. While it is true that this portent of the "Great Mystery of the Holy Grail" was hidden in the "sack of Benjamin," we know that the silver chalice itself was actually Joseph's cup. Mary Magdalene and probably the Bethany sisters were represented by Joseph's silver cup, which by inheritance became his son Ephraim's cup.

It was Joseph's, not Benjamin's, chalice. The significance of the cup far transcends the importance of the sack. The Mary and Martha of Bethany would have been a living vessel (cup) of Ephraim, a "daughter of Shiloh," residing in Benjaminite land, or "Benjamin's sack" (Bethany). This sack was used to catch Judah (Jesus Christ). She is the silver cup and Bethany is the sack.[21] Its purpose was to unify Israel.

Why was the kingship even given to Saul the Benjaminite in the first place, rather than to someone of the royal tribe of Judah? It should be remembered that Benjamin the son of Jacob was the second child from Rachel. Thus he was not in line for either the birthright, which went to Rachel's eldest son, Joseph, or for the scepter, which went to Judah, Jacob's fourth born. Therefore there were no promised leadership roles prophesied for Benjamin's descendants, even though Ehud, one of the first judges, was a Benjaminite. But of course each of the twelve tribes of Israel had a representative judge. Descendants of Benjamin were not considered "rightful" heirs to the throne.[22]

The tall and handsome Saul was a most charismatic military leader who had much success against the invading Philistines, Amalekites, and the Ammonites. There was also growing unrest among the tribes of Benjamin and Ephraim and a fear among them for the people's cry for a king in that troubled time. The Ephraimite prophet Samuel was opposed to a king, but relented to popular demand and presided over Saul's formal election at Mizpah (1 Samuel 12) Why? Because the tribe of Benjamin had always been a buffer between Ephraim and Judah, and Saul was a welcome compromise and battle leader, but eventually he proved to be a disaster. Even though Ephraim and Benjamin had always been the closest of tribes, Starbird weighs in with the opposite report:

> Israel's first anointed King Saul was of the tribe of Benjamin, and his daughter Michal was the wife of King David. Throughout the history of the tribes of Israel, the tribes of Judah and Benjamin were the closest and most loyal of allies. Their destinies were intertwined. A dynastic marriage between a Benjaminite heiress to the lands surrounding the Holy City and the messianic Son of David would have appealed to the fundamentalist Zealot faction of the Jewish nation. It would have been seen as a sign of hope and blessing during Israel's darkest hour.[23]

Starbird believes that since the tribe of Benjamin was given possession of the lands around Jerusalem and since Mary Magdalene was from Bethany, then she "must" automatically have been a Benjaminite.

The key issue of the marriage of Christ and the Magdalene was its dynastic implications. But, according to Starbird, it assuaged the friction between the royal families of David, son of Jesse (tribe of Judah), and Jonathan, son of Saul the Benjaminite, both pretenders to the throne.[24] Dan Brown blindly follows: "By marrying into the powerful House of Benjamin, Jesus fused two royal bloodlines, creating a potent political union with the potential of making a legitimate claim to the throne and restoring the line of kings as it was under Solomon."[25]

But Saul was an elected king, while his son, Jonathan, and only surviving grandson, Mephibosheth, always paid obedience to David—there was no successional friction (1 Samuel 19). Any political marriage of Jesus with a Benjaminite would have been of no significance in the big picture.[26]

By the time of Christ the tribes of Judah and Benjamin had intermarried to such a degree that any breach was already mended for all practical purposes. There were also no prophecies about a Benjaminite king to be on the throne—nothing but total silence from the scriptures and Rabbinic literature. The so-called Jonathan succession was not an issue, but the longtime break between Judah and Ephraim (Israel) was real and devastating. There are numerous scriptures that deal with this breach and an eventual reconciliation. One scripture will suffice to make the point:

> *The envy also of Ephraim shall depart,*
> *and the adversaries of Judah shall be*
> *cut off: Ephraim shall not envy Judah*
> *and Judah shall not vex Ephraim.*
>
> —ISAIAH 11:13

Benjamin was merely an intermediary between Judah and Ephraim. When the land was divided by Joshua, the tribes of Ephraim and Judah received territory first.[27] The tribe of Benjamin being the most trusted by both tribes, it was assigned land lying between them in sort of a buffer zone.[28] Indeed the whole tribe seems to be a liaison between Judah and Ephraim. It was only logical that through the tribe of Benjamin a *rapprochement* between Judah and Ephraim was or would be affected.

There are therefore no prophetic reasons why either Mary of Magdala or Bethany should be of the tribe of Benjamin, Judah, or Levi.[29] Scriptural arguments for representatives of these tribes marrying to solve problems besetting the Hebrews simply don't exist. Furthermore, these three had already combined, through intermarriage and politics, to create the Jewish Kingdom of Judea. What was needed was to reconcile the Northern Kingdom and peoples of Israel with the Southern Kingdom and peoples of Judea. If the Benjaminite King Saul and Judaic Kings David and Solomon had ruled in righteousness, then the dividing of the land into two separate kingdoms, Judah and Israel (Ephraim), would not have occurred. But it did. Thus a prophetic reconciliation and healing was needed and actually achieved through the marriage of Judah and Ephraim—Christ and His wives.[30]

MENDING THE BREACH, HEALING THE WASTELAND

Ephraim also is the strength of mine head; Judah is my lawgiver.

—PSALM 60:7

There has been a breach between God, man, and the planet since the time of the fall of Adam to the point that all suffer. While this has a significant probationary purpose in the Second Estate, it will not be the final state of the world. This chapter deals with the two-fold plan of the Sacred Marriage and the Atonement of Jesus Christ that begins the process of mending the breach and healing the wasteland of the two houses (kingdoms) of Israel.

There are legends that in Neolithic times the world was a much better place. In this "Golden Age" men and women, neighbors, and even the animals lived in peace. Latter-day Saints would note that these were the times between the paradisiacal Garden of Eden and the Great Flood. After the expulsion of Adam and Eve into the "lone and dreary world" and the inundation of Noah, paradise was lost. But it was lost in degrees.[31] For six thousand years this world was decreed a wilderness. If it were not for the Grail knight, Perceval, only bad things would happen, as in T. S. Elliot's *The Wasteland*: "And you know what will happen because that king will not now rule his land or be healed of his wounds? Ladies will lose their husbands as a result; lands will be lost; and girls who will be left orphans, will be without guardians; and many knights will die because of it."[32]

Faithful men and women of God would heal the world by degrees and finally an exaltation would make perfect this celestial planet. Before Adam and Eve were cast into the wasteland, they received curses, which created a breach between the scepter and the birthright, or rather between the sovereignty (jurisdiction) of men and of women. Eve's curse from God was that she must obey her husband and conceive in pain, while Adam was given responsibility of directly obeying God and working by the sweat of his brow—meaning that they and their posterity would not have easy lives.

Just as there were a number of "falls" to arrive at the benighted state the earth now endures, there will be a number of restorations in order to heal and mend this planet. In a larger context, the work of the Savior upon this earth at the Meridian of Time established the basis for the healing of a wounded world. It included five decisive elements:

1. The Atonement came through Christ: his suffering at Gethsemane, death at Calvary, resurrection at the tomb, and ascension into heaven (Mosiah 18:2, Hebrews 9).

2. The creation of a living royal bloodline, binding Judah and Ephraim through a sacred marriage of Jesus Christ to Mary Magdalene and the Bethany sisters. They were sealed by the patriarchal-matriarchal "Holy Order." This would carry the seeds of regeneration (the Bloodline) to the last generations of the earth's 6,000 year wasteland stage.

3. The foundation of the original true Church and kingdom of God, with Prophets and Apostles, and so forth (the priesthood line).

4. The teachings and example which Christ left the world, with an inspirational and ethical standard irreproachable and unmatched through any other of the earth's "Great Souls."

5. The restoration of the true Church and kingdom in the last days, His second coming and millennial reign.

But for our study the second element is of central importance. Ultimately the breach of sovereignty would be healed by Christ's posterity and they would eventually heal the wasteland. Isaiah 58:11–12 speaks of the spring of water of the royal generations: "Like a watered garden, and like a spring of water, whose waters fail not. And they that shall be of thee [and] shall build the old waste places: thou shalt raise up the foundations of many generations; and thou shalt be called, The repairer of the breach, The restorer of the paths to dwell in."

Water from the generational fountain was judiciously sprinkled among the Gentiles to bring forth a garden in the latter day. It would take 1,800 years before the fruit of this meridian marriage would surface at a time called "the fulness of the Gentiles" (Romans 11:25–27). During the dispensation of the fulness of time, many marvelous things were accomplished by the seed of His loins and her womb through the sacred marriage of Mary and Christ.[33]

Then Ephraim, often called Israel (the lost ten tribes), and Diaspora Judah shall be reunited in a latter-day restoration by a descendant of this sacred marriage. This will happen in a time when Israel shall come to its senses: "Ephraim shall say, 'What have I to do any more with idols?'" (Hosea 14:8). There are numerous prophesies concerning the return of the house of Israel (Ephraim) to heal the wasteland:

And I will bring again [from] the captivity of my people of Israel [Ephraim], and they shall build the waste cities, and inhabit them; and they shall plant vineyards and drink the wine thereof; they shall also make gardens and eat the fruit of them. And I will plant them upon their land and they shall no more be pulled up out of their land which I have given them, saith the Lord thy God."

—AMOS 9:14–15

Behold the days come, saith the Lord, when I will make a new covenant with the house of Israel [Ephraim] and with the house of Judah.

—HEBREWS 8:3

In those days the house of Judah shall walk with the house of Israel [Ephraim], and they shall come together out of the land of the north to the land that I have given for an inheritance unto your fathers.

—JEREMIAH 3:18

The terms *I will bring* and *In those days* emphasize the latter-day healing of the Ephraim-Judah breach that is symptomatic of the rift between the divine feminine and the divine masculine. It began with Jesus' sacred marriage in circa A.D. 20 and began anew with the restoration of the gospel in 1830. Taken together this trajectory will, in process of time, cause the wasteland to be healed. This reunion of the scepter and bloodline seems to find its type in Jacob's wives, Rachel (Joseph/Ephraim), and Leah (Judah/David), weeping together. As the scripture states:

> *In those days, and in that time, saith the Lord, the children of Israel [Ephraim] shall come, they and the children of Judah together, going and weeping; they shall go, and seek the Lord their God. They shall ask the way to Zion with their faces thitherward, saying, Come, and let us join ourselves to the Lord in a perpetual covenant that shall not be forgotten.[34]*

—JEREMIAH 50:4–5

Rachel's hope for the return of her children to the Lord (Jeremiah 30:9) while Leah's cried for that son of David in whom Judah and all Israel would dwell in safety (Jeremiah 23:6). Other scriptures tend to confirm this analysis. A new interpretation of Ezekiel 37:15–17 is enlightening to our topic.

These verses are usually examined in how they make reference to the combining of the Bible with the Book of Mormon. However, verse 22 of Ezekiel 37 speaks clearly of the making of two nations into one kingdom. Perhaps a uniting of the genealogical records is a valid reading of Ezekiel as well as the uniting of scriptures and the uniting of nations. The Book of Mormon has been called "the stick of Joseph" but could also be referred to as "the [genealogical record of the] stick of Joseph in the hands

of Ephraim."[35] Brigham Young said as much: "But where is the stick of Joseph? Can you tell where it is? Yes. It was the children of Joseph who came across the waters to this continent and this land was filled with people, and The Book of Mormon or the stick of Joseph contains their writings, and they are in the hands of Ephraim. Where are the Ephraimites? They are mixed through all the nations of the earth. God is calling upon them to gather out, and he is uniting them, and they are giving the gospel to all the world"[36] (see Hosea 7:8).

The Ezekiel scripture may, in this line of reasoning, refer to the uniting of the genealogical branches of the "sticks" of the tribes of Judah and Ephraim. From the time of Christ these sticks have been joined and have become "one in thine hand." In Doctrine and Covenants 27 we learn that the "keys" to the stick of Ephraim were, in fact, given to Joseph Smith.[37]

Again we have reference of the uniting of Judah and Ephraim branches in some form of family tree. Lehi prophesies of the uniting of the fruit of the loins of Judah and Joseph: "Wherefore, the fruit of thy loins [Joseph] shall write; and the fruit of the loins of Judah shall write; and that which shall be written by the fruit of thy loins, and also that which shall be written by the fruit of the loins of Judah, shall grow together, unto the confounding of the false doctrines and laying down of contentions, and establishing peace among the fruit of thy loins" (2 Nephi 3:12).

The following list of scriptures gives evidence of the necessity of the reconciliation of these two tribes: Psalm 60; Psalm 108:8; Isaiah 11:13;[38] 2 Nephi 21:13; Jeremiah 31:6–9; Hosea 10:10–11; and Zechariah 10:6–7. Historically Joseph (Ephraim) held the birthright of the priesthood, while Judah held the scepter of kingly rule. Considerest thou not the two [Grail] families which the Lord hath chosen? (see Jeremiah 33:24).

Only when "Shiloh" (the Messiah) came were the two houses, blessings, and lineages, bridged in the spirit of Shalom. The fecundity of Israel was restored, and many nations came forth. Ultimately the blessing pronounced by Ezekiel (36:24) will reign: "For I will take you from among the heathen, and gather you out of all countries, and bring you into your own land."

THE BULLOCK AND UNICORN OF EPHRAIM

Let the blessing come upon the head of Joseph, and upon the top of the head of him that was separated from his brethren. His glory is like the firstling of his bullock, and his horns are like the horns of unicorns: with them he shall push the people together to the ends of the earth: and they are the ten thousands of Ephraim and they are the thousands of Manasseh.

—DEUTERONOMY 33:16–17

Our picture of Mary Magdalene is not flat or pale. Her very name colorfully challenges our imagination. Since the eleventh century, she has become a potent symbol of her gender. Though often depicted as an ascetic penitent in a cave with a skull, a beautiful red-haired woman with a unicorn best represents her image.[39] The Italian Renaissance master Raphael painted a portrait of a woman fitting this description. Once provocatively titled *Portrait of Maddelena Doni* the painting depicts a beautiful young woman holding a small unicorn on her lap (see Plate 10).[40] Behind her are what could represent the Jachin and Boaz columns, symbolizing the houses of Judah and Ephraim.[41] It is with Raphael's image in mind that we begin our study of this elect lady and the unicorn.

The marriage of Mary and Jesus has been allegorically alluded to in art and scripture through the union of two special animals—the unicorn and the lion. The mythical unicorn was supposedly the first animal named by Adam.[42] It was not some magical beast left off Noah's ark, but was actually a wild ox or white bull, as in the constellation Taurus. The Hebrew animal *re' em* might have been the same as the Greek *monokeros* or Latin *unicornis*. The unicorn has been identified with an Indian wild ass the size of a horse with a white body. Or, as most etymologists think, it was a gigantic wild ox, *aurochs* or *urus*, an extinct ancestor to the domesticated cattle of today. Aurochs were depicted in Assyrian bas-reliefs in profile with only one horn visible.

According to the book of Numbers the unicorn was the strength of Jacob without any enchantment or divination (Numbers 23:22–23). It was a sign of Ephraim's spiritual strength and gift of being a seer.[43] Furthermore, Ephraim's horn was prophesied to be exalted like a unicorn's (Psalm 92:10, 29:6) The early Christians likened the unicorn to a figure of Christ.[44] This was a tradition that persisted into medieval times. Yet Christ's tribe, Judah, was scripturally never called a unicorn/bull but was rather identified with the lion. These two animals are mentioned together in Balaam's prophecy of Israel's blessing: "God brought him forth out of Egypt; he hath as it were the strength of a unicorn: he shall eat up the nations his enemies, and shall break their bones, and pierce them through with his arrows. He crouched, he lay down as a lion, and as a great lion: who shall stir him up? Blessed is he that blesseth thee, and cursed is he that curseth thee" (Numbers 24:8–9).

It seems from this prophecy that all of the Israelites together were symbolized by these two animals and the power of each. Later, in about 975 B.C. when the kingdom of Israel was divided into the House of Judah and the house of Israel, the southern house took the emblem of the lion and the northern house took the unicorn.[45] The heraldic unicorn was specially appointed as a symbol of the tribe of

Joseph/Ephraim. But somehow, through Christ's marriage to Mary Magdalene, a pure Ephraimite, He too became associated with the unicorn.[46]

The unicorn was the emblem of the Grail throughout the medieval period. The unicorn's head lying on the pure maiden's lap in a walled garden often symbolized the Holy Grail myth.[47] The beast in the garden with the beautiful virgin is often linked with the Songs of Solomon (Canticle of Canticles) 1:16: "Behold, thou art fair, my beloved, yea, pleasant: also our bed is verdant." The unicorn represents pure love within this garden setting.

Medieval legend has it that all but a few unicorns were ruthlessly hunted and killed.[48] Where did the last few unicorns go? Into hiding. Allegorically this hunting represents Satan's vain attempt to completely eradicate the unicorns of God, the true vine, the living water, the bread and the stone, or the lineage of Jesus Christ and Mary Magdalene and the Bethany sisters. The unicorn and maiden in the garden are another symbol of healing of the wasteland. The bloodline was eventually to become a fruitful vine, a horn of plenty—a cornucopia, a verdant garden. Psalm 92:10 prophesies: "But my horn shalt thou exalt like the horn of an unicorn: I shall be anointed with fresh oil."

The marriage of Christ and Mary (Judah and Ephraim) is emphasized by the fact that the unicorn is often united symbolically with the lion. Perhaps the earliest known version can be seen at Les-Saintes-Maries-de-la-Mer in the Camargue delta of the Rhône River in Southern France. There at the eleventh-century Church of the Maries can be seen, embedded into the south outside wall, two carved animal statues in deteriorated white marble, of much greater antiquity (see Plate 11).[49] A lion on the left and an ox or unicorn to the right—the veritable symbol of the Holy Grail Shiloh Dynasty.[50]

The so-called *Stuttgart Psalter* is thought to have been painted in northern France in the early ninth century (see Plate 12).[51] It depicts the crucifixion of Christ, and to the right is seen the unicorn and a lion with a floating Holy Grail chalice between them. It is a miniature illustrating Psalm 22:21: "Save me from the lion's mouth: for thou hast heard me from the horns of the unicorns." This image is a clear representation of the warring Houses of Ephraim and Judah, united by the Grail vessel symbolizing Mary Magdalene and the Bethany sisters, who are not otherwise shown. Below can be seen Nicodemus with a knife to scrape the sacred blood of Christ and Joseph of Arimathea with a blanket to receive the crucified Savior.[52]

Is Ephraim the "fair one" in the Song of Songs, who is wooed by Judah? (Song 2:10–13). Was the coupling of these two tribes the advantage needed to thwart the evil one? The unicorn did not symbolize the new line alone but the two animals together. In more arcane circles, it was represented by a woman sitting between the Jachin and Boaz pillars, holding a scroll with a crown on her head and a moon at her feet (see Plate 13).[53]

Deuteronomy 33:17, mentioned above, has long been associated with Joseph Smith Jr. by the LDS Church[54] (see D&C 110:9). The ingathering is associated with the latter-day prophet Joseph, as in Job 39:9–12: "Wilt thou believe him [the unicorn], that he will bring home thy seed and gather it into thy barn?" Moreover he shall trump the saving sound in the day of judgment from the horn of a unicorn as is prophesied, "For thou hast heard me from the horns of the unicorns" (Psalm 22:21; Isaiah 34:7–8). Could this be the "horn of salvation" mentioned in Luke 1:69?

It should be remembered that the new dynastic line is an equal mixture of Judah and Ephraim, for in an earlier Hebraic parlance, the female bloodline dominates as the male inheritance line does as well. The royal inheritance goes through the male's "Y" chromosome, while the birthright goes through the female's mitochondrial DNA. Therefore Ephraim tribal lines dominate from the time of Christ's earliest church to the present day.

Then in the Millennium, Judah's lion shall rule. Later we shall examine how this emblem of the lion and the unicorn, the symbol of the Holy Grail, rested in Britain. This is the same order as they are seen in the Tudor English royal regalia and coat of arms. It is the quintessential symbol of the Holy Grail.

NOTES

1. Butler, *Gospel of John*, 159. Butler believes that the city of Ephraim was fourteen miles northeast of Jerusalem. It could also be the city of Ephraim or Ephron (2 Chronicles 13:19) or Ophrah (1 Samuel 13:17).

2. Olson and Miesel, *Da Vinci Hoax*, 104. An earlier hagiographer from the tenth century sermonized in Cluny, saying that Mary Magdalene was an "heiress."

3. Taylor, *Coming of the Saints*, 28.

4. Olson and Miesel, *Da Vinci Hoax*, 104. Taylor, *Coming of the Saints*, 28, has relied on *Life of Rabanus*, chap. 1, as his source. Syro (Syrus or Cyrus) is a different name from Theophilus mentioned by Olson and Miesel, *Da Vinci Hoax*.

5. Taylor, *Coming of the Saints*, 18, from *Life of Rabanus*, chap 1. Taylor states, "Mary of Magdala was the daughter of a Syrian and a Jewess, her father, a Syrian prince or ruler, having married a Jewish maiden who traced her descent from the royal family of David." The Syrian, if this legend is true, might have been an Ephraimite. Collins, *Twenty-First Century Grail*, 148, notes that Rabanus's work, although ascribed to his lifetime (d. 856), was almost certainly of mid–twelfth-century construction.

6. Gardner, *Bloodline of the Holy Grail*, 116. Voragine in his *Legenda Aurea* says that the royal house of Israel, specifically of the Hasmoneans, were Maccabeans of the House of Levi. He further states that Mary owned the fortress of Magdala, Lazarus was lord of part of Jerusalem, and Martha owned part of Bethany.

7. Gardner, *Bloodline of the Holy Grail*, 116.

8. Unknown author, "Magdalene the Bride of Christ" (2000, paper) in author's possession.

9. Olson and Miesel, *Da Vinci Hoax*, 104. Interestingly, present-day Syria is not a maritime country.

10. Taylor, *Coming of the Saints*, 83.

11. Picknett, *Mary Magdalene*, ix. See Olson and Miesel, *Da Vinci Hoax*, 180.

12. Thiering, *Jesus the Man*, 367. She notes that Mary Magdalene was attached to the regional "Order of Dan" and that Helena her mother was of the "Order of Asher." Interestingly, in Revival Centres International Articles and Bible Studies <www.rci.org.au/bible_studies/articles_plan02_emblemsintro.htm> notes that Asher is associated with a "goblet" and with Great Britain.

13. Blake and Blezard, *Arcadian Cipher*, 131–32. Luke 8:42 says that she was only twelve at her "raising," which the above authors say was synonymous with her "elevation" in status to wife or promised one. Blake and Blezard and Gardner say this transpired in 17 C.E, and that she was fourteen at the time (because in Freemasonry rituals girls were so "conducted" at the age of fourteen). The entire text of Luke 8 deals with healing and not the secret rituals of marriage, as they believe.

14. Brown, *Da Vinci Code*, 248.

15. Others include Dan Brown; Knight and Lomas; Baigent, Leight, and Lincoln; L. Gardner; Wallace-Hopkins; and almost everyone else who has written on the subject.

16. Laidler, *Head of God*, 137.

17. Ibid., 77–78.

18. Strong, *New Strong's Exhaustive Concordance of the Bible*, 122. Strong says it is "a title for a worthless person."

19. Eisenman, *James the Brother of Jesus*, 298. This is seen in Rabbinic literature and certainly in the Essene War Scroll at Qumran.

20. Starbird, *Woman with the Alabaster Jar*, 7, 49.

21. Hall, *Secret Teachings of All Ages*, cxxx. Hall noted that in the Tarot deck, the first numbered major trump card is called Le Bateleur, the Juggler or magician. He stands behind a table upon which are spread several objects. Most prominent among them, Hall claims, is a cup, the "Holy Grail, the cup placed by Joseph in Benjamin's sack" (Genesis 44:2). Here we have the first mentioning of this silver cup having anything to do with the Holy Grail. Of course, it has everything to do with it. Also see Knight and Lomas, *Second Messiah*, 90, regarding the tarot card.

22. Olson and Miesel, *Da Vinci Hoax*, 103. It should be noted that the king took wives from all the tribes of Israel.

23. Margaret Starbird, in Burstein, *Secrets of the Da Vinci Code*, 20.

24. Starbird, *Woman with the Alabaster Jar*, 7. Other than this significant episode itself the scriptures are silent

about any ongoing problem between the descendants of David and those of Jonathan.

25. Brown, *Da Vinci Code,* 249.

26. The incident of the Benjaminite, Shimei, son of Gera, was of little significance (2 Samuel 16:5–13); however, King David noted "Sheba the son of Bichri shall do us more harm than did Absalom" (2 Samuel 20:6). This Benjaminite lived in the mountains of Ephraim (Belial) and was the last chief of the Absalom insurrection. It almost seems to anticipate the revolt of Jeroboam in the north. With his death there were no further grinding conflicts between the tribes of Judah and Benjamin.

27. The square encampment had four brigades: west with the bull, Ephraim (also Benjamin and Manassah); north with Dan (also Asher and Naphtali); east with Judah (also Issachar and Zebulon), and south with Reuben (also Gad and Simeon). See Numbers 2. In a sense it could be said that earlier Benjamin was actually in Ephraim's sack, while later, after the partition, it was in Judah's. According to Collins, *Twenty-First Century Grail,* 191, "Although the lion, bull, eagle and man in this connection do represent the Evangelists, they also signify the four elements as well as four of the twelve tribes of Israel: Judah, Ephraim, Dan and Reuben." They each had one of the four sides of the tabernacle.

28. Barnum, *Comprehensive Dictionary of the Bible,* 112.

29. There was a problem with Benjamin in a war with the rest of Israel. "And the people repented them for Benjamin, because that the Lord had made a breach in the tribes of Israel" (Judges 21:15). But this was, for the most part, solved with the "Daughters of Shiloh" being given to Benjamin from Ephraim.

30. It is true that when Palestine was partitioned in 925 B.C., between Jeroboam the Ephraimite and Rohoboam of the tribe of Judah, Benjaminite lands were ceded to the House and Kingdom of Judah. This had more to do with geography than anything else. For in the period of traveling in the wilderness in Israel's encampment around the tabernacle, the tribe of Benjamin was found in Ephraim's Brigade, with the tribe of Manasseh. Opposite to Ephraim was Judah.

31. Skousen, *Earth,* 261–64.

32. As quoted in Barber, *Holy Grail,* 205.

33. The dispensation of the fulness of times is a period of time that transpires in the thousand years before the Millennium, when Christ returns to the earth. Joseph Smith Jr. was the dispensational head for this thousand years.

34. See Jeremiah 31:15; cp. 9:18. Here we see bitter lamentation for Rachel weeping for her children.

35. Joseph Smith Jr., *History of the Church,* 1:84.

36. Brigham Young, in *Journal of Discourses* (29 May 1870), 13:174. See also Widtsoe, *Discourses of Brigham Young,* 127.

37. Shute, Nyman and Bott, *Ephraim,* 60. Doctrine and Covenants 27:5 notes that Moroni was entrusted with the "keys of the record of the stick of Ephraim." This refers to the Book of Mormon as the record, not the stick of Ephraim, which would be the bloodline of that tribe.

38. Another translation by Keil and Delitzsch, *Commentary on the Old Testament,* 7:290. Isaiah 11:13 reads: "And the jealousy of Ephraim is removed, and the adversaries of Judah are cut off; Ephraim will not show jealousy towards Judah, and Judah will not oppose Ephraim." Hostility will then end between the two tribes.

39. Often the unicorn has been wrongly associated with the Virgin Mary instead of Mary Magdalene. But the Magdalene and the unicorn are both associated with the tribe of Ephraim within a verdant garden.

40. Raphael (1483–1520), Italian, *Portrait of a Lady with a Unicorn* (ca. 1505–1506, oil on wood transferred to canvas, 67.8 x 53 cm). From the Museo Galleria de Villa Borghese, Rome (inv. 371). Its former title, *Maddelena Doni,* relates to Mary Madeleine/Magdalene.

41. In the temple of Solomon two great columns stood just outside the entrance to the temple, these pillars were named Boaz and Jachin. They symbolized the two great tribes of Israel, Ephraim and Judah represent God's channels for bringing salvation to the world. These columns represent both the kingly power of Boaz *mishpat* (judgment) on the left side and the priestly power of Jachin *tsedeq* (righteousness) on the right. In the temple of Solomon they are missing a lintel or an arch to connect them, but one day when united it would symbolize the mending of the breach and healing the wasteland. The pillar on the left would represent Judah, because of our knowledge of Boaz as the great-grandfather of David, the king of Israel. The other pillar is known as Jachin, who was the first high priest of the temple.

42. Raphael (1483–1520), Italian, *Portrait of a Lady with a Unicorn* (ca. 1505–1506, oil on wood transferred to canvas, 67.8 x 53 cm). From the collection of the Museo Galleria de Villa Borghese, Rome (inv. 371). It was once titled *Portrait of Maddelena Doni.*

43. Aldebaran, a first-magnitude star is located at the eye of the bull, Taurus, and is noted for being the "seer" star. See John P. Pratt, "The Lion and Unicorn Testify of Christ, Part 1: The Cornerstone Constellations," *Meridian Magazine,* at www.meridianmagazine.com (2005).

44. St. Ambrose, bishop of Milan, noted as early as the fourth century, "Who is the unicorn but the only begotten Son of God . . . Christ." He is the unicorn with the Father because Christ said, "I and the Father are one" (John 10:30). See http://www.unicornlady.net/christianity.hlml (2004).

45. Bennett, *Symbols of Our Celto-Saxon Heritage,* Figure 1.

46. This, in much the same way as He became Shiloh by marrying a "daughter of Shiloh" (Proverbs 15:4).

47. One medieval legend has it that the Son of God was not ready to become a mortal man, as required of him. He was therefore compelled to do so by the unicorn at God's command, which chased Jesus' spirit to the garden where the Virgin retreated.

48. Could this also mean that a number of the Grail children were found and killed?

49. Side of Church of St. Sarah, Les-Saints-Maries-de-la-Mer in the Camargue delta of the Rhône River, France. Embedded into the south wall of this eleventh-century fortress church are two carved animals in a much older marble, set into an indented arch.

50. While very obliterated through time, the animal to the right, upon close personal examination was definitely not a lion, as the lion and cub are to the left. It is much taller with its hind leg not being a cat's paw. It is likely to be an ox, horse (unicorn), or oryx.

51. Unknown artist, Northern France, *The Stuttgart Psalter: Crucifixion of Christ* (820–830, painted miniature). From Wèrttemburgische Landesbibloiothek, Stuttgart, Germany. (Bibl. fol. 23, fol. 27r) The Grail chalice can be seen between unicorn of Ephraim and the lion of Judah. The Psalter probably illustrates Psalm 22:21.

52. Nicodemus collected the clotted blood from Christ's wounds and preserved it carefully. Supposedly when he died he gave it to his nephew Isaac, who, obeying a voice from heaven sealed it in lead and put it in the trunk of a fig tree, which he threw into the sea. It washed up in Normandy at Fécamp where an abbey was built for the relic. See Barber, *Holy Grail,* 129.

53. Unknown artist, *The High Priestess* (fifteenth century, tempera on paper). Supposedly this card is from a tarot pack. See Knight and Lomas, *Second Messiah,* 90.

54. Conversation with Richard L. Anderson (May 1982). He believes that Joseph Smith Jr. was specially called to gather the righteous together in the last days.

CHAPTER TEN
SHILOH, MAGDALA, AND BETHANY

And the Lord appeared again in Shiloh . . .

—1 SAMUEL 3:21

The towns of Shiloh, Magdala, and Bethany may seem to have no particular association. The affinity between them seems tenuous; however, this study hypothesizes that they have a profound interrelationship. Not that there is any broad connection, but in the person of Mary Magdalene and the Bethany sisters, they touch one another in a mysterious and consequential way. Just how tangential they are we shall now examine.

MAGDALA, A TOWN OF TWO FACES

Can there any good thing come out of [Magdala]?

—JOHN 1:46

Mary Magdalene supposedly hails from the seaside town of Magdala of Galilee, about 120 miles north of Jerusalem, in the land parceled to Naphtali by Joshua (19:32–39). Some scholars believe that Mary was from Magdala on the northwestern bank of the Sea of Galilee.[1] It is located about four miles north of Tiberias and south of Capernaum.[2] Magdala was a flourishing little place where Jewish and Hellenistic culture coexisted. It was certainly not off the beaten path.

According to Margaret Starbird, Magdala is a title or epitaph, not a location.[3] Micah 4:8 is used for support.[4] Of course a name could be a toponym and have added meaning. While the scriptures do not mention "Mary of Magdalene," neither do they reference "Mary the Magdalene." The epitaph idea is to bolster the "one Mary theory"; otherwise we open the door to two anointings by separate wives. So the Galilean nativity of Mary Magdalene must, in a politically correct fashion, be avoided by feminists at all costs.

But what kind of town was Magdala that produced such a significant resident? The literature shows its many sides. First it was an ancient fishing village at the site called in Aramaic, *Migdal Nunayah,* meaning the "Tower of the Fishermen," or the "Tower of Salted Fish."[5] In Hebrew the word *migdal* translates to tower, stronghold, or castle keep.[6]

Others cite that Magdala or Migdal was known as a village of doves, a place where sacred doves were bred for the temple.[7] According to Esther de Boer, the sages give an extensive description of the piety of the town. Supposedly there were some 300 stalls where one could buy the doves necessary for ritual purification.[8] Given Mary Magdalene's sexual connotations, we are hardly surprised to learn that the dove was "a sexual emblem sacred to love and mother goddesses."[9] In this respect Magdala had a religious cast to it, as did Shiloh.

Yet, Talmudic literature offers a very different perspective. We read that the town met with a terrible end, being destroyed because of its fornication and adultery. It may come from a Talmudic expression meaning "curling women's hair," which the Talmud (*Tosefta* or the *Tosafoth*) compares to the profession of an adulteress.[10] Alfred Edersheim notes of Magdala that "according to Jewish authorities it was famous for its wealth, and for the moral corruption of its inhabitants."[11]

Apparently this notoriety and licentious behavior led to its destruction, either at the time of Lamentations 2:2 or in A.D. 75.[12] Magdala was therefore associated with piety and also with adultery. This dual reputation may have later tainted the name and supposed character of Mary Magdalene.[13] It was in essence, a town of two faces. Again we see that the city of Shiloh too was destroyed because of its wickedness.[14]

Bishop Jacobus de Voragine, in his imaginative work *Legenda Aurea* (*The Golden Legend*) first published about 1260, notes Mary's relationship to Magdala and other regions of Palestine: "[Mary Magdalene] with her brother Lazarus, and her sister Martha, possessed the castle of Magdalo, which is two miles from Nazareth, and Bethany, the castle which is nigh to Jerusalem, and also a great part of Jerusalem, which, all these things they [divided] among them. In such wise that Mary had the castle Magdalo, whereof she had her name Magdalene. And Lazarus had the part of the city of Jerusalem, and Martha had her part in Bethany."[15]

Realizing that de Voragine incorrectly collapsed the two Marys into one person, these regions in relation to Mary Magdalene, Lazarus, and his sisters are explained as follows:

1. Castle Magdalene: The term probably meant the stone battlement watchtower in Magdala. From its coign of vantage the two-by-four-mile Fertile Crescent for grazing sheep was plainly observable. It was given to Mary Magdalene.

2. Bethany: This area was possessed by Martha and was located in Bethany in Benjaminite land.

3. Part of Jerusalem: This was in the possession of Lazarus when his Ephraimite ancestry returned from the Babylonian exile and settled here (1 Chronicles 9:3, 5; Nehemiah 11:5).[16]

Furthermore, these strategic positions proved to be very important, as explained in the next chapter. Like Mary in Magdala, Jesus spent most of His short life along the shores of the Sea of Galilee. And to the west of Magdala, just six miles away, lay Cana, where it is claimed that Christ married Mary Magdalene and the Bethany sisters.[17] But why would the Magdalene be from the lands bestowed to Naphtali, if she were a high-born Ephraimite with Shiloh descendants?

Why did they live in this green and pleasant land in contrast to dry and stony Judea, where they put Him to death? The question, "Why on the margins of Palestine?" could later be asked of the fledgling Church in Britain: Why on the margins of the Roman Empire and even of Christianity itself? For safety's sake. Not everything happened in Jerusalem or Rome; there were other "promised lands" (see Mark 6:7).[18]

While Magdala was Mary's birthplace, it is posited that Shiloh in Mount Ephraim was her ancestral home, as it was for the two Bethany sisters. Ultimately the ancestral home shall play a more important role than her native home. We will now examine the significance of Shiloh in the life of Jesus and his wives. The Holy Grail went and came from many lands.

"DAUGHTERS OF SHILOH"

O' daughter of Shiloh
Revered of Joseph
Silver Cup in Benjamin's Sack

Sacred vessel of the Grail
Blessed of Ephraim
Wife of Shiloh[19]

The town of Shiloh lay in Ephraimitic lands, just east of the route connecting Bethel to Shechem. Its sacred name and fame was vouchsafed with the holy tabernacle "tent" from the days of Joshua to a more permanent "temple" during the time of Samuel. In this city the ultimate inanimate vessel, the ark of the covenant, was kept in earliest times.[20] With adequate water and pasturage, it was the perfect site of religious pilgrimages and festivals.[21]

It is here stated that Mary Magdalene and the Bethany sisters' progenitors were originally from Shiloh, the City of Ephraim, in much the same way as Jesus was from Bethlehem, the City of David (Luke 2:4). The *abduction of the maidens* motif now takes center stage (see also Mosiah 20:1–23, 25:12). Very little has been written about the strange and obscure abduction occurrence in the little town of

Shiloh during the time of the Judges. But much hinges upon it.

Because of an incredibly tragic dispute, the tribes of Israel, including Ephraim and Judah, fought together and decimated the tribe of Benjamin to near extinction.[22] After the devastating war, the defeated tribe of Benjamin numbered just under 600 men. Since almost all of their wives and children had been killed, there were not wives enough for the remaining men. Yet, an the oath sworn during the heat of the conflict by all Israel at Mizpeh "saying, Cursed be he that giveth a wife to Benjamin" (Judges 21:18) needed to be kept intact.[23]

The Tabernacle at the time of the last Judge was in Shiloh in Ephraim, while later the ark of the covenant was at Kirjath-Jearim in Benjamin lands. Because of the sanctity of these two places and the love between the sons of Rachel (Joseph and Benjamin), an interesting and secret arrangement was struck between the tribes of Benjamin and closest kin, Ephraim and Manasseh (sons of Joseph).

A certain city in Manasseh, Jabesh-Gilead, did not heed the call to assembly and the oath of Mizpeh. Because of this and for not helping in the war against Benjamin, the Judges had killed all the married men and women of Jabesh-Gilead.[24] They then gave 400 virgins of that city for wives to the remnant of Benjamin. Yet this was not a sufficient number of wives for the decimated Benjaminites.

Since there were not quite enough wives, certain Ephraimite leaders secretly instructed the remaining 200 wifeless Benjaminites to go to Shiloh at the time of the Feast of Jehovah and capture the requisite number of maidens from the dancing females. So the beautiful virgins of Shiloh came out to dance at the appointed time: "And see, and, behold, if the daughters of Shiloh come out to dance in dances, then come ye out of the vineyards, and catch you every man his wife of the daughters of Shiloh, and go to the land of Benjamin" (Judges 21:21, also 22–23).[25]

Benjamin was preserved, the somewhat oath kept, and the capture "winked at" by Ephraim. The seizure of these Ephraimite daughters for the preservation of Benjamin's lineage was altogether fitting. Ephraim's only full uncle was Benjamin, the brother of their father, Joseph through Rachel. No wonder their remorse at slaughtering their brethren was doubly felt.[26] Symmetry demanded that Joseph's birthright heir should provide wives for his brother in their time of need as the Levirate law decreed.

However, the offspring of this marriage would be Benjaminite by inheritance but not by bloodline, since in Hebraic tradition tribal blessing was determined by the father, while the national bloodline identity is through the mother.[27] This study seeks to make the case that Mary Magdalene and the Bethany sisters were literal "Daughters of Shiloh." They were related to, though not descendants of, these particular women given to Benjaminites. They were distant relatives of those families that were a part of this transaction, while they themselves were full-blooded Ephraimites.[28] Thus, according to theory, a certain direct lineage of the undiluted blood of Ephraim was protected and preserved by the Lord's own hand through the centuries until the time of Christ.

This is ideologically close to Brigham Young's statement that Joseph Smith's lineage was protected by "God's own hand." Not all of the "Daughters of Shiloh" were tinged with the DNA of these Benjaminites. The interconnectedness between those daughters that were captured and those that were not allowed certain lines to be pure Ephraimite. While part of Mary and Martha's ancestral branches were taken to Benjaminite lands and thus her connectedness, her direct lineage was not.

In the wilderness, during the exodus from Egypt, it was Ephraim with Manasseh and Benjamin who camped on the west side of the Tabernacle. In this study, where divine symmetry and sacred geometry are of importance, it is essential that Mary

Magdalene and the Bethany sisters were quintessential "Daughters of Shiloh." For this will fully explain the proverbial "Ephraim's cup in Benjamin's sack" mentioned earlier.

A final question plagues us with regard to Mary Magdalene and the Bethany sisters each being a pure Ephraimite of noble birth. How was it possible for her progenitors to avoid seizure when the Assyrian King Shalmanezer took away the elite families of the Kingdom of Israel in 723 B.C.? The answer may lie in their being "Daughters of Shiloh." Because of the above-mentioned historical episode, their heritage, through historical genealogical relationships, was in Shiloh, Bethany, and in Galilee of the Kingdom of Israel.

When the Assyrians came to conquer Israel in 723 B.C., the family simply moved south to the Kingdom of Judah where they had inheritance and holdings in Bethany and Jerusalem. Then when it was safe, they returned to their ancestral homes in the north.[29] Thus they avoided the mass deportation affecting the rest of the ten tribes, including their own tribe of Ephraim. Then later in 586 B.C., when the Babylonians took Jerusalem into captivity, they directly returned to Samaria and Galilee in the north to avoid the exile.

The "Daughters of Shiloh" circumstance helped preserve a small but well-traced noble lineage of Ephraim for the Savior to marry. It was, in a sense, a dual citizenship, which afforded them protection. It is very possible that some of the daughters of Shiloh were even a part of the *Shiloni* ("Men of Shiloh"), an Ephraimite family of exiles who returned from the Babylonian Captivity and settled in Jerusalem[30] (see 1 Chronicles 9:3, 5; Nehemiah 11:4, 5).

In this sense, it is possible that part of the Shiloh family was not spared the exile in Babylon, but returned to this area of Judea. Either way we can see how Mary came to be in this part of Palestine. This allowed for the preservation of a pure, noble

Ephraimite lineage that would heal the breach with Judah through a strategic Grail marriage with the Messiah.

"UNTIL SHILOH COME"

The sceptre shall not depart from Judah, nor a law giver from between his feet [loins], until Shiloh come; and unto him shall the gathering of the people be.

—GENESIS 49:10

The above verse from Genesis is one of the most enigmatic passages in all scripture.[31] It is possible that the correct meaning has been lost. Various interpretations of Jacob's blessing abound without any resolution.[32] But as the reader may have gathered, the new paradigm in this study allows a fresh explication of this verse. By thinking outside the traditional box, we examine a startling new exegesis, presented here for the first time.

When shall the royal scepter depart from Judah? How will it be taken? W. Ewing suggests, "It [Genesis 49:10] contemplates the ultimate passing of the power of Judah into the hands of an ideal ruler." [33] Only when "Shiloh come" will an *atonement* and/or "gathering" be made, and until then the tribe of Judah will have kingly dominance. After that time, a new loin, bloodline, or dynasty will predominate in an eventual ingathering. We postulate that Ephraim (later called gentiles or nations) will provide that leadership. Then the "people" will be gathered through the missionary efforts of Ephraim (see D&C 133:6).

What more can we learn about Shiloh that will help us understand the dynamics that occurred in about A.D. 20–30? Shiloh was one of the earliest and most sacred of the Hebrew sanctuaries in Canaan.[34] It was a secluded and favorable place for worship and pious study. The enigmatic word or title Shiloh has been variously interpreted:

1. Shiloh: Literally means "tranquillity," a place of rest, peace, and quiet.

2. Shiloh: May also be rendered as "He whose right it is to rule."[35]

3. Shiloh: In the *RV* it is explained thus: "till he come to Shiloh," in reference to an event that fulfilling the assembling of Israel to Shiloh in Joshua 18:1, when the tribe of Judah nobly relinquished the preeminence it had formerly enjoyed.

4. Shiloh: By a revocalization of the Hebrew, the phrase may be interpreted to mean, "until that which is his shall come," or "the things reserved for him," or "so that tribute will come to him" (to Judah). See also an echo in Ezekiel 21:27, which perhaps points to the Hebrew word *shelloh* (short for asher-lo, "that which is to or for him").[36]

5. Shiloh: It is not a name or a simple word, but rather a compound composed of the relative pronoun *she*, the preposition *l*, and the pronominal suffix of the third person masculine *oh*. This phrase has been interpreted as meaning "that which is his," "whose it is," or "his own one" or child.[37]

6. Shiloh: Traditionally, it was understood to refer to or mean the Messiah, or Prince of Peace. See the Inspired Version (JST) (Genesis 49:10), which says it is Jesus Christ (see also Luke 1:30–33).

7. Shiloh: The Home of the Tabernacle of the congregation and ark of the covenant. Joshua the Ephraimite moved the Tabernacle from Gilgal to Shiloh after the conquest (Joshua 18:1), and it was from there that he divided the land of Israel with a portion going to each tribe except Levi. The ark of the covenant stayed at Shiloh, until it was captured by the Philistines during the time of Samuel (ca. 1050 B.C.).

8. Shiloh: During the time of the Judges, it was the location for the annual Feast of Jehovah, which was probably the Feast of Ingathering.

9. Shiloh: The actual name of the "House of God" (Judges 18:31) in which Eli and his sons officiated at the town of Shiloh.

10. Shiloh: A town in Mount Ephraim. The Ephraimite town on the north side of Bethel on the east side of the highway that goes up from Bethel to Shechem, and south of Lebanon on the road to Shechem (Judges 21:9). The modern town of Seilun. "Others assume that the city itself is intended: 'until he [the king of Judah or the Judean empire] comes to Shiloh' [expansion of Judah over Israel]."[38]

11. Shilonites: A native of Shiloh, as with the prophet Samuel, to whom God appeared in Shiloh (1 Samuel 1:9; 3:1), and the prophet Ahijah the Shilonite.

12. Shiloni: A family of exiles, "men of Shiloh" who returned from the Exile of Babylon and settled in Jerusalem[39] (1 Chronicles 9:3, 5; Nehemiah 11:5).

13. Shiloh: The words *Shiloh* and *Pool of Siloam* meant "sent" (John 9:7; Luke 4:18; Deuteronomy 22:7).

Joseph Smith's Inspired Version (JST) (Genesis 50:24) adds to our understanding of Shiloh when it states, "Not the Messiah who is called Shilo."[40] This seems to indicate that Jesus Christ was "called" Shiloh, but why would he be called after an Ephraimite town noted not for its scepter but for its priesthood and the ark of the covenant? And when was he first called Shiloh?

According to this theoretical paradigm, the tribe of Judah was to hold sway until Jesus Christ (*Messiah ben Judah or David*) married a daughter of Shiloh, and then it rightfully passed to his son (*Shiloh ben Jesus*). The new "house" would come through his wife, matrilineally; that is, through the tribe of Ephraim by virtue of the sacred birthright, and through Judah by Divine Right of Kings through inheritance.

But one could ask why to the wife's bloodline tribe and not only to the husband's? As noted previously, in Israelite custom Judaism is always ascribed through the bloodline of the wife, not the husband. For example, if a Jewish man is married to a gentile woman, the child is not Jewish, but if a Jewish woman marries a gentile man, the child is Jewish.[41] It stems from the injunctions in the Bible (Deuteronomy 7:3) and the temple scroll "Statutes of the King" not to marry gentiles. One should marry only an Israelite woman, a wife from his father's own tribe.[42]

Rabbinical law was more generous; the king could take a wife from any Israelite tribe, whereas Essene law was much stricter. For them to take "A wife from the house [tribe] of his father" meant just that—such as Judah was to marry Judah, Levites to marry Levites, Danites to marry Danites, etc.

This comes from Abraham's instruction to Isaac as recorded in Genesis 24:37: "You shall not take a wife for my son from the daughters of the Canaanites . . . but you shall go to my father's house and to my kindred, and take a wife for my son."[43] It would seem that the command was more severe for the king than for the high priest, because the high priest Aaron of the tribe of Levi married Elisheba, of the tribe of Judah (Exodus 6:23).[44] Of course, in those days of polygamy, the king or priest could take wives of Israel, but the preferred bloodline came from the wife of the father's tribe, usually the first wife.

This reasoning then leads us to the true King, Jesus Christ himself. By marrying outside His tribe, Jesus was acting in an atypical fashion for one having true and full authority. Yet, He purposefully broke tradition in order to mend the breach between Judah and Ephraim. For Christ, traditional convention was made for man. It wasn't just any tribe He intermarried with, but the right person in the one tribe that made all the difference. By doing so, He created a new dynasty or house, which we may call the *Shiloh line*. It was a pure blend of the House of Jesse through David to Jesus Christ and the House of Joseph through Ephraim to Mary Magdalene and the Bethany sisters (see D&C 113:4–6).

The scepter departed Judah in the same sense that the birthright also departed Ephraim when the two tribes united through a strategic marriage. Christ broke the custom of the King of the Jews in order to become the King of All Israel. His wife was Ephraimitic, so his children were all descendants partially of the birthright of Joseph/Ephraim and partially with the inheritance of Judah/Jesse through the mtDNA and Y-Chromosome (see D&C 113:3–6). How wise it was to marry a "daughter of Shiloh" in order to bring in *Shalom* to heal the wasteland through the Holy Grail.

Now Christ and Mary Magdalene, through their intertribal marriage, united the blood of the scepter and of the birthright. This union formed a new dynasty. But all this was hidden from the world until the last days in a time when the tribe of Ephraim, held sway (D&C 133:30–32). Only among

Latter-day Saints is this secret known today. Nearly every other scholar, cult, and religious persuasion has Christ as either a celibate bachelor or married to a Benjaminite.

Perhaps Jesus was called "Shiloh" in prophecy because of two events. First, He married two Shiloh women living in the Benjaminite city of Bethany.[45] Their lineage was probably through the *Shiloni*, and thus He was called "Shiloh," as He was also called "Nazarene" after His hometown or sect. Second, the purpose of His mission on earth was to sprinkle His blood on the heavenly ark's Mercy Seat to atone for the sins of the world. He came to the heavenly "Shiloh" (or tabernacle where the ark was kept) to perform the final act of the atonement (Hebrews 9:11–14).

The term *until Shiloh come* probably meant that the royal bloodline should not pass from Judah until Christ's marriage to the figurative "daughter of Shiloh" and the birth of their son, *Shiloh ben Jesus*. It may be that when Jesus and His disciples came to the town in Ephraim (Shiloh) just before His death, the Savior may have officially transferred the prerogatives of Judah to Ephraim (John 11:54).

This is when "Shiloh came." At this point the tribal lines were melded and Jesus Christ moved beyond being a High Priest after the Order of Melchizedek, and by virtue of this sacred marriage, advanced to the position of Head Patriarch in the *Holy Order* with his chosen Matriarch.

Sadly, Rev. J. H. Allen believes that the scepter will depart from Judah at Christ's second coming, not at his first coming during the Meridian of Time.[46] Rather, after Jesus and the destruction of the temple, the scepter passed to Ephraim, then known as the *gentiles*, such as "first to the Jews, then to the Gentiles." Then, in the very last days it will go in the opposite direction (1 Nephi 13:42, D&C 90:9). It literally passed to the combined new tribe of Judeo-Ephraim, thus combining scepter and birthright.

This new tribe, or the Shiloh Dynasty, will be guided by the Lord: "It shall come to pass, that like as I have watched over them, to pluck up, and to break down, and to throw down, and to destroy, and to afflict; so will I watch over them, TO BUILD, and TO PLANT, saith the Lord" (Jeremiah 31:28).

NOTES

1. Barnum, *Comprehensive Dictionary of the Bible,* 609. She is called Mary of Magdala, not Mary of Taricheae (in Greek, *Meidel*), which strengthens the view that she is a Hebrew. Esther de Boer, "Mary Magdalene: Beyond the Myth," in Burstein, Secrets of the Da Vinci Code, 39. De Boer notes that a few of the oldest manuscripts for Mark 8:10 and Matthew 15:39 read "Magdale" where the official text has Dalmanutha and Magadan. The Sea of Galilee is sometimes called Kinneret, or Chinnereth.

2. Magdala lies equidistant between Tiberias and Tabga, a place close to Capernaum. Magdala or Mejdel was on the road to Nazareth, which lies twenty miles away. Capernaum was about six miles from Magdala. It should be noted that Jesus made Capernaum, not Nazareth, his home base during His ministry.

3. Margaret Starbird, "Mary Magdalene: The Hidden Bride," Salt Lake City Sunstone Symposium workshop (28 July 2005).

4. Starbird, Goddess in the gospel, 147–48. We are not exactly sure why she adds "Magdal-eder" to her quotation, except to say that the Hebrew word for tower is migdol and the tower of Edar (Genesis 35:21) is located near Jerusalem. She claims that the name "Magdal-eder" (Magdalene) is a title given to Mary and means "watchtower of the flock." Magdala, however, is mentioned in the Jerusalem Talmud as a village near Tiberias on the southeast corner of the Plain of Gennesaret.

5. Starbird, Magdalen's Lost Legacy, 129, believes this to be a mistake, thinking the site was named by later Christians. A Discovery Channel TV special (2003) noted that a translation might be "The Tower of Salted Fish." In the ancient system of Gematria each letter has a number, and each number value carried a symbolic meaning. The Greek name Maria is by Gematria 152. One unit, called in Hebrew a *colel*, may be added or subtracted to a sum without changing its symbolic significance. By adding 1 to 152, it equals 153, the sacred canon number of the Vesica Pisces or the "measure of the fish."

6. Barnum, *Comprehensive Dictionary of the Bible,* 580. The Hebrew name for the town Mejdel, or Magdale (Migdol), literally means "tower-stronghold" or "elevated place." The town is now called el-Mejdel where the ruins of an ancient watchtower remained into the nineteenth century, lying on the water's edge near the Plain of Gennesaret. Interestingly, the very name Magdalen means "tower for watching flocks of sheep."

7. According to Quinn, Early Mormonism and the Magic World View, 91, "The dove was the one form neither devils nor witches could assume."

8. Esther de Boer in Burstein, Secrets of the Da Vinci Code, 40. It is also said that the religious tax from Magdala was so heavy that it had to go to Jerusalem by wagon. Such was the religiosity of the town.

9. Jobes, *Dictionary of Mythology,* 1:466. The dove and the olive branch were sacred to Venus and Jupiter.

10. See *Catholic Encyclopedia.* In the Talmud the "dressing of woman's hair" was an appellate 1290 given to Miriam, the mother of Jesus. It was considered a shameful profession because hair had strong sexual connotations in first-century Judea.

11. *Midrash Rabbah on Lamentations* 2, 2. See also *Edersheim, Life and Times of Jesus the Messiah,* 1:571; Hastings, *Dictionary of the Bible,* 284.

12. Esther de Boer says it occurred at the time of Lamentation (*Midrash Ika Rabbah II,* 2,4); Haskins said it happened at about A.D. 75; in Burstein, *Secrets of the Da Vinci Code,* 30 and 40, respectively. Haskins, *Mary Magdalen,* 15, notes: "Its apparent notoriety in the early centuries of Christianity—it was destroyed in A.D. 75 because of its infamy and the licentious behaviour of its inhabitants—may have helped later to colour the name and reputation of Mary Magdalen herself."

13. J. E. Fallon, "Mary Magdalen," in NCE, 9:387.

14. Taylor, *New Bible Dictionary,* 1105. God's judgments upon the people and city of Shiloh are noted in Psalm 78:60; Jeremiah 7:12, 14, 26:6, 9. This probably happened about 1050 b.c.

15. Voragine, *Legenda Aurea,* published in Genoa in 1275. See www.fordham.edu/halsall/basis/goldenlegend/GoldenLegendvolume4.htm for its analysis. This source is late thirteenth century and can be relied upon not in a historical sense but as undocumented legend. See Gardner, *Bloodline of the Holy Grail,* 117. There was probably no castle in Bethany per se, but there was a battlement tower on the Plain of Gennesaret in Galilee until the end of the nineteenth century.

16. The "Men of Shiloh," or Shiloni, an Ephraimite family of exiles who returned from the Babylonian Captivity and settled in Jerusalem. See Wigoder, *Illustrated Dictionary and Concordance of the Bible*, 925–26: "Men of Shiloh were among those who returned from the Babylonian Exile" (Nehemiah 11:5). Yet other commentaries seem to indicate that Nehemiah was referring to those of the tribe of Judah, not Ephraim. See Barnum, *Comprehensive Dictionary of the Bible*, 1022; Davis, *Dictionary of the Bible*, 754; Hastings, *Dictionary of the Bible*, 845; and *New Bible Dictionary* (Tyndale), 1102.

    However, a parallel account in Chronicles 9:3, 5 reads that Ephraim was among those involved in the resettlement of Jerusalem after the Babylonian Captivity, whereas in Nehemiah 11:4, it is left out. Therefore the "Shiloni" must refer to men and women of Shiloh, not to Judah itself. Because Nehemiah 11:4 conflicts with Chronicles 9:3, we may conceive of the Shiloni as not being Shelah, or, a man of Judah, but of Ephraimites from the city of Shiloh. The author realizes that the ancient Syriac version gives "Shelanite" for "Shilonite" in Nehemiah 11:5, but he believes that 1 Chronicles 9:5 reverses it.

17. Quoting Apostle Joseph F. Smith, as quoted in Wilford Woodruff Journal, 8:187 (22 July 1883).

18. This land was not in the kingdom of King Herod the Great, but rather that of one of his sons, Herod Antipas (ruled A.D. 4–39), the tetrarch of Galilee and Peraea; thus it was somewhat safer for the Savior's ministry.

19. Vern Swanson, "Oh Daughter of Shiloh" (2004, poem).

20. With the wicked sons of Eli, the high priest, and Shiloh's people, the temple and city were probably destroyed by the Philistines and the Ark was captured. Shiloh apparently ceased to be significant even after its return (Jeremiah 7:12–14, 26:6–9). A terrace, with a rock-hewn quadrangle, approximately 400 feet by 80 feet, may have been the site of the ancient temple precinct housing the Ark.

21. Neusner, *Invitation to the Talmud*, 6. It was there that the annual Festival of Jehovah or Feast of the Lord was held. Perhaps this was the Feast of Ingathering-Tabernacles-Covenant mentioned in Exodus 23:16. Jacob Neusner finds rabbinic support for a similar celebration, with dancing maidens, at the close of the Day of Atonement on the 10th of Tishri.

22. The war, recorded in Judges 19–21, was caused because the Benjaminite "sons of Belial" raped and killed the concubine of a Levite. The Benjaminites would not give up the perpetrators to the authorities from the other tribes. Thus they fought a civil war with the warlike tribe of Benjamin, who were renowned with the bow and the sling. Eventually only 600 Benjaminite men, who took refuge in the cliff Rimmon, survived.

23. In a sense the tribes of Ephraim and Manasseh were eventually cursed for giving wives to Benjamin. They were cursed to be driven out of Israel and to be lost to history.

24. This area of Gilead included half the tribe of Manasseh as well as the tribes of Gad and Reuben (see Judges 21:8–14; Barnum, *Comprehensive Dictionary of the Bible*, 421).

25. The dancing maidens came out either on the 15th of Av or at a similar celebration near the close of the 10th of Tishri (Day of Atonement). Rather than the beautiful daughters, perhaps Ephraim palmed off its least-pleasing daughters, the most difficult to give in marriage, to the Benjaminites; thus the Ephraimites did not receive much credit for their "gift." Surely the virgins were forewarned and willing.

26. To this day, Israelis place a rock on the grave of the departed in memory of this event.

27. Kleiman, DNA and Tradition, 41.

28. Just as the Virgin Mary (a pureblood Davidian) was related to Elisabeth (an Aaronite of the tribe of Levi), so these "Daughters of Shiloh" were related to those who took part in the abduction, but "by God's own hand" were carefully maintained as "pure Ephraimites." We should remember as well that Manasseh also provided wives and thus would have heirs.

29. The move from Shiloh in Samaria to Galilee was probably necessitated by the wickedness of the Kingdom of Israel.

30. Wigoder, *Illustrated Dictionary and Concordance of the Bible*, 925–26: "Men of Shiloh were among those who returned from the Babylonian Exile (Nehemiah 11:5)."

31. The *Targum Onkelos* states, "The transmission of domain shall not cease from the house of Judah, nor the scribe from his children's children, forever, until Messiah comes" (Boren and Boren, Following the ark of the covenant, 45).

32. Many have noted that Genesis 49:10 meant that Judah must "go" to Shiloh until the Tabernacle with its Ark was removed to Jerusalem. For this and other interpretations, see Barnum, *Comprehensive Dictionary of the Bible*, 1021–22.

33. Ewing, "Shiloh," in *Dictionary of the Bible*, 848.

34. Barnum, *Comprehensive Dictionary of the Bible*, 1022.

35. Hagee, *Final Dawn over Jerusalem*, 203.

36. Boren, *Messiah of the Winepress*, 45.

37. Davis, *Dictionary of the Bible*, 753. This is an old

interpretation having been entertained in ancient translations of the Bible, including; the Septuagint, Targums of Onkelos and Jonathan, Syriac, and Jerome. This may mean "his child" or "family."

38. Wigoder, *Illustrated Dictionary and Concordance of the Bible*, 925.

39. Ibid., 925–26.

40. The 1970 printing of the Inspired Version says, "A prophet (not the Messiah who is called Shilo)," page 114. Several questions come to mind. Why are the parentheses around this remark? Was it written by Joseph Smith or by another hand? And does it mean "the Messiah who is Jesus Christ" or another Messiah, like a prophet who is called Shilo? We are left to wonder.

41. Kleiman, *DNA and Tradition*, 41. The female mitochondrial DNA, which changes very little from generation to generation, carries the lineage code and is passed on to both male and female children, whereas the Y chromosome passes only to males.

42. Yadin, *Temple Scroll*, 198. Actually the word is "house," not "tribe," but the meaning remains the same.

43. Ibid., 198–99. This did not mean intermarriage, as attested by Nehemiah 13:25. Also see Leviticus 21:14, which states that a high priest "shall take a virgin of his own people." Curiously the Septuagint translation, after the words "in her virginity" (v. 13), adds "of his own family."

44. It may be that the Virgin Mary's "Aaronite" cousin Elisabeth was somehow of this lineage. As long as the Aaronite Y chromosome was preserved it was enough for priesthood authority.

45. It was possible that some of those living in the area around Jerusalem, near Bethany in Benjamin lands might not have been from that tribe but rather related to those whom the Benjaminites took as wives.

46. Allen, *Judah's Sceptre and Joseph's Birthright*, 351.

PART FIVE

ZION—THE LOST GRAIL KINGDOM

*In relation to the kingdom of God, the devil always
sets up his kingdom at the very same time in opposition to God.*

—JOSEPH SMITH JR.[1]

ealing the wasteland through the marriage and children of Jesus Christ should be seen as the literal planting of seeds that would eventually grow into a beautiful garden. However, the opposite effect occurred, and things became dormant. Shortly after Jesus' ascension, an apostasy began to create a new wasteland or wilderness and with it the loss of the Holy Grail promise of renewal. Apparently before things could get better they had to get worse. The scriptures call this the "falling away first" (see 2 Thessalonians 2:3; Amos 8:12).

In Revelation 12:6 the Church is likened to a woman who flees into the wilderness, where she hath a place prepared of God, that they should nourish her for 1,260 days or years. Why must this "going underground" happen just when things should have gotten better? Jesus explained in parable: "Except a corn of wheat fall into the ground and die, it abideth alone: but if it die, it bringeth forth much fruit" (John 12:24). We must look at a dormant timeframe of nearly thirteen hundred years before the restoration and eventual millennial paradisiacal garden would begin to "cover the earth" with much fruit. The restoration during the meridian of time would only see a generation or two of flame before beginning its long process of decay and final flickering out.

The hollow husk of the true faith found in Judaism at the time of Christ would be superseded by the equally hollow husk of the Catholic and Orthodox faiths of Christianity. Nothing is harder to obey than a celestial faith in a mortal telestial world. We now examine how primitive Christianity fell from being God's official to His unofficial organized religion. This is important because the true Grail seed and the true Grail church are inseparably connected.

CHAPTER ELEVEN
THE JERUSALEM CHURCH

Woe unto you, lawyers! [scribes] For ye have taken away the key of knowledge, the fullness of the scriptures; ye enter not in yourselves into the kingdom; and those who were entering in, ye hindered.

—JST INSPIRED VERSION, LUKE 11:52

etween the death of Jesus Christ and the destruction of Jerusalem by the Romans a generation later, the Jewish sect of Saints began to simultaneously experience growth and apostasy. "Numerous persecutions," writes Starbird, "were carried out against the Christians by the Jewish authorities in Jerusalem."[2] In ca. A.D. 35, Stephen, one of the seven deacons, was stoned, heralding a malignant persecution for the Saints in Jerusalem (Acts 7:55–60). Later that year, Joseph of Arimathea took the entire Holy Family, including the Virgin Mary, Mary Magdalene, the Bethany sisters, and their children out of Palestine.[3]

The center of the Church in Jerusalem was run by Peter, the Apostles, and Church Patriarch and Presiding Bishop, James the Just. Being closer to Jewish roots, they taught a "low Christology," denying that God the Father and His son Jesus Christ were one and the same being, nor were they equal in some respects. But gnostic Hellenizers, even at this early date, began to "spiritualize" the gospel away, saying that Jesus was the God of light rather than the son of the Father through Mary of Nazareth.

The Church grew rapidly, "not simply among the poor and oppressed or common people, but also among the Jewish priests, as we read in Acts 6:7, 'A great multitude of the priests were obedient unto the faith.'"[4] Then in A.D. 62–63, Simon Peter was crucified upside down, and James the Just was murdered near the Temple Mount.[5] These pummeling losses rocked the nascent Christian Church, a blow from which it would never fully recover.

By A.D. 63–65, Herod's temple was finished, leaving 18,000 to 20,000 men out of work. The ensuing economic difficulties undoubtedly contributed to the outbreak of the war against the high priests and Rome.[6] Discontent incited the politico-religious Zealots who seized the country. Thus began the four-year First Jewish Revolt against Roman rule.

For the most part, the bitter conflict ended in A.D. 70, when Titus, the son of the Roman Emperor

Vespasian, destroyed Jerusalem and Herod's temple. Hundreds of thousands of Jews were killed, and most of the rest fled. The Jewish *Diaspora* had begun in earnest, as had the gentilization of the Christian Church. These times and circumstances caused a break in the connection between the bloodline of the Holy Family and the priesthood line of the Apostles.

This disconnection had a deleterious effect on the early Church. Neither could stand unless they both stood together. The dark night of the Great Apostasy was already beginning to fall between the time of the Holy Family's departure and the destruction of the temple thirty-five years later. Few saw the significance of a new breach between the two lines that subtly appeared.[7] But the scriptures foresaw the dismal prospects for the kingdom of God at that time (2 Peter 2:1–2; 2 Thessalonians 2:1–12; 2 Timothy 4:1–4; Matthew 24; D&C 112:23).

Then after the fall of the Holy City in A.D. 70 and the dispersion of the Christian community in Jerusalem, matters only worsened. Paul's teachings to the outside world saved the Church, in much the same way that Joseph Smith's sending missionaries to Britain saved the nascent LDS Church in this dispensation. Although the nature of Christ became misunderstood in the confusion, a true latter-day church would eventually enlighten the world through the true bloodline of the Holy Grail.

JOSEPH OF ARIMATHEA AND THE DEATH OF CHRIST

Someday our posterity shall burn to remember when simple honesty was known as courage!

—YEVTUSHENKO[8]

Joseph of Arimathea's life forms the undergirding framework that ties together the most salient elements of our Grail narrative. He is the nail upon which all else hangs. If he did not exist, then we would, of necessity, have to invent him, by fact or by fiction. Logical momentum demands Arimathean guidance in our storyline. He is the quintessential "Grail Guardian" and upon him rests the drama of the Holy Grail.[9] Robert M. Price believes that though he was unhistorical and essentially an ideological tool:

> We might compare Mary Magdalene, gnostic apostle, to Joseph of Arimathea, pressed into service as the apostle of an indigenous Celtic Christianity ostensibly planted by this New Testament figures centuries before Roman Catholic missionaries set foot on the British Isles bearing their popish evangel.[10]

For many the tale of the Holy Grail begins with the Last Supper, where Christ drank deeply from the chalice. While deep, we know that the implications of the Grail are even deeper than this. However, the supper holds great interest for nearly everyone. The presence of our guardian, Joseph of Arimathea, at this and subsequent events enlightens us of the true meaning of the Grail.

The evening of the Last Supper begins the cycle of suffering and death of our Lord Jesus Christ. Where did this most hallowed meal take place? Grail enthusiast Tony Fieldsted noted that the upper chamber for the Last Supper was actually Joseph of Arimathea's Jerusalem abode.[11] Isabel Elder notes that as a member of the Sanhedrin Joseph would have had a house in Jerusalem.[12] However, some medieval legends, particularly Robert de Boron's *Joseph d'Arimathie* have noted that it was actually the house of Simon the Leper.[13]

The upper chamber may have been on the Hill

of Zion (upper city) in western Jerusalem some distance from the Garden of Gethsemane.[14] In Luke 22:7–13, we learn that the Passover meal was to be held in the City. The disciples Peter and John were to enter Jerusalem, where a servant man with a water pitcher was to meet them.[15] They were to follow him to his Master's house, to a guest chamber in a large furnished upper room. Hugh J. Schonfield's radical translation of the New Testament is interesting: "As you enter the city," he told them, "a man will meet you carrying a water-pot. Follow him into the house he enters, and say to the master of the house, "The Teacher asks you, which guest room am I to have to eat the Passover with my disciples?" He will then show you a large upstairs dining room already laid out. There prepare."[16]

Tony Fieldsted reasoned that since Joseph of Arimathea was on the Council, he would need a Jerusalem house, and since he was rich, he could afford a palatial one. Because Joseph was a secret follower of Jesus, "for fear of the Jews" (John 19:38), he might have been personally unknown to His disciples. The disciples probably would not have conceived of using the famous Arimathean's guest chamber. Subterfuge was used to hide the householder's involvement. Since Jesus was already under suspicion, the servant's anonymity and the relative anonymity of Peter and John would have protected the goodman of the house—Joseph of Arimathea.[17]

There at Joseph's house, possibly with Mary Magdalene present, Jesus and the disciples partook of a passover meal, for Jesus said, "With desire I have desired to eat this [P]assover with you before I suffer" (Luke 22:15). Then, at Joseph's magnificent round table, He took the cup, saying, "This cup is the new testament in my blood, which is shed for you" (Luke 22:20). Thus begins a type of "Fellowship of the Round Table" consisting of the Twelve Apostles, plus Christ and Joseph.[18]

Was Mary Magdalene present at the Last Supper?

There is a painting by the Spanish master Pedro Berruguete and workshop depicting the Supper with John's head on Jesus' breast and Mary Magdalene kneeling in front of the table.[19] Before her on the floor is either the Holy Grail or her alabastron; we cannot be sure. The artist must have reached into some deep source that allowed him to place the Magdalene at the Last Supper.[20]

From a secondary source we learn that Joseph of Arimathea might have been present at the Last Supper, which also supports the supposition that it was his house. Recorded in *The Sweet Old Poem of Joseph of Arimathea* and paraphrased by Elizabeth C. Prophet, we read: "After the conclusion of the feast Joseph, contemplating the words of Jesus, decided that he must have a keepsake of the event. He returned to the upper room where he found the table still set with the remains of the Passover feast. Taking the cup from which all had drunk, he hid it in the folds of his garment. As he stood in the darkness at Calvary the following day, he still had Jesus' cup in the folds of his garment—a treasure."[21]

It was reported in another version of the legend that after Christ's apprehension by the Roman guard, the cup was taken to Pontius Pilate. According to Robert de Boron, it was recovered from Pilate by Joseph of Arimathea just before the Crucifixion or during the burial sequence.[22] In another medieval legend, Joseph of Arimathea took the vessel himself from the house of Simon the Leper.[23]

However, during the Crucifixion it was Joseph who is credited with collecting the blood and sweat that poured from Christ's wounded side as a result of the centurion's spear. It may be here that the idea of the two cruets, one containing the blood and the other the sweat, came from[24] (John 19:34). The sacred blood seems to have been collected in several ways: the spear point, the two cruets, the cup or Grail, a washbasin, Magdalene's hair, and a bloodstained stone. The blood was gathered through flowing, scraping, dripping, wiping, and washing of the blood.[25]

Legend has it that Joseph then caught the bloody water from Jesus' side at Calvary in this self-same urn or cup of the Last Supper[26] (see Plate 14).[27] There is a miniature from an early twelfth-century gospel showing the Deposition of Christ with Joseph of Arimathea collecting the blood (see Plate 15).[28]

Robert Grosseteste wrote a tract which said that Joseph collected the blood that flowed from Christ's wounds when he washed the body after taking the Savior down from the Cross. The washbasin's bloody water was then kept. Other stories have Nicodemus using knives to scrape the dried blood from Christ and keeping it in a cloth.[29] Then, at the cross, Mary Magdalene wiped the blood from Christ's feet, collecting it with her hair and hands. [30]

After the Crucifixion we are told that Joseph "went in boldly unto Pontius Pilate and begged the body of Jesus" (Matthew 27:57–60; John 19:38). The reason for his boldness was his high position as provincial senator of Rome. In an expanded translation of scripture we learn, "This man, having gone in to Pilate *asked a personal favor* for the body of Jesus" (Luke 23:52).[31] His stature and wealth undoubtedly persuaded Pilate. Also, Jewish custom and Roman law held that it was the duty of the senior nearest-of-kin to bury the dead.[32]

In the midst of all this was Nicodemus, Joseph's friend, colleague, and confidant, "a master in Israel," actually a doctor of the Law. He spoke as a lawyer and as a Levite.[33] It is striking that two of the richest people in Jerusalem, Nicodemus and Joseph of Arimathea, stood up for Jesus when they had so much to lose. They were also the ones to lay the Savior to rest.

In other versions, the collection of blood into the Grail occurred at the time of the preparation of the body with the seventy-five pounds of "myrrh and aloes."[34] Robert de Boron's account explaining

how Joseph of Arimathea and Nicodemus worked with the body is as follows: "While they were washing [Jesus], the wounds began to bleed, which made them very afraid, for they remembered the stone at the foot of the Cross that was split open by the falling blood. Then Joseph thought of his vessel and decided that the drops would be better preserved there than in any other place. So he took it and collected the blood from the wounds . . . he took the vessel with the blood home with him."[35]

This gives rise to the tradition of the Grail as a stone, at the foot of the cross, upon which the "dead Jesus bled." When this solid stone split, the blood was able to trickle down into a cavern below in which the ark of the covenant was secretly stored. Thus the Savior's blood was sprinkled on the Mercy Seat to atone mankind from the sins of the world.[36] However, the blood on Passover was not intended for the Mercy Seat, but for the altar of incense.[37]

Be this as it may, we should remember that in all three cases the blood was derived from a dead corpse, not a living sacrifice. All Grail legends are based on blood from Christ's dead body; thus we may infer that this blood was of lesser import than the bloody sweat from his living body at the Mount of Olives. The Bitter Cup vessel with which the angel Michael-Adam caught the living blood in Gethsemane, far exceeds in value the Last Supper vessel and blood which Joseph of Arimathea, Nicodemus and Mary Magdalene may have caught during and after Calvary. One was infinitely spiritual whereas the other was temporal.

After the burial, according to the noncanonical *The Gospel of Nicodemus*, the Jewish elders expressed anger at Joseph for having buried Jesus.[38] They captured Joseph and imprisoned him. A seal was placed on the door to the cell and a guard posted in front. He was left to starve in a high tower, but the Grail cup that he had hidden fed him for forty years until he was released.[39] Barber knows of no source before de Boron that names the Grail as a vessel.[40]

The exaggerated "bardic" forty years was probably forty months.[41] Furthermore, according to de Boron, Christ himself taught Joseph the mysteries of the Grail. Sinclair explains: "Jesus gave esoteric teaching to Joseph of Arimathea, who established the mysteries of the grail under the guardianship of its hereditary knights."[42]

Another apocryphal account is *The Narrative of Joseph* that coincides with the Nicodemus accounts. Several details are added, such as Christ coming to the jail with the saved robber, Demas. It also states that Joseph spent three days with Jesus in Galilee, presumably to learn the mysteries mentioned above.

Later, when the elders returned, the seal was still in place but Joseph was gone.[43] They later learn that he is in Arimath to the north, have a change of heart, and send a letter of apology to Joseph via seven friends. He returns to Jerusalem and is civilly questioned by the elders. The *Gospel of Nicodemus* continues with Joseph stressing to the elders, specifically to Annas and Caiaphas, that Jesus Christ had risen from the dead and ascended into heaven. He also says that others were resurrected and identifies to the elders the two resurrected sons of the high priest Simeon, Charinus and Lenthius.

Cardinal Caesar Baronius (1538–1607), Vatican librarian from 1596 to 1601, published his influential twelve-volume historical work *Annales Ecclesiastici*. It describes that following Joseph's seizure by the Sanhedrin, he decided to go to Britain in A.D. 35. Of this we shall hear more later.

Scripture does not mention Joseph again, but legend now begins to abound with his name. Joseph of Arimathea went on to be the guardian of the Grail cup and keeper of its contents until his death. While the Holy Grail became a venerated relic, it was actually an encoded symbol for something much more important. In fact, Joseph of Arimathea becomes, with the Virgin Mary and Mary Magdalene, the central figure in Celtic and Gaelic Christianity.

Manly P. Hall in his *A New Encyclopedia of Freemasonry* called Joseph of Arimathea "the first bishop of Christendom."[44] This is a term generally reserved for James the Just, the first Bishop of Jerusalem. However, this loosely ties the two together because James the brother of Jesus was undoubtedly the first bishop to the circumcised (Jews), while Joseph of Arimathea was possibly the first bishop to the uncircumcised (gentiles). His bishopric was undoubtedly second to James' but was the first in the "Land of the Gentiles."

Both Joseph of Arimathea and James the Just were to become entrusted with the "secret Church of the Holy Grail." It was the invisible and hidden receptacle—the patriarchal bloodline of Christ. It says in the *Didcot* and *Vulgate* scriptural versions that Joseph knew "the secret words of Jesus." [45] In this higher knowledge, Joseph of Arimathea joins four others: Simon Peter, the prophet and president of the Church; John the Evangelist; James the Just; and Mary Magdalene.[46] None of them heard "all" of the secret words, but together they were the embodiment of the fulness of the inner gospel and Grail message.

THE CHURCH AND FAMILY PROBLEMS?

But a small cadre of feminist scholars—especially those tutored and credentialed at Harvard Divinity School—go much further. Their headline-making claim is that in the early church there was a party of Magdalene and a party of Peter—again, men versus women, as in the case of Miriam [and Moses]—and that the party of Peter not only won but also proceeded to expunge the evidence and memory of the Magdalene faction from the New Testament and to tarnish the reputation of Magdalene to boot.

—KENNETH WOODWARD[47]

It was through the descendants of Jesus Christ that the kingship of Judah and the birthright of Ephraim were united. But this lasted, in an official sense, but for a fleeting moment. Soon after the ascension they were separated again as the Church was forced one direction and the bloodline another. The political situation in Palestine caused the separation, which eventually led to the downfall of the twin sources of authority within Church and kingdom.

Some submit that even before the Grail family and the Church were fully disconnected, problems of personality and conflict of opinions began to mount. In the minds of many feminists, the ecclesiastical and the family branches of the true gospel began to fray soon after the Pentecost. Laurence Gardner exaggerates the problem: "Mary's legacy remained the greatest of all threats to a fearful church that had bypassed Messianic descent in favour of a self-styled Apostolic succession."[48]

However, before the destruction of the second temple and the rise of Christian-Gnosticism in the latter first century, no such division was known. Turf battles ensued within the Church, not regarding succession, but rather between the Jewish vs. Gentile natures of the Church. This coupled with persecution and acceptance of insidious Hellenistic philosophy led to the eventual fall of The Church of Jesus Christ of the Meridian of Time.

It is noted in the apocryphal *Gospel of Philip* that there supposedly was a forgotten gender battle between the President of the Church, Peter, and Mary Magdalene[49]:

[Peter says] "Has the Savior spoken secretly to a woman and not openly so that we would all hear? Surely he did not wish to indicate that she is more worthy than we are?"

Mary wept and said to Peter . . . "Do you think that I thought this all up myself, or that I am not telling the truth about the Savior?"

Levi answered, and said unto Peter . . . "You have always been hot-tempered, now I see you arguing with the woman as if you were enemies [like these adversaries]. But if the Savior found her worthy, who are you, indeed, to reject her? The Savior surely knows her well enough."[50]

Of course this apocryphal codex was written by a gnostic fundamentalist and was ideologically motivated but not factually grounded. However, it is reminiscent of the animosity that existed between President Brigham Young and Emma Hale Smith, the wife of the Prophet Joseph Smith.[51] Only in Mormon times, it was the conservative Emma who was angry with Brigham over esoteric doctrinal points rather than Peter being angry with Mary in the first century for the same reason.

Early Christian gnostics of the late first century could not accept the literalism of the official Church, but in reality did not have any descendants of Mary Magdalene to offer instead. Why would they promote a succession that they could not find? At least the RLDS dissenters from the Mormon Church had Joseph Smith III to offer for leadership. The apocryphal *Gospel of Mary* (Magdalene) demonstrates gnostic antipathy to the apostolic church by promoting that Peter had strained relationship with Mary Magdalene, saying, "Would he really have spoken privately to a woman, and not freely to us? Why should we change our minds and listen to her?[52]

What teachings was Peter rejecting? While this

papyrus acknowledges the "spiritual" reality of Jesus' death and resurrection, it rejects His atonal suffering and death as the path to eternal life. It also rebuffs the notion of the immortality of the physical body, attesting that only the soul will be saved. Numerous "watchers" and levels of spiritual attainment may faintly resound to LDS ears, but not to the gnostic's favorite straw man, the "hothead" Peter.

The gnostic text *Pistis Sophia* [The Wisdom of Faith] also shows Peter complaining about Mary's preaching and dominating the conversation; finally Peter asks Jesus to quiet her. Jesus rebukes Him and later Mary confides, "Peter makes me hesitate. I am afraid of him because he hates the female race."[53] Then Jesus interrupts, "Whatsoever the Spirit inspires is divinely ordained to speak, whether man or woman"[54] (1 Timothy 2:11-12). The Gospel of Thomas has Peter objecting to the Magdalene's presence: "Simon Peter said unto them, Let Mary leave us, for women are not worthy of life."[55]

The conjectured conflict between Peter and the Magdalene possibly split the Church between the "adherents of the message" (Church) and the "adherents of the bloodline" (Family). Again this is not unlike the problem that existed between the Brighamites and the Josephites, between the "Kingdom" and the "King."[56] The first thing Lucifer sought to destroy was the unity of gospel ministers. If he could make them "not One," then they are "not Mine," according to the words of the Lord in Gethsemane (John 17:21-23).

Simon Peter, with James and John (the sons of thunder), the apostles, and others, were given the priesthood to lead an earthly Church. But because it was not united with the bloodline of Christ's progeny, it was eventually destined to fail. It did so, slowly leading to the Great Apostasy. While the vestigial husk of the true Church continued to grow worldwide as Eastern Orthodox, Catholicism, and later as Protestantism, it was not the fulness of the gospel.

Although there were many "lateral members" of the nuclear family of Jesus, none were literally related to the special blood he had, because the Savior's brothers and cousins were actually his stepsiblings and the rest were related only through marriage. His immediate progeny left Palestine.

The only *True* (priesthood) and *Living* (bloodline) Church of God would eventually need to be restored. Similarly roots, limbs, and branches of the true vine (bloodline) grew in the wilderness, but the particular genealogical branches would be the chosen origin of the restored gospel (John 15:1, 5; Isaiah 5:7). Interestingly, John records that the woman and her child had to flee the power of Satan in the Levant. Perhaps they are symbolized by Mary Magdalene and her child[ren]: "And the woman fled into the wilderness, where she had a place prepared of God, that they should feed her there a thousand two hundred and threescore years. . . And to the woman were given two wings of a great eagle, that she might flee into the wilderness, into her place, where she is nourished for a time, and times, and half a time, from the face of the serpent" (JST, Inspired Version, Revelation 12:5, 14).[57]

In Hugh J. Schonfield's translation of Revelation 12:15, he writes, "So the Dragon was enraged against the woman, and went off to make war *with the remainder of her offspring*."[58] Are these offspring the Grail children? Could this be the reason why the children had to flee into the British wilderness?

It is believed by many Latter-day Saints that the woman is the "church of God" and the "man child" is Jesus Christ or the priesthood[59] (D&C 86:3). While not contradicting this argument, there is another line of reasoning which postulates that "the Church" or woman is the *tribal* heritage of the House of All Israel. The child is not specifically the priesthood but is the posterity through that tribal lineage.[60]

In another way of thinking, the Church (Chosen People) gave birth to Jesus Christ the

FIGURE 6
SACRED LINES

CHRIST REPRESENTS THE PRIESTHOOD LINE.......................THE TRUE
MAGDALENE REPRESENTS THE BLOODLINE.......................THE LIVING
THE WOMAN ....THE TRIBAL LINEAGE
THE CHILD/OFFSPRING ....THE POSTERITY

"man child" with "the rod of iron" or scepter (see Revelation 12:3, 5). Then that scepter passed from the tribe of Judah to the tribe of Ephraim, via Mary Magdalene and the Bethany sisters. Parley P. Pratt noted the close relationship between the Church and the lineage:

> In the lineage of Abraham, Isaac, and Jacob, according to the flesh, was held the right of heirship to the keys of Priesthood for the blessings and for the salvation of all nations. From this lineage sprang the Prophets, John the Baptist, *Jesus, and the Apostles; and from this lineage sprang the great Prophet and restorer in modern times [Joseph Smith], and the Apostles who hold the keys under his hand."*
>
> From the days of Abraham until now, if the people of any country, age, or nation have been blessed with the blessings peculiar to the everlasting covenant of the gospel, its sealing powers, Priesthood, and ordinances, *it has been through the ministry of that lineage, and the keys of [that] Priesthood held by the lawful heirs according to the flesh.*
>
> But no man can hold the keys of Priesthood or of Apostleship, to bless or administer salvation to the nations, unless he is a literal descendant

of Abraham, Isaac, and Jacob. Jesus Christ and his ancient Apostles of both hemispheres were of that lineage. . . . The world has from that day to this been manufacturing priests, without any particular regard to lineage.[61]

Thus the fairytale of Princess Aurora (Sleeping Beauty), who sleeps until the true Prince awakens her, is true when interpreted from this gospel standpoint. Sleeping Beauty may be a metaphor for the sleeping, unconscious and unknowing, lineage of Jesus' posterity. "The Woman" (the Church) remains dormant (asleep) for 1,260 years, until it is awakened with a kiss by the Prince, Joseph Smith Jr. This is the "lineage of your fathers" spoken of in Doctrine and Covenants 86:8–10.

In this Dispensation, the scepter and the birthright were restored through the King's Son, Joseph Smith Jr. Though he lived only fourteen years after restoring the Church, he "rolled off" the authority to the rightful priesthood and lineage found within the Quorum of Twelve. The major difference between the gospel at the meridian of time and at the fulness of time was that all the prophets, apostles, and seventy of the dispensation of the fulness of times were deeply imbued with the blood of Jesus Christ, just as Joseph Smith was. This would be enough to carry off the kingdom. At the death of Jesus Christ only his few children had "the Grail lineage," and they were being hidden away.

JAMES THE JUST, REGENT PATRIARCH— PRESIDING BISHOP

Known for his faithful observance of the law . . . Apart from his belief in the exceptional status and mission of Jesus and some specific ritual practices, nothing distinguished him from many of the Jews of his time. He regarded himself as a pious Jew, a member of the Israel of the end-time. He would certainly have been surprised had someone told him that he adhered to a new religion.

—PIERRE-ANTOINE BERNHIEM[62]

James (*Ya'akov* or Jacob) the Just (*Zadok* or Teacher of Righteousness, in Hebrew *Moreh-zedok*) is often called "James the brother of the Lord." He is the most significant of all the *Desposyni*, or children of Joseph and Mary. His importance is of utmost consequence to this study. James was a regent Patriarch acting for and in behalf of Christ's own eldest son. One of Christ's male offspring eventually was supposed to become presiding patriarch, priest, and king of the faith. Non-Mormon Dr. M. Zvi Udley explains this idea: "It would be only natural for Jesus' son, when he was old enough to succeed James, the brother of the Lord, on his death, to the Presidency of the Church."[63]

The gnostic *Apocalypse of James* denies that James was a literal sibling of Jesus, saying, "[James is] said to be the Lord's brother only in a purely spiritual sense."[64] Eusebius refers to James as "one of the alleged brothers of Jesus."[65] James the Just was, according to some Epiphanian sources, the eldest stepbrother of Christ from Joseph the carpenter's earlier wife.[66] As mentioned above in the section on the conception of Christ, Origin quotes the *Proto-Evangelium of James* (8:2–9; 17:1) which probably goes beyond the mark:

"But some say, basing it on a tradition in the Gospel according to Peter, as it is titled, or the Book of James, that the brothers of Jesus were sons of Joseph by a former wife, whom he married before Mary."[67]

This has become the orthodox position today in order to perpetuate Mary's eternal virginity.[68] This might mean that all the *Desposyni* (family of the Lord) stepbrothers and stepsisters of Christ—James, Joses, Simon, Jude, and Mary (Matthew 13:54–56, Mark 6:3)—were older than himself.[69] If the names are in age order, James would be the oldest of Joseph's children, perhaps older than Jesus; however, at least some of these other children might have been born of Mary of Nazareth. In fact, Helvidius, a contemporary of Jerome, argued that James and the other brothers were the children of Mary and Joseph.[70]

Regardless of his birth order, as one of the eldest and most spiritually devout and observant of all the extended "Holy Family," James would have been accorded much deference. Probably before but certainly after the resurrection, James' conversion to the mission of Jesus Christ was total, his leadership ability unchallenged, and his pedigree flawless. James led by spiritual piety, official position, and priesthood authority.

His righteousness, kinship to Christ, and charisma were a central beacon to the primitive Church, especially Pharisaic Jewish Semitic Saints. The first three or four decades after the crucifixion, the vast majority of Christians was still Jewish. They practiced a mixture of Judaism and Christianity, as Taylor says, a *via media*.[71] He was a "Hebrew of the Hebrews" attending the temple and blameless before the Law. Likewise, James is often considered the author of the New Testament book Epistle to the Hebrews.

When Paul returned from his missionary work, James said, "Thou seest, brother, how many thousands of Jews there are which believe; and they are all zealous of the Law" (Acts 21:20). The early Christian chronicler Hegesippus (ca. A.D. 110–ca.

180) wrote that James was the leader of the fledgling Jerusalem church. Hegesippus noted, "Those who did believe, believed because of James."[72] Shanks and Witherington III believe that James the Just was also numbered among the Nazarites.[73] (Acts 21:24) Eusebius, quoting Hegesippus' *Memoirs*, notes James' Nazarite traits: "[James] was holy from his mother's womb; drank no wine or strong drink, nor ate animal food; no razor came upon his head; he neither oiled himself nor used the bath; he alone was permitted to use the holy places, for he never wore wool, but linen. . . . Indeed, on account of his exceeding great righteousness he was called "the righteous" and "*Olbias*," which means in Greek "defense of the People" and "righteousness."[74]

The crosscurrents of conflict swirling in Jerusalem at the time were immense. The aristocratic priests, like Annas and Caiaphas, who were responsible for the crucifixion of the Savior, still claimed Christ an imposter. Then, "mingling with them, devout, strict and blameless—if possible out-rivaling them in all religious ceremonial and observances—were the early Jewish Christians."[75]

It was all gall and wormwood to these culprit families to have the presence of Jesus' brother, James the Just, within their midst. He was too popular and too honorable to be summarily murdered, so they bided their time and perhaps even gave begrudging respect. The adage "Hypocrisy is the homage which vice pays to virtue" applies here.

The Sadducees were in charge of the temple, which Jesus Christ prophesied would soon be "thrown down" (Matthew 16:1). Later, in Matthew 26:61, Jesus said, "I am able to destroy the temple of God." Such threats against the temple may have been one of the reasons the Sadducees and the temple's own imperial Sanhedrin sought to have Jesus executed. "It is also unlikely," writes G. Shapiro, "given the support of the Pharisee Gamaliel for James, that the Sanhedrin *Gadol* had anything to do with Jesus' trial."[76]

Unlike the traveling apostles, who were sent to the Jews and gentiles, James remained in Jerusalem to "hold down the fort." Epiphanius of Salamis in his *Panarion* (ca. A.D. 370) indicates that James was the first bishop of Jerusalem.[77] Hegesippus notes that James succeeded Christ and was ordained bishop by Him.[78]

According to the most primitive part of the Clementine *Recognitions* (1.27–71), Jesus nominated James first bishop of Jerusalem.[79] Eusebius quotes Clement of Alexandria as saying that Peter, James, and John, shortly after the ascension of Christ, chose James as the first bishop of Jerusalem.[80] However, James likely replaced Stephen as bishop somewhat later than this. Stephen was the head one of the seven deacons chosen by the disciples to care for the widows and needy[81] (Acts 6:1–5). Eusebius himself believed that after Stephen was stoned (ca. A.D. 35–36), James became the bishop of the Jerusalem Church.[82] The position was probably renamed bishop rather than presiding deacon; thus, James was technically the first bishop.

All this is certainly true but might be pushed somewhat further. We can claim that not only was James the presiding bishop of the Church but regent patriarch as well. His authority did not impinge upon the very active and tiring work of the younger Simon Peter and the Twelve apostles. Rather there was a bicephalous-type arrangement between the patriarch and the Twelve.

Holding both the spiritual patriarchal and the temporal Bishopric positions for the fledgling Church would have placed James in a most powerful position. His seniority undoubtedly placed him in much the same position as Father Joseph Smith Sr. but only more so. In fact the first bishops and patriarchs of Jerusalem were all circumcised Jews and most, if not all, claimed a blood relationship to Jesus through his brothers and uncles.[83] "The notion of a dynastic Christianity is certainly nothing new," writes Bernheim. He quotes Maurice Goguel: "It is extremely significant that in the earliest days of Christianity, as in Islam and Mormonism, as soon as the prophet had died, a dynastic element appeared and tried to assert itself."[84]

Most non-Mormon exegetes have not understood the office of Patriarch of the Church or its dynastic implications and have reversed Peter's and James's positions. However, since the office of a bishop was an ecclesiastical position within the church, it came under the jurisdiction of Peter and the Quorum of the Twelve Apostles. Furthermore, James' position as Regent-Patriarch or "father" over the whole Church and bishop of Jerusalem within the Church, would not have placed him above its head, Simon Peter, despite his pedigree. Eusebius reads thus, "Together *with the apostles*, James the Lord's brother succeeded to the Church."[85] Such an arrangement was made with the agreement and blessings of both the Holy Church and the Holy Family.

Truly, if James the Just's position was regent Patriarch over the charismatic Church he would be, in essence, Jesus' successor, though no more than Peter. Hegesippus emphasized James' preeminence in the primitive church: "Control of the church passes together with the apostles, to the brother of the Lord, James, whom everyone from the Lord's time till our own has named the Just, for there were many Jameses, but this one was holy from his birth."[86]

Because of persecutions by King Herod Agrippa I, Peter quit the Holy City by A.D. 43–44, giving James the Just more local jurisdiction[87] (Acts 12:17). Roman Catholic scholars believe that "The Church" moved from Jerusalem to Antioch and finally to Rome. It seems as though Peter was the supreme authority of the Church. And if Peter and James did not agree on every aspect of the Law, it only reflected the diversity of thought in Palestinian Judeo-Christianity of the first century.

Matthew 6:19 gives Peter preeminent ecclesiastical authority (Melchizedek Order) over Christ's Church but does not mention anything about bloodline authority (patriarchal order). But between A.D. 44 and 62, this seems to have continued until their deaths in A.D. 62. This loss might be compared in Christianity to the Jewish loss of the temple eight years later. By the third century A.D., James the Just's position had slipped out of the minds of most Christians, and Peter was singularly accorded the most prominent position in the original Church.

Not only this, but James the Just was said to be the chief authority on doctrinal issues and "all teachers in the Church were expected to match and correlate their teachings with those of James."[88] In the seventh book of Clement's *Hypotyposes*, quoted by Eusebius, we read: "James the Just, John and Peter were entrusted by the Lord after his resurrection with the high knowledge [or *gnosis*]. They imparted it to the other apostles and the other apostles to the Seventy."[89]

At the Council of Jerusalem, James seems to be in charge in formulating that Council's Apostolic Decree, which is not inconsistent with the idea of his being the doctrinal scholar of the early Church.[90] The *Clementine Homilies* continue to equate James the Just with being the Church Theologian of his day: "That is why, above all, remember to flee every apostle, doctor or prophet who has not previously submitted his preaching carefully to James called the brother of my Lord, and charged with governing the church of the Hebrews in Jerusalem."[91]

In Switzerland is located Codex I, which contains the *Apocryphon of James*, which also tells of a revelation granted by Jesus to both James and Peter.[92] Codex V, the *First Apocalypse of James*, has the resurrected Jesus granting a special revelation to James but not Peter who plays no role. Logion 12 of the Coptic *Gospel of Thomas* demonstrates the second-century gnostic departure from a Peter-centered Church: "The disciples said to Jesus: 'We know that you will go away from us. Who will be great over us?' Jesus said to them: 'In the place to which you have gone, you will go to James the Just, for whose sake the heaven and the earth came into existence.'"[93]

Thus we see that the patriarchal authority of James seems nearly equal to that of the ecclesiastic authority of the First Presidency. LDS scholar S. Kent Brown in his 1973 article on the subject notes that James the Just was a "chief guarantor of Jesus' resurrection" and "the guardian of the true doctrines of salvation."[94] James, with Peter and Mary Magdalene, seem to be among the first unto whom Jesus appeared after His resurrection in an individual way (see 1 Corinthians 15:5–7). Brown accurately notes that none of the extra-scriptural documents gave James the Just much position before A.D. 150 and those were of gnostic origin.

Secular history informs us that James was martyred during political unrest of the Jews, during the interregnum between the unexpected death of the procurator Festus and the appointment of his successor, Albinus, in A.D. 62. The growth of the Christian movement greatly disturbed the aristocratic high priests. Many of the lesser priests (Levites) had already converted, and the Sadducean higher priests irresistibly felt that some far-reaching conspiracy "subversive of the national custom and religion of the Jews" was undermining their authority.[95]

Anan ben Anan (Ananus the Younger), the bold-tempered and insolent Sadducean had recently been appointed high priest, but his tenure lasted only three months. Ananus seized the moment to strike at the heart of the Jewish Christian community.[96] He was very rigid in judging offenders and now saw a propitious moment to rid himself of his opponents, especially the thorn in his side, James the Just. James was a constant reminder of the shabby legalisms employed by most Sadducees and a few Pharisees to murder his brother, Jesus Christ (Acts 5:17). James' incendiary oration at the temple during Passover proclaimed the eminent return of the Messiah with "Great Power" in the clouds.[97] According to Josephus: "[Ananus] followed the school of the Sadducees, who are indeed more savage than any of the other Jews. . . . So he [Ananus] assembled the Sanhedrin of Judges and brought before them the brother of Jesus, who was called Christ, whose name was James, and some others and when [Ananus had] formed an accusation against them as breakers of the law, he delivered them to be stoned."[98]

Before his successor arrived, Ananus had a death sentence pronounced by the imperial Sanhedrin (*synedrion*) in conformity with Sadducean code.[99] John the Baptist had earlier called this supreme council, "You brood of vipers!" (Matthew 3:7-10). It was mostly the Sadducees and the Romans who were responsible for the death of Christ, not the Jews as a whole. James the Just was killed at the Temple Mount in Jerusalem in A.D. 62.[100]

This martyrdom caused the Pharisees to be greatly angered and they made their discontent known to the Jewish King Agrippa II and Albinus. Flavius Josephus recorded that the inhabitants of Jerusalem were greatly offended by the killing of James and that they secretly urged King Agrippa II to punish the Sadducean high priest Ananus.

Stoning was a punishment reserved for those accused of blasphemy, adultery, or being a false teacher leading the faithful astray. Richard Bauckham shows that it was a normal Jewish procedure for this punishment to first push offending persons off a high place and then to stone them[101] (see Luke 4:29).

James the Just was impulsively cast down from the wall of the Temple Mount's southeast corner (not the sanctuary's pinnacle) and tumbled into the Kidron Valley, just north of Silwan. Miraculously surviving the fall, he was pelted with stones, and then dispatched with a blow to the side of his head from a fuller's (laundryman's) club.

Flavius Josephus' account, above, notes that

"some others" were accused and stoned. Who were they? Probably other lesser-known but still dangerous brothers of the Lord: Joses, Simon, and Jude. This would be the typical progression to kill the family line, to get at the "root" of the problem. Interestingly, it was Symeon, son of Clopas (Cleopas), the first cousin of Jesus, who seems to have been assigned to be the new leader of the Church in Jerusalem after James' death, not one of his brothers.[102] Evidently there was a strong need to keep the leadership of the Jerusalem Church within the Grail family of Jesus.[103] The immediate family that remained in Jerusalem had been virtually wiped out.

But this miscarriage of justice created a backlash of monumental proportions. For Origen of Caesarea (ca. A.D. 185 to ca. 254), Eusebius and Jerome explain that Josephus records the, "fall of Jerusalem was attributed to his [James] death."[104] The early Church Father Origen wrote: "James was of such great Holiness and enjoyed so great a reputation among the people that the downfall of Jerusalem was believed to be on account of his death."[105]

The third-century church historian Eusebius gives this passage of the same cause and effect:

> The account is given at length by Hegesippus, but in agreement with Clement. Thus it seems that James was indeed a remarkable man and famous among all for his righteousness, so the wise even among the Jews thought that this was the cause of the siege of Jerusalem immediately after his martyrdom, and that it happened for no other reason than the crime that they committed against him.[106]

Eusebius notes that after the death of James the Just and the onset of the Jewish War, Christians in Jerusalem were warned by a prophecy to flee.[107] They escaped to Pella, north of Jerusalem and Judea, east of the Jordan and south of Galilee. About A.D. 65 the Jewish Christians fled the deteriorating situation in Jerusalem.[108] With the Christians gone, and food shortages and infighting among Jews increasing, the end of Israel was in sight.

THE REX DEUS LINE

And he beheld Satan; and he had a great chain [lineage] in his hand, and it veiled the whole face of the earth with darkness; and he looked up and laughed, and his angels rejoiced.

—MOSES 7:26

This section deals with a subset of the *Desposyni* ("belonging to the Lord"), those descendants of Jesus' mother called the *Rex Deus*, the descendants of Jesus himself. In Malcolm Godwin's book is an interesting layout across two pages. It shows the supposed genealogies of two major families. One he calls The Grail Guardians: the Western Realm and the other The Sons of Cain: the Eastern Realm.[109] According to him, "The sin of Cain . . . was to rob Earth of her virginity by spilling his brother's blood. Cain sinned against the Earth and yet remained united with the earth, and must eventually redeem the Earth."[110] Since Adam and Eve, it has always been a contest between two *Rex Deus* families, one righteous, and one wicked. This would be the beginning of the contest between the Shiloh Dynasty and the Master Mahon or Gadianton conspiracy of the evil *Rex Deus*.

Let us examine what might be one of the false *Rex Deus* lines, the Sadducean priestly families. They claimed descent from Zadok, the high priest who had anointed King Solomon. The Sadduceans were probably an admixture of the tribe of Judah and the tribe of Levi. They were one of the three most influential parties or schools in Judaism until just before their purge in ca. A.D. 64 and the destruction of the Second Temple in A.D. 70.[111] They were the most affluent and intellectual strata of society, with most of their members in the temple priestly class, holding the keys to the temple. They sought accommodation with Roman rule and Herodian kingship, for a mysterious purpose that we shall later see.[112]

The books of Christopher Knight and Robert Lomas dealt with this topic and were as influential at the end of the 1990s as the writings of Baigent, Leigh, and Lincoln were during the 1980s and early 1990s.[113] Most of the New Age *Holy Blood, Holy Grail* "follow-up" books insist that Christ survived the Crucifixion to foster children, who were protected by guardians of the illusive *Priory de Sion*. However, Mormon logic requires that if Jesus had children, they would be born before, not after, His crucifixion. Knight and Lomas offered an alternative view to the *Priory de Sion* hegemony for tracing the bloodline, replacing it with the *Rex Deus* theory instead.

While their understanding of a *Rex Deus* lineage has a slim chance of existing, the *Priory de Sion* has none. According to neognostics Wallace-Murphy and Marilyn Hopkins, this new theory had merit and might explain the whereabouts of the temple secrets and a bloodline:

> Another far more plausible, but little known legend speaks of a hidden, hereditary group of families who have exerted great influence over European life from before the time of Jesus to the present. They call themselves "*Rex Deus*" and claim direct descent from the twenty-four priestly families of the Temple in Jerusalem and from Jesus himself.[114]

Wallace-Murphy, Simmans, and Hopkins do not believe that God Himself is the father of Jesus but that He was descended from one of these twenty-four aristocratic priestly temple families.[115] Amazingly, none of these popularizing authors relate these families with the ancient Sadducees—but that is who these temple priests would have been. Nor do Wallace-Murphy and Hopkins accept Jesus as the major scion of the family; only later in history, they believe, because of the preachings of Paul, does this come about. According to Wallace-Murphy and Hopkins, these families were descended from the combined pedigree of the Levitical temple priests and royalty of Judah.

The Sadducees (Sons of Saddoc, Zadoc) were probably formed during the Levitical Hasmonean dynasty (142–37 B.C.) in an attempt to blend the top priestly echelons of Aaron with the remnants of the royal Judaic-Davidic political base, in order to synthesize the power of olden times.[116] "These successive rulers combined in their persons," writes Morgenstern, "the office of king and high-priest."[117] The idea was a Jewish theocracy through inter-marrying the tribes of Levi and Judah. An example of this might be the Virgin Mary, who was a rare and pure member of the House of David, while her cousin, Elizabeth, was in fact a "daughter of Aaron" (Luke 1:5). Thus we see an overlapping of tribal genealogies as planned by the Sadducees.

As discussed earlier, the bringing of the Virgin Mary from Britain, where the Sadducees knew there was a pocket of the full blood of Judah through the House of David, was possibly an orchestrated event. It could be supposed that she held great theocratic value for *Rex Deus* genetic engineering by conniving Sadducees. Significantly, Mary of Nazareth, according to Catholic legend, was raised in the temple from the age of three.[118] Perhaps this was with the view of eventually finding her a suitable husband of the House of David. The Sadducees possibly believed that with such a son from this marriage God would make him the Messiah, prophet, priest, and King to liberate Israel, restore the monarchy, and heal the desolate and waste places.

They would collaborate with the Romans until they had the perfect "Son of David" worthy to sit on the throne and usher in the age of peace and plenty. However, their carefully laid plans collapsed when Mary became pregnant out of wedlock. In their view Jesus was the bastard son of a Roman soldier, Panthera (Pandira, Panther).[119] This would have completely disqualified Him from being the Messiah and King.

This may have been the real reason why they rejected Him, even before they heard His message—which they rejected as well. Any subsequent children from Mary would also be disqualified because they would not be firstborns. The Sadducean genetically engineered program could not compare with Heavenly Father's strategy of being the father of Jesus Christ Himself. The Sadducees looked too low for the proper mate for the Virgin Mary.

The Sadducees planned to engineer a pure strain of Davidic lineage under their own auspices. This is not unlike the genetic breeding today of a perfect unblemished red heifer for a sacrifice that will lead to the rebuilding of the third temple. They would then raise a number of such "heir apparents" in the temple and in the manner they would have them raised. Then hopefully one of the firstborn children would be given the gift, talent, and charisma to be the Messiah "chosen of God." Below are four ways the *Rex Deus* lineage program would or would not work:

1. False *Rex Deus*: Uniting ever purer strains of the tribe of Judah (David) under Sadducean control, until one was worthy enough to be chosen of God to be the Messiah, prophet, priest, and King.

2. False *Rex Deus*: The Sadducean mixing of the tribes of Judah (David) and Levi (Aaron) helping to create a theocracy.

3. Non *Rex Deus*: Uniting the tribes of Judah (David) and Benjamin. Not really in the Sadducean program, but a popular idea today with most writers, who call Mary Magdalene a Benjaminite.

4. True *Rex Deus*: Uniting the purest strains of the tribes of Judah (David) and Joseph (Ephraim).

The Sadducees were involved in rationales numbers 1 and 2, attempting to establish a legitimate line of kings and priests to rule and reign in all Israel. They believed in an afterlife only through dynastic continuity, that is, by means of their posterity through chosen lineages of God. Thus this aristocratic sect, holding the temple keys and secrets, claimed to be "the" *Rex Deus* ancestry. However, the true *Rex Deus* was the lineage of Jesus Christ, but we now concentrate on the counterfeit group of the same name in order to understand how the Grail could be perverted.

One can see the Sadducean point of view, if indeed the Virgin Mary was of the lineage of All-Judah (Zerah and Perez), while Joseph was a Davidic member of one of the twenty-four aristocratic families. While rejecting Jesus as Messiah because he was illegitimate, perhaps his older brother James might have been acceptable within the inner councils,[120] if it were not for his testimony of Christ's divine parentage. Such parentage was completely alien to their theology.

While the Sadducees believed in one infinite and unknowable God, they did not believe that God might foster mortal children as Greek mythology alludes in the myths dealing with Jupiter mating with mortal women. They did not believe in angels or demons but believed that the soul died with the body. Thus they did not believe in heaven, hell, or the resurrection. In this they were somewhat similar to the gnostics and deists. They did believe in a form of "living in grace" or *karma* by obedience to purifying rituals, similar to Catholics. They were also the ancient "moral relativitists." Yet the Sadducees did not believe in fate but only free will. Flavius Josephus says of them: "Now the Sadducees, the second party, deny destiny altogether and place God beyond doing or seeing anything bad. They say that good and bad are dependent on human choice; and one may allow each of these according to one's own decision. They deny the soul's permanence as well as rewards and punishments in the underworld."[121] In this they were a little like Korihor in the Book of Mormon:

> And many more such things did he say unto them, telling them that there could be no atonement made for the sins of men, but every man fared in this life according to the management of the creature; therefore every man prospered according to his genius, and that every man conquered according to his strength; and whatsoever a man did was no crime.
>
> —ALMA 30:17

Like many Knights Templar and Fascists after them, they believed in the power of the will against fate. Neither did they believe in the atonal redemption, nor in the literal bodily resurrection of the dead.[122] They did not hold a place for the blood except as an expiation sacrifice, not a redemptive one. In all this they philosophically differed greatly from the Pharisees (elders). The chief priests supervising the temple, its maintenance, ordinances, and worship, were almost exclusively Sadducean.

Sadducean doctrines were based inclusively upon the Written Law, Torah, the Pentateuch, while the oral law of Moses and Prophets was not. They did believe in the five books of Moses and not in

continuing revelation or miracles. Because of their strict adherence to the letter of the Written Law, the Sadducees acted severely in cases involving the death penalty. They maintained the exclusive centrality of temple and constituted the religious establishment of their day.

Few have pondered the question of what happened to the Sadducees after the destruction of Jerusalem. This fugitive people disappeared from the scanty paragraphs of history. The author also wondered how the Sadducean *Rex Deus* crossed lines with the true *Rex Deus* claimants. Instead of their being part of the Zealots fleeing the clutches of Rome in 67–70 A.D., the author has another theory.

After the sycophant Sadducean (Herodian high priest, Anan ben Anan) murdered James the Just in 62–63 A.D. and the goading practices of the governor, Gessius Florius, increased, a revolt ensued against Rome and their *quislings*, the temple priests.[123] In the Dead Sea Scrolls' *Thanksgiving Hymns* the Teacher of Righteousness refers to the Sadducees as "those who seek smooth things during the last days, who walk in lies and falsehood." He continues: "I praise You, O Lord, because Your eyes remains upon me, and You deliver me from the zeal of false advisors. From *the party of the Seekers of Accommodation* have You rescued the life of the poor ones whom they plotted to destroy [the children of Jesus?], whose blood they planned to spill over the issue of Your Temple service."[124]

According to another source: "They were identified with the aristocracy and sought to ingratiate themselves with the Roman rulers by collaborating with them in keeping the populations quiescent and obedient. They were consequently less popular than the Pharisees with the ordinary people."[125]

Members of the radical separatist Pharisaic faction were called Zealots. They were followers of Judas the Galilean and one called *Sadduc*. Following the murder of James the Just, the patriotic Zealots, who Flavius Josephus called "the fourth philosophy," killed many of the collaborating Saducean temple priests. This then ushered Palestine into a rebellion against Rome and the corrupted Herodian temple (A.D. 64–73).

However, a select number of priests from the Jewish sect of Boethusian Sadducees (Zadokites) and certain imperial Sanhedrin members, who controlled the temple, escaped the Zealot and Essene purges. "Later," notes Eisenman, "they also burned all the palaces of the High Priests appointed by Herodians, all of whom appear finally to have been slaughtered, including James' nemesis Ananus."[126] We presume that not all were killed and a number of representatives from each of the aristocratic priestly families conceivably escaped.

Just before and after the destruction of the temple, the Sadducees quickly disappeared from history. On the other hand, a form of the Pharisees called Rabbinic was preserved and continues today in mainstream Judaism. It sought to reform and purify the religious practice of Judaism. But what became of the Sadducees?

The rapid disappearance of the Sadducees from the historical record may have been caused by several reasons, i.e., their extermination by the Zealots; the Roman Emperor Titus's holocaust of over 1,350,000 Jewish men, women, and children; the destruction of the temple; their assimilation into Roman culture; and later the Christianization of the Mediterranean world.[127] It is said that the Karaites hold doctrines that are, with few exceptions, the same as those of the Sadducees.[128] But in the end, the Sadducees had lost touch with what was deepest in the soul of the Jew.

Even after the Jewish-Roman War, the aristocratic Sadducees were not safe from the militant *Sicarri* assassin remnants of the defunct Zealot movement. Those remaining Sadducees concealed their identity and fled to join earlier migrations. For years the

Sadducees must have salted away places of refuge against just such a scenario as this.[129]

It is postulated that they escaped Jerusalem for Russia, Austria, and the West, especially Italy. Probably they secretly fled, first to Greece in the future Constantinople area, and then to the Calabria region, in the isolated eastern mountains of the boot in southern Italy.[130] Calabria has links between the Ordre de Sion and the Carmelites which relate to Grail studies. St. Berthold, the founder of the Carmelites, originated from Calabria.

Speculatively, a few of the Saducean leadership may have retreated to Liguria in northwest Italy. The hilltop village of Seborga, in an area two miles north of Bordighera, between Ventimiglia and San Remo was a likely hideout (see Plate 16).[131] There, on top of a small mountain, now called the Principato Seborga, they found a seductive little Eden in the Italian Flower Riviera, more notable for its rare flowers than for desert codices and underground conspiracies.[132] Its ancient name of "Castrum Sepulcri" was later changed to "Sepulcri Burgum," then to "Serporca" and ultimately to the contemporary name of Seborga (Cambiato in Sebolcaro).[133]

To this place, it is proposed, our conniving remnant secretly took their families, some inestimable sacred temple records, a few holy relics, and a large portion of their temporal wealth. Such stories of dramatic escape with sacred objects from impending destruction have been heard of many times, for example, with the lost tribes, Tephi Tea, and the Lehites. It is a recurring leitmotif.

Possibly these surviving fragments of priestly *Rex Deus* Saducean families went underground and then allegedly assimilated into the Jewish, pagan, and Christian aristocracy of Europe throughout the centuries. They ostensively "blended" into European culture. However, with their tight family connections and written records, they were able to keep their identity alive for over a millennium. Seborga once again returned to being a sleepy tiny hilltop town as the Diaspora Sadducees fanned out across the Western world.

Even as they blended in and "accepted" Christianity, they continued to have a firm resolve to return one day and reclaim Jerusalem in the Levant and establish a theocracy. Details became forgotten or twisted with time, but certain facts and energies remained clear for many centuries. Too many things in history are quickly forgotten, while others are burned indelibly into a people's psyche. The false *Rex Deus* lineages would contaminate the Grail heritage and be confused with it by a number of contemporary gnostic writers.

NOTES

1. Smith, *Teachings of the Prophet Joseph Smith* (2 May 1844), 365.
2. Starbird, *Magdalen's Lost Legacy*, 88. In fact, persecution of the Christian faith by the Jews extended beyond the A.D. 70 holocaust, deep into the Diaspora.
3. Many believe that they left in A.D. 63 or just before the Jewish uprising. I think otherwise, see below. By this time, Jesus' wives would be dead or quite elderly and could conceivably have had some great-grandchildren, which doesn't seem likely given the legends. If Jesus was married at twenty (ca. A.D. 14), then it is possible his children had children by the age of sixteen to twenty.
4. Taylor, *Coming of the Saints*, 72.
5. Eisenman, *James the Brother of Jesus*, xxxii. Eisenman dates Peter's death at A.D. 62, somewhat different from Ambelain.
6. Bernheim, *James, the Brother of Jesus*, 65.
7. Having only mended the breach through the new dynasty, that dynasty now separated from the main body of the Church, as it fled into the wilderness. By doing so, for its own safety, it inadvertently created yet another breach between the bloodline and the priesthood line.
8. Yevgeny Yevtushenko, Ukrainian poet and anti-Soviet patriot, second half of the twentieth century.
9. There is a painting that reflects this concept. See Bartolommeo de Giovanni, Italian, *The Lamentation*, courtesy of Art Gallery of Ontario, Toronto, Canada. This painting depicts Joseph of Arimathea with the Grail (jar or cruet).
10. Price, *Da Vinci Fraud*, 218. See also Perkins, *Gnostic Dialogue*, 136.
11. Tony Fieldsted is a researcher in the field of the Holy Grail from Springville, Utah.
12. Elder, *Joseph of Arimathea*, 38.
13. Rappoport, *Medieval Legends of Christ*, 291. See Collins, *Twenty-First Century Grail*, 43, and Barber, *Holy Grail*, 41. It may also be noted that Simon the Leper was reportedly the father of the Bethany sisters. Others say that it was the house of Mary Magdalene or rather Lazarus. See Voragine, *Legenda Aurea (The Golden Legend)*, Genoa (1275).
14. The Upper Chamber may mean "upper city," which was on the southwest part of the old City. To get to the Mount of Olives, they might pass to the lower city, cross the Tyropoeon Valley, head eastward across the Kidron Valley and up the Mount of Olives. The more probable is the route was over Wilson's arch across the temple mount and then across a narrow causeway to Gethsemane. The House of Caiaphas was also in the Upper City.
15. This was quite unusual because the carrying of water is considered "women's work" in the Middle East to this day. Even in twenty-first-century Russia, such is still the rural custom.
16. Schonfield, *Radical Translation and Reinterpretation*, 186.
17. It is said that one Rhoda was the servant who kept the entrance to the house upon Mount Zion. While Joseph of Arimathea was Christ's great-uncle, it was a relationship little known by most.
18. In Robert de Boron's *Joseph d'Arimathie*, Joseph is told by the Lord to recreate the Last Supper in a "[round?] table of the Grail." Later, Merlin makes a round table for King Arthur, which may possibly be the same table as that of the Last Supper and Joseph of Arimathea's table.
19. Another painting depicts this scene. See Pedro Berruguete and Workshop, Spanish, *The Last Supper* (ca. 1500) Location of artwork is unknown. Interestingly, Mary Magdalene with her jar is present in front of the company at the table.
20. Picknett and Prince, *Templar Revelation*, 20–21, 52–53. One thing we know is that Leonardo Da Vinci did not include Mary Magdalene at the table in his famous *Last Supper* fresco in Milan.
21. Prophet, *Lost Years of Jesus*, xvii–xviii. Prophet's source for this poem and its date are not given.
22. Robert de Boron, *Joseph of Arimathie*, as quoted in Prophet, *Mysteries of the Holy Grail*, xvii. Supposedly Pilate gave it

to Joseph because of years of military service.

23. Rappoport, *Medieval Legends of Christ,* 291.

24. The first mention of two cruets was from an anonymous poem published by royal printer Richard Pynson in 1520: "Thys blode in two cruettes/Joseph dyd take." It also mentions the thornbush but not the staff. There are two nearby springs at the base of the Glastonbury Tor, one called White Spring and the other Blood (Red) Spring. Supposedly Joseph of Arimathea placed the cruet of blood in one (which is high in iron content) and the cruet of sweat in the other (which is high in calcium carbonate). Supposedly one was of gold and the other of silver. See Morgan, *Holy Grail,* 55–56.

25. Perhaps one purpose for doing this would be that the sang raal would be discovered in a time when science using DNA testing would prove the Jesus Christ to Joseph Smith Jr. genealogical connection.

26. Barber, *Holy Grail,* 171. "Joseph preserved the water which he had used, which was mingled with blood, 'in a most pure vessel.'" Voragine provides yet one more version of the story. He claims in *Chronicon Januense* (ca. 1277), as quoted in Dunlop, *History of Prose Fiction,* 1:465, that a "certain vessel of emerald" used at the Last Supper was taken by Nicodemus to collect "the sacred gore [blood] which was still moist, and which had been ignominiously spilled about."

27. Unknown artist, France, *Utrecht Psalter: Catching the Blood at Calvary* (Universiteitsbibliotheek der Rijksuniversiteit, Utrecht MS 32, f. 67). A miniature ink drawing illustrating Psalm 115 from Reims in the mid-ninth century (ca. 830). Illustrated in Barber, *Holy Grail,* 121. See Van der Horst, *Utrecht Psalter in Medieval Art.* They depict a man, possibly Joseph of Arimathea, catching the blood at Calvary. This was long before the first Grail romance. The first representations have the vessel either sitting on the ground or floating in the air. However, most Italian paintings from the thirteenth to the fifteenth centuries depict the blood from the side, hands, and feet of Christ being caught by flying angels. Only a few have Joseph of Arimathea doing it, some from Christ's side and others from His hands and feet.

28. Unknown artist, *The Deposition* (twelfth century, miniature). From the collection of Abbey of Weingarten, Landesbibliothek Funda South Germany (MS Aa35, fol 81: Bildarchiv Foto Marburg). This miniature from a gospel book depicts the Deposition with Joseph of Arimathea collecting Christ's blood. This is, according to Barber, *Holy Grail,* 124 (illustration), the first evidence of this tradition, nearly a hundred years before Robert de Boron.

29. Begg and Begg, *In Search of the Holy Grail and the Precious Blood,* 43–49. Amazingly Nicodemus puts the dried blood scrapings in a leather glove, which is a symbol of Mary Magdalene, who is the patron saint to glove makers. See also Sinclair, *Discovery of the Grail,* 80. The name Nicodemus means "innocent of blood" in Hebrew. He was a Pharisee, a ruler among the Jews and a teacher of Israel (John 3:1, 10). Nicodemus was a member of the Jewish Sanhedrin, who secretly interviewed our Lord. He had a constitutional timidity that caused him to oppose, in a cautious and general way, the Sanhedrin's inquisition against Jesus.

30. Sinclair, *Discovery of the Grail,* 42, 117, 120. A seventeenth-century painting by Antoine Coypel of France, *Death of Christ,* in the Art Gallery of Ontario, Toronto, Canada, depicts Mary Magdalene collecting the blood in her hair.

31. Wuest, *New Testament,* 203.

32. Because of ritual uncleanliness, it was given to women to actually prepare the body for burial.

33. Elder, *Joseph of Arimathea,* 16.

34. Joseph placed the body in his own new tomb, located in a garden near the place where Jesus was crucified (Matthew 27:60, John 19:41). He and Nicodemus prepared the body according to Jewish burial customs, by wrapping it in linen along with seventy-five pounds of "myrrh and aloes" (John 19:40). He then rolled a stone in front of the tomb, thus sealing it. For all this, the Roman Church eventually made Joseph the patron saint of undertakers.

35. Sinclair, *Discovery of the Grail,* 49, who quotes Robert de Boron, who was probably inspired by the Apocryphal Gospel of Nicodemus, which was written in Greek sometime after the second to fifth century.

36. The Mercy Seat was the lid to the ark of the covenant box, which contained sacred relics and was placed in the Holy of Holies of the tabernacle/temple. Legend has the ark of the covenant buried at Golgotha instead of the temple mount under the Holy of Holies.

37. Another story has it that at Yom Kippur, when the blood was sprinkled on the spot where the Ark used to stand, that a crack in the foundation stone allowed the blood to trickle down to the hidden Mercy Seat in a cavern below. The blood of Gethsemane was for the mercy seat.

38. "Gospel of Nicodemus," *Lost Books of the Bible,* 75. Some had dated this Greek text to as early as the second century, but most toward the fifth century. Gregory of Tours, writing in the sixth century, references this writing.

39. As noted by Prophet, *Lost Years of Jesus,* xviii. Robert de Boron's *Joseph d'Arimathie* notes that Joseph was jailed.

40. Barber, *Holy Grail*, 119.

41. It would be improbable that he was imprisoned for forty years. It is more likely that it was forty months, which would coincide nicely with the date of his departure from Palestine with the Holy Family in A.D. 36–37.

42. Sinclair, *Discovery of the Grail*, 8.

43. John of Glastonbury, John Capgrave, the Apocryphal Acts of Pilate, and Bishop Gregory of Tours. The *Magna Glastoniensis Tabula* note that he escaped and was later pardoned.

44. Hall, *Secret Teachings of All Ages*, clxxx. Interestingly, Joseph's son-in-law, Josephus was also called the "first bishop" according to the Grail romances. See Barber, *Holy Grail*, 166.

45. Knight and Lomas, *Second Messiah*, 112. See Phillips, *Search for the Grail*.

46. Taylor, *Coming of the Saints*, 167, notes that, according to Bishop Ussher (vols. v, vi and xvii, on the authority of Valdes), St. Patrick drove the venomous snakes from Ireland through the wisdom and advice of Joseph of Arimathea. "If St. Patrick was the Saint who accomplished the work, the source of his knowledge is directly attributed to St. Joseph."

47. Kenneth Woodward in Burstein, *Secrets of the Da Vinci Code*, 53.

48. Gardner, *Illustrated Bloodline of the Holy Grail*, 90. Yes, it did become this way, but there was little problem at first.

49. The Gospel of Mary [Magdalene] [Evangelium Marie] describes a similar event to that in the *Coptic Gospel of Philip*, where Mary is explaining some doctrinal point, "But Peter loses his temper: he suggests that Mary has herself imagined what she is relating; at which she bursts into tears. Levi interposes to defend her." Doresse, *Secret Books of the Egyptian Gnostics*, 88.

50. Nag Hammadi Codes BG 8502.1, as quoted in Gardner, *Bloodline of the Holy Grail*, 99. It was presented to show that Peter was denying Christ one more time by rejecting the Magdalene.

51. The close relationship between the Virgin Mary and Mary Magdalene reminds one of the closeness of Lucy Mack Smith and Emma Hale Smith.

52. As quoted in Gardner, *Bloodline of the Holy Grail*, 122. See Nag Hammadi Codex BG 8502–1. The Gospel of Mary (Magdalene), BG, I.17: "In her book *Mary Magdalene, the First Apostle: The Struggle for Authority*, Anne Brock draws upon this tradition of conflict between Peter and Mary Magdalene to paint a chauvinistic male authoritarianism over the divine feminine nature."

53. Pistis Sophia 2.72. Another translation has it, "I am afraid of Peter because he threatened me and hateth our sex." The confrontation of Peter and Mary Magdalene is also found in the Coptic Gospel of Thomas and The Gospel of the Egyptians. See Knight and Lomas, *Second Messiah*, 91. It should be remembered that most forms of Gnosticism are anti-organized church and not particularly pro-woman.

54. Pagels, *Gnostic Gospels*, 65. Also see Gardner, *Bloodline of the Holy Grail*, 122.

55. Gardner, *Bloodline of the Holy Grail*, 122, as quoted from Nag Hammadi Codex II, 2.

56. Perhaps this is one reason why Mary Magdalene's name had been besmirched by the Catholic Church in later times.

57. The 1,260 years might mean the years from the loss of the Grail until Joseph Smith restored the Living Church in 1830. This would put the date of the Lost Grail at about A.D. 570, just after the Arthurian period and the rise of the Merovingians. This date might denote the last vestige of the priesthood line of authority on earth. King Arthur was the last known Grail king (see D&C 86:3).

58. Schonfield, *Radical Translation and Reinterpretation*, 569.

59. McConkie, *Doctrinal New Testament Commentary*, 3:516. Bruce R. McConkie says that this is backward, "[It] is refuted by the obvious fact that the Church did not bring forth Christ; [for] he is the Creator of the Church." He goes on to say that "the man child is the priesthood, a seemingly persuasive speculation, which again however must be rejected by the same line of reasoning."

60. By defining the Church of God in genealogical terms we understand it as a kingdom with the man child being the King by birthright.

61. Parley P. Pratt, in *Journal of Discourses* (10 April 1853), 1:261, either a literal descendant or specially adopted into that lineage.

62. Bernheim, *James, the Brother of Jesus*, 259.

63. M. Zvi Udley, Ph.D., quoted in Kraut, *Jesus Was Married*, 92. Christ's son would not necessarily assume the presidency but rather the office of Patriarch. This author is uncertain who Zvi Udley is and has been unable to ascertain his identity.

64. Robinson, *Nag Hammadi Library in English*, 260. See also Freke and Gandy, *Jesus and the Goddess*, 226 ff156.

65. Eusebius, *Historia Ecclesiastica* 1.12.4–5.

66. See Bernheim, *James, the Brother of Jesus*, 19.

67. Wellnitz, *Christ and the Patriarchs*, 157.

68. Matthew 1:25 does not prohibit sexual relations after Jesus' birth between Mary and Joseph.

69. Hall, *Secret Teachings of All Ages*, clxxix. According to the

Gospel of Pseudo-Matthew, Joseph the Carpenter even had grandchildren older than the Virgin Mary! That would make him old indeed.

70. Shanks and Witherington, *Brother of Jesus*, 202.

71. Taylor, *Coming of the Saints*, 73. They believed "the Messiah had come, the types and worship pointing to His advent were valued all the more perhaps on account of this, and were in no sense cast aside."

72. Robert Jones; see robertcjones@mindspring.com (2004).

73. Shanks and Witherington, *Brother of Jesus*, 113. See also Laidler, *Head of God*, 68.

74. As quoted in Laidler, *Head of God*, 69.

75. Taylor, *Coming of the Saints*, 73.

76. G. Shapiro, "The Sadducees and Jesus' Trial" (1997); see www.geocities.com. The Gadol was the people's council.

77. Epiphanius, *Panarion* (treatise on the heresies) 29.3–4, 66.21–22. This is an old tradition as seen in Epiphanius, *Panarion* 78.7, "to whom the Lord entrusted His throne on earth as first bishop."

78. Lawlor and Oulton, *Eusebius, The Ecclesiastical History and the Martyrs of Palestine*, 2:74. See also LDS scholar S. Kent Brown, "James the Just and the Question of Peter's Leadership," *Sperry Symposium*, 15, ff8. Brown also notes that he became bishop, which means to oversee. James could have become the "fatherly overseer of the Kingdom," perhaps meaning Presiding Bishop of the Church.

79. Bernheim, *James, the Brother of Jesus*, 221.

80. Eusebius, *History of the Church (Historia Ecclesiastica)*, 2.1.3; see also 4.5.3–4; 5.12.1–2.

81. Stephen was the James the Just, before James the Just. He is called "a man full of faith and the Holy Spirit" (Acts 6:5). Stephen did great wonders and miracles among the people (Acts 6:8). He was intellectually brilliant and very wise (Acts 6:9–10). He, like James three decades later, was accused before the Sanhedrin with false witnesses and stoned.

82. Eusebius, *Historia Ecclesiastica*, 2.1.2.

83. "Magdalene the Bride of Christ"; see www.spiritbride. com (2004).

84. Bernheim, *James, the Brother of Jesus*, 218. He quotes Goguel, *Birth of Christianity*, 113 n.6.

85. Eusebius, *Historia Ecclesiastica*, 2.23.4. He is quoting Hegesippus.

86. Shanks and Witherington, *Brother of Jesus*, 185, from Book 5 of the *Hypomnemata*, as quoted by Eusebius of Caesarea, *Historia Ecclesiastica*, 2.23.4.

87. Bernheim, *James, the Brother of Jesus*, 192. James, the brother of John, was martyred by Agrippa with the sword (Acts 12:2).

88. Brown, "James the Just and the Question of Peter's Leadership," *Sperry Symposium*, 11, is citing Clement of Alexandria.

89. Eusebius, *Historia Ecclesiastica*, 2.1.4. We can also add Joseph of Arimathea and Mary Magdalene to this list.

90. Bernheim, *James, the Brother of Jesus*, 193. James spoke last at meetings and summed up the discussion and announced his decision with the word *krino*, a term often used in legal writings to signify "I decree," "I decide."

91. Clementine Homilies XI:35.4. Also see Pseudo-Clementine Recognitions IV:34–35, as quoted in Bernheim, *James, the Brother of Jesus*, 270. Again, James' local not general authority is recognized.

92. See Brown, "James the Just and the Question of Peter's Leadership," *Sperry Symposium*, 11, 15. He quotes Malinine, et al., *Codex Jung—Epistula Iacobi Apocrypha*.

93. William R. Schoedel's translation in Grant, *Secret Sayings of Jesus*, 128. The phraseology seems similar to 2 Baruch 15:7, "And with regard to the righteous ones, those whom you said the world had come on their account." See also Shanks and Witherington, *Brother of Jesus*, 178–79. Another translation of this Logion in the Gospel of Thomas is an even more controversial statement, as quoted in Knight and Lomas, *Second Messiah*, 233.

94. Brown, "James the Just and the Question of Peter's Leadership," *Sperry Symposium*, 12. Brown's Ph.D. thesis from Brown University in 1967 was "James: A Religio-Historical Study of the Relations between Jewish, gnostic and Catholic Christianity in the Early Period through an Investigation of the Traditions about James, the Lord's Brother."

95. Taylor, *Coming of the Saints*, 74.

96. Shanks and Witherington, *Brother of Jesus*, 167.

97. Eisenman, *James the Brother of Jesus*, 417.

98. Josephus, *Antiquities*, 20.9.1.

99. Bernheim, *James, the Brother of Jesus*, 249. This was the Roman imperial court, called synedrion in Greek, on which the Sadducees served. The other Sanhedrin was called *bet din (Gadol)* in Hebrew, which was based on and dealt with Jewish law. See Freudmann, *Antisemitism in the New Testament*, 33.

100. Eisenman, *James the Brother of Jesus*, 413, notes Clement's Box Seven saying that it was a fuller's club, but Eisenman concurs with Josephus in saying that James was stoned and martyred.

101. Bauckham, "For What Offence Was James Put to Death?"

in Chilton and Evans, *James the Just and Christian Origins,* 202–4.

102. Schonfield, *Passover Plot.* See Eisenman, *James the Brother of Jesus,* 416, for a description of the election of Simeon bar Cleophas to succeed James according to Eusebius' account of Hegesippus. This might bolster the idea that other family members were already dead.

103. Bauckham, *Jude, 2 Peter,* 5–133. Also see Shanks and Witherington, *Brother of Jesus,* 194.

104. This does not appear in any present copies of Josephus's *Antiquities of the Jews;* these early exegetes may have had other Josephus sources. See Bernheim, *James, the Brother of Jesus,* 3, and Eisenman, *James the Brother of Jesus,* 415.

105. Origen, vir ill 2, cited in Eisenman, *James the Brother of Jesus,* 395.

106. Eusebius, *Historia Ecclesiastica,* 2.23.1–3.

107. Eusebius, *Historia Ecclesiastica,* 3.11.1.

108. Shanks and Witherington, *Brother of Jesus,* 172.

109. Godwin, *Holy Grail,* 170–71.

110. Ibid.

111. The others were the Pharisees and Essenes.

112. Joezer ben Boethus, representing the Sadducean "establishment" opposed the patriotic Zealot (Saddok) militant Pharisaic wing, which resisted the Roman rule, taxes, and moral laxity.

113. Knight and Lomas, *Hiram Key;* Baigent, Leigh, and Lincoln, *Holy Blood, Holy Grail,* and *Messianic Legacy,* and Baigent and Leigh, *Temple and the Lodge.*

114. Wallace-Murphy and Hopkins, *Rosslyn,* 97.

115. Hopkins, Simmans, and Wallace-Murphy, *Rex Deus.*

116. The books of the Maccabees are our most significant source of information about this period, in which the Jews revolted in 167 B.C. against the Syrians, Seleucids, and their allies. The dynasty commenced with Simon, the Levite brother of Judas Maccabeus, and lasted until Mark Anthony captured Jerusalem in 37 B.C.

117. Ferm, *Encyclopedia of Religion,* 325. The section on the Hasmoneans was written by Julian Morgenstern.

118. Catholic teaching, noted in the apocryphal Proto-Evangelium of James. Also see Rabbi Chaim Richman Temple Institute, "The Order of Burning the Red Heifer" (2001).

119. Quoted in Crossan and Reed, *Excavating Jesus,* 39–40. See also Laidler, *Head of God,* 134–35, which quotes Osman, *House of the Messiah,* 170. Laidler notes that in the tenth century Tol'doth Yeshu, a certain Rabbi named Jochanan was betrothed to Miriam but a man, Jesu ben Pandira (Panther; ben Stada says the *Gemara* is the same as *den Pandira*), came to her and was the true father of Jesus Christ. Laidler further explains that the Hebrew word *Pa-ndi-ra* in Egyptian is transliterated as *Pa neter ra,* which is the title of the sun god, Ra. Thus, Jesu Ben Pandira literally means "Jesus, son of Ra," the old pharaohonic title for King and God. This is quite accurate, given the nature of his miraculous conception from Heavenly Father. See Klausner, *Jesus of Nazareth,* 51–53, who says it does not mean "son of the virgin [parthenos]." Also see Hereford, *Christianity in Talmud and Midrash.* The Tol'doth Yeshu is not a part of the Talmud, but rather the "References from the Rabbis."

120. But Joseph was the descendant of Jechonias, whose sons were never to sit on the throne (Jeremiah 3:17). Perhaps the mother would have been another Mary (earlier wife of Joseph). The name Miriam (Mary) was prophesied would be the name of the Messiah's mother.

121. Josephus, *Jewish War,* 2.164–65.

122. However, some may have believed that the soul might quickly be transferred (transmigration of souls, a kind of reincarnation) to another body but would be released one day to a "nothing" existence.

123. Josephus, *Antiquities of the Jews* (200). Eisenman, *James the Brother of Jesus,* 485–86. The high priests established (appointed) by Herod, were of the Sadducean sect. The lower priests were called by some "Levites" (see page 291). These priests elevated their rank by wearing the white linen of the high priests. This brings up the question, "Were the Sadducees solely of the tribe of Levi?" It may be that many were also of the tribe of David.

124. Parentheses mine. See Robert Jones, see robertcjones@ mindspring.com (2003). Jones quotes Wise's *First Messiah* as believing that this is referring to the Pharisees, but this author believes it is dealing with the Sadducees.

125. Wigoder, *Illustrated Dictionary and Concordance of the Bible,* 876.

126. Eisenman, *James the Brother of Jesus,* 291.

127. Milman, *History of the Jews,* as quoted in Knight and Lomas, *Second Messiah,* 17. This according to various reports from Josephus.

128. Eisenman, *James the Brother of Jesus,* 16, says, "so-called Jewish 'Karaites' in the Middle Ages, who considered themselves latter day heirs to the Sadducees." They had nothing to do with "the Sons of Zadok" from the Essene Qumran community; therefore we call Sadducees "Zadokites" to distinguish between them.

129. There is no known evidence of any safe haven for the Sadducees. But given their intelligence, wealth, and particularly their unpopularity, they would have thought of some ancient Swiss-type escape route.

130. The Sadducean Rex Deus families probably landed her

first before going onward, with several staying in this region. Italy, either north or south, was ideal because of the sanctuary afforded the Sadducees by the Roman Empire.

131. Principato di Seborga, an independent principality near Bordighera. In the distance can be seen the French Riveria. This was the supposed hiding place for the Sadducees after their escape from Jerusalem.

132. "Riviera of Flowers" is noted for cultivating and exporting flowers, especially carnations, roses, mormosa, broom and violets.

133. Seborga, Mille anni di storia (Seborga Agosto Booklet, 1963, 3rd reprinting, 1995), 17. The name means "city of sepulchers," or cemetery, perhaps because a king or important dignitary of unknown identity died in the vicinity and they made a sepulcher for him.

CHAPTER TWELVE

THE PATRIARCHAL GRAIL BLOODLINE

*Immediately after the passion of Christ, Joseph of
Arimathea . . . proceeded to cultivate the Lord's
Vineyard, that is to say, England.*[1]

The Holy Grail, or patriarchal bloodline, of Christ became lost even to its
own birthright lineage. God tended
the vineyard with a subtle hand. As the
secret progeny grew, it lost memory of its own heritage.
However, the Grail's mystique continued, and it engendered a veneration, which led to a search or quest for
its roots. Unfortunately, its meaning became obscured
and when its Seekers lost the vision of what they were
after, they redoubled their efforts. John Matthews
notes that Grail author Wolfram von Eschenbach
". . . also indicates that the disposition of the Grail
lineage is a secret known only to the angels."[2] Its protection came not only from anonymity but also in
increasing its numbers, as Wolfram attests: "Maidens
are given away from the Grail openly, men in secret,
in order to have progeny . . . in the hope that these
children will return to serve the Grail and swell the
ranks of its company."[3]

Eventually the veneration of the Holy Grail became a mystery religion or secret gospel in its own
right, prone to the distortions of men and devils. On
one hand this worship became the basis for knighthood, which stressed these concepts: sacrifice, duty,
care of the poor, courtesy, and the idealization of
women.[4] On the other we find cultic cabals and corrosive conspiracies.

Before the true Grail blossomed, this treasure
first needed to be buried in rich soil. Quietly planted
deep, the Grail seed began to germinate and take
root. Slowly it began to cover the rocky wilderness.
Its roots, stems, and branches can only be discovered
through patriarchal blessings, Urim and Thummim,
and eventually scientific DNA analysis.

JESUS' SEED SECRETED AWAY

"Non dice reil lese crita abboce." (Do
not say the secret out loud.)[5]

Religious writer Dean F. W. Farrar aptly remarked,
"We seem to trace in the Synoptists a special reticence

about the family at Bethany."[6] All became "hush, hush" for this family among the followers of Jesus after the crucifixion. Does fear for their personal safety explain why the Magdalene and Bethany sisters' story is so deeply shrouded in mythology? If political and religious circumstances had been different, the eldest son of Jesus Christ would have been King of All Israel and quite possibly the entire world. The Holy Grail, more than just being a precious chalice, was the royal bloodline through Christ's progeny.

Needless to say, these descendants would be costly cargo and of absolute importance to our story and the history of the world. The chief custodians of that secret and sacred lineage were the mothers, John the Beloved, then Joseph of Arimathea, and several generations of Grail guardians. John was the only one of the Twelve Apostles not to desert Jesus after His arrest. This loyalty prompted the Savior to place His mother in his protective household (John 19:26–27).

On the other hand, it may be that Joseph's guardianship began when the Virgin Mary's husband died, some years before. Or, as we read in the *Cotton. MS. Titus* manuscripts, "St. John, while evangelizing Ephesus, made Joseph *Paranymphos*."[7] *Paranymphos* is a Greek term for "Guardian," and one could assume that it meant the steward of the Holy Family. The guardianship of the bloodline was placed in Joseph of Arimathea's hands by Apostle John the Revelator and not by some secret society.

Because of persecution from the Sadducees, scribes, Herodian tetrarchs and the fearsome Romans, the members of the Holy Family were forced to flee Palestine. The stoning of Stephen in A.D. 35 was the signal for the onset of anti-Christian persecutions, which forced the Holy Family and others to flee Jerusalem.[8] (Acts 6–8) During this period of unrest the family possibly escaped northward toward Ephesus. Although popularizing writers such as Hopkins, Simmans, and Wallace-Murphy were

willing to make up stories, this one has some small resonance of truth: "However, as the family of a criminal known as 'the King of the Jews', Mary Magdalene and her children would have been forced to flee in order to escape the vengeance of both the Romans and the House of Herod. The *Rex Deus* sagas recount how the children of Jesus were parted in an attempt to ensure their security and the continuation of his bloodline."[9]

It may be that some of the Grail children were split up at this early date. The killing of the children of Jesus would be Pharaoh's attempt to kill Moses and Herod the Great's earlier "Massacre of the Innocents." It was the prime directive of both the Romans and the Sadducees. "But, whenever possible," writes Gardner, "they were pursued to the death—hunted down like outlaws and put to the Roman sword by Imperial command."[10] In 1854, Orson Hyde powerfully speaks of Christ's children and this distinct possibility:

> They had no father to hold them in honorable remembrance; they passed into the shades of obscurity, never to be exposed to mortal eye as the seed of the Blessed One. For no doubt had they been exposed to the eye of the world, those infants might have shared the same fate as the children in Jerusalem in the days of Herod, when all the children were ordered to be slain under such an age, with the hopes of slaying the infant Savior. They might have suffered by the hand of the assassin, as the sons of many kings have done who were heirs apparent to the thrones of their fathers.[11]

It would be essential, after having killed Jesus for being "King of the Jews," to also destroy any potential heirs. The Virgin Mary's painful memories of this slaughter must have haunted the Holy Family as they prepared to escape. Mary Magdalene and the Bethany sisters surely knew of these stories and keenly felt anxiety for their children. Micah 4:8–10 gives a poetic cast to their plight:

> As for you, O Magdal-eder, watch-
>   tower of the flock, O stronghold of
>   the daughter of Zion,
> The former dominion will be restored
>   to you;
> Kingship will come to the daughter of
>   Jerusalem.
> Why do you now cry out aloud?
> Have you your king?
> is thy councilor [husband] perished?
> for pangs have taken thee as a woman
>   in travail.
> Be in pain and labor to bring forth, O
>   daughter of Zion,
> like a woman in travail:
> for now shalt thou go forth out of the
>   city,
> and thou shalt dwell in the field.
> And thou shalt go even to Babylon
>   [the world];
> there shalt thou be delivered;
> there the Lord shall redeem thee,
> from the hand of thine enemies.

This scripture seems to be directed to Mary Magdalene, who has lost her husband and is pregnant. She must flee her adversaries and go into the world and wait her time until her posterity regains Zion from their enemies. The mystery of the Holy Grail is an epic play with several acts and many actors. So complex, enigmatic, profound, and cryptic is its message that to the unknowing it is merely the confusing miasma of bygone prophets, troubadours, and romancers. Even the poets of this holy drama were never quite sure what the script meant.

Starbird concludes, "Was it too dangerous to speak aloud about this woman in the first generation of Christianity?"[12] In one of the earliest gentile references to the sacred marriage and lineage, the noted mythographer Robert Graves wrote a novel entitled *King Jesus* in 1946. Starbird summarizes its plot: "That Jesus' lineage and marriage were concealed from all but a select circle of royalist leaders. To protect the royal bloodline, this marriage would have been kept secret from the Romans and the Herodian tetrarchs, and after the crucifixion of Jesus, the protection of his wife and family would have been a sacred trust for those few who knew their identity. All reference to the marriage of Jesus would have been deliberately obscured, edited or eradicated."[13]

The unknown author of "Magdalene the Bride of Christ" romance offers this cautionary note, "We have seen from history that the physical danger to his family and followers would have been reason enough to remove Jesus' marriage from the record."[14] Similarly, just two years after Jesus' resurrection, the Grail Seed had to be hidden to avoid danger, otherwise they would perish. The medieval Grail romancers did not understand the Grail's plain and precious meaning.

The Grail guardian (*paranymphos*) Joseph of Arimathea now takes center stage. After being targeted by the Romans and Sadducees, they speedily fled the persecutions, which were now beginning to fully rage.[15] Though a number of Jewish Christians probably fled north into Syria, Lebanon, and Ephesus, leading members of the Grail family, according to legend, were captured by the Jews (Sadducees).

These priests did not have the authority to outright put the family to death, a right reserved for Romans. Supposedly the Holy Family were put adrift into the

Mediterranean Sea near Caesarea Maritima in a ruinous boat without sails, oars, rudder, or drinking water by the vengeful Sadducees.[16] One could hazard a guess that their reasoning went something like this: "If they are of God, He will save them, and if not, the bottom of the sea will have them, but at least we are rid of them." Perhaps their consciences were lightly salved by this machination.

Legendary sources state that they traveled in a rudderless boat named *Stella Maris* ("Star of the Sea") guided by providence. Being cast out to sea was fortuitous for the traveler Joseph of Arimathea who was at home at sea. First they probably came to Cyprus, which had trade connections with Joseph of Arimathea.[17]

Then they supposedly went to Alexandria, Egypt.[18] Perhaps, as Taylor believes, they then sailed to Cyrene in North Africa,[19] and then toward the seaport of Marseilles (Massilia) in southern France or just west of it. Finally after various adventures they arrived in Britain.[20] The fourth-century manuscripts *Vindicta Salvatoris* and *Evangelium Nicodemi*, both in the Vatican Library, attest that Joseph of Arimathea and companions fled Palestine and settled outside of the Roman Empire, somewhere in the far north.[21]

Some say the route they took began in the southern part of Jaffa (Joppa), or even Ephesus, depending upon the version cited.[22] Ephesus is appealing because supposedly John and the Virgin Mary went there to preach. Even the Frankish historian, Bishop Gregory of Tours (544–595), supports the idea that Mary Magdalene went to Ephesus.[23] But placing the Holy Family in the rickety boat was no problem for the skilled mariner, Joseph of Arimathea. Joseph had often plied the shipping lanes and was undoubtedly familiar with sailing. Legend has it that he was steeped in the tin trade and probably followed the familiar Phoenician or Asherite route for tin in which he had many contacts and friends for support.

All versions trace the Holy Family and disciples to the area of Marseilles, where the apostle Philip would later go. According to the late *Annales Ecclesiasticae* (1601), the Vatican librarian Cardinal Caesar Baronius found a pertinent ancient manuscript. Baronius described the voyage of a company of the Lord's family and friends.[24] It recorded that they first went to Marseilles in A.D. 35 and then to the nearby port of Narbonne with its large Jewish population. Narbonne was also a center of the tin trade, with which Joseph of Arimathea was, of course, well acquainted.[25]

Joseph of Arimathea, the Virgin Mary, Mary Magdalene, Martha her sister, and at least twelve others found their way out of Palestine. Other sources place the number at exactly seventy-two.[26] This number does not include the names of any of Jesus' children, who were probably called the "Children of Joseph of Arimathea." But ultimately the escape for the safety of Christ's offspring was the *raison d'etre* of the expedition. Following is a partial passenger manifest drawn from several legends:[27]

1. Joseph of Arimathea, as the leader, proceeds to Wales and the west country of Britain.

2. The Virgin Mary continues on to her homeland in western Britain.

3. Mary Magdalene also goes to Britain and possibly returns to Aix-en-Provence at St. Baume.[28]

4. Mary of Bethany (perhaps the same person as Mary Magdalene) continues to Britain and then possibly back to southern France.

5. Martha went to Britain and then possibly back to Tarascon in Southern France.

6. Lazarus, the brother of the Bethany sisters, stayed on in Marseilles and became its first Christian bishop.

7. Mary Jacobe, the wife of Cleopas and mother of James "the Less" and Joseph. She stayed at Les-Saintes-Maries-de-la-Mer.

8. Mary Salome (Helena), a midwife, stayed at Les-Saintes-Maries-de-la-Mer.

9. Trophimius stays on in Marseilles. Is this the Triphonius who goes to Britain?

10. Maximin (Maximinus), moved to the vicinity of Auvergne in Aix-en-Provence and accompanied Mary Magdalene in preaching in this area.

11. Cleon goes to Britain.

12. Eutropius goes to Orange in southern France.

13. Sidonius (Restitutus, Cedon, and Sedonius), "the man born blind," lives in Auvergne and then goes to Britain.

14. Martial, with his parents Marcellus and Elizabeth, were perhaps the last [family] to break off from the group. They tarried in Limoges (Lemovices) in Aquitaine in France.

15. Saturnius goes to Toulouse and finally to Britain.

16. Marcella, the handmaid of Mary and Martha, goes to an unknown location.

17. Zachaeus, the publican in the gospels, remained at the romantic town of Rocamadour to spread the Good News.

18. Sarah the Egyptian (gypsy), handmaid of Mary Jacobe and Mary Salome, stayed at Les-Saintes-Maries-de-la-Mer.[29] It is said that when the ship was set adrift, she cast herself into the sea to join her mistresses

and by the help of Salome was brought into the boat.[30]

They landed in Provence safely at the tiny seaside village of Ratis (Les-Saintes-Marie-de-la-Mer) in the wetlands of the Camargue delta of the Rhône River (see Plate 17, general view of town).[31] The beach was sandy, making for secure landing on a forlorn and isolated region. Nobody would be looking for them there, and they organized themselves. Then, after ascertaining their safety and acquiring necessities, they began to preach the gospel in the region of Arles (Arelate), Marseilles (Massilia), and Narbonne in Provence.

One of the earliest visual references of Mary Magdalene's life in France is found in the stained glass windows of the Gothic masterpiece, Chartres Cathedral. It depicts her arriving by boat. Divine providence saved her and others as they landed at Les-Saintes-Maries-de-la-Mer. A few stayed on in Provence, while others pressed onward to Britain. It should be noted that the word for Grail, *graal*, is a Provençal word.

And what of these events in the minds of those left behind? Insiders purposefully denied that Jesus was married and had a family. As the years receded, and events became obscured in memory, the "lost Grail family" at first was secret history, then an obscure memory, then a myth, and finally a heresy.

ON TO GLASTONBURY AND GLAESTINGABURH

Joseph brought with him to Britain the Pledge, or the Chalice used by the Savior.[32]

We need not believe that the Glastonbury legends are records of facts; but the existence of those legends is a very great fact.[33]

The safety of the Holy Family could not be guaranteed in Roman Gaul (France). They had to escape the clutches of the Imperial Roman and Jewish prejudice. The first concern of the troupe was for the Grail children and second for the Virgin, Mary Magdalene, and the Bethany sisters. As the group traveled on, their numbers dwindled. They would leave Mary Salome and Mary (Jacobe) Cleopas with Sara the servant at Les Saintes-Maries-de-la-Mer.[34] For safety's sake they could not all remain together.

Early legend has Lazarus becoming the first Bishop of Marseilles, and Maximinus becoming the first bishop of Aix (Aquensem). Supposedly, Maximinus had special protectorship of Mary Magdalene, while Parmenas the first bishop of Avignon, took care of Martha.[35] Martha, legend has it, quelled the dragon of the Rhône at Tarascon.[36] While we hear little of her, most sources cite that she continued to live in Tarascon of Provence for the remainder of her life.[37] However, it is difficult to ascertain precisely the specific details of the Holy Family's movements.[38]

It is believed that the small party headed by Joseph of Arimathea went up the Rhône River past Arles. Elizabeth Clare Prophet notes that they went from Marseilles and quickly left the Rhône River to Figeac, Rocamadour, Limoges, and then to Morlaix.[39] In some reports they proceeded onward to Morlaix in Brittany, France, while other legends say they went slightly east to Mont-Saint-Michel.[40]

Then perhaps, they crossed the Channel, to Cornwall's St. Michael's Mount, called Ictis (or Mictis, Michel), near Penzance and Marazion. This was certainly a logical step.[41] This was not unlike the Arthurian voyage to these same Cornish coasts, of Tristan with La Belle Iseult (Isolde, Isould) to King Mark[42] (see Plate18).[43]

As with almost everything dealing with the Holy Grail, there are competing arguments and legends.[44] A new theory, forwarded by Steve Blake and

Scott Lloyd, says that the "real" Avalon is "Located in the ancient region of Gwynedd in North Wales, in an area referred to as the Realm of Affalach that was also the geographical location associated with Annwn."[45] It proclaims that the Glastonbury in Somerset was a medieval fraud and absorbed traditions of Glaestingaburh on the Dee River.[46] We shall first examine the traditional theory.

Joseph's party probably chose not to travel overland through Cornwall because of the large number of relatives they had there. This was a secret mission and the fewer that knew about Christ's children, the better. They very well could have sailed around Land's End, making for the Jesus Well near Padstow. Then they continued onward to the Paradise area of the Severn Sea, entering the estuaries of the Parrett and Brue Rivers, then through the waterway to Godney, the Port of Glastonbury. From there it is but a short distance to a cluster of islands known as Glastonbury in Somerset, not far from the tin mines owned by Joseph of Arimathea in the nearby Mendip Mountains.[47]

These twelve Glastonbury islands along the Brue and Parrett stream made up the legendary Isle of Avalon.[48] There is a nineteenth-century stained-glass window at the All Saints Church in Langport in the West Country, depicting Joseph of Arimathea on his way to Avalon. Here the Holy Family found Glastonbury's Holy Tor and Chalice Well.[49] These sites were, in an earlier period, revered to be manifestations of Annwn, the Other-world and Gwynn ap Nudd, the British god Nodens, King of the Fairies, and Lord of Glastonbury Tor.[50]

Legend states that the Holy Family's boat made final landfall in the vicinity of what is now Bridgewater Bay, near Highbridge, after a disastrous excursion into Wales.[51] Another tradition has it that they arrived at Barrow Bay in Somerset and continued the eleven miles inland to Glastonbury.[52] They proceeded in a straight tract, perhaps using geomantic divination, cross-country, "following a route of antique ancestry, a route originally used by Phoenician or Asherite tin traders."[53]

When the Holy Family stepped from the boat in early January of A.D. 37, they were exhausted from their long journey. This gave the name of the location as "Wearyall Hill." There Joseph of Arimathea reportedly thrust his staff into the ground. This walking staff may have been Jesus' very own staff, for Joseph as "His nearest male relative had the disposal of our Lord's belongings. It was certainly not Joseph's staff for by Israel law his staff must pass to his eldest son and was often made in a death-bed ceremony."[54] Like Aaron's budding and blossoming rod, Joseph's staff was also planted (Numbers 17:8). From it sprang the white thorn that never failed to blossom at Christmas[55] (see Plate 19). It flowers at the old Christmas day, around January fifth and sixth (see Plate 20).[56]

When Joseph of Arimathea and his twelve companions arrived at Glastonbury,[57] they were greeted cordially by Celtic King Gweirydd (Gweyreidd) of Siluria (Cornwall, Somerset, and Gloucester).[58] The name of the location of this island (*ynys*) in the Welsh documents sometimes is given as *Aballach*.[59] *Ynys Wydrin* meant glassy, as in vitreous.[60] Thus "glassy island" probably meant Glastonbury.[61] It was here that Joseph of Arimathea came on his mission (see Plate 21).[62]

Because of his prestige, Joseph was granted by the king twelve hides of land around Glastonbury, one for each of his companions.[63] There he and his brother disciples settled in Avalon (Glastonbury).[64] These twelve hides, the "Hallowed Acres of Christendom," remained holdings of free land for many centuries, as corroborated by the *Domesday Book* of 1086:

> The Home of God, in the great Monastery of Glastonbury, called the Secret of The Lord. This Glastonbury Church possesses in its own Villa XII hides of land which have never paid tax.[65]

Another tradition declares the Glastonbury is a twelfth-century fraud and absorbed the traditions associated with Avalon in North Wales and that the Somerset location assumed an unmerited significance. The Welsh name would be Yny Wytherin (Wydrin), which was the original name of the town before it received its Saxon name.[66] Geoffrey Ashe believes it was derived from the Saxon tribe who colonized the site in the seventh century, calling it "burh of the Glaestings."[67] It was often called Glastonia or Glaestingaburh.[68]

This theory has Joseph of Arimathea coming to the Wirral peninsula and the Realm (Isle) of Avalon, nearly two hundred miles from Somerset. Joseph and his troupe supposedly landed in the Wirral Peninsula then traveled up the Dee River.[69] According to the Cistercian *L'Estoire del Saint Graal*, Joseph was imprisoned by Crudel, a tyrannical king of North Wales. They were released and given land in Avalon at what became Glaestingaburh.

It might be that Joseph first landed in Somerset, but after the invasion of the Romans he migrated to North Wales and thus the legends became melded. Joseph of Arimathea came to Glaestingaburh in about the same time, A.D. 63, as some legends attest, and Glastonbury in Somerset in A.D. 37. This synthesis of the two positions may be the best "holding pattern" until further information comes available.

Tradition has it that Joseph carried two cruets (vessels or vials), one of gold and lead and the other of silver and lead. Together they formed the Holy Grail and were called "Red" and "White," symbolizing the blood and water that issued from the wounds of Christ's side at the crucifixion. Supposedly these were buried near Chalice Hill in Glastonbury.

The two cruets may represent the two families of Jesus Christ, the Red for Mary of Magdalen and the White for Mary and Martha of Bethany.[70] In a sense, these bloodlines rightly explain that the Holy Grail was plural, not singular. There were at least two vessels holding the patriarchal bloodline of Christ not one. Another way of looking at it has the Y chromosome of the *white* male side (Christ's) and the mitochondrial DNA of the *red* female side. Each cruet in turn filled other vessels in the expanding descendancy of the Savior.

THE LORDSHIP OF THE GRAIL

On whom is laid much power.

—D&C 113:4

The history of the descendants of the royal Grail bloodlines of Christ begins to assert itself at this point. These bloodline histories were preserved for centuries in a land said to be saturated with the lineage of Ephraim and the Davidic–Scarlet Thread Judah. Sacred and profane legends attempt to delineate what happened in that remote time, but still it remains in obscurity. We have the unenviable position of working from the ambiguous to the vague. Perhaps the confusion was intentional to give protective cover to the Grail children. Which leads to the question, who were the children of Jesus Christ that Joseph brought to Glastonbury?

In a bizarre book, *Jesus the Man*, published in 1992, Dr. Barbara Thiering claims that Jesus and Mary Magdalene were married and she bore Him a girl and two boys.[71] According to Thiering's preposterous assertion, the Magalene abandoned Him after the failed crucifixion attempt, which he survived by about thirty years.[72] Then Christ supposedly remarried. Thiering, a lecturer at the School of Divinity at Sydney University, bases her claims on a new reading of the Dead Sea Scrolls, which did not directly apply to Jesus Christ.

According to the equally unreliable Laurence Gardner, Mary Magdalene had three children from Jesus; a daughter named Tamar and two sons, Jesus Justus the Younger, and Josephus (Josephes).[73]

Thiering, Gardner, and the authors of *Holy Blood, Holy Grail*, like so many in this field, bend to their own purpose whatever material crosses their path.[74]

Margaret Starbird produces the same ideological engineering when she proclaims with no proof that Jesus Christ and Mary Magdalene had a single child named Sarah (Hebrew for "princess") and at the age of twelve she was taken to southern France.[75] She believes that the child proved that Jesus was a normal person. Sarah, she claims, probably did not have any children.[76] The illusive M. Zvi Udley somehow found evidence that Martha had children by Jesus as well:

> Orthodox Christians have purposely destroyed valuable historical evidences which would prove embarrassing to them; that such was probably the case here is suggested by the fact that several ancient writers imply that Simeon the Bishop of Jerusalem, and President of the Church (died c. 106 A.D.), was of the family of Jesus.
>
> It would be only natural for Jesus' son, when he was old enough to succeed James, the brother of the Lord, on his death, to the Presidency of the Church. In all probability Simeon was a son of Jesus and Martha, and was that child who appeared at the crucifixion.[77]

As is common among some pseudohistorical writers, only stating the proposition is considered proof enough. However, although Udley gives no evidence, the suggestion of a child between Jesus and Martha plausibly hints at a polygamous marriage. Other names from the Grail romances then begin to crop up. No other figures after Joseph of Arimathea are more noticed than his supposed sons: Adam, Josephus

(Josephes), Brân the Blessed, and his son-in-law Bron, (Hebrons) husband to his daughter Enygeus (Anna).[78] These "children of Joseph of Arimathea" may have been, in reality, Jesus' literal offspring, thus called for their own protection. Then confusion sets in, as there are conflicting accounts of the identity of each of these characters of the Shiloh Dynasty.

A leading candidate for "son of Jesus" may be Josephus, the "son" of Joseph of Arimathea.[79] Josephus crossed the sea to come to Britain. According to the Romances, the Lord Himself consecrated Josephus as the first bishop of the church, "as sovereign pastor, after Me, to watch over my new sheep."[80] When the devil attacked some people who refused baptism, Josephus tried to protect them. In doing so his thigh was wounded by an angel for interfering.[81]

In the *Quest of the Holy Grail,* it is Josephus who grants Galahad's petition to view the Grail. Here Josephus opens the ark containing the Grail and has a vision. Galahad does not know him until Josephus reveals who he really is: "Learn then," he said, "that I am Josephus, son of Joseph of Arimathea, whom Our Lord has sent you for companion. And do you know why he has sent me rather than another? Because you have resembled me in two particulars: in that you have contemplated the mysteries of the Holy Grail, as I did too, and that you are a virgin (pure) like myself."[82]

Sir Thomas Malory of Warwickshire (–1471), wrote a tale of the White Knight. Josephes informs King Evalach that he will die unless converted to the true faith. The King is baptized and given the *Shield of the Most Worthy* (azure and silver shield with the red cross of Joseph of Arimathea as noted in *Perlesvaus*), which was supposedly the supernatural white shield of the Savior Jesus Christ Himself.

Contrary to the united belief of all scholars dealing with the subject of the *Shield of the Most Worthy,* we are not talking about a piece of armor for battle. Rather, it is probably the white cloth temple garment, "the shield" of Jesus Christ, which the White Knight wears. By wearing these "robes of the priesthood" of "white samite," Tolleme would be unable to kill King Evalach, because if he were worthy the robes would be a protection and shield.[83]

Josephes went on a mission to Britain where the tale was undoubtedly told and worked itself into the folklore of the Briths. Malory notes in *Le Morte d'Arthur* that eventually the shield was retrieved by Sir Galahad.[84] "Thereafter," in the dying words of Bishop Josephus, "the last of my lineage shall have it about his neck, that [he] shall do many marvelous deeds."[85] Does "have it about his neck" mean to wear it, as in a garment? Could we be talking about a temple garment and is Joseph Smith Jr. the "last of my lineage"?

The medieval poet Robert de Boron of Burgundy writes that Joseph of Arimathea was joined in Britain by a small company including his daughter, Anna (Enygeus) and her husband Brân.[86] According to tradition, Anna was a cousin to Mary, the mother of Jesus.[87] Anna supposedly married into the royal line of the Silurian Arch-druid the elder, Brân the Blessed (Bendigeidfran), from which it is theorized the Welsh House of Tudor descended.[88]

It is difficult to delineate exactly who or which Brân is being spoken of when we say Brân the Blessed.[89] Legend states that Joseph entrusted the Grail to Brân, who may as a child have been one of his companions and the son of Jesus and Mary.[90] This may be the same figure as the great Celtic hero and protector of Britain, also called Brân the Blessed.

The Castle of the Fisher King, according to Loomis and Godwin, would have been that of Castell Dinas Brân near Llangolan in Denbighshire, North Wales, by the sacred River Dee and near the "Spoils of Annwn."[91] This ancient town was called Glaestingaburh, and quite possibly named after Glastonbury, in Somerset[92] (see Plate 22).[93]

Brân was probably, after Josephus, the next "Guardian of the Grail." He may have been, in fact,

Josephus's son. In the Grail romances it notes that Sir Perceval realizes the Grail and *serves the father of the Fisher King* (who is never mentioned before or afterward in the account)."[94] In many accounts, Brân is called the "Rich Fisher" or the "Fisher King." Although other authors do not pick up on this idea, the Grail serves Jesus Christ, the father of the Fisher King.

It was in Robert de Boron's ca. 1212 poem, *Joseph d'Arimathie* (sometimes called *Merlin*), that Christ appears to Joseph of Arimathea in prison with the Grail cup, telling him that he will be the guardian of the vessel and is instructed in its mysteries. "However," writes Grail scholar John Matthews:

> These [mysteries] were not to be spoken of aloud or passed on to everyone, but were to be kept as part of the "Secrets of the Savior" and relayed only to those who formed the "family" of the Grail. Later, as Joseph is dying, the voice of the Holy Spirit speaks to him, *telling him that he has established a lineage which will continue until, in a far-off time, one will come who shall achieve the Grail.*[95]

He is then told by Christ that the vessel is to be called "calice."[96] Then a voice from the "calice" warns Joseph that one among them is guilty of lust and also instructs him to find a round table to commemorate the Last Supper and for Bron to catch a fish. Thus Bron or Brân becomes the Fisher-King guardian of the Grail by instruction from Joseph of Arimathea.[97] When Joseph names Bron as his successor, the Fisher-King, an Angel commands him to tell Bron: "The holy words which are sweet and precious, gracious and full of pity, whose proper name is to be called *the secrets of the Grail*"; Joseph does so and also writes them down.[98] He then demonstrates the secrets to Bron "very privately." The fact that

Joseph "demonstrates" the secrets implies that there is a ritual at the heart of the matter.

Knowledge, authority, and sealing are best conveyed through ritual. The ultimate source of such ritual must come from heavenly intervention. Legend has it that the Fisher-King lived only on the communion host, which came directly from Heaven and the Holy Spirit and not from or through the Church of Rome.[99] Thus this King had another line of authority to sustain his spirituality, a line not stemming from Italy.

A generation later, Robert de Boron writes, Joseph of Arimathea, by power of investiture or seneschal, took Christ's place at the table. One chair at the table was kept empty, the "seat perilous," the one originally vacated by Judas. Graham Phillips explains: "In each romance the Grail or Grails are kept by the family of Perceval, the direct descendant of Joseph of Arimathea. The [Grail] authors go to considerable lengths to explain this lineage and its significance—Joseph is appointed as Grail guardian by Christ himself. Here lies the Grail's importance—it is a visible, tangible symbol of an alternative apostolic succession."[100] In truth it is not an "alternate" apostolic succession, but rather the "other" half of the double lineage (bloodline and priesthood line) of authority and succession.

This stewardship was only to be filled by a son, Alain (Alein le Gros) or a grandson (Perceval/Parzifals/Peredur) of Bron. The Grail guardianship was handed from Josephus to Alain.[101] Eventually Bron's wife gave birth to twelve children, thus quickly extending the Grail family. Alain was the foremost of Bron's twelve sons.[102] After the death of his uncle (grandfather?) Josephus, he became the keeper of the Grail.[103] Alain was destined to be the father of a paramount Grail knight, Sir Perceval. When Bron departed from the world, Perceval became the keeper of the Grail.[104] The following genealogy figure is presented, realizing that the whole subject is convoluted and impossible to prove.

Most Grail legend authors have Galahad, the son

FIGURE 7[105]

POSSIBLE GENERATIONS OF THE SHILOH-DYNASTY

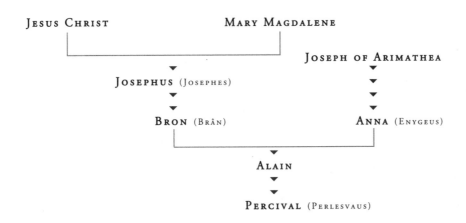

of Lancelot de Lac and Lady Elaine, as being a direct descendant of Joseph of Arimathea.[106] Robert de Boron insists that Perceval (Percival) was the grandson of Bron.[107] Confusion of genealogy is to be expected with the plethora of legends that exist. Nevertheless, Joseph of Arimathea was the Grail Guardian, not the Grail Father—Jesus Christ, Himself was that.

There were four major knights of the Grail legend, including Gawain (the forerunner of Perceval), Galahad, Lancelot, and Bors. Three actually achieve the quest, Galahad, Perceval and Bors. Lancelot is disqualified because of his affair with Guinevere. The ordinary man, Bors, strives to reach the infinite and succeeds, which is the true meaning of the Grail Quest.

Most romances have Bors, Perceval, and the pure Galahad as cousins. Interestingly, the once Queen of the Waste Land predicted that all three were destined to find the Grail. Only he, the red armored knight Galahad, will sit upon that terrible throne at the Round Table. This young untutored lad whose father was killed in battle and is therefore called the "Son of the Widow Lady," impetuously sits upon the seat (Siege Perilous), which instantly splits. Although

he will suffer greatly for his rashness, because he is of the Grail Lineage, he was spared the pit.

Galahad is able to sit on the Perilous Seat. The imposter, Moyses, is the only one who does not feel nourished by the fish (Christ?), and insists on sitting on the empty seat and is swallowed up promptly.[108] Only the one who achieves the Grail may sit there.

The confused environment of the first generations after Christ is to be expected. So much has been lost to bardic symbolic expression. But to what use or effect were these Grail children? What purpose did the Lord have for them? The always-intelligent Richard Barber surmises they were leaven to the world: "The function of this chivalric brotherhood is not only to guard the Grail, but also to maintain order in lands where the succession was in doubt because there was no male heir: knights were sent secretly from the Grail to marry the heiresses of the lands and restore peace. Girls chosen to serve the Grail were given openly in marriage. . . . The Grail company acts as a stabilizing influence in an unstable world."[109]

Perhaps they helped legitimize the royal pedigrees for the Welsh of Henry Tudor, the Plantagenets, and the Scottish Stuart lines of British kings.[110] The blood of Christ may well have been spread to most of the royal families of Europe by the end of the eighteenth century. This is the "reasoned leadership" that leavened Europe and then America and led to the restoration of the grail in the *Novis Orbis*.

NOTES

1. Lewis, *St. Joseph of Arimathea at Glastonbury,* 35.
2. Matthews, *King Arthur and the Grail Quest,* 130. Von Eschenbach was the German author of Parzival.
3. Wolfram, as quoted in Matthews, 130. The quotation continues: "As to those who are appointed to the Grail, hear how they are made known. Under the top of the Stone an inscription announces the name and lineage of the one summoned to make the glad journey [to the temple]. Whether it concerns girls or boys, there is no need to erase their names, for as soon as a name has been read it vanishes from sight! Those who are now full-grown came here as children. Happy the mother of any child destined to serve here. . . . Such children are fetched from many countries and forever after are immune from the shame of sin and have a rich reward in heaven."
4. These were the codes of chivalry, which permeated Western Europe where the blood of Israel was the strongest. The rights of men and women and tolerance of opinion began through the mixture of Hebrew blood and the Grail heritage of Christianity.
5. A paleo-Christian inscription of Comodilla catacomb, scratched in a scrambled code in Vulgar Latin (in transition to Italian). My thanks to artist Alex Bigney of Salem, Utah.
6. Farrar, *Life of Christ,* 483, as quoted in Talmage, *Jesus the Christ,* 523 n. 6.
7. Laidler, *Head of God,* 160, notes that two ancient chronicles, the *Magna Glastoniensis Tabula* and the *Cotton MS Titus,* both relate that while John was the first guardian, Joseph of Arimathea was to be a second guardian, or *paranymphos* (*Magna Glastoniensis Tabula* at Naworth Castle, as quoted in Jowett, *Drama of the Lost Disciples,* 134). Of course, Jesus from the Cross offers his mother to John's keeping. I would assume that John never lost this role, but rather shared it with Joseph of Arimathea.
8. Wigoder, *Illustrated Dictionary and Concordance of the Bible,* 957. Stephen was a Diaspora Jew, one of the original seven deacons then presiding over the Jerusalem Church.
9. Hopkins, Simmans, and Wallace-Murphy, *Rex Deus,* 79. They have been unable to produce or publish such Rex Deus sages. They, like the promised but yet-to-be-seen Priory de Sion documents, are probably like the postulated Quelle "Q" gospel.
10. Gardner, *Illustrated Bloodline of the Holy Grail,* 83. See Martin, *Decline and Fall of the Roman Church,* 44.
11. Orson Hyde, in *Journal of Discourses* (6 October 1854), 2:82–83. Hyde continues, "History is replete with circumstances of neck-or-nothing politicians dyeing their hands in the blood of those who stood in their way to the throne or to power" (2:83).
12. Starbird, *Magdalen's Lost Legacy,* 133.
13. Margaret Starbird, in Burstein, *Secrets of the Da Vinci Code,* 20. As usual, Starbird overstates Robert Graves' understanding of the Grail family and inserts her own ideas.
14. Unknown author, "Magdalene the Bride of Christ," www.spiritbride.com (2004).
15. Ralls-MacLeod and Robertson, *Quest for the Celtic Key,* 159. Taylor, *Coming of the Saints,* 56–57, states, "After the first persecution, when St. James [the Greater] was slain by the sword, [ca. A.D. 44] those who had followed him were thrust into a boat." Other commentators have noted that fourteen years after the ascension they were set adrift. But A.D. 44 and 47 would be far too late. The date of A.D. 35 would better suit the circumstances.
16. Dobson, *Did Our Lord Visit Britain,* n.p. In this group were Lazarus with his two sisters, Martha and Mary; Maximin, one of the seventy-two disciples, from whom they had received baptism; Sedonius (Cedon, the blind man); and Marcella, the handmaiden who attended on the two sisters. Taylor, *Coming of the Saints,* 175, notes that the residence of St. Philip and sender of Joseph of Arimathea to Britain was in Caesarea.
17. Although there is no evidence of Joseph of Arimathea and retinue going on the boat to Cyprus, Barber mentions that Joseph had founded a Lydda and Cyprus congregation. See *Holy Grail,* 39.
18. Starbird, *Magdalen's Lost Legacy,* 132. She writes this with no supporting evidence or source.
19. Taylor, *Coming of the Saints,* 177.
20. Appleby, *Hall of the Gods,* 216.
21. Ralls-MacLeod and Robertson, *Quest for the Celtic Key,* 159.
22. Taylor, *Coming of the Saints,* 70. Taylor believes that it was Caesarea, which he calls "the most important centre,

23. See Gregory of Tours, *De Miraculis*, I, xxx, and *Glory of the Martyrs*, 47. Remember that ironically it is Gregory of Tours who is our main source for Merovingian history. Greek tradition says that Mary Magdalene was buried in Ephesus in Asia Minor and her bones were supposedly taken to Constantinople by Emperor Leo in A.D. 886.

24. Ralls-MacLeod and Robertson, *Quest for the Celtic Key*, 158. Just what manuscript he found is unknown, but we assume it was the apocryphal Gospel of Nicodemus.

25. Diodorus Siculus, a Roman historian in the first century before Christ, wrote, "This tin metal is transported out of Britain into Gaul, the merchants carrying it on horseback through the heart of Celtica to Marseilles and the city called Narbo," as quoted in Prophet, *Mysteries of the Holy Grail*, xxxiii. See also Taylor, *Coming of the Saints*, 143. Why the Rhône River is not mentioned or why the tin goes to Marseilles before it goes to the Port of Narbonne, out of the way to each other, is not addressed.

26. Picknett, *Mary Magdalene*, 93–98. Also see Gospel of Nicodemus. This number is more likely.

27. Aristobolus (Peter's father-in-law), Simon Zelotes, and possibly Triphonius (who might be Trophimius, who supposedly stayed in Marseilles) are not on this list, but are associated with Joseph of Arimathea's trip to Britain.

28. Mary Magdalene and Mary of Bethany were treated in all lists as the same person, according to Western tradition. This may or may not be the case. My study has them as separate people.

29. Another explanation is found in Paul Guérin's "Life of the Saints" published by the Paris Benedictines: "In it we discover a group of Persian martyrs, among whom Martha, two Maries, and a Sara were martyred on 10 December 352. Their shrine(s) were brought to Gaul between the fifth and eighth centuries." The Benedictines believed, inaccurately, that they were witnesses of the Resurrection, thus adding glory to the sanctuary of the Saintes-Maries. See tourist booklet, Les-Saintes-Maries-de-la-Mer, *Le Mystère de Sara-la-Noire*, 6.

30. Prophet, *Lost Years of Jesus*, xxxi, undoubtedly quotes Taylor, *Coming of the Saints*, 105. The earliest legend of the arrival of Mary Magdalene in France is the early eleventh-century *Apostolic Life of Mary Magdalene*. It adds Mary the Egyptian (the Alexandrian reformed prostitute) to Mary Magdalene's persona. See Newman, *Real History behind The Da Vinci Code*, 155–56. Yet according to the Gypsies of the Carmague, she was a native of the area and the first to be converted to Christianity. See Le mystère de Sara-la-Noire (n.d.) page 7. It should also be noted that the Gypsies never passed through Egypt and the veneration of Sara in Les Saintes-Maries-de-la-Mer began before the Gypsies came in the fourteenth century.

31. General view of Les-Saintes-Maries-de-la-Mer in southern France.

32. Humpherys, *You and I, Who Are We?* 163. Was the "Pledge" actually the children of Jesus Christ?

33. Freeman, *Avalonian Quest*, 131.

34. To this day their landing is celebrated in the Camargue delta of the Rhône River from the 23rd to the 25th of May.

35. Taylor, *Coming of the Saints*, 89, 94. Perhaps this was an arrangement similar to the marriage of Eliza R. Snow and Brigham Young.

36. Sinclair, *Discovery of the Grail*, 115.

37. Taylor, *Coming of the Saints*, 99, quoting from Rabanus. Supposedly, Martha had a "book of the Passion of Christ, written in Hebrew, which she brought with her from Jerusalem." If she had such a book, it might have been the basis of St. Luke's gospel, according to Taylor.

38. Robert de Boron's *Joseph d'Arimathie* states that one companion of Joseph of Arimathea traveled ahead to the vaus d'Avaron (probably Avalon) to prepare a place for the Grail. In *The Romance of the History of the Grail*, Joseph of Arimathea, after giving Bron the guardianship of the Grail, sends a lieutenant, Petrus, to Avalon to report that the Grail stewardship has been handed to another. Petrus says, "I shall go to the land in the west which is wild and harsh, to the vaus d'Avaron." See Barber, *Holy Grail*, 132. This is the only place where the Vale of Avalon is mentioned, though the cross found with King Arthur's body in 1191 said, "insula Avallonia" (Isle of Avalon). Some think it may refer to an Avallon in Burgundy, not far from Robert de Boron's home.

39. Prophet, *Mysteries of the Holy Grail*, xxxv.

40. Taylor, *Coming of the Saints*, 140. The present construction on Mont Saint-Michel dates back only to A.D. 708 when Aubert, Bishop of Avranches, built a sanctuary. But the island's importance extends back long before this date.

41. According to Prophet, *Lost Years of Jesus*, xxxiii, the island of Ictis is almost certainly St. Michael's Mount just off Cornwall. Elder, *Joseph of Arimathea*, 9, notes that the tribe of Asher, sometimes called the Phoenicians, probably named the mount after Mishael in Canaan, one of the four cities of refuge (Joshua 21:30). It was a Levitical place of refuge. Marazion, where the island is located, means "bitter Zion." Another legend notes that

Joseph of Arimathea was accompanied by Nicodemus and a small retinue. They sailed to the White Isle in Britain. Godwin, *Holy Grail*, 72, 87. Could this be the Isle of Wight? This comes from the first *Continuation of Le Conte del Graal.*

42. Barber, *Holy Grail*, 198–202. The twelfth-century *Roman de Tristan en Prose (Prose Tristan),* unlike Grail literature, is not given to Chivalric exploits, spiritual ideals, and chaste self-denial of the troubadour poetry of southern France. The hero, Tristan, is the greatest lover and knight and shares with Lancelot and Galahad descent from Joseph of Arimathea. The story has Tristan winning the fair Iseult in Ireland on behalf of King Mark. Tristan and Iseult fall passionately in love on the way home to Cornwall but are torn by loyalties. It reflects the Lancelot, Guinevere, and Arthur story in parts.

43. John William Waterhouse (1849–1917), British, *Tristan and Isolde* (1916, oil on canvas, 42" x 32"). Courtesy of Frederick C. and Sherry L. Ross, New Jersey. The Celtic legend was retold by Sir Thomas Malory. It tells of the couple who accidentally drank a love potion from the sacred Grail. Tristan's name means "sadness." He was killed by the jealous King Mark, husband of Isolde. She died of grief and was buried beside Tristan, and a vine grew entwining their graves. Here the Grail cup of love became as much *eros* as it was *agape.*

44. The Bard, Melking lived in the middle of the sixth century. He gives the bare bones to the narrative, suggesting that the legend of Joseph of Arimathea was already in existence at that time. See Blake and Lloyd, *Keys to Avalon*, 208.

45. Ibid., 167.

46. This is near modern-day Llangollan in North Wales.

47. Sinclair, *Discovery of the Grail*, 18. The smelting town of Priddy is located in these gentle mountains.

48. Others feel that the two great Christian centers of Glastonbury Abbey in England and Fe'camp Abbey on the Normandy coast were founded by Rome after the sixth century. See Goodrich, *Holy Grail*, 11.

49. See Jowett, *Drama of the Lost Disciples*, 72–88. According to Morgan, *Holy Grail*, 61–62, 64, there is a grove of yew trees in Chalice Well, growing there from at least Roman times. They are a Celtic symbol of death and rebirth with their bright red berries that have toxic qualities, while their evergreen nature suggests renewal and vigor.

50. Sinclair, *Discovery of the Grail*, 17; Prophet, *Lost Years of Jesus*, lii; Ralls-MacLeod and Robertson, *Quest for the Celtic Key*, 207. Morgan, *Holy Grail*, 65, notes that Gwynn ap Nudd means "White Son of Night."

51. E. J. Watson, "The Legend of Crewkerne" *Somerset County Herald* (1920), noted in Roberts, *Glastonbury*, 38. However, Blake and Lloyd, *Keys to Avalon*, believe that the group first landed not in southern but in northern Wales. Interestingly only four churches in Wales are dedicated to Mary Magdalene. See ibid., 83, 262.

52. Blake and Blezard, *Arcadian Cipher*, 116.

53. Roberts, *Glastonbury*, 38.

54. Elder, *Joseph of Arimathea*, 24.

55. Treharne, *Glastonbury Legends*, 5, suggests that this detail was not added to the Glastonbury legend until after the sixteenth century and then commercialized by an eighteenth-century innkeeper. The thorn tree itself, however, is a genuine Levantine variety (a freak hawthorn or applewort) named *Crataegus oxyacantha* (or *Crataegus monogyna praecox*). Normally it cannot be struck, only budded. Alfred Lord Tennyson's poem "The Holy Grail" commemorates this event: "To Glastonbury, where the winter thorn blossoms at Christmas, mindful of our Lord." March 17 is Joseph of Arimathea's Day in the area. A rhyming couplet relates this day to the fertility of the land round about:

> If Saint Joseph's day is clear,
> We shall get a fertile year.

56. Brian Kershisknek (1960–), Kanab Utah, *The "Children" of Joseph of Arimathea* (2003, oil on board). Courtesy Diane and Sam Stewart collection. The painting depicts Joseph of Arimathea with a blossoming staff and the children of Christ, who were called the "children of Joseph of Arimathea" for their own protection.

57. The "twelve" were probably all men, since they had staffs to stick into the ground. Women and children would have come, but were not generally mentioned. My list notes some of the women who we believe possibly came to Britain:
    1. Joseph of Arimathea
    2. Virgin Mary
    3. Mary Magdalene
    4. Mary of Bethany
    5. Martha of Bethany
    6. Aristobulus (or Aristoabulua, Peter's father-in-law)
    7. Simon Zelotes
    8. Triphonius (could be Trophimius, who supposedly stayed in Marseilles)
    9. Cleon
    10. Saturninus
    11. Sidonius (Cedon or Sedonius, the "man born blind")
    12. Marcella, the maid of Mary and Martha

58. The King was the Arviragus or High King (Paramount). It was said that they are also greeted by Kings: Lud, Lyr, Arvigatus, and Beli.

59. This might be a derivation of "Joseph of Abarimacie" (Arimathea), Joseph ab Arimacie. The name relates to "Ynys Wydrin of Afallach (Afalla)," or "Ynys Avalon" (Island of Apples). Ynys Afalla (Isle of Apples) is consistently linked by legend to Glastonbury, "the Blessed Isle in the West."

60. Appleby, *Hall of the Gods*, 216. See also Gardner, *Bloodline of the Holy Grail*, 370 ff.10, who notes that Glastonbury, earlier Glastonia, might have an etymological connection with blue vegetable dye woad. In old British *glaist* means "woad" and Scots-Irish Gaelic *glas* means "translucent blue" (blue-green). Some have misconstrued the "Isle of Glais" as "the Isle of Glass." *Ynes* can mean "island" in Welsh, and *Wydrin (Vytrin, Witrin)* was assumed to mean "glassy" as in vitreous.

61. Gilbert, *Holy Kingdom*, 129. Note the spelling change. According to Gilbert it could also mean "island of faith." While Gilbert, Wilson, and Blacket do not believe that this refers to Glastonbury in Somerset, the author and almost all other scholars of the legend do.

62. William Blake (1757–1827), *Joseph of Arimathea Preaching to the Inhabitants of Britain* (nd, tempera painting). Blake's portrayal of the Arimathean was one of a number he painted of Joseph of Arimathea. Courtesy of Sir Geoffrey Keynes Coll., Cambridgeshire, UK, and Bridgeman Art Library International.

63. Gardner, *Bloodline of the Holy Grail*, 134. A hide is an area of land reckoned agriculturally to support one family for one year with one plough, equal in Somerset to 120 acres (48.5 hectares). In 1619, Liber Soliaco stated that one hide of land equaled 160 acres (Elder, *Joseph of Arimathea*, 25). Humpherys, *You and I, Who Are We?* 161, surmises that each hide equals 160 acres of land, or 1,920 acres altogether. Prophet, *Lost Years of Jesus*, xxv, calculates it to be about 1,400 acres.

64. Barnum, *Comprehensive Dictionary of the Bible*, 500. His source for this statement is not mentioned.

65. Morris, *Domesday Book: 8, Somerset*, 8; see also Sinclair, *Discovery of the Grail*, 18.

66. Blake and Lloyd, *Keys to Avalon*, 168.

67. Castleden, *King Arthur*, 197. He quotes Ashe, *King Arthur's Avalon*, 19–20, 93. Blake and Lloyd, *Keys to Avalon*, 169, note that in the later interpolations of *De Antiquitate* that Glas(t) was a great-grandson of the Welsh king Cunedda Wledig (ca. A.D. 370). The name was probably Saxonized to Glastingaburi by the seventh century.

68. The Harleian MS. 3859 genealogical manuscript dates from 958 (surviving document ca.1100). It says that Glast's descendants were called Glaestings and their city was named Glaestingaburh in North Wales. This would be somewhere between the Valle Crucis Abbey and the present-day town of Llangollen (Church [Llan] of St. Collen [Gollen]) four miles away. It is on the Dee River near Eglwyseg Valley, bordering the domain of Dogfeiling, Glast's ancestors. Thus, according to this theory, the Somerset Glastonbury appropriated Glaestingaburh's story of St. Collen and the fairy king Gwyn ap Nudd, which rightfully belong to Wales.

69. Blake and Lloyd, *Keys to Avalon*, 201. *Wirral* and *Wearyall* became synonymous.

70. Or it may be that the gold cruet represented the blood from Gethsemane while the silver one represented the blood shed at Calvary?

71. Thiering, *Jesus the Man*, ii–xi. As a side note, there is an 1899 treatise by Hazrat Mirza Ghulam Ahmad(as), an Islamic writer, who claims that Jesus actually went to India after his crucifixion.

72. Haskins, *Mary Magdalen*, 374. See also Haskins in Burstein, *Secrets of the Da Vinci Code*, 33. Haskins questions why Thiering pushed the envelope of credulity.

73. Gardner, *Bloodline of the Holy Grail*, 115, 236, 243. Josephes, by some accounts, is the son of Joseph of Arimathea. The author disagrees with Gardner on all these points. Picknett and Prince mention the pseudohistorical *The Montgomery Document*, which is used by Baigent, Leigh, and Lincoln. This nineteenth-century document (after a supposedly earlier document) is from the Montgomery family. It claims that Miriam (Mary) of Bethany was arrested by the Romans and released because of pregnancy. She fled to Gaul, where she gave birth to a daughter, "Tamar." She is described as "a priestess of a female cult" (Diana?). See Picknett and Prince, *Templar Revelation*, 50–51.

74. Haskins, *Mary Magdalen*, 375. Gardner often quotes Thiering and relies on her analysis of Jesus Christ's life. I disagree with Gardner's genealogy because Gardner provides no evidence to prove the names of these children.

75. Starbird, *Woman with the Alabaster Jar*, 60–63. She now says Jesus had several children.

76. Personal interview, August 2004, Sunstone Symposium, Salt Lake City. She was strongly opposed to the idea that there was a special lineage established by Jesus and Mary Magdalene. The "dynasty," she believed, stopped at their daughter and only existed to prove the normality of Christ through the family condition.

77. M. Zvi Udley, Ph.D., as quoted in Kraut, *Jesus Was Married*, 92. While other writers quote him often, it

is difficult to know exactly who Dr. Udley was. He is writing about the discovery in the 1870s of a tomb of a certain Simeon linked to a person named Jesus in first-century Jerusalem. This would be the only non-LDS source saying affirmatively that Jesus was married and had children. Two other sources say this as well, though in a more obscure way: the ancient critic Celsus and anti-Cathar, Pierre des Vaux-de-Cernay.

78. Barber, *Holy Grail*, 212, lists "Adam" as a son of Joseph of Arimathea. It may be that Bran and Bron (Brons) were the same person. *Bran* is the Welsh word for "raven."

79. The question, Is Josephus the son of Christ, is unanswerable at present. Barber, *Holy Grail*, 113, says that Josephus (Josephes) was the son of Joseph of Arimathea, but of course, this may be the "cover story" in play.

80. Lancelot-Grail, I [1?], 51, as quoted by Barber, *Holy Grail*, 68. Joseph of Arimathea and James the Just also have the same title "first bishop of the church." John of Glastonbury notes, "In the fifteenth year after this he went to St. Philip in Gaul, taking with him Josephes, whom the Lord had consecrated a bishop in the city of Sarath [Sarras] . . ." published in *Cronica sive Antiquitates Glastoniensis Ecclesie* in the fourteenth century.

81. Barber, *Holy Grail*, 158. This is like the injury to Joseph of Arimathea and Brons. The "wound in the thigh" may mean a person who walked with a limp. This may be a sign of the Grail guardians. Joseph Smith Jr. supposedly suffered from a non-healing osteomyelitis from an operation to his leg, which he had as a child. Sometimes the Prophet walked with a limp or hitch.

82. Comfort, *Quest of the Holy Grail*, 282–84 (*La Queste del Saint Graal*, 277–79), as quoted in Barber, *Holy Grail*, 64. The term *virgin* certainly meant not celibacy, but rather purity of heart and soul.

83. Barber, *Holy Grail*, 98. Josephus "put on his vestments" or garments; see ibid., 113.

84. Supposedly after the Shield's use by King Evelake it was placed for safe keeping with the holy hermit Nacien. The De Sancto Joseph describes Nacien or Nacion not as a hermit but Prince of the Medes (i.e., Ephraimites).

85. Malory, *Morte d'Arthur*, XIII.10.

86. He is not to be confused with Brân the father of Caradoc. In fact, the child might have been given the name Brân after Caradoc's father, who was so helpful to Joseph of Arimathea, Virgin Mary, and Mary Magdalene. He is alternately called the son of Joseph of Arimathea or his son-in-law. Often he is called Bron.

87. Blake and Lloyd, *Keys to Avalon*, 125. In early Welsh genealogies, Beli Mawr ap Mynogan, a legendary King of Ynys Prydein, husband of Anna, a cousin of the Virgin Mary. Anna was supposedly the daughter of Joseph of Arimathea.

88. Whitehead, *House of Israel*, 205–8. Also see Gardner, *Bloodline of the Holy Grail*, 144. LDS author John H. Cox, lecture transcript (1999), page 3, gives a contrary version: "He [Joseph of Arimathea] is greeted by his daughter, Anna who was already living in Glastonbury as the wife of Prince Belinus, youngest son of King Brân the Blessed." Anna as the daughter of Joseph of Arimathea is recorded in *Genealogies of the Welsh Princes* (Harieian MS) 3859.

89. Gilbert, *Holy Kingdom*, 123. Gilbert has St. Ilid (Joseph of Arimathea) as the tutor of Brân the Blessed. Not far from St. Ilid's church in Wales was Trefan, or "The Manor of Brân."

90. Ashley, *Chronicles of the Holy Grail*, 5. In this case then, Eurgain (Anna) would have in fact been the Arimathean's daughter.

91. Loomis, *The Grail*, 132–34, and Godwin, *Holy Grail*, 42. The "Spoils of Annan" are the mountainous grave sites north of Llangolan.

92. This is the town of Glaestingaburh (Llangolan) that claimed the legendary Brân, King of Britain.

93. The eleventh-century Cistercian Valle Cruses Abbey on the Plain of Maelor in Valley Eglywsey very near Llangolan is on the sacred Dee River in North Wales. It was here that the Virgin Mary was supposedly taken for safety. Reproduction courtesy of Tony and Traci Fieldsted, Springville.

94. Collins, *Twenty-First Century Grail*, 14.

95. Matthews, *King Arthur and the Grail Quest*, 127. Matthews would think that the "far-off time" would be the A.D. 530s at the time of King Arthur. But Mormons can only assume that this was the Latter-day Galahad—Joseph Smith Jr.

96. As reported in Godwin, *Holy Grail*, 88. Robert de Boron wrote the poem between A.D. 1191 and 1202. The word *calice* probably means chalice.

97. Barber, *Holy Grail*, 132. Also see Fanthorpe and Fanthorpe, *World's Greatest Unsolved Mysteries*, 106.

98. Barber, *Holy Grail*, 164. He is quoting Roman du Graal 70, which should be compared to Joseph d'Arimathie 322, 328.

99. Sinclair, *Discovery of the Grail*, 18. The "host" is usually considered the sacramental bread (wafer) and water (wine), but in this case it may be a larger revelation.

100. Phillips, *Search for the Grail*, as quoted in Knight and Lomas, *Hiram Key*, 112. Taylor, *Coming of the Saints*, 170, notes that "nearly all his Table Round are represented as

having Hebrew relationship and being for the most part of Hebrew lineage."

101. Blake and Lloyd, *Keys to Avalon*, 200. Alain, son of Bron (Hebron) continued to Terre Foraine where he built the Castle of Corbenic to house the Grail, up to the time of Arthur, when it became lost.

102. Godwin, *Holy Grail*, 88. Joseph of Arimathea's sister or daughter bears Bron twelve sons, one of which, Alein le Gros, is to be the (chief) guardian of the Grail. The Vulgate Cycle says that the Grail was brought to Wales by Joseph of Arimathea's nephew, Alain le Gros. (Howard Reid, 2001, 92) Eleven of the brothers die attempting to bring in the "New Law" to the realm, and the role and title pass on to his brother Josue.' Alein has a son named Percival (Perlesvaus) and Mortal and a sister named Dandrane. Percival on his father's side is the grandson of Nicodemus. It is Percival who fails to ask the all-important question which will heal the Grail Fisher King, thus the realm is in a dolorous languor. See Phillips, *Search for the Grail*, 199.

103. Barber, *Holy Grail*, 71.

104. Ibid., 45.

105. I realize that this is a speculative and inaccurate genealogical chart. Certainly the largest leap is showing Bron as the son of Josephus. I present this figure to generate scholarly research on the pros and cons of the role of Jesus' generations. It is interesting that, if Josephus was the first child of the Lord, his name was tribally related to Joseph of Egypt.

106. Ibid., 200.

107. Laidler, *Head of God*, 161. This because the Grail seed all claimed Joseph of Arimathea as *pater familias*, because he became the guardian, or father, of the children of Christ.

108. Moyses may be a metaphor for Moses, which the anti-Semitic romances use to symbolize Jewry.

109. Barber, *Holy Grail*, 184.

110. Hansen, *Whence Came They?* 85.

CHAPTER THIRTEEN
THE EARLY CHURCH

he quest to find the Grail has always riveted popular imagination around King Arthur. The search for the Holy Grail has been synonymous with the eternal inquiry for truth. Symbolically it has become the earthly receptacle for the living essence of a superior world—salvation and heaven on earth.

The Grail Quest, like that of King Arthur, began in the far reaches of time and continued into late-Roman and Dark Age Britain. Our journey will not be delineated by photographic means, but must of necessity be done by small pixels coming together. Hopefully enough dots will be found that a pattern or perhaps even an image might emerge. As John Matthews wrote: "What had once been perceived as a cycle of stories and legends took on a patina of mystical awareness. This led to a search for the inner meaning of the story, and hints and clues were sought among the pages of the medieval manuscripts."[1]

EARLY MISSIONARY WORK: THE FIRST CENTURY

Then the apostle [Philip], desiring that the word of God should be spread abroad, sent twelve of his disciples to preach in Britain, placing at their head his favourite disciple Joseph of Arimathea, together with his son Josephus.

—JOHN OF GLASTONBURY[2]

The idea of Christianity in Britain during the first century is radical thinking. We have been led to believe that Britain did not become Christianized until St. Patrick in the west and St. Augustine in the east during the fifth and sixth centuries. Yet legend has it that from the safety of this island, Joseph of Arimathea and his twelve companions spearheaded missionary campaigns. They founded a form of Celtic Christianity, which would profoundly differ from that of Rome. And because of this, the British church has claimed from earliest times to be the first church or See in Europe.[3]

About A.D. 37, Joseph and companions built of wood or "withies and reeds" a circular church. This was the first in Britain and perhaps the first above ground church in all Christendom. F. Bligh Bond figured that this "first church was circular, having a diameter of 25 feet, with the twelve huts of the other disciples forming a circle around it"[4] (see Plate 23).

The Reverend Lewis notes that Joseph of Arimathea, himself, built a circular wattle church to St. Mary after he brought the Holy Family to Britain about A.D. 36–37.[5] Supposedly this unique little church was a scale model of the ancient Hebrew tabernacle-temple.[6] It would be the second above ground Christian church in the world, if we count Christ's own little chapel booth, built in his youth, as the first. It is possible that this later church was built around the original wattle booth to protect it.[7]

The *De Sancto Joseph ab Arimathea* mentions that Joseph's wattle-and-daub church was built at the bidding of the archangel Gabriel. It was supposedly dedicated "in the 31st year after our Lord's Passion" (A.D. 63–64).[8] John W. Taylor agrees:

> These holy men, thus dwelling in this desert place, were in a little time admonished in a vision by the Archangel Gabriel to build a church in honour of the Blessed Virgin, in a place to which they were directed. Obedient to the Divine precept, they immediately built a chapel of the form of that which had been shown them: the walls were of osiers [willow] wattled together all round.
>
> This was finished in the one-and-thirtieth year after the Lord's Passion, and though rude and misshapen in

form, was in many ways adorned with heavenly virtues; and being the first church in this region, the Son of God was pleased to grace it with particular dignity, dedicating it Himself in honour of His Mother.[9]

Gildas Badonicus III (516–570) in his A.D. 560 book *De Excidio et Conquestu Britanniae* (*The Ruin and Fall of Britain*), wrote that the precepts of Christianity were carried to Britain during the end of Emperor Tiberius Caesar's reign, who died in A.D. 37. The initial Christianization of Britain, according to St. Gildas the Wise, and the early historian Freculpus (Freculuphus), took place only four years after the crucifixion. Although in the earliest versions they don't mention Joseph of Arimathea by name, this was presumably who carried it to Britain.[10] Gildas writes:

> Meanwhile, these islands received the beams of light, that is, the Holy precepts of Christ, the true Sun, as we know, at the latter part, as we know, of the reign of Tiberius Caesar, in whose time this religion was propagated without impediment and death threatened to those who interfered with its professors.[11]

Early Church Father Eusebius gives support to the validity of this quotation by noting:

> Tiberius . . . threatened death to the accusers of the Christians: a Divine providence infusing this into his mind, so that the gospel, having freer scope at its beginning, might spread everywhere over the world.[12]

Small first-century Celtic Christian communities were scattered upon a sea of Druidism and paganism. The Druids taught a form of the doctrine of the atonement and the need for a Savior. They even worshipped one who possessed the Messiah's appellation—"Yesu," which was the same as Jesus' name.[13] Although unnoted by other writers, it is likely that the Druid priests of ancient Britain were descended from the united tribe of Judah.[14] The Arch Druid apparently wore a breastplate (*ephod*) similar to that worn by the Jewish high priest.[15] Thus the gospel of Jesus Christ found fertile ground, while at the same time becoming tinctured by Druidism itself.

The mission to convert the people of England on "The Isles of the Sea" first started with a visit to Britain from the youthful Jesus to his maternal family. Then after Christ's resurrection, his mission was continued by his great-uncle, Joseph of Arimathea, in Wales and western Britain. It may be that Wales had the gospel slightly earlier than *Lloegres* (England). According to Adrian Gilbert, Joseph of Arimathea and his companions had come first to the Khymric Kingdom of Essylwg to Llantwit Major on the southern coast of Wales called the Vale of Glamorgan in A.D. 36.[16]

Amateur researchers Alan Wilson and Baram Blacket believe that St. Ilid is the Welsh name for Joseph of Arimathea.[17] The name was derived from "Gilead," which means the "Galilean" and was a nickname of affection. Saint Patrick called him by a different name, "There [in Wales] Joseph de Marmore, named 'of Arimathea' took everlasting sleep."[18]

Caradoc's son, Cyllinus (Cyllin), became regent when his father was taken prisoner to Rome. He is credited with introducing into Britain the christening of infants with Christian names and a blessing.[19] Not long after organizing a Christian church in the Vale of Glamorgan in southern Wales, Joseph of Arimathea (St. Ilid) left to convert the king of Lloegres (England), Guiderius. But Guiderius was killed in battle and King Gweirydd, better known as Arviragus (Lord), succeeded his brother. This was during the period of the invasion of the Roman Caesar Claudius about A.D. 43.

George, as in St. George, is the Anglicized form of Gweirydd or Arviragus, but his conversion does not appear in the histories of Gildas, Nennius of Bangor, nor Geoffrey of Monmouth. They also do not mention Joseph of Arimathea or St. Ilid; however, another important source does. According to the Medieval British *Chronicles of Hardynge*, Arviragus was converted by St. Ilid, and the Khymric royal family was instrumental in establishing Christianity both in Britain and later in Rome.

Other missionaries joined St. Ilid in spreading Christianity. According to Taylor, the old Welsh records mention another missionary in Britain, his name Arwystli Hen, which translates into "Aristobulus the Aged," because supposedly he lived until he was 99 years old.[20] Some scholars have identified him as the brother of apostle Barnabas and the father-in-law of St. Peter.[21] He was one of the Seventy (missionaries) chosen by Jesus himself, when the Savior organized the original church.

About A.D. 59, Paul arrived in Rome under house arrest and met with Caradoc and his family. Together they planned a mission for some family members to preach the gospel to the British. By about A.D. 60, with the financial aid of St. Eurgain, a mission was prepared to travel north to bring salvation to Cambria in Wales. Thus Brân, the father of Caradoc, and Aristobulus with their supporters left Rome for Britain. Paul mentions in Romans 16:10, "My greetings . . . to the household of Aristobulus." It is believed that Aristobulus had already been in Britain before the apostle Paul finished writing the epistle to the Romans and was one of the original companions of Joseph of Arimathea.

Britain was sufficiently Christianized by the time of Eusebius, bishop of Caesaria (260–340), and St. Hilary of Poitiers (300–367) that they recorded early apostolic visits to Britain with Philip and Paul being the most noted. Theodoretus says, "Paul preached the gospel to the Britons and others in the West."[22] In 1931 Pope Pius XI noted "that St. Paul, not Pope Gregory, first introduced Christianity into Britain."[23] He visited London (Londinium) and preached from the site of the present-day St. Paul's Cathedral. In *Druidism in Britain* a remarkable story speaks of a Greek manuscript which asserts that the "Apostle after visiting Spain, came to Britain and preached upon the Mount Lud Ludgate Hill, London, and that the Druids came to Paul and showed him that their rites and ceremonies were descended from the Jews and the Apostle accorded them a kiss of peace."[24]

Clement of Rome spoke of St. Paul arriving "at the extremity of the West" and in A.D. 435, Theodoret said that "St. Paul brought salvation to the islands that lie in the ocean [Britain]."[25] However, it should be remembered that St. Philip was the chosen apostle to the Britons and he either came in person or was instrumental in sending Joseph of Arimathea in his stead.

Dorotheus of Tyre also states that Simon the Zealot, one of Jesus's twelve apostles (Matthew 10:1–4), was "killed in Britain soon after arriving in A.D. 60, at the height of the savagery of the Boudiccan rebellion."[26] If true, this may have contributed to the apostasy from the standpoint of the priesthood succession. Without the proper apostolic chain of ordination to the priesthood, authority to organize and maintain the Culdee church was no longer available.

Since Imperial Rome occupied Britain only in a general sense, Christianity grew in Britain from the first years of the apostolic ministry. However, a few key martyrdoms cut the Celtic church loose from its Jerusalem headquarters and the political center of Rome. The Holy Land itself was, conversely, cut off from the bloodline of the Grail Seed with disastrous results. The ties that bound the two were becoming tenuous.

Only seven years later, in A.D. 43–44, the Roman Emperor Claudius (?–54), brought his legions to invade Britain as far as Colchester. These were turbulent and desperate times. As a result of this attack on Britain, and in spite of the arrangements mentioned above, perhaps Mary Magdalene may have left the Celtic land and imigrated back to southern France for the balance of her life, though this, like so much from this obscure period, is mere speculation.

Though Gaul was a Roman province, it was oblivious to the "Grail question" which was then boiling in Britain. Mary Magdalene's leaving Wales and Somerset would have reduced the heat the Romans were bringing to bear upon the Grail children. However, Andrew Collins strongly takes exception to this position: "The medieval legends implying that the Magdalene ended her days in France appear to have been the fabrications of medieval churchmen, wishing to earn capital out of the thousands of pilgrims who flocked to see her holy relics."[27]

The appearance of Christianity in Britain at this early date helps to intimate Joseph of Arimathea's and the Grail family's presence there. We leave Joseph because of his death but continue to follow his secret "children." These descendants of Jesus, preserved by this great man, are the core of our continuing story of the Holy Grail.

CULDEE CELTIC CHRISTIANITY

It is a remarkable fact, that Druidism never opposed Christianity, and eventually became voluntarily merged with it.

—REV. C. C. DOBSON[28]

The debate continues as to the meaning of a "Celtic" or "Culdee" community.[29] Certainly it was not a single, cohesive church. Rather it must have been a diverse number of Christian communities, not a unified organization.[30] Many have come to think of Culdees as devout romanticized "holdouts" and keepers of the "old ways," against the encroaching Roman church.[31] It appears that the Culdees were the vestige of the bloodline church in much the same way that Catholicism was the vestige of the priesthood church.

Good King Lleirwg (Lucius) Mawr, the grandson of both Caradoc and Arviragus, sent an envoy to the Greek Pope Eleutherius (A.D. 174/5–192) to discuss religious matters.[32] Supposedly, King Lucius at the National Council of Winchester (Caer Winton) in A.D. 156 had already proclaimed Britain to be Christian as the "natural successor" to Druidism.[33] Mr. Godfrey Higgins believes that the Culdees were the last remnants of the Druids who had been converted to Christianity.[34]

The Venerable Bede of Jarrow and Nennius note that Lucius sent to the bishop of Rome for missionaries. As a result these two missionaries, Fagan (Phaganus) and Dyfan (Deruvianus), visited the "Old Church" of Glastonbury in A.D. 167.[35] It was at this time the forlorn area about the Isle of Avalon was reinhabited. The missionaries were successful in spreading the gospel and organizing the Culdee church. Although Geoffrey Ashe believes that King Lucius was fictional, the mission of Fagan and Dyfan certainly was not.[36]

It seems that not until after the Gallican persecution of the saints at Lyons and Vienne in A.D. 177 that statements exist as to a Celtic Christianity.[37] A number of the Christians of Gaul fled northward and found refuge in Britain.[38] The Christian Carthagenian, Tertullian, in his *Adversus Judaeos* (200–206 A.D.), that in the extremities of Spain, various parts of Gaul, and "places of the Britons, which are inaccessible to the Romans, but all subdued to [the worship of] the true Christ."[39]

Sabellius, an early Christian theologian from Rome, wrote in A.D. 250, "Christianity was privately confessed elsewhere, but the [first] nation that proclaimed it as their religion and called it Christian, after the name of Christ, was Britain."[40] Origen, a renowned early Church Father, refers to Britain in *Against Celsus* (ca. 245 A.D.): "The land of Britain has received the religion of Christ."[41] Again, Origen wrote, "The power of our Lord is with those who in Britain are separated from our coasts."[42]

The bishop of Caesarea, Eusebius (ca. A.D. 260–340) wrote in his ecclesiastical history, "The Apostles passed beyond the ocean to the isles called the Britannic Isles."[43] Saint John Chrysostum (A.D. 247–307), the Patriarch of Constantinople, then wrote: "The British Isles which are beyond the sea, and which lie in the ocean, have received virtue of the Word. Churches are there found and altars erected. . . . Though thou shouldst go to the ocean, to the British Isles, there thou shouldst hear all men everywhere discoursing matters out of the scriptures, with another voice indeed, but not another faith, with a different tongue, but the same judgement."[44]

The cruel edicts persecuting Christians by emperors such as Nero (A.D. 59) and Diocletian (A.D. 303–313) kept the two halves of Christianity separate long enough to lead to the Great Apostasy. Diocletian's reign of terror against the Christians began about A.D. 303 and was described by Gildas: "[During] the nine years' persecution by the tyrant Diocletian . . . the Churches throughout the whole world were overthrown. All the copies of the Holy Scriptures, which could be found were burned in the streets and the chosen pastors of God's flock butchered, together with their innocent sheep, in order that [if possible] not a vestige might remain in some provinces of Christ's religion."[45]

The Venerable Bede named St. Alban as the first Christian martyr in Britain. Surely this must mean the first "Diocletian martyr," who died in 304 A.D. Among the ablest of the "Pillars of the Faith" were the bishop of Llandaff, Presbyters of Caerleon, the archbishop of York, the archbishops of London, the bishop of Penrhyn (Glasgow), bishop of Carlisle, and thousands of others. In 313 A.D. the "Edict of Milan" was issued by Constantine the Great after his vision of the cross at the Battle of Milvian Bridge, to give toleration to all religions. The British church must have been reasonably well established by the fourth century because it sent three bishops to the Council of Arles in A.D. 314.[46]

After so much persecution, the connective tissue between the bloodline and the priesthood lines had become frayed. They had been separated long enough for the bond between them to be broken. With the Council at Nicea in A.D. 325 under the rule of the newly Christianized Constantine the Great, the two halves of Christianity continued to split, to the detriment of both. Once Christianity gained "official" status in A.D. 381, it continued to fall precipitously.

Interestingly, at the Council of Nicea in 325 A.D., legend has it that the British bishops were given precedence "as representing the church said to be founded by Joseph of Arimathea, causing a degree of jealousy among other churchmen, especially those from Gaul."[47] The priority of antiquity was questioned, on political grounds, by the ambassadors of France and Spain. The Council of Pisa in 1409, Constance in 1417, Sienna in 1425, and Basle in 1434 attempted to establish the seniority among the churches of Europe.[48]

These councils found that "the Churches of France and Spain (the area west of the Rhône Valley to Iberia proper) must yield in points of antiquity and precedence to that of Britain as the latter church was founded by Joseph of Arimathea immediately after the passion of Christ."[49]

The controversy was decided in support of England, because the church at Glastonbury was founded by Joseph, *statim post passione Christi* (shortly after the Passion of Christ). Britain won because Joseph of Arimathea was apparently buried in Glastonbury at the Abbey of Glais.[50] Polydore Virgil also believed that "Britain, partly through Joseph of Arimathea . . . was of all kingdoms the first that received the gospel."[51] Perhaps this was because the true Grail seed was present, leavening the pagan tribes with its influence.

The falling of Celtic Christianity can be seen in the Synod of Ariminum (Rimini), summoned by the Emperor Constantius in 359 A.D. to formulate a unity of faith for the whole church. Both Hilary of Poitiers and St. Athanasius the Patriarch of Alexandria stated that they were able to count on the Britons present to combat Arianism. Arianism was a troublesome heresy in the fourth century and had been officially declared heretical at the Council of Nicea thirty-four years earlier.

Arius, an Alexandrian priest and theologian, did not believe in the Trinitarian belief that God was essentially "three in One." He believed that at some point the Son had to have been begotten by the Father. This implied that there was a time in which the Son did not exist. "In doing so," wrote Ralls-MacLeod and Robertson, "he denied the true divinity of Christ in the eyes of the Church, although he felt he was upholding true monotheism."[52] The Arians were not gnostics and neither did they believe that Jesus was not a god, just that he was a lesser, or perhaps younger God than Heavenly Father. Inexplicably, the Culdee community sided with the Roman Church in its fight against Arianism. In doing so they rejected principles that allowed for a begotten Savior who in turn could beget children Himself. Were the Culdees too far into apostasy or were they still protecting the bloodline?

Even with doctrinal "accommodations" such as the one noted above, native British Christianity flourished. Archaeologists have discovered a *Chi-Rho* cross in a Roman mosaic in a small chapel in Lullingstone, Kent, dating from A.D. 360.[53] It is also known that St. Ninian was probably at Whithorn as early as 397 A.D. St. David accomplished the general conversion of Wales, and St. Patrick converted the pagan Irish (ca. A.D. 432). St. Columba of the Irish Church, by ca. A.D. 563 began to reintroduce the gospel to the non-Christian parts of Britain, the Pictish tribes and the new Anglian kingdom of Northumbria. Even though pre-597 Christianity in Britain is somewhat controversial, most scholars accept the fact that Christian communities did exist in the Isles.

Another death knell came in A.D. 381, during the reign of Emperor Theodosius (379–395) when Christianity was made the state religion at the Council of Constantinople. As might be expected, a year later the Roman Church decreed that anyone convicted of heresy would not only be excommunicated but also liable for execution. This is the first time that capital death was applied by a Christian organization. However, it would be almost two hundred years before the "church" had widespread civil authority to carry out this punishment. The inner Grail church, all the while, slowly became subsumed into the apostate outer church.

PELAGIUS THE HERESIARCH

A Saintly Man.

— ST. AUGUSTINE

Did Joseph of Arimathea actually found a Christian Church in Britain? He undoubtedly did as much as any missionary and senior priesthood bearer would, he organized branches of the Church in that part of the "Lord's vineyard." It was not a separate or alternative Church to that in Jerusalem but rather a mission-field organization in the Lord's kingdom of Saints.[54] Only later, during the Great Apostasy, did the British church become alienated.

The apostolic line from Peter was challenged by a British-Celtic Culdee monk named Pelagius called "Brito" (Morgan or Morien), who was born around A.D. 350.[55] He was a tall, portly, and well-educated Welshman who spoke and wrote in Latin and Greek and was well-versed in theology. Pelagius was a smiling, reserved, and modest man of great character, possibly a Grail descendant himself. He was, according to Orosius and Pope Zosimus, a practical ascetic and a lay monk. Even his famous rival, St. Augustine of Hippo, was led to call him a "saintly man."[56]

Sometime between 380 and 400 he made a pilgrimage to Rome. However, he seemed as out of place in Rome as James the Just in Jerusalem in A.D. 62. He was dismayed at the "lax morals of professing Christians and endeavored earnestly to raise the ethical standards by affirming the responsibility which men have before God for their actions."[57] A quiet man, he was more of a pastor than preacher. He professed obeying the commandments of God and the need of faith coupled with works.[58] He saw that Rome was not Christianizing the people, but rather making "conforming pagans."

While in Rome about A.D. 405, he heard someone reading from St. Augustine's *Confessions*, "Give me what you command and command what you will." Annoyed, Pelagius came into conflict with Augustine's professions of man's absolute lack of free will, irresistible power of grace, infant baptism, depravity, and predestination. Pelagius found all these doctrines to be pernicious and a culpable abdication of the spirit of the early Church fathers.[59]

Pelagius differed with the Pope on a number of teachings, most particularly the apostolic succession. He claimed his authority did not come through St. Peter's priesthood line of Roman bishops. Rather, his spiritual succession, he claimed, came directly from Joseph of Arimathea in an even more ancient Celtic church.[60] According to Knight and Lomas: "This version of the story is interesting because it raises the suggestion that there is an alternative apostolic succession through Joseph of Arimathea and his family. Moreover, this line is claimed to have secret knowledge, unknown to the established Church.[61]

Pelagius probably drew most of his early followers from the remnants of Joseph's original Grail bloodline church. The doctrine of the Pelagians was blatantly opposed to St. Augustine's established doctrines, according to Will Durant:

> From England came his [Augustine's] ablest opponent, the footloose monk Pelagius, with a strong defense of man's freedom, and of the saving power of good works. God indeed helps us, said Pelagius, by giving us His law and commandments, by the example and presents of His saints, by the cleansing waters of baptism, and the redeeming blood of Christ. But God does not tip the scales against our salvation by making human nature inherently evil.
>
> There was no original sin, no fall of man [Adam of course]; only he who commits a sin is punished for it; it transmits no guilt to his progeny. God does not predestine man to heaven or hell, does not choose arbitrarily whom He will damn or save; He leaves the choice of our fate to ourselves. The theory of innate human depravity, said Pelagius, was a cowardly shifting to God of the blame for man's sins. Man feels, and therefore is, responsible; "if I ought, I can."[62]

These beliefs were put forward in Pelagius' now lost *Commentary on the Pauline Epistles.* His doctrines display an enlightened outlook perhaps provided by Christ's own children in Britain. The words of Pelagius and his companion, the Celtic monk, Celestius (Coelestius) are today known mostly through their enemies. They cannot speak for themselves, but what we hear them say is music to Latter-day Saint ears.[63]

Pelagius and Coelestius were banned from the Holy City for calling into question the apostolic succession of the Roman church from St. Peter. How did Pelagius know about the Joseph of Arimathea origins of the Celtic church?[64] Precisely because he came from that part of the world, Wales, in which remnants of the Celtic or Culdee church still persisted.

We immediately see that there were two lines of authority or succession needed in order to maintain the Church of Christ. One would be the apostolic line of succession through St. Peter and the apostles, and another was ostensibly through the patriarchal Grail guarded by Joseph of Arimathea.[65] Actually, it is by Jesus' own patriarchal bloodline, not through His uncle Joseph of Arimathea, that the Celtic church could claim authority.

However, as we noted earlier the literal descendants of Christ were often referred to as "the children of Joseph of Arimathea." The kingdom would go through Peter's priesthood and the King through the bloodline. The two were split, leading to the general apostasy of both. Therefore, through asserting his authority, Pelagius may actually have been claiming his own descent from Christ.

Fearing the threatening attack of the Visigoths, he departed for Palestine in A.D. 409. There he was greeted with hostility by Augustine's theological ally, Jerome.[66] Pelagius's teaching of the perfection of man, *impeccantia* (sinlessness), sounded to Jerome like the Stoic notion of *apatheia,* which Origen had adopted. So Jerome had Pelagius formally charged with heresy and brought before the bishop Hon of Jerusalem at the Synods of Jerusalem and Diospolis in 415.

In 413 while living in Palestine, Pelagius wrote a treatise on living, long attributed to St. Jerome, entitled *Letter to Demetrias*.[67] It is one of the "jewels of Christian literature," full of practical moral advice. In it he wrote, "The body has to be controlled, not broken" (21:2).

It would seem that the writings of Pelagius and those of Joseph Smith Jr. were in many ways similar. One could almost conclude that Pelagius was nearly a Mormon.[68] This doctrine of freedom of the church of Joseph of Arimathea continued on to Pelagius and was certainly part and parcel of the spirit engendered by the bloodline of the Holy Grail. It infected later religious reformers, the American patriots, and the Joseph Smith family as well.

Eventually the eminent Sts. Jerome and Augustine heavily castigated Pelagius's critique of their teachings and outmaneuvered him. By 416, the Roman church proclaimed as heresy the teachings of Pelagius and his protegee, Celestius. The Roman emperor underscored this because at this late date the Catholic church was the binding power holding the Roman Empire together. Such strict teachings of Pelagius were unpopular with the masses and therefore detrimental to Rome's stability. By rejecting the teachings of the Spirit through the patriarchal bloodlines, the Roman church was certainly crumbling into apostasy.

Consequently the Emperor Honorius pressured Pope Zosimus in 418 to issue a command to the Pelagian bishops of Gaul to renounce their heresy before the bishop of Arles within 20 days or face severe penalties.[69] It is believed that Pelagius died that year, though some have speculated that he may have returned to Britain, first to Lérins and then to Wales.[70]

This then led to the reaffirming of the position of the previous pope (Innocent I) on the existence of original sin carrying with it the damnation even of unbaptized "parvuli" (baby infants). To implement the decrees of the Council of Carthage and of the Pope, a reign of terror was pronounced. However, in Britain, where the last of the Roman legions had left in 409–410, the Emperor Honorius had very little authority.

Therefore, Pope Celestine in 429 sent St. Germanus, the powerful bishop of Auxerre, on the first of two visits to Wales to combat the heresy in Britain. Germanus intellectually challenged the Pelagian chieftain Vortigern in the center of the Pelagian capital, Viroconium. Then when confronted with an invasion of Irish and Pictish Scots, Germanus's military acumen defeated the invaders near Mold in Flint by warriors shouting "Alleluia!"[71] After this victory Germanus was called Saint Harmon in Wales.

Though many were soon converted to orthodox Catholicism, Germanus failed to entirely clear out Vortigern's resistance to the rule of Rome. But eventually the Vatican, with the help of the Angles-Saxons, would spread the "Italian version of Christianity in Britain."[72] The beginning of the end was at hand for Celtic Britain and the Culdee community of Christianity.

Not everything attributed to Pelagius was in fact his message. He was more of a reformer than a systematic theologian. Yet at a time when King Arthur was coming onto the scene, the Celtic church was shriveling quickly into malaise. Little wonder that the devastation of the bleak and infertile wasteland would occur within a score of years. We do not know when Pelagius died, but when he departed, the Celtic church had lost its greatest advocate and the prominence of the bloodline authority would again become obscured.

NOTES

1. Matthews, *King Arthur and the Grail Quest,* 126.
2. John of Glastonbury, published in *Cronica sive Antiquitates Glastoniensis Ecclesie,* in the fourteenth century.
3. Godwin, *Holy Grail,* 81.
4. Unknown artist's rendering of twelve huts in circle, around the "old wattle church," depicts the settlement at Glastonbury sometime after Joseph of Arimathea's arrival in A.D. 37.
5. Lewis, *St. Joseph of Arimathea at Glastonbury,* 15–16.
6. Here the story diverges in detail because instead of being circular, the church is rectangular. Perhaps the difference is that Medieval Christians believed the Hebrew temple in Jerusalem was round.
7. It is said that a lead structure was eventually placed there sometime before the Glastonbury Abbey burned in the fire of 1184.
8. Gardner, *Bloodline of the Holy Grail,* 135. The first church (wattle booth) was built by Jesus about A.D. 14, Joseph's circular church was built in A.D. 37, and then a rectangular third church in A.D. 63. It is also probable that the *De Sancto* passage refers to a structure dedicated to the second Mary, the Magdalene, who died, according to the Chronicles of Matthew Paris, in A.D. 63. Thus there was the original wattle booth covered by a larger structure by Joseph of Arimathea and then another church in A.D. 63 dedicated to the Magdalene. It is also possible that this last church was built in Glaestingaburh in Wales and is now the Valle Cruses Abbey.
9. Taylor, *Coming of the Saints,* 152.
10. Wallace-Murphy and Hopkins, *Rosslyn,* 50–51. See Bede, *History of the English Church and People* (trans. Giles), 66.
11. Matthews, *Grail: Quest for the Eternal,* 87. Tiberius Caesar reigned from A.D. 14–37. This was more than five hundred years before St. Augustine, as we read in a different version: "Meanwhile these islands, stiff with cold and frost, and in a distant region of the world, remote from the visible sun, received the beams of light that are the holy precepts of Christ—the true Sun, as we know, at the latter part, of the reign of Tiberias Caesar" (see *History of Gildas,* sect. 8, 9, p. 20).
12. As quoted in Taylor, *Coming of the Saints,* 141. Interestingly it was near the end of Tiberius' reign that the Holy Family fled to Britain.
13. Strachan, *Jesus the Master Builder,* 51.
14. House of Zerah and the House of Perez, which had combined six centuries earlier, yet were in an apostate state.
15. Ralls-MacLeod and Robertson, *Quest for the Celtic Key,* 311. It might be possible that the ephod was the one carried by Jeremiah from Jerusalem to these Isles.
16. Gilbert, *Holy Kingdom,* 61–68.
17. Ibid., 123.
18. Sinclair, *Discovery of the Grail,* 126. Prophet, *Mysteries of the Holy Grail,* xl–xli, uses a different translation from Maelgwyn of Avalon: "The Isle of Avalon greedy of burials . . . received thousands of sleepers, among whom Joseph de Marmore from Aramathea by name, entered his perpetual sleep. And he lies in a bifurcated line next [to] the southern angle of the oratory made of circular wattles by 13 inhabitants of the place over the powerful adorable Virgin" (see Elder, *Joseph of Arimathea,* 38). *Marmore* is probably derived from the eastern word *Mar,* which means "lord." *More* or *Mawr* signifies "great." Thus together it might read, "The Great Lord Joseph of Arimathea."
19. Jowett, *Drama of the Lost Disciples,* 184.
20. Taylor, *Coming of the Saints,* 157. See Rees, *Essay on the Welsh Saints,* 81.
21. Jowett, *Drama of the Lost Disciples,* 159.
22. *De Curandis Graecorun Affectionibus* Lib. IX. Bishop Burgess writes, "Of St. Paul's journey to Britain we have as satisfactory proof as any historical question can demand." (anonymous, Independence of the British Church, n.d.). However, other books, such as McBrien, *Harper Collins Encyclopedia of Catholicism,* 974, and Wigoder, *Illustrated Dictionary and Concordance of the Bible,* 766, do not mention a trip to Britain.
23. Jowett, *Drama of the Lost Disciples,* 40.
24. Roberts, *Druidism in Britain,* 18.
25. Ussher, *Britannicarum Ecclesiarum Antiquitates,* 54.
26. Gilbert, *Holy Kingdom,* 138. Aristobulus seems to have died at about this same time. See Jowett, *Drama of the Lost Disciples,* 189.
27. Collins, *Twenty-First Century Grail,* 150–51. He also condemns the medieval cult of Joseph of Arimathea in Britain for the same reason.
28. Dobson, *Did Our Lord Visit Britain,* 37. However, Taylor, *Coming of the Saints,* 142, says it was a difficult matter to convert the British to Christianity.
29. *Culdee (Keledei, Celi De)* means "servants of God."
30. Ralls-MacLeod and Robertson, *Quest for the Celtic Key,* 107.
31. Ibid., 152, 155. The Culdees and Catholics were distinct from each other over two issues, one of which was the

tonsure, which means the specific manner in which they wore their hair upon being initiated into holy orders. In 1972, Pope Paul VI eliminated the tonsure altogether. The second problem was the dating of Easter. It should also be mentioned that most Celtic clergy were permitted to marry. The word *holdouts* is found in manuscript references in Ireland, Scotland, Wales, and England, but not outside the British Isles.

32. This first appeared in an extract from the *Liber Pontificalis* (also known as *Catalogus Felicianus*). See Baring-Gould and Fisher, *Lives of the British Saints*, 3:353, and Jowett, *Drama of the Lost Disciples*, 200. It appeared in Bede's *Ecclesiastical History* of A.D. 731. King Lucius was the son of Coel, who was the son of St. Cyllinus, who was the son of Caracatus, the son of Brân, the son of Llyr.

33. Jowett, *Drama of the Lost Disciples*, 80. There is some discrepancy in the date of A.D. 156, since the pope didn't reign until A.D. 177. Other accounts have it at A.D. 166. This is a legendary account and cannot be perfectly relied upon. It was King Lucius who supposedly made Christianity the state religion in A.D. 179.

34. See Ralls-MacLeod and Robertson, *Quest for the Celtic Key*, 292.

35. Mann, *Isle of Avalon*, 41. This event was recorded by the Venerable Bede around 720. Tysylio, Geoffrey of Monmouth, Urban, and John of Teignmouth all mention this mission. Strachan, *Jesus the Master Builder*, 21, 26 believes the date was closer to 174–179. Alternate spellings for *Fagan* include *Phaganus* and *Fugatius*; while for *Dyfan* we have *Deruvianus, Donatianus,* and *Damianus*. See Blake and Lloyd, *Keys to Avalon*, 212.

36. Ashe, *King Arthur's Avalon*, 37, 40. This can hardly be true, given the early recordings of King Lucius's name. See Davies, *Cymmrodor* 30 (1920): 143–46. He notes Giraldus Cambrensis's *De Invectionibur* (ca.1203) recording of a letter from the Chapter of St. Andrews and St. David to Pope Honorius II between 1125 and 1130, reiterating the story of King Lucius's conversion.

37. Ralls-MacLeod and Robertson, *Quest for the Celtic Key*, 158.

38. Taylor, *Coming of the Saints*, 159.

39. Taylor, *Coming of the Saints*, 222, who quotes *Life of Tertullian, Patrologia Latina*, vol. i. (A.D. 199). Strahan states that the gospel has gone to the "Places of the Britons, unreached by the Romans, but subject to Christ." See Strachan, *Jesus the Master Builder*, 17. In Prophet, *Mysteries of the Holy Grail*, xxxv, it is translated, "the extremities of Spain, the various parts of Gaul, the regions of Britain which have never been penetrated by Roman arms have received the religion of Christ."

40. Jowett, *Drama of the Lost Disciples*, 81. The Sabellian heresy said that the Father and the Son were different aspects of one Being, rather than distinct persons.

41. Chadwick, *Age of the Saints*, 12.

42. Jowett, *Drama of the Lost Disciples*, 81.

43. Prophet, *Lost Years of Jesus*, xxxv.

44. Ibid. St. Jerome in A.D. 378 wrote, "From India to Britain all nations resound with the death and resurrection of Christ" (Jowett, *Drama of the Lost Disciples*, 81).

45. Prophet, *Lost Years of Jesus*, xxxvii. One source says this persecution killed 889 communicants in Britain alone and destroyed all written records of Christianity in that country. Other emperors also persecuted the Christians in Britain, Decius (ca. A.D. 251) and Valerian (ca. A.D. 257), plus locally inspired persecutions.

46. Cox, "Influence of the English-Speaking People in Preparing the Way for the Restoration," 4.

47. Ralls-MacLeod and Robertson, *Quest for the Celtic Key*, 157.

48. There was some confusion as to the dates of these councils; for instance, Pisa is sometimes given as 1417, Constance as 1419, Sienna as 1423, and Basle as 1431. Possibly these later dates are how long the councils ran.

49. Theodore Martin, *Disputatio super Dignitatem Angliae et Calliae in Concilio Constantiou* (Lovan, 1517), as quoted in Strachan, *Jesus the Master Builder*, 30. Sinclair, *Discovery of the Grail*, 164, notes that Spain has the legend of Saint Lawrence who carried the Pope's gift of the Grail to that land.

50. In the other "Scotland" (West Country settled by early Scots), whereas the far north was called Caledonia.

51. Ussher, *British Ecclesiastical Antiquities* (1639), as quoted in Strachan, *Jesus the Master Builder*, 31. Polydore Vergil in the reign of Henry VII affirmed this in Parliament in his address regarding Philip of Spain and Queen Mary.

52. Ralls-MacLeod and Robertson, *Quest for the Celtic Key*, 157. This "heresy" has continued until today, with such well-known men as Sir Isaac Newton and Joseph Smith Jr. subscribing to this belief system.

53. Ibid., 158.

54. The sixteenth-century *Vindicta Salvatoris* (see Phillips, *Search for the Grail*, 120) says that Joseph of Arimathea founded a church in the far north of the empire. This would certainly have been Britain, which was slightly north and west of the Roman Empire.

55. *Pelagius* means, in Greek, "of the sea." Ferguson, "In Defence of Pelagius," 115; Nicholson, "Celtic Theology," 386. We do not know when he was born, probably between 350 and 360, and his death occurred about 420.

56. Rees, *Letters of Pelagius and His Followers,* 2.

57. Ferm, *Encyclopedia of Religion,* 569–70: "Pelagianism denied original sin and man's hereditary guilt. Physical death whether in the case of Adam or of his descendants is not the result of transgression, but is necessarily involved in nature. Spiritual death is not the inherited consequence of Adam's sin, but comes to each individual who misuses their power of free choice by choosing to sin. All men by virtue of their reason and free will have the power to avoid making this unrighteous choice. If in the exercise of his free and morally responsible will man so chooses, he may grasp the external aid of divine grace, which is bestowed according to man's merit. Divine grace is variously and ambiguously described as being the natural constitution of man, or as being God's Law which reveals the divine will, or again, as being the grace of Christ which works through His assurance of forgiveness to those who are baptized and through the teachings of the Church. The unassisted human will, however takes the determining initiative in the matter of salvation."

58. Rees, *Pelagius,* 20.

59. Pelagius believed that "if sin is a man's own, it is voluntary; if it is voluntary, it can be avoided" (see Newman, *Manual of Church History,* 1:364.) Pelagius did not believe in the Traducianist belief that the spirit and the body are created together at the period of procreation. We do not know if he believed in the premortal existence of the spirits of man, but he might have.

60. Phillips, *Search for the Grail,* 200. Phillips called him a gnostic priest, but this does not seem to be true. He rejected strict dualism and the antipathy toward the material world of the gnostics.

61. Knight and Lomas, *Second Messiah,* 102.

62. Durant, *Age of Faith,* 69. Latter-day Saints teach the same heretical doctrine, as the Articles of Faith: no. 2 states: "We believe that men will be punished for their own sins, and not for Adam's transgression." The Council of Ephesus (A.D. 431) condemned as a heresy the Pelagian view that man can be good at all outside the grace of God. Mormons believe that while goodness comes from God, man must strive to be good as the Father is good, within himself, through the gospel plan of happiness.

63. Augustine, *On the Grace of Christ,* XXVI, 602, as quoted in Barker, *Apostasy from the Divine Church,* 466. Augustine wrote, "How can this arrogant asserter of free will [Pelagius] say, that we are able to think a good thought comes from God, but that we actually think a good thought proceeds from ourselves."

64. Ashley, *Chronicles of the Holy Grail,* 6.

65. Phillips, *Search for the Grail,* 154.

66. Geoffrey O. Riada, "Pelagius: To Demetrias," http://www.brojed.org/pelagius.html (2001).

67. Named after a daughter of a prominent Roman family.

68. We should note that Pelagius' defense of the Nicene Trinitarian and Christological doctrines, the *Libellus Fidei,* are preserved in the Vatican because they were once thought to be writings of St. Augustine. Mormons do countenance the Nicene doctrine of three distinct individuals in the Godhead. However, the "one substance" dogma is interpreted differently by Latter-day Saints.

69. Phillips, *Search for the Grail,* 119.

70. Ferguson, "In Defence of Pelagius," 392.

71. Sinclair, *Discovery of the Grail,* 15.

72. Ibid.

PART SIX

THE GREAT APOSTASY

Though I or an angel preach another gospel, let them be accursed.

—Galatians 1:8

hen Paul said that there must be "first a falling away" before the coming of the Lord, he referred to the Great Apostasy, which was already beginning to threaten the early Church (2 Thessalonians 2:3). This was not to say that there was no longer a zeal for God, but it was not according to true knowledge (Romans 10:1–3). By the end of the first century, fragmentation riddled the Church. Proto and early orthodox Christianity may be seen as the equilibrium point between the true and living Church and its more radical apostate schisms. Hugh Nibley tells us that "in ancient times apostasy never came by renouncing the gospel but always by corrupting it."[1] This "tainted" settling level created a form of stability that could be maintained after A.D. 70, for five hundred more years, until the last vestiges of the original Christian Church were driven into the wilderness by its counterfeit.

CHAPTER FOURTEEN
ON THE TRAIL OF THE HOLY GRAIL

*Lord! How that San Graal story is ever in my mind
and thoughts continually. Was ever anything in the
world more beautiful as that is beautiful?*

—SIR EDWARD COLLEY BURNE-JONES[2]

Thus wrote the nineteenth-century British artist regarding the inspiring romance of Sir Thomas Malory's *Morte D'Arthur*. Few legends have captivated the western psyche more than the quest of the Holy Grail. Novelty adds authenticity to any legend. More than any other country, Victorian England fell under the spell of the Grail legends. Artistic interest was kindled by Malory's epic work that was published in 1471 and reprinted during the mid-nineteenth century.

Finished in 1469–70, *Morte D'Arthur* was written from London's Newgate Jail, with Malory's main source being the *Queste del Saint Graal*.[3] It was a propaganda bonanza for the Welsh Tudor dynasty, which reveled in the legend of Camelot.[4] The romance was first encountered by William Morris and Edward Burne-Jones whilst undergraduates at Oxford in 1855. From that time forward its effect on the Pre-Raphaelite and Arts and Crafts Movement was particularly profound.

The story was told and retold, painted and sculpted, sung and acted into a veritable tapestry of Western culture. Somehow it caught hold of both popular and scholarly imagination, and for the past millennia has never let go. The Grail was found, then hidden, then lost, then searched for, but always eluded the grasp of the questers who could never quite possess it. The central leitmotif of the Grail legend is "the blood in the vessel" which courses through all living and breathing things, as does this romance.

There is no real contradiction, notes Godwin, "between the vessel containing Christ's blood, *San Greal*, and a royal blood line, *Sang Real*, stemming from Jesus."[5] John Hardyng, a contemporary of Malory, happily misreads "*sang real*" for "*san greal*" so that the Sangraal (Holy Grail) becomes a double entendre, "royal blood."[6] However, this does not mean that there was ever a statement in medieval belief that Jesus and Mary were married with children.[7]

In fact the phrase, Holy Grail, is of medieval, not ancient, origin. The expression simply did not exist in any literature before the twelfth century. While the phrase is effectively used in its modern context, we should not assume that its various original meanings directly equate to or suggest its contemporary usage, such as the bloodline of Jesus and Mary Magdalene. The mythos of the Grail stories tends to bring antiquity forward by a thousand years to a more recent time. Non-LDS author Robert M. Price relates this to Mormonism:

> The legends of the grail serve a purpose analogous to that of the Book of Mormon, which extends the biblical tradition to a latter-day Christian community far removed from either the time or the place of the Bible. What the Book of Mormon does for American Latter-day Saints the grail sagas do for Western Europeans.[8]

The Middle Ages were intent upon the idea of a pure lineage of the "house of David" being through "the children of Joseph of Arimathea," not through any lineage of Jesus Christ. The latter insinuation would have totally repulsed them. None of the Celts, Merovingians, Cathars, supposed Priory de Sion, Knights Templar, or later Masons had conveyed any idea of the Holy Grail being the bloodline of Jesus.[9] Rather, all dealt with a bloodline flowing logically from the Hebrew throne of David to the kings of Western Europe. In this was carried much of the potency of its message.

KING ARTHUR

Rex quondam rexque futurus: "the once and future king."

The legend of King Arthur is the basis of all Grail romances. While not absolutely revealing, his story does push the Grail epic forward in time to the sixth century. The eighth-century historian Nennius, in his *History of the Britons*, records one of the earliest references to a war leader who defends his country against the Saxons.[10] The most likely dates for a historical Arthur would be A.D. 470–542.[11]

Tradition states that King Arthur's father, Uther Pendragon, could not have children from his wife. He found a married woman, Igraine (Eigyr, Igerna), the wife of Gorlois, the Duke of Cornwall, who, he believed, was of the proper bloodline. Gorlois, sensing Uther's interest in his wife, withdrew from the court, taking Igraine with him to Tintagel Castle on a coastal headland.[12] Anger seized Uther, who laid siege to the Duke's castle and eventually killed Igraine's husband in battle.

But Uther had Merlin disguise him in the form of the Duke. By enchantment Uther went to the sleeping Igraine and impregnated her. Their child was Arthur. Why was it so important for Pendragon to have a child through this particular woman, who initially disliked him?[13] Her lineage may have had something to do with his desire to mate with her. Could it have been a preferred Grail line? Blake and Lloyd ask a similar question: "This raised the question as to why Uthyr went to such lengths to marry Eigyr. Was it that the right to rule passed down through the female line and Eigyr held the royal bloodline of Ynys Prydein [Wales]. Was it only by marrying Eigyr that Uthyr could guarantee the crown for his heirs?"[14]

Certain strains of the sovereign "seed" of Christ were planted throughout Britain and the continent, both for its own protection and as "sifted leaven" for the European royal families. Perhaps a select number of white-clad Grail queens, such as Guinevere (meaning "white woman"), promulgated the mitochondrial DNA bloodline and the legend long after it had lost its meaning to the masses. The male side of the royal genealogical equation, attests Norma Goodrich, was well known: "Both [Arthur and Galahad] boast pedigrees that are at the same time 'Royal and Sainted.' In plain words, Lancelot and Perceval are descendants of the Kings David and Solomon."[15]

King Arthur's Round Table at Camelot, devised by Merlin, represented the democratic governance used to maintain the kingdom. The search for the family ancestry, the *Great Mystery of the Holy Grail*, became Arthur's greatest quest, and the sad affair of his wife, Guinevere, with Lancelot became his greatest tragedy. He was supposedly taken after his death to a cave in the Isle of Avalon to be healed and someday, when needed most, return, thereby becoming the "Once and Future King." Could the cave represent a dormant stage of a planted seed that would germinate one day into a living tree?[16] This seems to be the undergirding theme of the Grail.

In a painting of the dying King Arthur, we see him passing the sword Excalibur on to Galahad to be cast back into the lake (ocean?) (see Plate 24).[17] Perhaps Excalibur represents the Sword of Judah in the same fashion that the Sword of Laban represents the Sword of Joseph-Ephraim? It might have been taken by St. Brendan to the promised land in A.D. 570.

In Mendlesohnian fashion, the Grail must have been a true descendant from a true seed. The persistent legends of Joseph of Arimathea leading a band of twelve intrepid travelers escaping the Holy Land for "the Isles of the Sea" is intriguing. Isabel Elder noted, "Every one of the knights [of King Arthur] descended from Joseph of Arimathea."[18] John W. Taylor agrees: "These companions and relations are said to have intermarried with the families of the British kings or chieftains, and from them, by direct descent, in something like four hundred years, are said to have arisen the greater heroes of King Arthur's Court—the Knights of the Round Table."[19]

"Traditionally," writes Hansen, "Arthur and some of his knights are claimed as direct descendants of Joseph of Arimathea, Arthur being the eighth or ninth generation from Joseph."[20]

The Grail Castle was a Christianized temple. It had a "Holy Place" with a (round?) table possessing twelve loaves of shew bread. Could this have been the ancient table from Solomon's temple or from the Castle of Souls? Or perhaps it represents King Uther Pendragon's Round Table made by Merlin the wizard and used by King Arthur's knights.[21] Was this the original Fellowship of the Round Table?

Malcolm Godwin notes that there might have been as many as three "Round Tables."[22] The first was the table of Christ at the Last Supper, with its thirteenth "perilous Seat of Judas." As mentioned in a preceding chapter, the house of the Last Supper may have been owned by Joseph of Arimathea.[23] Joseph of Arimathea's "Round Table," because of his study of Essene practice, might have been a high table with upright chairs. It was different from the Greco-Roman, Jewish, and Bedouin custom of a low table with guests lying beside it.[24]

Then, according to Godwin, there was the "Table Round devised by Merlin, symbolizing the earth, the planets, the stars and the spheres, a true epitome of the universe." This may have something to do with the twelve planets of this system or eternity, of which the LDS prophet John Taylor speaks.[25]

It too had a thirteenth chair, the "perilous Seat of Dread," which only the true leader could sit upon. According to Michell and Rhone, "Sir Galahad is said to have founded the order of the Holy Grail, appointing 12 knights as guardians of the Round Table which St. Joseph first established in Britain."[26] This table and the outward emblem of the Grail, a chalice, were apparently fashioned in Jerusalem.

Thus we see that all trails lead to Joseph of Arimathea, King Arthur's distant relative, as the creator of the Round Table(s). The Queen of the Waste Land describes three great fellowships: "That of the Last Supper, that of the Holy Grail and that of the Round Table, instituted by Merlin."[27]

Finally the Grail and Round Table were lost

again but later found by Sir Perceval, who was also of the lineage of Joseph of Arimathea.[28] For Perceval and the other knights, the search for the Grail meant that the right man should find the right woman, to "keep pure" and perpetuate the chosen patriarchal bloodline.

Sirs Hector and Lancelot signify the futility of the quest for many knights as they mounted two powerful steeds, saying, "Let us seek what we shall never find."[29] Knights Gawain, Bors, and the pure Galahad, among others, go questing individually for the Grail, which weakens Arthur's Fellowship of Knights. The quest was serious business with high stakes. An ancient hermit declares to Arthur's court, "For this is no search for earthly things, but a seeking out of the mysteries and hidden sweets of Our Lord."[30]

Arthur's knights set out together, but they soon choose separate paths for the Grail. Only when they let the reins of the horse go free were these knights errant guided by the hand of God to the right mate, trusting in the compass (Liahona) as much as in the square (Iron Rod).[31] As Godwin notes: "Eastern mystics can never seem to understand Christ's saying, *'Seek and ye shall find.'* They insist that this is not the way to enlightenment, to the Ultimate State."[32]

The reason for this dichotomy comes from the fact that this was in a time of apostasy and one did not, until the Restoration, have anything more than "hints and suggestions" to go by. The harder facts of truth just weren't available at that time. Thus intuition and the Spirit had to suffice. As the genealogy of the Holy Grail continued for generations becoming less and less a known fact, it became more like the swirling mists of Avalon. In truth, the bloodline of Christ was never found again until it was rediscovered and recognized in Joseph Smith Jr. at the Sacred Grove (Enchanted Forest) in 1820. It was there that the right question was finally asked.

This epiphany was a *Holy Grail* icon, dealing as it did with the coronation of the united bloodlines of Judah and Ephraim. All artifacts relating to the heirship and blood descent of True Israel were automatically relics of the Grail vessel. They tend to follow the peoples of the true birthright lineage. It was the Eucharistic chalice of the Last Supper, brought to Britain by Joseph of Arimathea.[33] Then, perhaps, this silver cup was brought to America with the "Fruitful Bough" of Ephraim and St. Brendan, as we shall see later.

The idea that the Holy Grail refers to a castle (the temple) is widespread.[34] A corollary to this idea is that the temple refers to the body of Jesus Christ.[35] Thus a search for the Holy Grail led one to the temple, which in turn led one to the living Christ. During the Great Apostasy, the temple, the great intermediary between heaven and earth, was lost, not to be recovered until the latter days by a Fisher King and brave Knight, Joseph Smith Jr.

MEDIEVAL GRAIL LEGENDS

Hear ye the history of the most holy vessel that is called the Grail, in which the precious blood of Jesus was received on the day that He was put on the Cross.

—ANON, *PERLESVAUS*

The Grail legend is the richest of all East-West myths and still has a powerful allure. However, according to Goodrich, the ten major authentic Grail manuscripts are "winging it" regarding the mystery and the romance.[36] Its Christian version, by consensus, begins with Joseph of Arimathea. Some say that he put the Grail cup into a well in Glastonbury and that the well-spring issues red-colored water in honor of the blood of Christ ever since.[37] Others say that it was secreted in the Glastonbury Abbey or the crypt of Rosslyn chapel.

It is not coincidental that the idea of the Holy

Grail should suddenly revive after A.D. 1100 Dr. Walter Johannes Stein's research led him to believe that the first written references to a search for the Holy Grail date from the late ninth century.[38] If this is true, it lends credence to a pre-Templar and perhaps even an ancient origin of the Grail quest accounts. The initial tales rested on pagan prototypes such as *Peredur*, a part of a collection of Welsh legends known as the *Mabinogion*.

In 1094, the Crusades were begun under Pope Urban II, at Bari, France, with the charismatic revivalist Peter the Hermit, who had just returned from a pilgrimage to Palestine.[39] When the Crusaders returned from Islamic lands with sacred and miraculous early Christian relics, the first written Grail Legends began to be published. It was from this charged era of the troubadours, trouveres, and *raconteurs*, long after the San Graal (holy blood) was lost, that a loosening of the bloodline secret was broached. Mind you, not one had even an inkling by this time that the Grail might have meant the literal bloodline of the married Christ.

The exotic religious atmosphere allowed a totally distorted version of the story to be mentioned for the first time. This occurred during the Crusades of the militant Knights Templar. Likewise the white-mantled Cistercian Order romanticized what had earlier been pagan and early Christian Celtic myths. The Order felt that the Grail legends were originally Hebrew ideas that had come to the pagans, and the monks felt obliged to powerfully reclaim and embellish them to fit the new Christian reality.

Certainly by the end of the twelfth century, from France, Flanders, Germany, and England literature promoting the quest of the Grail began to flood popular imagination. Laurence Gardner and others believe that "Grail lore was born directly out of this early Templar environment."[40] In a sense it was an attempt to link the dim remembrances of the Grail experience of Arthur with the Crusader Grail Quests of the twelfth century.

Also instrumental were the activities surrounding Glastonbury Abbey at the time.[41] After 1184, when a fire severely damaged the Glastonbury Abbey, funds were sorely needed to rebuild. The abbots eventually began to revive and embellish for their own use the ancient legends of Christ visiting Britain and of the Holy Family later coming to Somerset and Cornwall.

The earliest literary source for the Grail romance rested with the poet Chrétien de Troyes (fl.1160–1190), who came from the Champagnes region of France. His epic *Perceval: Le Conte de Graal* (*Perceval: The Story of the Grail*) became the rage of Europe and possibly sparked the Grail idea at Glastonbury. The Grail craze boiled in 1191 when Joseph of Arimathea's body was supposedly unearthed at Glastonbury Abbey with the bodies of Arthur and Guinevere (see Plate 25).[42]

Throughout Europe, and especially France, the Grail legend of Mary Magdalene flourished in the medieval period. In fact the village church at Beckery was first dedicated to the Magdalene before being rechristened to the Virgin.[43] It seemed that her cult was never far from well-known Grail sites. Yet it should be emphasized that nowhere in literature is there any hint of the Holy Grail being a person but rather an exquisite idea and a venerated object.[44] Nowhere is a sacred marriage of Christ or His children ever even hinted at, no matter how provocative the Grail literature.[45]

In these legends, hero and heroine both possessed high valor, virginal purity, and an exemplary family pedigree as the source of their spiritual powers. They only had this power when they used their authority wisely and in the cause of good. Their great innocence caused them to be named, like Percival (Perceval), "the Great Fool." They became awkward misfits, like Forrest Gump, in a sophisticated cosmopolitan society that was embarrassed by them. Like Parzival's unreflecting and unquestioning behavior, "don't ask questions," he falls back on rote conduct by not asking the one question that would heal the Fisher King, "What ails thee, Uncle?"

This would have also broken the enchantments of both realm and king. The goal never really was the Grail hallow itself but the reconciliation which heals the wasteland and restores paradise found within the Holy Grail. In this the knights were not worldly, but rather pure and loyal. Their quest, while real, was spiritual, not secular.

Galahad found the Holy Grail and sat upon the Seat Perilous, as was predicted. Malory has twelve nuns with Galahad at the Round Table with fresh golden letters on the seats saying *"Here ought he to sit, and he ought to sit here."* But on the Siege Perilous or Judas Seat was written that the seat would only be filled 454 years after the passion of Christ. This would make it about A.D. 487 when Galahad sat down upon the Grail seat.[46] Certainly Galahad had certain rights, but he had no recorded children. After him the lineage became secreted again. This was, then, the quest of King Arthur—to find the bloodline Grail again.

Galahad seemed to be the right person (lineage) at the right time. Could it be that he found the Holy Grail because he was, in fact, the Holy Grail itself? He was born to it and knew no other task.[47] Although unnoticed by other Grail scholars, it is possible that while Joseph of Arimathea was a Jew of the united Zerah-Perez house, Galahad was a selected Grail Son from the united Judah and Ephraim Shiloh-Dynasty. Later the wasteland would be cured when another "desired knight," Joseph Smith, stemming from this same new dynasty of Shiloh, restored the gospel of Jesus Christ to the world (see D&C 113:2–6). The New Jerusalem would then be planted at the Center Stake of Zion and grow like Daniel's Rock until the whole world is filled.

Few doubt that Wolfram von Eschenbach's *Parzival*, the German version of the legend, is the best of the subsequent Grail texts. Eschenbach believed that Chrétien's work did not do the Grail justice. Unlike Chrétien's *Perceval: Le Conte du Graal*, it had the Knights Templar defined as the Guardians of the Grail and Grail family.[48] Throughout his text Wolfram maintained the importance of a genealogical connection between the Grail and the coming of Christ. Malcolm Godwin writes: "From a belief in the forces of heredity he was able to reconstruct a family tree of the grail. *'And the sons of baptized men hold It and Guard It with humble heart and the best of mankind shall those knights be.'* These are the Grail Guardians, whose lineage and destiny stretch as far back as Cain, the son of Adam."[49]

Wolfram maintained that the Grail was a stone. This emerald stone fell from the crown of Lucifer to the earth, as Satan plummeted to hell after the war in heaven. As it fell, one tradition states, it changed from a stone to a sword, then to a spear, and finally into the Grail chalice.[50]

Thus we see from the earliest legends the emphasis which was placed on bloodlines. The major motif rests upon the heirship of the House of David to underscore the royal right to reign for the kings of Britain. While not specifically identifying the Grail children of Christ, or the dual bloodlines, the literature is very provocative to our contention.

BOOK OF JESUS CHRIST: "BOOK OF THE HOLY VESSEL"

Wherefore, I will that all men shall repent, for all are under sin, except those which I have reserved unto myself, holy men that ye know not of.

—D&C 49:8

The fall of King Arthur's realm came with his death in about A.D. 542. A year before this we are told that Arthur personally saw the Grail lying "open and discovered" before him.[51] What form the Grail took we are not told, but his royal Knight Parzifal called it a "revelation" or "apocalypse" (Greek for "lifting the veil"). This particular Grail may well have been a book, a receptacle of Christ's genealogy, rather than just a chalice alone.[52] On the cover of the book might have been an image of a chalice with a seer stone embedded in its binding, just to tidy up the symbolism.

The anonymous eighth-century Scottish author of *The Chronicle of Heliandus* notes that the book is a pedigree or genealogy of Jesus Christ.[53] These *Chronicles of Helinandus* give one of the earliest accounts of the Grail. The author tells of a hermit who had a remarkable vision of Joseph of Arimathea. On the eve of Good Friday in 717 Christ supposedly appeared to the hermit Waleran and said: "This is the book of thy descent, Here begins the Book of the Holy Grail, Here begin the terrors, Here begin the marvels."[54]

According to the document, the Lord gave him a small book "no larger or wider than the palm of a man's hand," containing "greater marvels than any mortal heart could conceive. Nor will you have any doubts that will not be set straight by this book. *Inside are My secrets, which I Myself put there with My own hand.*"[55] Grailologist Nora Goodrich notes: "To think that there may once have been a book of the Bible actually written by Jesus Christ, in his own handwriting, and that it contained his genealogy, brings shivers to the reader; for the genealogy of Christ takes us afar, to Bethlehem and Jerusalem, and to Kings David and Solomon."[56]

Goodrich assumes that it was Christ's genealogy back to Solomon; however, it is possible that the book was His genealogy backward and forward, from Michael-Adam to, at least, the author of *Grand Saint-Graal*. The "holy men that ye know not of" noted in the Doctrine and Covenants may have been the secret lineage of Jesus Christ (D&C 49:8).[57] Again we

read in *Doctrine and Covenants* 86:8–10 of the *raison d'etre* of these hidden holy men: "[Ye] have been hid from the world with Christ in God—Therefore your life and the priesthood have remained, and must needs remain through you and your lineage until the restoration of all things spoken by the mouths of all the holy prophets since the world began." Sometimes we are those "holy men" with a purpose.

Arthurian knight Gawain told us that all forms of the Grail were associated with the blinding light of the Savior himself in beatific vision. The bright revelation of the Grail could cause temporary disorientation.[58] Perhaps the Grail was a transcendent vision of Christ with his brides coupled with the genealogy of His seed.

The French romance *La Folie Perceval* (ca. 1330) references and relies heavily upon much earlier material, particularly the lost *Peveril* poem. It notes that Perceval, at a feast in the Grail Castle, received a box before the Fisher King and Queen. When they open it a sacred platter is revealed. "And upon the platter was the book of the holy vessel, but Perceval could not look upon it for it shone with so great a light."[59]

The *Fulke le Fitz Waryn* also quotes *Peveril* in describing one of the Grails as a book, "the book of the holy vessel." No other surviving romance uses this precise description. The "book of the holy vessel" seems to refer to the list of holy human vessels [grails] that are contained in Christ's hidden bloodline descendancy. But because Perceval fails to ask a certain decisive question he is unable to read the book. As the Bible says about such cases, "Ye have not, because ye ask not" (James 4:2; see also Luke 11:9–10). Sir Perceval realizes the consequences of his silence and takes it upon himself to carefully understand the mystery of the Grail.

Eventually, after many adventures, Perceval again finds the Grail castle, which has been struck down by devilish lightning bolts. The Fisher King (his grandfather) is feeble but cannot die. When the King breaks the bread and serves the wine (Holy Sacrament) the Grail procession begins again. The Hall is filled with good odors, and every knight had such meats and drinks as they loved best. Only this time, as the sacred book is opened, Perceval finally asks the right question, "Whom does the Grail serve?"[60]

The Fisher King now answers, "The Grail serves the father of the Fisher King," being satisfied that Perceval has met all the conditions to take over the Grail Guardian role.[61] Sir Perceval can now read the book, even though it shines brightly. The Fisher King is probably Jesus Christ and His Father is God Himself.[62] So Sir Perceval, himself, would be the "King's Son" literally and figuratively. The mystery of the book lies in the fact that it outlines the lineages of Christ's children to the very day it was revealed. Therefore, Perceval's own name was written in it. Furthermore, the *Vulgate Cycle* Grail legend includes, as one of its Grails, a book written by Jesus himself.[63] How precious are books.[64]

This interpretation seems better than the one forwarded by Dr. Graham Phillips in his 1996 book, *The Search for the Grail*. Phillips notes that the old King then teaches Perceval about the book, that it contains the secret words of Jesus Christ written down by His disciple Judas Didymos, called Thomas.[65] Discovered in 1945 in Egypt, the Nag Hammadi gnostic documents revealed the *Gospel of Thomas*, which purports to be the secret teachings of Jesus. Phillips believes this to be the true Holy Grail. But after carefully reading this gnostic text, it would be a major disappointment, as the Grail text for it carries nothing of Christ's lineage and just a few enlightening Logions.

The list of certain hidden "holy men [and women]" contained in this book will make great world history when their story is finally told. Christ's descendants, "hid from the world, with Christ in God" will be an honor roll of the greatest humans of the past two thousand years. It might also include a list of the most evil people as well. Most of Christ's

genealogy served mankind without the benefit of the priesthood until the latter days. Our story now enters the dark phase of the Great Apostasy, where priesthood was the right but not the blessing of these "holy men."

NOTES

1. Nibley, *Temple and Cosmos*, 395.
2. Quoting Burne-Jones in Nicola Redway's "The Quest of the Holy Grail," *Christie's International Magazine* (October-November 1994): 18.
3. With Perlesvas, it was the first Christianized version of the Grail legend. Completed between 1215–35 it drew heavily from the Song of Songs (Solomon) for its powerful symbolism. It was a part of the Latin-French Vulgate Cycle and supposedly relied upon writings by Jesus and Joseph of Arimathea.
4. Sinclair, *Discovery of the Grail*, 194. King Henry VII's son Arthur was born in Winchester, then thought to be Camelot.
5. Godwin, *Holy Grail*, 184.
6. Hardyng, *Chronicle*, 134–35. This is similar to Henry Lovelich's comments at around the same time. The earlier, long version of the chronicle is unpublished. It is in the British Library, Lansdowne 204. See Barber, *Holy Grail*, 227.
7. Hopkins, Simmans, and Wallace-Murphy, *Rex Deus*, 75, say this is so, but they do not footnote their sources. She falsely believes, in hindsight, that the accumulation of "hints" makes it perfectly obvious that medieval Europe was hiding the secret while at the same time revealing it through veiled codes.
8. Price, *Da Vinci Fraud*, 56.
9. This author has been unable to find any references in Freemasonry to the marriage and bloodline of Jesus. However, in the twenty-fifth degree, "Prince of Mercy," there appears the most blatant reference in Masonry to the blood of Jesus:

   Question: Are you a Prince of Mercy?

   Answer: I have seen the great light (Delta), and our Most Excellent, as well as yourself, in the "Triple Alliance" of the "Blood of Jesus Christ," of which you and I have the mark.

   Beyond this obscure comment, there is nothing at all

direct or even indirectly related to Jesus being married and having children. If the Masons believed in the Hieros Gamos of Jesus, they kept the secret perfectly from everybody. See Cain (pseud.), *Secrets of the Lodge*, 181.

10. MacInnes, "The Arthurian Legend," *World Mythology*, 189. King Vortigern around A.D. 450 invited the Angles/Saxons into Wales as his mercenaries. See Blake and Lloyd, *Keys to Avalon*, 59.

11. Radford, "Glastonbury Abbey," in Ashe, *Quest for Arthur's Britain*. According to Reid, *Arthur the Dragon*, 51, Geoffrey of Monmouth's chronology would place Arthur's reign somewhere between A.D. 480 and 520.

12. Ralls-MacLeod and Robertson, *Quest for the Celtic Key*, 221, note that excavations at Tintagel in 1990–91 prove that the location was not a monastery but a fifth- and sixth-century stronghold, used on a seasonal basis.

13. According to Arthurian scholar Robyn Lamm, most stories suggest that they eventually were so devoted to each other that they ignored everyone else, including their children.

14. Blake and Lloyd, *Keys to Avalon*, 117.

15. Goodrich, *Holy Grail*, 6.

16. Like the Sleeping Beauty legend, in which the maiden would awake or the woman in the wilderness would be discovered (Revelation 12:6).

17. Sidney Harold Meteyard (1868–1947), *The Passing of Arthur* (n.d., watercolor), sold Christie's London auction house (June 1999). In a painting of the dying King Arthur we see him passing the sword, Excalibur, on to Galahad to be cast back into the lake (ocean?). Perhaps Excalibur represents the Sword of Judah in the same fashion as the Sword of Laban represents the Sword of Joseph/Ephraim? It might have been taken by St. Brendan to the promised land in A.D. 570.

18. Elder, *Joseph of Arimathea*, 33.

19. Taylor, *Coming of the Saints*, 141. Also see Barber, *Holy Grail*, 200.

20. Hansen, *Whence Came They?* 103. Knight and Lomas, *Second Messiah*, 104, claim that King Arthur was also descended from a certain Constantine, possibly the same that was called "Great."

21. Goodrich, *Holy Grail*, 17.

22. Godwin, *Holy Grail*, 123.

23. Tony Fieldsted of Springville, Utah, conversation with the author (April 2002).

24. The modern idea of a high table for dining was also known among the Britons. The Essenes saw it as a more sanitary way of eating, as well as having individual servings of food, rather than eating from a common bowl or pot.

25. Taylor, *Mediation and Atonement*, 76–77: "And again, the 'twelve kingdoms' which are under the above-mentioned Presidency of the Father, Son and Holy Ghost, are governed by the same rules and destined to the same honor. . . . That is, each kingdom, or planet, and the inhabitants thereof, were blessed with the visits and presence of their Creator, in their several times and seasons."

26. Michell and Rhone, *Twelve-Tribe Nations*, 69.

27. Matthews, *King Arthur and the Grail Quest*, 106.

28. Godwin, *Holy Grail*, 74. Anonymous, "A Myth for Our Times," *The Grail* (n.d.), 167. He says that Perceval and Gawain are the same person. Grail scholar Robyn Lamm, Burnsville, Minnesota, takes exception to this, saying they should not be confused, for Perceval is one of three who finds the Grail, while Gawain fails in his quest.

29. Godwin, *Holy Grail*, 127.

30. Matthews, *King Arthur and the Grail Quest*, 106.

31. In the apostate world view, which is always ready to cast off the commandments of God, the gnostic author of "A Myth for Our Times," *The Grail*, 173, wrote: "Apparently for our time, life demands to be lived as a Koan question, as a continual searching; not, as before, in accordance with the dogmatically prescribed pattern of behavior and moral codes."

Godwin, *Holy Grail*, 151, observes that the Man of Tao follows the Watercourse Way, trusting in the flow of things. Latter-day Saints often believe the easiest way is not always the best way, and sometimes we must swim upstream or follow the rocky path uphill. Eastern religions tend to use the "drift to the sea" metaphor, while Mormonism is best described as the "climb to the mountain" mentality.

32. Godwin, *Holy Grail*, 154. He also states, " . . . the Grail Castle is strange, in that anyone actually looking for it will never discover its whereabouts." The two views of "seek" and "don't seek" collide in the Grail myth. It is said that Buddha made every effort for six years in his quest for the Ultimate State. "But it was only when he finally gave up all effort that he attained that which he had been seeking." I maintain that if Buddha had not sought long and hard for six years, it would not have come to him when he relaxed. If he had not sought the Ultimate State, he would have never striven, nor meditated . . . and consequently would not have "obtained."

33. Sinclair, *Discovery of the Grail*, 60, 149. St. Lawrence supposedly had the cup of the Last Supper, which he would not give up to the Roman Emperor.

34. Goodrich, *Holy Grail*, 21.

35. Ibid., 19.

36. Ibid., xxiv. In chapter 58 of *The Da Vinci Code,* we are told that the truth about Mary Magdalene and Jesus was preserved in the ingeniously conceived allegory of the Holy Grail. See Haag and Haag, *Rough Guide to The Da Vinci Code,* 22. But it was much more subconscious than that. No Grail writer knew exactly what it meant.

37. Chalice, or Bride's, Well, at the foot of the Glastonbury Tor, is a natural spring with deposits of iron ore. In 1906 a Mr. W. Pole found a blue glass bowl/cup in the well, which he had deposited there eight years earlier. See Barber, *Holy Grail,* 298–99.

38. Stein, *Ninth Century and the Holy Grail,* vi.

39. Most Crusades began in Reims and had an enlightening influence upon medieval Europe.

40. Gardner, *Bloodline of the Holy Grail,* 257.

41. Sinclair, *Discovery of the Grail,* 49. Under the inspired leadership of Henry of Blois, the nephew of the English King Henry I, the abbey underwent a Cluniac reform before it came under Cistercian control.

42. The Abbey Ruins in Glastonbury, Somerset.

43. Sinclair, *Discovery of the Grail,* 125.

44. Abanes, *Truth behind The Da Vinci Code,* 46.

45. This statement flies in the face of almost all popularizing Grail books of the late twentieth and early twenty-first centuries.

46. Since King Arthur died about A.D. 540, this would have been roughly the time of Arthur's birth, long before Galahad was supposed to have been born.

47. Matthews, *King Arthur and the Grail Quest,* 122.

48. Baigent and Leigh, *Temple and the Lodge,* 118.

49. Godwin, *Holy Grail,* 137. Wolfram claims Kyot's research had revealed a genealogical connection between the account of the Grail and the coming of Christ foretold by Flegetanis (his source). The murderous Cain was the founder of the cult of Master Mahan, a man of sin and founder of the false lineage. From the lineage of Cain came the cursed race. It is interesting that the genealogy would be traced back to Cain and not to Seth, Adam's other righteous son after Abel.

50. Godwin, *Holy Grail,* 53.

51. Goodrich, *Holy Grail,* xxvii.

52. Ibid., 1.

53. It was later rewritten by a monk of Froidmont in the twelfth century, in the French language and titled *Grand Saint-Graal.*

54. Godwin, *Holy Grail,* 10. The book *Le Seynt Graal* was supposedly famous in the time of King Ina of the West Saxons. Ina extended his kingdom to include Glastonbury, the ancient site of the first Christian church in Europe. Waleran's manuscript was referred to by Heliand, a French monk of the Abbey of Fromund, ca. 1200. It was also noted by John of Glastonbury in the *Cronica sive Antiquitates Glastoniensis Ecclesie* and later by Vincent of Baeauvais in his 1604 *Speculum Historiale.*

55. *Estoire del Saint Graal,* I, 4, as quoted in Barber, *Holy Grail,* 65.

56. Goodrich, *Holy Grail,* 5.

57. These would also include translated beings and other angels.

58. The Book of Mormon notes that when certain angels revealed themselves, their brightness shocked and caused people to appear dead (Alma 18:42, 22:18).

59. See Phillips, *Search for the Grail,* 152. La Folie Perceval survives in manuscript form in the Bibliotheque National, Paris (MS Fonds François 12577).

60. Phillips, *Search for the Grail,* 153. Though different from the question, "What ails thee?" it served the same purpose.

61. Collins, *Twenty-First Century Grail,* 14. The father of the Fisher King is certainly Jesus Christ.

62. Or going the other way, "the Son of Jesus."

63. Godwin, *Holy Grail,* 117–18.

64. One of the saddest occurrences of "book burning" happened when the English King Edward I, following the conquest of Wales, had all the great books of Welsh history taken to the Tower of London and burnt. Blake and Lloyd, *Keys to Avalon,* 164.

65. Phillips, *Search for the Grail,* 154. Altogether there were 114 sayings or Logions in the apocryphal Gospel of Thomas.

CHAPTER FIFTEEN
THE DEATH OF THE CELTIC CHURCH

Behold, verily I say, the field was the world, and the apostles
were the sowers of the seed; And after they have fallen asleep
the great persecutor of the church, the apostate, the whore,
even Babylon, that maketh all nations to drink of her cup,
in whose hearts the enemy, even Satan, sitteth to reign—
behold he soweth the tares; wherefore, the tares choke the
wheat and drive the church into the wilderness

—D & C 86:2–3

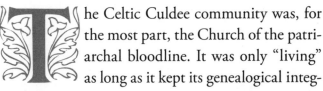

he Celtic Culdee community was, for the most part, the Church of the patriarchal bloodline. It was only "living" as long as it kept its genealogical integrity. This was the case in much the same way as the priesthood to be "true" must keep its own unbroken line by the laying on of hands. Of course, in both instances each side of the authority coin must worthily hold to gospel principles and practices (D&C 11:20). Few things on this mortal terrestrial earth after many generations are in a straight line and precisely dateable. But the ecclesiastical complexity does not totally obscure the pattern or template of the truth and order behind all things.

There are several clues worth examining that led us to believe that the Culdee, Catholic, and Orthodox churches finally fell into the Great Apostasy at about the same time. It seems that between A.D. 570 and 607 the last vestiges of Grail authority

joined the Lord's priesthood in the wilderness.

How can we reckon the significance of A.D 570 in light of Revelation 12:6? If 1830 signified the date of return of the woman fled into the wilderness, then how does 570 calculate into the equation? A number of significant implications for that date have been found. But ultimately it was the date of the revealing (birth) of the Man of Sin mentioned by Paul in II Thessalonians. And who was this man? In the author's opinion the "man of sin" was Judeo-Christianity's old nemesis.

The death of the Celtic Christian community led to its assimilation into the Roman Catholic Church. Finally in 664 at the Council of Whitby, the Celtic, or Culdee, native churches were dissolved and subsumed into the Roman Church. But this assimilation was just a recognition of what had happened decades before. The grail church finally succumbed and was forced into hiding in the wilderness.

THE LAST OF THE FISHER KINGS (A.D 537–570)

Subsumed within the larger context of the Grail Seed, there seems to have been a hidden line of Fisher Kings or patriarchs. These uncrowned patriarchs were the most direct *Rex Deus* blood heirs of Jesus Christ, called Fisher Kings. In difficult times they might be consulted by secular kings and later, when their pedigree was lost, sought after in Grail quests.[1] Britain was about to experience the demise of its aboveground native Celtic Christian community, with its succession of anonymous Fisher Kings.[2] The veil over the land was called Logres, which is the inner soul of the earthly Britain.[3]

Although the bloodline of Mary and Christ still continued to exist, their descendants lost the priesthood authority to run the Celtic Culdee Church. It should be remembered that by the sixth century most of Britain outside Saxon domination in eastern England was already Christian but not Roman Catholic.[4]

This schism, between the British and Italian branches of Christianity, first became apparent in A.D. 416, when the Welsh monk Pelagius was pronounced a heretic. It may be assumed that long before the Pelagian Heresy, there simmered a rift between the two early forms of Christianity. The adherents of the apostolic succession (through St. Peter) and the adherents of the bloodline (Fisher Kings through Joseph of Arimathea) were plainly at odds by the fourth and fifth centuries. During the Roman Empire, before the troop evacuations of A.D. 410, it might be surmised that the official Roman Catholic form of Christianity held some influence over many parts of Britain. Wales, while conquered, was never completely subdued, and the native Church had its strength there.[5]

By the fifth century, the indigenous Britons were being savaged by the Angles and Saxons and other invaders, while the Celtic Culdee community was under threat from Rome. Natural disasters at this time were creating catastrophic environmental problems, which signaled to many at the time the apostasy of the Church. These natural signs may have been portents of a spiritual falling away.

According to Mike Ashley there was a total eclipse of the sun in A.D. 538, which was clearly visible in Britain.[6] It was considered as an evil omen. Norma Goodrich cites the year of the eclipse as A.D. 536, which accords with the legends of the death of Merlin, King Arthur's advisor and prophet at the royal fortress in Snowdonia.[7] Also it relates to Arthur's death at Camlann.[8]

A.D. 538 was the year, according to Stothers and Rampino, of the "dim sun" or "dry fog" (dust veil) noted in contemporary annals.[9] Tree-rings for the years A.D. 536–545 window give evidence of radical narrowing. Now science has given some credence to legendary statements of such conditions, previously without scholarly foundation, such as the date of King Arthur's death.[10] Norma Goodrich has King Arthur as the sixth and last supreme initiate at the Grail Castle in Britain.[11] Thus King Arthur was supposedly the last of the Fisher Kings, the bloodline patriarchs who maintained the Church.

Other natural disasters coincide with the pivotal break in the patriarchal bloodline. Halley's comet came in A.D. 530, but a few years afterward came other close encounters with more menacing comets.[12] Edward Gibbon notes in 1788: "Eight years afterward [A.D. 538–39], while the sun was in Capricorn, another comet appeared to follow in the Sagittary: the size was gradually increasing; the head was in the east, the tail in the west, and it remained visible about forty days. . . . The nations, who gazed with astonishment, expected wars and calamities from their baleful influence; and these expectations were abundantly fulfilled."[13]

This must be the A.D. 540 comet postulated by Mike Baillie.[14] It was described as a fire-breathing dragon encircling the earth with its tail and claws. Cometary debris struck like atomic bombs in western Britain, Wales, and Ireland. It decimated the countryside, turning it into an environmental disaster zone similar to the wasteland mentioned in Arthurian legends. In *The Ruin and Fall of Britain* the near contemporary annalist, British monk Gildas, gave apocalyptic warnings, saying, "These things [catastrophic events] will happen again," meaning that the depredations of the previous generation would be revisited on the people.

The comet seemed to be a star fallen from heaven, and in conformance with the book of Revelation they called it wormwood (Revelation 8:11). Don Carleton of Bristol postulates that a comet landed in the Celtic (Irish) Sea, causing tectonic movement and belching out gases of sulfuric methane.[15] Its fragments poisoned the waters, polluted the air, killed the vegetation and animals, and caused floods throughout the region. Malory's *Le Morte d'Arthur* describes King Arthur's dream along these lines:

> [It] seemed that a dreadful dragon did drown much of his people, and he came flying out of the west, and his head was enameled with azure, and his shoulders shone as gold, his belly like mails of a marvelous hue, his tail full of tatters, his feet full of fine sable, and his claws like fine gold; an hideous flame of fire flew out of his mouth, like as the land and water had flamed all of fire.[16]

There are several reasons why this event comes down to us through mythologized legend instead of written history. The fact that the episodes were so spectacular and hard to describe made them difficult to believe.[17] The idea that "the sun shall he cause to rise in the West" was too strange to be understood; thus it eventually became discounted in the official record.

The events also coincided with similar descriptions mentioned in holy writ regarding the last days and the second coming of Christ. If such "signs" would precede the parousia, and Christians were commanded not to "look" for such signs, then a false sign should be ignored or rejected. When the Lord did not return, these events were censored from the official written records of their day because they were a confusion to the people. However, they could not be totally suppressed from mythology or obliterated from oral tradition, and thus they were passed on to the future in legendary form.

Shortly following the comet's destruction, British champion and battle-king Arthur died, sometime between 540 and 542 at Camlann (Camelot) in north Wales. This was then followed by a devastating yellow plague of A.D. 543.[18] In fact, the mighty Welsh king Maelgwyn died of the plague in A.D. 549. Deteriorating environmental conditions may have sparked the plague, yet it might have been the comet itself that brought the disease.[19] Magnusson notes that "the years around 550 were the real watershed for Britain. . . . [The plague provided] the impetus for another [Saxon] surge against the weakened natives . . . many libraries may have been destroyed, and the shape of England's political and *dynastic* landscape for centuries to come was formed."[20]

The bombardment of the earth with cometary debris was frightening to the populace. In the face of such trying circumstances, powerful emotions longed for the restoration of the Fisher King. It would be his archetypal "kingly fertility" which would heal the wasteland and clear the skies of its paroxysm and auroral displays. With so many portents and premonitions of destruction most people were clearly apprehensive about what was coming from the stars. These events were sufficiently momentous as to aid St. Patrick's mission to Christianize Ireland.[21]

The stage was also set for momentous struggle between Briton and Saxon, and between the British and Roman forms of Christianity. When nothing eschatological happened, the deterioration of faith following these natural disasters opened the door for Catholicism. There is an interesting side note in the commentary to the Middle English *The Story of Grisandol:* "Merlin digresses to prophesy that a dragon from Rome will come to destroy Britain and battle against a crowned lion, but that it [dragon] will be killed by a bull."[22]

Thus we begin to see events unfold. In eastern Britain in Kent after A.D. 550, the pagan English king Ethelbert married Bertha, the Roman Catholic daughter of the Merovingian king Charibert I.[23] The marriage was contingent upon Bertha being allowed to continue her faith among the predominately pagan English (Anglo-Saxons). Following Ethelbert's death, there was considerable strife in the land as Catholic Christianity was being established.

The semi-Christian, brutal Merovingians ruled as kings of the Franks (French) from A.D. 470 to 751, claiming, like most European aristocracy, to be descendants of King David.[24] They developed this claim to counter Celtic assertions of spiritual and royal sovereignty. Then over time they wound up believing it themselves.[25] Their myth would place the bloodline and priesthood succession within the hands of the Catholic Church. The Merovingians descended instead from European and not a royal Davidian lineage, but as often occurs, propaganda won out. According to Mike Ashley:

> It is quite possible that if the legend of the Merovingian descent had leaked out, then rumours of the true Grail being with the Saxons and not the Celts would have caused considerable confusion and consternation amongst the [native Celtic]

followers of Christ. Who were they to follow?[26]

Despite such legends, the Merovingians were not the true *Rex-Deus* bloodline of kings destined to heal the wasteland. Christ's descendants who lived in Britain during these turbulent times possessed that mantle. Between the native church and the Roman church people had to make a choice. The *quest*(ion) of Peredur/Perceval, "What ails thee?" or "Whom does the Grail serve?" was paramount. It was akin to Joseph Smith Jr.'s question, "Which sect is right?" and needed to be asked and answered by a member of the correct lineage (Joseph Smith–History 1:18). It was the lack of wisdom, which the biblical book of James 1:5 was the antidote, in the spirit of "Ask and you shall receive."[27] All depends upon asking the right questions and a willingness to receive the proper answers, but few did, and many Grail questers followed the wrong claim.

Was the Roman Church the "real harbour of the Grail of the natural Christ, or did it rest firmly with the British, through the Fisher King?"[28] Thus we see how science, history, and politics combined contemporaneously to create the Arthurian mythos. Oral traditions began to make empirical connections.[29] One legend with such a nexus is found in Thomas Malory's *Le Morte d'Arthur*. It deals with the story of the Knight of the Two Swords, Sir Balin. Mike Ashley recounts the story:

> Sir Balin was something of a hot-head, who killed almost anything that moved. He was a staunch supporter of Arthur, though he managed to incur Arthur's wrath by killing the Lady of the Lake in one of his wilder moments. Balin was always questing, and on one of his adventures he encounters an invisible knight, Sir

Garlon. He kills Garlon, which angers Garlon's brother, King Pellam. Pellam and Balin now clash. In the battle Balin's sword is broken, and as he is chased around Pellam's castle he finds the Spear of Longinus on the walls and, wrenching it free, turns and stabs Pellam.

Pellam is known elsewhere as Pelleam or Pellehan, and is the Maimed King whose health must be restored. It can only be restored if his wounds are avenged. The Maimed King is sometimes treated as the Fisher King, or the Fisher King's brother. Either way, we realize that it was Balin's action, using the very spear that had maimed Jesus on the Cross, that has brought destruction to the Land. His action has been called the Dolorous Stroke [comet]. It was this destruction that Perceval could have reversed had he asked about the nature of the Grail procession, which meant he had to gain an understanding of how the Maimed King came to be injured and who it was he needed to avenge.[30]

The contest between the British and Roman Church is apparent in this legend. The nature of the division between these ecclesiastical bodies now becomes apparent. The Roman spear which wounds the thigh of the now maimed Fisher King represents the Roman church injuring the Celtic church, which could not die, neither could it flourish (Christ's bloodline). The king reigned over a wasteland realm, "yet, paradoxically, he was guardian to a vessel of inexhaustible abundance and everlasting life."[31]

The Grail questers attempted to rescue the Celtic church and establish its preeminence over its Roman counterpart. But to do so they had to ask the right question ("Which church is true?") in order to find the true Fisher King or patriarch. This would prove an elusive quest for another twelve hundred and sixty years.

Another interpretation of the Arthurian legends might have validity. Perhaps the flinging of the Spear of Longinus (or the Dolorous Stroke of Balin) was not the Roman Catholic Church itself. Perhaps the spear was the flying comet of A.D. 540 and its aftermath, which ravaged the Celtic community's homeland, bringing the incurable wasteland and creating doubt amongst the people as to whether God was with them or not. Maybe it seemed a divine judgement upon those Grail keepers who had proved unworthy. They were unworthy because they had not converted the pagans in their midst or lived the covenants they had made.

Perhaps Sir Balin's "Dolorous Blow" or judgment was this comet that destroyed all in its path and was brought about by the apostasy of the people. The sword or spear that wounds the land is revealed as the horn of a unicorn, which was "as long as a spear shaft and as sharp as the sharpest thing." It devastated all live and growing things. Possibly the comet tipped the scales and helped bring on the apostasy, which in turn brought on the judgments. Arthurian, Grail, and Merlin writings speak of "a cessation of worship."[32] In the year A.D. 570 we mark the total eclipse of the Living Church of Jesus Christ—the final end of the "Birthright Church."

ST. BRENDAN AND THE CHURCH IN THE WILDERNESS

And the woman fled into the wilderness, where she hath a place prepared of God, that they should feed her there a thousand two hundred and threescore days [years].

—REVELATION 12:6

Great persecutor of the church, the apostate . . . and drive the church into the wilderness.

—D&C 86:3, 8–10

Much can be learned in the legends of the Blessed Isles in the Voyages of St. Brendan. St. Brendan's life (ca. 486–575) may be inextricably tied to the fall of the Culdee churches.[33] Just as success at converting the pagans was beginning to happen, the native Christian community began to go into eclipse. The two were inversely related to each other, perhaps due to accommodation.

As we grope for answers, tidbits of historical trivia flood our mind. Maybe this apostate shadowing had something to do with the supposed departure of Merlin the high priest in A.D. 570.[34] Or possibly it occurred with the rise of papism under Pope Gregory I, called "the Great," at about the same time.

Also in A.D. 570, the historian Gildas III recorded the fate of the "church in the wilderness" in his book, *The Ruin and Fall of Britain*.[35] He could have as easily titled the tome "Apostasy of the Celtic Church of Christ." Gildas, according to Alistair Moffat, gives an account "short on names and facts and long on blame and complaint."[36] Gildas, living in the churn of events, could only bemoan "something" being amiss.

We shall see in the next chapter how this dying church inexorably flickered out. A post-mortem reveals the apostasy and then the demise of the Lord's church in this part of the Lord's vineyard where the blood of Christ was found. It is true that the purer Irish Celtic Church was quite missionary-driven, but it lacked the central guiding authority of the true priesthood. That authority rested with the apostles who were long gone. The British saints forgot to spread the gospel and, when added to other wickedness, this caused their collapse. The Saxon Bishop Bede found this to be true: "Among other most wicked actions, not to be expressed which their own [British] historian, Gildas, mournfully takes notice

of, they added this—that they never preached the faith to the Saxons, or English [pagans], who dwelt amongst them."[37]

Before Gildas died in A.D. 570, he had a visit from the Irish monk St. Brendan. Though not sanguine about the dying Celtic church, he was impressed. Gildas hoped that Brendan, whom he thought of as "a second Peter the Apostle" might save or restore the church. But it had fallen too low, and Brendan was unable to do so. Legend has it that the dejected St. Brendan sailed on a mission to the "land of promise" about A.D. 570. He was perhaps the last authority or patriarch of the Church of the chosen bloodline before the subtle shadowing of the apostasy. While the message continued to spread, the authority to do so shrank.

St. Brendan, called "the Navigator," was born between 486 and 489 in Ciarraighe Luachra near Tralee in County Kerry, Ireland. His birth was said to have been marked by the hovering of angels over his house. He was baptized by Bishop Erc, at Tubrid near Ardfert. He received his earlier education from Saint Ita and later studied under St. Erc who ordained him in A.D. 512. Along with establishing a number of monasteries in Ireland, most importantly the Clonfert Abbey in County Galway around 560, he traveled to Scotland, Wales, and to Brittany with Saint Malo.

The *Navigatio Sancti Brendani Abbatis* written in the ninth or tenth century claims that he had a vision of a westward "land of promise of the Saints."[38] Brendan wrote in the *Book of Lismore* details of his travels, "that an angel appeared to him telling him that God granted him a special retreat beyond the shores of his native Ireland."[39] He built a large wooden ship that could carry sixty and set his course westward.[40]

On one of the several islands they encountered a hermit who told them the way to the "promised land." Brendan wrote that when they finally reached land, it was an "odorous, flower-smooth and blessed" place. Supposedly the voyage in search of the Isles of the Blessed land took seven years. Various scholars note that there is no proof that Brendan or his party made it the 3,500 miles to America, *la Merica*. But, this was the general direction of his voyage.[41]

Is Brendan's voyage just Irish folklore? Not according to Robert Sullivan, who notes that Canada's national archivist declared, "There is no doubt that Irish monks reached our shores before the Vikings."[42] It is believed that Brendan's "stepping-stones" of Scotland, the Shetlands, the Hebrides, the Faroes, Iceland, Greenland, Newfoundland, and Nova Scotia led to the western land of promise. Certainly between the years of A.D. 570 and 870, the Irish left remains in New England and south along the Atlantic coast. Was there evidence of the fabled St. Brendan's Isle noted in Columbus's map?[43]

Dennis Stone, vice president of the America's Stonehenge Foundation at Mystery Mountain in North Salem, New Hampshire, believes that the supposed Celtic ruins found there were visited by St. Brendan when he came to America.[44] He believes that St. Brendan brought sacred relics to the site, but since none have been found that he must have carried them to another place. Serious archaeologists question the Foundation's conclusions, believing that the site was mostly built after European settlers arrived in the early seventeenth century. But astrological assessments have shown that the ruins may have served as a Druidic sacred site.

It is not certain why the angel's vision directed Brendan to the New World. We do not even know what Brendan was doing in "The promised land." But we can imagine that it was something much more important than just wanderlust. It might, speculatively, have had something to do with protecting holy treasure—sacred relics and church records. We do know for certain that Irish Monks in A.D. 770 at the Faroe Islands sailed for "Iceland in their small craft, taking with them their religious objects and writings and their tools."[45] Could it be that St. Brendan earlier took religious objects and texts into the "wilderness" interior of eastern America, exactly two hundred years previous?[46]

This voyage might be the taking of the "woman" (Church) into the "wilderness" as mentioned in Revelation 12:6. Earlier we saw this same verse used as an illustration to the Grail children leaving the Holy Land for Britain; now we see the Church leaving Britain for the New World (wilderness). In a sense St. Brendan may have been a Celtic Moroni, depositing the records and relics of The Church in the vaults of the Hill Cumorah about 150 years after the Nephite record had been deposited there.[47] The popular book *How the Irish Saved Civilization* might be recast, using this theory as *How the Irish [Monk] Saved the Celtic Church* for posterity.

Joseph Smith and Oliver Cowdery twice visited in vision a large cave inside the Hill Cumorah (Ramah) being filled with sacred writings, instruments, and relics.[48] As Howard Carter said to Lord Carnarvon when looking into King Tutankhamen's tomb, "I see things, wonderful things!" the same could be said of the Cumorah trove. Upon condition of faithfulness, the three witnesses of The Book of Mormon in 1829 were promised a view of the golden plates, breastplate, sword of Laban, and other sacred objects[49] (D&C 17:1). Apparently they were not sufficiently faithful and did not see this vault, which was possibly filled with a vast and sacred treasure.

President Ezra Taft Benson reportedly said when asked, "How will we know where the true Church would be during the future apostasy?" He said, in effect, to stay with the majority of the Quorum of the Twelve and follow the records of the Church[50] (see Plate 26[51]). If Brendan and sixty fellows took the holy records and relics of the church, then it must follow that the "Church" went also. With the taking of church records from Britain, Pictland (Scotland),

Wales, and Ireland to the wilderness of America, we see the demise of the British or Celtic religion, the last glint of the "Living Church" to remain on the earth. The Cumorah cave may hide the "rich treasures" of the "woman" in the wilderness (see D&C 133:30).

Other organized branches of the Church had already withered, and in A.D. 570 began the Great Apostasy. Would the records of "lost sheep" of the Celtic church one day be joined to the records of the "Lost Sheep" of the Nephite Church? Is this one of the ways that Joseph Smith, the *Hierophant*, knew about the sacred marriage?[52] Had he an inkling of the import of his genealogy through these Celtic records?

At the convent of his sister Briga at Annaghdown in A.D. 577, the recently returned St. Brendan died. This was the same year as the final major defeat of the demoralized Celtic forces at the Battle of Dyrham. The Celtic church no longer had the Spirit, and it had precious little else to offer. After the battle, it just gave up. This was reminiscent of the Nephites before their final battles with the Lamanites. They had lost all zeal.

The date of A.D. 577 was exactly 1,260 years (Revelation 12:6) before the first LDS missionaries went to Britain to again pronounce the true gospel of Jesus Christ. Heber C. Kimball, reflecting on his missionary work in 1837 in the Ribble Valley near Preston, England, wrote, "When I returned, I mentioned the circumstance to brother Joseph who said, 'Did you not understand it? That is the place where some of the old Prophets travelled and dedicated that land, and their blessings fell upon you.'"[53]

THE GREAT APOSTASY BEGINS
(A.D. 563–664)

The significance of St. Columba (521–597), an Irish monk and abbot, is immense.[54] With twelve companions, he founded Christianity on the island of Iona (Icolmkill) in A.D. 563 after being given the island by King Conall Dalriada. His aggressive missionary efforts to the Picts proved crucial in converting these pagans to the gospel. St. Columba was called the "Dove of the Church" and built a famous library and monastery. His mission successfully taught the "old ways" until his death in 597, the year of Augustine's arrival at Canterbury.[55]

Pope Gregory I the Great of Rome, who had long coveted the Christian lands of Britain, now saw his opportunity. In A.D. 596, he sent St. Augustine as his emissary to Saxon-held Kent with the mission of converting pagan and Celtic Christian England to Roman Catholicism.[56] He was cordially received by the Anglo-Saxon King Ethelbert and was allowed to preach at Canterbury. He established the Roman Church diocese at Canterbury, and Gregory consecrated Augustine as archbishop of Canterbury in 601.

The Catholic envoy was visited by seven wise men representing the Celtic church from Bangor of S. Dunod. They came to test him to see if he was a humble servant of Jesus Christ. They wished to see if he would come to greet them or rise from his seat when they came to him.[57] St. Augustine failed this simple test, and the Celtic church gave considerable opposition to Augustine's efforts of converting them to Catholicism.[58] Roman sovereignty over the native British church failed at the Conference of Aust on the Severn River of Wales in A.D. 603.

Augustine's successor, Laurentius, spoke bitterly of the antagonism of the Scots to the Catholic papacy, "We have found the Scottish bishops worse even than the British."[59] At that time Western Scotland, called Dalriada, and the territory now called Argyll, were the hotbed of this opposition. For three more generations this futile conflict raged throughout Britain, until it was finally resolved with Wilfrid the Catholic bishop of York at the Synod of Whitby in Northumberland in A.D. 664. Ostensibly the Celtic Culdee and Catholic churches met to decide upon the date of Easter. The Celtic church said it was the date that John the last surviving apostle had said it was. The book on the Synod states: "Though the British Church [up to that point] steadfastly refused to recognize the recently instituted authority of the Pope, A.D. 610, flatly denying the worship of Mary or use the term "Mother of God" proclaimed by the Roman Church A.D. 431, at the Council of Ephesus, or the doctrine of purgatory, established by Gregory the Great about the year A.D. 593, they shared the same communion."[60]

Shortly before the great Synod's decision, there was a literal total eclipse of the sun. Night had passed over Whitby. Through capitulation and collapse King Oswy of Northumberland found in favor of the Roman church and the supremacy of the Roman rite in England. Now the two entities became one—Roman that is. After Whitby an epidemic of plague broke out in Britain and Ireland. Lehane states that "It must have killed thousands, for all the English Bishops save one were victims."[61] The continual encroachment on British lands by the Saxons and Norsemen ensured the demise of the primacy of the long apostate Celtic-British church.

There you have it, the Grail legends converge from two sides, each side preempting the other's position for its own gain until Rome won and the Celtic church went into the wilderness. The search for the Holy Grail now became the search for the Living Church and the understanding of its sacred teachings—the gospel of Jesus Christ. The quest for the secret of eternal life and the meaning of life itself is undertaken with the question "Which church is true and which should I join?" (Joseph Smith–History 1:18–19).

The date for the Great Apostasy, between A.D. 570 and 607, may seem to be arbitrarily set. Could it have happened a few years earlier or a few years later? Perhaps.[62] While these dates were probably fixed and were occasioned by some defining event, they would seem negligible to those "on the ground" at the time.

Even though they were seemingly inconsequential in themselves, they produced paradigmatic changes in God's garden.

Just short of one hundred years after the fall of the Roman Empire (A.D. 476) the wilderness apostasy happened not only in the north countries but also around the world.[63] According to Will Durant, the Dark Ages began about A.D. 566.[64] Between A.D. 570 and 607 the last vestiges of the Roman power fell with the invasion into northern Italy by Scandinavian barbarians called the Lombards.

As Paul says the "falling away" will start with the rise of the man of sin, "For there shall come a falling away first, and that man of sin be revealed, the son of perdition" (JST Inspired Version, II Thessalonians 2:3). The falling away, according to Maurice Jones, was "a religious apostasy on the part of either Jews or Christians, or of both and not a political revolt." And *the man of sin,* according to Jones, "This is not Satan himself, but some tool or emissary of Satan."[65] The lifting of the final impediment to the Great Apostasy came in A.D. 570. Paul says, "And now ye know that which restraineth, to the end that he may be revealed in his own season. For the mystery of lawlessness doth already work; only there is one that restraineth, until he be taken out of the way. And then shall be revealed the lawless one" (2 Thessalonians 2:6–8).

And who is it that "restraineth" or impedes the way of the wicked one? It could have been the Roman emperors and empire which was demolished by the Lombards between A.D. 568 and 570. Rev. Philip Allwood agrees with this date: "The north of Italy falling under the dominion of the Lombards, their kingdom became the tenth and the last of those which agreeably to the prophetic intimation, should arise within what had been the territories of the empire of the west. . . . now commenced the period of the one thousand two hundred and sixty years."[66]

On this question, Rev. Ira Case has commented: "Twelve hundred and sixty years is surely the period of these anti-Christian Gentiles' occupancy of the visible church, and of the true church's captivity, in spiritual Babylon, and of her abode in the wilderness. During that period, the true church can hardly be said to have any visible form or distinct organization."[67]

Thus we see that some Protestant scholars admit that none of the existing churches were the true "visible church." The western emperors jealously guarded and enforced the preeminence of Rome against every encroaching competitive force or influence.[68] But when they were overcome, the power of the pope greatly increased. Roman Catholicism now began to emerge as a temporal prerogative of the papacy. Pope Gregory the Great was the first ecclesiastical governing authority over Rome. Reverend Benjamin Slight noted: "Antichrist, then, was to take his rise at the removal of the hindrance. That hindrance was the Roman power, which would not permit the assumption of any temporal power; or of those high spiritual usurpations within its jurisdiction. When that was removed by the dismemberment of the Roman Empire, [the] Antichrist was to rise."[69]

But the unleashing of papal power in A.D. 570 was not enough in its own right to cause the Great Apostasy. Other events needed to accompany it. The beast that was to devour the child was not just one force but it seems to have been two, three, or more. In 588 A.D., John the Patriarch of Constantinople of the Eastern Church assumed the title of universal bishop. This led the jealous Pope Gregory to say "that whosoever in his elation of spirit called himself or sought to be called universal bishop, that man was the likeness, the precursor, and the preparer for Antichrist."

Yet this is exactly what happened in the west in A.D. 607, when Emperor Phocas "confirmed the right of the Roman See and bishops to the *headship of* all *churches*."[70] He decreed "that the name *Universal* was appropriate only to the church of Rome as that which was head of all churches and that it suited the dignity of the Roman pontiff alone."[71]

This was the year that the Anglo-Saxon or Celtic Church finally gave in to Catholic supremacy. H. Grattan Guiness, a non-Mormon scholar, wrote: "This year [607] constitutes a noble epoch in the rise of the papal apostasy, especially as it marked also the time at which both the Anglo-Saxon and the

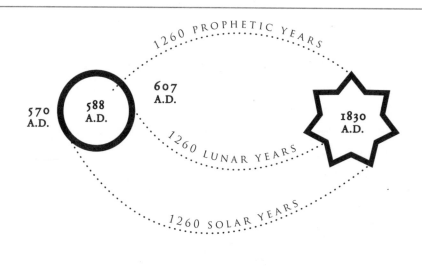

FIGURE 8

PROPHETIC TIMETABLE[76]

Lombard kingdoms, the last of the ten, gave in their formal submission to the religious supremacy of papal Rome."[72]

Thus we see three remarkable dates spanning thirty-seven years fulfilling 2 Thessalonians 2:6–8. First, by opening the way (A.D. 570); second, the eastern proclamation of supremacy (A.D. 588); and finally, the western churches "taking over" the Saints (A.D. 607), all of which lead to the forcing of the true Church into the wilderness. After this time the Roman Catholic and Greek Orthodox churches, both built upon seven hills, had the power to compel the saints to conformity upon penalty of death.[73]

If the Great Apostasy began about A.D. 570 and lasted for 1,260 years, as in John's revelation, then it would be restored in 1830. The gospel was in fact restored in 1830 through the Prophet Joseph Smith. Reverend J. A. Wylie was of the opinion that there might be a double or perhaps a triple commencement of the 1,260-year period.[74] The following analysis points to dates when the apostasy began and ended:

1. If one takes the first date, A.D. 570, and adds 1,260 solar years (each 365¼ days) to it, we arrive at 1830.

2. If we take the second date, A.D. 588, and add 1,260 prophetic years (each 360 days) to it, we arrive at 1830.

3. If we take the third date, A.D. 607, and add 1,260 lunar years (354⅓ days each) to it, we still arrive at 1830.

This "divine dating" might not be coincidental. The Reverend William Ward, a distinguished divine of the Church of England who predicted the restoration to occur in 1820, understood along similar lines. He even emphasized the important years in which the First Vision, the appearance of Moroni and the founding of the LDS Church happened: "In consequence of the Lombard invasion, 570 to 1830. . . A year of spiritual revival and triumph, the

greatest year in the calendar of the world. . . . I hope, through that grace, to see more glorious seasons in 1820, 1823 and 1830."[75]

And so it did happen as predicted. The latter-day work commenced in 1820 through 1830 and beyond. It was as the Savior said, "The kingdom of heaven is like unto leaven which a woman took and hid" or as "a treasure *hid* in a field" (Matthew 13:33, 44). Eventually the work would come forth out of obscurity.

NOTES

1. This would be *sub rosa*, an unconscious or merely intuitive reaction, for while the Culdee community still existed, its Fisher Kings had, for a long time, become lost.
2. This would be very much like the demise of Christianity in the Great Apostasy in the Roman Church, with the loss of the succession of the apostles through St. Peter.
3. Godwin, *Holy Grail,* 20.
4. Gilbert, *Holy Kingdom,* 127. Gilbert notes, "This original 'Church of Britain,' dating from centuries before the Saxon invasions, claimed to have been founded by the Apostles themselves."
5. For instance, Ireland and Scotland never came under the Roman yoke.
6. Ashley, *Chronicles of the Holy Grail,* 6.
7. Goodrich, *Merlin,* 335. See also Baillie, *Exodus to Arthur,* 183, 192. However, other sources place Merlin's death at A.D. 570, not 536. This later date would also have prophetic meanings, as we shall see.
8. The date for this is given variously as A.D. 537, 540, and 542 for Arthur's death. Goodrich, *Merlin,* 335, says Arthur, Gawain, and Lancelot all died in A.D. 542.
9. Baillie, *Exodus to Arthur,* 192.
10. Ice-core readings and Irish "narrowest-ring" work for the dates of A.D. 530 to 545 describe catastrophic conditions. These are not easily described by Stothers and Rampino's "dry fog" volcanic veil year of A.D. 536, but align more closely to a cosmic event. See Baillie, *Exodus to Arthur,* 156.
11. Goodrich, *Holy Grail,* xxvii. The author thinks that King Arthur was not a Grail guardian per se, but that the Grail had been lost and he was attempting to recover it.

12. Other parallels can be drawn between the Celtic bright god Lug (Yahweh) and Merlin (Myrddin). The word *Lug* actually means "God" and Merlin must have been his priest. According to Nikolai Tolstoy, they can both be associated with a comet. See Tolstoy, *Quest for Merlin*.

13. Gibbon's *Decline and Fall of the Roman Empire*. This was undoubtedly the circa A.D. 540 comet.

14. Baillie, *Exodus to Arthur*, 181–202. Independent researcher Don Carleton also felt that there was an impact-related event in the year 540. Baillie notes that in ancient Israel, the New Year Festival included aspects of Yahweh wounding the serpent Rahab. There was widespread association of dragon fights with New Year's festivals, especially in China and Ireland.

15. Baillie, *Exodus to Arthur*, 125–26. This caused a tsunami that inundated the land and poisonous gases that killed men and beasts. Dust clouds caused a nuclear winter effect and drought, which in turn caused disease and plague conditions. The sixth-century Byzantine historian Procopius appears to mention Britain's deadly western regions, as cited in Baillie, *Exodus to Arthur*, 153.

16. As recorded in Baillie, *Exodus to Arthur*, 242. Baillie notes that this might refer to a tsunami and that the Legend of Lyonesse, wherein the land between the Isles of Scilly and Cornwall were inundated in the same year as Arthur's death, might relate to the A.D. 540 events. Since Merlin's death came at the sign of the comet and eclipse, which "came from the West to the East," we often speak of him living his life backwards.

17. The comets, with their multicolored lights, like red and white dragons breathing fire and destruction, were beyond description.

18. Goodrich, *Merlin*, 335. Others say it was A.D. 547.

19. Astronomer Fred Hoyle and Chandra Wickramasinghe have suggested that comets actually bring plagues in the form of interstellar viruses (*Current Science*, January 2000). They also believe that it may have been the "seed of life" for this planet's early development.

20. Magnusson, *Scotland*, 33.

21. The idea of St. Patrick ridding Ireland of its serpents might have something to do with the dissipation of the comet (dragon with serpent's tail). That St. Patrick is traditionally given a fifth-century date instead of a sixth-century date is problematic to Baillie, who accepts the later date. See Baillie, *Exodus to Arthur*, 154.

22. Goodrich, "Story of Grisandol," in *Romance of Merlin*, 160. This is an interesting sidebar because it has the major elements of the legend. The Dragon (comet and Catholicism) attacks the crowned Lion (the Grail child of Judah), but the Dragon is killed by a Bull, i.e., unicorn (tribe of Ephraim).

23. Clovis is known in French history as the first "erstwhile" Christian King of France, through his wife Clotilda, the niece of Gondebaud, King of Burgundy. He was converted in A.D. 496 through an incident in a battle. Charibert I, the son of Chlotar I, was king of Paris from 561 to 567. See Blake and Blezard, *Arcadian Cipher*; facing 190 is a genealogical chart of the Merovingian kings which is entirely too speculative.

24. Newman, *Real History behind The Da Vinci Code*, 161. "Although nominally, as Christians, they were only allowed one official wife, this was usually ignored and the sons of concubines had rights of inheritance."

25. See Sinclair, *Discovery of the Grail*, 163. This may be the origin of the source of the modern Priory de Sion's fictitious claim of a Merovingian bloodline from Jesus and Mary Magdalene to prove their sacred role. For a profound rebuttal to this claim, see Putnam and Wood, *Treasure of Rennes-le-Château*, 76. In the History Channel's "Digging the Past" (25 March 2006), Dr. Jean-Jacques Cassiman of the Center for Human Genetics at KU in Leuven, Belgium, tested the bones of Merovingian queen Arugon (wife of King Clohthar) for mitochondrial DNA. They then compared it with members of the Syriac Orthodox Church in Jerusalem who claim to be descendants from the family of Jesus' parents. They found the queen was of typical European stock, while the Syriac DNA was of Middle Eastern descent. There was no genetic relationship between them.

26. Ashley, *Chronicles of the Holy Grail*, 7.

27. Matthew 21:22. In Jeremiah 33:3 we are commanded to ask and, "Call unto me, and I will answer thee, and show thee great and mighty things which thou knowest not."

28. Ashley, *Chronicles of the Holy Grail*, 7.

29. Baillie, *Exodus to Arthur*, 158–59. The Beowulf story, once thought to have been penned in the ninth century, actually deals with mid sixth-century events with definite Arthurian connections. The image of a serpent-decorated sword plunging into a lake, fighting dragons and the motifs of dragons and ponds are undoubtedly relating to actual historical events of this period.

30. Ashley, *Chronicles of the Holy Grail*, 7–8.

31. Godwin, *Holy Grail*, 67.

32. Baillie, *Exodus to Arthur*, 156. Or, "a cessation which in folk belief might be sufficient to account for any subsequent drought which might affect the land."

33. He was the abbot of Clonfert and other monasteries in western Ireland.

34. Goodrich, *Merlin*, 335, believes that Merlin died in A.D.

536, so this might not be the clue. Perhaps it was a result of the fulness of the wickedness of the Merovingians when King Chilperic I murdered his wife in ca. A.D. 570, even though they were not of the desired bloodline. But this is stretching credulity.

35. This was also the date of Gildas's death.

36. Moffat, *Arthur and the Lost Kingdoms,* 199.

37. Bede, *Ecclesiastical History,* I.xxii.

38. Lehane, *Early Celtic Christianity,* throughout; additional information gleaned from a number of Internet articles about St. Brendan.

39. http://beatl.barnard.columbia.edu/students/his3487/cole/brendan.html (2004).

40. He had earlier made three boats, called curraghs, of the skins of slaughtered animals, and with seventeen companions made an unsuccessful trip. He returned home, where his foster mother suggested that the animal skins rendered the vessels unfit for holy travel.

41. In 1976–77, the sea journey was reenacted by Tim Severin, called "The Brendan Voyage." He successfully sailed across the Atlantic, from Ireland to Newfoundland, in a currach (skinned leather) boat.

42. Robert Sullivan, "In Saint Brendan's Wake" http://www.ics.vilanova.edu/in_saint_brendan.htm

43. Mike McCormack, "America's First Christmas Card," acknowledges Celtic Irish monks being in West Virginia as early as the sixth century after Christ: http://www.catholicism.org/pages/brendan.htm

44. The History Channel, "America's Stonehenge," aired in Salt Lake City, 22 February 2004.

45. Patrick I. N. Bury, "Who Really Discovered America": http://www.nordzeit.de/discam.htm. The prominence called Mergech meant "repository" and denotes a place of buried treasure. These treasures of St. Brenden may have included the Title Deeds to Palestine and Evidences (believed to be deeds to the Temple mount, for the eventual rebuilding and restoration of the Temple).

46. Interestingly, the Irish monk St. Brendan, in the sixth century, supposedly was identified with an ancient temple site on the McIntosh farm, which adjoined Joseph Smith Sr.'s farm in Vermont. It was believed to have been established by Irish monks between A.D. 500 and 600 (see Boren and Boren, *Following the Ark of the Covenant,* 122). Also, not far from Joseph Smith's birthplace in Sharon is a town named Glastonbury. Like its counterpart in Somerset, England, it has a reputation as a mystical place.

47. Perhaps one day these Celtic records will come forth with the secrets of the grail lineage.

48. Nibley, *Witnesses of the Book of Mormon,* 173–75;

Smith, *Essentials in Church History,* 72–73.

49. The Sword of Laban may be "the legendary Sword of David, which Solomon's wife places in the ship of Solomon to be sent down the ages until the Grail knights [not Knights Templar] discover it." Godwin, *Holy Grail,* 47.

50. This was reported to me by friends, but I have no corroborating footnotes.

51. Don Thorpe's photograph of the Hill Cumorah in upstate New York. This may possibly be the location of the records of the Celtic Church as well as the Nephite peoples. Used with permission.

52. *Hierophant* means "one who reveals sacred things." See Knight and Lomas, *Second Messiah,* 96.

53. Heber C. Kimball, in *Journal of Discourses* (6 April 1857), 5:22b.

54. He is also known as Columcille, Colm, and Colum.

55. Ralls-MacLeod and Robertson, *Quest for the Celtic Key,* 111.

56. Gilbert, *Holy Kingdom,* 126.

57. Bede, *Ecclesiastical History,* II.ii. The six bishops and the abbot of Bangor, who conducted the conference with Augustine's Oak, A.D. 607, clearly demonstrate the gulf between the Celtic church and the change of the primitive Catholic church and the newly formed papacy.

58. After Augustine's death, Ethelfrid sent soldiers to massacre 1,200 unarmed Celts who had come to pray. See Scott, *Pictish Nation,* 182–85.

59. Anonymous, "The Introduction of Christianity into Britain" (April-June 2002).

60. Jowett, *Drama of the Lost Disciples,* 162, quoting the Minutes of the Synod of Whitby.

61. Lehane, *Early Celtic Christianity,* 210.

62. An example might be; a man is sitting on a chair in the dark of night, with his back to the east. He is asked to snap his fingers when it is daytime. He waits and waits. After some hours he can see that everything is a little brighter than it was before, but is it daytime yet? He continues to wait, the sky is a little brighter and still he does not snap his fingers. The transition between night and day has been so subtle that he is not sure when to snap his fingers but eventually he does because it is obvious that the day has come.

63. Romulus Augustulus was the last Roman emperor in A.D. 476 when Odoacer, a German mercenary deposed him. The Western empire was officially ended. In ancient America the apostasy of the Church happened in about A.D. 421.

64. Durant, *Age of Faith,* 423, 450–51. Durant says this is a

loose term and difficult to define, but notes that it would roughly begin between the death of Boethius in A.D. 524 and 566 when the Dark Ages began.

65. Jones, "II Thessalonians," *New Commentary on Holy Scripture,* 572. I will not say who the "Man of Sin" is that came (was born) in A.D. 570, because it is politically incorrect and dangerous for me to say so. But grievous wars, terrorism, deprivation of women, and torments have happened from his life until today have been caused by him and his followers.

66. Allwood, *Revelation of Saint John,* 1:16, 17.

67. Case, *Light on Prophecy,* 76, 264.

68. Macgregor, *Marvelous Work,* 69. This author is a member of the Church of Christ Temple Lot in Missouri.

69. Slight, *Apocalypse Explained,* 268. As far as we know the Pope neither held nor claimed any bloodline authority.

70. Elliott, *Apocryphal New Testament,* 3:163.

71. Allwood, *Revelation of Saint John,* 1:305.

72. Guiness, *Light for the Last Days,* 104.

73. Constantine the Great used the state church to wield unlawful power; now the Church was using state power to weld the same apostate power. The author is not at all anti-Catholic or Greek Orthodox; rather he admires these churches immensely.

74. Wylie, *Seventh Vial,* 153. Edgren noted that this period "evidently has two or more beginnings" (*Epiphaneia,* 90).

75. Ward, *Prophetic History,* 5:243, 240, 74; see also 6:266–67.

76. MacGregor, *Marvelous Work,* 90.

CHAPTER SIXTEEN
THE GRAIL QUAGMIRE

"They were deceived by ancient error."[1]

A number of fabricated stories have clouded our understanding of the true Holy Grail. These have infiltrated the *Zeitgeist* of society and demonstrate how broadly conspiracy theories pervade our culture. Clandestine organizations in our Ivy League universities, secret satanic cells, and even rogue Masonic lodges create a psychic aura of hidden patterns and meanings where none exist.

Paranoiac, we often give coincidences deeper significance, and every reality is seen merely as a facade of the "real" truth. For many there is a sinister guiding hand, or kismet of fate, driving everything. We are, according to conspiracy theory, mere pawns being moved or swept aside by "larger forces." Thus we only see portents in the hidden (occult) netherworld, where nothing is as it seems.

At times the trail goes cold and at other times it seems to diverge into too many directions. This part of our study, however, seeks to understand that intervening period of the Dark, Medieval, and Modern ages when the "seemed grail" lay in apostasy. In order to appreciate the true Grail epic we must understand the false. These include the Merovingians, Cathars, Rennes-le-château, Knights Templar, Rosslyn Chapel, and the Freemasons in the story of deceit and shabby hoaxes. It is the search for these dark tenuous threads that concerns our story now.

THE CATHAR MYTH

In matrimony no one can be saved.
—PIERRE DES VAUX-DE-CERNAY[2]

A religious sect, the Bogomiles, migrated from the Balkans to northern Italy and southern France in the early eleventh century.[3] They settled in the Languedoc-Roussillon and Provence regions of France and became known as the Cathars (the "pure ones"). They were gnostic dualists and anti-clerics in most respects, which marked them as a heretical sect in the Middle Ages. They were suppressed by Catholic forces in the Albigensian Crusade between 1209 and 1250. In early 1209 Pope Innocent III called for a crusade against the Cathars in southern France and a reformation of Catholicism, which had become corrupt.

In the nineteenth and early twentieth centuries the Cathars became identified with the Teutonic-Aryan race and in the late twentieth century with the Grail pedigree of Jesus Christ and Mary Magdalene. However, Giles Morgan firmly believes that "the Cathars' attitude toward Jesus Christ has led many historians to argue that they are an unlikely religious group to link with the Grail."[4] They were, in essence, a perversion of the Grail like the Merovingians, rather than representations of the true Grail.

So what does connect them to the Grail by the "Jesus was married" enthusiasts? It comes down to only two well-known quotations, which were spun from each other. An earlier tractate titled *An Exposure of the Heresies of the Albigenses and Waldenses* ascribed to Ermengaud de Béziers, a companion of Durand of Huesca, notes, "Also they teach in their secret meetings that Mary Magdalen was the wife of (the pseudo-) Christ, She was the Samaritan woman to whom He said, 'Call thy husband.'"[5] The 'repulsive' concept of a married Christ was the Cathar way of denigrating the earthly Christ who they thought was as devilish as John the Baptist.

Ermengaud was later relied upon by a rabid anti-Cathar Cistercian Crusader Pierre des Vaux-de-Cernay writing between 1213 and 1218. On July 22nd of 1209, Mary Magdalene's feast day, a massacre at Béziers in Provence, killed Cathars and sympathetic Catholics. Of these several thousand were murdered in the sacred precincts of the town's Madaleine Cathedral where they had gone for sanctuary. Chronicler Pierre de Vaux-de-Cernay claimed that the massacre was punishment for the supposed Cathar blasphemy against Jesus and the Magdalene:

> Béziers was taken on St. Mary Magdalene's day. Oh, supreme justice of providence! . . . The heretics claimed that St. Mary Magdalene was the concubine of Jesus Christ . . . it was therefore with just cause that these disgusting dogs were taken and massacred during the feast of the one that they had insulted.[6]

Did the Cathars secretly believe that Mary and Jesus had coitus in something less than a sacred marriage? [7] Even if it were a false charge, it would still be the first account noting Jesus' sexuality since the anti-Christian Celsus in the third-century. Another version of the above quotation goes:

> They held that all the Patriarchs of the Old Testament were damned, and declared that St. John the Baptist was one of the greatest devils. The heretics even affirmed in their secret assemblies that the Christ who was born in terrestrial and visible Bethlehem and crucified in Jerusalem was evil, and that Mary Magdelan was his concubine and the very woman taken in adultery of who we read in the gospel. [8]

Since the derogatory comment came from a highly partisan Cistercian monk, it cannot be trusted to accurately describe Cathar belief. Was it made to justify the cruel actions of Simon de Montfort, the Crusade leader? Or was it just an outrageous slur like the torrid accusations later made against the Knights Templars of worshiping Satan and kissing the anuses of cats?

The secret treasure of the elitist Cathars was supposedly their hermetic wisdom with a decidedly ascetic outlook.[9] From known documents we are to believe that either the Albigensi (Cathars) had an "evil" Jesus and Mary sexually engaged or that the two contemporary chroniclers were overly biased in their prejudices to the point of inaccuracy. A third alternative is that a sacred marriage was not revealed because the Cathars were "keeping it secret," but because it was contrary to their core beliefs, it was never in their consciousness and did not exist.

They were probably ignorant of any marriage and any thought of it would have been highly repugnant to their philosophy. To have Jesus and Mary Magdalene in some kind of a sexual union would run counter to their espoused beliefs, unless, that is, they secretly hated the Jesus Christ of the New Testament.[10] As devote reincarnationists, Cathars would not have their supposed *perfecti* (Jesus and the Magdalene) sexually "wallowing in the mud like pigs."

The restored gospel, The Church of Jesus Christ of Latter-day Saints, also claims sacred knowledge. However, they see marriage as a sacred obligation and the conception of children as a gift from God. Unlike the Catharists, it posits that this world is real, that matter is good, that absolutes exist, and that Jesus of Nazareth is the Christ. Furthermore, it claims to possess the true ancient priesthood and temple ritual. So why are the Mormons not mystics like the Cathars, Rosicrucians, Campagnie du Saint-Sacrament, Knights Templar, and Freemasons, etc.?

The major reason is that the non-elitist LDS Church is attempting to *teach* ancient saving truths, not *hide* them behind a cloak of secrecy. It does not seek a tight vanguard of adepts but rather seeks to carry the gospel message worldwide to every willing ear. Unlike the gnostics, Mormons believe in an orderly hierarchy of grounded leaders who volunteer without purse or script. Mormons do not cut new converts from their gentile families or from temporal society as so many cults do. Catharism is an empty vessel.

Through the last two millennia, numerous *Questers, Seekers, Reformers,* and *Restorers* have sought the Holy Grail contents of the temple, sometimes called the "inner chamber." They, like the Cathars, believed that they could find or had found the spiritual utopian panacea for "what ails the world." All but one such Grail Seeker have failed. We have picked up the threads of archaeology, history, legend, and mythology to tie our story together. It is a long and complicated narrative.

THE ORDER OF THE POOR KNIGHTS OF CHRIST AND TEMPLE OF SOLOMON

These fighting monks had an improbable conception, a controversial existence and a spectacular demise.[11]

The Knights Templar reshaped European history in a multitude of ways, some of which are only now being appreciated. They have been mentioned earlier in the text, but will now be discussed in some depth as pertaining to our search for the Holy Grail. Their origin is shrouded with secrecy and intrigue. At this time, Baldwin I (Baudouin), the younger brother of Godfroi de Bouillon (conqueror of Jerusalem in 1099, count of Flanders, and duke of Lower Lorraine), became the first Christian king of Jerusalem in A.D. 1100. Jerusalem was now secure and a Davidic claimant was on the throne of Israel, but he was a Christian not a Jew.

According to L-A de St. Clair, in 1104, Hughes 1, the Count of Champagne met in Troyes, France, for a secret conclave with members from certain noble families—Brienne, de Joinville, Chaumont, and d'Anjou.[12] Supposedly all were members of the conspiratorial false *Rex Deus* underground (Sadducean families) who escaped the destruction of Jerusalem during the Jewish Wars after A.D. 63 by fleeing to Europe.

It may be surmised that Hughes de Champagne's close relationship with the great Jewish Cabbalist, Rabbi Solomon ben Isaac (Rashi), who lived in his city of Troyes, had something to do with it.[13] Later, his militia, *la Milice du Christ* ("Soldiers of God") were called "The Order of the Temple." They were undoubtedly associated with Godfroi de Bouillon's "Order of Sion" with the secret agenda of restoring the Davidic line to the throne of Jerusalem as negotiated by the Count of Champagne.

Mystery also surrounds the founding and development of the Cistercian Order, a Benedictine offshoot that became associated with the Knights Templar. The order was instituted in 1098 by a group of Benedictine monks from the abbey of Molesme, not long before the capture of Jerusalem. They ostensibly wanted to return to the spiritual and temporal austerity of the original Benedictine rule. They may have been mostly aristocrats, possibly of the false *Rex Deus* lineage.

While this outward piety masked an inward secret, they were not Jewish Essenes as Knight and Lomas believe.[14] They were likely, at their very core, Jewish Saducean patricians and erstwhile Christians, lying low and "blending." They would often say, "we believe the same as you," in order to assuage any uncomfortable situation. This was the same philosophy of both the Knights Templar and later the inner circle of the Masons.

The young abbot Bernard de Fontain of Clairvaux (1091–1153) and thirty-two members of his influential family joined as novices the struggling and almost defunct Cistercian Order in 1112.[15] This bizarre event nearly doubled the size of the Order. Later, William of St. Thierry wrote about the Cistercians in 1140, "From that day God prospered the house, and that vine of the Lord bore fruit, putting forth its branches from sea to sea."[16]

Supposedly there was a secret Saducean *Rex Deus* archive in the principality of Seborga in

northwestern Italy. There are reports of discovered documents claiming that St. Bernard of Clairvaux, at twenty-two years of age, founded a Cistercian monastery there in 1113 to protect a "great secret."[17] A greater possibility is that remnants of the counterfeit *Rex Deus* line of priestly Saducean Jews were the keepers of a great temple secret that was located there.

The Templar movement was led by a Flemish nobleman from Champagne named Hugues de Payens along with eight laymen knights mostly from Champagne in the north and Languedoc in the south. Apparently St. Bernard nominated Hugues de Payens as the first grand master, and the Abbot Edouard of Seborga consecrated him in this position.

For eighteen years, Baldwin I du Bourg ruled Jerusalem as its king. Supposedly during this time Baldwin I allowed no excavation work to be done on the Temple Mount, perhaps fearing reprisals from Moslem assassins. The scenario was rather complex. A small contingent of *Rex Deus* members in Jerusalem surveyed the situation that was complicated by the Muslim building of the Dome of the Rock.[18] Their collective memories and notes could not make sense of the scene on the Mount.

In 1104, Hugues de Payen and Hugh de Champagne traveled to Jerusalem to examine things themselves. They consulted with Baldwin and made carefully documented reports regarding the Temple Mount, then left for Europe to consider further plans. But still nothing happened to change the impasse, that engulfed the entire project. Baldwin I would not be moved.

Then in 1113 a group of Christian knights formed a new order entitled "The Sovereign Military Order of the Hospital of St. John of Jerusalem of Rhodes and of Malta," generally called the Knights Hospitaller. They were to defend a hospital built in Jerusalem before the First Crusade. This may have planted an idea in the *Rex Deus* group. Immediately Hugues de Payen and Hugh de Champagne went on a second trip to Jerusalem with another plan for King Baldwin.

Finally in 1118, with Baldwin I's death, he was quickly succeeded by his cousin, Baldwin II du Bourg, who was much more receptive to the Templar plans. In 1119, Hugues de Payens, appeared unannounced before Baldwin II, requesting permission to excavate, with this cover story:

> Since they did not have a church, nor a settled place to live, the king conceded a temporary dwelling to them in his palace. . . . The first element of their profession . . . was "that they should protect the roads and routes to the utmost of their ability against the ambushes of thieves and attackers, especially in regard to the safety of pilgrims."[19]

So Baldwin II, the King and Patriarch of Jerusalem, readily supported the nine knights' request. Certainly the eighteen years of nonexcavation had lulled the minds of the Muslim people. Baldwin II provided quarters in the eastern part of his royal palace, which adjoined the al-Aqsa Mosque on the southern edge of the Haram al-Sharif or Temple platform.[20] It was this year, 1119, that they changed their name from *La Milice du Christ* to the *Paupers conumilitones Christi Templque Salomom* (Order of the Poor Knights of Christ and the temple of Solomon). They were called Knights Templar for brevity's sake. This knightly order would play a well-publicized role in the history of the Grail. But nowhere is there the slightest hint that they secretly held the view that Jesus was married and had children.

THE RISE AND FALL OF THE KNIGHTS TEMPLAR

The Templars' rise was meteoric and their fall was precipitous.

The avowed purpose of the knights, to save pilgrims from evil Muslim bandits, was a convenient ruse. According to Baigent and Leigh, this story hid a "more grandiose geo-political design which involved the Cistercian Order, Saint Bernard, and Hugues, Count of Champagne, and one of the first sponsors and patrons of both the Cistercians and the Templars."[21] Their true mission was to locate and secure the temple scrolls, relics, and treasures of their Sadducean forebears.

Who was behind their efforts and under what mission did they give such concerted exertion? Why would nine unlearned knights dedicate the best part of their lives and fortunes in burrowing around the Temple Mount in Jerusalem without immediate results? It is unthinkable that such dedication could have come from mere treasure hunters. Without doubt they were advisedly chosen and well instructed long before they ever left for the Holy Land.

A very young man, Bernard (1091–1153), from a noble family in Burgundy had everything to do with the project. Though only thirty at the time, Bernard believed that God had reclaimed Jerusalem for Christianity through the Crusade so that its secrets might bring on the expected millennium. This much-anticipated era was not just Bernard's thinking, but his inheritance from a milieu of like-minded thinking in Burgundy. He was a genius who solidified these lofty ideals through research, profound writing, and exhortation. From reading of secret hermetic documents, Josephus' writings, and the scriptures, Bernard had gathered ideas.[22]

His first thought was to organize the order to excavate the immense caverns or catacombs within the extended platform of the Jerusalem temple. Within these vaults, supported by rows of arched colonnades at the time of King Herod, were huge stables, erroneously called "Solomon's Stables."[23] These stables had remained sealed since biblical times and were discovered in their secret excavations on the Temple Mount. Beyond ostensibly keeping pilgrimage lanes open, these knights were on a quest for the great mystery of the Holy Grail.[24]

Second, Bernard's researches had led him to believe that the ark of the covenant lay hidden within these vaults.[25] He surmised that the Ark contained the stone tablets of the law of Moses and possibly even more precious writings, such as the legendary "Tables of Testimony."

Persistent legends claim that the Templars found many other sacred artifacts, including a considerable quantity of ancient documentation. One can speculate as to the exact nature of these documents, but "a reasonable consensus is emerging that they contained scriptural scrolls, treatises on sacred geometry and details of secret knowledge, art and science—the hidden wisdom of the ancient initiates of the Judaic/Egyptian tradition."[26]

Legend has it that Geoffroy de St. Omer, the second-in-command, was dispatched from Jerusalem to his home with a number of scrolls. He supposedly took them to his scholarly relative, Lambert de St. Omer, to be translated. We are told from an undocumented source that the aged cleric made a copy of one, without permission, and was killed because of it in 1128.[27] St. Bernard translated the "sacred geometry" of King Solomon's masons, which he concluded was an octagon contained within a circle—like the Dome of the Rock.

While the Poor Knights never found the ark of the covenant, they may have found other thaumaturgical treasures beneath the temple. These amateur archaeologists possibly acquired the precious scrolls purporting to be the secret and sacred endowment ceremony of the temple of Solomon. From the Knights Templar, this temple ceremony was somehow transmitted to modern Freemasons. Then in separate fashion, this time through revelation, it came to Joseph Smith and the Mormons, who restored it to its purity through divine intercession. French historian Gaetan Delaforge noted: "The real task of the nine knights was to carry out research in the area in order to obtain certain relics and manuscripts which contain the essence of the secret traditions of Judaism and ancient Egypt, some of which probably went back to the days of Moses."[28]

There is evidence that the Templars conducted extensive excavations under the ruins of Herod's temple.[29] The true temple of Solomon and Herod lay north of the Dome of the Rock. This misinformation probably saved the treasure from discovery during the Muslim habitation of Jerusalem. The secret of the Temple Mount lay hidden for centuries, and then, according to Laidler:

> This information on the "true treasure's" hidden whereabouts seems to have been lost to all but a few Jewish [Sadducean] families who fled Israel to Europe and who, over one thousand years later, in A.D. 1100, had formed new alliances and held power and lands in France. These families were instrumental in the setting up of the Knights Templar, whose function was said to be the protection of pilgrims but who . . . had in reality a very different agenda to follow—the recovery of whatever constituted the true treasure of the temple of Jerusalem.[30]

Therefore, whatever the Knights Templar encountered on the Temple Mount was of paramount importance. Some nine years after 1119, Hugues de Payens and his associates supposedly opened up a vault beneath the rubble of the floor of the Holy of Holies.[31] They apparently encountered the precious documents buried by the Sadducean high priests until about A.D. 63–64 and then by the Zealots between the springs of A.D. 68 and 70. This happened once the impossibility of fending off Roman armies under the emperor's son, Titus, was appreciated.

J. R. Church, among others, believes the Templars spent their time digging for buried treasure beneath the ancient Jewish temple:

> In 1953 a copper scroll was found in a cave near the Dead Sea that told of a fabulous Temple treasure, estimated at more than 138 tons of gold and silver that had been buried by the Jewish priesthood [Sadducean high priests] in 64 locations before the Romans destroyed the Temple in A.D. 70. Twenty-four of those hordes of gold and silver were buried under the Temple Mountain.
>
> It is believed that the Knights Templar plundered the treasure of the Temple and took it back to Europe. After nine years in Jerusalem, the Templars returned to Europe wealthy beyond belief. In the years following they built castles all over Europe and became famous as the guardians of the Holy Grail. Evidently they were successful, for they instituted an international banking system across Europe and had the resources to loan gold to kings and governments.[32]

Of all the secret treasure the Templars found beneath the sanctuary, the most important were twelve documents or scrolls relating to the sacred ordinances of the temple of Solomon[33] (see Jeremiah 32:14). Bernard of Clairvaux, the great Cistercian monk, had certainly brought the fledgling Order to the attention of Pope Honarius II sometime in 1127.[34] He implored the Pope to grant them a constitution that laid out requirements for conduct and practice which would give them legitimacy and status within the Church. They obtained a papal blessing and were chartered in a hurried fashion.

Bernard drew up the regulations, the monastic rule, as it was called, governing the Knights Templar. This constitution amazingly does not mention the protection of pilgrims, their apparent sole reason for existing![35] They took vows of poverty, chastity, and obedience and swore to generally protect the Holy Land. Entrants were forbidden to cut their beards, but were obliged to cut their hair.

This rule was granted on 31 January 1128, when Hugues de Payens appeared before the specially convened Council of Troyes under the auspices of Abbot Bernard of Clairvaux.[36] When drawing up the rule, Bernard laid down a specific requirement on Knights to make "obedience to Bethany and the house [castle] of Mary and Martha,"[37] thus attesting to the significance to the importance of the Bethany sisters. In 1146, Saint Bernard preached the Second Crusade to King Louis VII and many nobles at Vézelay in the Morvan district of France. In Vézelay was the Basilica of St. Mary Magdalene, which falsely claimed possession of her bones.[38]

The Order expanded rapidly in terms of a massive influx of inductees and massive donations of money and land. Within a decade they owned land in Austria, Constantinople, England, France, Germany, Hungry, Portugal, Scotland, and Spain. In 1185, they built the significant Temple Church just off Fleet Street on Inner Temple Land in London. By the mid-century mark they were perhaps the most powerful institution in Christendom outside the papacy.

Through playing off Islamic divisions, such as supporting the Assassins against the Sunni rulers in Syria and elsewhere, the Templar Knights were able, diplomatically, to maintain their position in the Holy Land. According to Gaetan Delaforge: "Templars believed that the integration of the different streams of the tradition—Christianity, Islam, and Judaism—stemming from the patriarch Abraham was successfully effected there by the Templars, and that the richness of today's Western esoteric tradition is due to this work. The Templars were given the task by St. Bernard of finding and reuniting the hidden and dispersed parts of these streams."[39]

Beyond this, what endeavor were they about? The answer: to set up a Judeo-Christian kingdom in Jerusalem, to build the third temple, and to establish conditions to usher in the Millennium. In 1140, the Abbey at St. Clair estates in Kilwinning in Ayrshire, Scotland, was completed and the Templar trove was reportedly removed to that location.[40]

In 1185, with the death of Baudouin IV (Baldwin) a dynastic fight over the title of King of Jerusalem commenced. It was caused by the betrayal of an oath by the Templar Grand Master, Gerard de Ridefort, to the dead monarch. Ridefort's cavalier attitude alienated the Saracens, causing the breakup of a longstanding treaty. By 1187, hostilities broke out, and Jerusalem was lost to the Muslims at the Battle of Hattin. All would not be well with these Knights who served Martha, Mary Magdalene, John the Baptist, and preeminently themselves.

While the Templars may have found the temple scrolls, they did not understand them and, therefore, did not possess the secret of the Holy Grail. In fact, they would be scandalized to hear that Jesus was married. Not one document attests to the Templars knowing anything about the sacred marriage.

Over the next century and several Crusades, bit by bit of the Holy Land was ceded to the Muslims. At last, Acre, the most important Knights Templar stronghold and port in the Levant, fell to the Mamluk army in April 1291.

Finally with total loss of the Holy Land in 1303, their martial spirit lagged and they lost their *raison d'etre*. The loss of a defining role made the Templars' riches and sacred treasure the envy of kings and the established church as "easy pickings." The exotic esoteric and mystic Orientalism of this unfettered small class of warrior monks now became spotlighted and intolerable.

Templar morals had eroded somewhat, and the kernels of corruption had gained for them a reputation for arrogance and avarice. Soon a secret plan was hatched in which the French king, Philip iv would enrich himself. The Church would be cleansed with the acquiescence of the papacy under the French Pope, Clement V, who was belatedly notified and shocked by the matter.

On Thursday, the Templars' grandmaster, Jacques de Molay, occupied a place of honor at the funeral of Catherine de Valois, the sister-in-law of the king. Then the trap was sprung the following morning, on Friday, 13 October 1307. This episode was commemorated by the saying, "Friday the thirteenth, unlucky for some."[41] That dawn, Jacques de Molay and sixty of his senior Knights of the inner circle were apprehended. Simultaneously more than six hundred of the three thousand Templars living in France were arrested.[42]

The treasure of the Knights Templar was never found. Legend has it that the Templar fleet spirited it away to Scotland as the trap was sprung on the Knights. Theories abound, but the crypt at Rosslyn Chapel six miles south of Edinburgh seems to have been the repository of this treasure. We now examine the true treasure of the architecture of that chapel.

THE KEY OF ROSSLYN

If every theory about what lies under Rosslyn Chapel in Midlothian were true, the church would sit on a mound of earth at least 150 ft. high![43]

There are many enigmatic icons inside the overly famous Grail site, Rosslyn Chapel. Built in 1450, it lies six miles south of Edinburgh. Though totally unappreciated, its foremost aspect is the modest center column between the penultimate pillars: the Boaz (apprentice) and Jachin (master) pillars.[44] Andrew Sinclair, Wallace-Murphy, and Phillip Coppens alone recognize some small value to this pillar, calling it the Journeyman's or Companion Pillar.[45] Unfortunately they do not elaborate on this finding or cite a source for this conclusion (see Plate 27).[46]

On top of the Master (Earl's) pillar, in the choir, is the head of the murdered apprentice.[47] Originally the head possessed facial hair, but someone who perhaps sought to hide the identity of this person later chiseled it off. Since, in medieval times, apprentice stonemasons were not allowed to wear beards, it is more likely that it was the Master's head, demoted to an Apprentice head,[48] meaning that the Apprentice pillar may, in fact, be the Master pillar. The head is possibly that of the Master Builder Jesus Christ Himself. The elaborate story of an apprentice carving the master pillar was probably a real incident that inadvertently changed the meaning.

In John Slezer's *Theatrum Scotiae* of 1693 the pillar "is called the Prince's Pillar so much talk'd of." In this case the prince talked about is not an apprentice, but perhaps the "Prince of Peace" Jesus Christ. So famous is the column that in the nineteenth century the master plaster-mold makers for the Victoria and Albert Museum made a copy of this and an adjoining part of Rosslyn Chapel. Ultimately, this pillar should be called *Jachin*, meaning "He will Establish" His kingdom.

The two flanking columns may have something to do with two major noble bloodlines.[49] Interestingly, gnostic Wallace-Murphy happens upon the true meaning regarding the two outside pillars by relating them to the Solomon's temple: "The lilies had been carved above the two pillars guarding the portal of the original temple in Jerusalem and are believed to signify the descending bloodline of the kings of Israel."[50]

These two flanking pillars are highly decorated, but the center Journeyman or Entered Apprentice Pillar is fairly anonymous, plain, and severe.[51] While the center pillar is not much different from the other columns in the aisle, it is somewhat dissimilar in that its base is turned 90 degrees to the side. So, while it looks much the same, except for its straight vertical ridges, it is also quite different. Its central position between the two much better known columns seems to manifest some grand meaning or message.

We are struck by the importance of the middle shaft's central position in the architectural scheme. It may represent the melding of the Grail lines of Jesus Christ and Mary Magdalene that was hidden by Joseph of Arimathea many centuries before. Not that the builders of Rosslyn Chapel knew anything about this concept. The columns are used here to make a point, which was lost on the Sinclair family. If the two outside columns exemplify the priestly and kingly bloodlines, then the central column might be the embodiment of spanning the breach between them through a new dynastic bloodline (Genesis 49:10).

We might call this the "Shiloh" shaft or column. We could argue that it represents the hidden and true *Rex Deus* line, which has been "kept from the world" until the time is right. This unassuming column may represent the real mystery of Rosslyn Chapel. Its meaning is being inexorably pried loose, shred by shred, "here a little, there a little." The combined paternal and maternal bloodlines epitomized by this polished shaft are the key to understanding the meaning of the secret of the Holy Grail.

The capital of this shaft in Rosslyn Chapel has an interesting problem. Just where a carved sculpture should protrude from the capital shaft, "editors" or censors have aggressively hammered and chiseled away a postulated image. The other two columns have their capitals intact, but the center one does not. It is the only place in the entire building that has been completely obliterated by vandals. On the other hand, the chapel's builder, William St. Clair, may have purposely left this area unfinished.

We may never know what or who this "missing piece" to the Rosslyn puzzle represents. Perhaps in the vault or crypt are the detailed plans and renderings of the chapel's original sculptural schema with explanations. Grail enthusiasts can only hope and wait (see the following page for an interpretation by the author of the column's significance).

This hitherto not fully recognized third "Journeyman" pillar is the true key to understanding the entire *raison d'etre* of Rosslyn Chapel. The central shaft's significance is only now beginning to be understood.

The key token of the edifice probably lies in the stone cells beneath.[58] They will unlock the answers. The town of Roslin was a manuscript manufactory of some note. In its heyday during the fourteenth and fifteenth centuries, Roslin was almost as important as that of d'Anjou in France. In fact, some of the Chapel's early manuscripts were from d'Anjou.[59] The connection between these two centers of manuscript production is of utmost importance, because both d'Anjou and Roslin figure in the Grail legends.

There may be a secret within Rosslyn Chapel, but all our knowledge about it is initial, preliminary, and preparatory. Before we leave Rosslyn, "the *arcanum* in stone," it should be noted that there are other half-forgotten but very memorable places in the world, much greater than this chapel. They are

the Hill Cumorah in upstate New York and a hill in Manti, Utah, with a Mormon temple on its brow. They may be the repository of much knowledge, as we shall later see. As the destruction of Mount Moriah may have led to the downfall of Israel, perhaps Cumorah and Manti will lead to its redemption.

THE RENNES-LE-CHÂTEAU AND PRIORY OF SION HOAX

The books we have looked at make astounding claims. It is a brave act to write a book which "could constitute the single most shattering secret of the last two thousand years," or "shed light on the origin of our species" or "end with the discovery of the greatest secret of all" on such fragile foundations.[60]

Now because of certain enormous influences on Grail studies since the late 1960s we must waste time on stupidity. Certainly the most famous of the late twentieth-century Grail deceptions surrounds the tiny village of Rennes-le-Château in the rugged, unspoiled area of Languedoc-Roussillon in the Department of Aude in the southwestern corner of France.[61] This region, comprising much of the old Jewish coastal principality of Septimania Midi, was supposedly identified with the Visigoths and later the Cathars and Knights Templar.

Much of the enigma surrounds the village's eccentric priest, Bérenger Saunière (1852–1917), who was born in the area and died in mysterious circumstances. The secret of buried treasure and earth-shattering conspiracies have been the engine of outlandish claims for Rennes-le-Château. Excavations in August 2003 at Rennes, conducted by Professors Eisenman and Baratollo, hoping to find traces of gold proved disappointing. Paul Smith unmasks the ludicrous pseudohistory and sensationalist waffle

FIGURE 9

THREE PILLARS
IN ROSSLYN CHAPEL

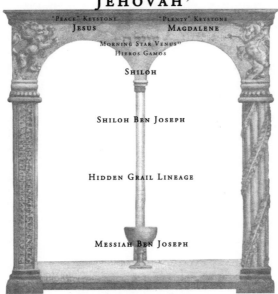

JEHOVAH[52]

"PEACE" KEYSTONE   "PLENTY" KEYSTONE
JESUS   MAGDALENE

MORNING STAR VENUS"
HIEROS GAMOS

SHILOH

SHILOH BEN JOSEPH

HIDDEN GRAIL LINEAGE

MESSIAH BEN JOSEPH

PILLAR	THE POLISHED SHAFT[54]	PILLAR
JACHIN "HE WILL ESTABILSH [BEAUTY]" (2 SAMUEL 7:16)	**SHILOH** "WISDOM"	**BOAZ** "IN STRENGTH [BANDS]" (PSALMS 60:7, 108:8)
(1) MASTER "FELLOW"	**(3) JOURNEYMAN** "ENTERED APPRENTICE"	**(2) APPRENTICE** "COMPANION"
KINGLY (SCEPTER)	PATRIARCHAL (BLOODLINE)	BIRTHRIGHT
JUDAH-JESSE-DAVID[55]	EPHRAIM+JUDAH	JOSEPH-EPHRAIM[56]
JESUS CHRIST	HIDDEN GRAIL LINEAGE	MARY MAGDALENE
TREE OF KNOWLEDGE	ROD AND ROOT OF JESSE	TREE OF LIFE
TSEDEQ (ZADOK)[57] (RIGHTEOUSNESS/LAW)	SHALOM (PEACE/BEAUTY)	MISHPAT (PSALMS 60:7) (STRENGTH/WISDOM)
MELCHIZEDEK (RIGHTEOUS KING)	JOSEPH (MAY [GOD] INCREASE)	SOPHIA (WISDOM/INTELLIGENCE)
BREAD	OLIVE	WINE
SOUTH/JUDEA	STRATEGIC MARRIAGE	NORTH/ISRAEL
SUN	EYE	MOON
LEFT	CENTER (AS WE LOOK WEST)	RIGHT
SOUTHEAST SOUTHWEST	EAST WEST	NORTHEAST NORTHWEST
WINTER SOLSTICE	EQUINOXES	SUMMER SOLSTICE
SATURN	FOUNDATION STONE (OMPHALOS, THE CENTER)	JUPITER

PEACE KEYSTONE   PLENTY KEYSTONE

surrounding Rennes-le-Château: "The negative results should not surprise informed researchers who have known for decades that no 'treasure' at Rennes-le-Château ever existed and is merely the fantasy of confidence tricksters and catchpenny authors."[62]

In outline the story notes that Saunière took up residence at Rennes-le-Château in 1885 as its parish priest. Supposedly during repairs of the Church of the Magdeleine he found some hidden parchments concealed in a hollow Visigothic pillar. Then in 1891 he found gold treasure in a grave. To support his ambitious building program and lavish lifestyle, Saunière began to sell masses at one franc apiece.[63] He also royally entertained rich older women with the idea of donating in his projects. By December 1910, Saunière was suspended from the right to celebrate mass because of abuse, which put him into financial straits.

Some believe that instead of finding treasure, he found information, "the greatest secret the world has ever known" which he used to blackmail the Roman Catholic Church.[64] With his newfound wealth he began to remodel the parish and construct Villa Bethania, an expansive belvedere and the fine stone Tower of Magdala, which housed his extensive library (see Plate 28).[65]

Forged parchments, such as *La Serpent Rouge* and *The Secret Dossiers* by Phillipe de Chérisey and Pierre Plantard, were fabricated to seem to reflect a deeper mystery, namely a Holy Grail of sorts.[66] They mention the last Merovingian king, Dagobert II, and Nicholas Poussin's painting *Et Tu Arcadia.*" Other hoaxsters have noted that the Visigothic treasure, originally from Jerusalem, was deposited at Rennes-le-Château after 410 A.D. from the sack of Rome. These spurious records mention the mysterious guardian of the Merovingian bloodline, the Priory of Sion—*Prieuré de Sion.* The Catholic Church, these documents allege, betrayed the Merovingian dynasty and sided with Pepin the

Short. The Church then crowned its destroyers, the Carolingians.

A puzzle lies in the redesign of Saunière's church, other building projects, and the very topography of the area. The parish church had been dedicated to the Magdalene in 1059. It had an upside-down Visigothic pillar underneath the altar stone, a statue of the demon Asmodeus guarding the door, and other bizarre inconsistencies. One carving shows a child swathed in Scottish plaid, or Pontius Pilate wearing a veil, or Joseph and Mary each holding a child (Christ and his twin, Thomas Didymus, as gnostics believe).

A businessman, Noël Corbu acquired the Villa Bethanie from Saunière's housekeeper, Marie Dénarnaud, who continued to live in the house until her death in 1953. Corbu remodeled it into the Tower Hotel and then began to release spectacular stories of treasure to the local newspaper, *La Dépâche du Midi* in March 1956. His goal was to ensure the success of his hotel.

In 1967, Gerard de Séde published his sensationalist book on the golden treasure of Rennes-le-Château, and soon the world came to the little hilltop village. Most influential in spreading the myth was Henry Lincoln, who swallowed Corbu's, Séde's, then Pierre Plantard's stories completely. Since Lincoln, Baigent, and Leigh's book, *Holy Blood, Holy Grail*, came out in 1982, Rennes-le-Château has unfortunately become a center of Grail studies.

Some three hundred books on the village and its mystery are said to have been published. Many of these publications, especially by Henry Lincoln, Andrews, and Schellenberger, have analyzed the topography and geometry of the area and supposedly discovered pentagrams or hexagrams and even the tomb of Jesus Christ![67] Ultimately these proved to be nothing more than a numerological conjuring trick. Putnam and Wood, in their exposé of the Rennes-le-Château hoax and delusion, have found that the "sacred pattern" overlaid by man on this area was patently unscientific.[68] Everybody involved seems to have had a motive:

> Four people with different characters, different interests and different motives together produced one of the most famous historical puzzles of the century: Noël Corbu, anxious to make his hotel a commercial success, and cleverly exploiting the strange life of Bérenger Saunière to attract the visitors; Pierre Plantard, believing himself to be of the royal line of France, spotting an opportunity to manufacture evidence in support of his claim and hijacking the Rennes-le-Château legend for his own ends; Philippe de Chérisey, playboy and joker, making puzzles for his own amusement; and Gérard de Sède, writer on historical matters, who was none too rigorous in his acceptance of evidence, but was happy to write a bestseller. . . . (Then) Henry Lincoln was captivated, and the mystery of Rennes-le-Château began to flourish even more.[69]

But what of the Priory of Sion itself? Surely diehards posit that it existed and flourished underground for centuries, protecting the sacred bloodline. It supposedly did this under the emblems of the cicada and the *fleur-de-lis* combined with the initials P.S. as their symbol.[70] Pathetically, all the evidence for their existence exists on a single fraudulent page in the *Secret Dossiers of Henri Lobineau*. Lobineau is a fictitious name, used by conspirators Pierre Plantard and Phillippe de Chérisey to enter it into the Bibliotéque Nationale under false circumstances in the 1960s. "The Priory Documents," writes Paul Smith, "is a historical fiction concocted by Pierre Plantard during the 1960s."[71]

We learn from this dishonest document that the religious order was first called *L'Order de Sion*, being founded in 1090 by the virulent anti-Semitic Godefroy de Bouillon. They were reportedly installed in the Abbey of Notre Dame on Mount Sion at Jerusalem, which is a small hill just to the south of the old walled city.[72] Then in 1306 the Priory of Sion supposedly replaced the little Priory of Mount Sion and Ormus, and went underground.

The Priory finally surfaced in the twentieth century. Citing "schism" within an older Priory, Pierre Plantard (1920–2000) registered the order in 1956 with the French bureau of organizations. Nothing is known about any older group from which the new Priory descended. Plantard eventually claims to have calmed the schism and reunited the group sometime later.

Between 1961 and 1978, Plantard and his associates began depositing mysterious documents in Bibliotéque Nationale, under pseudonyms like Henri Lobineau and "Anthony the Hermit." These all had to do with treasures of gold and parchment, Rennes-le-Château, Merovingians, white queens, Priory de Sion, and other hidden secrets. Interestingly, none of these documents dealt with Christ's bloodline, which Plantard later denounced upon hearing it from Henry Lincoln. Of course the Priory was supposed to be the guardians of the Grail lineage of Christ, but this was a later emendation from the authors of *Holy Blood, Holy Grail*.

Plantard began the arrant fraud with a list of Grand Masters, or *Nautonniers* (Helmsmen), of the Priory de Sion. All were called Jean, or Jeanne, for the four female Grand Masters. The list of the Grand Masters and the dates they presided is most eminent: Sandro Botticelli (1483–1510), Leonardo Da Vinci (1510–1519), Robert Fludd (1595–1637), Robert Boyle (1654–1691), Sir Isaac Newton (1691–1727), Victor Hugo (1844–1885), Claude Debussy

(1885–1918), Jean Cocteau (1918–1963), and Pierre Plantard "Chyron" (1981–1994). This list of Grand Masters of the dubious Merovingian cause was just too good to be true.

Sadly, many still believe that the Priory de Sion, with its list of grand masters and other *Prieure* documents, was authentic. Grailists, such as Lincoln, Baigent and Leigh, Dan Brown, Blezard, Picknett, and Prince, etc.,[73] even give some credence to them. Plantard claims to have been made Grand Master of the Priory of Sion in 1981, whereas before he was its "General."[74] In 1982 the book *Holy Blood, Holy Grail* finally linked it all together with the bloodline of Jesus Christ and Mary Magdalene. Henry Lincoln simply connected the imaginary dots to come to this conclusion.[75]

Yet authors like Picknett and Prince, in spite of false names, nonexistent addresses, inventions, falsehoods, and improbabilities still accept the faked documents supporting the Rennes myth as acceptable: "It is in our opinion, a great mistake to dismiss the *Dossiers secrets* simply because their overt message is demonstrably implausible. The sheer scale of the work behind them argues in favour of their having something to offer."[76]

From these and other publications, Putnam and Wood reveal: "From telling to telling, the story develops. Each little bit that has been added to make the story more entertaining becomes part of the accepted history and from a few dimly remembered facts grows an account full of persuasive detail."[77]

"A sensational story with little hard evidence to back it up . . . full of assumptions and possibilities, which when repeated often enough (and occasionally embroidered upon) become effectively the definitive account . . . not only dubious but fraudulent. They have gained authenticity simply by being repeated over and over again."[78]

The numerous books on Rennes-le-Château and the Priory de Sion, though detailed and clever, are not authentic history or science. Rather they are parodies of both. The lifetime work of professional scholars, archaeologists, and theologians is too often ignored or plundered with little care or respect. Texts are speculated upon out of their natural context until they are nothing more than self-serving pretext. Popularizing authors hate vacuums, and given the paucity of hard fact, they flood in to fill it with speculation, which becomes more orthodox by the telling.

The problem of citing evidence without footnoting its source presents data in a misleading way. Listing coincidences as proof, ideologically selecting information, disregarding or suppressing contrary evidence, and unethically smearing opposing views is the hallmark of most "alternative Christianity" publications. They have not wanted to let the allure of Rennes or the Priory go. Though pure hokum, it will continue as "fact" to inform gnostic texts on the Holy Grail for another generation. Gnosticism is not so much concerned with historical fact as it is with alternate truths. The way to the Grail is not found in falsehood, even when it is for a supposedly good cause.

NOTES

1. The 1307 confession of Jacques de Molay, Grand Master of the Knights Templar.
2. Pierre des Vaux-de-Cernay, *Historia Albigensis* no. 246, explaining the Cathar, not his own, position on marriage. See Christopher M. Kurpiewski, "Writing Beneath the Shadow of Heresy," *Journal of Medieval History* 31 (March 1905): 1–27. Another, expanded, translation goes as follows: "They [the Cathars] preached that Holy Matrimony was meretricious, and that none could be saved in it, if they should beget children." Raynaldus, *Annales* (trans. Maitland), *History of the Albigenses and Waldenses*, 392–93.
3. They were later called Albigenses because of a town they settled called Albi. These Cathars had connections with the Waldenses, Poor Men of Lyons, and especially the Bogomiles of Bulgaria, who had their roots in Egyptian Gnosticism. The label Cathars was not unique to the

Albigensians, for it was used in the third century to describe the Novatins, then the Manicheans, but was usually employed to describe this medieval dualist sect. See Clay Randal, "Were the Albigensians Primitive 2x2's?" www.angelfire.com. (2001).

4. Morgan, *Holy Grail,* 93. They believed that there were two Christs: an evil one born of Joseph and Mary (Adam and Eve reincarnated) in Bethelehem, who had disgusting sex with a harlot Mary Magdalene. The other was the good Christ who was born in the celestial world, was a spirit and did not lie.

5. Wakefield and Evans, *Heresies of the High Middle Ages,* 234. In footnote 35 on page 719, Wakefield and Evans explain this was the Cathar "pseudo-Christ," not their "good Christ," who was never married in this world. Starbird, *Mary Magdalene,* 107–8, gives the quotation and mentions the Samaritan woman at the well (John 4:16) as the "woman taken in adultery whom Christ exonerated. These spurious slanders of Mary Magdalene, ostensibly derived from Cathar doctrine, survived in a vastly distorted version well into the Reformation period, and were apparently believed by Martin Luther himself, who is quoted as saying that Jesus had sexual affairs with all three women."

6. Malcolm Barber, "The Albigensian Crusades: Wars like Any Others?" *Dei gesta per Francois: Estudes sur les croisades deditees a Jean Richard,* 1. Barber repeats this quotation slightly differently, as he got it from Peter of Les Vaux-de-Cernay, *Hystoria Albigensis,* edited by Guebin and Lyon, 1. 90–91, pp. 91–93. Vaux-de-Cernay, *History of the Albigensian Crusade* (trans. Silby and Silby), 50–51, 78–79.

7. Margaret Starbird at the 2005 Salt Lake City Sunstone Symposium (28 July 2005) claimed that Vaux-de-Cernay's quote was proof positive that the Cathars believed in a sacred marriage between Mary Magdalene and Jesus Christ. However, these Cathars did not believe it was a "sacred marriage" but thought that Christ was evil and not the loving Christ we worship. Furthermore, the Vaux-de-Cernay quotation says "concubine," not "wife," as in the passage attributed to Ermengaud. Concubines have a legally recognized position less than a wife. It is not a fully recognized marriage, but a sexual contract without rights going to the children. It usually relates to second or polygamous relations. The word *concubine* comes from the Latin *cubare,* meaning "to lie." The tenuous reasons to connect the Cathars with the Grail all come down to these two quotations, one relying on the other.

8. Wakefield and Evans, *Heresies of the High Middle Ages,* 238.

9. According to Durant, *Age of Faith,* 769, Albigenses or Cathar had echoes of Manichean dualism and Mazdakian communism. From Islam they inherited a hostility to images, an obscure fatalism, and distaste for priests. From the failure of the Crusades, they inherited a secret doubt as to the divine origin and support of the Christian Church.

10. The Cathars would not have condoned such sexual behavior in either contention. Maxine Hanks of the Mormon Women's Forum suggested (29 July 2005) that not all Cathars believed the same, and perhaps some saw Jesus married to Mary Magdalene. If this was the view of a splinter group or a secret "inner circle" and not the general or main body of the Cathars, then why is it claimed that they were persecuted for it? I would think the main body would have given denials right, left, and center, on this point, at least.

11. Knight and Lomas, "The Holy Grail," in Flanders, *Mysteries of the Ancient World,* 20.

12. L-A de St. Clair, *Histoire Genealogique de la Famille de St. Clair,* as quoted by Hopkins, Simmans, and Wallace-Murphy, *Rex Deus,* 110. The Count of Champagne was related by blood and marriage to the Capetian kings of France, the duke of Burgundy, and the Norman and Plantagenet kings of England.

13. Hopkins, Simmans, and Wallace-Murphy, *Rex Deus,* 110. While the origins of Cabalism extend into antiquity, its present form developed in the Rabbinical schools of Moorish Spain during the tenth and eleventh centuries.

14. Knight and Lomas, "The Holy Grail," in Flanders, *Mysteries of the Ancient World,* 75.

15. Wallace-Murphy and Hopkins, *Rosslyn,* 95, quotation from Michel Kluber, "Une Vie par reforme l'églisé" in the journal *Bernard de Clairvaux* (Les editions de l'Argonante, France).

16. See Claudia Cannon of Mapleton, Utah, MS, fn 109.

17. Hopkins, Simmans, and Wallace-Murphy, *Rex Deus,* 113–14. Nobody has any firm evidence that any documentary material exists. See http://alandpeters. tripod.com/knightstemplarera1188t013–12/id1.html

18. The Moslems, Knights Templar, and present-day Ultra-Orthodox Jews believe the Dome of the Rock is built on the Holy of Holies of the Second Temple. I do not believe this, but think that the Dome was built on the site of the apse of the Temple of Jupiter built by the Roman Emperor, Hadrian. The Temple is north of the Dome, with the Cupola of the tablets marking the spot of the Holy of Holies.

19. William of Tyre, *History of Deeds Done beyond the Sea.*

20. Knight and Lomas, *Hiram Key*, 27, and Laidler, *Head of God*, 167.

21. Baigent and Leigh, *Temple and the Lodge*, 72.

22. They wished for knowledge, relics, talismans, and treasure. Laidler, *Head of God* (throughout), believes that for a millennium a select cabal of Jews secretly harbored the idea of recovering the Temple treasure. These were the relatives of those Sadducees who had fled Jerusalem before Roman legions besieged the city.

23. See Galbraith, Ogden, and Skinner, *Jerusalem*, 187. They say, "Below the floor level to the north and west was earth fill, but to the south Herod supported the floor with vaults—twelve rows of arched colonnades with a total of eighty-eight pillars. The area under the floor of the southeast portion of the Temple courtyard therefore was hollow. This space is now occupied by a large, columned chamber. Because it was constructed by Herod, the place did not exist in Solomon's day, though it was later used by the Crusaders for stabling horses."

24. Hancock, *Sign and the Seal*, xi, speculates that they were looking for the Holy Grail, the lost treasures of the Temple, or perhaps the ark of the covenant. The location of the Ark, in fact, was the raison d'etre of Hancock's research, but the Templars were probably looking for treasure, religious and monetary.

25. Nibley, *Mormonism and Early Christianity*, 335. Nibley notes from Join-Lambert's book *Jerusalem*, 170, that the Holy of Holies was in a cave under the same Temple Rock. Another story has a cave under Mt. Nebo rather than the Temple Mount. See Bruce R. McConkie, *Doctrinal New Testament Commentary*, 1:382. Vilnay, *Legends of Jerusalem*, 1:123, also states that the ark of the covenant was directly below the Holy of Holies in a special chamber.

26. Hopkins, Simmans, and Wallace-Murphy, *Rex Deus*, 116. These authors are highly partisan to Gnosticism and predisposed to overreach what "consensus" might exist. Also see "Templars excavation of Solomon's Temple," http://alandpeters.tripod.com/knightstemplarera 188t01312/id15.html.

27. Knight and Lomas, "The Holy Grail," in Flanders, *Mysteries of the Ancient World*, 83. They offer no source.

28. Delaforge, *Templar Tradition in the Age of Aquarius*, 68.

29. Lieutenant Charles Wilson of the Royal Engineers, *The Excavation of Jerusalem*, as quoted in Knight and Lomas, *Hiram Key*, 29, 267: "The Templars may have been the first people to excavate below the Jerusalem Temple, but they were not the last. We mentioned earlier that in 1894 a group of British Army officers, with a budget of just five hundred pounds, set out to try and find the vaults below the ruins of Herod's Temple. The contingent of Royal Engineers led by Lieutenant Charles Wilson conducted some excellent work under very adverse conditions and they could confirm that the chambers and passageways they found were often vaulted with keystone arches."

30. Laidler, *Head of God*, 116.

31. Knight and Lomas, *Second Messiah*, 24.

32. Church, *Guardians of the Grail*, 24. He quotes Allegro, *Treasure of the Copper Scroll*, 107ff; see Baigent, Leigh, and Lincoln, *Holy Blood, Holy Grail*, 88. Knight and Lomas, *The Hiram Key*, believe that the Qumran Community and the Jerusalem Church were one and the same thing, and that the Templars had found the "mother lode" of the "purest" Christian documents possible (58).

33. Allegro, *Treasure of the Copper Scroll*, notes that there were "twelve scrolls and other scrolls."

34. His Cistercian Order was founded in 1098 as a part of the great monastic reform and crusades. He also vigorously championed the Second Crusade.

35. Their new Rule made joining members probationers for the first year and required from them an immediate vow of poverty.

36. Knight and Lomas, *Hiram Key*, 30–31. The papal legate, Cardinal of Albano, presided over the council, which was composed of the Archbishops of Rheims and Sens, no fewer than ten bishops, and many abbots. They granted the request, and the Templars were given the right to wear their own mantles, which at that time were pure white and later they received the red cross.

37. Wallace-Murphy and Hopkins, *Rosslyn*, 105. See Hancock, *Sign and the Seal*, 334.

38. Begg, *Cult of the Black Virgin*, 103. See Gardner, *Bloodline of the Holy Grail*, 257. Supposedly Gerard de Rousillon, the founder of the abbey, brought her bones from southern France in the eighth century for safekeeping from the Moslems. The first certain mention of pilgrimage to her relics there was in 1037. See Abbé Alexander Pissier, Le Culte de Sainte Marie-Madeleine a Vézelay (1923), 14, as noted in Newman, *Real History behind The Da Vinci Code*, 157. She was considered the same person as Mary of Bethany.

39. Delaforge, *Templar Tradition in the Age of Aquarius*, 68.

40. Ward, *Freemasonry and the Ancient Gods*, as quoted in Knight and Lomas, *Second Messiah*, 209. "Mother Kilwinning" is No. 0, as the very earliest Masonic Lodge in Scotland. See Ralls-MacLeod and Robertson, *Quest for the Celtic Key*, 143.

41. On Google under "Friday 13th, history" several sources

other than the Templar roundup are mentioned for this unlucky date.

42. Sinclair, *Secret Scroll*, 102.

43. M. Hannan, *The Scotsman* (Edinburgh newspaer), 14 September 1998.

44. The author has switched the names of these two columns and their meaning, see figure. 15 below. I use Coppens, *Stone Puzzle of Rosslyn Chapel*, as my major source for this change, but I also accept the internal logic this change makes in other interpretations. There is a pair of similar columns at the twelfth-century Dunfermline Abbey, although the more elaborate of the two is considered the work of the master. See Fawcett, *Scottish Medieval Churches*, 163; See also Newman, *Real History behind The Da Vinci Code*, 254.

45. Wallace-Murphy and Hopkins, *Rosslyn*, 9. Coppens, *Stone Puzzle of Rosslyn Chapel*, 53, also calls it the Journeyman's pillar. Coppens and then goes into greater detail on page 106. Laidler and Sinclair also mention the column.

46. Never before illustrated and little remarked upon, center "Shiloh" or "Salaam" column at Rosslyn Chapel in Roslin, Scotland, with detail of its capital. Its position between the Apprentice and Master columns is fraught with meaning regarding the Grail dynasty. Note the upper right of column's capital, where it has been chipped away. Perhaps this was the severed head of Brân the Blessed.

47. Jess Nisbet, "Secrets of Rosslyn Chapel," www.mythomorph.com (2004).

48. It should be noted that no Templar or Grail references in connection to Rosslyn were known exist before the nineteenth century. See Newman, *Real History behind The Da Vinci Code*, 254.

49. In the Temple of Jerusalem the two columns were freestanding, but at Rosslyn they are "bridged," intimating that Christ and Mary Magdalene may have spanned them and began a new dynasty.

50. Wallace-Murphy and Hopkins, *Rosslyn*, 10.

51. Coppens, *Stone Puzzle of Rosslyn Chapel*, 59, has speculated that the Journeyman's Pillar might be the "journeywoman."

52. Baigent and Leigh, *Temple and the Lodge*, 179. These authors note that Jehovah oversees the entire program.

53. A five-pointed star shining in the darkness between Boaz and Jachin. This is the "bright star of the morning," Venus. See Knight and Lomas, *Book of Hiram*, 19.

54. Sinclair, *Secret Scroll*, 98, mentions the center column: "The central undecorated pillar refers more to the tradition of the Templars, as on their seal of 1214, as to the usual pattern of Masonic Lodges with their three pillars, representing Beauty, Strength, and Wisdom. There are dozens of small Temples of Solomon carved on the Rosslyn walls, usually with the three pillars and two arches of the Templar seal." Further, Sinclair notes in *Secret Scroll*, 179: "The three pillars of Masonry were Jachin, Boaz and Mac-Benac, making up the initials J.B.M. or Jacq. Burg. Molay, the name of the martyred last Grand Master of the Order. Mac-Benac was also the pseudonym of Aumont, the Templar leader of those knights who had fled to Scotland."

55. There is a prophecy to David: "And thy house and thy kingdom shall be established forever before thee: Thy throne shall be established forever" (2 Samuel 7:16).

56. Most scholars, like Knight and Lomas, *Second Messiah*, 86, believe that the Jachin pillar represented Levi, "the priestly line." They do not even have in their consciousness that it might be Ephraim, the "birthright" line.

57. Traditionally, Tsedeq and Mishpat have been switched the other way. The author has likened Tsedeq with Melchizedek and Mishpat with Ephraim—and Judah with the Law (see Psalm 60:7).

58. This author does not fully subscribe to the Oak Island, Nova Scotia, theory. Perhaps some treasure was taken to the New World, but copies of the scrolls were left? I do not believe that Rosslyn Chapel really possesses any ancient documents.

59. Rene d'Anjou inherited from his father the title King of Jerusalem, even though the Holy Land had been lost to the Muslims in 1187.

60. Putnam and Wood, *Treasure of Rennes-le-Château*, 147.

61. The capital of this Department is the ancient walled city of Carcassonne.

62. Paul Smith, "Rennes-Le-Château Debunked: No treasure at Rennes-le-Château", 1, http://www.anzwers.org/free/rlcdebunked/ (2003).

63. Putnam and Wood, *Treasure of Rennes-le-Château*, 4. They record, "He had an enormous amount of mail. The postmistress in Couiza reported that he received as many as 150 letters a day." It is estimated that he probably sold on average of about 100 masses per day, although the Catholic Church guidelines allow for only three to be said per day. Obviously Sauniére took the money without saying all the individual masses.

64. According to the argument in *The Da Vinci Code* the Knights Templars, the keepers of the Grail secret, were already receiving money and privileges from the Vatican in exchange for not revealing the truth about Jesus and Mary Magdalene. See Haag and Haag, *Rough Guide to The Da Vinci Code*, 23. If the Templars were willing

to reveal the secret unless money was paid them, were they unworthy keepers? If the Catholic Church paid the Templars to keep quiet, then why did they attack them in 1307? Nothing in the immediate post-Templar world even hints at the idea. The above specious argument holds no credence.

65. Photograph of the Tower of Magdale at Rennes-le-Château, France. The entire hoax of Rennes has badly damaged Grail studies. Courtesy of Tony and Traci Fieldsted.

66. Phillipe de Chérisey was interested in surrealist and hermetic ideas and puzzles. The mystery was that the Merovingian dynasty had survived. No mention is given of Jesus' bloodline, which Henry Lincoln later imputed to the story.

67. Lincoln, *Key to the Sacred Pattern,* and *Holy Places;* and Andrews and Schellenberger, *Tomb of God,* are among the most famous.

68. Putnam and Wood, "The Geometry of the Pentagon," "Alignments," and "Units of Measurement," 211–33. It should also be noted that the Paris Meridian does not pass through Rennes, but is actually about six kilometers east.

69. Putnam and Wood, *Treasure of Rennes-le-Château,* 125.

70. The fleur-de-lis was not an emblem used by the Merovingians. See Hinkle, *Fleur de Lis of the Kings of France, 1285–1488,* 4–5. And far from being a Johannine Christianity, their favorite patrons were Saints Martin, Denis, Vincent, and Médard. John the Baptist is notably absent.

71. Paul Smith, "Priory of Sion Misconceptions—Robert Richardson and Steven Mizrach," 4. See http://home.graffiti.net/prioryofsion/posmis.html. The documents were forged by Phillipe de Chérisey, a one-time friend of Plantard. They include the Dossiers Secrets and LeRouge Serpent.

72. In truth the Priory de Sion was founded in 1956 and named after the nearby hill to Saint Julien-en-Genevois called Mont Sion, and had nothing whatever to do with the "Sion" in Jerusalem.

73. Other hoaxes include the Piltdown Man and the saga of Frank Watkins and his long-distance riding horse, Hidalgo. Some spurious myths are too good to let go of.

74. Paul Smith, http://templarchronicle.homestead.com/prioryofsion.html (2001).

75. The "dots" being this legend of Mary Magdalene coming to Provence in southern France, the newly published gnostic gospels, Phipps's *Was Jesus Married?* and now the Rennes and Priory stories.

76. Picknett and Prince, *Templar Revelation,* 58. What this something "is" is debatable. Perhaps it is a cautionary note to be careful not to ignore facts for ideology.

77. Putnam and Wood, *Treasure of Rennes-le-Château,* 106. This is similar to "false memory syndrome" where the mind subconsciously fills in "plausible" facts and reasonable details complete the psychological picture.

78. Ibid., 146–47.

PART SEVEN

RETURN OF THE KING'S SON

*[Joseph Smith was the] Last Prophet who is called
to lay the foundation of the great Last Dispensation
of the Fullness of Times.*

—BRIGHAM YOUNG[1]

New thinking and doctrines came with the Reformation and Protestantism, some positive and others negative. Though information is very scarce, the idea of the *hieros gamos* slowly was retrieved.[2] Little was known until the early Mormon references to Jesus' marriage to Mary and Martha and their having children. This unquenchable story had boiled to the surface in the twentieth century, for it is an eternal phoenix. The resurfacing of this tale begins with two *ascendant descendants* of Jesus Christ and his Ephraimite wife, Mary Magdalene. They were Joseph Smith Sr. and his wife, Lucy Mack Smith. The Lord carefully watched over the fountain of this bloodline, protecting it, to fulfill His purpose in the last days. The Grail seed had been planted deep in Britain and took nearly 1800 years in two directions to take root, to branch, and finally to blossom. The fruit was Joseph Smith Jr., the scion of Ephraim and the true King's Son. We now probe the story of the return of the royal heir in the nineteenth century.

CHAPTER SEVENTEEN

THE OUTRE CHURCH

For I deign to reveal unto my Church things which have been kept hid from the foundation of the world, things that pertain to the dispensation of the fulness of times.

—D&C 124:41

The mysteries of the kingdom, kept secret through the centuries, had trickled down in snippets of knowledge through the ages. The knowledge in its arcane form was called the *gnosis*. For Joseph Smith to restore the true Church in its pristine form, he understood the esoteric-hermetic tradition well enough to divide the Lord's business from that corrupted by man. And he followed the Lord's directions.

Our study of the Holy Grail has tightly woven various threads from which to tease out strands of knowledge from antiquity until today. This intertwining of truth and error, though ultimately unsatisfying, was inevitable given the clouded history and feeble mindset of mankind. Further research and then revelation will continue to ferret out truth from falsehood, history from legend, as our study of the great mystery of the Holy Grail has occasionally bordered on the occult, always with the idea of separating light from darkness and retrieving memory fossils from the strata.[3]

BRITISH-ISRAELITISM

Ephraim feedeth on wind, and followeth after the east wind.

—HOSEA 12:1

Early British-Israelitism, not the Knights Templar or the Freemasons, gave a foundational understanding to Joseph Smith's revelations on the tribal union between Judah and Ephraim. An east wind blows West, and Ephraim went westward. Eventually they were cast ashore far off to the West, first to the "Isles of the Sea" (Great Britain), then in time to *La Merika* in the Western hemisphere. There they built up their vigor a little at a time.

Keep silence before me, O islands, and let the people renew their strength.

—ISAIAH 41:1

Eventually the people of America were to become a mighty nation, the strongest in the history of the world.[4] The present state of Israel in Palestine (the Levant) is technically the *State of Judah* and not really of "all Israel." Other tribal descendants of Jacob living in Israel today are not accorded full rights given to the Jews (Judah, Simeon, Benjamin and half the tribe of Levi) living there. Many of the Israelite tribes are currently hidden elsewhere in the world. Most persistent of the various explanations of where the lost ten tribes of Israel are today are found in the legends about the Zorahic-Judah, Ephraimitic, and other Hebraic emigrants into "the Isles of the Sea."

The speculative antiquarianism of the eighteenth century and the Protestant British-Israelite Movement of the late nineteenth and early twentieth centuries had much in common. They romantically believed that "Tara of the Kings" in Ireland played a key role in establishing Britain as latter-day Israel. The imperialistic and patriotic theories of Charles Vallancey (1720–1812) helped shape British-Israelism as an organized movement.[5]

British-Israelism tended not to be scientific in its etymological gymnastics, trying to make the Celtic tongue into a Hebraic language. It was also archaeologically unscientific. Crew noted that "distorting history and archaeology in the service of myth had been a specialty of the Vallancey school of speculative antiquarianism. It was also a feature of British-Israelite doctrine."[6] In 1931, R. A. S. Macalister wrote negatively concerning British-Israelism, that it was an abortion begotten of unscholarly ignorance of the nature of the biblical historical record, upon unbridled national bumptiousness.[7]

On the other side of the equation, Denis Hanan speaking in 1898 said that British-Israelites "were used to ridicule in the defense of truth," but that "they must be strong enough to be superior to it."[8] What did the British-Israelites believe regarding the origins of a holy race in the British Isles? They theorized that early immigrants, perhaps descendants of Noah, Shem (and Japheth), and Eber, though unknown by name, settled in the British Isles.[9] The mystic poet and artist William Blake asked rhetorically, "Was Britain the Primitive Seat of the patriarchal religion?"[10]

Supposedly Blake was referring to those megalithic peoples who built Stonehenge and gigantic Avebury, at about the time of Enoch. As archaeologists now confirm, Stonehenge was begun as early as 3,000 B.C., four hundred years before the Great Pyramids of Gizah.[11] British-Israelite Walton Adams wrote of the "singular relation" that existed between the measurements of the "Ark, Pyramid of Egypt, and the site at Tara."[12] It was unimaginable, they believed, for such feats to have been accomplished by raw primitive peoples without the guidance of a superior will and intelligence, namely the Lord's chosen people, the Hebrews.

British-Israelites searched for similarities between the Hebrew and Celtic tongue. It was here in the "far off isles" that they supposed the Phoenician wanderers landed. They see in the scripture "For, with stammering lips and another tongue, will he [the Lord] speak to this people," a resonance with the Gaelic language (Isaiah 28:11; 32:4; 33:19). Indeed, there seem to be many crosscurrents that lead to our Grail story. LDS scholar Hugh Nibley said as much: "It all seems to be right out of the Egyptian or Babylonian epics, and indeed scholars have long since and often pointed out the extremely close resemblances between the Celtic epic literature, especially the Grail saga, and the Babylonian and Egyptian legends and rituals."[13]

The study of the transmittal of ancient and arcane knowledge to recent times is fraught with difficulties. Freemason Sir William Betham believed that the Celtic tribe *Cabiri* was a secret Phoenician society, which concealed from all but the initiated its knowledge of science and the arts. He considered Freemasons to be the successors of the Phoenician Cabiri. Mairéad Carew notes:

> The British-Israelites married the imperialistic logic of Ledwich with the Irish-patriot-Phoenicianist theories of Vallancey to arrive at a very distinctive collection of theories appropriate to the particular agenda of their own movement in the late nineteenth century. They celebrated the past of Tara as a British-Hebrew past and therefore as part of their own history as descendants of the ancient Hebrews.[14]

The history of "these islands" was, in theory, interwoven with the migration of "mighty men" from Israel, Egypt, Phoenicia, and Troy. Furthering the notion of great intellectual wealth in Great Britain are the stories of the *Hyperborean* geniuses, who came to Greece from the northwest—from an island opposite Gaul.[15] These mighty men therefore blessed the world. In the fifth century B.C. the Greek scholar Hecateus is quoted by Diodorus Sykeliotis as saying:

> That in the regions beyond the land of the Celts (Gaul) there lies in the ocean an island no smaller than Sicily. . . . [It] is situated in the north and is inhabited by the Hyperborean, who are called by that name because their home is beyond the point whence the north wind [Boreal] blows.
>
> Moreover, the following legend is told concerning it: "Leto (the mother by Zeus of Apollo and Artemis) was born on this island and for that reason Apollo is honoured among them above all other gods.

> There is also on the island both a magnificent sacred precinct of Apollo and a notable temple, which is adorned with many votive offerings and is spherical in shape. Furthermore, a city is there which is sacred to this God and the majority of its inhabitants are players on the citheria.[16]

We may logically deduce from these ancient documents that the island must be the British Isles. The Isles are called, according to Ralls-MacLeod, the temple of Apollo [the Celtic god, *Lugh*, the "Shining One"] of the Hyperborean. This name derived from an astronomical phenomenon, in which the moon's every nineteen- [18.61] year cycle, was called the "southern extreme of the major standstill." The moon stood still and appeared close to the earth. The natives therefore believed that, "The god (light) enters the earth every nineteen years."[17]

The Grail city, Glastonbury, rests on a straight ley line with Stonehenge (*Cor-Gawr*), which might be the "temple" mentioned above. More importantly, this theory may be hiding a higher truth. For instance, "The basic circumference of Stonehenge—3168—is also the numerical value of the most sacred name in Christianity—"Lord Jesus Christ."[18]

Direct and straight ley lines may relate symbolically to a meridian or kingship lineage, namely to a straight genealogical ley line of divine kings and queens. According to Paul Devereux, "In such mystical union with the land, with the goddess, the king infused the earth with his power, the divine power [through] the kingly line."[19] For the British-Israelites, and later neognostics, (ley lines) proved the Lord's presence in Britain and His connection with the early tribes that built the sacred sites.

In the legend mentioned above, could the Virgin Mary actually be the matrilineal Leto of Hyperborea? And did she from her eternal husband Zeus (Heavenly Father) become the mother of

Apollo—who is Jesus?![20] Graves in *The White Goddess* definitely believes that Yahweh of Israel and Apollo of the Hyperborean were the same person.[21] Thus we see that revelatory legend begins to imitate history and the beginning of a regal ley line between the Meridian of Time and the Fulness of Time.

These successive waves of immigrants fertilized the bloodlines already present in Great Britain, making it a fruitful ground for the royal rod, stem, and branch of Israel to take root. Of British-Israel and the Anglo-Saxon race, LDS Apostle Erastus Snow had much to say:

> The children of Abraham from among the kingdoms and countries of the earth [were] to first hear and then embrace the everlasting gospel; and the remnants of the seed of Ephraim who were scattered from Palestine and who colonized the shores of the Caspian Sea and thence made their way into the north of Europe, western Scandinavia and northern Germany, penetrating . . . among the first Elders of the Church; they and the fathers having been watched over from the days that God promised those blessings upon Isaac and Jacob and Joseph and Ephraim. And these are they that will be found in the front ranks of all that is noble and good in their day and time, and who will be found.[22]

A number of Mormon Church leaders in the first half of the twentieth century believed that Great Britain was a sacred repository of the blood promises of Israel. Most inclined for this idea were Andrew Jenson, B. H. Roberts, Melvin J. Ballard, Anthony W. Ivins, and James E. Talmage. Talmage writes in the *Millennial Star* in 1925:

Among the most recent claims as to the location of these tribes is the one so strongly and aggressively maintained by the British-Israel-World Federation. This organization held a great congress in London from October 12th to 17th inclusive. [1925] The present writer was privileged to attend several of the meetings. A wide range of topics was covered by the addresses delivered and papers read, all embraced under the general subject "The Greatest Discovery of the Age." This "Discovery", as affirmed at the Congress, is that the British people are the lost tribes of Israel.[23]

This confirms, to some degree, what Brigham Young had taught regarding the British and Anglo-Saxons as descendants of Ephraim.[24] This would have given a "fertile crescent" of sorts for the "chosen" people and the Savior's descendants to intermix. According to this reading, the British Isles were specially "prepared" to receive the Savior's seed. Non-Mormon British-Israelite J. H. Allen asks: "Is it possible that this little royal remnant (Tephi Tea's entourage) shall have gone to that same unknown land to which they of the ten tribes had previously gone?"[25]

To substantiate this contention, the British-Israel Association of London began to search for the ark of the covenant on the Hill of Tara in County Meath about twenty miles northwest of Dublin during the summer of 1899.[26] The excavation lasted until about 1902 and ended in failure. The most stalwart faction from among the secret fraternity of British-Israelites, Identitists, and Freemasons were The Knights of Tara. They were founded about 1885 and had a definite esoteric slant.[27] This maverick group, possibly led by Walton Adams and Charles Groom, believed that the Ark was concealed in the emerald Hill Tara and needed to be exhumed for the sake of the world.[28]

This Freemason wing of the movement theorized that the ark of the covenant was buried in Tephi Tea's tomb at Tara while others called it "a poetic illusion hatched in dreamland fancy."[29] Tara was, according to old Irish chronicles, the resting place of kings. British-Israelites felt that God had transferred from the Holy Land the symbols of Pan-Israel to the "Isles of the Sea," such as Great Britain and America. Finding these sacred relics at Tara would dramatically usher in the new millennium and serve as the capital of a millennial theocracy.

The British-Israelite movement was heavily imbued with Freemasonry and saw salvation in national terms rather than a personal redemption. They were interdenominational, Protestant, white supremacists, with an imperialistic worldview. British-Israelites clung to apocalyptic theories and had a romantic though fatalistic perspective. They believed that invading Gaels (half Canaanite-Phoenician, enemies of Israel) drove Irish Israelites into Scotland, leaving Ireland racially impure.[30]

British-Israelites believed that dormant Israel would be awakened, starting from Tara Hill. Furthermore, the gospel would be spread from Tara, where it would be "radiated round the world."[31] To them: "The concept of Tara as the centre of a spiritual, religious or cultural conquest of the world is a recurring theme in British-Israelite literature. Tara was regarded by them as an ancient royal site in the British Empire, the deposition of the Ark, there would be evidence that Tara was indeed the spiritual birthplace of the Anglo-Saxon nation."[32]

At the same time Irish nationalists, who believed that British-Israelism was an English Protestant plot to further subvert Catholic Irish independence, railed against the pseudo-archaeological desecration of Tara. For them Tara Hills represented the capital of Free Ireland and the qualities of verdancy, rusticity, and Gaelic innocence. For both groups, Tara epitomized quintessential positive aspects, one to the Hebraic provenance of Britain, and the other to Irish culture. "Tara, it seems," writes Carew, "was central to the concept of both the British-Israelite millennium and the Celtic millennium."[33] Rev. Allen continues: "[The original British] are in every way the greatest race on earth, but they do not know where they originated, nor who were their ancestors—they are lost."[34]

While British-Israelism may have been weakened by the general malaise of Christianity and its many inaccuracies, something of truth exists within the movement. That Christ's Grail children came to a "prepared land", not just to a pagan people, still has some resonance. A number of Latter-day Saint authors were energized by its concepts, including E. L. Whitehead, James Anderson, and Vaughn Hanson.

MORMONISM AND FREEMASONRY

The Secret of Masonry is to keep a secret.

—JOSEPH SMITH JR.[35]

I believe he [Joseph Smith] accepted Masonry because he genuinely felt he recognized true ancient mysteries contained therein. . . . Joseph was under the strong compulsion to embrace Masonry. The Prophet believed that his mission was to restore all truth, and then to unify and weld it all together into one. . . . My assumption is that Joseph Smith believed he was restoring Masonry's original pristine brilliancy, and that he was re-creating the Mysteries of the ancient Priesthood.

—REED C. DURHAM JR.[36]

As God's chosen prophet, Joseph Smith Jr. has had much criticism heaped upon him with the intention of discrediting the divinely inspired revelation he received regarding the Grail-based temple endowment. If Joseph was a fraud, he could not be the birthright descendant of Christ, the *Messiah ben Joseph*. The most misguided of these criticisms is the assertion that Joseph did not receive the endowment ceremony by revelation but rather stole it from the Freemasons, with some imaginative alterations. In order to vindicate the Prophet Joseph and the position he held, this presumptuous assertion will be challenged.

Joseph Smith explained in May 1841 to an early member of the Church, William Appleby, that the Lord revealed "the Grand key words of the Holy Priesthood to Adam in the garden of Eden, as also to Seth, Noah, Melchizedek, Abraham, and to all whom the Priesthood was revealed."[37] Thus we see that a form of Masonry existed from Father Adam. However, most Freemasons see their rituals descending from Solomon's temple.

In America, Freemasonry flourished with only some persecution and was instrumental in founding the United States. Masonry was a leading force behind the American Revolution. The Boston Tea Party of 1773 was organized by members of the St. Andrew's Lodge. Counted among its members were Samuel Adams and Paul Revere. Many of the founding fathers of the United States of America were Freemasons, including Benjamin Franklin, John Hancock, and George Washington, among others.[38]

The interest in Freemasonry began in the Joseph Smith Sr. home when Hyrum became a Mason during the early 1820s. Hyrum received the first three degrees of Masonry in the Mount Moriah Lodge No. 112 in Palmyra, New York.[39] This occurred during a period of rampant anti-Masonic crusades in western New York. Members of the Smith family were at times both pro and anti-Masonic, depending upon the issue in question. The younger Joseph Smith never rejected Freemasonry nor was he willing to accept it *in toto*.[40]

An interesting episode reveals something of Joseph's early involvement with Masonry. A certain Capt. William Morgan, who was about Joseph's own age, lived in the Palmyra area. Dr. Rob Morris, an American Masonic biographer of William Morgan, wrote that he "had been a half way convert of Joe Smith, the Mormon, and had learned from him to see visions and dreams."[41] Supposedly Morgan was kidnapped and perhaps martyred by the Masons. Joseph Smith Sr. was one of the committee of ten men who signed an impassioned plea for aid to Morgan's bereaved wife. It was printed in the "rabidly anti-Masonic" newspaper, *The Seneca Farmer and Waterloo Advertiser.*

In 1829, Pope Pius VIII issued an encyclical condemning the craft of Freemasonry. This tended to push the movement toward a Protestant membership, the same people most likely to join the nascent LDS Church. By the second year of the Church's organization a number of men deeply immersed with the pros and cons of Masonry had been baptized. Among the more influential were Heber C. Kimball, W. W. Phelps, Newel K. Whitney, and Brigham Young. Parallels to Freemasonry were rife from the first years of the Church with anointing with oil, *Book of the Law*, conferences, councils, Egyptian references, elders, high priests, priesthood, ordinances, initiations, and temples. By 1835, Joseph delivered a sermon with Masonic allusions, though in fact it was from the Bible, Isaiah 22:23 and Ecclesiastes 12:11: "I exposed their abominations in the language of the scriptures; and I pray God that it may be like a nail in a sure place, driven by the Master of Assemblies."[42]

Since Joseph had recorded the revelation, Doctrine and Covenants 124 on 19 January 1841, which generally outlined the temple ritual, he understood the endowment before he had much direct knowledge of Masonic secrets. B. H. Roberts, writing in the *Improvement Era* in 1921, noted that, "I believe the beginnings of God's revelation to him of endowment ceremonies began with his getting possession of the book of Abraham in the form of Egyptian papyrus manuscripts."[43] An apostolic epistle dated 15 November 1841 established the need for a temple and endowment: "God requires of his Saints to build Him a house wherein His servants may be instructed, and endowed with power from on high, to prepare them to go forth among the nations, and proclaim the fullness of the gospel for the last time. . . . In this house all the ordinances will be manifest, and many things will be shown forth, which have been hid from generation to generation."[44]

Joseph Smith and Sidney Rigdon were inducted into formal Masonry on 15 March 1842, the same day that the Illinois Grand Master Mason, Abraham Jonas, installed the Nauvoo Lodge by request of Joseph. The next day he advanced Joseph and Sidney to the Master Mason Degree. Joseph Smith was then a 32nd degree Mason and Master of the Nauvoo Lodge in Illinois. In June 1842, Heber C. Kimball wrote to Parley P. Pratt, who was in England at the time, regarding these events: "We have received some precious things through the Prophet on the Priesthood which would cause your soul to rejoice. I cannot give them to you on paper, for they are not to be written. So you must come and get them for yourself. We have organized a lodge here of Masons since we have obtained a charter. That was in March. Since that there have near 200 been made Masons."[45]

Within a few years there were five Masonic Lodges, with several others in the planning stage. Even an LDS temple with a few Masonic motifs was being constructed, and Mormon membership in the fraternal brotherhood soon numbered 1,366. What then motivated Joseph Smith, as Reed Durham says,

to "'grab on' to Masonry and then transcend it?"[46] According to Rudger Clawson's journal, the president of the Twelve, Franklin D. Richards, said in 1899 that:

> He desired to say a few words about Freemasonry. A Masonic Lodge, he said, was established in Nauvoo. . . . Joseph the prophet, was aware that there were some things about Masonry which had come down from the beginning and he desired to know what they were, hence the lodge. The Masons admitted some keys of knowledge appertaining to Masonry were lost. Joseph enquired of the Lord concerning the matter and He revealed to the Prophet true Masonry, as we have it in our temples.[47]

Some Masonic lodges have adopted the grade of Templar, and in America, according to J. R. Church, "Mormonism also has a philosophical connection to the order of the ancient Templars."[48] This could only be natural if the Masons had any semblance of the true endowment and temple ordinances. Freemasons, themselves, admit they do not have all the lost secrets, but have substituted many secrets until the genuine ones are found and do not understand all their meanings.[49]

The loss of memory for Masons was caused by centuries of changing and amending things without divine authority. "Without doubt," writes Knight and Lomas, "Freemasonry is guilty of concealing some great secret. Unfortunately, there may be no one alive today who knows what it is!"[50] The meanings and nuance of the Masonic rituals were later corrected and placed into perspective by Joseph Smith Jr.

One source says that the temple ceremony or

ritual "was explained, was revealed by an angel, and the Prophet only joined the lodge to see to what extent it had degenerated from its Solomonic purity."[51] Joseph knew what he knew, but he was inquisitive about what the Masons knew. He discovered that the Masons had some of the ceremony but little of its mysteries. Beyond this curiosity, Lorenzo Snow reports, "Joseph the prophet, and others of the brethren joined the Freemasons in order to obtain influence in furtherance of the purposes of the Lord."[52]

It was ultimately a "means to an end" to advance the acceptance of the LDS temple endowment, not an opportunity to copy the Masonic ceremony. John Taylor concluded, "Freemasonry is one of the strongest binding contracts that exists between man and man."[53] Thus it would have value in two ways—helping the saints to accept the LDS endowment and calming the hostility level of neighboring people. Joseph Fielding in December 1843 said as much: "Many have joined the Masonic Institution. This seems to have been a stepping stone or preparation for something else, the true origin of Masonry."[54] It was a "paving stone" for further light and knowledge from God for the Church and probably served to assuage the "strangeness" LDS temple rituals might have for "normal" people.

The ultimate purpose, beyond political considerations, was to create a mindset with the membership in which the ancient Orders could be restored without the "culture shock" that might otherwise exist.[55] Joseph Smith once said it was hard to get things into the heads of the Latter-day Saints.[56] Heber C. Kimball wrote that even this step was sometimes difficult: "Brother Joseph and Sidney were the first that were received into the Lodge. All of the Twelve have become members except Orson P[ratt]. He hangs back. He will wake up soon. There is a similarity of Priesthood in Masonry. Brother Joseph says Masonry was taken from priesthood, but has become degenerated. But many things are perfect. I think it will result in good."[57]

In May 1842, Joseph Smith instituted the true endowment itself with high expectation. But soon thereafter it become apparent that Freemasons were as likely to persecute Joseph and the saints as any other people.[58] Eventually Mormonism's embracing of the Masonic cult led, in some measure, to the death of its two founding prophets. Brigham Young firmly believed that Masons were to blame for Joseph and Hyrum's deaths: "And there were delegates from the various lodges in the Union to see that he was put to death. . . There are other Masons sent to this territory for the same purpose to establish a lodge here and try to get an influence with some here to lay a plan to try to murder me [and] the leaders of the Church."[59]

Latter-day Saint "perfection" of Masonry is just now being understood. Both had different ancestry, whereas Masonry relied upon traditions being passed down through the ages, Mormonism relied upon direct revelation from God. While they "touched and kissed" in 1842, they soon traversed radically different paths. Eventually Brigham Young rejected any further affiliation with Masonic society: "We have got to look to the God of Israel to sustain us and not to any institution or kingdom or people upon the earth except the kingdom of God."[60]

Reed C. Durham Jr. observed that Joseph Smith had no qualms about using Masonry for the Lord's own purposes. But Durham believed it was incorrect to say that Joseph just "modified" it.[61] Anti-Mormons, such as Jerald and Sandra Tanner say, "[LDS endowment] is the product of Joseph Smith's own fruitful imagination combined with his own personal knowledge of Masonry."[62] But the sophistication of the LDS endowment warrants a more concerted scholarly study than the off-hand remarks from those like the Tanners.

Joseph Smith did not "borrow" the ceremony, but rather the Masons did. Albert Mackey, the most famous of all Masonic historians, frankly admits that Freemasonry has "borrow[ed] its symbols from every source."[63] Although there are many pagan, Muslim, and Egyptian gnostic sources, the Bible was one of the most significant texts for Masonic ritual.[64] Utah traveler, John W. Gunnison wrote the Mormon view:

> [W]e are informed [that the priesthood has] working signs, and that Masonry was originally of the church, and one of its favored institutions, to advance the members in their spiritual functions. It had become perverted from its designs, and was restored to its true work by Joseph [Smith], who gave again, by angelic assistance, the key-words of the several degrees that had been lost; and when he entered the lodges of Illinois, he could work right ahead of the most promoted; for which, through envy, the Nauvoo lodge was excommunicated.[65]

It would be more accurate to say that Mormonism and Masonry had "overlapping" portions, but that Joseph's Masonry (endowment) was not particularly derived from or measured by Freemasonry's ceremonies. Matthias Cowley explained that the endowment really "superseded" rather than "morphed" from Masonry: "[The] fraternity sought for in [the Masonic] organization was superseded by a more perfect fraternity found in the vows and covenants which the endowment in the House of God afforded members of the Church."[66]

Edward H. Ashment, David J. Buerger, and George D. Smith incorrectly claim that Joseph Smith declared he restored the endowment keys "of Solomon's temple from corrupt, apostate Masonry."[67] Whatever synchronicities the LDS endowment had to Masonry were not fundamental but dealt with the mechanism of the ritual. In 1858, Brigham Young recorded Heber C. Kimball as saying: "We have the true Masonry. The Masonry of today is received from the apostasy, which took place in the days of Solomon and David. They have now and then a thing that is correct, but we have the real thing."[68]

This is quite different than saying Joseph borrowed (stole) it from apostate Masonry. Michael Quinn stated: "Therefore it seems more appropriate to regard as superficial the similarities existing between Freemasonry and Mormonism."[69] The early saints believed that the Masonic "institution dates its origins many centuries back, it is only a perverted Priesthood stolen from the temples of the Most High."[70] Benjamin F. Johnson once noted that Joseph Smith told him, "Freemasonry, as at present, was the apostate endowments, as sectarian religion was the apostate religion."[71]

As the Knights Templar of old were able to dig on the Temple Mount and perhaps find treasure of gold artifacts and writings, so Joseph Smith Jr. entered by vision the bowels of the Hill Cumorah (Mount). There he also found a room of treasure of the most precious relics, e.g. writing, swords, temple relics, etc.[72] As Hugh W. Nibley said, "[We need not] rummage in a magpie's nest to stock a king's treasury!"[73] This was more than a mere assortment of sacred mementos collaged together, but crucial ingredients in restoring the Latter-day gospel and completing the winding-up scenario.

In Mormonism we find an enlightened similitude with Masonry, which creates a contextual basis for understanding the ancient temple endowment. James Cummings, a Master Mason in the Nauvoo Masonic Lodges, noted in Horace Cummings' autobiography that Joseph Smith seemed "to understand some of the features of the ceremony better than any Mason and that he made explanations that rendered the rites much more beautiful and full of meaning."[74]

The restoration of the temple in LDS society is certainly the reason for Joseph Smith's abiding interest in Masonry. He seems to have had a balanced view of Freemasonry in the sense that he at once sought to "use" it to bring about the purposes of the Lord, but never totally revered it as a sycophant might. Being both pro- and anti-Masonic, he saw the lodge as a means to an end.

Joseph's affinity with Masonry's priesthood placed him in a brotherhood of service unknown to his contemporaries. He transcended shady symbolism and obscure traditions to literally commune with angels regarding their true meaning. John Addinton Symonds, an historian of Renaissance Italy, wrote in 1875 something which we can relate to Joseph Smith and the Order of the Grail:

> O nobler peerage than thou
>   ancient vaunt
> Of Arthur or of Roland!
> Chivalry Long sought, last found!
> Knight of the Holy Grail!
> Phalanx Immortal!
> True Freemasonry![75]

Thus we see that the true Grail King, Joseph Smith, possessed the power to heal the present wasteland, and prevent the greater wasteland to come, by restoring the great mysteries of God, by resurrecting True Freemasonry, through the temple endowment ceremony. The temple was the *axial mundi* between God and man, sealing the living and the dead. As Malachi 4:5 announced: "And he shall plant in the hearts of the children the promises made to the fathers, and the hearts of the children shall turn to their fathers. If it were not so, the whole earth would be utterly wasted at his coming" (Joseph Smith–History 1:39).

RESTORING THE PATTERN: THE GARDEN AND THE GODDESS

Moreover I will appoint a place for my people Israel, and will plant them, that they may dwell in a place of their own, and move no more; neither shall the children of wickedness afflict them any more, as before time.

—2 SAMUEL 7:10

Look among the nations and watch; be utterly astounded! For I will work a work in your days which you would not believe, though it were told you.

—HABAKKUK 1:5 NKJV

Through Joseph Smith Jr. and his associates the Garden (Paradise) was in process of restoration and the Goddess (female sovereignty) came into it "like a watered garden" (Isaiah 58:11). Yet, in our day, many Mormon dissidents say that an LDS hierarchy of male domination has created a wasteland, not healed it. These *refuseniks* of sorts incorrectly say that the LDS Church is manipulative, divisive, stratified, and class structured.[76] Recent studies have brilliantly challenged their arguments.[77]

The hierarchy of the Melchizedek Priesthood is not the problem, but rather it is disobedience to the gospel of Jesus Christ which creates the wasteland (D&C 11:20). Joseph Smith, the Grail Knight, came to correct this evil and restore Eden by preparing the world for the paradisiacal Millennium. The cynical and carping dissenters will never bring it to pass.[78]

Indeed Joseph did restore the true lost Goddess by establishing the doctrine of our Mother in Heaven, the wives of Jesus, and women's own exalted motherhood. He rescued Mother Eve and Mary Magdalene from Christian disparagement. Then he reinstituted, by including women in the endowment, the promised "Queens and Priestesses" in our temple ceremony.[79] The lost "female principle" so beguiling to feminists and gnostics has already been restored by Joseph Smith in several unique ways.

1. Joseph restored the idea that we have a Mother Goddess in Heaven as well as a Father God. The two are not melded into one by androgyny but are distinct in gender, though one through marriage. Because of this union they are able to conceive spirit children. The truth of the eternal family was Joseph's greatest revelation. Today the Church has asked each member to quietly hold this sacred truth firmly in their hearts. However, pseudo-intellectual Mormon dissidents have used this concept to tear at our unity, while true Saints have found peace in what has been revealed and patiently await further light and knowledge.

2. Mother Eve has been promoted in LDS theology to an exalted place and role within the grand scheme of things. No longer is she berated for the "fall." The necessity of it was brought about by her perceptive understanding of its historic inevitability. Brigham Young proclaimed that "we should not have been here today if she had not [partaken]; we could never have possessed wisdom and intelligence if she had not done it. . . We should never blame Mother Eve, not in the least."[80] She is now an exalted Goddess ruling by Michael-Adam's side, as our hymn rejoices:

Mother of our generations,
Glorious by great Michael's side,
Take thy children's adoration;
Endless with thy Lord preside.[81]

3. Joseph Smith and his associates Brigham Young, Orson Pratt, Orson Hyde, etc., did not see Mary Magdalene as a wanton woman or prostitute but rather as the divinely chosen help-mate of our Lord, Jesus Christ. Her intelligence, chastity and reverence have been reclaimed in LDS theology. It was through her, and Mary and Martha of Bethany, that New Testament destiny should be traced. They were, according to the LDS prophets, all sacred companions of the Lord.

4. Even the priesthood in its highest form, the Holy Order, was promised to all righteous celestially married women in the LDS temple endowment and sealing ceremony. The right to be "queens and priestesses" with their "king and a priest" husbands is clearly pledged in the temple. When the highest order of the Melchizedek Priesthood is activated in the last days, it will be held by women and men together.

Again Mormon dissidents gnaw at the roots of the Tree of Life by insisting upon women being ordained into the Aaronic and Melchizedek orders of the priesthood right now. Of course, they seldom ask for the Highest or Holy Order, which comes with certain obligations.[82] They pressure and demand for their version of the priesthood, with little regard to the order and timing of latter-day events or the will of the Lord of which they are ignorant.

5. Joseph Smith restored the temple as the rightful place for women as well as men. Earlier Hebraic and Masonic temples excluded women. The center

point of God's transaction with mankind—the fountain in the center of the Garden—must have been in Joseph's mind. As the plans for ancient temples were revealed by God to His ancient prophets, so Joseph through revelation restored them in the Dispensation of the Fulness of Times. Brigham Young said of Joseph Smith: "Joseph not only received revelation and commandment to build a temple, but he received a *pattern* also, as did Moses for the Tabernacle, and Solomon for his temple; for without a pattern, he could not know what was wanting, having never seen one, and not having experienced its use."[83]

Because of this, for the first time in history women are now equal partners with their male counterparts in the most sacred precincts of the temple. The Song of Solomon sings of the joys of the garden. In the midst of the temple is found the bridal chamber, where God is the gardener.

> *My beloved is mine, and I am his: he feedeth among the lilies. . . Let my beloved come into his garden, and eat his pleasant fruits . . . My beloved is gone down into his garden, to the beds of spices, to feed in the gardens, and to gather lilies. I am my beloved's, and my beloved is mine: he feedeth among the lilies.*
>
> —SOLOMON'S SONG 2:16;
> 4:16; 6:2–3

Never since the City of Enoch has the true divine feminine of women become so elevated, and never before has the garden been so verdantly green. This is the pattern of God's millennial paradise and future celestial kingdom; it is a paean of praise. Isaiah 58:11–12 speaks of healing the wasteland, repairing the breach, and restoring the paths: "Like a watered Garden, and like a spring of water, whose waters fail not. And they that shall be of thee [and] shall build the old waste places: thou shalt raise up the foundations of many generations; and thou shalt be called, The Repairer of the Breach, The Restorer of Paths to dwell in."

The restoration of the Grail paradigm repairs and restores the essential balance of all things.

NOTES

1. Brigham Young, as quoted in *Wilford Woodruff Journal* (11 December 1869), 6:508.
2. Lisa McLaughlin and David Van Biema incorrectly reported in *Time* magazine, "Martin Luther believed that Jesus and Magdalene were married, as did Mormon patriarch Brigham Young." McLaughlin and Biema, "Mary Magdalene: Saint or Sinner?" *Time*, 11 August 2003, 55. Actually, Luther believed that Jesus was having sexual affairs with a number of women. See Phipps, *Was Jesus Married?* 12. He quotes Pastor John Schlaginhaufen, who records a comment by a friend of Martin Luther, "Christ was an adulterer for the first time with the woman at the well for it is said, "Nobody knows what he's doing with her" (John 4:27).
3. Joseph Smith's involvement with such things is propounded in Quinn's book *Early Mormonism and the Magic World View.*
4. This would be the Anglo-American federalism. Together they were superior to the Roman Empire or Han dynasty in China.
5. Richard Brothers in 1791 began the speculative antiquarianism aspect of the British-Israelite movement, while Charles Vallancey was its best early advocate. John Wilson of Brighton published his important *Lectures on Our Israelitish Origin* in 1840. The Reverend Glover published his pivotal book, *England, the Remnant of Judah and the Israel of Ephraim,* in 1860. The British-Israel Association was founded in 1889 by Edward Wheeler Bird (1823–?), while the British-Israel Association of Ireland (B-IAI) was founded in Dublin in 1897. Rev. Denis Hanan, rector of Tipperary, was president of the B-IAI and contributed articles to *Covenant People,*

Banner of Israel and co-edited a book entitled *British-Israel Truth: A Handbook for Inquirers.*

6. Carew, *Tara and the Ark of the Covenant,* 55.

7. Macalister, *Tara,* 32.

8. Denis Hanan, "Ephraim's Birthright," *Covenant People* 5 (1899): 203.

9. Boren and Boren, *Following the Ark of the Covenant,* 29–30. Heber, or Eber, was a descendant from Zarah's child Calcol. Nennius of Bangor in his Historia Brittonum in the ninth century says that Europe was peopled by Noah's son Japheth and Japheth's son Alanus and the children of Alanus (Alan = noble = Aryan).

10. Boren and Boren, *Following the Ark of the Covenant,* 30.

11. Dr. Lance C. Harding of American Fork, interview with author, 2 November 2002. Dr. Harding studied Stonehenge at the Prince of Wales School in London.

12. Walton Adams, *Covenant People* 9 (1903): 71. See Carew, *Tara and the Ark of the Covenant,* 32. The Freemasonry and Pyramidism of Adams led him to the archaeological site of Tara Hills. Carew says that Charles Groom's work at Tara was influenced by this Pyramidism.

13. Nibley, *Lehi in the Desert,* 397.

14. Carew, *Tara and the Ark of the Covenant,* 43. The Cabiri was an ancient British tribe.

15. Graves, *The Greek Myths,* 1:80.

16. Diodorus Siculus, II.46.4–47.1, 37, 39, as quoted in Strachan, *Jesus the Master Builder,* 232, 245. See also Boren and Boren, *Following the Ark of the Covenant,* 23. The spherical temple may be a roofed Stonehenge.

17. Ralls-MacLeod, *Quest for the Celtic Key,* 82. It has to do with an observation, the "Callanish," on the Isle of Lewis in the Scottish Hebrides. It may be that Jesus came to the Isles at the age of nineteen.

18. Starbird, *Magdalen's Lost Legacy,* 30. A painting by Dale Fletcher, *Another Treehouse* (1972, mixed media, Springville Museum of Art collection), uses this same number.

19. As quoted in Coppens, *Stone Puzzle of Rosslyn Chapel,* 100.

20. Sun gods in Egypt (Ra), Greece (Apollo), Rome (Sol Invictus), Persia (Ahura Mazda), and to Christians (Jesus Christ).

21. Graves, *White Goddess,* 414.

22. Erastus Snow, in *Journal of Discourses* (6 May 1882), 23:185–86.

23. James E. Talmage, editorial, *Millennial Star* 87 (29 October 1925): 696. Other LDS British-Israelites are James Anderson, E. L. Whitehead, Vaughne Hansen, and Leslie Pearson Rees.

24. Brigham Young, in *Journal of Discourses,* 10:188.

The Rev. John H. Allen, in *Judah's Sceptre and Joseph's Birthright,* 292, said, "The name Saxon, as it is the most general name of the race, really is the present generic name of the House of Joseph." The term "Isaac's sons" is operative in this case.

25. Allen, *Judah's Sceptre and Joseph's Birthright,* 200. The dispersed portion of Israel, according to Allen, seems to have followed the seven guiding stars of Ursa Major (the Great Bear; see Proverbs 9:1, Job 9:9; 38:32) and heavily settled in the British Isles and northern Europe.

26. Carew, *Tara and the Ark of the Covenant,* 11.

27. Ibid., 35.

28. The Tara Exploration Fund had been in existence since 1877 by the British-Israel Association of London.

29. Ibid., 33.

30. In *Covenant People* 8 (1902): 468–69, the stated aim of the (British-Israel Conference) Association was to "promulgate the important Truth, that the British Empire (Home and Colonial) and the United States of America, are the two Great Peoples into which it was predicted the House of Joseph, or Israel—not Judah—would be divided in these 'latter days.'"

31. *Covenant People* 1 (1895): 3.

32. Carew, *Tara and the Ark of the Covenant,* 15. The author thinks that the "United Judah" race began at Tara between the children of Tephi Tea and King Heremon.

33. Ibid., 56.

34. Allen, *Judah's Sceptre and Joseph's Birthright,* 296.

35. Smith, *History of the Church* (15 October 1843), 6:59. See also Smith, *Teachings of the Prophet Joseph Smith,* 329, and Ehat and Cook, *Words of Joseph Smith,* 257. Brigham Young noted, "The main part of Masonry is to keep a secret" (cited in *Wilford Woodruff Journal,* 5:418, 22 January 1860). By proving a person could keep a secret and by performing rituals and various tests of merit over many years was the endowment to be given. On 19 December 1841, Joseph Smith states that even though he could keep a secret, the Lord was not revealing more of his secrets to the general membership of the Church because they did not know when to refrain from revealing certain things, even to their enemies. See Smith, *Teachings of the Prophet Joseph Smith,* 194–95; Brown, "David John Buerger, 'The Mysteries of Godliness,'" 109. Joseph once said, "I can keep a secret till doomsday." See Quinn, *Early Mormonism and the Magic World View,* 93.

36. Durham, "Is There No Help for the Widow's Son?" 10.

37. William Appleby Journal (5 May 1841), LDS Church Archives, Salt Lake City, Utah. Even earlier Joseph explained to a Nauvoo Lyceum that the "great God has

a name by which he will be called which is Ahman—also in asking, have reference to a personage like Adam, for God made Adam just in his own image. Now this is a key for you to know how to ask and obtain." See also Ehat and Cook, *Words of Joseph Smith*, 64. William Clayton said, "He also spoke concerning key words. The g[rand] key word was the first word Adam spoke and is a word of supplication. He found the word by the Urim and Thummim." See Smith, *Intimate Chronicle*, 133–34. Freemasons believe that certain elements of their ritual are "lost" and have been substituted for, but will come back when "time or circumstance should restore the former." See Hamill, *The Craft*, 15–16.

38. In Europe such luminaries as James Boswell, François Voltaire, Andrew M. Ramsay, Robert Burns, and Jonathan Swift were Freemasons.

39. Durham, "Is There No Help for the Widow's Son?" These degrees include the Entered Apprentice (the initiation), Fellowcraft (known as the passing degree), and Master Mason (known as the raising degree). See Knight and Lomas, *Book of Hiram*, 15.

40. Knight and Lomas, in *Hiram Key*, x, explain: "This has led me to believe that perhaps there is some truth to the accusations levelled against Masonry that 'only the top (high) degrees know the truth.'"

41. Durham, "Is There No Help for the Widow's Son?" 2.

42. Smith, *History of the Church* (29 December 1835), 2:347. See also Durham, "Is There No Help for the Widow's Son?" 2. See Isaiah 22:23: "fasten him as a nail in a sure place."

43. Roberts, "Masonry and Mormonism," *Improvement Era*, August 1921, 937–39. Joseph Smith received the mummies with the papyrus in July of 1835.

44. Smith, *History of the Church* (15 November 1841), 4:449.

45. Heber C. Kimball letter to Parley P. Pratt in England (17 June 1842), Parley P. Pratt papers, Church Historical Department.

46. Durham, "Is There No Help for the Widow's Son?" 9.

47. Franklin D. Richards, cited in Journal of Rudger Clawson (4 April 1899), in Larsen, *Ministry of Meetings*, 42. Charles Charvatt knew the Prophet and reported, "There were some signs and tokens with their meanings and significance which we [Freemasons] did not have. Joseph restored them and explained them to us." Manuscript of Samuel C. Young (LDS Church Archives, Salt Lake City). Horace H. Cummings noted about the same things: "The Prophet explained many things about the rites that even Masons do not pretend to understand but which he made most clear and beautiful" ("True Stories from My Journal," *Juvenile Instructor*, August 1929, 441).

48. Church, *Guardians of the Grail*, 27. Joseph Smith realized that Masonry was but a shell of the true endowment.

49. Knight and Lomas, *Hiram Key*, 3, note that while Freemasons might have the symbols, they have lost the meaning: "Most people in the Western world are at least vaguely aware of Freemasonry, and its mysteries tantalize two large groups: those who are not Masons, who wonder what the secrets of the order are; and those who are Masons, who also wonder what those secrets are! A compelling reason for silence amongst Masons is not so much a compulsion to adhere to their sacred vows, or a fear of macabre retribution from their fellow; it is more that they do not understand a word of the ceremonies they participate in, and their only fear is that people would laugh at the apparently pointless and silly rituals they perform."

50. Knight and Lomas, "Holy Grail," in Flanders, *Mysteries of the Ancient World*, 67.

51. Arbaugh, *Revelation in Mormonism*, 160.

52. Larsen, *Ministry of Meetings*, 316.

53. John Taylor, in *Journal of Discourses* (1 March 1863), 10:125–26.

54. Joseph Fielding journal, 9 December 1843. See Andrew Ehat, "They Might Have Known That He Was Not a Fallen Prophet," *BYU Studies* 19, 2 (Winter 1979): 145.

55. Many of the most important figures of the United States of America were Freemasons. It had a membership throughout the country of hundreds of thousands. Because of this its "quirkiness" was overlooked. Noting that George Washington and John Adams were Masons somehow underscored its credibility. After initiation into a lodge, the LDS temple ceremony would now not seem so strange after all. It was used as a means of "bringing along" the brethren.

56. Ehat and Cook, *Words of Joseph Smith* (21 January 1844), 319. "But there has been a great difficulty in getting anything into the heads of this generation it has been like splitting hemlock knots with a corn dodger for a wedge and a pumpkin for a beetle. Even the Saints are slow to understand I have tried for a number of years to get the minds of the Saints prepared to receive the things of God, but we frequently see some of them after suffering all they have for the work of God will fly to pieces, like glass, as soon as anything comes that is contrary to their traditions, they cannot stand the fire at all."

57. Heber C. Kimball letter to Parley P. Pratt in England (17 June 1842), Parley P. Pratt Papers, Church Historical Department.

58. Times and Seasons 5 (15 July 1844), 585. See also *Woman's Exponent* 7 (1 December 1878), 98, and *Wilford Woodruff Journal*, 5:482–83. (19 August 1860) I believe that the entire Restoration of the gospel came with a "two steps forward and one step back" proposition.

59. Brigham Young, as quoted in *Wilford Woodruff Journal* (19 August 1860), 5:482–84.

60. Brigham Young, as quoted in *Wilford Woodruff Journal*, 5:483. Thanks to Matthew Brown for his research and his 1998 paper.

61. Durham, "Is There No Help for the Widow's Son?" 8. Brother Durham continues: "I wish to reiterate is that the Masonry as practiced in the Church under the Prophet's direction was daily becoming increasingly unorthodox as contrasted with Illinois traditional Masonry. Therefore, it appears that the Prophet first embraced Masonry and, then in the process, he modified, expanded, amplified, or glorified it."

62. Tanner and Tanner, *Evolution of the Mormon Temple Ceremony*, 28, 56, 58.

63. Mackey, *Encyclopaedia of Freemasonry*, 99.

64. Brown, "David John Buerger, '*The Mysteries of Godliness*,'" 118, has counted 115 elements in the three main initiation rituals alone that come straight from the Bible.

65. Gunnison, *Mormons*, 57, 59–60.

66. Cowley, *Wilford Woodruff*, 160.

67. Smith, *Journals of William Clayton*, xxxvii.

68. *Journal History of Brigham Young* (13 November 1858), 1085, with Heber C. Kimball speaking. See also Kimball, "Heber C. Kimball & Family, the Nauvoo Years," *BYU Studies* 15, 4 (1975): 458 (13 November 1858). St. George Temple President McAllister noted that "Pres. Young once said that Free Masonry is the corruption of the keys and powers of the Holy Priesthood" (3 September 1888). Church Archives vault, restricted document, Confidential Research files 1950–1974, Historical Department, CR 10014 #2 volume 8:34. In 1902, Apostle Matthias Cowley said, "Freemasonry as being a counterfeit of the true masonry of the Latter-day Saints" (in Larsen, *Ministry of Meetings*, 380, 8 January 1902).

69. Quinn, *Early Mormonism and the Magic World View*, 234. Quinn continues, "By contrast, the ancient occult mysteries manifest both philosophical and structural kinship with the Mormon endowment."

70. H. Belnap, "A Mysterious Preacher," *Juvenile Instructor* 21 (15 March 1886): 91. Thanks to Matthew Brown, "David John Buerger, '*The Mysteries of Godliness*,'" 115.

71. Johnson, *My Life's Review*, 96. This was written about 1902.

72. Joseph Smith and Oliver Cowdery twice visited the vaults inside Cumorah. See Nibley, *Witnesses of the Book of Mormon*, 173–75; Smith, *Essentials in Church History*, 72–73.

73. Nibley, *Message of the Joseph Smith Papyri*, xiii.

74. "Autobiography of Horace Cummings," BYU Library, Special Collections.

75. As quoted by Sinclair, *Discovery of the Grail*, 242.

76. See Godwin, *Holy Grail*, 218. But LDS pseudo-intellectual gnostics have no unified answers, only criticisms. They are led by the brilliantly unwise Toscano family, especially the divisive Paul Toscano.

77. See Cheryll May, education curator of Brigham Young University MOA, February 2004.

78. In my opinion, these dissenters know much and are intellectually very bright, but are not sure what is eternally true. I was struck by how little union there is between them on "the truth" but how tightly they are unified against "the Church." This is very reminiscent of nineteenth-entury ancient historian Eduard Meyer, who positively compared Mohammed's soul-searching struggles with his mission, against the cocksure literalist attitude of Joseph Smith. LDS dissenters are often hardwired for enigma and doubt and against obedience and logical clarity (see Nibley, *World and the Prophets*, 18–22).

79. Non-Mormon scholar Newman, *Real History behind The Da Vinci Code*, 5, states, "There is no evidence that I can find that women were ever ordained as priests [in the first centuries of Christianity]."

80. Brigham Young; see Doctrine and Covenants 29:40, which says that Adam partook, but it probably means Mr. and Mrs. Adam.

81. "Sons of Michael, He Approaches," *Sacred Hymns and Spiritual Songs for the Church of Jesus Christ of Latter-day Saints*, 375.

82. Among these is the reinstitution of the Order of Enoch, Law of Consecration and Stewardship, and United Order, in which of course they are not particularly interested.

83. Brigham Young, in *Journal of Discourses* (6 April 1853), 2:31a.

CHAPTER EIGHTEEN
EPHRAIM REMEMBERED

For there shall be a day, that the watchmen upon the Mount Ephraim shall cry, Arise ye, and let us go up to Zion unto the Lord our God. For thus saith the Lord; Sing with gladness for Jacob, and shout among the chief of the nations: publish ye, praise ye, and say, O Lord, save thy people, the remnant of Israel.

Behold, I will bring them from the north country, and gather them from the coasts of the earth, and with them the blind and the lame, the woman with child and her that travaileth with child together: a great company shall return thither.

They shall come with weeping, and with supplications will I lead them: I will cause them to walk by the rivers of waters in a straight way, wherein they shall not stumble: for I am a father to Israel, and Ephraim is my firstborn.

—JEREMIAH 31:6–9

In the last days the Lord will remember Ephraim and restore to this tribe its prominent leadership role. The gathering of this people of the Lord will one day commence:

I have surely heard Ephraim bemoaning himself thus; Thou hast chastised me, and I was chastised, as a bullock unaccustomed to the yoke: turn thou me, and I shall be turned; for thou art the Lord my God. Surely after that I was turned, I repented; and after that I was instructed, I smote upon my thigh: I was ashamed, yea, even confounded, because I did bear the reproach of my youth.

—JEREMIAH 31:18–19

The non-healing injury in the thigh of Ephraim is a reminder of the tribe's waywardness. In Grail lore, the Fisher-King's thigh was also wounded because of the apostasy of the Celtic Church. But here the symbol of the wounded thigh being healed is a token of Ephraim's repentance. Some have supposed that the Grail king's fertility was impaired through the wound, but it seems to have been more a suffering bloodline than a nonexistent one. The Lord has remembered Ephraim and is now restoring them:

Is Ephraim my dear son? is he a pleasant child? for since I spake against him, I do earnestly remember him still: therefore my bowels are troubled for him; I will surely have mercy upon him, saith the Lord. Set thee up waymarks, make thee high heaps: set thine heart toward the highway, even the way which thou wentest: turn again, O virgin of Israel, turn again to these thy cities.

—JEREMIAH 31:20–21[1]

Ephraim is the Grail lineage of the latter days and represents the Gentiles. In these last days the gospel went first to the Gentiles and then to the Jews. But Ephraim has not yet repented and come into its own, only a vanguard of the Grail seed has restored the movement. The latter-day tribulation must come forth before all the house of Israel repents and the millennium is ushered in.

EPHRAIM-SHILOH: "SUCH A ROOT-STUMP IS A HOLY SEED"

And is there still a tenth therein, this also again is given up to destruction, like the terebinth and like the oak, of which when they are felled, only a root-stump remains: such a root-stump is a holy seed.

—ISAIAH 6:13 [2]

For, verily I say that the rebellious are not of the blood of Ephraim, wherefore they shall be plucked out.

—D&C 64:36

Even though the Lord had removed the remnant of Israel "far away" and they apostatized, they would one day return (Isaiah 6:12). One should remember that as not all Israel is Ephraim, so not all of Ephraim is of the Shiloh Dynasty (the Holiest seed), the spearhead of the gospel in the last days.

Thus we see that a small proportion of the seed shall be a "Holy Seed" fit to redeem the kingdom. Each winter the deciduous teil and oak trees appear dead, but then during the spring they bring forth an abundance of new leaves. This is a metaphor for the Holy Seed (Isaiah 6:13). Shute, Nyman, and Bott interpret this verse in Isaiah as meaning that the leaves will spread among the Gentiles in the springtime of the restoration, and the holy seed (birthright holders) are the substance of a new life.[3] The RSV translates the final line of the 13th verse as "whose stump remains standing when it is felled. The holy seed is its stump" (see Plate 29).[4]

We see in the last days that Israel is journeying from being *Lo-ammi* (not my people) to *Ammi* (my people) by virtue of the infinite atonement and gospel restoration. The Lord will work with the vineyard, cultivating it until it becomes productive. This evolutionary process has been going on for a few millennia as Isaiah wrote, "That he may do his work, his strange work; and bring to pass his act, his strange act" (Isaiah 28:21).

The Lord's "marvelous work and a wonder" (Isaiah 29:14) was to bring to pass his will through the vines of his vineyard, which are fruitful lineages. As Hebrews 12:6 says, "For whom the Lord loveth he chasteneth." The "strange act," then, has God contending against his own willful people to bring to pass his purposes—a righteous generation, a noble race. This is the message of the Lord to Joseph Smith:

For the preparation wherewith I design to prepare mine apostles to prune my vineyard for the last time, that I may bring to pass my strange act, that I may pour out my Spirit upon all flesh.

—D&C 95:4

For the Ephraimite people to be remembered in the sight of the Lord they must first repent. Before they can repent, they must be called unto repentance, pruned, tried, and tested in the crucible. This was the mission of our Grail hero, Joseph Smith Jr., to be an ensign to the people to gather around.

One of Joseph's special missions was to lead the lost ten tribes of Israel from the North country.[5] Of Ephraim, President Joseph F. Smith wrote, "A striking peculiarity of the Saints gathered from all parts of the earth is that they are almost universally of the blood of Ephraim."[6] Apostle John A. Widtsoe later noted that the "Latter-day Saints are of the tribe of Ephraim, the tribe to which has been committed the leadership of Latter-day work."[7] Amplifying this sentiment, Brigham Young noted: "We are now gathering the children of Abraham who have come through the loins of Joseph and his sons, more especially through Ephraim. . . . The spirit in them is turbulent and resolute . . . [and] they are the Anglo-Saxon race."[8]

The stump is coming to life and is growing in the latter days, through the restoration of the gospel and the gathering of Ephraim's righteous Grail and adopted children. Joseph Smith, who we will now examine, is leading them. Just who he is will answer the question of why he was the catalyst of the Lord's dealing with the earth in the last days.

THE ARCHANGEL OF THE LORD

But there are no angels who minister to this earth but those who do belong or have belonged to it.

—D&C 130:5[9]

"Why is Joseph Smith worth writing about?" asks Hugh Nibley. "Only, apparently, because the Mormons are still going strong."[10] However, this prophet's earthly story was presaged by an incredibly significant premortal account, a record we know next to nothing about. We can imagine that in Joseph's first estate he was a person of extraordinary prominence. Orson F. Whitney, biographer and grandson of Heber C. Kimball, eloquently wrote of Joseph and his companions:

This, then, was the purpose, *the divine intending,* for which they were

now in conjunction; "noble and great ones," great in the heavens and great upon the earth, ordained as "rulers" ere morning stars sang gladsome greeting, or Sons of God shouted for joy around the cradle of the infant world. This, the object of their descent from celestial empires; to build up a Kingdom unto God, and prepare the world for the coming of Him "whose right it is to reign." Jewels from Jehovah's diadem, diamonds in the dust, unseen of saint or sinner in all their lustre, concealed from a world unworthy of the light it could not comprehend.[11]

Angels are not some breed of being apart from mankind, but are literally us, ourselves.[12] Joseph Smith was probably not just a ministering nor administering angel but an actual "angel of the Lord" of high status. Joseph remarked about his presidency of the restored Church, *"I suppose that I was ordained to this very office in that Grand Council."*[13] He understood that his earthly position was predicated upon his heavenly probation.

The most renowned and pivotal spirits in premortality were the archangels. Was Joseph Smith one of the seven archangels, and did each of them become one of the dispensation heads on earth? Most prominent of the archangels was the great prince Michael, who is known by Latter-day Saints as Adam.[14] (D&C 107:54) The second most significant archangel is Gabriel, whom we know in mortality as Noah.[15] It may be that the Elias of Doctrine and Covenants 27:7 was in fact Gabriel-Noah[16] (see Luke 1:13–19). It is possible that Enoch was the prominent apocryphal archangel Raphael.[17]

The archangel *Barchiel* (Uriel), who rules over Jupiter, may have been Joseph's premortal name.[18] In Doctrine and Covenants 128:21, Joseph Smith wrote, "And the voice of Michael, the archangel; the voice of Gabriel [Noah] and of Raphael [Enoch], and of divers angels, from Michael or Adam down to the present time." Since Joseph lists Raphael as an angel who speaks to him, it would seem that he himself was not Raphael.[19] But he leaves out the name of the fourth most important archangel, Uriel.

Could it be that Joseph Smith himself is Uriel? We know that Joseph Smith's code name is *Baurak Ale* in older editions of Doctrine and Covenants 103:21–22, 35 and 105:16, 27. Does this name relate to the archangel, *Barchiel*, or *Barakiel*?[20] What is the connection, because Barakiel was not listed as one of the seven archangels on most lists? However, Barakiel is counted by some as amongst the archangels and four ruling Seraphs. More pointedly Barakiel is the angel who governs the tribe of Ephraim, as well as the planet Jupiter.[21]

Could Uriel and Barakiel be the same angel?[22] Joseph Smith must have had pivotally significant premortal, mortal, and postmortal callings to serve as an archangel in the salvation of this planet (see D&C 135:3). It would make sense for Joseph to be an archangel, as all the dispensation heads appear to have been. As an "angel of the Lord" or archangel, Joseph Smith Jr. would wield immense power.[23]

JOSEPH AS DISPENSATION HEAD

Joseph Smith was the Elias, the restorer, the presiding messenger, holding the keys of the Dispensation of the Fullness of Times.
—PARLEY P. PRATT[24]

Next to being an Adam or a Savior to the world, being a dispensation head is the highest position that any person can obtain on earth.[25] As mentioned above, it is conjectured that the archangels in premortality became dispensation heads on earth.[26] Either

held singly or with councilors (Peter, with James and John) this position can only be eligible to those of the proper lineage. For all dispensation heads, including Joseph Smith Jr., it was inherited "from the fathers." Joseph received such authority:

> *For verily I say unto you, the keys of the dispensation, which ye have received, have come down from the fathers, and last of all, being sent down from heaven unto you.*
> —D&C 112:32

It is Joseph Smith who holds the keys to the dispensation of the fulness of times (D&C 90:2–3, 64:5). In the Grand Council during his first-estate, Joseph Smith Jr. was foreordained to this high commission. His insight was astounding: "Every man who has a calling to minister to the inhabitants of the world, was ordained to that very purpose in the Grand Council of Heaven before this world was."[27]

Along these lines Brigham Young cited the crucial points, which proclaim Joseph's legal and spiritual preeminence:

> It was decreed in the counsels of eternity, long before the foundations of the earth were laid, that he [Joseph Smith Jr.] should be the man in the last dispensation of this world, to bring forth the word of God to the people and receive the fullness of the keys and powers of the priesthood of the Son of God.
>
> Joseph [of old] was foreordained to be the temporal saviour of his father's house, and the seed of Joseph are ordained to be the spiritual and temporal saviours of all the house of Israel in the latter days. Joseph's seed has mixed itself with all the seed of man upon the face of the whole earth

. . . Joseph Smith [J]unior, was fore-ordained to come through the loins of Abraham, Isaac, Jacob, Joseph and so on down through the Prophets and Apostles; and thus he came forth in the last days to be a minister of salvation, *and to hold the keys of the last dispensation of the fullness of times.*[28]

Brigham proclaimed, "And Joseph will stand at the head of this Church and will be their President, Prophet and God to the people of this Dispensation"[29] (see D&C 64:5; 90:2–3). To give perspective, we could say that Joseph Smith was the prophet "of" a dispensation, while Brigham Young and his successors were prophets "within" a dispensation. In the end, spoke Brigham Young: "He is the Last Prophet who is called to lay the foundation of the great last Dispensation of the Fullness of Times."[30]

As the direct descendant of Jesus Christ, Joseph is the Grail King for this dispensation and all those of his millennium must file past him before they may progress to higher orders.[31] He is the judge of all people born in this dispensation and the keeper of the golden or pearly gate of heaven. Just as Saint Peter held the keys to the gate of heaven for those who lived during his dispensation, so Joseph Smith now holds those keys for his own dispensation.

No longer does St. Peter, the head of the dispensation of the meridian of time, stand there.[32] But since roughly A.D. 1000 Joseph Smith, as the head of the dispensation of the fulness of times, has stood at the pearly gate. The major difference is that Joseph Smith was of the pure patriarchal bloodline of Jesus Christ and Peter was not fully so. Therefore, Joseph was the greater prophet (see D&C 135:3).

Joseph Smith is one of the sentinels by whom every Latter-day Saint must pass before each one can proceed to the celestial kingdom.[33] Further to this Brigham Young announced: "No man or woman in this dispensation will ever enter into the celestial kingdom of God without the consent of Joseph Smith. From the day that the Priesthood was taken from the earth to the winding-up scene of all things, every man and woman must have the certificate of Joseph Smith, junior, as a passport to their entrance into the mansion where God and Christ are."[34] Interestingly, Brigham Young says that from the time the priesthood was taken from the earth (c. A.D. 570) was when Joseph would judge, rather than c. A.D. 1000. Perhaps some dispensations lasted longer than others.

Joseph said, in effect, "I stand at the gate, I admit you or keep you out."[35] Joseph Smith will be a judge in the Great Judgment and stand on the outside of the Holy Gate while God will be on the other side. As gatekeeper, Joseph will present whom he will at the veil. But as the dispensation head he gave all men who would receive them the keys of the endowment so they might pass through the gate in righteousness.[36]

Being a dispensation head has great responsibilities on both sides of the veil. Joseph is the Grail king who presides over his millennium-long kingdom on earth and into the eternities. But the world knew nothing of Joseph's great callings. Since they did not accept the gospel, nothing would have made sense to them. But to the Grail-Shiloh Dynasty vanguard, it all made sense.

"NO MAN KNOWS MY HISTORY"

You don't know me. No man knows my history. I cannot tell it: I shall never undertake it. . . . When I am called by the trump of the archangel and weighed in the balance, you will all know me then.

—JOSEPH SMITH JR.[37]

In a previous chapter we postulated that there was a great mystery about Joseph Smith that would be troubling to the world. Perhaps he was an archangel *incognito*, but certainly he was a dispensation head. Now and again we postulate that he was a direct descendant and heir of Jesus Christ.[38] Unquestionably, the prophet Joseph Smith was the most written-about unknown man of the nineteenth century. Even in his own day, many of those closest to the prophet could not take the extra step to know him. Heber C. Kimball believed that Joseph Smith was trying to tell us his "true" identity when he said: "Had not Joseph said many times—are no men now living who heard him say: 'Would to God, brethren, I could tell you who I am! Would to God I could tell you what I know! But you would call it blasphemy and there are men upon this stand who would want to take my life.'"[39]

When at the King Follett funeral Joseph Smith boldly uttered, "No man knows my history," the prophet Joseph plausibly had in mind a reference to his genealogy in the royal lineage cascading directly from Christ.[40] Orson F. Whitney, biographer and grandson of Heber C. Kimball, wrote of this: "Had Heber's inspired mind probed the secret of Joseph's thought, expressed in his own oft-quoted words: 'Would to God brethren, I could tell you who I am!'"[41]

Could Brigham Young have had Joseph's heritage in mind when he said, "If I was to reveal to this people what the Lord has revealed to me, there is not a man or woman would stay with me."[42] This has the familiar ring of John 10, in which Jesus told the Jews that He was the Son of God and they called it blasphemy and tried to kill him (John 10:18). Or when Jesus asked His disciples, "Whom do ye say that I am?" (Matthew 16:17). In effect, was Joseph saying that he was a son of the Son of God "by descent"?

Clearly, Joseph felt constrained from explaining this secret at that time. He knew that even the closest to him would buckle as to his true identity: "Brethren you do not know me, you do not know who I am

. . . I would to God that I could unbosom my feelings in the house of my friends."[43] Was he saying, "I am Jesus' direct heir?" Given the complete novelty of this teaching in the 1830s and 40s, it could hardly not scandalize. In 1905, during a lecture at Brigham Young Academy, Mary Elizabeth Lightner recalled a similar statement by Joseph Smith: "People little know who I am when they talk about me, and they never will know until they see me weighed in the balance in the kingdom of God. Then they will know who I am and see me as I am. I dare not tell them and they do not know me."[44]

Sister Lightner then says, "These words were spoken with such power that they penetrated the heart of every soul that believed on him." To clear up any confusion as to Joseph Smith's pedigree, Brigham Young issued this pronouncement about six months after Joseph's death: "I will first set in order before these relations the true order of the kingdom of God and how the families hereafter will be organized; *you have heard Joseph say that the people did not know him;* he had his eyes on the relation to blood-relations (genealogy). Some have supposed that he meant spirit (Holy Ghost), but it was the blood relation. This is it that he referred to."[45]

Brigham Young's remarkable statement gives a platform to understand the problem. By saying that Joseph was referring to blood relations, he undoubtedly meant genealogy. But our second Mormon prophet really did not fully express Joseph's intent. Instead he skirts the issue. Paul in Galatians may have been Brigham's source, "And if ye be Christ's then are ye Abraham's seed, and heirs according to the promise" (Galatians 3:29). Joseph's statements referred to "Abraham's patriarchal power."[46] Truman Madsen furthers this point in saying, "God by appropriate unions of ancestors, had watched over that blood until it came pure and unsullied into Joseph [Smith]."[47]

President Young had glossed over the "blood relations" issue, to protect the besieged Church and himself from yet more charges of sacrilege and blasphemy. Once safely in Utah, however, he fully notes that Jesus was married, was even a polygynist with many children, and that Joseph Smith was his direct descendant.[48] This was the blasphemy that would have people take Joseph's life even though it sounds tame today. Furthermore, Joseph Smith was the most direct descendant, seed, and royal heir of Jesus Christ.

If the true order of royal succession had been adhered to throughout history, Joseph Smith Jr. would have been declared King of Israel and Patriarch of the gospel by the righteous of the world. "And who shall declare his [the Lord's] generation?" asks Isaiah (53:8). The answer would be, "His descendant, Joseph Smith Jr., a Vermont native."

As Brigham Young noted in January 1845, "The human family will find out who are the saviors of the Earth. The world knew nothing of the office of saviors upon Mount Zion."[49] Very few appreciate that Joseph Smith is second only to Jesus Christ in the salvation of the human family (D&C 135:3).[50] When they do, the jubilant Mormon hymn, "Praise to the Man" will then be sung: "Wake up the world for the conflict of justice. Millions [Billions] shall know brother Joseph again."[51] He himself noted that he would be known for good and ill through out the world. This "best blood of the nineteenth century" will then become known to the world (D&C 135:6).

To the Lord's Church in the latter days, the Grail's meaning is clearly revealed through brother Joseph.[52] Now even "babes and sucklings" can know what was hidden from "the wise and prudent" of an earlier age (Matthew 11:25; Luke 10:21). President George Q. Cannon said as much, "The Lord has hid the chosen seed in this way (among the poor and humble)."[53] The farm boy will soon be known.

THE GENETIC TRUE SEED

Thy [genetic] seed will I establish forever.

—PSALM 89:4

The birthright went through Ephraim and the inheritance (scepter) through Jesse. Therefore, Christ's own children must have partaken of both bloodlines, if they were to lead His Church. The story of this enigmatic bloodline of Jesus has a number of interesting aspects. One would be the Y-chromosome line, which would be derived from Judah-Jesse through the Savior Himself. Another would be the mitochondrial DNA from his wife(s), which in following the logic must be of Ephraim.

Thus two lineages would proceed from the male and the female children of Jesus Christ. This new house may be called the *Shiloh Dynasty* and through it the whole world would be blessed. Can enlightenment be carried in the genes?[54] Well, yes and no. Some peoples are athletically or intellectually superior to others. For instance, Ashkenazi Jews and the Chinese people test higher on standard IQ tests than Caucasian people.[55] While much can be credited to sociological conditions, not everything can. Some things are in the genes. Added to this may be one other component: Could there be a chosen genetic lineage through which noteworthy premortal spirits are directed for birth? If these conditions apply, then enlightenment could in a sense be carried or transferred in the genes.

As Christ's descendant, Joseph Smith could have inherited a variety of enlightening aspects. His goal was to bless the earth by restoring the gospel and uniting the house of Israel, and to do it he needed a special power. The blessings of Ephraim were directed to this mission. LeGrand Richards spoke of this great cause: "I do not know how the enmity and the envy between Ephraim and Judah [Isaiah 11:13] can disappear except that we of the house of Ephraim, who have the custody of the gospel, should lead out in trying to bring to this branch of the house of Israel the blessings of the restored gospel."[56]

According to Rabbi Kleiman, national lineage goes through the mother's lineage, while the tribal lineage came through the father.[57] This might be just the opposite of the way it truly is, with the tribe being ascribed by the mother and the inheritance through the father. Still, descent from the tribe of Joseph-Ephraim to Joseph Smith is documented, the significance of Ephraim was so little understood by the world. Nevertheless this lineage too was protected, "by God's own hand" as it came down from Mary Magdalene and the Bethany sisters without admixture or mutation.

The hand of the Lord preserved Joseph of Egypt's seed, for it was promised to Joseph, "that his seed should never perish as long as the earth should stand" (2 Nephi 25:21). We understand through the Book of Mormon that Joseph Smith Jr. was the direct heir and seed of Joseph of Egypt (2 Nephi 3:15). But how can that be, when with every generation fifty percent of the DNA material changes? There seem to be two explanations for this to happen:

1. The Lord ensures that only the unmixed male seed of Joseph marries the unsullied female seed of Joseph. Thus the purebred lineage is maintained.

–OR–

2. Through the non-recombining Y-chromosome (NRY) for the male line or the mitochondrial DNA (mtDNA) for the female line, is passed down virtually unchanged through the generations.[58] These "markers" might connote the true channel for spirits awaiting mortal birth.

Every living thing, from the most primitive microbe to human beings, are all part of a unified information system based on DNA. In contemplating this, the scripture "How manifold are your works: You have made them all in wisdom" (Psalm 104) comes to mind. We are living in a time of rapid progress in comprehending the human genome and the power of DNA markers as an "archeological" or "anthropological" tool tracking the history of maternal and paternal genealogies.[59]

Significant to our study is the genetic research done on the Levitical "sons of Aaron," the priestly *Kohanim* lineage, by molecular genetics scientists. They have successfully traced the *Kohanim* back to a Most Recent Common Ancestor (MRCA), to Aaron the High Priest and brother of Moses, by discovering a common set of genetic markers, called the standard Cohen Modal Haplotype (CMH) within a haplogroup.[60]

The importance of knowing one's family history is of immense importance to Jewish and Mormon priesthood bearers.[61] In Judaism, those of uncertain genealogy were not allowed to minister as priests. For example, "A man who had no knowledge of his tribe or clan was under a serious disability, and was specially excluded from the priesthood."[62] Only those who could prove their descent from Aaron, according to Numbers 16:40, were admitted.

Since most genealogical records have been lost on earth, one way of following the lineages of the *Kohanim* is through genetic studies.[63] There is not really a "Cohen gene" but rather a combination of neutral mutations indicating a common lineage or genetic signature. These studies have shown the MRCA based on variable markers date calculation or "genetic clock" (coalescence time) yield 106 generations or approximately 3,300 years, roughly to the lifetime of Aaron.[64]

Thus the keys of the Levitical-Aaronic authority come by virtue of inheritance as well as righteousness. We know that, in LDS parlance, a literal descendant of Aaron has the legal right to the presidency of the (Aaronic) priesthood, to the keys of this ministry, to act in the office of bishop without counselors (D&C 107:76). We also understand that the "literal descendants of the chosen seed" will have the right of serving in the priesthood (D&C 107:40).[65]

Aaron should have had the same paternal Y-chromosome genetic signature as his fathers back to Levi, Jacob, Isaac, Abraham, and Adam. This, with various maternal mtDNA, established the basic Hebraic or Israelite gene pool. Though there would be genetic affinity with the Hebrews, it is hypothesized that a new Grail haplogroup would be formed through this Shiloh Dynasty of Jesus Christ and Mary Magdalene. In all this we say that Jesus' Y-chromosome has "marked" about sixty-six to seventy-two generations for about 1800 years.[66]

Jesus' wives, on the other hand, were of pure Ephraimite descent from Joseph and Ephraim, coming through the generations in a protected manner.[67] We can assume that an Ephraimite mtDNA signature came directly from Jesus' wives to His children. Though there was a diversity of matriarchs in Judaism generally, within the new *Shiloh Dynasty* one female branch of Jesus lineage was kept pure Ephraimite. Thus Jesus and Mary Magdalene would have to have had at least one male child and one female child, to create both Y-chromosome and mtDNA lineages. This would be repeated with Jesus and the Bethany sisters to give nucleus DNA diversity while keeping the Y and mtDNA singularity.

It should be noted here that the regions of non-coding DNA (Y-chromosome and mtDNA) do not register any visible physical results. Only nucleus DNA does this, and it recombines every generation, constantly reshuffling DNA information.[68] Therefore any bodily characteristics or attributes would quickly dissipate within three or four generations. The appearance of a direct descendant may be quite diverse, even though the human genome sequence is almost exactly (99.9 percent) the same in all people and the mtDNA and Y-chromosome were much more exact.[69]

We have no Urim and Thummim (*seer stones* or interpreters) to certify our lineage as they did anciently (see Ezra 2:63; Nehemiah 7:65). However, it is possible that Joseph Smith discovered his own ancestral pedigree during the time he held possession of a Urim and Thummim[70] (Ether 3:21–28). Thus as a Seer with these *seer stones* (Mosiah 8:13; 28:13–16), he may have understood his Grail heirship from as early as 1827.[71]

How can Latter-day Saints in general know of their pedigree? Fortunately, the Lord has blessed the Church with patriarchs who pronounce lineage upon the heads of the Saints.[72] With this, the major houses or tribes are delineated. Joseph Smith's lineage of Ephraim was revealed in this manner. But there is another indelible method of recording one's lineage, which God imprinted on our very bodies—genetic testing.[73]

If Christ's posterity continued through Mary Magdalene and the Bethany sisters, then certain inherited genotypes or markers distinctive of tribal Judah and Ephraim should be found together. Fast-forwarding, it is possible that the properties of the "birthright" can be found in a Judaic Joseph Smith Sr. and Ephraimite Lucy Mack Smith. To those who have been "marked" by this DNA signature, certain promises and rights were generally made but conditionally given. Brigham Young in 1845 spoke of these matters: "Ephraim is the character who has the [genetically] pure blood of promise in him. The Lord has respect unto it. This doctrine is perfectly plain and simple. Those who have the right will redeem the nations of the Earth."[74]

We can only imagine that Christ's genetics would have had a dynamic impact on the hereditary roots of Joseph Smith's parentage. Joseph Smith Jr. was a Son of David through the lineage of his father's Y-chromosome, for it is written:[75] "Ought ye not to know that the Lord God of Israel gave the kingdom over Israel to David for ever, even to him and to his sons by a covenant of salt?" (2 Chronicles 13:5).

A number of molecular DNA researchers have

attempted to examine the Mormon idea of a connection between Native Americans and Israelites.[76] Much more interesting to our study is the genetic research project that Sorenson Laboratories in Salt Lake City have begun on father Joseph Smith Sr.'s family. Buddy Youngren, at a Smith Family Reunion of 2003, orchestrated the taking of buccal mucosal swabs of nearly four hundred members of the family. The purpose was to find a DNA signature for the Smith family to trace that lineage.

Genealogist Michael (Smith) Kennedy of Alpine, Utah, has researched the Joseph Smith Sr. family bloodline for thirty years.[77] He has been working with molecular geneticists to uncover the DNA markers connoting the Smith ancestral heritage. He hopes to verify which lines are related to the prophet and the Most Recent Common Ancestor (MRCA) of these people and to extend

Joseph Smith's lineage deeper into the past.

Genetic scientist Ugo Perego of West Valley City is conducting research on the Joseph Smith Sr. and Lucy Mack family DNA samples at the Sorensen Molecular Genealogy Foundation (SMGF).[78] Molecular biologist, Scott Woodward of Brigham Young University is also deeply involved on the project.[79] Funded by Jim Sorensen Sr. and Jr. of Salt Lake City, the project's mission is to "give meaning to" the information generated by the powerful scientific tools of genetic molecular genealogy.[80]

This enterprise under Dr. Perego's hand has already yielded some startling results. He has successfully traced Joseph Smith's inferred Y-chromosome, a major key in identifying his paternal lineage.[81] The following figure compares the haplotypes of Joseph Smith with his sons Joseph Smith III and Alexander Hale Smith:

FIGURE 10

JOSEPH SMITH, JR., INFERRED Y-CHROMOSOME HAPLOTYPE[82]

Locus	Joseph Smith III	Alexander Hale Smith	Joseph Smith Jr.
1. DYS 19	14	14	14
2. DYS 385	11, 13	11, 13	11, 13
3. DYS 386	12	12	12
4. DYS 389I	14	14	14
5. DYS 389II	30	30	30
6. DYS 390	24	24	24
7. DYS 391	11	11	11

LOCUS	JOSEPH SMITH III	ALEXANDER HALE SMITH	JOSEPH SMITH, JR.
8. DYS 392	14	14	14
9. DYS 393	13	13	13
10. DYS 426	12	12	12
11. DYS 437	16	16	16
12. DYS 438	12	12	12
13. DYS 439	12	12	12
14. DYS 447	25	25	25
15. DYS 454	11	11	11
16. DYS 455	11	11	11
17. DYS 460	11	11	11
18. DYS 461	11	11	11
19. DYS 462	11	11	11
20. GGAATT1B07	10	10	10
21. YCAII	19, 23	19, 23	19, 23
22. Y-GATA-A10	13	13	13
23. Y-GATA-C4	23	23	23
24. Y-GATA-H4	12	12	12

The above figure is reckoned by the author to be exactly (unmutated) to the Savior's own Y-Chromosome Haplotype. But just as important is Joseph Smith Jr.'s maternal lineage. "Yes," wrote Perego to the author, "I was able to isolate and identify Lucy Mack's mtDNA sequence."[83] This breakthrough represents the matrilineal genealogy of the Grail king, Joseph Smith Jr., through his mother's mother's mother back to Mary Magdalene or the Bethany sisters.[84]

DNA INHERITANCE CHIASMAS PATTERN

Y-CHROMOSOME
(MALES ONLY)
JUDAH LINEAGE

X ◀ JOSEPH SMITH, JR. (1805–1844)

▶

1. JOSEPH SMITH, SR. (1771–1840)

2. ASAEL SMITH (1744–1830)

3. SAMUEL SMITH (1714–1785)

4. SAMUEL T. SMITH (1666–1748)

5. ROBERT SMITH, JR. (1626–1693)

6. ROBERT SMITH, SR. (1589–)

7. EDWARD SMITH (1553–1590)

8. ROBERT SMITH (1526–1585)

9. THOMAS SMITH (c. 1500–)

1. LUCY MACK SMITH (1775–1856)

2. LYDIA GATES MACK (1732–1817)

3. LYDIA FULLER GATES (1709–1778)

4. HANNAH CROCKER FULLER (1688–)

5. HANNAH HOWLAND CROCKER (1661–)

6. MARY LEE HOWLAND (1630–)

7. MARY ____ LEE (1606–)

JESUS CHRIST
PATRILINEAL

MARY MAGDALENE
MATRILINEAL

MITOCHONDRIAL DNA
(PASSES THROUGH FEMALES)
EPHRAIM LINEAGE

Of course the chiasmatic chart can only be proven so far. Rather it is a snapshot of the theory upon which this book is based—the claim of Joseph Smith's rights "through the fathers [and mothers]." However there is another way to test the validity of the propounded hypothesis. Easy! Just find the Holy Grail chalice, carbon date the blood of Christ inside it, and analyze it for its Y-chromosome haplotype! If it matches Joseph Smith Jr.'s, then Joseph's pedigree to the Savior is confirmed and his other claims of spiritual authority and wisdom are true. How easy is that?

While the Autosomal DNA of all Church members is generally diverse, the *Shiloh-Dynasty* Y-chromosomes and mtDNA are homogeneous. It would be interesting to estimate the time at which *Shiloh-Dynasty* DNA was derived from a Most Recent Common Ancestor (coalescence time). If so, would we arrive at the time of the Savior and the Magdalene, two thousand years ago? Were both the Y-chromosomes of Joseph Smith Sr. and the mtDNA of Lucy Mack Smith kept unmutated over these centuries?[86] Brigham Young seemed to say as much: "The decrees of the Almighty will be exalted—that blood which was in him was pure and he had the sole right and lawful power, as he [Joseph Smith] was the legal heir to the blood that has been on the earth and has come down through a pure lineage. The union of various ancestors kept that blood pure."[87]

"He [Heavenly Father] has watched that family and that blood as it has circulated from its fountain to the birth of that man . . . Joseph Smith, Jr."[88]

Having the "pure" blood (unmutated Y and mtDNA) is something different from being a thoroughbred from nuclear DNA.[89] Being called the seed of Christ, carries with it a potential for vanity or worse.[90] (D&C 84:34, 124:58) Alma's mission to the apostate Zoramites who have a false concept of election, "We thank thee, O God, for we are a chosen people unto thee, while others shall perish [at death]"

(Alma 31:28). Genetic search into one's genealogy requires an "avoidance of intellectual pride, [which] allows the person of traditional religious faith to work comfortably within the framework of rigorous scientific hypothesis and empiricism."[91] The goal of such genetic research is to understand and give meaning to our precious heritage and not allow DNA to become the master of our social destiny.[92]

Our genetic makeup does not predetermine our destiny. Being of the house of Israel is a spiritual and metaphysical state, not merely a physiological DNA condition. For all, through faith, can join the family of Christ and receive the same blessings as those who are naturally born that way. Elder McConkie ties the law of adoption into the seed of Christ: "Indeed, the faithful are adopted to the family of Christ; they become 'the children of Christ, his sons, and his daughters'; they are 'spiritually begotten,' for their 'hearts are changed through faith on his name,' thus being 'born of him,' becoming 'his sons and his daughters' [Mosiah 5:7]."[93]

While this is absolutely true, another factor plays a part. The acceptance of genetic predeterminism is well appreciated by LDS sages (Abraham 3:22–23). As the plan of salvation was initially laid out, certain noble premortal spirits were to come to this earth in certain official authoritative ecclesiastical positions. They were foreordained to be born in specific times and places to accomplish the Lord's will. Thus literal direct descendants of the Chosen Grail Seed fill the highest Church leadership roles (D&C 107:40).

NOTES

1. Another scripture expounds the same idea: "I will hiss for them, and gather them; for I have redeemed them: and they shall increase as they have increased. And I will sow them among the people: and they shall remember me in far countries; and they shall live with their children, and turn again" (Zechariah 10:8–9).

2. Translated by Keil and Delitzsch, *Commentary on the Old Testament*, 7:201. Keil and Delitzsch note on 7:203: "And this remnant would become a seed, out of which a new Israel would spring up after the old had been destroyed." (See also 2 Nephi 16:13.)

3. Shute, Nyman and Bott, *Ephraim*, 48.

4. Jan Van Scorel (1494–1562), Dutch, *Mary Magdalene* (1530, oil on canvas, 26" x 30"), Rijksmuseum, Amsterdam. Mary Magdalene is in center; to the right can be seen the root-stump of promise.

5. Oliver Cowdery, "A Patriarchal Blessing" to the Prophet Joseph Smith at Kirtland, Ohio (22 September 1835), patriarchal blessings book (Church Historian's Office, Salt Lake City) 2:28, pars. 21–22. Also see Diary of Charles L. Walker (typescript, BYU Special Collections, 28 January 1881). This with John the Revelator (see D&C 77:14). See Joseph F. Smith, "Editor's Table," *Improvement Era*, May 1905, 547.

6. Smith, *Gospel Doctrine*, 115.

7. Widtsoe, *Evidences and Reconciliations*, 322. It has become evident that while the growth of Church membership has lately come from outside Ephraim, leadership has been slow to come from non-Ephraimitic people, even though the Church has tried diligently to develop such leadership. Black Africans received the priesthood in 1978, and baptisms among people of color have now far outstripped baptisms among white Caucasians.

8. Brigham Young, in *Journal of Discourses* (8 April 1855), 2:268–69. President Young is not talking about racial superiority but rather the demonstration of resolute leadership.

9. Latter-day Saints believe that all those who minister to this earth are those who are of this earth. Both Heavenly Father and Michael-Adam, while born on another world, "belong" to this earth, since they, with Jehovah, created it and have visited it. Adam and Eve actually lived on this earth in the Garden and thus belong to it.

10. Nibley, *On the Timely and the Timeless*, 213.

11. Whitney, *Life of Heber C. Kimball*, 32.

12. Angels are leaders, messengers or servants of God, who are either premortal spirits, mortal living people, spirits of just men made perfect, translated persons, or resurrected beings. See McConkie, *Mormon Doctrine*, 35–37. The devil, we should know, also has his angels or minions.

13. Smith, *Teachings of the Prophet Joseph Smith* (April 1844), 365. The Grand Council(s) in Heaven organized the outline history of the earth and those who would be leaders in it.

14. Some early sources claim that Adam was different from the other archangels because he was much older and was born on another world. When he came to this earth he already had an exalted resurrected body. The author postulates that he was from an earlier Round of Eternity and not of our own Eternal Generation. See Brigham Young, in *Journal of Discourses* (9 April 1852), 1:46–51, and Tullidge, *Women of Mormondom*, 177–81: "Michael was a celestial, resurrected being from another world."

15. Smith, *Teachings of the Prophet Joseph Smith* (2 July 1839), 157.

16. Joseph Fielding Smith: "Elias came and restored the gospel of Abraham. Who was Elias? That question is frequently asked. Well, Elias was Noah, who came and restored his keys" (Conference Report, April 1960, 72; see also Andrus, *Doctrinal Commentary on the Pearl of Great Price*, 367, n. 48). There are other Eliases, such as John the Baptist, Christ himself, and John the Revelator.

17. Brown, *All Things Restored*, 42. He notes that Bruce R. McConkie believed that the archangel Raphael of Doctrine and Covenants 128:21 may have been the patriarch Enoch (see McConkie, *Mormon Doctrine*, 618).

18. Astrologically, 23 December makes Joseph's birth sign a Capricorn, which is ruled over by Saturn, but this is deceiving. Joseph's emphasis is on his birth-Decan governing planet, which is Jupiter. See Quinn, *Early Mormonism and the Magic World View*, 71–72 (414n41): "Therefore, Jupiter ruled both his birth year and his birthdate within the zodiacal sign. Joseph was born in the first of three 10-degree arcs (Decans) of Capricorn. This Decan is ruled by Jupiter. In addition, a specific planet governed each year and Jupiter ruled 1805."
That would be like saying a person was an American (Capricorn) but was from Utah (Jupiter). In some quarters the Decan sign was considered more important (fateful) than the birth sign. To say that the Decans "thus preside" is thus an accurate statement. Some see the Decans as angels who preside over the thirty-six subdivisions of the Zodiac. Joseph felt that Jupiter was even more important than Saturn to him.

19. "However Smith's letter eliminated Uriel as one of the angels who ministered to him" (Quinn, *Early Mormonism and the Magic World View*, 225). Thus he might be Uriel, himself. Doctrine and Covenants 128:21 is the only place in scripture that *Raphael* appears.

20. The original Hebrew word for *Barchiel* can be transliterated as *Baraqui'el*, *Barak-el*, *Baurak Ale*, or *Barakh El*. See Quinn, *Early Mormonism and the Magic World View*, 224–25. Moise Schwab identified the

meaning of *Barakh El* as "God bless you" and specifically designated for Jupiter.

21. Quinn, *Early Mormonism and the Magic World View*, 224–25. This was Joseph Smith's Israelite tribe and governing planet in astrology. Joseph Smith was known to possess a Jupiter Talisman, which he carried on his person at his death in Carthage Jail in 1844.

22. According to Davidson, *Dictionary of Angels, Barakiel* ("lightning of God") was one of the seven archangels and one of the four ruling seraphim. Encyclopedias of Joseph Smith's generation, according to Quinn, specified that the "Jews reckon four orders or companies of angels," each headed by Michael, Gabriel, Raphael, and Uriel. See Quinn, *Early Mormonism and the Magic World View*, 225. These four ruling angels presided over the four elements, directions, and winds. It could be that each of the four ruling angels presided over a quarter of the twelve tribes, planets, zodiacal signs, and months.

23. Just one of his missions, but not the least, was being the gathering of the lost tribes in the dispensation of the fulness of times.

24. Pratt, *Key to the Science of Theology*, 81. Pratt was commenting on the verse from Malachi 3:1. However, Bruce R. McConkie noted that the "Elias" in the passage referred to John the Baptist, while the "messenger" referred to Joseph Smith (*Doctrinal New Testament Commentary*, 1:115). Joseph Fielding Smith said that it had a double meaning and could refer to both Joseph and the Baptist (*Doctrines of Salvation*, 1:193).

25. The list of who these dispensation heads are is debatable. Enoch, Noah, Abraham, Moses or Elijah, Peter, Joseph Smith, and Jesus Christ are one list. Some place Jesus on this list at the meridian of time, instead of Peter, but I would put Jesus on it at the Millennium instead. Others have Adam on the list as the founding dispensation head.

26. It might also be that the devil has his "dispensation heads," or Master Mahans, such as Cain, Lamech, and Judas. (Moses 5:16–55).

27. Smith, *Teachings of the Prophet Joseph Smith* (13 June 1844), 365. "I suppose that I was ordained to this very office in that Grand Council." Joseph Fielding Smith expressed a similar view in speaking of his father, Joseph F. Smith, son of Hyrum Smith: "The child was destined to walk in the steps of his beloved father [Hyrum] and his illustrious uncle [Joseph] as the vice-regent of Jesus Christ upon the earth." From Smith, *Life of Joseph F. Smith*, 117.

28. Brigham Young, in *Journal of Discourses* (9 October 1859), 7:290.

29. Brigham Young, as quoted in *Wilford Woodruff Journal* (16 February 1847) 3:132; Kelly, *Journals of John D. Lee* (16 February 1847), 83. "Those that are adopted into my family and take me for their counsellor, if I continue faithfully I will preside over them throughout all eternity and will stand at their head."

30. *Wilford Woodruff's Journal* (11 December 1869), 6:508.

31. Brigham Young, in *Journal of Discourses* (9 October 1859), 7:289.

32. The apostle Peter stands at the pearly gates for those born during his dispensation.

33. Brigham Young, in *Journal of Discourses* (8 March 1857), 4:271.

34. Brigham Young, in *Journal of Discourses* (9 October 1859), 7:289. Orson Hyde taught the same thing in *Journal of Discourses* (3 January 1858), 6:154–55: "I tell you, Joseph holds the keys, and none of us can get into the celestial kingdom without passing by him. We have not got rid of him, but he stands there as the sentinel, holding the keys of the kingdom of God; and there are many of them beside him. I tell you, if we get past those who have mingled with us, and know us best, and have a right to know us best, probably we can pass all other sentinels as far as it is necessary, or as far as we may desire. . . . We see the position that brother Joseph stands in; we see that he has overcome, and that he has power over the nation."

Brigham Young, in *Journal of Discourses* (21 October 1860), 8:224: "As I have frequently told them, no man in this dispensation will enter the courts of heaven without the approbation of the Prophet Joseph Smith jun. Who has made it so? Have I? Have this people? Have the World? No, but the Lord Jehovah has decreed it. If I ever pass into the heavenly courts it will be by the consent of the Prophet Joseph. If you ever pass through the gates into the Holy City, you will do so upon his certificate that you are worthy to pass."

35. Brigham Young noted: "If you can pass Joseph and have him say, 'Here: you have been faithful, good boys; I hold the keys of this dispensation; I will let you pass'" (*Journal of Discourses*, 7 October 1857, 5:332).

36. Brigham Young, in *Journal of Discourses* (6 April 1853), 2:29, said: "Your endowment is, to receive all those ordinances in the House of the Lord, which are necessary for you, after you have departed this life, to enable you to walk back to the presence of the Father, passing the angels who stand as sentinels, being enable to give them the key words, the signs and tokens, pertaining to the Holy Priesthood, and gain your eternal exaltation in spite of earth and hell."

37. Smith, *Teachings of the Prophet Joseph Smith* (7 April 1844), 195, 361–62. See also Ehat and Cook, *Words of Joseph Smith,* 355 (Thomas Bullock report). Here the quotation is quite different: "You don't know me; you never knew my heart. No man knows my history—I cannot do it. I shall never undertake—if I had not experienced what I have I should not have known it myself."

38. Pratt, *Key to the Science of Theology,* 81.

39. Whitney, *Life of Heber C. Kimball,* 34, 322, 333.

40. *Times and Seasons* (15 August 1844), in Smith, *Teachings of the Prophet Joseph Smith,* 361–62.

41. Whitney, *Life of Heber C. Kimball,* 32; see also 322.

42. Brigham Young, in *Journal of Discourses* (25 May 1862), 9:294a. We are not sure what Brigham Young had reference to, but the quotation underscores the idea of hidden and mysterious identities which would rattle the testimonies of the Latter-day Saints.

43. Joseph Smith as quoted by Wilford Woodruff, in *Journal of Discourses* (10 Oct. 1880), 21:317. From the earlier context of the speech, Woodruff was clearly talking about Joseph's role as a dispensation head and possible relationship with Jesus Christ's posterity.

44. Andrus and Andrus, *They Knew the Prophet,* 26. See also Lightner, *Life and Testimony of Mary Lightner.*

45. Brigham Young, in "A Family Meeting in Nauvoo: Minutes of a Meeting of the Richards and Young Families Held in Nauvoo, Ill., 8 January, 1845," *Utah Genealogical and Historical Magazine* 11 (July 1920): 104–8. Most apostate fundamentalists believe that Joseph Smith is the Holy Ghost. This was the gist of Brigham Young's refutation as it came to be believed after the release of John Taylor's Doctrine and Covenants 134. Joseph Smith did *not* mean that he was the "Holy Ghost" or spirit, as most Mormon apostate fundamentalist believe. See Vern G. Swanson's typescript, "Who Is the Holy Ghost?"

46. Ehat and Cook, *Words of Joseph Smith* (27 August 1843), 245. "The Lord covenanted with Joseph of old, that his branch of Israel would one day run over the wall" (Genesis 49:22).

47. Madsen, *Joseph Smith the Prophet,* 107. See Genesis 49:22–26 and 2 Nephi 3:6–15. See also statements collected in *Our Lineage,* a 1933 lesson manual for genealogy classes.

48. Brigham Young, in *Journal of Discourses* (13 November 1870), 12:309a. The quotation goes: "The scripture says that He, the Lord, came walking in the Temple, with His train; I do not know who they were, unless His wives and children." Most Latter-day Saints are accepting of Jesus Christ being married, but His being polygynist and having children strains even Mormon minds. Remember that plural marriage was not announced to the world until the Saints were in Utah.

49. Brigham Young, as quoted in an address 8 January 1845, *Utah Genealogical and Historical Magazine* 11 (July 1920): 107; emphasis added. This is the first time such an "Office" has been mentioned. It has reference to those who "save their dead" through temple work.

50. What is meant is obscure. Did Joseph's dispensation have more people live in it than any other dispensation; thus he did more? See Smith, *Teachings of the Prophet Joseph Smith* (29 September 1839), 157.

51. This is from "Praise to the Man," *Hymns,* no. 27.

52. The term *Holy Grail* is not in the Mormon lexicon, but is an appropriated phrase to denote what the Church knows about the royal bloodline and Joseph Smith's and our own sacred heritage.

53. Journal of Rudger Clawson, 374–75; ellipses in original; see Larsen, *Ministry of Meetings,* 72. See also journal of Anthony W. Ivins (2 July 1899), LDS Archives.

54. Godwin, *Holy Grail,* 193. He notes that while bloodlines can come to a dead end, myths are more recyclable and renewable. Ever the gadfly, he questions: "So what? Even being the son of the son . . . of the Son of God still doesn't make anyone a Christ. Enlightenment has yet to be proved to be carried in the genes. And even if it had created a Savior he would be unlikely to be recognized any more than was his great, great . . . grandfather."

55. Michelle Malkin, editorial in *Conservative Chronicle,* 2004.

56. LeGrand Richards, Conference Report, October 1956, 23.

57. The Torah-based tradition is that Jewish nationalism is determined by the mother's status and that tribal membership follows the father's lineage. The matrilineal definition was established very early in Jewish history (Deuteronomy 7:3). The son of a non-Jewish father and Jewish mother remains "your son" while the son of a Jewish father and non-Jewish mother is to be considered not a son of the Jewish nation (see Kleiman, *DNA and Tradition,* 41).

58. A recent book by Kleiman, *DNA and Tradition,* outlines many of the ways the "Cohen Gene" and genetic matriarchs, etc. are being discovered by modern science and technology. mtDNA is passed on only from the mother to both male and female offspring, unchanged except for neutral mutations in the non-coding area. Only the Y chromosome passes on from father to son and has a higher mutation rate, which is random and unpredictable.

59. Preface by Karl Skorecki to Kleiman, *DNA and Tradition,*

14; Kleiman, *DNA and Tradition*, 29.

60. A haplotype is a set of closely linked genetic markers present on one chromosome, which tend to be inherited together and can be used to indicate lineage. Of those tested, who called themselves Kohanim, 98.5 percent had the YAP (Y Chromosome Alu Polymorphism) insert sequence, which is not at all common in other populations. There were also six chromosomal markers found in about 94 percent of the Kohanim's group. There are 18 major haplogroups known worldwide. See Kleiman, *DNA and Tradition*, 19, 29.

61. We read in Ezra that after the return from Babylonian exile a number of people feigned to be priests but were proven not to be by genealogical record: "And these were they which went up from Tel-Melah, Tel-Harsa, Cherub, Addan and Immer: but they could not shew their father's house, and their seed, whether they were of Israel. . . . These sought their register among those that were reckoned by genealogy, but they were not found: therefore were they, as polluted, put from the priesthood" (Ezra 2:59–62; see also Nehemiah 7:64; Titus 3:9).

62. Carson, et al., *New Bible Commentary*, 21st century edition, 399. Ezra the Scribe, a Cohen and member of the Great Assembly, examined the genealogy of his contemporary Kohanim. Those unable to bring proof of their lineage were refused the privilege of serving in the Temple. See Kleiman, *DNA and Tradition*, 109.

63. Malcolm Ritter, "Jewish Priesthood Is Inherited, Scientists Confirm," *Salt Lake Tribune*, 11 July 1998, describes how scientists have discovered that members of the Jewish Levite priesthood, "are [genetically] part of an unbroken line extending back thousands of years . . . Scientists who studied the Y chromosome in modern-day Cohanim [Jewish priests] reported evidence that the designation truly has been passed from father to son." Ritter quotes *Nature* magazine and researcher David Goldstein of Oxford University.

64. Kleiman, *DNA and Tradition*, 20. Studies have also shown a high degree of fidelity among the wives of Kohanim, a scientific testimony to the historical integrity of Jewish family faithfulness.

65. Kleiman, *DNA and Tradition*, 24: "The results do reinforce the rabbinical position that today's Kohanim are indeed the continuation of the ancestral Cohen line and should be granted full rights of Kohanim in regard to such practices as Redemption of the Firstborn and Blessing the Congregation." These studies confirm thousands of years of written and oral tradition indicating Jewish historiography originating from the ancient Middle East.

66. Jesus was given heavenly nuclear DNA with a Y chromosome marker from Heavenly Father. It is blatant heresy with many people to say that God the Father has a "Y" or "X" chromosome. They believe that God is beyond any such scientific description. However, others believe that Heavenly Father is a resurrected man, who is married to a wife, and has spirit children and one mortal child (Christ). This child would not be male if He did not have a Y chromosome inherited from His father. Yet, Jesus was fully a man in all physical and spiritual respects. Most naysayers believe that Joseph the Carpenter, not God, was Jesus' literal father, or that the conception was immaculate and needed no sperm. Except for the Y chromosome's determination of maleness, it is almost entirely of a non-coding DNA.

67. There were not, in this one branch of Ephraimites, any exogamous marriages (where an outsider marries in). It is possible that these wives' mtDNA and also that of the Virgin Mary, were pure (unmutated) from mother Eve. Thus the Shiloh Dynasty is merely a reiteration of the DNA of Adam and Eve and our Heavenly Parents before them.

68. The total DNA makeup of a human being consists of over three billion nucleotides; sixty million are in the Y chromosome. Human DNA is packaged in the 23 pairs of chromosomes residing in the nucleus of each cell of the body. It is like a gigantic document, book or map, written in a small alphabet in linear, one-dimensional, and one- directional form. The DNA protein molecule is shaped like a spiral staircase, the famous "double helix" with the steps being complementary nucleotides. Four chemical bases spell out the words of the alphabet, A, C, G, and T., are translated into a twenty-word code of amino acids, the building blocks of proteins. Rabbi Jonathan Sacks, Chief Rabbi of Great Britain states:
The human genome does seem to me to be one of the rare scientific discoveries that is poetical and even mystical. The Kabbalists actually maintained that everything that exists is the result of tzerufim—various permutations of the letters of an alphabet. It now turns out that this is not a metaphor at all. It is actually, literally true . . . the DNA string of those characters is all a series of letters—A, C, G and T—which, as it were, extend to perform this huge language that is the DNA. All life is exactly as the Bible said, a matter of language, of instructions, of letters, and words. We suddenly realize the deep resonance of the biblical idea: "and God spoke and there was" (Professor Jonathan Sacks, Forum, 6 February 2001, as quoted in Kleiman, *DNA and Tradition*, 172).

69. My friend and half-brother, Dr. Robert D. Hill, believes that DNA proves that we are less descended from Joseph of Egypt than from the Chimpanzee. He writes (1 June 2005) in an email to the author: "Did you know that 98 percent of human DNA is identical with the DNA of a Chimpanzee? I just don't believe a bloodline is important. The fact that the DNA of a Chimp is so close to human DNA proves evolution and that we evolved from the apes. Not to mock you but maybe someone should write about the "sacred bloodline of the apes." What Dr. Hill does not appreciate is that the DNA, in the long run, is an identification marker, not necessarily a magical codebook, which transmits super powers. Long-term evolution of humanoids does not alter the fact that subtle DNA markers may distinguish certain people of "promise" to receive certain premortal spirits.

70. This Urim and Thummim (meaning Lights and Perfections) of the brother of Jared, was separate and distinct from the one held by Abraham and the prophets of Israel. These are described as two stones set in silver bows from a breastplate. Joseph's Urim and Thummim was taken back by the angel as punishment sometime after he lost the 116 pages of the Book of Mormon in 1828. See Quinn, *Early Mormonism and the Magic World View,* 171, 248. Dr. Richard L. Anderson believes they were returned in the winter of 1828 (D&C 3 and 10 seem to confirm this). Joseph Smith also had a chocolate-colored seer stone as well, which he found while digging a well at the Chase home in Palmyra. He completed the translations of the Book of Mormon and probably used it in like manner to the Urim and Thummim. After 1830 Joseph possessed the priesthood and no longer needed these instruments in the revelation process. The stone is still in the Church's possession.

71. Joseph also seemed to have genealogical knowledge about other early saints. Probably the knowledge of his ancestry came about through early use of the Urim and Thummin, while the other seerstone in Joseph's possession perhaps gave the genealogy of the Cowderys and Whitmers and others.

72. Smith, *Doctrines of Salvation,* 3:169–72.

73. This is not to say that there is an "Ephraim gene" or a "Benjamin gene," but coupled with the best genealogies available, the Sorenson Molecular Genealogy Foundation of Salt Lake City can ascertain one's lineage.

74. Brigham Young, in "A Family Meeting in Nauvoo: Minutes of a Meeting of the Richards and Young Families Held in Nauvoo, Ill., 8 January, 1845," *Utah Genealogical and Historical Magazine* 11 (July 1920): 112.

75. Heavenly Father and King David would have the same Y DNA, as would Ephraim.

76. So far they have had no success, and the consensus is that all Native American tribes descend from common ancestors in Siberia. Thomas W. Murphy, chairperson of the anthropology department at Edmonds Community College in Lynnwood, Washington, raised as a Mormon, did not find any correlation. See W. Lobdell and L. B. Stammer, "Anthropologist may be Ousted for Questioning Teachings about Native American ancestry," *Los Angeles Times,* 8 December 2002. It may be that the very small pocket of Laman's and Lemuel's Hebraic DNA that entered the Native American population was swallowed up in the existing sea of DNA gene pool. The Nephite (Hebraic) DNA was exterminated. Thus only small amounts of Hebrew DNA among the more aboriginal natives, could or would be found to analyze. See Simon G. Southerton, *Losing a Lost Tribe* (2004).

77. Author's interview of Michael Kennedy, Thursday, 22 March 2005, at his home in Alpine, Utah. Brother Kennedy also noted that Bruce R. McConkie directly told him that his heritage came down from the married Christ. Of Joseph Smith Jr's. direct line we know that in 1956, Gracia Smith was the first to be baptized into the Church. Michael Kennedy was the first priesthood holder and joined the Church in the early 1970s. He is descended through Alexander Hale Smith.

78. Ugo Perego is director of operations and senior project administrator examining the DNA sequence of both Joseph Smith Jr.'s father and mother. The James Sorenson family of Salt Lake City began this foundation in 2001 to study the posterity of the larger Smith family. Their major goal, however, is to link family trees together on a cross-cultural and worldwide basis.

79. The Sorenson Molecular Genealogy Foundation has concentrated on one of the two major ways of looking at the genetic code. For isolating Joseph Smith Jr.'s code, they have followed the STR (Short Tandem Repeats) method where the 60 million piece long Y chromosome is grouped in segments. This is particularly good for practical recent ancestral genealogy. The other method was followed by the Jewish researchers of the Cohen haplotype. They used SNPS (Single Nucleotide Polymorphisms) where the indicators are placed one above another for matches. This is particularly good for deep past ancestral anthropological research. The Genographic Project sponsored by IBM and National Geographic are looking back in terms of 60,000 years ago and more.

80. Traditional genealogy and molecular genealogy relate to each other in the following fashion:

    *Name ——————— Haplotype
    *Gender ——————— (r) Y Chromosome
    *Birth Date——————— (r) Mutation Rate
    *Birth Place ——————— (r) Gene Pool

81. See Ugo Perego, "Reconstructing Joseph Smith Y Chromosome: Genealogical Application," *Journal of Mormon History,* August 2005: "In that article we discuss how we were able to reconstruct a small part of Joseph Smith Jr.'s DNA and use it to verify if Joseph Smith was the father of three boys that some people claimed were born of him through polygamous relationships" (Perego, email to Swanson, 18 July 2005, in author's possession). The paternity of these children proved negative.

82. With thanks to Ugo Perego and Sorenson Molecular Genealogy Foundation of Salt Lake City (used with permission). Using the Cambridge Standard Sequence, this partial chart of the Inferred Y Chromosome Haplotype (MRCA) sequence of Joseph Smith Jr. Reconstruction comes from an analysis of Joseph's sons (Joseph Smith III and Alexander Hale Smith) and was presented on 30 July 2005 at the BYU Genealogy Conference in Provo, Utah.

83. Email from Ugo Perego to Vern G. Swanson, 20 July 2005. Perego understandably declined to share this with the author because it had not yet been published by the Sorenson Molecular Genealogy Foundation

84. As in the case with the Virgin Mary's lineage back to Abraham, so Lucy Mack Smith's genealogy must have been every bit as compelling as that of Joseph Smith Sr.

85. This genealogy (not this figure) was gleaned from Michael Kennedy's website, Googled at "Joseph Smith Sr. and Lucy Mack," July 2005.

86. According to Ugo Perego, the Y chromosome has a mutation rate of about 10 percent per generation and is very good at shorter time intervals. But the mutation is random and does not affect everybody's Y chromosomes in the same way. Thus some Y chromosomes can be transmitted for thousands of years with little or no mutation, whereas others will have high mutation rates.

87. Brigham Young, in "A Family Meeting in Nauvoo: Minutes of a Meeting of the Richards and Young Families Held in Nauvoo, Ill., 8 January, 1845," *Utah Genealogical and Historical Magazine* 11 (July 1920): 104–8. The word "pure" may mean that God protected the Y chromosome and mtDNA not to mutate at all over the centuries.

88. Brigham Young, in *Journal of Discourses* (9 October 1859), 7:289–90.

89. We do not know of any physical traits, other than gender, that are bestowed by the Y chromosome and none from the mtDNA. Thoroughbred means to combine physical and other traits through nuclear DNA (recombining DNA) selective breeding.

90. Lynn Picknett and Clive Prince, as quoted in Burstein, *Secrets of the Da Vinci Code,* 292. Some have questioned the viability and the very divinity of this lineage: "A great many people have missed this point, and this has led to theories that there is something inherently, perhaps even genetically, different about this bloodline. Indeed, we regard the notion as potentially dangerous, just like any elitist system that upholds certain people for their physical characteristics over all others. This may take the form of Hitler's master race or white supremacists or those who believe some carry the Jesus bloodline gene, making them automatically superior to the rest of us." Hundreds of millions of people may be genealogically related to Jesus Christ (see Picknett and Prince, *Sion Revelation,* 279). Yet if we only follow the Y and the MtDNA directly, this number falls dramatically, and if we only follow the true Y and MtDNA combined, it is quite rare. At the August 2004 Sunstone Symposium, a panel made of five members of the Mormon Women's forum and Paul Toscano all lambasted the idea of a genetic heredity in the Church.

91. Preface by Karl Skorecki to Kleiman, *DNA and Tradition,* 14.

92. Ibid., 15. After all, it is not the DNA of the physical body per se, but the spirit housed in the body that counts. The genealogy of the spirit body may have greater significance. Were we the sons and daughters of the great Father, or the "children of a lesser god?" Even that does not matter but rather faithfulness does.

93. McConkie, *Mormon Doctrine,* 23. Biological sons and daughters of Christ, if unfaithful, would lose all.

CHAPTER NINETEEN

"Art Thou That Prophet?"

Joseph Smith Jr. discovered the meeting place between the logres of the inner and outer world—heaven and earth. It was his finding of the bridge (axial mundi) between the two worlds, locating the sacred fountain and piercing the veil that made Joseph the hero of the Grail romance. His identification with "who we are" reestablished the precious links between the female and male sovereignty in this earthly realm.

With unrelenting fortitude Joseph, the knight unerrant, found the sacred precincts of the Palace of God and communed with Him there. His prophetic voice was the wellspring that healed the barren wasteland of the two kingdoms. The wasteland was the Great Apostasy; Joseph Smith was its antidote as he restored the gospel at the time of "the fulness of the Gentiles."[1]

THE SHEPHERD, THE STONE OF ISRAEL

Joseph is a fruitful bough. . . . But his bow abode in strength, and the arms of his hands were made strong by the hands of the mighty God of Jacob; (from thence is the shepherd, the stone of Israel).

—GENESIS 49:22, 24

In the middle of Jacob's blessing to his twelve sons, he places his hands on the head of Joseph with this utterance ("from thence is the shepherd, the stone of Israel") (Genesis 49:24; ellipses in original). Most scholars believe this is an enigmatic parenthetical note dealing with Jesus Christ. But if so, why were Jacob's hands placed on Joseph, not Judah? This riddle may be a key to unlocking great wisdom regarding the latter days.

Doctrine and Covenants 50:14 was given to Joseph Smith in 1831. In this revelation, Jesus Christ clearly identifies Himself, "Wherefore, I am in your midst and I am the good shepherd, and the stone of Israel. He that buildeth upon this rock shall never fall." Yet in 1832 the Church's first official publication, *The Evening and the Morning Star,* quotes the Genesis scripture and explains:

But the most profound is, *From thence is the Shepherd, the Stone of Israel.* It could not mean the birth of the

Savior, for Paul says, it is evident our Lord sprang from the tribe of Judah. But when Paul said to the Romans, *There shall come out of Sion the Deliverer, and turn away ungodliness from Jacob,* he must have meant the Deliverer which is to come and gather his sheep into his fold, and becomes the good Shepherd: and according to the blessing of Moses, Joseph is the firstling of his bullock.[2]

The periodical seems to say that the birth of a latter-day "Shepherd, Stone of Israel" would be born out of Joseph's Ephraimite lineage. Who is referenced here, Jesus or Joseph Smith? It was probably Martin Harris who began the rumor of Joseph Smith being the Shepherd, the Stone of Israel. In 1853, Brigham Young tried to squelch the idea: "There is a man named Martin Harris, and he is the one who gave the holy roll to Gladden. When Martin was with Joseph Smith, he was continually trying to make the people believe that he (Joseph) was the Shepherd, the Stone of Israel. I have heard Joseph chastise him severely for it, and he told me that such a course, if persisted in, would destroy the kingdom of God."[3]

Yet the notion persisted. Was Joseph Smith just being politically correct in the face of mounting persecution? It is interesting to note that the Bethel Stone, upon which all the Judaic kings of Israel were crowned, made covenants, took oaths or made vows, is sometimes called "The Shepherd" stone.[4] This stone of the sceptered tribe is the only one to be anointed with oil; thus it preeminently was called "the anointed one." This Stone of Israel would therefore refer to a member of the tribe of Judah. Isaiah 28:16 mentions a special stone which might answer the above description: "Therefore thus saith the *Lord God,* Behold, I lay in Zion for a foundation a stone, a tried stone, a precious corner stone, a sure foundation: he that believeth shall not make haste."

The "foundation stone" relates to God, because it is Jesus Christ (Deuteronomy 32:4). Yet, in the Genesis 49:24 verse we have another scripture in which Joseph (Ephraim) and Judah are being connected. Verse 24 is interesting in this respect, according to Edward King: "If a scholar, entirely free from the preconceived notions of either Jew or Christian, were set to interpret this Prophecy of Jacob, he would, I think, infer that while there was a promise of a Messiah to Judah (verses 8–12) there was at least an equally clear one to Joseph (verses 22–26), especially in the words from thence is the Shepherd the Stone of Israel."[5]

The connection is made because Judah's foundational stone in verse 24 is being referenced in a blessing being given to Ephraim. Then in "cross-over" fashion, we again have in Genesis 49:10, a blessing for Judah which references Ephraim's "Shiloh." Does the "Shiloh come" noted earlier in verse 10 refer to some connection between the two tribes? *Strangely, both tribes appears in each other's blessings.* It is difficult to imagine a more important connecting point for the course and history of the world. The "stone of Israel" and "Shiloh" may both refer to Judah and to Ephraim, after the sacred marriage of Jesus.

From this marriage's progenitors came our latter-day prophets and apostles. In February 1875 Orson Pratt correctly notes that this scripture has reference to a blessing placed on the head of Joseph, not Judah. This intimates that Joseph Smith, as Jesus' *ascendant descendant,* was also the stone:

Now who can explain and tell us what this means? Can any of the wise commentators of the day? Can any of those who have studied theology in their life-time, tell us why it is from Joseph that the Shepherd, the Stone of Israel is to be made manifest? Says one:

"It cannot have reference to his birth, because Jesus descended from Judah, instead of Joseph, out of the loins of Judah, through the lineage of David. He is the Lion of the tribe of Judah."

Why then this peculiar saying of the old Prophet Jacob, about the tribe of Joseph, that from thence is the Shepherd, the Stone of Israel, if he was not born of Joseph, and did not descend through that tribe? This is a very curious kind of a saying. But he will be made manifest in the character of a shepherd, and that shepherd will lead Joseph (the tribe) as a flock and he will stir up his strength and will save the house of Joseph. But it will be in his own time and way.[6]

Pratt does not cite the pertinent Psalm 80:1–2 in the above quotation, "Give ear, O shepherd of Israel, thou that leadest Joseph like a flock." Others, who are not of the Mormon faith, share Pratt's conclusion:

> If the phrase [the Shepherd, the Stone of Israel in Genesis 49:24] be an interpolation as we suggest, it would be better to regard the whole of the preceding passage as the antecedent, and to make it mean that the Messiah will spring from the persecuted tribe of Ephraim, that is from Joseph, who is here the object of Jacob's blessing. *We regard the verse therefore as a prediction of the Messiah ben Joseph.*[7]

Both the Christian Knights Templar and the Islamic Shiites "awaited the *Mahdi*, the 'Desired Knight,' to reestablish paradise on earth, halting the spreading desert wasteland brought about by the loss of the Goddess."[8] In Mormon parlance the *Mahdi*, might be "the one mighty and strong" (D&C 85:7). Perhaps the Prophet Joseph Smith and the "Goddess" is the bloodline itself. The seed and lineage come straight from Abraham: "Abraham received promises concerning his seed, and of the fruit of his loins—from whose loins ye are, *namely, my servant Joseph [Smith]*" (D&C 132:30; 124:58; 2 Nephi 3:5–6).

The name of Eschenbach's hero Parzival, or "Perce à Val," has been translated as "piercing the valley" but might be translated "parting the veil." Joseph Smith was "that prophet" who pierced the veil of darkness covering the world and established the True and Living Church (Grail Castle) in the last days. Joseph the martyr gave his life that the world's wasteland might be healed. As John Taylor was inspired to say, "[It] cost the best blood of the nineteenth century to bring them forth for the salvation of a ruined world" (D&C 135:6).

There seem to be two individuals named "Shepherd, the Stone of Israel," with Jesus Christ being one and Joseph Smith being the other. Next to the Lord Jesus, Joseph Smith gave the most in this the most important of all dispensations for the salvation of man. Again we rely upon John Taylor: "Joseph Smith, the Prophet and Seer of the Lord, has done more, save Jesus only, for the salvation of men in this world, than any other man that ever lived in it" (D&C 135:3).

MESSIAH BEN JOSEPH

And that my name should be had for good and evil among all nations, kindreds, and tongues, or that it should be both good and evil spoken of among all people.

—JOSEPH SMITH– HISTORY 1:33

Jacob became the last of a line of patriarchs who held the full power of the blessings of the firstborn. We know that before Jacob died, the old patriarch blessed his sons Judah with the scepter and Joseph's son Ephraim with the birthright (Genesis 49:10 and 22-26). This divided the blessings of the children of God in two halves, leading to an eventual breach between the children of Judah and Ephraim.[9] Joseph of Egypt also gave a father's blessing in which we are told that the world would be blessed through Ephraim's posterity: *"I die, and go unto my fathers; and I go down to my grave with joy. The God of my father Jacob be with you, to deliver you out of affliction in the days of your bondage; for the Lord hath visited me, and I have obtained a promise of the Lord, that out of the fruit of my loins, the Lord God will raise up a righteous branch out of my loins"* (JST Genesis 50:24).

Joseph knew that the Lord would raise up a choice seer in the latter days. He would be named "Joseph," the son of "Joseph" out of "a righteous branch" from his loins (Genesis 50:33 JST; 2 Nephi 3:15). This has reference to an anointed leader, usually called *Messiah ben Joseph* or *Messiah ben Ephraim*.[10]

Cleon Skousen notes that this answers a puzzling Jewish tradition: "From the most ancient times, Jewish tradition has proclaimed that a great servant of God from the House of Joseph would come in the latter days to prepare the way for the coming of Shiloh, the Great Messiah."[11]

This precursor or Elias shall come as a messiah (anointed one or deliverer) in his own right. "The doctrine of the two Messiahs holds an important place in Jewish theology," writes Charles Torrey, a Yale University religion professor, "more important and more widely attested than is now generally recognized. It is not a theory imperfectly formulated or only temporarily held, but a standard article of faith, early and firmly established and universally accepted."[12]

Rabbi Solomon Zeitlin concurs with this assessment: "According to a Talmudic statement the Jews believed in two messiahs, one of the tribe of Joseph, or rather who was an Ephraimite, and the other a scion of David."[13]

Dr. Joseph Klausner, formerly of Hebrew University in Jerusalem, comments on Zechariah 12 in his book *The Messianic Idea in Israel*: "But the Talmud and the New Testament saw in these words a reference to the Messiah—the former to Messiah sons of Joseph who was slain and the latter to Jesus of Nazareth who was crucified." [14]

In the *Encyclopedia Judaica*, Joseph Klausner and then Cleon Skousen note the attributes of this *Messiah ben Joseph*, who would come forth in the latter times: [15]

1. He will rise up shortly before the coming of Shiloh the great Messiah ben David or Messiah ben Judah.

2. He will be a descendant of Joseph through Ephraim. Of course this is the message of Genesis 50:33 JST and 2 Nephi 3:15 mentioned above.

3. Messiah ben Joseph's mission will commence about the time the prophet Elijah returns, as promised in Malachi (Malachi 3:1).[16] According to Louis Ginzberg (1911), 6:339, "Elijah's chief activity will consist in restoring the purity of the family."

4. He will be given the keys to the gathering of Israel, and he will restore temple worship.

5. In the heat of his contest with his enemies the mortal Messiah ben Joseph would be "pierced" and killed.

6. Then, at the end of the course of the present world he will (as a resurrected being) rebuild the temple in Jerusalem.

7. While preparing mankind for the coming of Shiloh, (a resurrected) Messiah ben Joseph will enter into a great contest with the anti-Christ forces and destroy the enemies of Israel.[17]

In this list, we find striking parallels with the life of Joseph Smith Jr. LDS scholar Victor L. Ludlow writes about the Jewish tradition of an anticipated two "saviors" or "messiahs." He quotes the *Encyclopedia Judaica* (11:1411), which states, "A secondary messianic figure is the Messiah son of Joseph (or Ephraim), whose coming precedes that of the Messiah, son of David, and who will die in combat with the enemies of God and Israel. Joseph Smith and his martyrdom could already be a fulfillment of this role."[18]

Dix notes that he will be from the injured tribe of Joseph, "The Messiah [*ben Joseph*] will spring from the persecuted tribe of Ephraim, such as from Joseph, who is here the object of Jacob's blessing."[19] Joseph Smith is, according to Joseph F. McConkie, the "suffering Servant."[20] Raphael Patai testifies to the same: "Talmudic legend unhesitatingly identifies him with the Messiah, and understands specially the descriptions of his suffering as referring to Messiah ben Joseph."[21]

According to the early Jewish writing, *baraithot* of Zechariah, this *Messiah ben Joseph* was to be martyred and his death caused by being "pierced."[22] As Jesus was pierced by nails, so Joseph Smith was pierced by bullets, thus fulfilling this prophecy. Joseph's death came while combating a lawless mob on 27 June 1844. Anti-Mormons have insisted that Joseph was not martyred because he fought to his last breath.[23] The idea of Joseph "going down fighting" rather than letting the evil mob have their way is an acceptable form of martyrdom.

What Klausner and others do not say is that *Messiah ben Joseph* (Joseph Smith) would be a literal direct descendant of *Messiah ben Judah* (Jesus Christ)[24] (see D&C 113:3–6). The idea that in the last days, one would come to prepare the way for the second coming of Christ, as John the Baptist [*Messiah ben Aaron*] did for the first coming, seems appropriate.[25] But in the last days all three would come, as Joseph Fielding McConkie writes: "If we let 'the Prophet' have reference to Joseph Smith (*Messiah ben Joseph*), the 'priestly messiah' to John the Baptist (*Messiah ben Aaron*), and the 'lay messiah' to Christ (*Messiah ben David*) then all the parts of the puzzle fit snugly together."[26]

Jeremiah 30:21 sets the tone for this pattern, "His Mighty One shall proceed from himself and his Ruler come forth from his own midst (loins)." Edward G. King's commentary on this scripture remarks, "Certainly we could not blame any Jew who should see in these words a *Messiah ben Joseph*. This shall be 'in the latter days.'"[27] There is an extrabiblical prophecy by Joseph's mother, Rachel, "That Joseph would be the ancestor of the (Ephraimitic) Messiah, who would arise at the end of days."[28]

There is, a Samaritan tradition that the name Joseph is *Taheb* or "The Restorer."[29] Pharaoh gave Joseph the Egyptian name of *Zaphnath-paaneah*, which means "he who reveals that which is hidden" (Genesis 41:45; see 2 Nephi 3:7, 15). This latter-day restorer would be a revelator as well. His name Joseph in Hebrew, *Asaph*, means "God gathereth," or in Hebrew, *Yosef*, means "he shall add." Edward G. King notes that the restoration of the ten tribes and the return of Elijah were both "always associated with the Messiah ben Joseph."[30] We associate *Messiah ben Joseph* with Joseph Smith Jr.

Messiah ben Joseph is a direct descendant of Joseph of Egypt and of King David in that "far country" called *la Merica* (America). Thus with him the ingathering of the exiles has begun. He has come to prepare the way for the second coming of Jesus Christ, the true Messiah, against the formidable opposition of the anti-Christ. Although the Antichrist succeeded in martyring Jesus, the kingdom of God has been established and is now rolling forth. This breathes life into the idea that the Vermont native was a truly chosen Grail vessel of God to restore the gospel.

JOSEPH SMITH, "THE ROOT OF JESSE"

And there shall come forth a rod out of the stem of Jesse, and a Branch shall grow out of his roots.

—ISAIAH 11:1; 2 NEPHI 21:1

And in that day there shall be a root of Jesse, which shall stand for an ensign of the people; to it shall the Gentiles seek: and his rest shall be glorious.[31]

And it shall come to pass in that day that the Lord shall set his hand again the second time to recover the remnant of his people which shall be left. . . .

And he shall set up an ensign for the nations, and shall assemble the outcasts of Israel and gather together the dispersed of Judah from the four corners of the earth. The envy also of Ephraim shall depart and the adversaries of Judah shall be cut off: Ephraim shall not envy Judah and Judah shall not vex Ephraim.

—ISAIAH 11:10–13; 2 NEPHI 21:10–13

Isaiah 11:1 is confusing to many scholars. The identities of the "Rod," "Stem," "Branch," and "Roots" are highly speculative. Some LDS apostates such as Francis M. Darter incorrectly believe that the root of Jesse was John the Revelator.[32] Rev. J. H. Allen quotes Isaiah that "He (*God*) shall set up an ensign" and that this means the "root of Jesse."[33]

Most LDS scholars believe that Joseph Smith Jr. is both the rod and the root of Jesse.[34] Another smaller group believes that Joseph Smith is the rod but not the root.[35] Finally there is a group that thinks that the rod (verse 4) is a direct ancestor of the root (verse 6], who is Joseph Smith.[36] In Old Testament and Near Eastern texts, "root" is often used to mean "offspring," not "ancestor."[37] Sidney B. Sperry correctly believes that the "root of Jesse" spoken of in Doctrine and Covenants 113:5–6 was a direct reference to Joseph Smith Jr.[38]

To confuse the issue, McConkie uses Revelation 5:5, "the Lion of the tribe of Juda, the Root of David," to say that the "root of David" is Jesus Christ himself.[39] The Revelation 22:16 states: "I, Jesus have sent mine angel to testify unto you these things in the churches. I am the root and the offspring of David, and the bright and morning star."

The "root of Jesse" and the "root of David" are very close metaphors, but are they talking about the exact same person? It seems that from this root of the tribe of Judah sprang the "Stem," who according to Doctrine and Covenants 113:1–2 is Jesus Christ. The "Branch" which sprang from the "root of Jesse" is The Church of Jesus Christ of Latter-day Saints.[40] We know of no "Branch" springing from the "root of David." Therefore the "root of David" (Jesus Christ) is different from the "root of Jesse" (Joseph Smith).

Given as revelation in March 1838, Doctrine and Covenants 113:5–6 explains that the "root of Jesse" mentioned in Isaiah 11:10 would be a specific descendant of Jesse (Judah) and Joseph (Ephraim). Historically all Church general authorities and most LDS scholars clearly state that the "root of Jesse" has reference to Joseph Smith Jr. himself. In this sense, the Branch, or Church, grew out of Joseph's restoration of the gospel in 1830:

Behold, thus saith the Lord, it [the root of Jesse] is a descendant of Jesse, as well as of Joseph, upon whom rightly belongs the priesthood, and the keys of the kingdom, for an ensign, and for the gathering of my people in the last days."

—D&C 113:6

Joseph Smith specifically restored the "keys of the kingdom" in the last days (D&C 27:12–13; 81:2; 97:14; 115:19; 128:20). Thus it is certain that the "root of Jesse" is Joseph Smith Jr. But do we know or are we sure that Joseph was also the "rod of Jesse" of Doctrine and Covenants 113:3–4? No, for Hyrum Andrus gives the possibility of their being separate individuals:

> Since the Prophet said the priesthood and the keys of the kingdom would rightly belong to the figure symbolized as the root of Jesse, then, like the rod of Jesse, the person so represented would descend through the presiding lines of both Joseph and Judah. Therefore he would have a legal claim to the birthright over Israel and political power within the patriarchal order.[41]

Amazingly, the Grail knight Sir Galahad also had to establish his genealogical tree through two lines of descent. These were from Jesse (father of David) and Joseph (father of Ephraim) before he could take up the mystic sword of David (Kingship of All Israel).[42] It might be deduced that Galahad, like Joseph Smith, was of the royal Grail lineage. Andrew Sinclair notes: "Galahad, the son of Lancelot by the daughter of the Fisher King and *the descendant of [both] King David and Joseph,* had sat in the Siege [seat] Perilous at the Round Table, the Judas seat which tipped any imperfect knight into hell."[43]

Thus we see that, as in Doctrine and Covenants 113:3–6, it must be a descendant of Jesse and Joseph who by right could sit at the head chair (Seat Perilous). It was Joseph Smith Jr. who as the latter-day Sir Galahad, by descent through two lineages, found the Great Mystery of the Holy Grail. He too put together the two pieces of the broken sword, which had wounded the Fisher King.[44] The "wound in the thigh" is a signature limp or lameness sign or stigmata of the true Fisher King. The wasteland turned green (starting the Millennial paradisiacal process), or as Isaiah 35:1 says, "The desert shall blossom as a rose." With this sword Galahad-Joseph Smith cut loose and restored the "woman in the wilderness" (the lost or hidden Church) (see Plate 30).[45]

The malefic enchantments cursing the earth began to diminish once Joseph Smith, as Sir Galahad, found his Holy Grail family through revelation. In the *Quest of the Holy Grail* we read of the true knight's quest:

> For this is no search for earthly things but a seeking out of the mysteries and hidden sweets of Our Lord, and the divine secrets which the most high Master will disclose to that blessed knight whom He has chosen for His servant from among the ranks of chivalry: he to whom He will show the marvels of the Holy Grail, and reveal that which the heart of man could not conceive nor tongue relate.[46]

Joseph Smith as such, is a Grail knight chosen from chivalry. And, like Galahad, he too saw the Grail openly and did not remain on the earth afterward for very long. He too could say as Galahad did upon seeing the Holy Vessel: "Lord, I worship Thee and give Thee thanks that Thou has granted my desire, for now I see revealed what tongue could not relate nor heart conceive. Here is the source of valour undismayed, the spring-head of endeavour; here I see the wonder that passes every other!"[47]

It should also be remembered that his right to such a vision comes from the "Stem of Jesse," which has reference to the Savior, Jesus Christ (D&C 113:1–2). From the Messiah's lineage would come two descendant knights. The first personage, the "rod or branch," in this model, would be the son of Jesus Christ and Mary Magdalene, "the rod of Jesse" the first of the *Shiloh-Dynasty* (D&C 113:3–4).[48]

Second, would come a latter-day personage, a dispensation head, called the "root of Jesse" (D&C 113:5–6). The "root" is therefore a literal descendant of the "rod." Thus there are two separate patriarchs, whom we might call *Shiloh ben Jesus* and *Messiah ben Joseph* respectively.[49] They are directly connected by a long chain of descendants, stretching some eighteen hundred years and accounting for an estimated sixty-six and seventy-two generations.

Through the genealogy of Jesus Christ and the birthright lineage of Mary Magdalene (the chalice) to this very day, this bloodline has had a noble purpose. Brigham Young once announced, "You understand who we are; we are of the house of Israel, of the royal seed, of the royal blood."[50] Can we postulate the identity of the legitimate heir, the King's Son, in the last days, across the vast reaches of time? We can, by projecting evidence and argument along logical paths. While this is not proof, it does give indications of plausibility.

The significance of Brigham Young's observation of the royal seed and blood was underscored by Orson Pratt who said, "It being expressly declared that the children of one of His [Christ's] wives shall be made Prince in all the earth."[51] The second personage, "root of Jesse," or *Messiah ben Joseph,* will be possessed of four gifts: 1) the priesthood, 2) the royal keys of the kingdom, 3) be an ensign (leader), and 4) be the gatherer of Israel in the last days.

This person is Joseph Smith Jr. (*Messiah ben Joseph*). One day when all the branches of this lineage are made known, it will be seen that this is the most prestigious family in all the annals of world history. Erastus Snow, in 1882, when he spoke of the seed of Ephraim, followed the same reasoning:

> Their blood has permeated European society and it coursed in the veins of the early colonists of America. And when (the) books shall be opened and the lineage of all men is known, it will be found that they have been first and foremost in everything noble among men in the various nations in breaking off the shackles of king-craft and priest-craft and oppression of every kind, and the foremost among men in upholding and maintaining the principles of liberty and freedom upon this continent (America) and establishing a representative government, and thus preparing the way for the coming forth of the fullness of the everlasting gospel.[52]

Who is the righteous *branch,* which will grow from the *root* in the last days and be gathered? It is the LDS Church membership, who are the seed of the *root of Jesse,* Joseph Smith, and the *root of David,* Jesus Christ. Orson Hyde spoke along the same lines as Erastus Snow:

> And he who has not the blood of Abraham flowing in his veins, who has not one particle of the Savior's [blood] in him, I am afraid is a stereotyped Gentile, who will be left out and not be gathered in the last days; for I tell you it is the chosen of God, the seed of the blessed [Savior] that shall be gathered. . . .

That seed [of Christ] has had its influence upon the chosen of God in the last days. The same spirit inspires them that inspires their father, who bled and died upon the cross after the manner of the flesh.[53]

In the last days the Lord raised up one who would restore the proper balance.[54] Yet, there is much more to it than that. In Doctrine and Covenants 110:11 we are told that Joseph Smith received from Moses the keys of the gathering of Israel in the latter time. This is one of the ensigns of the root of Jesse.

Consequently we see the significance of the angel Moroni quoting the entire eleventh chapter of Isaiah to the young Joseph Smith, emphasizing his lineage. Thus Joseph, the scion of Ephraim, was a precious part of the lost lineage of the Grail family that separated from England and came to America. He was the proverbial Masonic "widow's son"! The Inspired Version (JST) of the Bible notes that through the loins of Joseph a righteous branch would arise. Joseph of Egypt speaks of an event in the last days and expressly identifies Joseph Smith Jr.:

> And it shall come to pass that they shall be scattered again; and a branch shall be broken off, and shall be carried into a far country; nevertheless they shall be remembered in the covenants of the Lord, when the Messiah cometh; for he shall be made manifest unto them in the latter days.
>
> —JST Genesis 50:25
> (See also v. 33)[55]

Thus we see Joseph Smith's lineage as the "root of Jesse," allowed for him to receive the Holy Grail, the priesthood, the ordinances, the revelations, and the genealogy. The Church of Jesus Christ of Latter-day Saints grew as a *branch* out of this *root* and its faithful members are its seed.

JOSEPH CAME WITH CREDENTIALS AND POWER

I will build on the foundation of his [Joseph Smith's] claims and rights.

—BRIGHAM YOUNG[56]

The *bona fides* of any true prophet rest in their ability to restore lost knowledge and authority, heal the breach in the soul, and build Zion upon the earth. The veracity of any prophet rests in validating their claims. The Egyptian restoration concept of *Ma'at* feather comes to mind. It is a bundle of ideas around "truth, justice, fairness, harmony, and moral rectitude as symbolized by the regular purity of the perfectly upright and square foundations of a temple."[57]

These ideas are blended in Joseph Smith's values of "promoting the kindness of society, the knowledge of Science, the beauty of art, and the spirituality of theology.[58] For Joseph, truth was a shining purity, not something between unnourishing poverty and the encrustation of false traditions of the fathers. Joseph Smith, like Mark Twain, believed that "loyalty to petrified opinion, never broke a chain or freed a human soul" (see Plate 31).[59]

The complexities of the world were not for enigma's sake but for variety to gladden the eye. To be sure, his mission was to bring the understanding and revelation of God and the kingdom to these last days in a clear not mystical fashion. John Locke knowingly wrote as much: "To know that if any revelation is from God, it is necessary to know that the Messenger that delivers it is sent from God, and that cannot be known but by credentials given by God himself."[60]

The Lord set his hand to recover Zion a second time through Joseph Smith Jr. who came with credentials. What exactly were they? At least five original concurrent lines of authority intersected to verify Joseph's license to restore the rejected gospel:

1. The high position he held in premortality for the salvation of the world (Archangel).

2. His ordination in premortality for his mission on this earth (Dispensation Head and Prophet).

3. He was born through a special bloodline channel, which qualified him to receive certain promises (combined Ephraim and Judah lineage).

4. The keys, blessings, revelations, and instruments he received by divine intervention and angelic ministration (priesthood, endowments, scripture, and Urim and Thummim, and so forth).

5. His personal worthiness and valiance in carrying out his duties. (He restored the gospel, passed it on, and sealed his testimony with his life.)

All told, he was the antidote to what ailed the earth. That false priests and professors had formulated dogmas, which defined their conflicting creeds, was proof that an apostasy had occurred. "The fact that Christianity has split into over 20,000 denominations worldwide is evidence of this tendency."[61] The need of a true prophet to initiate the restoration of the true gospel was now greater than ever before. Ralph Waldo Emerson wrote along these lines during the same generation as Joseph Smith:

> The need was never greater for new revelation than now . . . [there has been] a universal decay and now almost death of faith in society. The soul is not preached. The church seems to totter to its fall, almost all life extinct . . . Men have come to speak of revelation as somewhat long ago, given and done, as if God were dead. The injury to faith throttles the preacher, and the godliest of institutions becomes an uncertain and inarticulate voice.
>
> We are now so far from the road of truth, that religious teachers dispute and hate each other. . . . The forgoing generations beheld God and nature face to face; we through their eyes. Why should not we have a poetry and philosophy of insight and not of tradition, and a religion by revelation to us?
>
> I look for the hour when the supreme beauty, which ravished the souls of those eastern men and chiefly of those Hebrews, and through their lips spoke oracles to all times, shall speak in the West also. . . . I look for the teacher that shall follow so far those shining laws that he shall see them come full circle. . . . And shall show that the right, and the duty is one thing with science, with beauty and with joy.[62]

How close Emerson was to the mark! The world had suffered for centuries in a great apostasy. Yet, the Spirit of God continued to manifest itself, but not the true Church of God. Then, in Emerson's own generation came Joseph Smith Jr., who had authority vested in him. He brought the church out of hiding or captivity by the restoration of the priesthood, which he was privileged to through his vaulted lineage.

This flesh-and-blood inheritance which was "hid from the world" during the Great Apostasy was the lineage of the royal and birthright chosen seed. The scriptures, particularly Doctrine and Covenants 107:40, amplify this understanding: *The order of this priesthood was confirmed to be handed down from father to son, and rightly belongs to the literal descendants of the chosen seed, to whom the promises were made.*

Hyrum Smith was appointed to take his father's place as patriarch by blessing and also by right (D&C 124:91). This dual basis for patrilineal priesthood authority is manifested in "Abraham's patriarchal power."[63] All other keys of ecclesiastical and family government are subsumed within this highest authoritative power. Thus Joseph Smith, with the help of Oliver Cowdery, was able to restore the Aaronic Order of the Melchizedek Priesthood, both by blessing and by right.[64] This highest command of the powers of heaven, writes Joseph Fielding Smith, comes through lineage, righteousness, and ordination: "Joseph Smith, father of the Prophet, received the birthright in Israel which he inherited through his fathers back to Ephraim and Joseph and Jacob and Abraham. For that reason the patriarchal priesthood was conferred upon him with the commandment that it should be handed down from father to son."[65]

Yet, anti-Mormons are forever pointing out that Joseph Smith could not hold this priesthood because he was not of the tribe of Levi nor a descendant of Aaron. They also challenge the means by which this order of the priesthood was bestowed. But Joseph had the full birthright authority of the patriarch Jacob, later divided between Judah (David), Joseph (Ephraim), and Levi (Aaron).[66] Not until Joseph Smith was the authority of the three tribes was the full authority centered again in one patriarchal person. Centuries earlier, before Aaron possessed the rights of priesthood that were given to Levi by assignment, it was found in Jacob.

Thus Joseph had the right, upon command of the angel, to baptize Oliver Cowdery.[67] We do not have all the details of their baptism and ordination. But it should be noted that numerous ancient individuals performed the duties of an Aaronic priest without actually being of that Cohen lineage.[68] Hyrum Andrus focuses on Joseph's claims and credentials:

These facts suggest that by right of lineage he was a natural heir in the flesh to the powers, promises, and blessings of the eternal family. The question could be asked, Would God choose a man to initiate and direct such a work who did not meet these qualifications? . . .

The fact that the persons represented by the rod and the root were to descend from both Ephraim and Jesse indicates that the presiding blood lines of those two families would have to merge into one, and that the right to the keys of both the birthright and of political power within the divine family order would center in one man, of family, in the last days.

This suggests that to identify the presiding family of Ephraim was also to identify the presiding line of Judah. If Joseph Smith was born in that line which had a right to the birthright of Ephraim, he must also have had the right by lineage to royal, or political, power within the divine patriarchal order.[69]

Thus we see that Joseph's credentials came partially through his "Shiloh" lineage of Ephraim and Judah. God has always worked through birthright inheritance conferred from father to son, like the priesthood. The fact that God required a living, breathing, modern spokesman necessitated that He work through a well-defined channel or chain of command. The prophets, seers, and revelators of God are the Grail seed and inheritors of the authority of God. God's house is a house of order.

NOTES

1. The angel Moroni appeared to Joseph Smith in September of 1823 and announced "that the fulness of the Gentiles was soon to come in" (Joseph Smith–History 1:41.) A multitude of nations (posterity of Joseph of Egypt) was established when Joseph Smith restored the gospel to the gentiles (see D&C 45:24–30; JST Luke 21:24–32; 3 Nephi 16:7–11; D&C 21:10–12; 85:8–11; 90:6–9).

2. *Evening and Morning Star* 1, 6, (November 1832).

3. Brigham Young, in *Journal of Discourses* (17 April 1853), 2:127a.

4. Allen, *Judah's Sceptre and Joseph's Birthright*, 242.

5. King, *Yalkut of Zechariah*, 85–86.

6. Orson Pratt, in *Journal of Discourses* (7 February 1875), 17:302b.

7. G. H. Dix, "The Messiah Ben Joseph," *Journal of Theological Studies* 27 (1926): 132–33.

8. Godwin, *Holy Grail*, 160. See also page 204: the Shiites (Islamic sect) still await the Virgin Pairidaeza (Paradise?), who will give birth to the Mahdi, the moon-guided messiah and savior known as the Desired Knight. Through the Shiite order, the Assassins, the Templars adopted this idea. Thus this heresy was spread to Europe.

9. Later it would be divided again with Levi and the sons of Aaron.

10. See *Encyclopedia Judaica*, 1:11: "According to the Talmud, the Messiah will be a descendant of the House of David and will be preceded by a secondary Messiah from the House of Joseph. When the Chief Rabbi, Avraham Hakohen Kook, was appointed in Palestine in the 1920s, he was asked if the Jews could now build the temple (destroyed since the year A.D. 70). His response was that the priestly rights were gone and referred to the great twelfth-century Rabbi Moses Maimonides. Maimonides said, in effect, "'We are waiting for the Messiah Ben Joseph, to him will be given the keys to the gathering of Israel, He will restore temple worship.'"

11. Skousen, *Third Thousand Years*, 156.

12. Charles C. Torrey, "The Messiah Son of Ephraim," *Journal of Biblical Literature* 66 (1947): 253, as quoted in McConkie, *His Name Shall Be Joseph*, 16. I am indebted to Brother McConkie for his excellent treatise on the subject.

13. Solomon Zeitlin, "The Essenes and Messianic Expectations," *Jewish Quarterly Review* 45 (1955): 107. The Messiah ben Joseph is, according to this tradition, to be killed, following which the Messiah ben David is to make his triumphant appearance. See McConkie, *His Name Shall Be Joseph*, 17.

14. Klausner, *Messianic Idea in Israel*, 204. The idea of Zechariah 12:10 being a messiah from the tribe of Joseph and being killed by the House of David was used to counter Christian attacks that the Jews had killed their own Messiah. The Yalkut Talmud was written to refute such arguments.

15. Klausner, *Messianic Idea in Israel*, 486–87, 498, 496; Skousen, *Third Thousand Years*, 156 onward. The author has relied upon Cleon Skousen's interpretations, realizing as Skousen does, that Klausner had other explanations for these same traditions. Skousen quotes Joseph Klausner extensively, and chapter 9 of *Third Thousand Years* is devoted exclusively to this subject.

16. Also noted in Burrows, *More Light on the Dead Sea Scrolls*, 299–311. In fact, Elijah did return on 3 April 1836 to the Kirtland Temple to restore the keys of sealing families.

17. Hebrew Book of Enoch (45:5). See Odeberg, trans., *3 Enoch or the Hebrew Book of Enoch*, 44.

18. Ludlow, *Isaiah*, 177. Interestingly, Joseph Smith died fighting the mob.

19. G. H. Dix, "The Messiah Ben Joseph," *Journal of Theological Studies* 27 (1926): 131–33.

20. McConkie, *His Name Shall Be Joseph*, 28, 116–18.

21. Patai, *Messiah Texts*, xxiii.

22. Moore, *Judaism in the First Centuries of the Christian Era*, 2:370. See Baraithot of Zechariah 12:10. The idea that Jesus Christ was also "pierced" at his death adds a parallel to this analogy.

23. One should remember that Jesus Christ's acquiescence to the mob was because he was a "willing sacrifice" of the Atonement, not just as a martyr for the cause.

24. Joseph Smith was an Ephraimite through the mtDNA and Judah through the Y chromosome directly from the Christ.

25. Bernheim, *James, the Brother of Jesus*, 71. The texts at Qumran speak of two Messiahs, a royal David Messiah and a priestly Messiah descended from Aaron. Certainly

this would be Christ and John the Baptist in the Meridian of Time.

26. McConkie, *His Name Shall Be Joseph,* 161.

27. King, *Yalkut of Zechariah,* 87. (See Genesis 49:1.)

28. Parentheses in original quotation. Ginzberg, *Legends of the Jews,* 5:299; see also Patai, *Messiah Text,* 165, as quoted in McConkie, *His Name Shall Be Joseph,* 162. Jesus was not a descendant of Joseph of Egypt, but Joseph Smith was a direct descendant of this Joseph and of Jesus Christ.

29. Bruce, *Biblical Exegesis in the Qumran Texts,* as quoted in McConkie, *His Name Shall Be Joseph,* 161. Other meanings include "he who returns" or "he who causes to return."

30. King, *Yalkut of Zechariah,* 97. He mentions a "very old Jewish tradition that Edom (i.e., 'the world power,' Arab) can only fall by the hands of Joseph" (91).

31. Keil and Delitzsch, *Commentary on the Old Testament,* 6:288, translates it thus: "And it will come to pass in that day: the root-sprout of Jesse, which stands as a banner of the peoples, for it will nations ask, and its place of rest is glory."

32. Darter, "Root of Jesse," in *Zion's Redemption,* 30–37. It "appears that John the Revelator is to be the latter-day prophet, referred to by Isaiah, as the 'Root of Jesse'" (30). Darter believes that the priesthood rightly belongs to John the Revelator and that Doctrine and Covenants 113:5–6 mentions the priesthood rightfully belonging to a person; therefore, John is the "root of Jesse." He says that since Salome was John's mother, who supposedly was Mary's sister, that John had the right to the priesthood and that he came from the same root of Jesse. His research does not hold up to modern scholarship.

33. Allen, *Judah's Sceptre and Joseph's Birthright,* 351.

34. McConkie, *Millennial Messiah,* 339–40. See also Shute, Nyman, and Bott, *Ephraim.* The anonymous writer of a manuscript (in author's possession) on the subject of the LDS Holy Grail, writes: "Joseph was the rod during his first ministry and will be the root during his second—or perhaps it is the other way around" (55). Or perhaps this is not true at all.

35. Andrus, *Doctrinal Commentary on the Pearl of Great Price,* 463–64.

36. These include Matthew Brown, Cleon Skousen, Vern G. Swanson, and Martin Tanner. The Rod is a child of Jesus Christ, according to this theory.

37. Jackson, "Revelations Concerning Isaiah (D&C 86:113)," in Jackson and Millet, *Studies in Scripture,* 1:332 n.7.

38. Sperry, *Doctrine and Covenants Compendium* 616–17.

Like Bruce R. McConkie, Sperry believed that the Rod and the root were the same person.

39. Bruce R. McConkie says that "Christ is the Root of David" (*Mormon Doctrine,* 657) and *Doctrinal New Testament Commentary,* 3:472.

40. Shute, Nyman, and Bott, *Ephraim,* 57, write, "The branch is apparently The Church of Jesus Christ of Latter-day Saints established in these the last days."

41. Andrus, *Doctrines of the Kingdom,* 536.

42. Sinclair, *Discovery of the Grail,* 53. According to Sinclair, the Sword of David was made by his son Solomon. It had a stone pommel which contained all the colors found on earth, each with its own virtue in magic and science. The hilt had two ribs, one made from the (white?) salamander or serpent of wisdom, the other from a Euphrates fish, a symbol of induced forgetfulness and purpose (the veil?).

43. Sinclair, *Discovery of the Grail,* 52. Sadly, Sinclair does not follow up this insight, not realizing the significance of his statement regarding "David and Joseph."

44. Some say it was the spear from Balin's delorous blow" that wounded the Fisher King.

45. Sir Frank Dicksee (1853–1928), England, *Chivalry* (1885, oil on canvas, 72" x 53 ¾"). Courtesy of John Schaeffer, Sydney Australia. M Girouard's book *The Return to Camelot* shows the ideal of chivalry preoccupied the Victorians. The author has imputed this meaning to this painting. See also John Everett Millais (1829–1896), British, *Knight Errant* (1870, oil on canvas) in the Tate Gallery, London. Here the woman is depicted nude as a representation of purity and innocence in the primitive Christian church. In both pictures the knight frees the Church (woman) from the bondage of the apostasy and "restores" her to her rightful place.

46. *Quest of the Holy Grail,* 47, and *Queste del Saint Graal,* 19, as quoted in Barber, *Holy Grail,* 165.

47. As quoted in Barber, *Holy Grail,* 220–21.

48. Most LDS scholars note that both the stem and root of Jesse allude to Joseph Smith Jr. McConkie, *His Name Shall Be Joseph,* 42, incorrectly concludes, "The servant spoken of in verses four and six of this revelation clearly appears to be Joseph Smith." This author, however, disagrees with him and other scholars, noting that these verses refer to two separate people from two ends of the same lineage.

49. Instead of Shiloh ben Jesus, we might also call the son of Jesus and Mary Magdalene Joseph bar Jesus (Shalom ben Joseph).

50. Brigham Young, in *Journal of Discourses* (8 April 1855), 2:269b. See also ibid. (14 April 1867), 12:33; (7 February 1858), 6:199; (25 May 1873), 16:75.

51. Orson Pratt, *The Seer* 1, 11 (November 1853): 172 (Psalm 45:16). It has been asked, Who is "David the Prince" who is to come forth through Joseph in the last days? In my opinion it will be a descendant of Joseph Smith Jr. or Joseph himself as a resurrected being.

52. Erastus Snow, in *Journal of Discourses* (6 May 1882), 23:185–86. This is one of the first times that a rehearsal of the dispersion of Ephraim was expounded in the British-Israel sense by a Church leader.

53. Orson Hyde, in *Journal of Discourses* (6 October 1854), 2:82–83.

54. See Jeremiah 31:9: "and Ephraim is my firstborn."

55. Later, in JST Genesis 50:31, we have reference to Joseph and Judah "grow[ing] together." Perhaps this is a reference to Ezekiel 37. The prophesied branch will be a servant of the Lord (Zechariah 3:8). This branch will be raised up to David (Jesse's son) (Jeremiah 23:5, 33:15). Joseph Smith as a premortal spirit coming to earth took up the lineage of both Joseph and Judah.

56. Brigham Young, in "A Family Meeting in Nauvoo: Minutes of a Meeting of the Richards and Young Families Held in Nauvoo, Ill., 8 January, 1845," *Utah Genealogical and Historical Magazine* 11 (July 1920): 109.

57. Knight and Lomas, *Hiram Key,* 144.

58. Ibid. Knight and Lomas are not LDS; in fact, they are anti-Christians, and I have borrowed their terminology only because it adequately expresses the essence of Joseph Smith's teachings.

59. John Henri Moser (1876–1951), Logan, Utah, *Portrait of Joseph Smith* (1930, oil on canvas, 32" x 26"). Courtesy Springville Museum of Art, Springville, Utah.

60. Locke, *Discourse of Miracles,* in *The Works of John Locke,* 9:250–65.

61. Freke and Gandy, *Jesus and the Goddess,* 10, 212 ff9. These gnostic believers, however, fail to say that their Gnosticism has no absolute doctrine or creed and is interpreted in many conflicting ways by each believer. It is a personal approach to religion but not a religion per se.

62. Carpenter, *Ralph Waldo Emerson,* 79–80. Statement to the Cambridge Divinity School.

63. Ehat and Cook, *Words of Joseph Smith* (27 August 1843), 245.

64. As a patriarchal head, the Prophet Joseph united the prerogatives of the birthright; priesthood (Melchizedek and Aaronic), and kingship.

65. Smith, *Way to Perfection,* 128.

66. Of course, if Oliver Cowdery was a Levite of the lineage of Aaron, then criticism would be muted or assuaged. It should be remembered that "all priesthood is Melchizedek," and according to Doctrine and Covenants 107:5, "All other authorities or offices in the church are appendages to this priesthood" (see D&C 107:14; 84:29–30).

67. Joseph Smith, by birthright inheritance, had the right to baptize Oliver Cowdery and confer the Priesthood of Aaron (since he was commanded by John the Baptist, an angel holding that authority) even though he had not yet received this ordinance himself (see Joseph Smith–History 2:69–71). Brigham Young was adamant that one could not officiate in an ordinance that one had not already received. In this case the authority was there. I do not believe that Oliver Cowdery would have had sufficient authority within himself to have baptized Joseph first.

68. The Sons of Zadoc (Sadducean temple high priests) may have also been of the tribe of Judah, not just of the priests of Levi.

69. Andrus, *Doctrines of the Kingdom,* 537–39.

PART EIGHT

LATTER-DAY ISRAEL

*Go into your gardens and take a cucumber vine,
and do you not know that in the latter part of the
season you will find the largest and longest at the
most extended part of the vine?*

—HEBER C. KIMBALL[1]

 n old Pentecostal hymn "There's Power in the Blood" boldly announces that it is through the blood of Jesus Christ that all men are saved. Non-Latter-day Saint Christians believe it was the blood shed on the cross of Calvary that is the salvation of man. Mormons have added the blood shed in Gethsemane as having equal or perhaps superior atonal value. There is a third place in which the blood of Jesus Christ has atonal worth for the salvation of mankind. It was not only in the blood He shed but also in the bloodline He perpetuated through his royal seed that had power to "save."

It is with respect and honor that we now focus on Joseph Smith Jr. In John 8:56, Jesus declares, "Your father Abraham rejoiced to see my day: he saw it, and was glad." We could say the same thing about Jesus: He saw Joseph Smith's day "and was glad." In September 1842, the *Times and Seasons* predicted that the world would eventually "prove Joseph Smith a true prophet."[2] Brigham Young speaks for us all: "I feel like shouting hallelujah, all the time, when I think that I even knew Joseph Smith, the Prophet whom the Lord raised up and ordained, and to whom He gave keys and power to build up the kingdom of God on earth and sustain it."[3]

Plate 1: Sir Lawrence Alma-Tadema (1836–1912), *Joseph, Overseer of Pharaoh's Graneries* (Opus CXXIV, 1874, oil on board, 13" x 17"). Collection Dahesh Museum of Art, New York City.

Plate 2: Steven Adam (?–1910), British, *The Marriage of the Lamb and His Bride* (c. 1906–1910, stained-glass window). Located at St. Mary's Kilmore Church in Dervaig, Isle of Mull, Scotland. The window was probably meant to represent Christ and the Church, but its verisimilitude gives the impression that it is an actual marriage between Mary of Bethany and Jesus Christ. An inscription quotes Luke 10:42, mentioning Bethany.

Plate 3: John Melhuish Strudwick (1849–1937)
British, *The Ten Virgins* (1883, oil on canvas, 29" x 60").
Courtesy of John Schaeffer, Melbourne Australia.

Plate 4: Unknown artist, Spanish-colonial, *Joseph of Arimathea with a Child of Jesus* (seventeenth-century, oil on tin, 10 1/8" x 8 ½"). Painting in the possession of Brian Kershisneck of Kanab, Utah. The work possibly represents Joseph of Arimathea with the son of Jesus and holding a budding or flowering staff, or perhaps Jesus Himself with His son.

Plate 5: Nicolàs Rodriguez Juarez (1667–1734) Mexico City, *The Holy Family* (1690, o/panel, 13" x 17 ½"). Courtesy of Christie's New York Old Masters. The painting is meant by the artist to portray the Virgin Mary and Joseph with the Christ child. However, it is used here to represent Mary Magdalene and Jesus with their firstborn son in their hands.

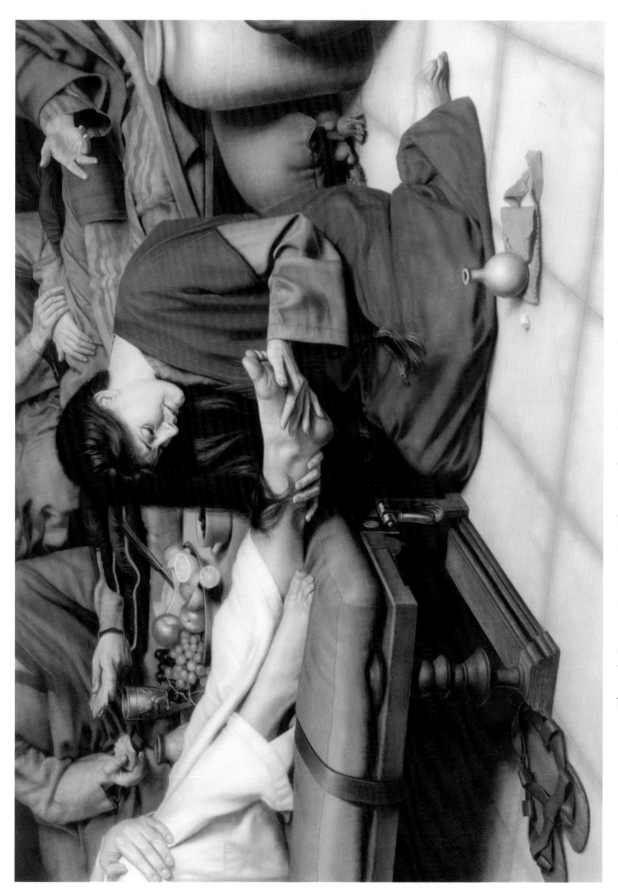

Plate 6: Simon Dewey, *For She Loved Much* (2001, acrylic on canvas). Courtesy of the artist. Here is Mary Magdalene washing and anointing Christ's feet at the House of Simon the Pharisee in Galilee.

Plate 7: Gustave Moreau (1826–1898) French, *La Licorne* (1884–85, oil on canvas, 19 7/8" x 13 3/8"). Christie's London, 24 November 2004 (23). We are not sure of the woman's identification, but for our purposes she perfectly fits the image of Mary Magdalene, crowned and robed, with the symbol of her tribe, the white unicorn. Her nudity represents the bride as chastity and the Christian church.

Plate 8: Michel Sytal, *Mary, Mother of Jesus* (sixteenth-century, oil on panel) from a reproduction in Bruce E. Dana book written in Chinese (ZITO, 2003) page 90. It originally depicts the Virgin Mary, but could just as easily be Mary Magdalene kneeling in a garden before the throne of God, receiving her crown and benediction of exaltation from the Father and the Son.

Plate 9: William Blake (1757–1827) British, *Christ the Mediator: Christ Pleading Before the Father for St. Mary Magdalene* (c. 1799, pen and grey ink and tempera on canvas, 10 ¾" x 15 ¼"). From the collection of the late George Goyder, C.B.E., his sale at Christie's London, 14 June 2005 (10). There is no biblical text for the subject, but in general it is derived from 1 Timothy 2:5, "For there is one God, and one scripture." 1 John 2:1 notes, "My little children, these things write I to you, that ye sin not. And if any man sin, we have an advocate with the Father, Jesus Christ the righteous." In this picture Mary Magdalene may represent all mankind as a whole.

Plate 10: Raphael (1483–1520) Italian, *Portrait of a Lady with a Unicorn* (c. 1505–06, oil on wood transferred to canvas, 67.8 x 53 cm) From the collection of the Museo e Galleria de Villa Borghese, Rome (inv. 371). It was once titled *Portrait of Maddelena Doni.*

Plate 11: Side of Church of St. Sarah, Les-Saints-Maries-de-la-Mer in the Camargue delta of the Rhône River, France. Embedded into the south wall of this eleventh-century fortress church are two carved animals in a much older marble, set into an indented arch. To the left is a she lion and cub, and to the right is possibly a unicorn or a male lion.

Plate 12: Unknown artist, Northern France, *The Stuttgart Psalter: Crucifixion of Christ*, (820–830, painted miniature). From Württemburgische Landesbibliothek, Stuttgart, Germany. (Bibl. fol. 23, fol. 27r) The Grail chalice can be seen between unicorn of Ephraim and the lion of Judah. The Psalter probably illustrates Psalm 22:21.

Plate 13: Unknown artist, *The High Priestess* (fifteenth-century, tempera on paper). Supposedly this card is from a tarot pack. See Knight and Lomas, *The Second Messiah*, 1997, 90. The columns represent Boaz and Jachin, the families of Judah and Ephraim

Plate 14: Unknown artist, France, *Utrecht Psalter: Catching the Blood at Calvary* (Universiteitsbibliothek der Rijksuniversiteit, Utrecht MS 32, f. 67). A miniature ink drawing illustrating Psalm 115 from Reims in the mid-ninth century (c.830). Illustrated in Richard Barber, *The Holy Grail: Imagination and Belief*, 2004, 121. See K. Van der Horst (editor), Utrecht Psalter in Medieval Art (1996).

Plate 15: Unknown artist, *The Deposition* (twelfth-century, miniature). From the collection of Abbey of Weingarten, Landesbibliothek Fulda, South Germany. (MS Aa35, fol 81: Bildarchiv Foto Marburg). This miniature from a gospel book depicts the Deposition with Joseph of Arimathea collecting Christ's blood. This is, according to Richard Barber, 2004, page 124, (illustration), the first evidence of this tradition, nearly a hundred years before Robert de Boron.

Plate 16: Principato di Seborga, an independent principality near Bordighera. In the distance can be seen the French Riveria. This was the supposed hiding place for the Sadducees after their escape from Jerusalem. The Church of St. Barnard can be seen to the lower right.

Plate 17: General view of Les-Saintes-Maries-de-la-Mer in southern France. The Church of St. Sarah can be seen in the middle of the town.

Plate 18: John William Waterhouse (1849–1917) British, *Tristan and Isolde* (1916, oil on canvas, 42" x 32"). Courtesy of Frederick C. and Sherry L. Ross, New Jersey. The Celtic legend was retold by Sir Thomas Malory, of the couple who accidentally drank a love potion from a Grail. His name means "sadness." He was killed by the jealous King Mark, husband of Isolde. She died of grief and was buried beside Tristan; a vine grew entwining their graves.

Plate 19: Gloria Montgomery, Utah *"Joseph of Arimathea's Budding Rod of Glastonbury"* (2004, pencil drawing).

Plate 20: Brian Kershisknek (1960–   ) Kanab Utah, *The 'Children' of Joseph of Arimathea* (2003, oil on board). Courtesy Diane and Sam Stewart collection. The painting depicts Joseph of Arimathea with a blossoming staff and the children of Christ, who were called the "children of Joseph of Arimathea" for their own protection.

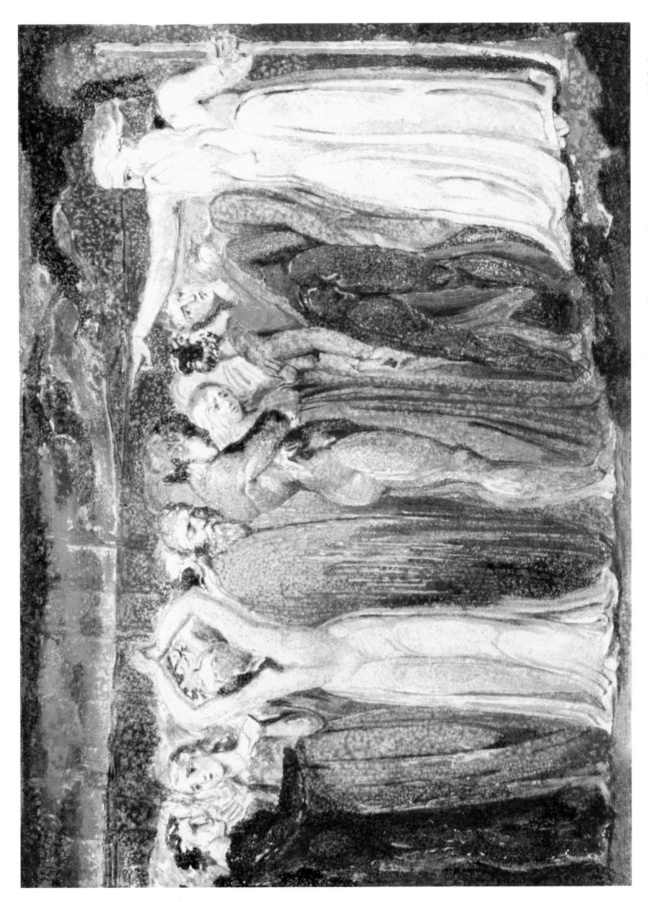

Plate 21: William Blake (1757–1827), *Joseph of Arimathea preaching to the inhabitants of Britain* (nd, tempera painting). Blake's portrayal of the Arimathean was one of a number he painted of Joseph of Arimathea. Courtesy of Sir Geoffrey Keynes Coll., Cambridgeshire, UK, and Bridgeman Art Library International.

Plate 22: The eleventh-century Cistercian Valle Cruses Abbey on the Plain of Maelor in Valley Eglywsey very near Llangolan, is on the sacred Dee River in North Wales. It was here that the Virgin Mary was supposedly taken for safety. Reproduction courtesy of Tony and Traci Fieldsted, Springville.

Plate 23: Unknown artist's rendering of twelve huts in a circle, around the "old wattle church" depicts the settlement at Glastonbury sometime after Joseph of Arimathea's arrival in A.D. 37.

Plate 25: The Lady Chapel at the Abbey Ruins in Glastonbury, Somerset.

THE·PASSING·OF·ARTHUR·

THOU·THEREFORE·TAKE·MY·BRAND·EXCALIBAR·
AND·FLING·HIM·FAR·INTO·THE·MIDDLE·MERE·
WATCH·WHAT·THOU·SEEST·AND·LIGHTLY·BRING·
ME·WORD·

Plate 24: Sidney Harold Meteyard (1868–1947), *The Passing of Arthur* (nd, watercolor), sold Christie's London auction-house (June 1999). In a painting of the dying King Arthur we see him passing the sword, Excalibur, on to Galahad to be cast back into the lake (ocean?). Perhaps Excalibur represents the Sword of Judah in the same fashion as the Sword of Laban represents the Sword of Joseph/Ephraim? It might have been taken by St. Brendan to the promised land in A.D. 570.

Plate 26: Don Thorpe's photograph of the Hill Cumorah in upstate New York. This may possibly be the location of the records of the Celtic Church as well as the Nephite peoples. Used with permission.

Plates 27a & 27b: Never before illustrated and little remarked upon, center "Shiloh" or "Salaam" column at Rosslyn Chapel in Roslin, Scotland with detail of its capital. Its position between the Apprentice and Master columns is fraught with meaning regarding the Grail dynasty. Note the upper right of column's capital, where it has been chipped away. Perhaps this was the severed head of Brân the Blessed.

Plate 28: Photograph of the Tower of Magdale at Rennes-le-Château, France. The entire hoax of Rennes has badly damaged Grail studies. Courtesy of Tony and Traci Fieldsted.

Plate 29: Jan Van Scorel (1494–1562) Dutch, *Mary Magdalene* (1530, oil on canvas, 26" x 30"), Rijksmuseum, Amsterdam. Mary Magdalene in center and to the right can be seen the root-stump of promise.

Plate 30: Sir Frank Dicksee (1853–1928) England, *Chivalry* (1885, oil on canvas, 72" x 53 ¾") Courtesy of John Schaeffer, Sydney Australia.

Mark Girouard's book The Return to Camelot (1981) shows the ideal of chilvalry preoccupied the Victorians. The author has imputed this meaning into this painting. Also see John Everett Millais (1829–1896) British, *Knight Errant* (1870, oil on canvas) in the Tate Gallery, London. Here the woman is depicted nude as a representation of purity and innocence in the primitive Christian church. In both pictures the knight frees the Church (woman) from the bondage of the apostasy and "restores" her to her rightful place.

HENRI MOSER 1930

Plate 31: John Henri Moser (1876–1951) Logan, Utah, *Portrait of Joseph Smith* (1930, oil on canvas, 32" x 26"). Courtesy Springville Museum of Art, Springville, Utah.

Plate 32: David Wilson (1980–   ) Provo, Utah, *Joseph Smith, Proclaimed King of All Israel by Hosannahs* (2005, o/c, 24" x 18"). Courtesy of the Artist.

Plate 33: Charles Z. Landelle (1812–1908), France, *Angel of the Holy Grail* (1812, oil on canvas). Courtesy collection of Frederick C. and Sherry Ross, New Jersey.

Plate 34: James C. Christensen (1944–) Orem, Utah, *The Shiloh-Dynasty of the Holy Grail* (2005, acrylic on board, 12" x 11"), in possession of the artist. Between the arches of Rosslyn Chapel can be seen Jesus and Mary Magdalene. The lion represents the kingly scepter of Judah while the unicorn represents the birthright of Ephraim.

CHAPTER TWENTY
LEGAL HEIRS ACCORDING TO THE FLESH

He [God] has watched that family and that blood
as it has circulated from its fountain to the birth of
that man [Joseph Smith].

—BRIGHAM YOUNG[4]

The question remains, "Why did *God* the Father and the Son appear to Joseph Smith and not to someone else?" The answer is as fresh today as the spring morning in 1820 when they appeared to the barefoot lad. He was special because he was the family heir, "according to the flesh" (biologically), of the promised blessings. He was the legal successor of the inheritance of Israel. The scripture underscores this stream of logic:

> *Therefore, thus saith the Lord unto you, with whom the priesthood hath continued through the lineage of your fathers—For ye are lawful heirs, according to the flesh, and have been hid from the world with Christ in God—Therefore your life and the priesthood have remained, and must needs remain through you and your lineage until the restoration of all*

> *things spoken by the mouths of all the holy prophets since the world began.*
> —D&C 86:8–10
> (SEE ALSO D&C 113:8)

The vision of the Father and the Son was foretold in Isaiah, "The father to the children shall make known thy truth" (Isaiah 38:19). Joseph was "the lost sheep" about whom Christ said, "I am not sent but unto the lost sheep of the house of Israel" (Matthew 15:24). Joseph Smith was the lost birthright son and as such the legal heir according to the flesh. To whom else would Heavenly Father and the Son appear in the spring of 1820?

PURE EPHRAIMITE AND PURE JUDAH

Joseph [Smith Jr.] is a father to Ephraim and to all Israel in these last days.

—BRIGHAM YOUNG[5]

*The Book of Mormon came to Ephraim,
for Joseph Smith was a pure Ephraimite.*

—BRIGHAM YOUNG[6]

Joseph Smith is a biological descendant of Joseph (Ephraim) and Judah (Jesse). A particular "remnant of the seed of Joseph" was to be preserved "by the hand of God" for the purposes of God in the last days (Alma 46:24). While many lines of the remnant fell by the wayside, at least two remained pure, though somewhat benighted. Captain Moroni, an Ephraimite, wrote of a certain line being of the remnant of Joseph, which would remain true. He also spoke prophetically of the possible fall of the Nephite remnant:

Yea, let us preserve our liberty as a remnant of Joseph; yea, let us remember the words of Jacob, before his death, for behold, he saw that a part of the remnant of the coat of Joseph was preserved and had not decayed. And he said— Even as this remnant of garment of my son hath been preserved, so shall a remnant of the seed of my son be preserved by the hand of God, and be taken unto himself, while the remainder of the seed of Joseph shall perish, even as the remnant of his garment. . . . And now who knoweth but what the remnant of the seed of Joseph, which shall perish as his garment, are those who have dissented from us? Yea, and even it shall be ourselves if we do not stand fast in the faith of Christ.

—ALMA 46:24, 27

The lineage of Joseph through Ephraim prospered in the northern European clime. Though they were ignorant of the gospel they prospered

according to the word they possessed until the day that a restoration would occur. "Yea, and surely shall He again bring a remnant of the seed of Joseph to the knowledge of the *Lord* their *God*," writes Mormon (3 Nephi 5:23).

The lineages of the Messiah began to realize Joseph's dream in which Joseph became the most favored son of all the children of Israel (Jacob). Until the family tree could blossom through many generations and millions of people, exceptional care had to be taken to protect the "fruitful bough." Special royal lineages, called the true *Rex Deus*, were kept secret and anonymous until the time was ripe that it should bear fruit. Three very important quotations from Brigham Young, in 1845 and 1859, respectively, set the tone for this chapter:

That promised blood has trickled down through our parents until now we are here. I know who has the right to the Keys—the Prophet has!

That blood has been preserved and has been brought down through father to son, and our heavenly Father has been watching it all the time and saw the man that had received the blood pure through descent—that is what Joseph meant.[7]

His descent from Joseph that was sold into Egypt was direct and the blood was pure in him. That is why the Lord chose him and we are pure when this blood-strain from Ephraim comes down pure. The decrees of the Almighty will be exalted—that blood which was in him was pure and he had the sole right and lawful power, as he was the legal heir to the blood that has been on the earth and has come down through a pure lineage.

The union of various ancestors kept that blood pure. There is a great deal the people do not understand, and many of the Latter-day Saints have to learn all about it.[8]

The Lord had his eye upon him, and upon his father, and upon his father's father, and upon their progenitors clear back to Abraham and from Abraham to the flood, from the flood to Enoch, and from Enoch to Adam. He has watched that family and that blood as it has circulated from its fountain to the birth of that man . . . Joseph Smith, Jr., was foreordained to come through the loins of Abraham, Isaac, Jacob, Joseph, [Judah] and so on down through the Prophets and Apostles.[9]

Thus by virtue of inheritance Joseph was able to restore, from heaven, all the rights pertaining to the priesthood and kingship. England's symbol, the Lion and the Unicorn, are reminiscent of Joseph Smith's patriarchal order of the bloodline (see Numbers 24:8–9). As declared in Doctrine and Covenants 113:6, he is a descendant of Jesse (Judah/David) and Joseph (Ephraim) in the last days who would possess the priesthood and the keys of the kingdom and be an ensign to gather the Lord's people. This *ascendant descendant* was the farm boy and the prophet of God. An anonymous LDS writer of a manuscript on the married Christ enlarges on this idea:

> It is a very interesting idea that the *Lord* preserved the purity of the blood through the union of Joseph's ancestors. It means that the Lord was specifically involved in the marriages and the birth of children in his ancestral line, guiding certain people to marry each other over the generations, eugenically preserving a pure blood-line. He "kept his eye" on all Joseph's progenitors through the years so that the time would come when the lines would merge, producing Joseph the Prophet—who held the keys of the kingdom by right of lineage.

The providential union of Joseph's parents, Joseph Smith Sr. and Lucy Mack, is reminiscent of C. S. Lewis's *That Hideous Strength*. In this book, Merlin the magician has been restored to life to support Ranson, who is known as the "Director," in his fight against evil. A certain couple, Mark and Jane Studdock, were married but had no children due to their practice of birth control. Merlin has just entered Ransom's house and sees that Jane Studdock is there. Merlin discerns that she is the one who should have conceived an uncommon child, but has failed to do so. In the exchange between Merlin and Ransom, in an old form of Latin, the dialogue becomes unpleasant:

> "Sir, you have in your house the falsest lady of any at the time alive."
>
> And Dimble heard the Director answer him in the same language:
>
> "You are mistaken. She is doubtless like all of us a sinner: but the woman is chaste."
>
> "Sir," said Merlin, "know well that she has done in Logres [world] a thing of which no less sorrow shall come than came of the [dolorous] stroke that Balinus struck. For, sir, it was the purpose of God that she and her lord should between them have begotten a child by whom the

enemies should have been put out of Logres for a thousand years."

"She is lately married," said Ransom. "The child may yet be born."

"Sir," said Merlin, "be assured that the child will never be born, for the hour of its begetting is passed. Of their own will they are barren: I did not know till now that the usages of Sulva were so common among you. For a hundred generations in two lines the begetting of this child was prepared: and unless *God* should rip up the work of time, such seed, and such an hour in such a land, shall never be again."[10]

We are fortunate that our couple of promise, Joseph Smith Sr. and Lucy Mack Smith, fulfilled the promise and conceived of "such a child" that would eventually put out of *Logres* the enemies for a thousand years.[11] We see in Joseph's parents "a hundred generations in two lines the begetting of this child was prepared."[12] This is reminiscent of the scripture, "Considerest thou not the two families which the *Lord* hath chosen?" (Jeremiah 33:24).[13]

In 1803, Mother Smith had an unusual, vivid dream of two beautiful and majestic trees growing on the edge of a lovely meadow beside a clear stream.[14] The first tree was surrounded by a "bright belt that shone like burnished gold but far more brilliantly." It moved gracefully with the breeze, the belt moving in unison with the tree and "partook of the same influence . . . refulgence and magnitude until it became exceedingly glorious."

The second tree in stark contrast was like a pillar of marble and would not bend regardless of the strength of the "mighty storm." She wondered about these trees and their meanings and decided that the first represented her husband and the second his stubborn brother, Jesse. But perhaps we might be permitted to revisit this dream and reinterpret it in light of the thesis presented here.

Perhaps the first tree symbolized Lucy Mack's own family tree of Ephraim, epitomized by the gentle feminine willow, swaying with life. In comparison, the other tree exemplified her husband's family tree of Judah, like a mighty unbending masculine oak. The one had a golden girdle, zone, or royal belt at its waist, while the other was like a shaft of marble.[15] Shall we say the Shiloh column? This allegorical dream could be open to such an interpretation.

The purpose of this line of reasoning is to establish that Joseph Smith Jr. is the direct posterity of masculine (oak) and feminine (willow) family trees descending from both Jesus Christ and Mary Magdalene. This establishes Joseph as the legitimate successor of the King's Son in the last dispensation. "Therefore," wrote Shute, Nyman, and Bott, "Joseph Smith had both the literal blood of Judah and the literal blood of Ephraim in his veins."[16] So the Father and the Son didn't appear to just anyone in the spring of 1820, but rather to the *rightful heir* of the family.

Joseph, like Abraham of old, "sought for the blessings of the fathers, and the right whereunto I should be ordained to administer the same; . . . even the right of the firstborn . . . through the fathers unto me. I sought for mine appointment unto the Priesthood according to the appointment of God unto the fathers concerning the seed" (Abraham 1:2–4, also see 18, 31).

It may be asked how Joseph could be pure Ephraimite when we know that the blood of Judah, also flowed through his veins? Doctrine and Covenants 113:5–6 makes pointed reference to Joseph Smith being of both the Houses of Jesse and Joseph. In 1947, E. L. Whitehead stated, "It is possible for Joseph Smith to actually be descended from Judah and Ephraim, and yet retain the characteristics of a pure Ephraimite."[17] Whitehead quotes President Brigham Young regarding this principle of this (Grail) inheritance:

> We want the blood of Jacob and that of his father Isaac and Abraham which runs in the veins of the people. There is a particle of it here, and another there, blessing the nations as predicted. . . .
>
> Take a family of ten children, for instance, and you may find nine of them purely of the Gentile stock, and one son or one daughter in that family who is purely of the blood of Ephraim. It was in the veins of the father or the mother and was produced in the son or daughter, while all the rest of the family are Gentiles. You may think that is singular, but it is true. It is the house of Israel we are after and we care not whither they come from. . . .
>
> The Book of Mormon came to Ephraim, *for Joseph Smith was a pure Ephraimite*, and the Book of Mormon was revealed to him, and while he lived he made it his business to search for those who believed the gospel.[18]

The distinguishing markers on Joseph's Y-chromosome help ascertain his kingship and right to the promises of the father. At the same time these distinguishing markers on his mtDNA possibly determine the Grail lineage through his mother, Lucy Mack. To this combined bloodline came a noble and great spirit. His lineage was chosen to serve, not to be served.

JOSEPH SMITH'S ANCESTRAL LINEAGE

Object not, therefore, too strongly against the marriage of Christ, but remember that in the last days, secret and hidden things must come to light, and that your life also (which is the blood) is hid with Christ in God.

Abraham was chosen of God for the purpose of raising up a chosen seed, and a peculiar people unto His name. Jesus Christ was sent into the world for a similar purpose, but upon a more extended scale.

—ORSON HYDE[19]

This chapter seeks to demonstrate that Joseph Smith's ancestral genealogy was the true font of his authority in the latter days. Saints can trace many of their blessings through the ancient patriarchs, through Jesus Christ, and now through the discovered lineage of Joseph Smith Jr.[20] In 1859, Brigham Young said as much: "Hidden in the blood of many LDS runs the blood of Israel from numerous directions, including that of the Savior. But it is specifically through the divine blood-right of Christ through Joseph Smith Jr. that all members of the Church are lawful heirs of the promise."[21]

Organizationally, there is an important reason for being a rightful heir "according to the flesh" through the bloodline. It allows waiting premortal spirits to be born through certain channels or lineages. These "noble and great" spirits have been premortally ordained to the highest levels of work for the Lord and are usually blessed to be born into a covenanted family.[22] Possibly through DNA markers, the Lord keeps track of those "hid with Christ in God . . . hid from the world" (D&C 86:9). In May 1843, Joseph put his hand on the knee of William Clayton and said,

"Your life is hid with Christ in God, and so is many others."[23] Since there are numerous mentionings of this, it must refer to Clayton and other leaders of the Church.[24] Parley P. Pratt, after referring to Doctrine and Covenants 86:9, wrote:

> This is to say, they have been held in reserve during the reign of Mystic Babel, to be born in due time, as successors to the Apostles and Prophets of old, being their children, of the same royal line. . . . They are of the royal blood of Abraham, Isaac and Jacob, and have a right to claim the ordination and the endowments of the Priesthood, inasmuch as they repent, and obey the Lord God of their fathers.[25]

A secret order exists in a world of chaos.[26] Beyond just wanting to be connected to our genealogical roots, the primary LDS world-view maintains that God is the gardener of His vineyard and the Father of His family. "Joseph's entitlement to the priesthood was," according to an anonymous LDS author, "derived from the lineage of his fathers. He received the priesthood because of his descent."[27] This could be said of some but not all members of the Church who received the gospel ordinances.

John D. Lee recorded a sermon from Brigham Young with a similar report: "Jos. Smith was entitled to the keys of the P.H. [priesthood] according to blood."[28] The next day Lee recorded an address by Heber C. Kimball: "Jos. [Smith] had a vision and saw and traced back our blood to the royal family."[29] Apostle Wilford Woodruff, speaking in October 1875, repeats this refrain: "Our lives have been hid with Christ in *God*, and we are heirs of the eternal Priesthood, through the lineage of our fathers. Thus saith the *Lord* through the mouth of the Prophet Joseph Smith,

who sealed his testimony with his blood."[30]

Thus we can see that the priesthood rightfully belonged to those of the blood (genetic lineage) of the "royal family." Joseph taught that most of the Church qualified to hold the priesthood because of lineage (see D&C 113:7–8). While neither Joseph, Brigham, or Heber identified which royal family from which they descended, we can surmise that it was not one of the crowned heads of Europe, but rather our King, Jesus Christ and His true *Rex Deus* posterity. President Young's sermon in February 1847 elaborates:

> I am entitled to the Keys of the Priesthood according to lineage and blood. So is Brother H. C. Kimball and many others. [They] have taken Kingly power and grades of the Priesthood. This we would have taught in the Temple if time had permitted. Joseph Smith was entitled to the Keys of the Priesthood according to Blood. Still he was the fourth son. But when we get another Temple built then we will teach you concerning those things.[31]

In August 1842, Joseph Smith recorded that with "the keys of the Priesthood a double portion of the spirit heretofore (was) conferred upon my fellows with all gifts possessed by my progenitors who held the Priesthood before me anciently."[32] We are talking about an inheritance that comes through the family of God. While others not of the family may become beneficiaries through faith and adoption, the literal line must not be marginalized, forgotten, or lost.

These successive waves of the Children of the Promise have landed in northern Europe, especially Britain. It was the opinion of Joseph Fielding Smith that the tribe of Ephraim intermarried with indigenous inhabitants of the northern countries, creating a prepared land for the gospel.[33] Brigham Young recognized the efforts of Ephraim to create a fertile baseline: "No hardship will discourage these men [descendants of Ephraim] they will penetrate the deepest wilds and overcome almost insurmountable difficulties to develop the treasures of the earth, to further their indomitable spirit of adventure."[34]

The British Isles were a choice land to hold and spread the holy blood of the bifurcated lineage of Jesus Christ and Mary Magdalene (Judah + Ephraim). Heber C. Kimball had great success as a missionary and felt a spiritual aura in England. "When I returned," he wrote, "I mentioned the circumstance to brother Joseph who said, 'Did you not understand it? That is the place where some of the old Prophets travelled and dedicated that land, and their blessings fell upon you.'"[35] In speaking of Ephraimite Britain as being a fruitful missionary ground, the Prophet Joseph Smith wrote in a letter to Isaac Galland: "In England many hundreds have of late been added to our numbers; but so, even so, it must be, for 'Ephraim he hath mixed himself among the people.' And the Savior He hath said, "My sheep hear my voice."[36]

Brigham Young added to the chorus: "Ephraim has become mixed with all the nations of the earth, and it is Ephraim that is gathering together. . . . It is Ephraim that I have been searching for all the days of my preachings, and that is the blood which ran in my veins when I embraced the gospel. If there are any of the other tribes mixed with the Gentiles we are searching for them. . . . Do you understand who we are; we are of Israel, of the royal seed, of the royal blood."[37]

LDS writer E. L. Whitehead asks the question, "Who is the Royal Seed?" His answer is a typical British-Israelite comment: "They are the descendants of those hearty Anglo-Saxon people."[38] But it went much deeper than that catechism, which obscures as much as it illuminates.

While all the above is important, the idea that Joseph Smith himself was a blessed combination of certain sacred bloodlines is what really counts. While it is significant that the blood of Israel in the lost ten tribes was dispersed across northern Europe, it misses the main point in this more narrow study. The paramount and essential claim is that Joseph Smith Jr. *possesses the true birthright within the living bloodline* (see 1 Chronicles 5:1–2; 2 Nephi 3:4; 4:1–2). Joseph F. McConkie established the unique but essential context for Joseph's claim: "There have been countless religious leaders and reformers, but one alone who thought it necessary to establish his claim to authority by virtue of lineage."[39]

Authority issues from the "King's Son," or the proverbial "Widow's Son"—the Shiloh dynasty and inheritance of Jesus Christ, which was first hidden and then lost.[40] Typically when we hide something, we often lose it. Lost, because the lineage was kept secret through the first few generations of the Christian era. The Holy Grail became missing because it was planted beneath the permafrost.

The royal seed of the Savior was buried deep, with its roots penetrating even deeper. There is a legend of the Hidden King, who after many generations comes forth. In Tolkien's *Lord of the Rings*, Aragon is the lost king whose "vine" waits for generations. Of this hidden patriarch Tolkien writes:

> *All that is Gold does not glitter,*
> *Not all those who wander are lost.*
> *The old that is strong does not wither,*
> *Deep roots are not reached by the frost.*

Certain branches were preserved because their roots were planted deep underground. Only in this latter day, during the information revolution, have we begun to dig into the particular origins of Joseph Smith's family. Searching not just the general milieu of the blood of Israel, but directly into the mysterious molecular secret—Joseph Smith as the most direct heir of Jesus Christ.

Unfortunately we are unable to find or connect the intervening "lost" generations. Presumably the straight line of Joseph's lineage was simple and unassuming Celts, Britons, Anglo-Saxons, Normans, and Englishmen, but some of the branches we may surmise were quite noteworthy. The details have been shrouded in the mists of time, but the general outline is certain.

Then, after many generations, because of the persecutions, adventure, and a desire for religious freedom, the Puritans and other immigrants came to the New World in the seventeenth century. In a kind of spiritual "Manifest Destiny," the sons of Ephraim felt the tug to come to America, the land of promise. Brigham Young saw that in the last days the bloodline of Ephraim would be gathered to this continent: "By and by the Jews will be gathered to the land of their fathers, and the ten tribes, who wandered into the north, will be gathered home, and the blood of Ephraim, the second son of Joseph, who was sold into Egypt, which is to be found in every kingdom and nation under heaven, will be gathered [to America] from among the Gentiles."[41]

Eventually Europe and England give way to the new world and America, for that is where the promises of Ephraim were given. The Book of Mormon speaks of a *Remnant of the Seed of Joseph* coming to America and building the New Jerusalem. "And that a New Jerusalem should be built up upon this land, unto the remnant of the seed of Joseph, for which things there has been a type" (Ether 13:6). Ether notes that Joseph went into Egypt that they might not perish: "Wherefore, the remnant of the house of Joseph shall be built upon this land; and it shall be a land of their inheritance; and they shall build up a holy city unto the *Lord*, like unto the Jerusalem of old; and they shall no more be confounded, until the end come when the earth shall pass away" (Ether 13:8).

Some of the more direct Grail descendants also came to America. The great English-Puritan reformer, John Lathrop (1584–1653), a fifth great-grandfather of the Prophet Joseph came to New England. Another ancestor who came on the Mayflower, was Humphry Howland, from whom so many of our general authorities are descended. During a particularly bad storm at sea, Howland's son John was washed overboard. All that could be done was to throw the lad a rope, because the attention of the crew was on saving the ship. John Howland held onto the rope for some time before finally being pulled aboard. He became the direct ancestor of both Joseph Smith and his wife Emma.

One of the earliest known direct relatives from Joseph Smith Sr.'s side of the family was Robert Smith Sr., born about 1599. He was the father of Robert Smith Jr., who was born in 1623 or 26 in Kirton Lincolnshire, in northeastern England.[42] Robert Jr. moved to Kent and from there, in 1638, he emigrated at the tender age of twelve or fifteen to Topsfield in Essex County, Massachusetts. Conceivably he was a member of the Protestant Baptists or Non-Conformists who had split from the Church of England in 1609.

It is difficult to imagine the motivation for such a move; perhaps religious persecution and a sense of adventure brought him to the New World, where the promises to Ephraim might be fulfilled. In 1656, Robert Smith Jr. married Mary French, daughter of Thomas French, to whom were born ten children. Robert Smith Jr. was a tailor until he died on 30 August 1693.

Robert's fifth child (third son) was Samuel Smith Sr. (born 26 January 1666). Samuel continued to live in Topsfield as a prosperous carpenter and held various public offices.[43] He married Rebecca Curtis in 1707 and had nine children. The third child was a son named Samuel "Capt." Smith Jr., born in Topsfield on 26 January 1714. Captain Smith married Priscilla Gould in 1734 and had five children. The Honorable

Samuel Smith Jr. died 14 November 1785.

Captain Smith's fifth child was Asael, born in Topsfield on the 7 March 1744. He married Mary Duty of Windham, New Hampshire, in 1767. They lived in Topsfield until the birth of their third child, then moved to Windham, New Hampshire. It was there that he fought in the Revolutionary War. Like his father, he was a religious man with liberal views, somewhat like the Universalists.[44] Later he moved near Tunbridge in Sharon County, Vermont where his grandson Joseph Smith Jr. the Prophet was born. Asael Smith prophetically declared about the "glorious revolution[ary war]" in a letter of 1796: "And I believe that the stone is now cut out of the mountain, without hands, spoken of by Daniel, and has smitten the image upon his feet by which the iron, the clay, the brass, the silver and the gold (viz. all the monarchial and ecclesiastical tyranny) will be broken to pieces and become as the chaff of the summer threshing floor; and the wind shall carry them away and there shall be not place found for them."[45]

In Asael Smith was first seen the prophetic inklings of the future seer. Asael believed that "God was going to raise up some branch of his family to be a great benefit to mankind."[46] Asael and his wife Mary Duty had eleven children, of whom Joseph Smith Sr. was the third born. Asael was blessed to live long enough to see the only true and living church restored before his death in October 1830.[47]

Joseph Smith Sr., a fifth-generation American, was born on 12 July 1771 in Topsfield, Massachusetts. In 1845, Brigham Young spoke of the Smith entitlement: "There is the same blood of Ephraim running in the veins of this [the Smith] family—and I know who has the blood and the Priesthood to carry the keys to the world."[48]

While God is no respecter of persons, He was deeply invested in the Smith family. A number of the ancestors of Joseph Smith Jr. were pioneers, builders, patriots, and ministers. Seven of his progenitors were on the *Mayflower*; three signed the Mayflower Compact. Ivan J. Barrett notes: "For the most part, Joseph Smith's ancestors were religiously inclined. Many of them were Seekers. Becoming dissatisfied with the Christianity of their day, they were seeking the religion once taught by Christ and his apostles. Some of them endured persecution because in conscience they were unwilling to subscribe to the tenets of the religious sects of their day."[49]

This great Ephraimite heritage was held by many members of the Church. But who are the lawful heirs? Joseph Smith's family as "the purest of a pure set of lineages" was the only one to hold the chosen Grail birthright by right. This is our quest to know more about this family.

PATRIARCHAL LINEAGE

An Evangelist is a Patriarch, even the oldest man of the blood of Joseph or the seed of Abraham. Wherever the Church of Christ is established in the earth, there should be a Patriarch for the benefit of the posterity of the Saints, as it was with Jacob in giving his patriarchal blessing unto his sons, etc.

—PROPHET
JOSEPH SMITH JR.[50]

I have thought when the Prophet Joseph began to trace his genealogy I should learn some things.

—JOHN SMITH,
CHURCH PATRIARCH[51]

The Prophet Joseph Smith said that the oldest son of the patriarchal bloodline of the seed of Abraham, or of Joseph, was to be the Patriarch of the Church. Thus the question of why Joseph Smith Jr. became the prophet of the Church, instead of his older brother Hyrum, is often asked. Seldom in the history of recorded scripture do we find the older brother ever obtaining the ultimate ecclesiastical status. Not with Cain, nor Ishmael, nor Esau, nor Reuben, nor Laman, nor Lemuel. Joseph Fielding Smith outlined the office of Patriarch of the Church: "[It] was conferred upon the father of the Prophet as a divine right, coming from the *Lord*, as the rightful descendant of Joseph, son of Jacob, who, because of transgressions of his older brothers, received the birthright in Israel. This office descends by the law of primogeniture."[52]

It seems that the law of primogeniture, while fully in force, is undermined by the fallen nature of the inhabitants of this earth during its second estate. On the other hand, sometimes the older children are righteous, as in the case of Manasseh, and still his younger brother, Ephraim, received the birthright. Joseph Smith Jr. was the third son of his parents, not even the second. Margaret Starbird noted, "and often in such stories it is the third son who is the hero, like the simpleton in *Puss in Boots*."[53]

It is not difficult to understand that the younger Joseph was called to the birthright heir status in the premortal councils in heaven. It may seem a distinctly *outré* reference, but Brigham Young said as much four years before his death:

> I can merely say this, however, that we see that the Lord makes his selection according to his own mind and will with regard to his ministers. Brother Joseph Smith, instead of being the first born, was the third son of his father's family who came to maturity, yet he is actually the heir of the family; he is the heir of his father's house. It seems to us that the oldest son would be the natural heir; but we see that the Lord makes his own selection.[54]

Alvin and Hyrum were older, but precedence was given to the younger brother. However, neither of these brothers lost any blessings in not being chosen Firstborn. Joseph said of Hyrum that he would "stand in the tracks of his father and be numbered among those who hold the right of patriarchal priesthood, even the Evangelical Priesthood and power shall be upon him."[55]

We have seen throughout the history of God's dealings with mankind that the firstborn hardly ever receives the mantle, even though it was the prescribed pattern. Neither was Abel, Abraham, Isaac, Jacob, Judah, or Joseph of Egypt firstborn. Neither was Moses or David the primogenitor, and even with Perez, the firstborn of Judah, there was a question. But God saw fit to give them all first-born status. Only Jesus was a literal firstborn. It must be that the law of the firstborn works perfectly only in heaven, not on earth.

The office of Presiding Patriarch was first filled by Father Joseph Smith Sr. (1833-1840). He received a blessing from his son Joseph that he would "be called a prince over his posterity, holding the keys of the patriarchal priesthood over the kingdom of *God* on earth" and that Father Smith would sit in the general assembly of patriarchs, in council with the Ancient of Days.[56] Then in return Father Smith gave his son a patriarchal blessing, which proclaims: "Shall a choice seer arise, whose bowels shall be a fountain of truth, whose loins shall be girded with the girdle of righteousness . . . and thou shall stand on Mount Zion when the tribes of Jacob come shouting from the north, and when thy brethren, the Sons of Ephraim, crown them in the name of Jesus Christ."[57]

In a stroke Joseph Smith Jr. established the concept of a patriarchal wing of the Mormon Church. Max Weber defined the authority of the Church as being charismatic.[58] It boasted two basic subdivisions of traditional authority, one being inherited "familial charisma," which rested upon hereditary bloodlines

---

FIGURE 12

MELCHIZEDEK PRIESTHOOD[63]

1. MELCHIZEDEK ORDER (KINGS AND PRIESTS)
ELIJAH'S KEYS AND POWER TO KINGDOM OF ENDLESS LIVES[64]

2. PATRIARCHAL ORDER (PROPHET, APOSTLE, PATRIARCH)[65]
GOSPEL OF ABRAHAM AND ELIAS, INNUMERABLE POSTERITY

3. LEVITICAL [AARONIC] ORDER (MINISTER)

---

and may be called patriarchal. The other is called church "office charisma" and is centered upon priesthood calling. Though both were divinely ordained, they were sometimes at variance with each other.

Father Smith was replaced because of health by his son Hyrum Smith (1841–1844), who was also assistant President of the Church. He was the only Patriarch of the Church to be ordained by his father. Hyrum worked in near perfect unity with his brother the Prophet. On 27 May 1843, the Prophet Joseph announced, "The patriarchal office is the highest office in the church, and father Smith conferred this office on Hyrum Smith, on his deathbed."[59] However, these statements regarding the supremacy of the patriarchal office may have been superseded on 28 September 1843, when Joseph Smith was ordained as "priest and king."

In the afternoon of 27 May, Joseph explained, "I would not prophesy any more, and proposed Hyrum to hold the office of prophet to the Church, as it was his birthright"[60] (see D&C 124:124). Hyrum Smith, the righteous elder brother of Joseph, was the Associate President of the Church and Presiding Patriarch of the Church under Joseph Jr.[61] The martyred Hyrum held "in concert" with Joseph all the keys of the kingdom (D&C 124:95). Interestingly,

in Hebrew the name *Hyrum* means "my brother is exalted."

On 27 August 1843, Joseph spoke of "three grand orders of priesthood," Melchizedek, patriarchal, and Levitical.[62]

Franklin D. Richard's account of Joseph's sermon references it in reverse order:

1. Levitical which was never able to administer a blessing but only to bind heavy burdens which neither they nor their father [were] able to bear.

2. Abraham's patriarchal power which is the greatest yet experienced in this church.

3. That of the Melchizedek who had still greater power even power of an endless life of which was our Lord Jesus Christ which also Abraham obtained by the offering of his son Isaac which was not the power of a Prophet nor Apostle nor Patriarch only, but of King and Priest to God to open the windows of Heaven and pour out the peace & Law of endless Life to man & No man

can attain to the Joint heirship with Jesus Christ without being administered to by one having the same power & Authority of Melchizedek.[66]

The patriarchal priesthood was conferred on 4 May 1842 to Brigham Young, Willard Richards, Heber C. Kimball, and Newel K. Whitney among others.[67] Then the "fullness of the Melchizedek" priesthood order was conferred upon them on the 28 September 1843 when Kings and Priests were ordained. Just one month before this date Brigham Young remarked, "If any in the Church had the fullness of the Melchizedek Priesthood, he [Brigham] did not know it. For any person to have the fullness of that priesthood, he must be a king and priest."[68] Now the patriarchal priesthood was no longer the highest authority in the Church.

The impulsive and meddlesome third Patriarch, William Smith, the younger brother of the Prophet, was ordained in 1845 and excommunicated later the same year. This summed up the difficulty of having a line of Patriarchs by descent. This was the same difficulty the RLDS Church encountered in order to find a superior quality, constant, and profoundly spiritual leader for its top ecclesiastical positions of president and patriarch. Eventually both churches, LDS and Community of Christ (RLDS), abandoned the direct descent model.[69]

The RLDS now has no blood relative of Joseph Smith holding the title of president. Wallace B. Smith (1931–   ) announced in September 1996 that he would retire in April 1997. He named his successor, W. Grant McMurray (1949–   ), to be president of the RLDS Church.[70] He was the first non-descendant of Joseph Smith to be leader of a church which claimed such bloodline "descendance" as the keystone of their authority. He resigned in November, 2004. He was replaced by Steve Veazey, a younger member of their Quorum of Twelve.

Other problems included the job description of Patriarch, which amounted only to giving blessings, counseling stake patriarchs, and sustaining the First Presidency. If they did too little, they were accused of not magnifying their calling; if they did too much they were a direct threat to the office of the President. William Smith wrote Brigham Young in July 1845 claiming the right to be the patriarch and to "attend to all of the ordinances of *God*, no man being my head."

"I want all men to understand that my Father's family are of the royal blood and promised seed and no man or set of men can take their crown or place in time or eternity."[71]

Brigham Young wrote back, with the blessing of Mother Smith, that William had the right of the Patriarch, but that the Twelve had the ultimate right to preside over the ordinances. William Smith did not have the right to act independently from the President of the Church and the Twelve Apostles. Ultimately, the Melchizedek Order presides over the patriarchal order, and the Church Patriarch is subservient to the president of the Church, who presides over the Melchizedek Order. Sealing by proxy was under the direction of the president of the Church, and rested with only one man at any time.[72] Later we shall see that all the patriarchs, apostles, and church presidents were select members of the Grail royal blood and promised seed.

The fourth Patriarch, Uncle John Smith (1847–54) was Joseph Smith Sr.'s brother. His temperament tended toward quiet devotion and unquestioned obedience to the more ecclesiastic side of the equation. In his 1853 blessing of his son, George Albert Smith, he included the concept of the Smith family as a "chosen" family.[73] President and prophet, George Albert Smith, in tracing his family back in time, said, "I come of a race of men whose lives have been devoted to the work of the *Lord*."[74]

Next came John Smith, who was the son of the

Patriarch of the Church, Hyrum Smith. He became the fifth Presiding Patriarch and held that office for fifty-six years, from 1855–1911. Throughout his long tenure, there simmered various personality conflicts between the familial charisma and the office charisma authority.[75] John Smith's relations with the presidency and apostles were strained, and in 1875 they voted to replace him with his brother Joseph F. Smith.[76] But Joseph F. intervened and convinced Brigham Young to give the patriarch six more months, "to see if he would magnify his calling any better than he had done in the past."[77] John Smith then remained faithful in his position for the remainder of his life.

The sixth patriarch, Hyrum Gibbs Smith (1912–1932) was the great-grandson of the Prophet's brother Hyrum and grandson of John Smith, whom he followed as patriarch. He was, appropriately enough, also the director of the Genealogical Society of Utah. Hyrum G. Smith gave the tantalizing suggestion that the patriarch become the "interim president" between the death of the prophet and the sustaining of a new one.[78]

Unlike the succession of the President of the Church, who was chosen by the Twelve from its ranks, the Presiding Patriarch was chosen by the Prophet and the Quorum of Twelve. The proving ground for the patriarch was never as exacting as that for the prophet and president of the Church. After Hyrum G. Smith, two acting Patriarchs of the Church were named, Nicholas Groesbeck Smith (1932–1934), the son of Apostle John Henry Smith, and George Franklin Richards (1937–1942). For some reason, G. F. Richards (1861–1950), who was not a direct Smith family member, was allowed to serve in this position.

This decade-long period of limbo left the office in uncertainty over its filling. Finally a cousin, Joseph Fielding Smith (1899–1964); (not the apostle and later prophet) filled the hereditary position (1942–46). Not including the "acting patriarchs," he was the seventh first Patriarch of the Church. On 6 October 1946, J. F. Smith suddenly resigned his office for serious health reasons, even though he lived another eighteen years.

He was soon replaced by Hyrum Gibbs Smith's son, Eldred Gee Smith. Called to fill the office, Eldred served with great energy from 1947–1979.[79] However, Eldred Gee Smith's occasional "murmuring" caused problems, making him and the troublesome office once again expendable to the Church. In October 1979, Patriarch Smith, though deeply spiritual and faithful to the gospel, was given emeritus status. With him the ancestral office of Presiding Patriarch became vacant and dormant. However, Eldred Smith has remained a responsible advocate of the Grail status of the Smith family. It should be mentioned that the office of Church Patriarch is of importance because of its revelatory value in pronouncing lineages. The patriarch was, at one time, sustained after the LDS prophet in General Conference.[80] As last to be named, his position was considered lofty. The Church Patriarch's chair was also raised higher than that of the Church President's. The office signified the bond between the Bloodline and the Priesthood line, the King and the Priest.

Joseph Smith Jr. comprehended the significance of the patriarch in sustaining the Church's authoritative viability. He probably understood, by virtue of creating this hereditary position, the importance of both the *patriarchal bloodline* and the *Melchizedek Priesthood line* within the Church. The difficulties of succession experienced after his death were both exacerbated and resolved through the office of Patriarch. The patriarchal family of Hyrum and John Smith in Utah is significant, because it definitely filled the void left by Joseph Smith III's joining the RLDS Church.

However, the Church's "Royal Family," as demonstrated by its Presiding Patriarchs, has been ill-defined in terms of who is included on the genealogical list, the prerogatives, means of succession, and integral responsibilities. At the very core the problem was two-fold:

1. Not all family members were chosen because of personal premortal worthiness or devotion to the LDS gospel, just some of them. They are merely born into the royal Smith or related families. Therefore petty bickering, hurt feelings, and even personal unworthiness permeate these chosen Smith and related families.

This is not unusual, for it is the same for one hundred percent of the other families in the world. Even biblically, the families of the great Patriarchs had their share of "black sheep." Only in today's environment, such behavior is all too public and distracting to the gospel issues at hand and can no longer be tolerated.

2. Even if the selected representatives of the royal Smith families had been sufficiently worthy, the general Church membership is unprepared to be instructed by a kingly line of authority. The controlling paradigm of the gospel today is the ecclesiastical, or office, charisma of the Church. The patriarchal order, which rests on the family, is not really in place and probably won't be until we near the Millennium. Today the Church and kingdom is dominated by the first and third orders of the Melchizedek Priesthood: the Aaronic (Levitical), and the Melchizedek orders.

The temple promises of members actually becoming Kings and Priests and Queens and Priestesses in the Melchizedek Order still lies in the future. Yet, it is a testimony to the Prophet Joseph Smith Jr. that he foresaw all needful elements in the gospel. But because the supposed failures of such premature plans as the United Order (Order of Enoch), he and we were unable to fully implement the promises of the Lord's richest blessings. Tradition implies that a great patriarch will lead the Church in the last days, toward the Holy or Patriarch Order[81] (see Isaiah 11:1, D&C 113:1–6).

The ancestral office of Presiding Patriarch will one day be filled by the President of the Church, and the two *charismas* will be united again. How would the history of the early Church been changed if Joseph had been able to fully make this transition to a higher realm of Prophet, King, and Priest? This royal kingship will one day be placed upon the most worthy direct ancestor of Jesus and Mary Magdalene, through the Smith family.

SEER, PROPHET, PRIEST, AND KING

Wherefore, Joseph truly saw our day. And he obtained a promise of the Lord that out of the fruit of his loins the Lord God would raise up a righteous branch unto the house of Israel; not the Messiah, but a branch which was to be broken off, nevertheless, to be remembered in the covenants of the Lord that the Messiah should be made manifest unto them in the latter days, in the spirit of power, unto the bringing of them out of darkness unto light—yea, out of hidden darkness and out of captivity unto freedom. For Joseph truly testified, saying:

"A seer shall the Lord my God raise up, who shall be a choice seer unto the fruit of my loins."

—2 NEPHI 3:5–6;
SEE ALSO VERSES 7–16

The Lord said that Judah and King David should never lack a man of his seed to sit upon that throne.[82] Such a Seer and King the Lord raised up in December 1805 on a small farm between Sharon and Royalton townships in Vermont.[83] Joseph Smith was also the theocratic *King of All Israel* throughout the world, being nobility of both Ephraim and Judah. In his prophetship we saw the marriage of those two tribes, the birthright and the scepter, making him both Priest and King.

As the birthright heir from the loins of Jesus Christ he was in the direct line of succession. Just before his death, Joseph was ordained to the high honor of "Prophet, Seer, Revelator, Priest, Ruler and King." Church clerk, William Clayton, on the 11 April 1844, noted in his journal that in a secret Council of Fifty meeting, "Joseph [was] chosen as our prophet, Priest, & King by Hosannas"[84] (see Plate 32).[85] This was no regular *Second Anointing* to be a heavenly "King and Priest," but an unqualified acceptance of Joseph Smith Jr. as King of All Israel on earth.[86]

The Diary of George A. Smith in May 1844 notes that Joseph Smith had been ordained "King over the Immediate house of Israel" by the Council of Fifty.[87] The *History of the Church*, on June 25th 1844, records an interesting statement regarding Joseph's elevation: "Dan Jones heard Wilson Law, whilst endeavoring to get another warrant against Joseph Smith for treason, declare that while he (Mr. Smith) was once preaching from Daniel 2nd chapter, 44th verse, said that the kingdom referred to was already set up, and that he was the king over it."[88]

A month later a veiled reference to this kingship was addressed by the statement of Apostles Lyman Wight and Heber C. Kimball to Joseph, "You are already President Pro Tem of the world."[89] This passage from the statement was deleted from the official *History of the Church* (7:139) for the obvious reason that the world would misconstrue the affair into something sinister.[90] After the Prophet's martyrdom, John C. Bennett produced a pseudo-revelation, but one that revealed an interesting element. Bennett hailed Joseph Smith as one to be "a great king and imperial primate over all Israel."[91]

Later the *Nauvoo Neighbor* in January 1845 declared that Joseph Smith was "crowned and anointed king" of Israel.[92] William Marks in 1853 wrote that

the Council of Fifty performed an ordinance "in which Joseph suffered himself to be ordained a king, to reign over the house of Israel forever."[93]

Joseph Smith's ordination was inherently a part of the gospel plan, as Parley P. Pratt explained in 1855: "This Priesthood . . . holds the keys . . . to appoint kings . . . to ordain or anoint them to their several holy callings."[94] In a meeting held by the Council of Fifty on the 27 June 1882, a revelation from President John Taylor reminded those present that Joseph Smith had been called "to be a Prophet, Seer and Revelator to my Church and Kingdom; and to be a King and Ruler over Israel."[95]

In the minutes of a very similar ceremony on 4 February 1885, John Taylor was the Council of Fifty's standing chairman. The Franklin D. Richards diary expands on the ritual which must have been similar, excepting the "hosannahs" to Joseph Smith's ordination in April 1844: "L[orenzo] Snow consecrated a bottle of oil. Counselor [George Q.] Cannon anointed President John Taylor & all laid hands on the Prest. [and ordained him] a King [,] Priest and Ruler over Israel on the Earth."[96]

The Abraham H. Cannon Journal of December 1885 speaks of a parallel or perhaps the same event, "Council of Fifty met . . . to anoint John Taylor as Prophet, Priest and King."[97] Greater detail of the Taylor anointing is given by Franklin D. Richards. He describes a revelation given to John Taylor: "Requiring him to be anointed and set apart as a King, Priest and Ruler over Israel on the Earth—over Zion and the Kingdom of Christ our King of kings . . . we clothed in our Priestly attire . . . after the usual ceremony . . . prayed in the circle . . . consecrated a bottle of oil . . . we all laid hands on the Pres . . . sealed the anointing according to a written form which had been prepared."[98]

What was this "Council of Fifty" that witnessed these sacred ordinations? It was originally a political organization of the kingdom of God over which

Joseph Smith presided. It was established to govern the temporal affairs of the kingdom on Earth. After unsuccessful attempts in the Mormon quest for theocracy in Jackson County, Joseph believed that the kingdom was now nigh at hand. There is no doubt that had Joseph Smith lived, he would have attempted to establish a theocracy somewhere in the West.[99]

On 14 April 1844, just three days after his ordination to the Kingship of Israel, Joseph Smith, as a politician, wrote to the *Daily Globe,* a non-Mormon newspaper:

> As the "world is governed too much," and there is not a nation or dynasty, now occupying the earth, which acknowledges Almighty God as their lawgiver, and as "crowns won by blood, by blood must be maintained," I go emphatically, virtuously, and humanely for a THEO-DEMOCRACY, where God and the people hold the power to conduct the affairs of men in righteousness, and where liberty, free trade, and sailor's rights, and the protection of life and property shall be maintained inviolate for the benefit of ALL.[100]

To create a Mormon civil theocracy, even within the United States, was the dream of Joseph, who saw the need of such a beacon to a benighted world. A religious sovereignty perfectly combined with the civil sovereignty of America was his aim.[101] An enlightened theo-monarchy-democracy with a constitutional foundation, would be the best system of government.[102] The Book of Mormon said as much:

> *Therefore, if it were possible that you could have just men to be your kings, who would establish the laws of God,*

> *and judge this people according to his commandments, yea, if ye could have men for your kings . . . I say unto you, if this could always be the case then it would be expedient that ye should always have kings to rule over you.*

—MOSIAH 29:13

But of course this could never happen or last for long with a secular king, who ascended or grabbed the throne without proper proving or experience. The Mormon scripture continued, "For behold, how much iniquity doth one wicked king cause to be committed" (Mosiah 29:17). Therefore Joseph sought to make an entire kingdom of priests and kings to govern themselves through the spirit of the Lord. Joseph Smith himself would be a theocratic king. He publicly announced, using Daniel 2:44 as his text, on 12 May 1844: "I calculate to be one of the instruments of setting up the kingdom of Daniel by the word of the Lord, and I intend to lay a foundation that will revolutionize the whole world."[103]

He stressed that it would not be by gun or sword but by conversion and not coercion.[104] At the time the members of this temporal association were called Princes.[105] But it was the very Council of Fifty, which ordained the prophet a king, which had certain betraying members. These traitors told apostate Wilson Law, whose *Nauvoo Expositor* threatened to make it public. Law said, "That the kingdom referred to [Daniel's stone] was already set up, and that he was the king over it."[106] In June 1844 Joseph had the offending *Nauvoo Expositor* destroyed, which led directly to his martyrdom on day 27 of that month.

Bruce R. McConkie continued this line of reasoning when he said, "The Church is a kingdom. The Lord Jesus Christ is the Eternal King, and the President of the Church. . . is the earthly king . . . the king of the kingdom on earth."[107] Joseph would not just be king of the Jews; he would be *King of All Israel* worldwide.

The tribe of Ephraim would eventually come to rule over the other tribes (Genesis 37:5–10; 49:22–26). But this would not negate the promises to the House of David, which would be fully encapsulated into the Ephraimite cause, that of ALL ISRAEL (2 Samuel 7:16; Psalm 89:3–4; and 1 Chronicles 28:4–5).

All the lost tribes will come, in the last days, to Ephraim and there receive their promises and blessings:

> *And there shall they fall down and be crowned with glory, even in Zion, by the hands of the servants of the Lord, even the children of Ephraim. . . . Behold this is the blessing of the everlasting God upon the tribes of Israel, and the richer blessing upon the head of Ephraim and his fellows.*
>
> —D & C 133:3, 34

In this dispensation, Joseph Smith Jr will be their Seer, Prophet, Priest and King.[108] What more kingly powers could one enjoy than being judge over all those born on earth during your thousand-year dispensation? Even unto the sitting down in the place which I have prepared in the mansions of my Father.

NOTES

1. Heber C. Kimball, in *Journal of Discourses* (6 September 1856), 5:214a. Brother Kimball was making reference to the Saints at the end of the vine in the latter-day, stretching back to antiquity. These were the choicest.
2. *Times and Seasons* (September 1842), 3:922. This book, *Dynasty of the Holy Grail*, in the author's opinion, is one of the proofs of the Joseph Smith prophecy.
3. As quoted in McConkie, *His Name Shall Be Joseph*, 4.
4. Brigham Young, in *Journal of Discourses* (9 October 1859), 7:289–90.
5. Brigham Young, *Journal History* (9 April 1837).
6. Brigham Young, as quoted in Smith, *Way to Perfection*, 128.
7. Brigham Young, in "A Family Meeting in Nauvoo: Minutes of a Meeting of the Richards and Young Families Held in Nauvoo, Ill., 8 January, 1845," *Utah Genealogical and Historical Magazine* 11 (July 1920): 112.
8. Ibid., 104–8. Most apostate fundamentalists believe that Joseph Smith is the Holy Ghost. This was the gist of Brigham Young's refutation as it came to be believed after the release of Doctrine and Covenants 134.
9. Brigham Young, in *Journal of Discourses* (9 October 1859), 7:289–90.
10. Quoted by an anonymous LDS author. See Lewis, *That Hideous Strength*, 278–79. Thus the "Dolorous Blow," or stroke, lays waste two kingdoms, according to Barber, *Holy Grail*, 71. Godwin, *Holy Grail*, 154, reminds us of the need to marry within the Grail stock in Wolfram's *Parzival*: "For while [Parzival] was born of a line of Grail Guardians he lacked the resolve needed for such a spiritual responsibility. He had fallen in love with the beautiful Orgeluse who was outside the Grail line."
11. On Joseph Smith's paternal side, Robert Smith came from England in 1638, and on the paternal side of his maternal line is John Mack, an immigrant from Scotland who came in 1680. From this stock a choice seer was raised (3 Nephi 3:7). The true maternal side would be Lucy Mack's mothers, her mother's mother, and so on. (See figure 8.)
12. Actually, it is something like 66 to 72 generations from A.D. 30 to 1805, between a child of Jesus and Joseph Smith. Rabbi Yaakov Kleiman, *DNA and Tradition*, notes that the lineage of the Sons of Aaron (the Cohen) goes back 106 generations or 3,300 years according to DNA dating. Malcolm Godwin, *Holy Grail*, 154, pleads, "The ideals of the Christian Church of a heavenly 'super nature' had overwhelmed all natural responses." Thus the will of God for some, had overwhelmed any "natural man" instincts of marrying outside the Grail family.
13. Allen also believes that it refers to Judah and Ephraim (*Judah's Sceptre and Joseph's Birthright*, 49–50).
14. Proctor and Proctor, *History of Joseph Smith by His Mother*, 59–60. See also Preston Nibley, *History of Joseph Smith by His Mother Lucy Mack Smith*, 44. Lucy Mack Smith begins her narrative: "The first thing that attracted my special attention in this magnificent meadow, was a very pure and clear stream of water, which ran through the midst of it; and as I traced this stream, I discovered two trees standing upon its margin, both of which were on the same side of the stream. These trees were very beautiful,

they were well proportioned and towered with majestic beauty to a great height. Their branches, which added to their symmetry and glory, commenced near the top, and spread themselves in luxurious grandeur around."

15. The "golden zone" or belt mentioned by Lucy Mack Smith may relate to the golden girdle of Daniel 10:5 and Revelation 1:13, 15:6. The "curious girdle" of Exodus 28:8 was made of the colors of the ephod. Isaiah 11:5 speaks of a girdle of righteousness and faithfulness, which probably represents the belt around the tree.

16. Shute, Nyman, and Bott, *Ephraim,* 65.

17. Whitehead, *House of Israel,* 541. Whitehead persuasively answers this question by using the argument of G. G. Mendel's law of heredity. After many generations, the right combinations would appear in the offspring. For example, if a person had a strain of the blood of the House of Ephraim, married outside the tribe to someone who also had some trace of Ephraim in them, they could have several children who were not pure Ephraimite and one who was. It could be that all the direct and unmutated descendants of Adam and Eve had the same genetic signature.

18. Brigham Young, in *Journal of Discourses* (8 April 1855), 2:268–69.

19. Orson Hyde, in *Journal of Discourses* (March 1857), 4:260. The parenthetical portion is found in the original. The above quotation begins with this paragraph, dealing with the very highest chosen or elected: "How much soever of holy horror this doctrine may excite in persons not impregnated with the blood of Christ, and whose minds are consequently dark and benighted, it may excite still more when they are told that if none of the natural blood of Christ flows in their veins, they are not the chosen or elect of God."

20. Orson F. Whitney, Conference Report, October 1905, 91.

21. Brigham Young, in *Journal of Discourses* (9 October 1859), 7:290.

22. It should be noted that not all of the noble and great spirits are ordained to be born into the covenant lineages. And, not all those born into these select lineages are specially ordained to mortal ecclesiastical missions on earth. But all who hold major positions in the Lord's latter-day kingdom are premortally ordained and born into these lineages.

23. William Clayton Journal (16 May 1843), in Smith, *Intimate Chronicle,* 102. See also Smith, *History of the Church,* 5:391–92. This may refer to his being sealed to eternal life, or his lineage, or both. Bruce R. McConkie equates "being hid in Christ in God" as receiving one's

calling and election blessings and the more sure word of prophecy (see *Doctrinal New Testament Commentary,* 3:34). While this may be one aspect, the intent of the language refers to being a descendant of Christ, unbeknownst to the world.

24. Heber C. Kimball, in *Journal of Discourses* (6 September 1856) 5:215.

25. Parley P. Pratt, *Journal of Discourses* (10 April 1853), 1:262. Wilford Woodruff spoke similarly; in ibid. (26 June 1881), 22:234: "We are called of God. We have been gathered from the distant nations, and our lives have been hid with Christ in God, but we have not known it. The Lord has been watching over us from the hour of our birth. We are of the seed of Ephraim, and of Abraham, and of Joseph, who was sold into Egypt, and these are the instruments that God has kept in the spirit world to come forth in these latter days to take hold of this kingdom and build it up."

26. This is symbolized by the magic square, which totals the number 15 in every direction, perhaps representing the 15 prophets, seers, and revelators on earth. It looks random or even chaotic, but has organization and order:

$$8\ 1\ 6$$
$$3\ 5\ 7$$
$$4\ 9\ 2$$

27. Anonymous LDS author, manuscript in author's possession (date unknown), 35. For many years I have wondered why Joseph Smith was able to baptize Oliver Cowdery, when he himself had not received this ordinance. That Melchizedek entitlement came by Joseph's descent, through his inheritance of the patriarchal priesthood from the fathers, which allowed him, by the command of the angel, to baptize. This unorthodox manner of bestowal would not be countenanced under any other circumstance.

28. Kelly, *Journals of John D. Lee* (16 February 1847) 82.

29. Kelly, *Journals of John D. Lee* (17 February 1847), 91. Lee did not say which royal family he was referring to, but given Kimball's later teachings, he certainly meant the Savior's. This passage does declare that a revelation was involved.

30. Wilford Woodruff, in *Journal of Discourses* (8 October 1875), 18:127b. He is loosely quoting from Doctrine and Covenants 86:8–10.

31. *Wilford Woodruff Journal* (16 February 1847) 3:131–32. See also Staker, *Waiting for the World's End,* 107; spelling standardized.

32. Author unknown, "Revelations in Addition to Those found in the LDS Edition of the Doctrine and

Covenants," *New Mormon Studies CD-ROM.* The anonymous LDS author's manuscript notes its source was Church Historical Department Ms f490 #2.

33. Smith, *Way to Perfection,* 1.

34. Brigham Young, in *Journal of Discourses* (31 May 1863), 10:188.

35. Heber C. Kimball, in *Journal of Discourses* (6 April 1857), 5:22 b.

36. Joseph Smith letter to Isaac Galland (11 September 1839), in Smith, *History of the Church,* 4:8.

37. Brigham Young, in *Journal of Discourses* (8 April 1855), 2:268; also quoted in Smith, *Way to Perfection,* 128, as quoted in Whitehead, *House of Israel,* 533.

38. Whitehead, *House of Israel,* 533. Erastus Snow also speaks as a true British-Israelite in *Journal of Discourses* (6 May 1882), 23:183–86, as does Brigham Young, in *Journal of Discourses* (31 May 1863), 10:188.

39. McConkie, *His Name Shall Be Joseph,* 202. Many claim to be Jesus Christ, but none claim to be descended from the Savior until Joseph Smith did just that.

40. Wilford Woodruff, in *Journal of Discourses* (25 February 1855), 2:199: "The Messiah, the Shiloh, their Savior." See also Orson Hyde, ibid. (6 October 1854), 2:82. Anciently, Jesus claimed authority through his lineage, and other kings have done the same.

41. Brigham Young, ibid. (14 April 1867), 12:38, as quoted in Widtsoe, *Discourses of Brigham Young,* 121.

42. Anderson, *Ancestry and Posterity of Joseph Smith and Emma Hale,* 51, 52, says he was born about 1623. She also notes that nothing is known about his ancestry before that time, "However this may be, it appears that Robert, either by accident or design, successfully destroyed all records, coats of arms, or other evidence of his English life and ancestry." The later date is preferable because the age of twelve appears too young to immigrate, whereas age fifteen is more likely.

43. The guilds of joiner (carpenter or Nager) and mason (operative freemason) were closely connected in the Middle Ages and the Renaissance.

44. Bushman, *Joseph Smith and the Beginnings of Mormonism,* 5.

45. Anderson, *Ancestry and Posterity of Joseph Smith and Emma Hale,* 61.

46. Quoted in Petersen, *Where Have All the Prophets Gone?* 345. Also in Church Education System manual, *Church History in the Fulness of Times,* 17, citing George A. Smith, *Memoirs of George A. Smith,* 2; see also Anderson, *Joseph Smith's New England Heritage* (1971), 124, 125, 129.

47. Smith, *History of the Church,* 2:443 (17 May 1836):

"My grandfather, Asael Smith, long ago predicted that there would be a prophet raised up in his family and my grandmother was fully satisfied that it was fulfilled in me. My grandfather . . . declared that I was the very Prophet that he had long known would come in his family." See also Anderson, *Joseph Smith's New England Heritage* (2004), 148–51, fns 215, 216, 218.

48. Brigham Young, in "A Family Meeting in Nauvoo: Minutes of a Meeting of the Richards and Young Families Held in Nauvoo, Ill., 8 January, 1845," *Utah Genealogical and Historical Magazine* 11 (July 1920): 108.

49. Barrett, *Joseph Smith and the Restoration,* 22.

50. Smith, *Teachings of the Prophet Joseph Smith* (27 June 1839), 151. See Smith, *History of the Church,* 3:379–81; Ehat and Cook, *Words of Joseph Smith,* 6.

51. Father John Smith, in "A Family Meeting in Nauvoo: Minutes of a Meeting of the Richards and Young Families Held in Nauvoo, Ill., 8 January, 1845," *Utah Genealogical and Historical Magazine* 11 (July 1920): 115. Just when Joseph started to trace his genealogy is unknown. Possibly it was when he received the Urim and Thummim of Jared.

52. Smith, *Life of Joseph F. Smith,* 417.

53. Starbird, *Magdalen's Lost Legacy,* 42.

54. Brigham Young, in *Journal of Discourses* (4 September 1873), 16:187b.

55. Smith, *Teachings of the Prophet Joseph Smith* (18 December 1833), 40.

56. Bates and Smith, *Lost Legacy,* 34.

57. *Utah Genealogical and Historical Magazine* 23 (October 1932): 175.

58. Max Weber, as quoted by Bates and Smith, *Lost Legacy,* 9.

59. Minutes of meeting of Joseph Smith, Hyrum Smith, James Adams, Newel K. Whitney et al., at Nauvoo (27 May 1843), in Miscellaneous Minutes, Brigham Young Collection, Church Archives, quoted in D. Michael Quinn, "The Mormon Succession Crisis of 1844," *BYU Studies* 16, 2 (Winter 1976): 202.

60. Smith, *History of the Church,* 5:510 (27 May 1843); emphasis added. This statement comes from the William Clayton journal in slightly different verbiage that suggests that Hyrum already held the office of prophet because of his lineage: "He [Joseph] stated that Hyrum held the office of prophet to the church by birth-right." See Ehat and Cook, *Words of Joseph Smith,* 232, 233. Later, men went to Joseph to complain about this turn of events, and Joseph reversed his statement. See Smith, *History of the Church,* 5:517–18; *Teachings of the Prophet Joseph*

Smith, 317–18. "I will advance your Prophet to a Priest, and then to a King." Alvin Smith (1798–1823) was dead by this time.

61. Corbett, *Hyrum Smith*, 320.

62. Smith, *Teachings of the Prophet Joseph Smith* (15 June 1842; 1974), 244, 322; *History of the Church*, 5:27.

63. Smith, *Teachings of the Prophet Joseph Smith*, 180. Joseph taught that "all priesthood is Melchizedek, but there are different portions or degrees of it."

64. This is synonymous with "The Priesthood after the Order of the Son of God" (D&C 107:3).

65. Smith, *Teachings of the Prophet Joseph Smith* (27 August 1843), 323. See also Smith, *History of the Church*, 5:554–56. Of the patriarchal priesthood, according to the version of the sermon published in the *History of the Church* and *Teachings of the Prophet Joseph Smith*, Joseph stated: "The 2nd Priesthood is patriarchal authority. Go to and finish the temple, and God will fill it with power, and you will then receive more knowledge concerning this priesthood."

66. Franklin D. Richards, "Scriptural Items" (27 August 1843), in Ehat and Cook, *Words of Joseph Smith*, 245.

67. Smith, *Teachings of the Prophet Joseph Smith*, 237. They were not ordained as kings and priests at this time, but only anointed to become such.

68. Smith, *History of the Church* (6 August 1843), 5:527; Ehat and Cook, *Words of Joseph Smith*, 304 n. 21.

69. In 1979, The Church of Jesus Christ of Latter-day Saints made emeritus the position of Church Patriarch, then held by Eldred Gee Smith, and announced it would not be filled after his death.

70. "RLDS Church to Go outside Smith Family for Next President," *Sunstone*, March 1996, 74. RLDS Church Director of Women's Ministries, Gail Mengel, noted, "The Church has never been without a Smith at its head, but it is not an overriding mandate." There were approximately 250,000 RLDS church members as of 1999, a drop of about 15 percent since the 1984 decision to ordain women to the priesthood. She notes that the RLDS church is not ready for a female relative of Joseph Smith to be its president. The 1861 church has now changed its name to Community of Christ.

71. Dean C. Jessee, ed., "The John Taylor Nauvoo Journal," *BYU Studies* 23, 3 (Summer 1983): 66. See also Smith, *Intimate Chronicle*, 170–71.

72. See E. Gary Smith, "The Patriarchal Crisis of 1845," *Dialogue*, 16, 2 (Summer 1983): 34.

73. John Smith patriarchal blessing, typescript in Church History Department (1853).

74. Smith, *Sharing the Gospel with Others*, 53.

75. Another son of Hyrum, Joseph F. Smith, became the sixth president and prophet of the Church after Lorenzo Snow. His grandson Joseph Fielding Smith became the tenth president of the Church.

76. Interestingly, Joseph F. Smith was ordained by his half brother John Smith.

77. Peter Scarlet, "Church's Lineage of Patriarchs Ties Mormonism to Old Testament Days," *Salt Lake Tribune*, 19 November 1994, C2.

78. Bates and Smith, *Lost Legacy*, 163. This suggestion was not taken seriously.

79. At ninety-nine years of age, he continues to be healthy and kindly holds regular office hours in the Joseph Smith Memorial building.

80. Peter Scarlet, "Church's Lineage of Patriarchs Ties Mormonism to Old Testament Days," *Salt Lake Tribune*, 19 November 1994, C2.

81. Ehat and Cook, *Words of Joseph Smith* (10 March 1844), 331: "And the throne and kingdom of David is to be taken from him [King David] and given to another by the name of David in the last days, raised up out of his lineage." Joseph Smith Jr. and this descendant, according to this model, partook of the royal stock of David. See 2 Samuel 7:12: "And when thy days be fulfilled, and thou shalt sleep with thy fathers, I will set up thy seed after thee, which shall proceed out of thy bowels, and I will establish his kingdom." This means that a Davidic descendant, like Joseph Smith Jr.'s posterity, will have the priesthood in the last days (see Ezekiel 34:24).

82. Allen, *Judah's Sceptre and Joseph's Birthright*, 182. He is quoting from 2 Samuel 7:16: "And your house and your kingdom shall be established forever before you. Your throne shall be established forever." See also Luke 1:30–33.

83. Interestingly, the Irish monk St. Brendan, in the sixth century after Christ, supposedly was identified with an ancient temple site on the adjoining McIntosh farm, believed to have been established by Irish monks between A.D. 500 and 600 (see Boren and Boren, *Following the Ark of the Covenant*, 122). Not far from Joseph Smith's birthplace in Sharon is a town named Glastonbury. Like its counterpart in Somerset, England, it has a reputation as a mystical place.

84. William Clayton Diary (1 January 1845; his entry for 11 April 1844 was more abbreviated: "voted our P, P and K with loud Hosannas"), as quoted in Quinn, *Origins of Power*, 124. See Smith, *Intimate Chronicle*, 154, 129. The term *seer* is not mentioned but implied.

85. David Wilson (1980–) Provo, Utah, *Joseph Smith, Proclaimed King of All Israel by Hosannahs* (2005, oil

on canvas, 24" x 18"). Courtesy of the artist.

86. Gordon C. Thomasson, "Foolsmate," *Dialogue*, 6 (Autumn-Winter 1971): 148–51. Thomasson challenges that Joseph was made King. He incorrectly claims that William Marks and others have confused or misrepresented Joseph's purely religious second anointing as making the Prophet a political "King and Priest."

87. Diary of George A. Smith (9 May 1844) as quoted in Kenneth W. Godfrey, "The Road to Carthage Led West," *BYU Studies* 9, 2 (Winter 1968): 212–13.

88. Smith, *History of the Church*, 6:568–69 (Tuesday 25 June 1844).

89. Lyman Wight and Heber C. Kimball letter to Joseph Smith (19 June 1844), LDS Archives.

90. While Joseph was running for President of the United States, he did not want the Kingship ordination made public.

91. Andrew Ehat, "Joseph Smith's Introduction of the Temple Ordinance and the 1844 Mormon Succession Question" (master's thesis, Brigham Young University, 1982), 220–22, n. 660.

92. *Nauvoo Neighbor* (1 January 1845).

93. William Marks to "Beloved Brethren" (15 June 1853) in *Zion's Harbinger and Baneemy's Organ* (St. Louis, July 1853), 3:53. As quoted in Quinn, *Extensions of Power*, 124, 361. Quinn also notes a number of other accounts which undoubtedly relied upon William Marks as a resource. Hansen, "The Theory and Practice of the Political Kingdom of God in Mormon History, 1829–1890" (master's thesis, Brigham Young University, 1959), 114, noted that George Miller was allegedly quoted as saying, "In this Council [of Fifty] we ordained Joseph Smith as king on earth." Quinn believes that this was forged by one John Zahnd, as an addition to a 27 June 1855 letter from Miller to James J. Strang. See Quinn, *Origins of Power*, 361. Strang had already assumed the title of "King" and thus the addition to the bottom of the letter was timely. It does lend credence to the idea of Joseph Smith as "King on Earth" rather than "King of the Earth."

94. Pratt, *Key to the Science of Theology*, 66.

95. Quinn, "The Council of 50 and Its Members 1844–1945," *BYU Studies* (Winter 1980): 186. Quinn's *Origins of Power*, 361, notes that this John Taylor revelation of 27 June 1882 was noted in the Annie Taylor Hyde notebook (page 64).

96. D. Michael Quinn, "The Council of 50 and Its Members 1844–1945," *BYU Studies* (Winter 1980): 188; and

Origins of Power, 361, quoting Franklin D. Richard's diary and miscellaneous papers, 4 February 1885, Church Archives. Franklin Richards lists President John Taylor as King and notes, "Attended council at Endowment House where we had prayers, consecrated oil and Prest. John Taylor was anointed K.P.R. of C. Z. & K." See Franklin D. Richards Journal, LDS Church Archives (4 February 1885). The abbreviations may stand for, "King, Priest, Ruler of Church, Zion & the Kingdom."

97. Abraham H. Cannon Journal, LDS Church Arcives (2 December 1885 or 95?), 198.

98. Manuscript in Franklin D. Richards Miscellaneous Papers (4 February 1885), Church Archives. See D. Michael Quinn, "The Evolution of the Presiding Quorums of the LDS Church," *BYU Studies* 20 (Fall 1979): 187; and "The Council of 50 and Its Members 1844–1945," *BYU Studies* (Winter 1980): 188. See also Quinn, *Origins of Power*, 124, 361.

99. William Clayton Diary, Hologram, LDS Church Archives (25 April 1844): "This government was about to be overthrown and the Kingdom which Daniel spoke of was about to be established somewhere in the west and he thought [not?] in Illinois."

100. Quinn, *Origins of Power*, 124–25, 362.

101. Ibid., 80.

102. The best of such systems has a tried and true head, selected from a quorum of elders (Twelve?) as a proving ground and a democratic republic beneath it to handle the functioning of governance.

103. Underwood, *Millenarian World of Early Mormonism*, 109.

104. Quinn, *Origins of Power*, 137, 371, quoting John E. Hallwas, "Mormon Nauvoo from a Non-Mormon Perspective," *Journal of Mormon History* 16 (1990): 60.

105. "In Joseph Smith's life-time it had been organized into the Council of the fifty Princes of the Kingdom." See George Miller, Journal History (4 January 1847), as quoted in Andrus, *Joseph Smith and World Government*, 83.

106. Smith, *History of the Church* (25 June 1844), 6:568–69.

107. McConkie, *Mormon Doctrine*, 415–16.

108. Godwin, *Holy Grail*, 179. Wolfram von Eschenbach notes that written upon the sacred Grail were the following words: "If any Templar of this community should, by the grace of God, become the ruler of a foreign peoples, let him ensure that they are given their rights."

CHAPTER TWENTY-ONE

THE LITERAL DESCENDANTS OF THE CHOSEN SEED

*The order of the priesthood was confirmed to be
handed down from father to son, and rightly belongs
to the literal descendants of the chosen seed, to whom
the promises were made.*

—D&C 107:40

The lineages of Jesus Christ and Mary Magdalene connecting again at Joseph Smith Jr. was the conduit through which the Lord channeled His blessings in these last days. Through Joseph's genealogy, the LDS Church was founded upon the principle of a priesthood line and bloodline authority, with its saving ordinances and living oracles. As early as 1835 the Prophet understood this principle, and Brigham Young understood its import: "If our progenitors had kept their records as the Jews anciently did they would be able to tell exactly where they came from—and where they run down in one straight line."[1]

Actually, it would be *two straight lines,* one through a male Y-chromosome and the other a female mtDNA. In spite of this sacred pattern, some accept Moses but not Christ; others confess Christ but not Joseph Smith; others Joseph but not Gordon B. Hinckley or intervening prophets. How can one accept the fountain but not the stream? The source of this "rosy stream" began with Adam, and continues to

Abraham, then to Jesus Christ, and naturally flows to Joseph Smith and beyond. Brigham Young believed that true Christianity came with the acknowledging of Joseph Smith as Christ's Prophet:

And every spirit that does not confess that God has sent Joseph Smith, and revealed the everlasting gospel to and through him, is of Antichrist, no matter whether it is found in a pulpit or on a throne, nor how much divinity it may profess, nor what it professes with regard to revealed religion and the account that is given of the Savior and his Father in the Bible.

[The world could acknowledge Christ] until doomsday, and He will never own them, nor bestow the Holy Spirit upon them, and they will never have visions of eternity open to them unless they acknowledge that Joseph Smith is sent of God. Such people I call unbelievers.[2]

Only through confessing and professing Jesus Christ and His latter-day prophet, Joseph Smith Jr., can we access the saving ordinances and powers of heaven found in the temple. In the LDS temple endowment ceremony, we are promised, upon conditions of faithfulness, to become Kings and Queens, Priests and Priestesses. This hints at a dominion, principality, or kingdom over which we will reign with Jesus Christ. In the spirit of family unity, the Lord said that we become heirs and joint-heirs (Romans 8:17) of all that is His. Thus we have and share a mighty realm indeed by right of our heritage in the Grail family, which family invites new members.

THE LORD'S LATTER-DAY DESCENDANTS

The Prophet Joseph Smith, and my father, Hyrum Smith, Brigham Young, John Taylor, Wilford Woodruff, and other choice spirits who were reserved to come forth in the fullness of times to take part in laying the foundations of the great latter-day work. I observed that they were also among the noble and great ones who were chosen in the beginning to be rulers in the Church of God. Even before they were born, they, with many others, received their first lessons in the world of spirits and were prepared to come forth in the due time of the Lord to labor in his vineyard for the salvation of the souls of men.

—D&C 138:53–56

Orson Scott Card once defined the premortal life as, "Where you committed all the sins you're being punished for now."[3] Your spiritual development in premortality greatly influences your life and sometimes your bloodline channel on earth.[4] The pure and protected patriarchal and matriarchal lineages combined in him were the choicest blessings and greatest burden Joseph Smith possessed.

Even though Abraham and Joseph Smith, unlike Pharaoh, had the right to the priesthood through lineage, they still needed a specific ordination and personal righteousness (see D&C 112:32). A rather large and consequential posterity flowed from the loins of Jesus Christ and in them, when pure and properly organized, rested the hope for the only true and living Church of God.[5] The most direct linear birthright line, the chosen heirs of the Savior and Mary Magdalene, however, was hidden more than other branches of the Grail Family. Locked so long in oblivion, the motto "patience under suffering" could apply to them.

The lost dynasty of the Holy Grail was found in the associates of Joseph Smith: the Cannons, Cowderys, Harrises, Johnsons, Kimballs, Knights, Partridges, Pratts, Richardses, Snows, Whitmers, Whitneys, Youngs, and many other early saints. Joseph Fielding Smith Jr. said as much: "The Lord reserved the right to send into the world a chosen lineage of faithful spirits who were entitled to special favors based on premortal obedience."[6] Wilford Woodruff concurred: "We are the seed of Ephraim, and of Abraham, and of Joseph, who was sold into Egypt, and these are the instruments that God has kept in the spirit world to come forth in these latter day to take hold of this kingdom and build it up."[7]

Ezra Taft Benson clearly stated this similar position: "There is a major difference this time. It is that God has saved for the final inning some of his strongest children, who will help bear off the Kingdom triumphantly. And that is where you come in, for you are the generation that must be prepared to meet your God."[8]

There is a "chosen people" reserved in premortality to come to this earth in the last days through certain lineages. There is also a "chosen family" in the latter days for Joseph Smith declared, "but few of them [gentiles] will be gathered with the chosen family."[9] The "chosen" were not all Jews, but also Ephraimites of the *Shiloh Dynasty*, who were called and ordained before the foundation of the earth to this work, and for the most part have admirably accomplished their missions.[10]

We have attempted to show how the patriarchal and matriarchal bloodline of the Lamb's chosen family presently flows through the veins of Joseph Smith, and because of it he was the Grail king and inheritor of the promises of the dispensation of the fulness of time. Because of this extended family the gospel could flourish where it was planted. In this regard, speaking of New York and by extension New England, the Lord declared:

Behold, and lo, I have much people in this place, in the regions round about; and an effectual door shall be opened in the regions round about in this eastern land.

—D&C 100:3

He also spoke in like manner of people in Salem, Massachusetts (D&C 111:2). America was veritably rife with "the family." The Puritan ancestors who settled New England were among God's chosen seed, and they were transplanted from Britain, the greatest nation this earth has ever known. But how are they associated with the restoration of the gospel in the last days? Were they also connected to the royal succession? We shall now see the inter-relatedness.

If the noble blood of Jesus Christ and His wives was present in America's founding fathers and specifically in Joseph Smith's lineage, might it also be present in other members of the Church leadership at all levels? If the blood of Israel was richly concentrated in England, Wales, and Scotland, was this not the ancestral base of most of our highest LDS leaders? It should be noted that all the latter-day prophets trace their pedigree to the British Isles.[11] Heber C. Kimball in 1856 saw the royal blood (*sang real*) or ancestry identified with "aristocracy":

The aristocracy—that is, those that are called the aristocracy, came out of the old country; they came as far as Lehi came from Jerusalem, and so on, till they came into this country [America]; but still those that remained behind considered themselves the aristocracy. But let me tell you those men that came here were the true aristocracy; they were of the original stock. . . . I have looked into the visions of eternity, and I know that I am true, and that I am [of] the true vine. I am one of the sons of those old veterans, and so is brother Brigham. . . .

Now, I will refer to brother Brigham, brother Heber, brother Joseph Smith, Oliver Cowdery, Bishop N. K. Whitney, and lots of other men. Brother Joseph actually saw those men in vision; he saw us in a day when we were all together. We have been separated by marriage and thrown apart; but he saw the day when we all came out of one stock, and that was out of the aristocracy. Yes, we came directly down through the Prophets, and not only us, but lots of others—the whole Smith race. I could remember probably twenty or thirty that Joseph mentioned came down through that channel. . . .

There is another thing that brother Joseph said—viz., that we were positively heir of the Priesthood; for he had seen us as such in his vision; yes, just as much so as my children are that have been born since I received my endowment. Our fathers were heirs to that Priesthood which was handed down from father to son, and we came through that lineage. . . .

Joseph told us these things, and I know them to be true. I know them by the revelations of Jesus Christ, and so do a great many men. We are and we were heirs when we were called and ordained to the Apostleship: we were of that class; yes, we were the sons and daughters of those that came down through that lineage.[12]

In scripture, the "true vine" is usually used as a reference to Jesus Christ (John 15:1, 5). However, it is also a metaphor for God's chosen people, as Heber C. Kimball has used it (Isaiah 5:7; Psalm 128; Ezekiel 19:10–14). It should be noted as well that later genealogical research has shown that many members of the early LDS Church leadership were distantly related to the Joseph Smith family.[13] Brigham Young, speaking in 1845 of a shared genealogy, noted: "When we come to the connections we discover that we all sprung back to the settlement of New England about 200 years ago. It is but a little more than that time when Father Smith, the Goddards, Richards, Youngs and Kimballs were all in one family—as it were."[14]

Brigham's statement regarding the reunion of the Young and Richards families in Nauvoo included them in the larger Smith family and, by inference, the Savior's family as well, "We are all relations. It is only three generations back that Brother Joseph Smith's family were related to this family."[15]

Other lines descending from Jesus Christ may be included in the Church's royal family. For instance Benjamin F. Johnson had four sisters married to the Prophet Joseph.[16] Their bloodline must have attracted the Prophet's interest. In Johnson's autobiography he states: "In Macedonia the Johnsons [family of Julia Hills and Ezekiel Johnson] were quite numerous and influential and the envious dubbed us the 'Royal Family.' When Joseph [Smith] heard of this 'honor' conferred upon us by our neighbors, he said the name was and should be a reality; that we were a royal family."[17]

A few common ancestors in Britain seem to have been a crucial pivot in the family tree, which spread its branches to other founders and apostles in the LDS Church. Dealing with this issue, an interesting letter written in 1853, referencing a speech from Brigham Young, from Orson Pratt to Parley P. Pratt has come to light: "You will recall that Joseph had a vision and saw that our families and his all sprang from the same man a few generations ago. . . . The Lord had his eye upon him, and upon his father, and upon their progenitors, clear back to Abraham and from Abraham to the flood, and from the flood to Enoch and from Enoch to Adam."[18]

Truman Madsen paraphrases Pratt's letter a little differently: "You will recall that Joseph had a vision in which he saw that our ancestral line [meaning the Pratt brothers] and his [the Smiths] had a common ancestor a few generations back."[19]

The letter, according to Truman Madsen, remained in an attic until about 1930. Then a granddaughter took it to Archibald F. Bennett (1896–1965), Church genealogist, who did research on the question. Bennett discovered that several generations back Joseph did have a common ancestor with the Pratts. This ancestor was the English reformer, John Lathrop (1584–1653), the fifth great-grandfather of the Prophet Joseph Smith.

John Lathrop was a minister in the Church of England who broke from his church and formed a small dissident congregation. He was persecuted and imprisoned and eventually emigrated to America. Thousands of his descendants are LDS, as Richard W. Price wrote in his biography and genealogy of Lathrop: "In the [LDS] Church I would say probably 25 percent of the original Church members in America were descended from him [Lathrop]. . . I don't think there's any recent, common ancestor that has more descendants in the Church."[20]

According to genealogy, early Church leaders related to Lathrop include Oliver Cowdery, Orson and Parley P. Pratt, Wilford Woodruff, Frederick G. Williams, Joseph Smith Sr., Joseph F. and Joseph Fielding Smith, Harold B. Lee, and others. More recently are included Nathan Eldon Tanner, Marion G. Romney, and Bishop H. Burke Peterson, to name a very few. From this astonishing discovery, one can reason that Joseph selected many of the general authorities, not because of nepotism, but because he knew them through revelation to be descendants of Jesus Christ.[21]

Besides LDS leaders, the Lathrop line has produced other noted Americans, namely Ulysses S. Grant, Franklin D. Roosevelt, Eli Whitney, Henry Wadsworth Longfellow, Oliver Wendell Holmes, and Dr. Benjamin Spock. More recently we have President George Bush, Utah Congressman Dan Marriott, former Secretary of Education T. H. Bell, former LDS Michigan governor George Romney and his son, Mitt Romney, governor of Massachusetts.

We are reminded of Pelagius, the fifth-century British monk, who left the Catholic Church to pursue a truer vision of the gospel. He claimed descent from the "children of Joseph of Arimathea" (a code name for the children of Jesus Christ). In like manner, Lathrop left the Church of England to live as he felt the scriptures taught. He was thrown into prison and eventually banished to New England where he was able to teach and practice a more Puritanical life. Interestingly, there are many similarities between the early Pilgrims, Puritans, and the LDS Church. "Half of what the Puritans believed," writes Cureton, "is what Mormons believe also."[22]

The converging genealogical lines point to Joseph Smith and the immediate leadership families of the Church as having a special calling. Joseph's lineage in Christ was very potent and was shared by many early Latter-day Saints. Among these are Judge James Adams, George Q. Cannon, and Heber C. Kimball.

The Oliver B. Huntington journal records an account of how Joseph Smith sealed a Sister Repshire to Judge James Adams of Springfield, Illinois. The entry notes that, "The Prophet stated to her (Repshire) that Judge Adams was a literal descendant of Jesus Christ."[23] Another example is brother Joseph saying to Edward Hunter, his scribe for section 128 of the Doctrine and Covenants, "I know who you are, we are near kin, I know your genealogy."[24]

These noted instances help to establish Joseph Smith's understanding of the concept of a genealogical link between the royal lineage of the Savior to living Latter-day Saints of the early Church. The genealogy of the family of the first Church bishop, Edward Partridge (1793–1840) indicates that they are related to the *Rex Deus* ancestry of the Plantagenets, d'Anjou, Stewarts of Scotland, and the Dukes of Normandy.[25]

The Isaac Morley lineage was supposedly through the Möres of the Orkneys, Sinclairs of Scotland, Madoc ab Owain Gwynedd (the Welsh Knight Templar), John Dee (1527–1608), the occult alchemist, and others of the Grail bloodline.[26] Isaac Morley was the Mormon patriarch who established the first pioneer settlement in Sanpete Valley in 1849 and baptized Ute Indian chief "Joseph" Walker in 1855.

The apostle Heber C. Kimball, grandfather of president Spencer W. Kimball, also claimed ancestry from Jesus Christ. A number of quotations from the early brethren confirm this concept. Orson F. Whitney, of the Grail seed himself, writes: "So was it with this servant of Christ [Heber C. Kimball], this brother of Jesus in the British Isles. . . . His, also, was the Savior's lineage; in his heart a kindred spirit; in his veins the self-same blood."[27]

This was not some metaphorical blood, but literal and living blood, with the Savior's DNA signature flowing through Kimball's very veins. Brother Kimball, in the Tabernacle in March 1857, spoke along these lines:

> Did you actually know Joseph Smith? No. Do you know Brother Brigham? No. Do you know Brother Heber? No, you do not. Do you know the Twelve? You do not; if you did, you would begin to know God, and learn that those men who are chosen to direct and counsel you are near kindred to God and Jesus Christ, for the keys, power, and authority of the kingdom of God are in that lineage.[8]

Heber C. Kimball's recent biographer, Stanley B. Kimball, wrote:

> In his own mind Heber was not only a follower of Christ, but a literal descendant. In his last public sermon, two months before his death, he said, 'You do not know who Heber C. Kimball is,' or you would do better.' If one can accept the possibility of Christ's marriage, then such a descent is possible.[29]

There are those who find this presumptuous at best and sinister at worse. Most left-leaning and liberal Mormons find any discussion of a "special"

or "chosen" bloodline repugnant and dangerous.[30] They believe it will lead to a "master-race" syndrome of racial superiority. They see a waning of bloodline and chosen-race rhetoric as the chief reason for the proclamation of 1978 regarding the Blacks and in the demise of the LDS Church Patriarch's office.[31]

It is at variance with Mormon tribalism, as given in patriarchal blessings. The idea of blood, ancestral inheritance, genealogy, and bloodlines is noted in scripture in almost every chapter. It is particularly evident in the statements of Joseph Smith, and early Church leaders made Grail claims for themselves. However, without understanding and appreciating its message and meaning, it is "unto the Jews a stumbling block, and unto the Greeks foolishness" (1 Corinthians 1:23).

THE NEW FISHER KING?

> *For this anointing have I put upon his [Joseph Smith Jr.] head, that his blessing shall also be put upon the head of his posterity after him. And as I said unto Abraham concerning the kindred of the earth, even so I say unto my servant Joseph: In thee and in thy seed shall the kindred of the earth be blessed.*
>
> —D & C 124:57–58

A root or branch is mentioned in the Old Testament referring to a righteous king who will unite the throne with the bloodline of God (Jeremiah 23:5–6; Isaiah 11:1–5; Zech.3:8–10; 6:12–15). This particular branch was probably Jesus Christ, although earlier we noted that the branch was the Church.[32] However, the righteous Branch might also refer to the Prophet Joseph Smith Jr. For as Zechariah wrote, "These are the two anointed ones" (4:14). Joseph Smith was well aware that he, an Ephraimite, would also represent the House of David.[33]

We have seen how the bloodline coming down in two lines upon Joseph Smith was protected pure and direct. But how it proceeded after Joseph is questionable. According to Michael Kennedy, shortly before his death Joseph was visited by an angel, telling him that his children would leave the Church.[34] This is reminiscent of Doctrine and Covenants 109:68–70, where Joseph prayed that his family's prejudices would be broken up and "swept away as with a flood."

After his death, none of Joseph's family stayed with the Church.[35] President George Q. Cannon in 1884 lamented that no posterity of Joseph Smith Jr. was in the Church:

> There may be faithful men who will have unfaithful sons, who may not be as faithful as they might be; but faithful posterity will come, just as I believe will be the case with the Prophet Joseph's seed.
>
> Today he has not a soul descended from him personally, in this Church. There is not a man bearing the Holy Priesthood, to stand before our God in the Church that Joseph was the means in the hands of God, of founding—not a man today of his own blood—that is, by descent—to stand before the Lord, and represent him among these Latter-day Saints.[36]

The vexing of the Church of the Firstborn (D&C 76:54) between the "adherents of the message" (priesthood) and the supposed "adherents of the bloodline" (birthright) will one day be reconciled.[37] The problem between the Brighamites and the Josephites, that is between the "kingdom" and the "king," will eventually be resolved.[38] Old and New Jerusalem will unite, but by who or by whom? President George Q. Cannon confirms this idea:

But will this always be the case? No. Just as sure as God lives, just as sure as God has made promises, so sure will someone of Joseph Smith's posterity rise up and be numbered with this Church. And bear the everlasting Priesthood that Joseph himself held. It may be delayed in the wise providence of our God. . . .

God made them [the promises] to Joseph during his lifetime; and they will be fulfilled just as sure as God made them. He [Joseph] will have among this people, some one descended from his own loins, who will bear the everlasting Priesthood, and who will honor and magnify that Priesthood among the Latter-day Saints.[39]

Whether Joseph Smith himself or one of his descendants will take up a leading role for the Church in the last days, we do not know. There is an interesting prophecy from Joseph Smith which gives us an inkling or portent of the future, "the throne and kingdom of David is to be taken from him [King David] and given to another by the name of David in the last days, raised up out of his [Joseph's] lineage."[40] Who is the King's Son, called "David" who would close out the last days when the "winding up scene is at hand?" This "Branch" would be named after "David, a prince" according to Ezekiel:

> *And I will set up one shepherd over them, and he shall feed them, even my servant David; he shall feed them, and he shall be their shepherd. And I the Lord will be their God, and my servant David a prince among them; I the Lord have spoken it.*
>
> —EZEKIEL 34:23–24

Emma's son who was most likely to head the Church was Joseph Smith III (1832–1914). One source indicates that he had been blessed to be the Prophet's successor as head of the Church on January 17, 1844, by his father.[41] But Emma's and Brigham's bitter interpersonal relations squelched this possibility. Joseph Smith III had completely apostatized by the time he accepted the mantle of president and prophet for the Reorganized Church of Jesus Christ of Latter-day Saints (RLDS, now known as the Community of Christ Church) in 1860.

Newell and Avery weakly claim that Brigham Young had told the Saints that "while the sun shines, the water runs, the grass grows, and the earth remains, young Joseph Smith [III] never will be the leader of the Latter day Saints!"[42] However, Brigham Young did remark to his brother Phineas in February 1860: "[Young] Joseph . . . will be a good latter-day saint; in time it may want a revelation from the Lord; but blessings will rest upon the posterity of Joseph Smith the Prophet."[43]

If Joseph III would not be the new Fisher King, who would be? The Utah Church did not seem to harbor negative feelings toward the concept of Joseph's children taking the reins of the Church. Brigham once said, "If one of Joseph's children takes the lead of the Church he will come and place himself at the head of this Church, and I will receive him as willing as any one here."[44]

The last son, David Hyrum (November 1844–1904), who was born five months after the prophet's death, seems to have had some *bona fides* for the succession. David was a fine person and a portrait artist by avocation, but he was mentally unstable.[45] Tradition has it that one "David the Prince" who is "The Branch out of the root of Jesse" will again unite in the last days, the priesthood and the patriarchal church. Oliver B. Huntington recorded: "At the time of his birth, it was intimated by old Mrs. Durphee and the others that Joseph the prophet had said that

he (David Hyrum which name Joseph gave him before his death) was to be the David the Bible speaks of to rule over Israel forever, which David spoken of most of the people took to be old King David."[46]

One Phebe Woodworth recorded:

> Smith came to her house and said, Emma was going to have a son of promise; and if a son of promise was walled in with granite rock, when the power of the Holy Ghost fell upon him he would break his way out. He knew the principle upon which a son of promise could be obtained, he had complied with that principle and Emma should have such a son. [That] November [1844] David H. was born . . . When Prest. Young announced the fact that in Joseph's posterity the keys of the Priesthood should rest and that upon young David [Hyrum] the blessing should descend.[47]

Perhaps the prophet entertained hopes for David Hyrum because he was the first male heir after Joseph and Emma were sealed in eternal marriage. Brigham said that in the spring of 1844, the Prophet Joseph expressed that David might possibly lead the Church: "Joseph [the Prophet] said to me, 'I shall have a son born to me, and his name shall be called David; and on him, in some future time, will rest the responsibility that now rests on me.'"[48]

When it became obvious that Joseph Smith III would not join the Church, Brigham looked to David Hyrum in general conference of October 1866: "I am looking for the time when the Lord will speak to David (H. Smith); but let him pursue the course he is now pursuing, and he will never preside over The Church of Jesus Christ of Latter-day Saints in time or in eternity. . . It would be his right to preside over this Church, if he would only walk in the true path of duty."[49]

One can only assume that Brigham kept sacred Joseph Smith Jr.'s prophecy. In August 1872 as he spoke in Farmington, Brigham Young continued to hold out some hope for David: "I have told the people times enough, they never may depend on Joseph Smith [III] who is now living; but David, who was born after the death of his father, I still look for the day to come when the Lord will touch his eyes. But I do not look for it while his mother lives."[50]

Clearly Joseph Smith Jr. saw in the lineal succession of his sons Joseph III and David something that also meant much to Brigham's way of thinking. President Young was not naturally hostile to the sons, but only to their mother, Emma, who, he deeply believed, betrayed her husband. David married Clara Hartshorn in May 1870. In spite of poor health, by November they were in Utah. He stayed for two months and in a letter to his brother Joseph III wrote that the Brighamites were favorable to him and his wife, but were not trying to convert him.[51]

In March 1871 David and Clara had their only child, a son called Elbert Aoriul Smith. The Prophet Joseph's grandson might have been the King's Son except he died in 1959 unmarried and without any known posterity. This would seem to be the end of David's line of succession. Sadly David Hyrum, from 1878 until his death in 1904, was mentally ill and lived in an asylum.[52]

Joseph III, on the other hand, had seventeen children, Alexander Hale Smith had nine, and the daughters of Joseph Smith had many children as well. Still, one of Joseph and Emma Smith's direct descendants might, one day, join the LDS Church and rise to high Church leadership. On the other hand, the Reorganized LDS Church was built upon the idea of lineal patriarchal succession.

This splinter church seems to be shrinking in size, while continuing to reject the peculiar parts of Mormon doctrinal and historical heritage, as it has done since 1860–61. At this point its new name, Community of Christ Church, underscores its becoming a mainstream Protestant religion. The Book of Mormon is no longer regarded as divine scripture, and the faith does not see itself as the "only true and living" Church. Thus it cannot be maintained that the diminishing Community of Christ Church will be a key spiritual player in latter-day events.[53]

If Emma had come west with her sons and taught them the gospel and had them receive the ordinances, it is almost certain that Brigham Young would have named them to the Quorum of the Twelve. He did this for Hyrum's eldest son with Mary Fielding, Joseph F. Smith. Joseph III, instead of his cousin Joseph F. Smith, might have become president of the Church following Lorenzo Snow in 1901 and would have served until his death in 1914.

Did Joseph Smith have a child through Eliza R. Snow, one of his plural wives? "No" notes Maureen Ursanbach Beecher, Snow's biographer.[54] Richard Van Wagoner gives the more tentative response of "possibly," from his research on polygamy.[55] If the "seed" of the Savior is carried on through Eliza's line, then there is possibly a hidden son, though never a hint of this was ever mentioned in the nineteenth century.

None of the above scenarios need necessarily be the events as they actually occurred in Church history. The reason? While the Joseph Smith III lineage was the purest font of Christian blood, it was by no means the only font from which a prophet, seer, and revelator might arise.[56] We are therefore not required to trace birthright authority just through Joseph Smith Jr., but rather through the larger lineage of the Savior.[57] The Mormon Church is rife with the blood of Christ coursing through its leadership's veins.

There is enough of the blood of the Savior and Joseph Smith's larger family within the general authorities of the Church for the kingdom to be governed by the "Lord's anointed." Jesus Christ has carefully watched over His children and His lineage to these last days to ensure this was the case. That is why this Church has, since 1838, appended to its title, "of Latter-day Saints." They are the modern descendants of the early-day Saints, and one of these descendants could be the Prince David spoken of by Joseph Smith.

THE LAW OF GRAIL ADOPTION

Therefore your life and the priesthood have remained, and must needs remain through you and your lineage until the restoration of all things spoken by the mouths of all the holy prophets since the world began.

—D&C 86:10

In this 1832 revelation, Joseph relayed God's word that the members of the Church were the under-girding power of the gospel on earth. Thus the name, The Church of Jesus Christ of *Latter-day Saints.* The gospel always seeks to draw the circle larger, to be more inclusive. When gentiles join the LDS Church they are adopted into the family of Abraham in order to receive the blessings of that lineage.[58] However, to receive the blessings of the literal seed of Christ, one must receive the ordinance of adoption into His family line. This *law of priesthood adoption,* which we might call *Grail adoption,* shall now be considered.

There were two kinds of sealing ordinances, one through the family (blood) and another through the priesthood (blessing). The law of priesthood adoption was an ordinance among the early Saints. It was initiated by Joseph Smith in Nauvoo and continued until a revelation by Wilford Woodruff halted the practice in 1894.[59] In it righteous men were not sealed to their own ancestors, but to the

priesthood-holding ancestors of others, usually a member of the Quorum of Twelve or First Presidency. This was different from today's temple sealings, which tie us to our own blood relations or family.

The purpose of sealing men to nonancestral men was to form a "chain of Priesthood" from Adam to us and not necessarily a sealing to our bloodline progenitors. Brigham Young told the brethren in 1847 that "their kingdom consisted of their own posterity and it did not diminish that at all by being sealed to one of the Twelve but only bound them by the perfect chain [of Priesthood] according to the law of God and the order of Heaven that will bind the righteous from Adam to the last Saint. And Adam will claim us all as members of his kingdom we being his children."[60]

Why would individuals be sealed to the Prophet, or a member of the First Presidency, or to a member of the Quorum of the Twelve Apostles? In the next chapter we shall see that the Twelve were all chosen from the bloodline of Jesus Christ. The Priesthood Chain has Adam to Noah to the Savior as its chief links.[61] Then within our Dispensation, Brother Joseph was the chief link by virtue of "lineage and blood."[62]

People were being adopted (sealed) into this sacred lineage of Christ because that lineage had full priesthood privileges. They therefore become a part of Grail history and an inclusive family. A temple ordinance was explained in 1873 by Brigham Young regarding the "chain" mentioned above. By this ordinance, he said, "Men will be sealed to their fathers, and those who have slept clear up to father Adam. . . . This Priesthood has been restored again, and by its authority we shall be connected with our fathers, by the ordinance of sealing, until we shall form a perfect chain [of Priesthood] from father Adam down to the closing up scene."[63]

Joseph Smith taught that there must be a "welding link" between the fathers and the children (D&C 128:18).[64] The Prophet is the "welding link" of this dispensation to Jesus Christ, adopting us into His royal family. Through lineage and through blessing, Brother Joseph is the indispensable man of this Dispensation.

Brigham Young taught that there were key links and that Joseph Smith was the first link for this dispensation and that every Latter-day Saint must descend from Joseph Smith through the law of adoption.[65] The law of Grail adoption likely had to do with sealing men to the family of the Great High Priest after the Order of Melchizedek, Jesus Christ. It was intended to bring all Latter-day Saints, from whatever gentile pedigree, into a common "chosen" lineage, that of Jesus Christ to Joseph Smith Jr. Claiming descent from Abrahamic Israel was sufficient for salvation but not for exaltation. "The saints also need[ed] to be adopted into an even more sacred lineage: the lineage of Christ."[66] This could be through Joseph Smith's lineage or other members of the Quorum of the Twelve, who are also descendants of Jesus Christ.

Gordon Irving of the Church Historical Department noted that "seventy-four percent of those adopted, excluding natural children and relatives, were linked to Apostles Heber C. Kimball, Willard Richards, John Taylor, or Brigham Young."[67] These were Grail lineages directly related to Joseph Smith, a descendant of the Savior. For everyone in this dispensation, Joseph Smith is the ultimate link in the patriarchal chain.

While we are not fully instructed in the law of priesthood adoption, we know that it has something to do with the lineage and blood of those Prophets and Apostles set over us. It is in some way essential to our highest salvation and exaltation. As Orson Pratt proclaimed that all men had to be "adopted into the Priesthood in order to become sons and legal heirs of salvation,"[68] the chain of priesthood descends from Father Adam, to those born-again of Jesus Christ, and then onward to those who accept the Grail King, Joseph Smith Jr.

THE QUORUM OF THE TWELVE, "KNIGHTS OF THE GRAIL"

I say unto you, that the Quorum of the Twelve have the keys of the kingdom of God in all the world. . . . [The Twelve are] an independent body who have the keys of the priesthood—the keys of the kingdom of God to deliver to all the world.

—BRIGHAM YOUNG[69]

The kingdom of God upon the earth could not solely rest upon the shoulders of one, two, or three men, if it was to cover the entire world.[70] Therefore, on 14 February 1835 he created an ecclesiastic Quorum of the Twelve Apostles and the Seventy to help in this matter (D&C 107:22–25). During the dedication of the Kirtland Temple, Joseph Smith had the assembly acknowledge the Twelve Apostles as "Prophets and Seers and special witnesses to all the nations of the earth."[71] Thus the Church has, in the First Presidency and Quorum of Twelve, at least fifteen "prophets, seers, and revelators" at all times. They are fifteen Grail knights.

Not long before his and Hyrum's deaths, Joseph made what was called the "last charge." In post-martyrdom statements, it is anecdotally noted that the Prophet said, "Brethren, I am tired [of] bearing the burden of the church, you must round up your shoulders, and bear it till I rest."[72] Elizabeth Lightner, one of the Prophet's plural wives, heard Joseph say, "I have rolled this Kingdom off of my shoulders onto the shoulders of the Twelve so they can carry out this work and build up His kingdom."[73] Mosiah Hancock recalled the same occasion: "Brethren, I now roll this work onto the shoulders of the Twelve; and they shall bear and send this gospel to every nation under heaven."[74] With the Twelve and the three members of the First Presidency working in concert, the kingdom would be in safe hands.

Though unclear at the time, after the martyrdom of Joseph Smith the keys of authority reverted to the Twelve Apostles, with Elder Brigham Young as the president and chief of that Quorum. In August 1845, Brigham Young again set the burden upon the heads of the Quorum of the Twelve Apostles to carry off the kingdom:

You are now without a Prophet present with you in the flesh to guide you; but you are not without Apostles, who hold the keys of power to seal on earth that which shall be sealed in heaven, and to preside over all the affairs of the Church in all the world: being still under the direction of the same God, and being dictated by the same spirit, having the same manifestations of the Holy Ghost to dictate all the affairs of the church in all the world, to build up the kingdom upon the foundation that the prophet Joseph has laid, who still holds the keys of this last dispensation, and will hold them to all eternity, as a king and priest unto the Most High God, ministering in heaven, on earth or among the spirits of the departed dead, as seemeth good to him who sent him.

Let no man presume for a moment that his place will be filled by another; for remember he stands in his own place and always will; and the Twelve Apostles of this dispensation stand in their own place and always will, both in time and in eternity, to minister, preside and regulate the affairs of the whole church.[75]

Through this blessing Brigham Young and the Twelve obtained through "the fathers" the right to reign. The Twelve Apostles hold all the keys of the kingdom severally, not personally, as a quorum not as individuals. Moreover, like Joseph and Hyrum, they possess such an authority because they possess the sacred blood of the Holy Grail. This power is embedded within the top two quorums, the First Presidency and the Twelve Apostles of The Church of Jesus Christ of Latter-day Saints, which blossoms as the Grail Church.[76]

An interesting incident occurred in the Salt Lake Temple after the death of President Wilford Woodruff that supports this conclusion. His natural successor was the president of the Quorum of Twelve, the aged Lorenzo Snow. Yet President Snow felt that his advanced age was a detriment to his serving as prophet of the Church. He retired to the temple to offer up a prayer that he might be taken in death, or that a younger man might serve in his stead. The Lord Jesus appeared to President Snow, saying that He came to him because Snow was of the proper lineage.[77] Thus Snow was entitled to the presidency by the Grail paradigm, and because he had served faithfully through the ranks of the Twelve.

Later, during the presidency of Lorenzo Snow, at a solemn assembly in the Salt Lake Temple, apostle George Q. Cannon divulged more concerning the familial relations existing in the Church to the Savior Jesus Christ. After Cannon spoke, Lorenzo Snow confirmed his testimony. Spoken on the 2nd of July 1899 it was recorded by two apostles:

"There are those in this audience who are descendants of the old Twelve Apostles—and shall I say it, yes, descendants of the Savior Himself. His seed is represented in this body of men."

Following Pres. Cannon, President Snow arose and said that what

Bro. Cannon had stated respecting the literal descendants among this company of the old apostles and the Savior Himself is true—that the Savior's seed is represented in this body of men.[78]

Another apostle at the same meeting recorded Lorenzo Snow as stating: "There are men in this congregation who are descendants of the ancient Twelve Apostles and shall I say it, of the Son of God Himself, for He had seed, and in the right time they shall be known."[79]

Perhaps this is the deeper meaning of Doctrine and Covenants 86:2: "the field was the world, and the apostles were the sowers of the seed." Proper authority rested in their own ancestors back to Jesus Christ Himself. Ultimately the Savior's blood, like that of Abraham, was to be a leaven and a blessing to the earth, "that in them and their children the whole world would be blessed"[80] (D&C 124:57–58).

As Orson Hyde so aptly put it, "remember that in the last days, secret and hidden things must come to light, and that your life also is hid with Christ in God."[81] Heber C. Kimball attempted to emphasize that a number of the Twelve were of the bloodline of Christ and therefore were "chosen to direct and counsel you." "Did you actually know Joseph Smith? No. Do you know Brother Brigham? No. Do you know Brother Heber? No, you do not. *Do you know the Twelve?* You do not; if you did, you would begin to know God, and learn that those men who are chosen to direct and counsel you are near kindred to God and Jesus Christ, for the keys, power, and authority of the kingdom of God are in that lineage."[82]

Parley P. Pratt noted the close relationship between Jesus Christ and the birthright lineage of the Apostles:

In the lineage of Abraham, Isaac, and Jacob, according to the flesh, was held the right of heirship to the keys of Priesthood for the blessings and for the salvation of all nations. From this lineage sprang the Prophets, John the Baptist, Jesus, and the Apostles; and from this lineage sprang the great Prophet and restorer in modern times [Joseph Smith], and the Apostles who hold the keys under his hand. . . . it has been through the ministry of that lineage, and the keys of [that] Priesthood held by the lawful heirs according to the flesh. . . .

But no man can hold the keys of Priesthood or the Apostleship, to bless or administer salvation to the nations, unless he is a literal descendant of Abraham, Isaac, and Jacob. Jesus Christ and his ancient Apostles of both hemispheres were of that lineage. . . . The world has from that day to this been manufacturing priests, without any particular regard to lineage.[83]

Victor L. Ludlow is the only contemporary official LDS scholar to mention how the lineage came to the Prophet. Ludlow noted that there were occasions "when a number of the brethren, including Joseph Smith, claimed that they shared lineage with Jesus in the tribe of Judah."[84] Even though it is not explicitly stated, they also shared the lineage of Ephraim through the mothers from Mary Magdalene.

Doctrine and Covenants 49:8 speaks of "holy men that ye know not of," who may well be the very leaders, the prophets, seers, and revelators, the Lord has placed over us. The sacred lineage and royal blood is thick amongst the Quorum of the Twelve Apostles. These fifteen Grail knights collectively have the right to administer the gospel to the entire world, because they are the "literal descendants of the chosen seed" (D&C 107:40). It is because of them that the *Sang Real* pulses through the veins of this only living Church (D&C 1:3).

NOTES

1. Brigham Young, in "A Family Meeting in Nauvoo: Minutes of a Meeting of the Richards and Young Families Held in Nauvoo, Ill., 8 January, 1845," *Utah Genealogical and Historical Magazine* 11 (July 1920): 108.

2. Brigham Young, in *Journal of Discourses* (9 September 1860), 8:176–77. "What good would it do to acknowledge Christ and not the servants He has sent?"

3. Card, *Saintspeak*, 40.

4. In the film *The Sound of Music,* Julie Andrews sings about how nothing comes from nothing, nothing ever could. This means that today depends upon yesterday.

5. That is when they receive the proper priesthood authority through The Church of Jesus Christ of Latter-day Saints (D&C 1:30).

6. Smith, *Way of Perfection*, 127–30.

7. Wilford Woodruff, in *Journal of Discourses* (26 June 1881), 22:233.

8. Ezra Taft Benson, "In His Steps," in *BYU Speeches of the Year, 1979.*

9. Smith, *Teachings of the Prophet Joseph Smith,* 15; Smith, *History of the Church* (4 January 1833), 1:312–16. The DNA markers that identify the chosen family do not pass on characteristics. Therefore, while most are Caucasian, some of the Grail lineage may now be of the other races or colors of mankind.

10. The author thinks that the very worst of mankind also came through this lineage.

11. Latter-day prophets Joseph Smith Jr., Joseph F. Smith, George Albert Smith, and Joseph Fielding Smith are all from English stock. Brigham Young, John Taylor, Wilford Woodruff, Lorenzo Snow, and Spencer W. Kimball are all related to Joseph Smith, according to *Church News,* 23 December 1984, 14. Heber J. Grant, David O. McKay, Harold B. Lee, Ezra Taft Benson, and Gordon B. Hinckley all trace ancestry to Scotland, Wales, and England.

12. Heber C. Kimball, in *Journal of Discourses* (6 September 1856), 5:215–16. Elder Kimball is relating a vision that Joseph Smith received on 8 February 1835 and recorded on 14 February 1835 at Kirtland just before the organization of the quorums of the Twelve and of the Seventies. See Doctrine and Covenants 107:93, received the following month, 28 March 1835.

13. See various writings by Archibald Bennett, Andrew Jensen, E. L. Whitehead, John A. Widtsoe, and Anthony W. Ivins. Noted in *Church News,* 23 December 1984, 14.

14. Brigham Young, in "A Family Meeting in Nauvoo: Minutes of a Meeting of the Richards and Young Families Held in Nauvoo, Ill., 8 January, 1845," *Utah Genealogical and Historical Magazine* 11 (July 1920): 107.

15. Ibid.

16. Two were married in life and two sealed to the Prophet after his death. As far as we know, none of these sisters had children with Joseph Smith. My thanks to Rebecca and Clay Wagstaff for pointing this out to me (letter, 4 April 2004).

17. Johnson, *My Life's Review,* 83.

18. Orson Pratt to Parley P. Pratt (11 October 1853), quoted in Keith W. Perkins, "John Lothropp, Forbear of Prophets, Presidents and Others," in *British Isles,* 56. See also Bennett, *Saviors on Mount Zion,* 86. See Kelly, *Journals of John D. Lee* (17 February 1847), 91: "Joseph had a vision and saw and traced back our [Joseph's, Brigham's, and Heber's] bloods to the royal family."

19. As quoted in Madsen, *Temples in Antiquity,* 107.

20. Nancy Cureton, "Many LDS Have Common Ancestor," *Church News,* 23 December 1984, 14. See Price, *John Lathrop;* see also Archibald F. Bennett, "The Ancestry of Joseph Smith the Prophet," *Utah Genealogical and Historical Magazine,* 20 (April 1929): 66–69; *Saviors on Mount Zion,* 85–90.

21. See D. Michael Quinn, "Organizational Development and Social Origins of the Mormon Hierarchy" (master's thesis, University of Utah, 1973), 1. It made Mormon hierarchy, in effect, an extended family. He notes that 22.6 percent of all Church hierarchy between 1832 and 1932 were directly related.

22. Nancy Cureton (23 December 1984), 14. The author, Vern Swanson, was a member of the Pilgrim Holiness Church before he converted to Mormonism. That church is a part of the larger Puritan, Quaker, and Friends movement.

23. Oliver B. Huntington Journal (29 December 1886), 2:259, 265. This marriage would be some time before 1843, the date of Judge Adam's death.

24. Madsen, *Life of Joseph Smith*, tape 2, side 2. The LDS prophet Howard William Hunter (1907–1995) came from this line.

25. Pedigree charts in author's possession from the Partridge family genealogy.

26. See Boren and Boren, *Following the Ark of the Covenant*. Their contention is that the Sanpete Valley is a very sacred place. They claim that the Mormon temple on Temple Hill in Manti was built upon at least two earlier temples and that the ark of the covenant is hidden in this hill or in the adjacent region.

27. Whitney, *Life of Heber C. Kimball,* 185. Elsewhere we note that the Whitney family are also of this sacred bloodline.

28. Heber C. Kimball, in *Journal of Discourses* (1 March 1857), 4:248a.

29. Kimball, *Heber C. Kimball,* 274. A letter from J. Golden Kimball, a son of Heber C. Kimball, states that "Heber believed he was descended from Christ" (274, n. 28). In *Journal of Discourses* (12 April 1868), 12:191, Heber C. Kimball says: "While brother Pratt was talking with me a voice spake to him and said 'Orson, my son, that man will one day become one of my apostles.' I did not know this till afterwards. A voice also spoke to me and told me my lineage, and I told my wife Vilate that she was of the same lineage, and she believed it."

30. See Salt Lake Sunstone Symposium, August 2004.

31. This may be vice versa. Foremost among those who feel this way are excommunicated LDS Church members Paul Toscano, Janice Allred, and Maxine Hanks. Others include Margaret Toscano and Armand Mauss.

32. McConkie, *Mormon Doctrine,* 102.

33. Smith, *History of the Church* (10 March 1844), 6:253.

34. Swanson interview with Michael Kennedy of Alpine, 22 March 2005. When the Prophet asked the angel, "Will this always be the case?" the reply was, "No, they will be restored, as it were a flood" (see D&C 109:70).

35. They believed in the familial, not apostolic, succession of the Church and followed a number of successors other than Brigham Young, until finally settling on the Reorganized LDS. Today only a few of Joseph Smith Jr's. descendants are members of the RLDS or Community of Christ Church.

36. George Q. Cannon, in *Journal of Discourses* (16 November 1884), 25:367, spoken in Ephraim in Sanpete County, Utah.

37. This is reminiscent, according to Collins, of what happened in the ancient church. See Collins, *Twenty-First Century Grail,* 41: "Despite a noble attempt at reconciliation between the two communities by John, and even by Paul, the rift remained and eventually the Gentile Church severed its links with the Christian Jews, many of whom were members of Jesus' extensive family."

38. "The kingdom was in one church: the line of kings in the other," as quoted in Newell and Avery, *Mormon Enigma,* 283. Flanders first used this phrase in his address "Brother Brigham and Sister Emma" (manuscript, Utah State Special Collection, ff362 #10).

39. George Q. Cannon, in *Journal of Discourses* (16 November 1884), 25:367.

40. Ehat and Cook, *Words of Joseph Smith* (10 March 1844), 331. Concerning the David of the last days to rule in Jerusalem, see 2 Samuel 7:8–19; Ezekiel 34:23–25; 37:21–28; Zechariah 3:8, 6:12–13; Jeremiah 30:9; Doctrine and Covenants 133:26–32.

41. Newell and Avery, *Mormon Enigma,* 169. Hill, *Joseph Smith,* 421. She says that Emma claimed Joseph III was blessed in 1839 at Liberty Jail to be his successor.

42. Newell and Avery, *Mormon Enigma,* 294. The source of this quotation is not footnoted in their otherwise well-documented book and must be held in suspicion.

43. Journal of Brigham Young, 1858–63 (28 February 1860), LDS Church Archives, Salt Lake City.

44. Quoted in D. Michael Quinn, "Joseph Smith III's 1844 Blessing and the Mormons of Utah," *Dialogue* 15, 2 (Summer 1982): 84–85. See also Andrew Ehat, "Joseph Smith's Introduction of Temple Ordinances and the 1844 Mormon Succession Question" (master's thesis, Brigham Young University, 243–44).

45. He painted pictures on commission and also painted Emma's portrait and himself as a young babe in the spring of 1871. See Newell and Avery, *Mormon Enigma,* 288.

46. Oliver B. Huntington Journal, typescript, 1:53. See also D. Michael Quinn, "Joseph Smith III's 1844 Blessing and the Mormons of Utah," *Dialogue* 15, 2 (Summer 1982): 74–75. Scriptures relating to David in the last days include 2 Samuel 7:8–29; Ezekiel 34:23–25; 37:21–28; Zechariah 3; Isaiah 55:3–5; Jeremiah 30:4–9; and Psalm 89:1–4.

47. Church Historian's Office Journal (1 September 1861), LDS Church Archives, Salt Lake City. Quoted in D. Michael Quinn, "Joseph Smith III's 1844 Blessing and the Mormons of Utah," *Dialogue* 15, 2 (Summer 1982): 74.

48. As quoted in Newell and Avery, *Mormon Enigma,* 285, from "Addresses of Brigham Young October 1863–1864: Remarks by President Brigham Young, G.S.L. City Bowery" (7 October 1863), as reported by G. D. Watt,

Brigham Young Collection, LDS Archives. Unpublished sermon of Brigham Young (7 October 1863), quoted in Quinn, *Origins of Power*, 230. Also see *Wilford Woodruff Journal* (12 June 1860) and Church Historian's Office Journal (15 August 1880 and 6 June 1868).

49. Brigham Young, unpublished sermon (7 October 1866), as quoted in D. Michael Quinn, "Joseph Smith III's 1844 Blessing and the Mormons of Utah," *Dialogue* 15, 2 (Summer 1982): 84–85. Joseph Smith said: "The priesthood that he received and the throne and kingdom of David is to be taken from him and given to another by the name of David in the last days, raised up out of his lineage." Ehat and Cook, *Words of Joseph Smith*, 331.

50. Brigham Young, in *Journal of Discourses* (24 August 1872), 15:136b.

51. David Smith to Joseph Smith III (12 November 1870) RLDS Library-Archives. They probably were subtly trying, and he was anxious that his brother not think him susceptible.

52. David was placed in the Illinois State Hospital for the Insane in Elgin in January 1877 and died there on 29 August 1904 at the age of fifty-nine. His wife raised their son near her father's family in northwestern Iowa.

53. Its first non–Joseph Smith line president and prophet, W. Grant McMurray, resigned in November 2004. Its new president, Steve Veazey, is a younger member from their Quorum of Apostles.

54. Personal interview with the author, March 1990.

55. Author's conversation with Richard Van Wagoner, March 1990.

56. We speculate that Lucy Mack Smith was of the precise matriarchal lineage, but this might not be the case with Emma Hale Smith. It could be, however, that Hyrum's wife Mary Fielding was and therefore Joseph F. Smith was the true heir.

57. Joseph Smith as dispensation head needed to be a direct descendant of Jesus Christ, both patrilineally and matrilineally, but perhaps the presidents and apostles of the Church need only be of the larger Grail family.

58. Smith, *Teachings of the Prophet Joseph Smith* (27 June 1839), 149. See also Smith, *History of the Church*, 3:380. "The effect of the Holy Ghost upon a gentile, is to purge out the old blood, and make him actually of the seed of Abraham." In a DNA sense this has not been proven, but in an adoptive sense it is literally so. The "old blood" may mean the curse of the natural man, now being brought into relationship with God.

59. Wilford Woodruff, "The Law of Adoption," *Deseret Evening News*, 14 April 1894. See also Woodruff, "The Law of [Priesthood] Adoption," *Latter-Day Saints' Millennial Star* 56 (21 May 1894; 28 May 1894): 321–25; 338–41.

60. Brigham Young, as quoted in *Wilford Woodruff Journal* (16 January 1847), 3:117–18. See also Staker, *Waiting for the World's End*, 102.

61. Until the Millennium, Adam holds the keys of the priesthood on this earth, at which time he will deliver them up to the Savior Jesus Christ. See Wilford Woodruff, *Deseret Weekly News*, 38:389, "Adam holds and reveals the Keys of the Ever-lasting Priesthood to men."

62. *Wilford Woodruff Journal* (16 February 1847), 3:131–32.

63. Brigham Young, in *Journal of Discourses* (4 September 1873), 16:186. "Sealed to their fathers" means "spiritual fathers," not necessarily earthly fathers.

64. Latter-day Saints may be grafted into the patriarchal order, thus becoming "legal heirs" and thereby possessing the "fathers in the priesthood."

65. Brigham Young, in *Journal of Discourses* (4 September 1873), 16:186.

66. Unknown LDS author, manuscript on the marriage of Christ in author's possession, (date unknown, probably late 1990s or early 2000s), 113, given to me by artist James C. Christensen.

67. Gordon Irving, "The Law of Adoption: One Phase of the Development of the Mormon Concept of Salvation 1830–1900," *BYU Studies* 14, 3 (Spring 1974): 295, 309.

68. *Wilford Woodruff Journal* (15 August 1847), 3:260.

69. Brigham Young, as quoted in Smith, *History of the Church*, 7:233 (8 August 1844).

70. Quinn, *Origins of Power*, 60–61. Quinn believed that the Nauvoo Standing Stake High Council presided over all organized stakes only, and the Quorum of the Twelve Apostles presided over missions and branches only. In a sense they were different but equal in authority under the First Presidency. One is reminded of the ancient twelve and James the Just, Bishop of Jerusalem. Some believe that James was the real ruler of the central Church, while Peter was over the worldwide missionary effort. But in the author's opinion, this is not the case.

71. Joseph Smith diary (27 March 1836), in Jessee, *Personal Writings of Joseph Smith*, 173. Smith, *History of the Church*, 2:417, has added "revelators."

72. Samuel James to Sidney Rigdon (28 January 1845), *Latter Day Saints' Messenger and Advocate* 1 (1 March 1845): 130, as quoted in Quinn, *Origins of Power*, 194. This was at a meeting of the Council of Fifty, which

included the First Presidency and Twelve Apostles.

73. Andrus and Andrus, *They Knew the Prophet*, 26. See also Lightner, *Life and Testimony of Mary Lightner.*

74. Andrus and Andrus, *They Knew the Prophet*, 103.

75. Brigham Young, in *History of the Church*, 7:250 (15 August 1844).

76. It is also thought by this author that the Grail lineage is liberally sprinkled in the Seventy, which quorum is equal to the other two when properly organized (see D&C 107).

77. Eliza R. Snow's *Biography of Lorenzo Snow* was written too early (1884) to note this event, but at least four people have mentioned this incident to me.

78. Journal of Rudger Clawson (2 July 1899), 374–75. Minutes of the Solemn Assembly, Salt Lake Temple. The quotation continues: "President Snow further said in conclusion he hoped the brethren would take the spirit of these meetings home with them and impart the same to the people."
In a little different rendition, President George Q. Cannon elucidated on this topic in 1899: "The Lord has hid the chosen seed in this way (among the poor and humble). There are in this audience descendants of the old Twelve Apostles, and—shall I say it? Yes, descendants of the Son of God Himself. He has seed among us; the Apostles and the Prophets have; and their seed will be known after a while, for the Lord will reveal their genealogy." Referred to Queen Victoria as descending from ancient Saints and good people and other rulers of the nations. Ibid. See Larsen, *Ministry of Meetings*, 72.

79. Anthony W. Ivins Journal (2 July 1899), 21, LDS Archives.

80. All those who faithfully accept the divine heritage within them or who are adopted to be children of Abraham and those properly sealed to Christ will be saved to the celestial kingdom.

81. Orson Hyde, in *Journal of Discourses* (March 1857), 4:260b.

82. Heber C. Kimball, in *Journal of Discourses* (1 March 1857), 4:248a.

83. Parley P. Pratt, in *Journal of Discourses* (10 April 1853), 1:261.

84. Ludlow, *Isaiah*, 172.

CHAPTER TWENTY-TWO
DIVULGING THE GRAIL SECRET

*President Snow further said in conclusion [that] he
hoped the brethren would take the spirit of these
meetings home with them and impart the same to
the people.*

—RUDGER CLAWSON[1]

lawson was quoting President Lorenzo
Snow's comments that the Twelve
Apostles were of the lineage of Jesus
Christ (above). Here, nine years after
the Manifesto of 1890 but before the 1904 second
manifesto, the President of the Church still wanted
the people to know more about the sacred bloodline.
However, this would be the last public statement on
the subject.

Yet there has never been a public or private injunction by the Church against the idea of Jesus being married. Latter-day Saints have intuitively understood the necessity of restraint in speaking about this
esoteric subject. The topic became something "we just
don't talk about." Twentieth-century Mormonism
has been reverently tight-lipped about the marriage
of Jesus Christ. But now, at the beginning of the new
millennium, the silence has been shattered by gentile
forces. We now seek to understand where dialogue on
the Holy Grail has advanced over the last century.

REVEALING THE SECRET: GENTILES SINCE 1945

*In its search for prior meanings and
secret codes, current popular grail
writing makes use of assumptions
rooted in what was respectable academic discourse.*

*Many popular works assume that the
authors of medieval romance were privy
to some cosmic insight and used the
romance genre to conceal secret information from members of the establishment, which was seeking to suppress it.
When the code is eventually broken, the
secret will be revealed.*

—JULIETTE WOOD[2]

One of the early Grail scholars who began discourse on the topic was Alfred Trubner Nutt, president of the Folklore Society at the end of the nineteenth century. His 1888 book, *The Holy Grail: With Special Reference to Its Celtic Origin* held the thesis that the Grail myth existed in Celtic culture and that the medieval romances reworked this myth which they no longer understood. His final summation came in 1902 with *Legends of the Holy Grail,* with its analysis of this thesis having enormous influence on later Grail scholarship.

Other critical works, such as Jessie L. Weston's *Sir Lancelot* (1901), *Gawain and the Green Knight* (1903), and *The Quest of the Holy Grail* (ca. 1903), contributed continental European material from medieval French, German, and Dutch romances. Arthur Edward Waite's *The Hidden Church of the Holy Grail* (1909) gives a British occult interpretation. Rudolf Steiner's *Christus und die geistige Welt: Von der suche nach dem Heiligen Gral* (1925) saw the Grail as a personal odyssey or initiation experience.

Steiner was soon followed by another German, Walter Johannes Stein, whose studies saw the Grail as symbol, along the line of the currently popular symbolic mythological studies by Joseph Campbell. Steiner and Stein also saw the Teutonic Knights as a Grail paradigm. The suggestion that the "grail" is a person rather than a thing, a lost royal heir may have come from Stein's idea, presented in the 1930s, that the Grail lineage is linked to Charlemagne and his successors.[3]

These critical analyses, though often of a mystical type, were conducted with serious erudition. None of them, however, related the Holy Grail to a sexually active Christ. Yet a new non-Holy Grail-related genre appeared in the early twentieth century centering upon Christ as a sexual being. Upon extensive research of gentile (non-LDS) literature, the author has found only five mentionings of Jesus being sexually active, or married, or having children, before the twentieth century.[4]

At least three fictional accounts by mid-century are known to portray Jesus with an instinctual *Id*. Frank Harris, in his short story *The Miracle of the Stigmata* (1913), has Jesus surviving the crucifixion, marrying, and living under the name of Joshua.[5] Then in 1929, D. H. Lawrence's *The Escaped Cock* represents the risen Jesus being seduced by a priestess of Isis. The mythographer Robert Van Ranke Graves (1895–1985) wrote a controversial historical novel in 1946 entitled, *King Jesus*. In it he proclaims that Jesus had wives and perhaps offspring, which were concealed to keep them safe.[6]

This led on to Nikos Kazantzakis's powerful novel, *The Last Temptation of Christ,* of 1952–55 and 1960. Here, the Savior is first presented with sexual impulses, though strangely enough living as a continent bachelor. Then the idea is advanced that Jesus and the Magdalene were carnal lovers or paramours. Jesus' libidinous desires are given fanciful range by the author. Yet it fostered the idea, later seen in the play *The Passion Players* and Andrew Lloyd Webber's musical *Jesus Christ Superstar,* that Jesus was a sexually driven being.[7] In one scene from Kanzantzakis's novel, He is carnally tempted by a devilish voice: "Take her! God created man and woman to match, like the key and the lock. Open her. Your children sit huddled together and numb inside her, waiting for you to blow away their numbness so that they may rise and come out to walk in the sun."[8]

Sadly, Kazantzakis imposes a polarity between the "impure flesh and the pure spirit that is not Hebraic."[9] In one Protestant journal, Kyle Haselden expresses appreciation to Kazantzakis: "In a day when the sweet, lulling incense of docetism is heavy in the theological air, we need the artist's pungent reminder that our Lord was one 'who in every respect has been tempted as we are, yet without sinning.'"[10]

While most recent pseudo-historical authors proudly announce that "hundreds" of medieval chroniclers have proclaimed a sacred marriage, none has referenced a single reliable source for the assertions. For instance, in the 2004 and 2005 Salt Lake Sunstone Symposiums, Margaret Starbird asserted that there were numerous Merovingian, Cathar, Priory de Sion, Templar, and Masonic statements about Jesus' marriage. She offered the well-known diatribe against the Cathars by Pierre des Vaux-de-Cernay that Mary Magdalene was Jesus' concubine.[11] But this was not a Cathar source.

No one has yet produced any scholarly pre-1945 literature even intimating that Jesus had a sacred marriage and fathered children. Dan Brown's character Teabing shamelessly exaggerates, "I shan't bore you with the countless references to Jesus and Magdalene's union."[12] Which references? Where? Revisionist authors have yet to reveal any original sources for what they say is "a matter of historical record."[13]

The 1945 discovery by two peasants in middle Egypt of the *Nag Hammadi* codices of Coptic gnostic gospels slowly set off the "Jesus was married" craze. Forty-six different apocryphal works were found, and some, like the *Gospel of Philip, Gospel of Mary [Magdalene]* and *Gospel of Thomas*, suggest a personal relationship between Jesus and Mary Magdalene.[14] But they do not actually say that Jesus and the Magdalene were sexually intimate, married, or parented children.

However, because of these freshly published ancient sources, ideas of a possible sexual relationship began to percolate by the 1950s and 1960s. The earliest known "gentile" critical source for a married Christ came from John Erskine in 1945. He suggested that Jesus had a wife and children during that decade of young manhood.[15] In 1965, Tom F. Driver wrote at length on the topic, sharing Erskine's point of view, though not so romantically. He noted, "It is not shocking, to me at least, to imagine Jesus moved to love according to the flesh."[16]

Presbyterian minister and professor at Davis and Elkins College in West Virginia William E. Phipps first academically broaches the question of a married Jesus in a 1968 article, "Did Jesus or Paul Marry?"[17] Then in 1970, William E. Phipps released his scholarly book *Was Jesus Married?*[18] His was the first and remains the most critical study on the question of the sacred marriage.

This comprehensive study set the stage for most publications that came later with the marriage of Jesus as their thesis. Dr. Phipps published his follow-up book, *The Sexuality of Jesus,* in 1973, again establishing a married Jesus Christ. Interestingly, Phipps does not concern himself with questions regarding children or a Jesus bloodline. His books were, for the most part, ignored by sectarian Christianity who hoped that the books' popularity would subside.

The first authors to put the Grail romances together with a sexual Jesus published in 1982. Michael Baigent, Richard Leigh, and Henry Lincoln threw down the gauntlet with their best-selling pop New Age paperback, *Holy Blood, Holy Grail* (1982). Actually Richard Leigh's sister, Liz Greene, published a novel with the same theory in 1980 titled *The Dreamer of the Vine.*

Interest again peaked in the "holy marriage" only this time it came coupled with a "Holy Grail" nexus, which guaranteed its popularity. But unlike William E. Phipps's publications, this pseudo-historical book and their other follow-up volumes, *The Messianic Legacy* and *The Lodge,* were highly speculative with strongly corrosive agendas toward Orthodox Christianity.

In this respect they were more closely related to the novels mentioned earlier. Extravagant claims, conspiracy theories, secret societies, anti-Christian rhetoric, and anti-Catholic diatribe gave these books a suspense-like, action-packed, mystery feel. The public could not resist. "They are," writes Price, "avid readers of books that claim to 'blow the lid off Christianity' by means of new discoveries, real or imagined."[19]

Holy Blood, Holy Grail remains a major best-seller. The more conspiratorially oriented among us, believed the book's half-truths and false conscious-ness. But whereas Phipps was only interested in the marriage and existence of children, *Holy Blood, Holy Grail* was the first book to go fully into the secret bloodline, maintained through the centuries by ultra-underground orders. The book promulgated interest in what had previously been a French preoc-cupation with Rennes-le-Château and turned it into a worldwide mania.

So charged was the atmosphere of intrigue that *Holy Blood, Holy Grail* engendered that scores of writers spawned an avalanche of continuations. Quickly, numerous other authors began to swallow the false with the true. While it piqued interest in Holy Grail studies in general, it pushed the subject away from scholarly research and closer toward the occult, radical feminism, and Gnosticism. Because of its esoteric intrigue, the book was mostly ignored by the Christian academic community.[20] Of this book, folklorist and Grailist Juliette Wood notes: "These are detective story analyses in which similarities are taken as proof of influence and connection, and an increas-ing tendency to refer to other popular works on the subject rather than to original source material."[21]

Barbara Thiering's edgy publication, *Jesus the Man* (1992), sees Christ as only human (not divine), a practicing Essene, as married and divorced, and surviving the crucifixion. It provided much of the controversial material for Laurence Gardner's 1996 publication. On the other hand, Margaret Starbird's 1993 book, *Woman with an Alabaster Jar*, was not so vehemently militant, but touted the "divine femi-nine," giving it a decidedly mainstream take. In total her five books sold millions of copies and became the first "sacred marriage" publications to seep deeply into more normative and semi-orthodox society.

Now the idea of the Holy Grail has become a household word. Margaret Starbird's popularizing books quietly gnawed away at Catholic reticence on the topic of a Jesus-Magdalene marriage. Far from being ephemeral artifacts of most pop culture, the ideas expressed, like the Grail legends themselves, have staying power.

With regard to alabaster jars, Graham Phillips, *The Search for the Grail* (1995/1996), claims that a candidate for the Grail was a Roman alabaster cup in possession of the Vernon family of Hawkstone manor. The alleged story leads to a medieval Welsh poem dealing with Fulk le Fitz Warin, a romance entitled *La Folie de Perceval* (in B.M. Ms. 12577) and a fifth-century Greek historian regarding the Grail coming to Britain. But according to folk Grailist Juliette Wood, no such Welsh poem in this Anglo-Norman romance tells the story of the outlaw knight Fulk. Neither is there a *La Folie de Perceval* section, nor a grail in the writings of the Greek historian Olympiadorus. She continues: "But this work, like so many others, is full of mysteries, codes and exciting 'discoveries' overlooked by establishment historians and academics."[22]

Laurence Gardner's *Bloodline of the Holy Grail: The Hidden Lineage of Jesus Revealed* (1996) was certainly the most labyrinthine "Jesus and Mary Magdalene" book thus far. However, this and his later book's faulty documentation, hateful tone, and exaggerated claims weakened its acceptance among scholars.[23] Also in 1996, Robert Lomas and Christopher Knight published their immensely popular study, *Hiram Key*. It expansively dealt with the Merovingians, Cathars, Templars, Freemasonry, Rennes-le-Château, Rossyln Chapel, and the Holy Grail lineage. They uncritically accepted most of the assertions of *Holy Blood, Holy Grail* and added a few more theories of their own.

Richard Andrews and Paul Schellenberger's *The Tomb of God* (1997) continued to rivet attention on Rennes-le-Château, the Cathars in southern France, and the idea of Jesus surviving the crucifixion. It is estimated that since the late 1950s nearly three hundred books have dealt with Rennes-le-Château and its myths and mystery. Later in 1997, Lynn Picknett and Clive Prince published their highly controversial work, *The Templar Revelation: Secret Guardians of the True Identity of Christ*. It maintained that Jesus and Mary Magdalene were sex partners rather than a married couple and that Mary Magdalene was a black woman.

In 1998, Keith Laidler published *The Head of God: The Lost Treasure of the Templars*, which furthered the ideas mentioned above and focused on the severed heads of John the Baptist, Mary Magdalene, and James the Just. Margaret Starbird's follow-up books *The Goddess in the Gospels: Reclaiming the Sacred Feminine* of 1998 and *Magdalen's Lost Legacy: Symbolic Numbers and the Sacred Union in Christianity* of 2003 were also highly influential.

In these books, Starbird proposed a daughter named Sarah from Christ's marriage to Mary Magdalene. This single daughter was used to promote the idea of the marriage and normality of his life, but Starbird was against the idea of a "special" bloodline. However, in her latest book *Mary Magdalene, Bride in Exile* (2005) she inexplicably writes that Jesus was married in His youth and had several children before His wife died tragically.[24] This is fiction parading as fact, for no sources are cited to substantiate this statement. Then she writes that Jesus did not remarry until visiting a family in Bethany: "Finding her irresistible, he formed a dynastically suitable marriage alliance with Mary, the younger sister of this family. We don't know exactly when, or how, but rumors of their intimacy survive in the gospels and apocrypha, so we speculate that it was so."[25]

Most of these books had slavishly accepted as factual the Priory de Sion basis of the Holy Grail story. But when its underlying faults were realized, the *Rex Deus* theory was put forward. Marilyn Hopkins, Graham Simmans, and Tim Wallace-Murphy's

corrosive, *Rex Deus: The True Mystery of Rennes-Le-Château and the Dynasty of Jesus* (2000) opened another viewpoint other than the Priory de Sion paradigm. This thesis emphasized the royal family of God rather than Grail guardians.

Around the year 2000 a backlash against the burgeoning literature extolling the Grail virtues of the: Merovingians, Cathars, Rennes-le-Château, Templars, Rosslyn Chapel, Pierre Plantard, and the Priory de Sion, began to develop. This was so because of the lack of scholarly methodology and dubious agendas of the above-mentioned authors and literally scores of others. All were egregiously wanting in dispassionate scholarship. Internet bloggers like Paul Smith, devastatingly debunked the Plantard myth, and the Priory de Sion and Rennes-le-Château hoaxes which have so poisoned research on the true Grail.[26]

One of the first books to challenge this "house of cards" was Philip Coppens' 2002 paperback, *The Stone Puzzle of Rosslyn Chapel*. It examined a number of claims of Tim Wallace-Murphy, and Tim and Marilyn Hopkin's savagely anti-Christian volume, *Rosslyn: Guardian of the Secrets of the Holy Grail* of 1999. Coppens discovered that the documentation on the Rosslyn claims was either exaggerated or nonexistent. Then Bill Putnam's and John Edwin Woods' *The Treasure of Rennes-le-Château: A Mystery Solved* (2003) soundly discredited the hoax of Bernard Saunière, Pierre Plantard, the Priory de Sion, and Rennes-le-Château. With this fresh research the cards came tumbling down for about nine-tenths of the revisionist and popularizing Grail literature based upon pervasive intellectual hucksterism.

However, the pendulum quickly swung back in 2003 when Dan Brown's full throttle, ideological blockbuster novel, *The Da Vinci Code* exploded upon the scene.[27] He was Robert Graves-like, grabbing hold of every gnostic twist propounded by the above cited popularizing but intellectually bankrupt books. Or as M. and V. Haag say, "[He] regurgitated whole this plethora of distortion."[28] Except for a few fictional additions, the book's arcane "facts" come straight from these books. Its flawed sources, misshapen "data," pro-neognostic stew, were chosen to spice the theological thriller with intriguing premises and "verisimilitude." In essence the work was instructive as to the enormity of its self-induced ignorance regarding the promulgation of its central hypothesis.[29]

Its vexing message was essentially of smear campaigns, secret gnosis, and dangerous conspiracies—giving it a dramatic subtext. One character in the novel insists that "almost everything our fathers taught us about Christ is false."[30] Another claims that Jesus and Mary had a daughter.[31] This breakthrough book was loaded with propagandistic feminist ideology pulp and the ignorant public ate it up in twenty-eight plus languages. Many rejoiced to see sacred truths "deconstructed" by post-modernism, *al la* Jacques Derrida.[32]

Its intriguing yet disturbing text screamed of the Holy Grail and a secret bloodline of Jesus and the Magdalene. Millions of copies were eagerly read by mass audiences, and the question of Jesus and Mary Magdalene's relationship was whispered everywhere. Many conservative churches, like the Broadway Baptist Church of Fort Worth, Texas, even held meetings to decry its influence.

Dan Brown has, according to R. Abanes, "utterly warped Christianity" in order to disagree with it.[33] The book played loose with the facts and caused confusion in the ranks of many unsuspecting Christians. "The author spins one gossamer story of conjecture over another," writes Laura Miller, "forming a web dense enough to create the illusion of solidity. Though bogus, it's an impressive piece of work."[34] But to the gullible public, it was all true. Along these lines, Alyson Ward of Knight-Ridder Newspapers, while denying its literary excellence, exalted in its provocative nature: "No, Brown's novel—which makes an eye-opening list of claims about hidden truths, suppressed gospels and various conspiracies maintained by the Catholic Church—has got people thinking. . . . *The Da Vinci Code* has riled up religious scholars as well. The Internet is full of lengthy treatises about the book's many errors and assumptions."[35]

In November 2003, ABC televised "Jesus, Mary, and Da Vinci," its homage to Dan Brown's novel. Billed as an exposé, the program hosted Elizabeth Vargas, claimed to reveal "surprising truths" about the book's more bizarre elements. They admitted they could find but one art historian who believed that the figure of John in Leonardo's *Last Supper* painting was really Mary Magdalene. "Then," writes Brent Bozell, "they let the expert with whom everyone else disagreed expound on his oddball theories for five minutes."[36] Bozell maintains that "ABC's liberal political and cultural agenda clearly was more important than its reputation."

Many skeptics have said about *The Da Vinci Code*: "Excuse me, but its only a novel! It's fiction, OK!" Yet many of the world's most disturbing and controversial ideas are often packaged in art, fiction, poetry, legend, and allegory. Being a novel made it no less subversive to Christian ethics than if it were a scholarly polemic tome. But being high "entertainment" it would be read widely. This novel's powerful influence can be registered by the number of rebuttal books published since 2003.

Like Dan Brown, Daniel Defoe's *Robinson Crusoe* and later Edgar Baine's *The Autobiography of Miss Jane Pittman* also made claims of authentic history that don't stand up to scrutiny and then fall back on "It's only fiction!" A cottage industry of "debunking" books has sprung up to challenge Brown's "facts" at every turn.[37] One such publication is Darrell L. Bock's *Breaking the Da Vinci Code: Answers to the Questions Everybody's Asking* (2004), which reveals fundamental factual and logical problems of Brown's book and others like it.

Brock notes that they scrutinize with inquisitorial intolerance every infinitesimal detail of the traditional story of Jesus. Then he demonstrates how Brown proposes an elaborate treatise founded on wide-eyed speculation based on a few scraps of ancient writing that hardly support his grandiose claims that "you can't trust what you've read." That is, by others, of course, not by Brown.

While the left-wing counter-culturalists, pseudo-intellectuals, and esoteric philosophers controlled the topic of the Grail marriage of Christ and Mary Magdalene, normative Christianity was content to hold their tongues. But once the regular church-going public began to read Brown's novel, which spewed anti-Christian propaganda in a palatable page turner, a Christian response was inevitable. The number of these counter-argument books has reached more than eighteen thus far. Some are "neutral," such as Dan Burstein's collection of essays, *Secrets of the Code: The Unauthorized Guide to the Mysteries behind the Da Vinci Code* (2004). It offered a diverse selection of responses to the subject of Brown's novel and the question of Jesus and Mary Magdalene being married.

Burnstein's book is liberal and slightly left of center, meaning that it is tilted toward feminism and neognostic positions. Dr. Bart Ehrman's 2004 volume, *The Truth behind the Da Vinci Code: A Historian Reveals What We Really Know about Jesus, Mary Magdalene, and Constantine*, was also liberal, but more moderate in tone. Interestingly there was at least one book that staunchly defends the factual basis of Dan Brown's novel. Martin Lunn's *Da Vinci Code Decoded: The Truth behind the New York Times #1 Bestseller* (2004) was appropriately published by The Disinformation Company of New York. Another angle of approach comes from Robert M. Price, a liberal-gnostic Episcopalian, whose book *The Da Vinci Fraud: Why the Truth Is Stranger Than Fiction* (2005) separates itself from other rebuttals:

"Every time a book like Dan Brown's *The Da Vinci Code* makes waves in the religious public, one can be sure it will call forth a raft of books trying to refute it. This is one of them. But most of these books tend to be rejoinders in behalf of the oppressive orthodoxy that Brown's novel attacks. They are defenses of the party line, cranked out by spin-doctors for Mother Church. This book, however, is decidedly not one of *those*."[38]

While critical of Brown's methodology, Price arrogantly pushes the envelope way past the novel he criticizes. However, most of *The Da Vinci Code*-related books condemn in strongest terms Brown's novel. Among these, the most considered Christian responses come from Richard Abanes, *The Truth behind the Da Vinci Code: A Challenging Response to the Bestselling Novel* (2004), James L. Garlow and Peter Jones, *Cracking Da Vinci's Code: You've Read the Book, Now Hear the Truth* (2004) and two Catholic scholars, Carle E. Olson and Sandra Miesel, *The Da Vinci Hoax: Exposing the Errors in The Da Vinci Code* (2004).[39] Having now entered the fray on the question of the Grail marriage and lineage, the Christian counter attack has exposed the pseudo-scholarship, deconstructive agenda, and the mean-spiritedness of militant feminism and hardcore neognostics.

While the false Grail seekers have been seriously wounded, more of their books continue to fester the same infection. However, Rennes-le-Château, the base-camp for neo-Gnosticism and the Roswell of France, lay in scholarly ruins. In the end, however, it does not seem likely that the polemical arguments pitting orthodox Christianity versus neo-Gnosticism will arrive at the truth. One rejects the truth of the sacred marriage while the other rejects the truth in the sacred marriage.

The Da Vinci Code, more than any other publication has gotten people thinking and pondering the question of hidden bloodlines and sacred lineages. This is something the world had not one iota of interest in for centuries. It was not *The Da Vinci Code's* plot but its premise that captivated us. The Grail marriage has now become an "above-the-fold" news item. Where once the world was not ready or willing to countenance this most tender romantic tale, it now clamors for more. In the end, Mormonism has something significant to offer relating to the entire question.

In some ways popular culture was even more influenced through film than through the pulp media. The public was delighted with cinema like the silent film staring Lon Chaney Sr., *The Light of Faith* (1922); the hit movie *Monty Python and the Holy Grail* (1975); Marion Zimmer Bradley's *The Mists of Avalon* (1982); John Boorman's epic *Excalibur* (1981, 1984); Martin Scorsese's *The Last Temptation of Christ* (1988); or Steven Spielberg's blockbuster *Indiana Jones and the Last Crusade* (1989); and Terry Gilliam's film *The Fisher King* (1991). However, none of these, not even Andrew Lloyd Webber's *Jesus Christ Superstar*, have dealt with the *hieros gamos*, the sacred marriage of Jesus.

Now we have the movie version of *The Da Vinci Code*, directed by Ronald "Ronnie" Howard and starring Tom Hanks as the novel's leading man, Robert Langdon. This and Dan Brown's new deconstructive novel, *The Solomon Key*, dealing with the Masons and the Mormons, should keep the pot boiling. In scholarly or popular media the entire Holy Grail theme has been used as a device for a feminist assault on the whole of western culture and Christian religion.[40] Such motivation and ideology will not stop in this generation. Yet curiosity about spiritual matters as a part of the human condition will continue to move Grail studies. It's just too good a tool and a weapon.

REVEALING THE SECRET: SAINTS SINCE 1963

How can we expect another to keep our secret if we cannot keep it ourselves?

—LA ROCHEFOUCAULD

Between 1899 and 1963 nothing of significance regarding the sacred marriage and bloodline was mentioned within the LDS Church. From the cessation of the practice of plural marriage in 1890 onward, the Church has become increasingly reticent on the matter.[41] The submersing of the secret, or as James E. Talmage said, being "reverentially silent," came in a century that this confidence was being slowly discovered by the rest of the world.[42] Since about 1900, scholarship in the Church has become decidedly based on British-Israelitism and has remained so to this day. Scholars like James H. Anderson, Ernest L. Whitehead, Vaughn Hansen, Robert Smith, and R. Merle Fowler were founded on British-Israel-World-Federation literature and philosophy. But for sixty years the secret was kept by keeping the *hieros gamos* secret mum.

However, from about 1963 to 1973 little snippets began to percolate to the surface. Now we have enough information to let us know that there was a wink of understanding just behind the mask of reticence. For example, in a letter written 17 March 1963 to the president of the Quorum of the Twelve Apostles, Joseph Fielding Smith, J. Ricks Smith of Burbank, California, asked two questions. The first involves Isaiah 53:10: "What is meant by 'he shall see his seed?'" On the original letter, near the quotation of the scripture, President Smith placed a single asterisk after the word "seed." Then, below in the margin, in typical Joseph Fielding Smith fashion, he notes, "*Mosiah 15:10–12 Please read your Book of Mormon!"[43]

The letter continues: "Does this mean that Christ had children? In the temple ceremony we are told that only through temple marriage can we receive the highest degree of exaltation and dwell in the presence of our Heavenly Father and Jesus Christ. Christ came here to set us the example and, therefore, we believe that he must have been married. Are we right?"

This time President Smith uses two asterisks just after the word "married." Then below he notes "**Yes! But do not preach it! The Lord advised us not to cast pearls before swine!" He then signed the original letter and sent it back to Brother J. Ricks Smith.[44]

According to Cky J. Carrigan (Baptist minister):

> This letter does, however, stand as important evidence of two features of the LDS doctrine of the marital and parental status of the Son. First, this letter is evidence that a high rank-ing, highly respected, late twentieth century LDS authority taught that the Son was both a husband, and by reasonable extension, a father in the flesh. Second, this letter is evidence of a deliberate suppression of this doctrine.[45]

Another such incidence, again involving Joseph Fielding Smith, occurred the same year. On 18 October 1963 a number of new missionaries were be-ing endowed in the Salt Lake Temple before depart-ing on their missions. One missionary recorded:

> At the end of the session we were escorted to a large upper room and told to wait. [We] did not know what was happening. In a few moments, Joseph Fielding Smith walked in and stood behind the pulpit. He explained that since this was the first time through

the temple for each of us, he was there to answer any questions that we may have had.

> The first question came from an elder who asked, "President Smith, was Christ married?" I was appalled at the brazenness of that elder, but Brother Smith just paused for a few moments, and then replied; "Yes, Christ was married. To Mary Mag-dalene. But don't teach it." I wrote that in my journal that day, and have treasured it ever since.[46]

Of course the missionaries were instructed not to teach such things to investigators or in the mission field. While both incidences in 1963 are welcome reminders of the continued understanding of the sa-cred marriage, neither is forthcoming with any new information. It was old ground, but it was a pleas-ant relief from the silence of so many decades. The provenance of this teaching from Joseph F. Smith to Joseph Fielding Smith, father to son, is unmistakable. But others not privy to this direct knowledge were much less likely to spill the beans of the Mormon understanding on this topic.

Even in closed meetings and under controlled circumstances few Church leaders were willing to broach the subject of a married Jesus. On 10 October 1966 in a letter to a Sister Sharon Pokriots of Provo, the prophet David O. McKay gives a much less di-rect answer to her question, "Was Jesus married?" His secretary writes back on his behalf:

Dear Sister Pokriots,

President McKay, who is under a heavy schedule of duties and meetings associated with the general jurisdiction of the Church, in addition to doctor's orders to curtail his activities as much as possible, has asked me to acknowledge from him your letter of September 29, 1966, wherein you ask if "Christ is Married."

I have been directed to tell you that there is no scripture or revelation on this subject. The wisest presumption upon this and related subjects mentioned in your letter is that the status of Christ, a member of the godhead, so far transcends the status of human beings and what they can attain in a lifetime of utter and complete faithfulness and perfection, that we should suspend and defer all concern about His [marital] status.

Secretary: Claire Middleness[47]

In a sense President McKay was trying to skirt the question, knowing the possibility of the letter coming to light. The statement that there was no "scripture or revelation on this subject" is true in that none outright says Jesus was married. Of course the pronouncements of living prophets and apostles in earlier years can be considered authentic though not endorsed as official doctrine.

However, by the end of the second half of the 1960s, discussion on the topic began to grow. In an address, the third lecture in a class series sponsored by the faculty of the Church Educational System during June 1967, Elder Bruce R. McConkie of the Quorum of the Twelve Apostles referred to a July 1899 Solemn Assembly in the Salt Lake Temple, the last semipublic statement on the topic:

Well, since we are quoting the brethren, let's just say a little more— it's not a bit uncommon. They had meetings where the brethren got up and spoke in the name of the Lord and said: "There are present in this congregation people who are the descendants of Christ." Well sure! I know a man to whom a patriarch told this—[and] not meaning adopted into the family of Christ. Now, George Q. Cannon was one of these who they announced, as I remember, was a man who was a literal descendant of Christ. Well, I know some others who are.[48]

Of course, Elder McConkie was the son-in-law of President Joseph Fielding Smith, who firmly held this position. Things began to heat up in February 1969 when an apostate named Ogden Kraut (1927–2002) published a cut-and-paste booklet titled *Jesus Was Married*. His first book, it was filled with quotations from ancient and modern prophets and apostles on the matter.

Just after receiving the first few hardback copies off the press, Ogden Kraut and his wife, Anne Wilde, drove from Dugway to Salt Lake City to show the book to Joseph Fielding Smith, a counselor in the First Presidency and president of the Twelve. They hoped to get his endorsement so the book could be placed in the Seventies Bookstores along the Wasatch Front.

In those days it was relatively easy to gain access to general authorities. They walked up to President Smith's secretary and saw that his door was open. When President Smith saw the Krauts he waved them in. "He was very pleased with the book's topic," reveals Anne Wilde, "and was happy to receive a copy as a gift. He promised to read it and wished us well with the sale of the book."[49]

They immediately took a number of copies to the Seventies Bookstore in Provo, but the store was a little hesitant to take copies because of its provocative title. With the verbal assurance that President

Smith had condoned its subject matter, the store finally took ten copies and instantly sold them out. They sold so quickly that the bookstore couldn't keep them in stock. A second revised edition came out in December 1970, which included even more material from Presbyterian minister William E. Phipps, who was just then making a stir about a married Christ. Phipps may have had Kraut's booklet available to him, for he quotes a number of early LDS sources, including Orson Hyde, in his 1970 publication. Interestingly, after thirty-five years, Kraut's book, though outdated, is still in print and is selling well.

In July 1970, the erudite Dr. William E. Phipps published his seminal book, *Was Jesus Married?* LDS scholar Keith Norman reviewed the book, calling it "scholarly, well documented, persuasively argued and very readable."[50] Less than two years later, Phipps was asked to write an article in *Dialogue: Journal of Mormon Thought.*[51] Titled "The Case for a Married Jesus" (Winter 1972), the article excited renewed Mormon interest in the topic. Then a subsequent book by Phipps, *The Sexuality of Jesus* (1973), opened wide the door on this controversial subject.

Perhaps because of these publications a remarkable event occurred, possibly during the presidency of Joseph Fielding Smith (January 1970–July 1972). President Smith had promised Ogden Kraut that he would carefully read his book, which included some material by Dr. Phipps. We could assume that President Smith also read the Phipps's book, released in 1970. We suggest that he saw in them substantiation for what he already believed and took them to heart. As mentioned previously, President Smith had spoken and written on this issue a couple of times before—but privately and never at any length.

According to Anne Wilde, Joseph Fielding Smith did not know at the time that Ogden Kraut was a Mormon fundamentalist and polygamist.[52] The mere pointing out of this fact would have stymied President Smith's presentation.

Considering the controversial nature of the topic, that Ogden Kraut was out of the Church, and how the entire state of Utah was blanketed with his book, the Brethren began to feel a little defensive. "In mid-to-late 1971," Anne Wilde continues, "they [the Quorum of the Twelve] prohibited the Seventies Bookstore from carrying copies and forbade the BYU religion classes from discussing the matter."[53]

Because it was already in the back of many Latter-day Saints' minds, the liberal Mormon feminists began broaching the question. They melded it with the emergence of the "Mother-in-Heaven" goddess cult during the early 1970s. The Mormon Women's Forum constantly fumed about the LDS Church's "cover-up" of the *hieros gamos* (sacred marriage) of Jesus. Actually, the Church's real problem was not in any cover-up but in being unable to keep the secret. This gnostic-laden Women's Forum never criticized others whom they believed kept the secret—the Cathars, Templars, Masons, and maybe even the Utah Godbeites.[54] They only criticized the Lord's Church for doing so.

With these things in mind, according to Dr. Richard L. Anderson, a letter from the Church was sent to all religion professors, institute teachers and Church Educational System (CES) instructors in the early 1970s.[55] It forbade them, in strong terms, from teaching the "mysteries," most specifically the marriage of Jesus Christ. After the Quorum's decision, things really did get reverentially quiet. An LDS scholar ventured into why this was the case:

> This may be opening a Pandora's Box, but like me, you may constantly receive inquiries as to why Orson Hyde and other nineteenth century LDS taught, and, at times in my opinion, speculated so freely about Mary

M and Jesus while current leaders are so reticent. . . .

My own feeling may not be very persuasive and may be naive—the Lord did not inspire his ancient apostles to write about His family and similarly is not directing his modern apostles and prophets to teach about it because His personal life is not our business and would distract us from focusing on the salvific aspects of His mission.[56]

Because of the ambiguity of the June 1966 letter from President David O. McKay, I specifically asked a certain general authority about this prophet's stance on the Savior's marriage. "Yes," he responded, "he understood the idea well and affirmed it."[57] This elder noted that President McKay was adept at public relations and desired that every member be a missionary. Thus he was eager to keep any mention of the sacred marriage out of the limelight.

In 1982, Elder Bruce R. McConkie, writing on Doctrine and Covenants 113:4–6, stated, "Those whose ears are attuned to the whisperings of the Infinite will know the meaning of these things."[58] Back in June 1967 he had spoken more openly of this verse and its relationship to Joseph Smith's literal birthright descent from the Savior.

In that same year BYU religion professor Victor L. Ludlow wrote in a much less ambiguous fashion. In referring to Joseph Smith's lineage from Judah he noted that "a number of the brethren, including Joseph Smith, claimed that they shared lineage with Jesus in the tribe of Judah."[59] We know that Ludlow was not just saying that both Jesus and Joseph Smith were from the lineage of Judah, but that from Judah to Jesus to Joseph was the arrow of descent. We know this because in Ludlow's footnotes his statement is accompanied with explicit Holy Grail quotes.[60]

So for the past thirty-plus years, Church leaders and instructors have, for the most part, been silent on the subject.

In February and March 2004 the Brigham Young University Museum of Art sponsored a lecture series titled "Mystery, Meaning, and Metaphor: LDS Perspectives on *The Da Vinci Code*." The organizers of the series were education specialists at the museum Cheryll May and Rita Wright. The events were attended by overflowing crowds of intensely interested Grail enthusiasts. Dan Brown's novel was then drawing attention in Utah as it was across the nation.

The first two lectures were by professor Dr. Eric Huntsman of the BYU Religion Department and art historian Dr. Steve Buele of Utah Valley State College. They were held a fortnight apart, and while wonderful in their scholarship, they were unsatisfying to the audience, which wanted to hear the Mormon slant on the topic.[61] Huntsman poignantly spoke on the scriptures and early Coptic documents dealing with Mary Magdalene. Buele convincingly said that Leonardo Da Vinci's *Last Supper*, *Mona Lisa*, and *Madonna of the Rocks* had nothing to do with Dan Brown's Grail assertions. And neither was there any evidence, according to Buele, of Leonardo's association with a fictitious Priory de Sion.

I was the third lecturer in the series and was encouraged by organizers to speak openly on early LDS documents dealing with the marriage of Jesus and with his children.[62] After twenty-six years of keeping publicly silent, I finally broached the topic.[63] The only premise in Brown's novel that corresponded to unique LDS Grail pronouncements needed to be mentioned, while other ideas needed to be rejected outright.

So, in this important public forum, the concept of a Grail dynasty descending from Jesus Christ and His wives directly to Joseph Smith was examined. The assembly of about eight hundred people now heard what they had come to hear, an unvarnished Mormon perspective on the Holy Grail marriage and lineage, presented as research, not doctrine. The listeners had many questions after the presentation but no criticism. In the end and over the next few months, I was rewarded with much new and valuable information on the subject.

In August 2004, the Sunstone Symposium in Salt Lake City featured the famous Grail evangelist, Margaret Starbird, in a special workshop and a number of sessions on the topic of Christ's marriage and *The Da Vinci Code*.[64] She was thrilled to have been quoted in Brown's best seller and to see her own sales skyrocket.[65] Sunstone basically surrendered this topic to the Mormon Women's Forum (MWF), which controlled all the "divine feminine" sessions. The left-leaning MWF and Mormon Pagan Women packed the panels with worshipers of the goddess principle.[66]

In one workshop and under questioning from the author, Starbird said that Joseph Smith undoubtedly got the notion of a married Jesus from the Masons, who got it from the Knights Templar.[67] Yet there is no known original source that either the Masons or Templars ever conceived of the idea of a married Christ, much less passed it on to the Prophet Joseph.[68] Starbird repeated that the Cathars had written records of Jesus and the Magdalene being married, but upon questioning from Janice Allred was unable to produce any early documentary basis for this belief.[69]

One later session titled "Real Goddesses Have Curves (and Identities)" dealt with the divine feminine in which the panel members agreed that they spoke allegorically rather than literally.[70] While referencing a number of goddesses, they ultimately did not believe in them as actual characters but rather only as metaphorical principles and in a figurative archetypal sense. But because she is a historical person, Mary Magdalene is literally believed in as a reincarnation of Sophia, the heroine-goddess of the Coptic gospels. One panelist said afterward that Mary Magdalene, but none of the others, had curves (feminine body) but only until her death.[71]

Surprisingly, most panel members were not absolutely sure if gender identification would even exist in the next world. For Mormon Women's Forum member Holly Welker, Gnosticism informs her belief that the Divine Feminine will not exist as gender in the nebulous hereafter. We may assume she means androgyny or a neutered state. Others like gnostic Mormon Maxine Hanks express the idea that the Divine Feminine is superior to the Divine Masculine in this and the next life. Margaret Toscano believes we will have resurrected male and female bodies, but "God" will not because God is uncreated and with no gender as Orthodox Christians believe.

No one from the Mormon Women's Forum or Mormon Pagan Women, to my knowledge, has espoused hermaphroditism or that only the female gender exists in the next world. Certainly none would dare extol the idea that only the male gender exists after death, even though many accept the value of the gnostic *Gospel of Thomas*.[72] Most "rediscovering the goddess" stances of these groups seem geared to bring liberal Christianity into fellowship with neo-paganism.[73]

Most, such as Jana B. Remy, find pantheistic pagan imagery of a goddess such as Ianna, Isis, Athena, or Asherah, more "fleshed out" than the bland and anonymous Mormon Mother in Heaven.[74] It should be noted here, unlike at *Sunstone,* that Egyptian, Babylonian, Indian, Greek, and Roman pagan societies were overwhelmingly patriarchal and anti-matriarchal.[75]

In another session, "What's behind the *Da Vinci Code* Craze? Uncovering the Divine Feminine," all the panel members strongly denied the existence of any bloodline, although they strongly believed in the notion of a married Christ.[76] Paul Toscano believed it was genocidal and dangerous to think in terms of "chosen lineages." In essence this was Margaret Starbird's position as well, when she said at the workshop, "I believe that Jesus had a child, because that fills out the normal family relationship. But any descendants after that [is an idea that] has absolutely no meaning."[77]

This double-speak is contrary to the Mormon message.[78] It has become obvious that only a nebulous "spiritual truth" and no enlightening solid information on the Holy Grail will come of these pseudo-intellectual semi-Mormons and ex-Mormons. Once Latter-day Saints were way ahead of the curve in their understanding of what the bloodline of the Holy Grail actually meant. Now, our own self-censorship or growing Gnosticism has placed us within the mainstream of international interest. But in active Mormonism, we are still well ahead in terms of knowledge, perspective, and understanding.

Some argue, "Why not let others carry this controversial water for us?" Yes, it might not be so bad except for one thing. The world's theological ignorance and separate agendas are poisoning that very water. In late 2006 Dan Brown is scheduled to publish *The Solomon Key*, which will have the Mormons in the position of the Catholic Church and the Danites in the place of the Opus Dei in the *Da Vinci Code*.[79] Then we, as a Church and as a people, will face the critical onslaught the Catholics have suffered for more than two decades. Mormon theology can be of great assistance in adding perspective and knowledge to the errors and misinformation coming from secular sources about these sacred issues.

Therefore it would be wise to tell our own story in a considered and academic fashion. We are not saying that LDS scholars have all the answers, and certainly they have no direct revelation on the Holy Grail, but we should merely affirm that as we research this important question through gospel lenses, we see a little deeper and understand a little better than our gentile counterparts. This is not because we are smarter but because we have the blessings of the restored gospel and the perspective it affords.

Now, at the beginning of the twenty-first century, the prophecies by early Church leaders that one day the secret will be fully out is beginning to take on fresh meaning. After almost 150 years of public silence on the topic, a wise and correct statement from The Church of Jesus Christ of Latter-day Saints was given on 16 May 2006 in response to *The Da Vinci Code* book and movie:

> The belief that Christ was married has never been official church doctrine. It is neither sanctioned nor taught by the Church. While it is true that a few church leaders in the mid-1800s expressed their opinions on the matter, it was not then, and is not now, Church doctrine.

Though the latest word, it will not be the last word.

THE CHRISTIAN AND ANTI-MORMON RESPONSE

Am I therefore become your enemy, because I tell you the truth?

—GALATIANS 4:16

Mormons are considered satanic enemies by most conservative evangelical Christian ministries because of the truth we espouse. The Latter-day Saint public pronouncements regarding the marriage and children of Jesus Christ during the early 1850s naturally led to a theological backlash and attendant persecution. Anciently this happened when some were "laying wait for him [Jesus], and seeking to catch something out of his mouth, that they might accuse him" (Luke 11:54). Elder Orson Hyde's bold statements at Church general conference in October 1854 created an accusatory furor in American newspapers. In

March 1855, Elder Hyde said, "I discover that some of the Eastern papers represent me as a great blasphemer, because I said, in my lecture on marriage, at our last conference, that Jesus Christ was married at Cana of Galilee, that Mary, Martha, and others were his wives, and that he begat children."[80]

Unfortunately, none of these Eastern newspaper editorials have yet been discovered. However, from this time forward the "Jesus was married" blasphemy was leveled at The Church of Jesus Christ of Latter-day Saints by anti-Mormon detractors as proof positive that we are not Christians. Since the nineteenth century there have been few negative treatments of the Church that did not include at least a cameo appearance of this supposed "sacrilege."

A small smattering of anti-Mormon literature tells the story of why Mormonism is demonic because of the sacred marriage. J. W. Gunnison's *The Mormons* and J. H. Snowden's 1926 book, *The Truth about Mormonism*, cover the territory of the polygamous Christ.[81] The Moody Bible Institute Press of Chicago issued a paperback by Gordon H. Fraser titled *Is Mormonism Christian?* (1957). Of course the conclusion was negative partially because they said, "He was not married," regardless of what was taught by Latter-day Saint leaders.[82] Anthony A. Hoekema's *Mormonism* (1963) broke no new ground on the subject and followed Fraser closely.[83] One of the most famous of the diatribes against Mormonism was written by Walter R. Martin, *The Kingdom of the Cults* (1965). Yet Martin only briefly but disparagingly mentions the "marriage."[84]

The established Christian attack upon the LDS Church has exposed anti-Mormons' lack of scholarship, deconstructive agenda, and mean-spiritedness. What is the reasoning of their opposition to Jesus being married? A listing of reasons (with many made up by the author) for arguing against the marriage is now in order:

1. The scriptures and post-Apostolic fathers are totally silent on the topic. (The Protestant mantra, "Where the scriptures are silent, we are silent" should apply to those being critical of the LDS Church as well.)

2. The idea of marriage is beneath the dignity and divinity of the Savior Jesus Christ and is therefore sacrilegious, profaning, and blasphemous. (So, can we assume that holy matrimony is not quite holy enough?)

3. Because Jesus Christ is God, any separate existence from the Father and the Holy Ghost is inconceivable. The Trinity does not operate or exist in such fashion. (Of course, the incarnation does tend to distance the person of Jesus from the person of the Father.[85])

4. Because true Christians do not believe that gender, marriage, and sex exist in heaven, there is no compelling reason for Christ to practice it on earth (Matthew 22:30). Furthermore, "normative Christians" believe that in the heaven all sexual distinctions will be eliminated and we will become completely neuter (Galatians 3:38; 1 Corinthians 12:13). (This does not exactly increase our interest in heaven.[86])

5. Jesus is already married: He is the bridegroom and the Church is the bride (Matthew 9:15; 25:1–13; Mark 2:19; Luke 5:34; John 3:29; D&C 33:17–18; 88:92; 133:10, 19). Therefore, He would not need to take "other" brides. (But nowhere in scripture is there an injunction that He could not take a bride.)

6. It would not have been fair for Jesus Christ to marry and beget children, only to leave them husbandless, fatherless, and hunted by their enemies. (Yet, this happens with

other families; is Jesus' family exempt from suffering?)

7. There was no woman remotely worthy enough to be the mate of the sinless Jesus Christ. Even Mary Magdalene, while no prostitute, had seven devils, making her an unequal bride. (But what about the saving grace of Jesus Christ, which makes us white of all scarlet sin through faith and repentance?)

8. Jesus never thought about self-gratification, only about the welfare of others. He was above and beyond interest in marriage and sex. (But he was not above the first commandment of God to multiply and replenish the earth. He came to fulfill all righteousness.)

9. His own purely spiritual immaculate conception and virgin birth give no place for Him engaging in any carnal and lustful sexual intercourse. (For those who consider marriage and children disgusting, I suppose this is true. But really, how much do we know about Christ's conception?)

10. Although human in shape, He was God and may not have had an alimentary tract, bodily functions, or sexual organs for procreation. (This is a more Docetist view, which was called heretical by the early church.[87])

11. Jesus' devotion to His mission for the atonement and salvation of mankind could not be compromised or complicated by being in a marriage relationship. (Was Christ just too busy? But he found time to be with little children and to drink and eat with sinners. Is this something like the minister who is too busy with his flock to tend to his

family? This is an argument with Catholics for celibacy for all of Christ's ministers.)

12. Other followers of Jesus, such as the Apostle Paul, advocated celibacy in order to serve the kingdom. But most of them were or had been married. His "end times" predictions negated time to have a family, and still he said, "Neither is the man without the woman, neither the woman without the man, in the Lord" (1 Corinthians 11:11).

13. Mormons taught about Jesus' marriages only to bolster their own teachings about polygamy. When the practice of plural marriage was stopped, so was teaching about the marriage of Christ. They were stopped for convenience, though neither has been repudiated by the LDS Church. (The preaching of a married Jesus was stopped because anti-Mormons persecuted the LDS Church.)

14. Men have become so deceived by the seducings of evil spirits that they readily believe that Christ was married (see 2 Thessalonians 2:11–12). This grand self-imposed delusion condemns untrue believers. (Is this all just a test from God to see who will fall and be condemned? Is it another way for God to judge men to hell? I think not.)

15. Even the pseudepigraphal Coptic gospels of Mary, Thomas, and Philip do not mention Jesus being married or His having children.

16. The Jews rejected Jesus' message, in part, because he was not married. Thus the Jewish injunction for marriage inveighed against Jesus' mission.

17. The children of such a marriage would be superhuman demigods, which would muddle the entire gospel message. (Of course, Jesus' own incarnation muddled the minds of the Jews.)

18. The need of an ongoing Old Testament bloodline, which pointed to Jesus Christ, had ended with Him. He was not only the Alpha but also the Omega of all things. He fulfilled the messianic lineage prophesied in the Old Testament, and there was no further need of a prescribed lineage (Matthew 5:17).[88]

19. The "seed" that the Savior shall see are those faithful saved people who believe on his name (Isaiah 50:10; Mosiah 5:7; 15:10–13).

20. Joseph the carpenter was exempt from the duty laid down for a Jewish father of arranging a marriage for his son because Jesus was not really his son.

21. No one or religion, until the Mormons in the nineteenth century, promoted the idea of a married Jesus Christ or offspring. (Although numerous occasions have availed themselves, the LDS Church has not retracted this teaching.)

22. The *hieros gamos* topic has only been promulgated by neognostic anti-Christian occultists since about 1950. Those who believe in it do not consider themselves orthodox Christians.

All the above reasons are man's projection of his own image of Christ. God has other reasons. Interestingly, during a radio debate on the subject in 1981, Dr. Malachi Martin, a Catholic scholar and former member of the Vatican's Pontifical Institute, "conceded that there was ultimately no real theological objection to a married Jesus."[89]

However, no LDS apologetic books for the restored gospel ever trace this topic or rebut anti-Mormon caricatures of the sacred marriage.[90] The idea is to "let sleeping dogs lie" until it becomes front-page provocation. However, since 2000 the Internet has spread word of the Mormon concept of a married Jesus. Now hundreds of anti-Mormon "Christian" websites and bloggers berate the Church for having Jesus be a polygamist.

Anybody who has deeply studied Mormonism will know that our Church once taught that Jesus and Mary Magdalene were married. Perhaps we should publish what we know to the world. Anti-Mormons like J. R. Church publish it for us, from the housetops and in the worst possible light: "The [Merovingian] symbol of the bee is also used in Mormon temples today. The bee is the state symbol for Utah. Furthermore, Mormon doctrine teaches that Mary Magdalene was the wife of Jesus Christ. The religion of the Mormon Church of the Latter Day Saints is replete with Merovingian ideology."[91]

There has been precious little on the LDS side to counterbalance the sea of negative argument against the Church for once having taught that Jesus was married and failing to invalidate it now. Latter-day Saint apologists W. John Walsh ("Why Was Jesus Never Married?") and Michael T. Griffith ("Was Jesus Married?") do credible jobs forwarding considered LDS positions on the issue.[92] Daniel Peterson and Stephen Ricks write, "Some denunciations of Mormonism seem to betray a Neoplatonic and gnosticizing disdain for the material cosmos, a discomfort with the body and with sexuality that is utterly foreign to the Bible."[93]

Probably the most reasonable non-LDS airing of this theme comes from a Baptist minister, Dr. Cky J. Carrigan, in January 2004.[94] He dispassionately described the levels of officiality of different authoritative statements by five high-ranking Mormon leaders on Jesus being married. In doing so, he automatically outlines the basic LDS position of Christ practicing polygamy and having children. He concludes by saying, "There is no evidence that any LDS authority has ever officially repudiated or rejected the teachings of Hyde, Pratt, Grant, Joseph F. Smith and Joseph Fielding Smith on the marital and parental status of the Son."[95]

Carrigan is the kindest of our critics. Others, like the blogger Pat Zukeran in his "The Mormon Doctrine of Jesus: Jesus the Polygamist?" reject the "Jesus of Mormonism [who] is not the Jesus of the Bible." He notes, "Although Mormons today try to distance themselves from this teaching, it is clearly a part of their historical record. . . . For these reasons, we cannot consider the Mormon teachings on Christ to be consistent with the New Testament."[96]

While it is true that Latter-day Saints never considered a married Jesus as an official doctrine, their reticence to talk about it is well founded. Who likes to be called "blasphemer" or "profaner"? Who wants to be persecuted by or needlessly offend one's neighbor? So as not to appear sacrilegious amongst those of Christian faith, Mormons do not talk about these esoteric teachings.

Yet some like MacGregor Ministries: A Christian Outreach Group try to reach those "trapped" in cult groups and are often extreme in their religious bigotry. Their "Facts Mormons Won't Tell You" series includes many such hurtful statements as the following:

MORMONS WON'T TELL YOU

that they intend to have many wives in heaven, carrying on multiple sex relations throughout eternity, until they have enough children to populate their own earth, so they can be "Heavenly Father" over their own planet!

MORMONS WON'T TELL YOU

that they believe Jesus had at least three wives and children while he was on this earth.[97]

When the Southern Baptist Convention met in Salt Lake City in 2001, there were numerous confrontations about the polygamous Jesus. Members of the Baptist group took special delight in bringing up the most arcane teachings and making them the centerpiece of conversation with Latter-day Saints. Banners with provocative quotes such as, "Now the Spirit speaketh expressly, that in the latter times some shall depart from the faith, giving heed to seducing spirits, and doctrines of devils" were everywhere (1 Timothy 4:1).

But since the *The Da Vinci Code* phenomenon exploded in 2003 and 2004, the mainstreaming of the "Jesus was married" idea began to be accepted by the general population. What was once a surefire means of arousing ire among the laity has become a doctrinal plus of sorts. Now anti-Mormons seem to emphasize not so much that Jesus was married, but that Latter-day Saints believe He was a polygamist. Mormons are not out of the woods yet regarding this teaching. But some of the sting is gone from much of the anti-Mormon propaganda.

Now as the events of the winding-up scene are ready to transpire, the focus of anti-Mormonism—Joseph Smith Jr.—is ready again to take center stage. The enemies of the Church, both secularists and spiritualists, are soon to become more aggressive. No amount of appeasing or compromising will protect us from the oncoming holocaust, before and during the time of tribulation. The Grail messengers and message will again be targets of the gentile church and the state.

THE SECOND COMING OF JOSEPH SMITH

My servant Joseph still holds the keys of my kingdom in this dispensation, and he shall stand in due time on the earth, in the flesh [resurrected body], and fulfill that to which he is appointed.

—PARLEY P. PRATT[98]

Eschatologically (relating to the end of time), there is little in Mormon theology dealing with Joseph Smith's eminent return to establish a literal Zion. The Prophet's unique role as Head of this Dispensation of the Fulness of Times did not end with his death in 1844. Many promises were associated with his mission, which were not accomplished during his mortality. According to Brigham Young, it was through Joseph Smith Jr., that this day would come: "He will hold the keys: he will rule, govern, and control all things in the spiritual world pertaining to this Dispensation until he has finished his work."[99]

But what do we know of his further work on this side of the veil? What about his resurrected ministry and second coming? It was incorrectly believed by some, such as Wilford Woodruff, that Joseph Smith would return in 1890 and immediately lead the Church and kingdom in the days preceding Jesus Christ's glorious second coming.[100] While this did not come to pass at that time, certainly Joseph will be resurrected at some time. But by whom?

One Jewish tradition has Elijah restoring Messiah ben Joseph to life.[101] The resurrected Prophet Joseph will play a major role in the "winding-up scene" of the last days. This would help usher in the *Parousia* of the Lord Jesus Christ. Orson Pratt has noted:

God's arm is not shortened that he cannot raise him [Joseph Smith] up even from the tomb. We are living in the dispensation of the resurrection, and there may be some who will wake from their tombs for certain purposes and to bring to pass certain transactions on the earth decreed by the Great Jehovah; and if the Lord sees proper to bring forth that man [Joseph] just before the winding up scene to lead forth the army of Israel, he will do so.[102]

Parley P. Pratt in 1832 stated that it will be through Joseph's support, that Christ will succeed in the latter days.[103] President Brigham Young in January 1856 explained Joseph's work of the last days:

When we return to Zion and build the great Temple which Joseph saw and the center of Zion is established the glory of God will rest upon it by day and by night and those that are prepared will see the face of the Son of Man and they will see Joseph and Hyrum in the flesh in their resurrected bodies. Then will the armies of Israel be terrible to all Nations. Then will one chase a thousand and two put ten thousand to flight.

Who will resurrect Joseph's body? It will be Peter, James, John, Moroni, or some one who has or will receive the keys of the resurrection. It will probably be one of those who held the keys of this dispensation and has delivered them to Joseph and you will see Jesus and he will eat peaches and apples with you. But the world will

not see it or know [of] it for wickedness will increase. Joseph and Jesus
will be there. They will walk and talk
with them at times and no man mis-
trusts who they are. Joseph will lead
the armies of Israel whether he is seen
or not whether visible or invisible as
seemeth him good.

I tell you there will not be much
of this [resurrection and adoption]
until Joseph comes. He is our spiritual Father. Our hearts are already
turned to him and his to us. This [is]
the order of the Holy Priesthood and
we shall continue to administer in the
ordinances of the kingdom of God
here on Earth.[104]

It is quite possible that Alvin and Hyrum Smith,
whose lives were cut short, will also be resurrected with
Joseph Smith to help their younger brother accomplish
all that was promised.[105] Alvin was considered by the
family to be the future prophet, while Hyrum was
Joseph's first councilor and co-president of the Church.
Their role in this Dispensation is immense and it will be
fully recognized one day.

There is a man called the "one mighty and
strong" which is noted in section 85 verse 7 footnote
g, of the 1879 and 1890 editions of the Doctrine and
Covenants as "a future messenger promised."[106] We
cannot be sure of this person's identity, but he seems
to come with the power of a resurrected being. It may
be Jesus Christ, Elijah, Michael-Adam, or Joseph
Smith (or perhaps all four) coming to square things
in this last dispensation before the final scenario:[107]

*And it shall come to pass that I, the Lord
God, will send one mighty and strong,
holding the scepter of power in his hand,
clothed with light for a covering, whose
mouth shall utter words, eternal words;*

*while his bowels shall be a fountain of
truth, to set in order the house of God,
and to arrange by lot the inheritances of
the saints whose names are found, and
the names of their fathers, and of their
children, enrolled in the book of the law
of God.*

—D&C 85:7

Perhaps Joseph Smith Jr. will come to "hasten my
[the Lord's] work in its time" (D&C 88:73). Many
of these promises have to do with the events in the
Western hemisphere which will lead the Saints and
the ten tribes to Jackson County and redeem Zion.
Some of the things, which were "appointed" to the
Prophet Joseph, were recorded in an 1835 revelation
to Oliver Cowdery in the patriarchal blessings book
kept by the LDS Church. Included are these blessings, some of which did not fully come to pass during Joseph's mortality:[108]

In due time shall he go forth toward the north, and by the power of
his word shall the deep begin to give
way: and the ice melt before the Sun.
By the keys of the kingdom shall he
lead (the lost tribes of) Israel into the
land of Zion, while the house of Jacob
shouts in the dance and in the song.
. . .

His fame shall be sounded in foreign lands, even to the ends of the
earth, as well as nigh at home: for in
this the times shall change, [and] a
prophet shall have honor in his own
country. . . .

He shall be a law giver to Israel,
and shall teach the house of Jacob the
statues of the Most High. . . . He shall
partake of the blessings of Abraham,

Isaac, and Jacob: the chief things of the ancient mountains, the precious things that couch beneath, and of the treasures hid in the sand.

The records of past ages and generations, and the histories of ancient days shall he bring forth, even the record of the Nephites shall he again obtain, with all those hid up by Mormon, and others who were righteous; and many others till he is overwhelmed with knowledge.[109]

No precious thing shall slumber from his possession, for he shall be covered with the most choice things of all ages, till his soul shall be satisfied and his heart shall say, "Enough! Enough!"[110] In his hands shall the Urim and Thummim remain and the holy ministry, and the keys of the evangelical priesthood forever, even the patriarchal; for behold, he is the first patriarch in the last days [dispensation head].

He shall sit in the great assembly and general council of patriarchs [Adam-ondi-Ahman], and execute the will and commandment under the direction of the Ancient of Days, for he shall have his place and act in his station.

Behold my brother Joseph is blessed, blessed are all who bless him, and blessed are all those whom he blesses.

He shall remain to a good old age, even till his head is like the pure wool. Behold there is no end to the vision, of the multiplicity of blessings and glories, which shall come upon my brother Joseph. . . . Thus closes the vision, and thus it shall be. Even so: Amen.[111]

It would be difficult to imagine a more glorious blessing (see D&C 25:14). Yet not all the above blessings were fulfilled during Joseph's lifetime. The prophecy of him living to the good old age of eighty-five years (D&C 130:15), which would of course make his hair white like pure wool, did not come to pass in mortality. While Joseph received the promises of old age the blessing was superseded. This might have been because Joseph asked to be taken sooner than his blessings had dictated. However, in regards to Cowdery's blessing, much of what was written is yet to take place when Joseph is resurrected. As a resurrected being, he might indeed have hair as white as wool.

In a sermon given to the Relief Society in the upper room of the Red Brick Store in Nauvoo, Illinois on 28 April 1842, Joseph Smith stated "that according to his prayers God had appointed him elsewhere."[112] Did this mean that Joseph had prayed to be taken away, to return at some later date? One of Joseph's plural wives, Mary Elizabeth Lightner, heard him say:

I am tired. I have been mobbed, I have suffered so much, from outsiders and from my own family. Some of the brethren think they can carry this work on better than I can, far better. I have asked the Lord to take me away. I have to seal my testimony to this generation with my blood. I have to do it, for this work will never progress until I am gone for the testimony is of no force until the testator is dead.[113]

In a similar statement to Benjamin F. Johnson, Joseph further explains the situation:

Then with a deep-drawn breath, as a sign of weariness, he sank down heavily in his chair, and said, "Oh! I am so tired—so tired that I often feel to long for my day of rest. For what has there been in this life but tribulation for me? From a boy I have been persecuted by my enemies, and now even my friends are beginning to join with them, to hate and persecute me! Why should I not wish for my time of rest?"

His words and tone thrilled and shocked me, and like an arrow pierced my hopes that he would long remain with us. I said as with a heart full of tears, "Oh! Joseph, what could we, as a people, do without you and what would become of the great latter-day work if you should leave us?"

He was touched by my emotions, and in reply he said, "Benjamin, I would not be far away from you. . . . to roll on this kingdom."[114]

Was Joseph Smith cut off from mortality early to consummate and validate his mission? Joseph's mission in the spirit world was of utmost importance, "and if on the other side of the veil I would still be working with you, and with a power greatly increased, to roll on this kingdom."[115] Did he receive the promise that nothing would be lost to him, but that a future work would be performed, as a resurrected being? It might seem so. Certainly the promises and blessings made to him must come true in one fashion or another.

What are some of the roles Joseph Smith will fill after his resurrection? Will Joseph return before Adam-ondi-Ahman to lead the lost ten tribes from the North country, to destroy the enemies of Israel on this continent, to retrieve the "rich treasures" (records) of the earth, and to establish the Order of Enoch in Jackson County, Missouri? Will the "holy city" mentioned in Ether 13:3, 8, be built under his auspices? It is entirely possible and maybe even probable. As the representative of Christ's posterity for the end time in the last dispensation, Joseph the prophet may be called upon to resolve a "multiplicity" of things as *Messiah ben Joseph*.

Non-Mormon scholar Edward G. King notes that the restoration of the ten tribes and the return of Elijah were both "always associated with the *Messiah ben Joseph*."[116] God spoke through His prophet Malachi, "Behold, I send my messenger, and he will prepare the way before me: and the *Lord*, whom ye seek, shall suddenly come to his temple, even the messenger of the covenant, whom ye delight in" (Malachi 3:1–2).

Rabbi Saadia Gaon (A.D. ca. 900) and Rabbi ben Ezra (ca. 1080–1164) said that this "messenger" sent to prepare the way of the Messiah is the "messiah" ("anointed one") son of Joseph (*Messiah ben Joseph*]. That is, a descendant son of Joseph will go before the return of Jesus Christ, the true *Messiah ben Judah*, restoring true temple ordinances and leading the way in rebuilding the temple of God first in Jackson County, Missouri, and then on the Temple Mount in Jerusalem.[117]

According to a biblical commentary known as the *Malbim* (1809–1879), the "Messiah son of Joseph" was to lead the lost ten tribes in the period known as the "latter days," leading to their eventual reconciliation and reunification with Judah.[118] Joseph Smith's calling was to gather scattered Israel from the four corners of the earth to the center stake of Zion, the "New Jerusalem" and mystical Grail castle of the last days (Revelations 21:1–4, 9–27; 22:1–5). Weiser's commentary on Ezekiel 37 noted:

Our sacred sages had a tradition that in the beginning (of the End Times) would arise a Messiah ["anointed one" or deliverer] from the house of Joseph who will reign over the ten tribes. He will wage wars and all of Israel will be gathered together under his banner. [This will continue] until later on, a descendant of David will appear and he will reign over them. . . .

A transformation will take place. The ten tribes and the stick of Joseph will draw themselves closer unto the stick of Judah, and this too will be through the agency of a Prophet and by miracles.[119]

Joseph Smith Jr., forever the evangelist, may be the one to eventually lead the missionary effort among Esau, the Ishmaelites, Edomites, and Muslim peoples. A part of this may be as a general in defeating the radical militants and terrorists among them. Eventually the score between Isaac and Ishmael, Jacob and Esau will be settled through fire. The book of Obadiah verse 18 (and verse 21) now comes into play:

And the house of Jacob shall be a fire, and the house of Joseph a flame; but the house of Esau shall be stubble, and they shall kindle them, and devour them; and there shall not be any remaining of the house of Esau; for the Lord hath spoken it.

The Talmud says only the tribe of Joseph is able to defeat Esau on the battlefield.[120] The apocryphal Hebrew Third Enoch gives a similar end times scenario: "I saw Messiah, son of Joseph, and his generations and their works and their doing that they will do against the nations of the world" (Hebrew Book of Enoch

45:5). Thus it seems that a resurrected Joseph Smith will be the general in an army that defeats "Gog and Magog."[121] According to Ginsberg, "the bull [unicorn of] Joseph will subdue the horned beast, the kingdom of wickedness, before the Messianic time."[122] The Lord has spoken in Revelation 3:12: "If you conquer, I will make you a pillar in the temple of my God." Joseph Smith is that polished shaft in the Lord's quiver who will become a prey upon his enemies (1 Nephi 21:2; D&C 133:28). Joseph shall play an instrumental role in the unification of Israel with Ishmael and healing the breach between them.

Brigham Young said that the law of [priesthood] adoption could not be completed in its fulness until Joseph Smith returns.[123] In December 1869 President Young taught that the bulk of the work of sealing men to men back to Adam in a priesthood chain was reserved for the Millennium. He further said that Joseph as a resurrected person would dictate the progress of this important work:

[It] will be the work of the Millennium and Joseph Smith will be the man to attend to it or to dictate it. He will not administer in person but he will receive his resurrected body and will dictate to those who dwell in the flesh and tell what is to be done for He is the Last Prophet who is called to lay the foundation of the great last Dispensation of the Fullness of Times. Some have thought it strange what I have said concerning Adam, but the period will come when this people of faithful [sic] will be willing to adopt Joseph Smith as the Prophet, Seer, Revelator and God.[124]

. . . After Joseph comes to us in his resurrected body he will more fully instruct us concerning the baptism for the dead and the sealing ordinances. He will say be baptized for this man and that man and that man be sealed to that man and such a man to such a man and connect the Priesthood together.[125]

We fully believe that a resurrected Jesus and Joseph will return one day and set the principle of priesthood adoption straight. Therefore as President Woodruff said, "When you get to the end, let the last man be adopted to Joseph Smith, who stands at the head of the dispensation."[126] Joseph Smith is the final link in the last Dispensation.

Brother Joseph is the most literal and direct descendant of Jesus on the Earth at the time of the Restoration. Seeing he has so much to do with our salvation, pay heed to Doctrine and Covenants 6:18: "Therefore be diligent; stand by my servant Joseph, faithfully, in whatsoever difficult circumstances he may be for the word's sake." He is the scion of the office of Saviors upon Mount Zion. Brigham Young said as much: "The world knows nothing of the office of saviors upon Mount Zion. If Joseph Smith is not the man on whom the Keys of the Kingdom rest, I would not give the ashes of a rye straw for our Salvation."[127]

As Christ's most worthy descendant, Joseph Smith will appropriately come in the end time a second time as a resurrected being. This will precede his forefather, exemplar and Savior, Jesus Christ who is the head. These Grail Kings, with others of the chosen lineage, shall guide us to the Millennium and then to our salvation.

NOTES

1. Journal of Rudger Clawson (2 July 1899), 374–375. Minutes of the Solemn Assembly, Salt Lake Temple.
2. Juliette Wood, "The Search for the Holy Grail: Scholars, Critics and Occultists," The Folklore Society at www.

juliette.wood.btinternet.co.uk/holygrail.htm (30 June 2003).

3. Juliette Wood, "The Holy Grail: From Romance Motif to Modern Genre," *Folklore* 3 (October 2000): 170. Later this is moved from the Carolingian dynasty of Charlemagne back to the earlier Merovingian dynasty of the Capetian King Dagobert by Baigent, Leigh, and Lincoln, *Holy Blood, Holy Grail.* Early Grail romances always affirmed that the lineage anciently came from Joseph of Arimathea.

4. These are Celsus from the second century, the anti-Cathars Ermengaud de Beziers and Pierre des Vaux-de-Cernay in the thirteenth century, Martin Luther in the sixteenth century, and the elusive Zvi Udey in the nineteenth century. None of these sources is dependable for accurate information, but interesting for perspective.

5. Oliver Kamm, "Mad, Bad but Not Dangerous," *Times,* 21 March 2005. Joshua rejects the teachings of Paul, but when he dies the scars of the crucifixion are discovered and Paul declares a miracle, "the Stigmata." Both these characterizations have the events happening after the resurrection, which inexplicably becomes the mantra for later writers.

6. Graves, *King Jesus,* boldly announced that Jesus was the son of Mary and Herod's oldest son Antipater. He has Jesus marry Mary Magdalene, who, he says, is an elderly priestess of an earth goddess cult and a witch. He also implies that Jesus was married to "his cousin" Mary of Bethany. Interestingly he separates the persons of Mary Magdalene and Mary of Bethany. He is critiqued by Mordecai S. Chertoff, who notes: "Since this invention would invalidate Jesus' claim to the throne of Israel as a direct descendant of Herod, Graves secures the claim in another way: he has Jesus marry (without consummating the marriage) Michal, who is the youngest daughter of a youngest daughter of the royal house of David" (see http://www.commentarymagazine.com/Summaries). Graves' important book, *The White Goddess,* does not say anything about a sacred lineage, marriage, or sexual relationship of Jesus.

7. Edmund P. Murray stage play, *The Passion Play* irreverently casts Mary Magdalene as an ex-stripper who is married to Judah but who once had a torrid affair with Jesus. The billing says, "Too profane for even the seamiest of tank towns."

8. Kazantzakis, *Last Temptation of Christ,* 257.
9. Phipps, *Was Jesus Married?* 11.
10. Kyle Haselden, "The Inferno of Dreams," *The Christian Century* 70 (October 5, 1960): 1149. See Hebrews 4:15.

11. Starbird, *Mary Magdalene*, 107–8, using Wakefield and Evans, *Heresies of the High Middle Ages*, 230–41, as her source. She mentions Ermengaud de Béziers, another anti-Cathar who seems to be the source of Pierre des Vaux-de-Cernay's claim. Her lecture was delivered at the Salt Lake City Sunstone Symposium workshop, 11 August 2004, and at the Salt Lake City Sunstone Symposium, July 2005. Of course Starbird does not accept that the Magdalene was a concubine, but uses the source anyway.

12. Brown, *Da Vinci Code*, 247. See also Maier and Hanegraaf, *Da Vinci Code: Fact or Fiction?* 19.

13. Brown, *Da Vinci Code*, 244. There are no "pro" and only a couple of rare "con" sources. Everything regarding a sexual relationship of Jesus and the Magdalene comes from anti-"they believe" and none from "we believe" sources. Of course this could have been a "hidden truth" held tightly by the Cathars, if it did not so strongly conflict with their strongly held beliefs that the good Christ had no physical body, while the evil Jesus was a regular (not divine) man. Their anti-marriage stance would negate the idea that the Cathars approved of the Jesus of the New Testament. It all challenges credulity.

14. Price, *Da Vinci Fraud*, 239. Here Price suggests a sexual nature: "It is obvious that the erotic imagery [of these gospels] is being used metaphorically in such passages, and yet who can discount the possibility that here, as in other cases, some notion, originally taken in a physical, material sense, has been 'docetized,' its offense to squeamish readers removed by 'not taking it literally?'"

15. Erskine, *Human Life of Jesus*, 27–28. He notes: "It does not seem improbable that he [Jesus] did fall in love and had some experience of parenthood. . . . He understood women very well indeed, with the special understanding of a man who has been hurt by one of them."

16. Tom F. Driver, "Sexuality and Jesus," *Union Seminary Quarterly Review* 20 (1965): 243, 240.

17. William E. Phipps, "Did Jesus or Paul Marry?" *Journal of Ecumenical Studies* 5 (1968): 741–44.

18. Certainly Phipps was and has remained the best writer on the topic. Tom Driver's 1965 article on the marriage of Jesus Christ, Phipps's 1968 article on a married Paul and Jesus, and then Kraut's cut-and-paste booklet, *Jesus Was Married*, were the only significant studies on a married Jesus before 1970.

19. Price, *Da Vinci Fraud*, 9.

20. For an evangelical rebuttal of Baigent, Leigh, and Lincoln's *Holy Blood, Holy Grail* and its theories, see Paige Patterson, "Holy Blood, Holy Grail—Holy Mackerel," *Christianity Today* 26 (3 September 1982): 28–29.

21. Juliette Wood, "The Holy Grail: From Romance Motif to Modern Genre," *Folklore* 3 (October 2000): 170. I can see this charge being used against myself as well.

22. Ibid., 171.

23. These include *Genesis of the Grail Kings, The Illustrated Bloodline of the Holy Grail*, and *The Magdalene Legacy*.

24. Starbird, *Mary Magdalene*, 95.

25. Ibid., 96. None of this is given as mere speculation, which it is, and no footnotes are mustered. She is probably influenced by Thiering's and Gardner's writings. She might also have been motivated by the desire to "cut short" the Mormon view that Christ had multiple wives.

26. Paul Smith, "The 1989 Plantard Comeback," priory-of-sion.com/psp/id60.html (2003).

27. Brown was a former English teacher at Phillips Exeter Academy, New Hampshire. It was reported that by October of 2004 he had grossed $350,000 from his efforts.

28. Haag and Haag, *Rough Guide to The Da Vinci Code*, 202.

29. Jeremy R. Hammond, "Was Jesus Married?" *Yirmeyahu Review* (16 April 2004), www.yirmeyahureview.com/scripture/was_jesus_married.htm.

30. Brown, *Da Vinci Code*, 235. This is such a ludicrous statement, superseded only by Jacques Derrida's injunction, "There are NO absolutes!" Or perhaps we can add Lucifer's demand, "Do not believe the truth!" to the list.

31. Dan Brown made a concession to orthodox belief by not saying that the daughter was born after the crucifixion, which Brown believes Jesus survived. He possibly felt that it was too controversial without moving the story along. See Haag and Haag, *Rough Guide to The Da Vinci Code*.

32. Olson and Miesel, *Da Vinci Hoax*, 14. Richard Tomkins, "Do Not Believe a Word of What You Are about to Read," *Financial Times*, New York, 15 October 2004, 8, which outlines the ideas of the modern founder of deconstructionism. "Derrida declared historical knowledge to be impossible, dismissed reason as the dishonest pursuit of certainty and called the search for truth 'the ruling illusion of western metaphysics'— in short, attacking the basis of western thought." Postmodernism is very similar to the old Gnosticism.

33. Abanes, *Truth behind The Da Vinci Code*, 77.

34. Laura Miller, as quoted in Burstein, *Secrets of the Da Vinci Code*, 299.

35. Alyson Ward, "Surprising Fictions in 'The Da Vinci Code'" *Provo Daily Herald*, 31 January 2004, section B.

36. Brent Bozell, "ABC's empty assault on Jesus," editorial (5 November 2003), *Conservative Chronicle,* 12 November 2003, 28.

37. On the page before the prologue is written: "FACT: The Priory of Sion—a European secret society founded in 1099—is a real organization. In 1975 Paris's Bibliothéque Nationale discovered parchments known as Les Dossiers Secrets, identifying numerous members of the Priory of Sion, including Sir Isaac Newton, Botticelli, Victor Hugo, and Leonardo da Vinci . . . All descriptions of artwork, architecture, documents, and secret rituals in this novel are accurate."

38. Price, *Da Vinci Fraud,* 11.

39. Also see Welborn, *De-Coding Da Vinci,* and McDowell, *Da Vinci Code—A Quest for Answers.* The latter book is an attempt by the Campus Crusade for Christ to create "cultural discourse."

40. Haag and Haag, *Rough Guide to The Da Vinci Code,* 204. They continue: "But whatever one thinks of the feminist argument, it is unfortunate when history is misrepresented for the sake of narrowly advancing a cause."

41. There was a Solemn Assembly in the Salt Lake Temple (2 July 1899) in which George Q. Cannon and Lorenzo Snow spoke of the seed of Christ and the ancient apostles in the body of men assembled that day. The idea that Jesus was married and had wives was presented.

42. Talmage made reference to certain details of Jesus' life. It was used with regard to a sacred marriage in a CD entitled *What Da Vinci Didn't Know* by Brigham Young University religion professors Holzapfel, Wayment, Huntsman, and Skinner.

43. Here the idea is expressed that all who accept and live the gospel of Jesus are his seed.

44. J. Ricks Smith, "Letter to Joseph Fielding Smith, March 17, 1963, with Reply." This letter is in the BYU Special Collections. A photocopy is in the author's possession.

45. Cky J. Carrigan, "Did Jesus Christ Marry and Father Children?" (addresss, 2004), 8.

46. Harold D. Ethington of Salt Lake City, email to Vern G. Swanson (26 April 2004), from his journal of 18 October 1963. Photocopies of journal in author's possession.

47. President David O. McKay's official letterhead, addressed to Sister Sharon Pokriots of Provo, and signed by his secretary, Claire Middleness [indistinct signature, last name], 10 October 1966; photocopy in Matthew Richardson's office, associate dean, Religious Education, Joseph Smith Building, BYU, Provo, Utah).

48. Bruce R. McConkie, address to faculty of the Church Education System, conducted during the first term of Summer school, 15 June 1967. This excerpt was transcribed from a tape of the lecture on file in the Recording Library of the Church Education System in Salt Lake City. Marion D. Hanks also noted this patriarch in his 2002 interview with the author.

49. Anne Wilding Kraut, "What's behind the Da Vinci Code Craze? Uncovering the Divine Feminine," Sunstone Symposium, 371, 14 August 2004. Augmented by my discussion with her after the session. She called him the prophet, but he wasn't until 23 January 1970.

50. Keith Norman, "Book Review of *Jesus Was Married* by Ogden Kraut and *Was Jesus Married?* by William E. Phipps," *Sunstone* 1, 2 (Spring 1976): 87–92. Norman concludes, "Given the thoroughness of his scholarship and the general soundness of his reasoning, the question 'Was Jesus married?' might eventually be answered by Christians in the affirmative."

51. William E. Phipps, "The Case for a Married Christ," *Dialogue,* 7, 4 (1972).

52. According to Anne Wilde (29 July 2005 interview), in mid-1971 Kraut's stake president Johnson received a letter from Apostle Mark E. Petersen. He wanted President Johnson to call in Ogden Kraut to ask "why he thought he had the right to write a book on Jesus being married when it was not a Church approved doctrine?" (as remembered by Anne Wilde). I assume this was about the same time as Joseph Fielding Smith's presentation to the Quorum of the Twelve.
President Johnson disregarded the letter, until a second one came several months later. Petersen asked for a response, so Johnson was obliged to talk to Ogden Kraut. Even though Kraut had already secretly embraced fundamentalism, he was still an active member in good standing, holding five callings in his ward. Ogden defended his position to the stake president, who thought Kraut was reasonable and made the mistake of noting such to Elder Petersen. By September of 1972, Kraut was excommunicated.

53. Anne Wilding Kraut (in an audience response), "What's behind the Da Vinci Code Craze? Uncovering the Divine Feminine," Sunstone Symposium no. 371, 14 August 2004, and my discussion with her after the session. The Seventies Bookstore chain does not now exist.

54. This author knows of no Godbeite statements on the subject of Jesus' marriage, but it was only noted in conversations with Mormon Women Forum members.

55. Interviews with Richard L. Anderson, professor emeritus of Church history, Brigham Young University, June 2004; and Matthew Richardson, associate dean,

Religious Education, Brigham Young University, Joseph Smith Building, 19 July 2004. A copy of this letter has not been discovered, but it does comport with the statements of Anne Wilding.

56. A friend's email to Vern G. Swanson, 24 August 2005, in author's possession.

57. Elder S. (24 August 2004). He noted that he was great friends with President David O. McKay. Elder S. rehearsed a number of reasons why the Savior had to be married and even quoted all the pertinent passages from Doctrine and Covenants 113 and 132.

58. McConkie, *Millennial Messiah,* 340.

59. Ludlow, *Isaiah,* 172.

60. He notes Whitney, *Life of Heber C. Kimball,* 185; *Journal of Discourses,* 4:248 (1 March 1857); Journal of Rudger Clawson (2 July 1899), 374–75; Anthony W. Ivins journal (2 July 1899), 9:21.

61. A panel discussion two weeks later included Zina Nibley Petersen, Rita Wright, and me.

62. Swanson lecture "On the Trail of the Holy Grail" was given in March 2004. Because of its controversial nature, BYU rightly chose (with my permission) not to publish it with the others.

63. In preparation for the MOA lecture, Ellie Sonntag organized a fireside in January at the Park City home of the erudite Dr. Chase and Greta Petersen. Dr. Petersen is a former president of the University of Utah. He later sent a letter to me with a list of questions and suggestions that helped immeasurably in my MOA presentation.

64. *Sunstone Magazine* sponsors an annual summer symposium in Salt Lake City, which is in my opinion decidedly left of center and usually critical of the Mormon church. While the author has usually boycotted it for over a decade, he attended the sessions on *The Da Vinci Code* and marriage of Christ because of his research for this publication. The 2005 Salt Lake City Sunstone Symposium again invited Margaret Starbird to participate.

65. Starbird workshop lecture at Sunstone Symposium Salt Lake City, August 2004.

66. 2004 Salt Lake City Sunstone Symposium, 14 August 2004, session 362. Presenter Doe Daughtrey, of the Sunstone board of directors, read the paper "The Goddess Is Alive and Magick Is Afoot: Mormon Pagan Women in the 21st Century." According to them, wicca, paganism, and other "earth-centered" or "nature" religions are the fastest growing of the all 'new' (old?) religious movements in America. On the evening of 11 August 2004, Maxine Hanks and Margaret Starbird spoke on "Reclaiming Magdalene: The Lost Bride in Christian Mythology,"

session 91. That evening she again was unable to provide any scholarly references for her exaggerated claims. She was not challenged by doting Mormon Women's Forum advocates.

67. Sunstone Symposium, Salt Lake City, 11 August 2004, W5, "Mary Magdalene: The Greatest Story Never Told," by Margaret Starbird. Starbird told the audience that Joseph Smith got his ideas of the sacred marriage from the Freemasons. She offered no proof. The Masons do not have this in their literature, and Joseph Smith could not have acquired this knowledge from that empty well. In an email to the author (26 September 2005) Starbird honestly and kindly wrote: "I'm not a Freemason and am not privy to their 'lore' other than the fact that they derive it in part from the Knights Templar (who were the medieval guardians of the Grail heresy . . .). What exactly the Freemasons know, I'm not sure. One told me recently that they always knew they were custodians of something, but they weren't sure what! The masons have many connections with medieval 'Grail' symbolism, but I'm not sure at what point their knowledge becomes 'overt.'
"I found many connections with the 'Great Secret' of the Middle Ages in a book called 'The Lost Language of Symbolism' and related it to information about Freemasonry's connections with the Old French (*Born in Blood,* by John Robinson)."

68. In an email (26 September 2005) to the author, Margaret Starbird revealed, "I don't know where I read that Joseph Smith had Freemason connections, maybe you know? . . . I think Joseph Smith may have 'intuited' the connections himself—although it is not impossible that a Freemason in his acquaintance actually told him the 'secret.'" As shown earlier, there is not a shred of evidence that Masons believed in a married Christ.

69. The French writer René Guénon regarded the Theosophical Society with suspicion and developed an elaborate spiritual rather than physical version of a Celtic Grail. He was, in 1925, one of the first to relate the Cathars (Albigensians) to the Grail, but it had nothing to do with any marriage. In Margaret Starbird's 2004 Salt Lake City Sunstone Symposium, August 2004, session 131, "Truth or Fiction? Reading *The Da Vinci Code,*" she thanked Dan Brown for opening up the topic with no criticism of Brown for being such an idealogue or purveyor of unfactual information. Then, in the Sunstone Symposium held 29 July 2005 she again highly praised Dan Brown and said that his detractors and debunkers were wrong. Panelists in 2004 included Maxine Hanks and Rev. Dr. Lance S. Owens of the

Ecclesia Gnostica (Gnostic church) of Salt Lake City.

70. Sunstone Symposium, session 271, 13 August 2004, searched for meaning in divine female power from non-LDS traditions such as goddesses Shakti, Kali, Rhiannon, Venus, Athena, Spider Woman, White Buffalo Woman, Isis, Kuan Yin, and so forth. The panelist—who included Holly Welker, Doe Daughtrey, Maxine Hanks, Jana Bouck Remy, Mary Ellen Robertson, and Margaret M. Toscano— admitted to praying to these and other deities, not in a literal sense but as representatives of divine principles.

71. Most gnostics (except perhaps LDS ones) do not believe that spirits have bodies in the shape of men or women.

72. Gospel of Thomas, Logion 114. "Simon Peter said to them, 'Let Mary [Magdalene] leave us, for women are not worthy of life [the mysteries].' Jesus said, 'I myself shall lead her in order to make her male so that she too may become a living spirit resembling you males. For every woman who will make herself male will enter the Kingdom of Heaven.'" Interestingly, in Mahayna Buddhist scripture, Saddharma-Pundarika XI:51 (Lotus of the True Law), no woman becomes a Bodhisattava, but rather she disappears and reappears in the male sex to become a Bodhisattava. See Price, *Da Vinci Fraud,* 241 ff6. The Mormon view might be that in marriage the woman takes the name of her husband, "Mrs. John Doe" and thus becomes male, but not male in gender, because she retains her full womanhood.

73. Price, *Da Vinci Fraud,* 245.

74. Salt Lake City, Sunstone Symposium, August 2004. This, not because she is nearly as real, but that there are extensive stories about these goddesses. What heroic or even mundane stories can we say about Heavenly Mother, or Heavenly Father for that matter? We do not even have or know their real names! But we do have Jesus Christ with a myriad of scriptures, stories and art, both illuminating and inspirational. He is the focus of our veneration.

75. Most pagan pantheons had hundreds of gods but only tens of goddesses. There were cults in which women were priestesses, though most required total renunciation of sex, the Vestal Virgins being the most familiar. See Sawyer, *Women and Religion in the First Christian Centuries,* 128.

76. Salt Lake City, Sunstone Symposium, 14 August 2004, session 371. Margaret and Paul Toscano, Margaret's sister Janice Allred, and Jody England Hansen, the liberal daughter of the late Eugene England. At this session, again there was uncertainty of the existence of "womanhood" after death but a gnawing sense that it might be an androgynous, hermaphroditic, or neutered existence.

77. Sunstone Symposium workshop session, 12 August 2004, Salt Lake City, Starbird's answer to a question posed by Swanson. Starbird, *Woman with the Alabaster Jar,* 178, believes that "the bloodline issue is basically irrelevant, except as it applies to the question of the full humanity of Jesus." This changes somewhat in her *Mary Magdalene,* 95–96. Here she has Jesus married twice and having a number of children.

78. James E. Faust, "Fathers, Mothers, Marriage: First Presidency Message," *Ensign,* August 2004, 4. Faust notes, "Honoring the priesthood means following the example of Christ and seeking to emulate His example of fatherhood." Hopefully I am not pushing the sentence too much by saying that it might also mean that Jesus was a literal "father."

79. Haag and Haag, *Rough Guide to the Da Vinci Code,* 215. It is set in "symbology rich" Washington, D.C, and New England.

80. Orson Hyde, in *Journal of Discourses* (18 March 1855), 2:210. He referred to his 6 October 1854 address at general conference in the Salt Lake Tabernacle. The author has been unable to find these eastern newspapers citations; however, one newspaper did note God the Father's marriage: *New York Daily Times,* 19 July 1853, 3, "The Mormonites" (20 April 1853). "On another page is the following gem, set in brilliants, of course: 'God was married, or how could he begat His son, Jesus Christ, and do the works of the father.'"

81. See Snowden, 130.

82. Fraser, *Is Mormonism Christian?* 60–61. Fraser aptly says, "Thus, according to Mormon logic, if Jesus was not married during His earthly life, He could rise no higher than an angel in the next life. . . . This, of course follows in the Mormon line of reasoning; otherwise Jesus could not have complete exaltation in the next life."

83. Hoekema, *Mormonism.* Rather than check Fraser's sources carefully, Hoekema blindly quotes verbatim Fraser's citing of Orson Hyde's statement from *Journal of Discourses,* 2:81–82. It is a paraphrase, not a quotation.

84. Martin, *Kingdom of the Cults,* 192.

85. The Nicene Creed says, "Do not compound the persons, nor separate the substance."

86. The irreverent Mark Twain said that sitting on clouds in heaven for all eternities, made it the most boring of places. Also, why is God called Heavenly Father if he does not have gender?

87. It was explained to the author by a devout Christian that the Savior never defecated or urinated and did not have sexual organs. This is basically a Docetist view, that while

God (Christ) seemed to be in the shape of a human, He was not at all a fleshly human in reality and therefore did not suffer and die for us.

88. Actually this argues the other way. "Christ came not to destroy the law but to fulfill it" may mean that it may continue after him. If the bloodline meant something before him, would not it mean something after him?

89. Baigent, Leigh, and Lincoln, *Holy Blood, Holy Grail*, 17.

90. Some of the most important apologia books do not include reference to Jesus' marriage: Hugh Nibley, *The Mythmakers* (Salt Lake City: Bookcraft, 1961); Rodger S. Gunn, *Mormonism: Challenge and Defense* (Salt Lake City: Hawkes Publishers, 1973); Robert L. and Rosemary Brown, *They Lie in Wait to Deceive* (Arizona: 1982, and three subsequent volumes); Paul Hendengren, *In Defense of Faith;* Gilbert W. Scharffs, *The Truth about "The God Makers"* (Salt Lake City: Publishers Press, 1986); *A Sure Foundation: Answers to Difficult Gospel Questions* (Salt Lake City: Deseret Book, 1988).

91. Church, *Guardians of the Grail*, 82. The Barbarini family of Rome is also represented by the honey bee, and no one makes anything of it. The very tenuous connection between the Mormons and the Merovingians is, in the author's opinion, not viable. The bee is also prominent in Masonic lore. Kennedy, *Orbis Enigma*, also believes in a strong LDS and Merovingian connection: "Ultimately, this must be a drive toward political and economic domination by the LDS Church. It is clear that the Mormons see themselves as descended from Jesus Christ via the Merovingians. It has been reported that the LDS Temple in Saint Louis actually has a huge genealogical chart in its Temple which depicts the bloodline of Jesus and Mary of Bethany through the royal houses of France [Merovingians] to the rest of the ruling families of Europe down to contemporary Mormon leaders."

92. W. John Walsh, (www.lightplanet.com/mormons/response/qa/marriage_Jesus.htm) and Griffith (ourworld.cs.com/mikegriffith1/id179.htm).

93. Peterson and Ricks, *Offenders for a Word,* 129. They refer to Irvine Robertson, *What Cults Believe* (Chicago: Moody Press, 1983), 129–30 n. 439. Peterson and Ricks further note: "Orson Hyde speculated that Jesus was married (Irvine). Robertson finds the suggestion "horrifying." Gnosticism would respond so, as would a Christianized Neoplatonism. But where in Judeo-Christian scripture is such a horror of sex and materiality to be found? If Mr. Robertson takes the Incarnation seriously, he must allow for some pretty gritty physiological attributes—at least as much so as sexuality—to be predicated of Jesus. If he does not, he is a Docetist. And Docetism, as we have

seen, is the one heresy that our ancient sources might justify us in expelling from Christianity."

94. Cky J. Carrigan, "Did Jesus Christ Marry and Father Children? A Survey of Mormon Teachings on the Marital and Parental Status of the Son of God," presented at the annual meetings of the Evangelical Ministries to New Religions, New Orleans Baptist Theological Seminary, 30 January 2004. Carrigan is on the National Missionary, North American Mission Board and adjunct professor, Southeastern and Midwestern Baptist Theological Seminary. (See ccarrigan@namb.net, and www.ontruth.com.)

95. Ibid.

96. Pat Zukeran, www.probe.org/docs/mormon-jesus.html, 2003.

97. (http://www.macgregorministries.org/mormons/facts.html). These were chosen randomly from a long list, but are accurately quoted in the correct order.

98. Pratt, *Autobiography,* 333–34.

99. Brigham Young, in *Journal of Discourses* (12 June 1859), 7:174a.

100. *Wilford Woodruff Journal,* 4:390–91; 5:575; 6:436.

101. Ginzberg, *Legends of the Jews,* 6:340. The idea is that he joins in the flight into the desert, where he will remain until he joins Messiah ben Judah in his redemptive work.

102. Orson Pratt, in *Journal of Discourses* (9 March 1873), 15:263.

103. Parley P. Pratt, *Evening and Morning* Star 1, 6 (November 1832).

104. *Wilford Woodruff Journal* (13 January 1856), 4:390–91.

105. Smith, *History of the Church* (21 January 1836), 2:380–81, Joseph's revelation noting that Alvin was in the celestial kingdom of God.

106. Apostle Orson Pratt in 1876 divided the Doctrine and Covenants into chapters and verses, and in 1879 it was issued with footnotes. The identity of this long-awaited messenger is not definitely known, though there is much evidence to support the commonly held belief that it will likely be the Prophet Joseph Smith or possibly even Adam. See Short, *Questions on Plural Marriage,* 43.

107. Joseph received this revelation on 27 November 1832. The Jews hope that Elijah the prophet (and priest) will sort out genealogy and resolve tribal difficulties. See Kleiman, *DNA and Tradition,* 117.

108. Some of the earlier passages read as follows: "For with the voice of his thunder shall he strike terror to their hearts, as with the wings of an eagle shall my brother (Joseph) be carried beyond all harm by the power of the Anointed. . . . Go thou, and say to the

strength of my house, 'To your tents, O Israel: build up the wastes and raise up the foundation of desolation that this generation has made.'

"Thus shall he be honored of the Lord, and thus shall it be recorded of him, that the generation to come may bless his name, in Israel, saying, "The Lord make thee as Joseph [Smith] the Seer, who was of the house of Ephraim the brother of Manasseh [Hyrum] . . ."

"His loins shall be like iron, girded by the hand of the Lord; and his feet shall be swift to execute the commandment of the Most High when he shall say 'destroy.'"

". . . His learning and wisdom shall astonish the great for they shall acknowledge that by his intelligence he has far surpassed their learning and their science."

109. This may have reference to the records and relics possibly locked in the Hill Cumorah, supposedly by St. Brendan the Navigator.

110. These may well be the rich treasures of the world (see D&C 133:30).

111. Collier, *Unpublished Revelations,* 74–77. I have skipped from verse to verse, but kept the proper sequence. Also see patriarch Hyrum G. Smith, "The Prophet Joseph Smith was declared to be of the house of Joseph, a chosen vessel," quoted in Whitehead, *House of Israel,* 532.

112. Ehat and Cook, *Words of Joseph Smith* (Nauvoo Relief Society Minutes, 28 April 1842), 116. A fuller account reads: "That he did not know as he should have many opportunities of teaching them—that they were going to be left to themselves—they would not long have him to instruct them—that the church would not have his instruction long, and the world would not be troubled with him a great while, and would not have his teachings . . . that according to his prayers God had appointed him elsewhere." Bathsheba W. Smith recollected that he said, "According to my prayer I will not be with you long to teach and instruct you; and the world will not be troubled with me much longer" (*Juvenile Instructor* 27:345).

113. Andrus and Andrus, *They Knew the Prophet,* 26. See also Lightner, *Life and Testimony of Mary Lightner.*

114. The Journal of Benjamin F. Johnson (Church Historian's Library). Also see, "An Interesting Letter," from Patriarch Benjamin F. Johnson to George S. Gibbs, dated 1903, from the file of Benjamin F. Johnson Church Historian's Office, Salt Lake City. Also quoted in Andrus and Andrus, *They Knew the Prophet,* 97.

115. The Journal of Benjamin F. Johnson (Church Historian's Library).

116. King, *Yalkut of Zechariah,* 91, 97. He makes mention of a "very old Jewish tradition that Edom the world power, Arab) can only fall by the hands of Joseph."

117. Ginzberg, *Legends of the Jews,* 4:233.

118. See Wilhelm Bousett and Gressman, *Die Religion des Judentums* (3d ed.), 224–25. Messiah ben Joseph will restore the lost ten tribes to their own land.

119. Meir Leib ben Yechiel Michael (Weiser), in the Malbim. R.

120. Talmud, Baba Batra 123b.

121. See Odeberg, trans, *3 Enoch or the Hebrew Book of Enoch,* 144: "The end of the course of the present world is marked by the appearance of Messiah ben Joseph and Messiah ben David, in whose times there will be wars between Israel and 'Gog and Magog'; the final consummation will then, so it seems, be brought about by the Holy One Himself."

122. Ginzberg, *Legends of the Jews,* 2:147.

123. *Wilford Woodruff Journal* (13 January 1856), 4:385–391.

124. *Wilford Woodruff Journal* (11 December 1869), 6:508. See Staker, *Waiting for the World's End,* 299. The saying, "In the Temple resurrected beings dictate" will never be truer than when Joseph Smith returns.

125. *Wilford Woodruff Journal* (13 January 1856), 4:390–91. See also Staker, *Waiting for the World's End,* 168–69, quoting Brigham Young; Gordon Irving, "The Law of Adoption: One Phase of the Development of the Mormon Concept of Salvation, 1830–1900," *BYU Studies* 14, 3 (Spring 1974): 295.

126. Wilford Woodruff (7 April 1894), quoted in Stuy, *Collected Discourses,* 4:73–74.

127. Brigham Young, "A Family Meeting in Nauvoo," *Utah Genealogical and Historical Magazine* 11 (July 1920): 107.

CONCLUSION

*The vantage point from the mount of revelation is
far different from that of the valley of tradition.*[1]

ow we close this rather long and
somewhat tedious tome. As if
speaking of this book, Pierre
Antoine Bernheim surmises,
"While all these hypotheses seem
plausible, none of them can be proved."[2] Or as
Hugh W. Nibley wrote to BYU Fine Arts and Communications dean, Lorin Wheelwright, "A common
pitfall in reconstructions of the past is the illusion that if one has explained by a proper scientific
method how a thing COULD have happened, one
has explained how it actually DID happen."[3]

We have demonstrated the logic and wisdom
of a sacred marriage of Jesus Christ to Ephraimite
wives. From this union of the tribes of Judah and
Ephraim may have come a bloodline called the
Shiloh Dynasty. For over twelve hundred years, the
priesthood line and the bloodline of Christ have
been withdrawn and hidden, only to be revealed by a
latter-day descendant of the Savior in 1830—Joseph

Smith Jr. The Prophet Joseph, as *Messiah ben Joseph*,
was an Elias figure preparing the way for the second
coming of Jesus Christ, Messiah ben Judah.

Only more time, new information, or broader view-
points will verify this scattershot miscellany of random
thoughts. In all this I am enticed by the scripture, "It is
the glory of God to hide a matter [and] it is the glory of
kings to search out a matter" (Proverbs 25:2). We can
now say that we have begun to "distill the quintessential
juices of this myth."[4] Perhaps then we can squeeze them
into our vessel of understanding.

Buddha's begging bowl is filled to the capacity
of our understanding and is based upon the principle of receptivity. Those with a wounded spirit or
moral failures often experience a void needing to be
filled. It can be gently erased by the gospel light of
Jesus Christ, for it was prophesied by Isaiah 42:3, "A
bruised reed shall he not break, and the smoking flax
shall he not quench: he shall bring forth judgment
unto truth."[5]

Latter-day Saints believe that no vessels are entirely empty but are full of the Spirit, with all manner of experience, refined matter, goodness and creation—until we have a fulness of joy.[6] The blessings of God's Grail will fill you in "good measure, pressed down, and shaken together and running over" (Luke 6:38). President Thomas S. Monson in general conference spoke along these lines:

> Fill your mind with truth,
> Fill your heart with love,
> Fill your life with service.[7]

God's plan of happiness is that everyone in the process of time should become a "chosen vessel unto me" (Acts 9:15). The French word for Grail vessel is *gradual,* which was a plate by which food was brought to the table little by little (in courses). Our word "gradual" comes from this word and when applied to the Quest, means a step-by-step improvement until we reach fulfillment and perfection in Christ. The Grail Quest is eternal progression for sincere seekers; it is an everlasting pilgrimage toward the highest degrees of the celestial kingdom.

The Church of Jesus Christ of Latter-day Saints is a vessel of love and service to His people. Working together, it waters the wasteland—bringing to pass the promised Paradise. This is reminiscent of the story spoken of by Brigham Young, who said that if the Saints were sent to hell (the wasteland) they would irrigate it into a Paradise (celestial kingdom). In the center of paradise is found a "precious spring of pure refreshment."[8] Heaven and hell are what we make of them and the inheritance we deserve. Our destiny, like the Grail, is a kingdom of God inside us (Luke 17:21). Through the law of affinity, "light cleaves to light," we carry the kingdom of God within us or we find it not. Each individual will go to that kingdom that resonates with who he really is:

The Grail can be seen only by those who already contain its inner matrix. As a man with a treasure map inevitably finds the treasure, if motivated, so those who have woven the Grail into their tapestry of life will, as like attracts like (as inner causes eventuate in outer effects), magnetize it to themselves. Galahad could not be kept from seeing the Grail because it was an inseparable, preexistent part of him.[9]

Wolfram von Eschenbach's *Parzival* declares that "no man can ever win the Grail unless he is known in Heaven and he is called by name to the Grail." Galahad looked into the sacred cup and saw himself. One is calmed by Jesus' injunction, "No man hath ascended up to heaven but he that came down from heaven" (John 3:13). In Richard Wagner's "Wolfram," inspired by the opera *Parsifal,* we see this idea personified in the Holy Grail. In one translation Parsifal/Gawain asks, "Who is the Grail?" and Gurnemanz replies:

> If thou has of Him been bidden
> From thee the truth will not stay hidden.
> The land to Him no path leads through,
> And search but severs from Him wider
> When He himself is not the guider.[10]

So who or what is the guider? In the only true and living church every person is a sacred vessel, a Holy Grail! We need not travel far to find the Holy Grail, for it is here within us. We are the patriarchal/matriarchal bloodline of the Holy Grail, the leaven to the world. Through the Shiloh Dynasty, which is our seed, the whole world will be blessed. As John Wells spoke in the 1934 LDS General Conference: "We must not repeat the experience of the knight in the ancient tale, who left his home, when a young man, to find the Holy Grail, or cup, out of which our Savior drank, and came back an old white-haired man, only to find the grail in his own house, where it had been all those years."[11]

The Grail is found by the internal compass within ourselves, aligned with the "true north" of our testimony of the latter-day work. The answer lies in the true and living Church as the Bride, having received its best man [Joseph Smith], and now awaits the Bridegroom [Jesus Christ]. We might use a passage from Alfred Lord Tennyson's "The Holy Grail" in *Idylls of the King* to make reference to both Joseph's and Jesus' eminent return:

> He passes to be King among the dead,
> But after healing of his grievous wound
> He comes again.

Joseph Smith, under the authority of Jesus Christ, is the splendid Grail King with his twelve Knights or Apostles of the Round Table. As the wizened old man with the ash-wood staff who spoke of Galahad, so might it be said of young Joseph: "Here begins the mysteries of the Grail. Now begins the time of testing and of sorrow. For many shall go forth this day, but few shall return and fewer still shall discover what they seek. This youth is named Galahad. I recommend him unto you all."[12]

For Joseph the Prophet surely knew the "Mysteries of the Grail." In the Millennial promise there is no mere offer or a promissory note for the hereafter in some far-off world. For the kingdom of God is being built upon *this* earth right now! The search for the Holy Grail is an inquiry within to discover where we came from, why are we here, and where we are going. T. S. Elliot said it best:

> We shall not cease from exploration
> And the end of our exploring

> Will be to arrive where we started
> And know the place for the first time.[13]

We are going home. The basic unit of the Church is the congregation and the basic unit of the kingdom of God is home and family. Our family is the family of God stretching from Adam to today and home is this earth when it becomes a celestial kingdom. We are the spirit children of our Heavenly Father and Mother. This is the grand secret, which those outside the family circle do not know and cannot understand. Yet, it is a nuclear family, ever ready to adopt everyone and ever ready to draw the circle bigger.

The Holy Grail is the family of God, organized through the bloodlines of Ephraim and Judah in the last days. All who will sincerely join with the twelve tribes will be saved in the celestial kingdom at the great and last judgment. Salvation is a choice. Charles W. Penrose wrote that premortal diligence leads to birthright privileges on earth: "Now, (we) are naturally so disposed; that there is something with us that tends to our willingness to accept the truth when it comes from God. I do not mean to say that this is confined to us, but that particularly those who are of the house of Ephraim are ready to receive the word and act according to it as the Lord shall direct."[14]

It is the joy of every Latter-day Saint to save our kindred dead, "(To) pick up the end of the cord—like the miner's clue—that leads off into the mists of time to the mysteries surrounding the fabled Isle of Avalon . . . and follow the Grail."[15] Tying the threads of our lives and those of our forebears, in the "Grail Castle" (Mormon Temple), saves both them and us.[16] Here we arrive at the three-fold mission of the Grail Church:

> Proclaim the gospel,
> Perfect the Saints,
> Redeem the dead.

We have reached the *ne plus ultra* of our quest for the Grail. As I end this volume, it seems more like a chapter than a book. So much has been left unsaid; the remarkable has been left unaddressed. Yet, I relate to the words of the Grail knight, Parzival, who on Good Friday said, "I have hardly taken a step, yet I feel I have gone far."[17] Brigham Young relieved the perplexed mind that ponders about such conundrums lying at the utmost bound of human thought, as he said, "When we go through the veil we shall know much more about these matters than we now do."[18]

NOTE: The author would appreciate any comment, correction, or information that would improve this book. Please contact him at vern.swanson@nebo.edu.

NOTES

1. McConkie, *His Name Shall Be Joseph*, 164.

2. Bernheim, *James, the Brother of Jesus*, 113.

3. Hugh Nibley open letter to Lorin F. Wheelwright (16 September 1965), 3. In author's possession.

4. Godwin, *Holy Grail*, 241.

5. In another translation: "He will not break a bruised reed/or snuff out a dimly burning wick."

6. LDS theology has it that all hollow spaces are filled with the Spirit of God—no space exists without a kingdom of some sort (D&C 88:37).

7. Thomas S. Monson, general conference, October 2004. See Mosiah 2:17: "And behold, I tell you these things that ye may learn wisdom; that ye may learn that when ye are in the service of your fellow beings ye are only in the service of your God."

8. Goodrich, *Holy Grail*, 120.

9. Non-LDS author Prophet, *Mysteries of the Holy Grail*, xli. This is reminiscent of the brother of Jared. The Lord said that because of his exceeding great faith He could not withhold Himself from him (see Ether 3:26, 12:21).

10. As quoted in Prophet, *Mysteries of the Holy Grail*, v.

11. John Wells, Conference Report, October 1934, 31.

12. Matthews, *King Arthur and the Grail Quest*, 120.

13. As quoted by Valoy Eaton, in Vern G. Swanson, *In Natural Light*, 62.

14. Charles W. Penrose, Conference Report, October 1922, 21–22.

15. Prophet, *Mysteries of the Holy Grail*, iii.

16. We are not talking about useless and foolish genealogies but living lines of ancestors and the temple work that will bind their cords and seal their families for time and all eternity. "There are twenty-six sections in the Doctrine and Covenants," write Shute, Nyman, and Bott (*Ephraim*, 111) "that confirm the thesis that the literal blood of Israel is in the majority of the Church membership today." These are but an extension of the scripture, "In [Abraham's] seed shall all the kindred of the earth be blessed" (2 Nephi 20:27; Genesis 12:1–3). More precisely, the blessings are fulfilled through "the [adopted or] literal seed, or the seed of the body [children]" (Abraham 2:11; D&C 103:17; 110:1–10, 12).

17. Wallace-Murphy and Hopkins, *Rosslyn*, 19.

18. Brigham Young, in *Journal of Discourses* (3 June 1860), 8:279–80. See also John Taylor, *Times and Seasons* (1844), 5:662.

Chronology

B.C.

7000–3000 B.C.	Neolithic period, god (phallus) and goddess (womb) fertility cults were celebrated.
ca. 4004 B.C.	Adam and Eve began to have children, according to tradition.
ca. 3353 B.C.	Enoch ordained by Adam (D&C 107:48).[1]
ca. 3100 B.C.	Newgrange passage tomb built in Ireland.
ca. 3073 B.C.	Great conference at Adam-Ondi-Ahman. (D&C 107:53) Then Adam and Eve partook of the tree of life and resumed their glorified existence.
ca. 3000 B.C.	The structure of the Twelve Stones of Stenness on Orkney was built.
ca. 2477 B.C.	Noah begat Japheth (Moses 8:12).
ca. 2452 B.C.	Noah begat Shem.
ca. 2444 B.C.	Noah begat Ham.
ca. 2344 B.C.	Great Flood occurred. We know this date and event are problematic, because no such worldwide cataclysm happened at this time according to scientists, historians, and archeologists.
ca. 2277 B.C.	Salah begat Eber.
ca. 2022 B.C.	Terah begat Abram.
ca. 1892 B.C.	Abraham begat Isaac.
ca. 1887 B.C.	Isaac was weaned and Ishmael cast out.
ca. 1847 B.C.	Abraham died.
ca. 1842 B.C.	Shem died.
ca. 1832 B.C.	Isaac begat Esau and Jacob.
ca. 1741 B.C.	Jacob begat Joseph.
ca. 1689 B.C.	Jacob [Israel] shifts the birthright to Ephraim and the sceptre to Judah.

ca. 1680 B.C.	Judah through Tamar has twin sons. One, Zarah (the seed) had a scarlet thread put around his wrist, while the firstborn, Pharez (breach) was given the primogeniture.	ca. 570 B.C.	The marriage of King Heremon the Echolaid to Queen Tephi Tea [Tamar] in Tara Plantation in Northern Ireland.
1631–1635 B.C.	Joseph of Egypt died.	539 B.C.	Start of the building of Zerubbabel's temple.
ca. 1275 B.C.	Moses led the Exodus from Egypt.	516 B.C.	Jewish people returned to Jerusalem and rebuilt the second temple.
1020–1002 B.C.	King Saul ruled Israel.		
1002–962 B.C.	King David ruled Israel.	428–348 B.C.	Plato initiated into secrets of priests, philosophers and mathematicians.
962–922 B.C.	King Solomon ruled Israel and built a temple and a palace.	384–322 B.C.	Aristotle, Greek scientist and philosopher of reason, lived.
922 B.C.	Solomon died, leaving religious and financial chaos across Israel.	333 B.C.	Greek hegemony over Palestine.
722–707 B.C.	Sargon II, ruler of Babylon, first used gematria in Hebrew literature.	168 B.C.	The priestly caste of Hasmonaean Maccabees rebelled against King Antiochus IV Epiphanes of Syria.
722 B.C.	Fall of the northern Kingdom of Israel, the dispersion of the lost ten tribes at the time of Shalmaneser's Assyrian invasion. Members of the kingdom of Israel, or Ephraim, taken into captivity.	ca. 130 B.C.	Wilderness community of Qumrân began.
		118 B.C.	Narbonne founded as Roman colony "Narbo Martius" in southwest France.
597–538 B.C.	Jewish people enslaved in Babylon.	55 B.C.	Classical writer Diodorus Siculus wrote about legend of Hyperborean on the island "beyond the north wind." Perhaps speaking of Callanish in Scotland.
586 B.C.	Destruction of Solomon's temple in Jerusalem.		
ca. 584 B.C.	The Chronicles relate that Tamar Tephi and Jeremiah, carrying the holy Stone of Destiny with them, took ship for Egypt, Spain, and then Ireland in or around the year 584 B.C.[2]	41 B.C.	Supposed year of birth of Joseph of Arimathea.[3]
		37–4 B.C.	Reign of Herod the Great in Judea; Temple rebuilt on a grand scale.
580–500 B.C.	Pythagoras, Greek philosopher, developed canon of symbolic numbers.	31 B.C.	A violent earthquake occurred in Judea.

ca. 26 B.C.	Laurence Gardner asserts Virgin Mary was born this year.[4]	A.D. 43	Britain invaded by the Romans under Claudius.
ca. 4 B.C. (6 Apr.)	Jesus Christ was born in Bethlehem of Judea.	ca. A.D. 45	Supposed year of death of Joseph of Arimathea, according to Blake and Blezard. (See ca. A.D. 82)

A.D.

		A.D. 45–62	Apostle Paul's missionary journeys; epistles to various communities, trip to Britain.
A.D. 16–20	Jesus married at Cana to the Magdalene.		
A.D. 26	Pontius Pilate assumed post of procurator in Judea.	ca. A.D. 47	Apostle Paul's epistles began at this date onward, the earliest documents in the official canon of Christian Church known as New Testament.
A.D. 32	John the Baptist was beheaded.		
A.D. 33 (Apr.)	Death and resurrection of Our Lord, Jesus Christ.	A.D. 50	Wales occupied by Romans.
ca. A.D. 35	St. Stephen was stoned, becoming the first martyr for Christ.	ca. A.D. 51	Brân taken hostage to Rome along with Caractacus the Pendragon.
ca. A.D. 35	Date given by Cardinal Baronius for Joseph of Arimathea's arrival in Marseilles.	A.D. 54–68	Christians suffered persecution during reign of Nero.
		A.D. 60–61	Boudican rebellion occurred in Nero's reign.
ca. A.D. 36–38	Paul's conversion occurred on the road to Damascus.	A.D. 60	Roman legions destroy Druid strongholds in Anglesey (Isle of Mona Wales).
ca. A.D. 37	Joseph of Arimathea and companions arrived in Glastonbury in Somerset or Glaestingaburgh in North Wales.	ca. A.D. 62	For preaching Christ, James the Just was thrown off the pinnacle of the temple at the instigation of Sadducean high priests. He was then "dispatched" with a fuller's club (or stoned; see Eisenman).
A.D. 39	Herod Antipas died.		
ca. A.D. 42	Followers of Jesus began to be called Christians for first time at Antioch.		
ca. A.D. 42–44	Date Margaret Starbird ascribes to "a boat bearing the refugee family of Mary Magdalene arrived on the coast of Gaul."	ca. A.D. 63	Deaths of Mary Magdalene and Simon Peter occurred.
		ca. A.D. 63	St. Philip arrived in Britain.

ca. A.D. 63	Arimathean remnant quit Glastonbury and moved to Llangolan (Glaestingaburgh) on sacred Dee River in North Wales, where Brân the Blessed lived in the Grail Castle.
A.D. 65	The temple in Jerusalem was completed.
A.D. 66	Zealots and Sicarii (an extreme patriotic group) revolted against Roman rule in Judaea.
ca. A.D. 66	Many Sadducean *Rex Deus* high priests and families are murdered by *Sicarii* extremists. A remnant of these aristocratic families escaped to a location near where Constantinople would later be built, then Calabria in the heel of the "boot of Italy," then onward to Seborga in the Italian Riviera, with sacred Second Temple documents, relics and treasure.
A.D. 68	Destruction of Qumrân occurred.
A.D. 70	Sack of Jerusalem and destruction of Herod's Temple by the Romans under command of Titus, the son of the Emperor Vespasian. The pillage and removal to Rome of sacred Jewish treasure from the Temple of Herod occurred.
ca. A.D. 70–71	Gospel of Mark written.
A.D. 73	Fall of last Jewish stronghold at Masada.
ca. A.D. 80–85	Gospel of Matthew written.
A.D. 81–96	During reign of Domitian, Christians suffered persecution.

A.D. 81	Some disciples of Apostle John visited Caledonia and preached the gospel.
A.D. 82 (27 Jul.)	According to Cressy's *Church History,* Joseph of Arimathea died on this date. But he would have been much too old. (See ca. A.D. 45)
ca. A.D. 85	Gospel of Luke written.
ca. A.D. 90–95	Gospel of John written.
ca. A.D. 95–100	Apocalypse of John (Book of Revelation) written.
A.D. 98–117	Reign of Roman Emperor Trajan; Christians suffered persecution.
ca. A.D. 101	Supposed death of John the Beloved.
A.D. 117–138	Reign of Roman Emperor Hadrian; Christians suffered persecution.
ca. A.D. 130–202	Irenaeus of Lyons, author of *Against Heresies*, reprimanded Gnostics.
A.D. 132–135	Second Jewish Revolt led by Simon Bar Kochba, Prince of Israel and Rabbi Akiva, with hopes to build third temple and destroying the temple of Jupiter in Jerusalem.
A.D. 135	Emperor Hadrian expelled all Jews from Jerusalem.
A.D. 135	Hadrian rebuilt Jerusalem, which he called Aelia Capitolina, and renamed the province Syria-Palestine.
A.D. 138–161	Reign of Roman emperor Antoninus Pius; Christians suffered persecution.

A.D. 155–220 — The patristic Church Father Tertullian became a heretic and wrote a polemic against Gnostics and "numbers theology."

ca. A.D. 156 — Britain was said to have been proclaimed Christian by King Lucius at National Council of Winchester. (See ca. A.D. 179)

A.D. 161–180 — Reign of Roman Emperor Marcus Aurelius; Christians suffered persecution.

ca. A.D. 165 — Christian apologist Justin Martyr died.

ca. A.D. 170 — St. Cadval, a famed British missionary, going out from Glastonbury, founded church of Tarentum, Italy.

A.D. 170–180 — 22 of the 27 books of New Testament were collected.

A.D. 170–235 — Hippolytus of Rome, a Christian scripture exegete wrote a commentary on Song of Songs and a polemic against heretics.[5]

A.D. 174/5–192 — Eleutherius was Pope.

A.D. 175 — Anti-Christian Celsus wrote of the young Jesus working in Egypt.

A.D. 175 — Roman emperor Marcus Aurelius dispatched 5,500 Iazyges (Samatrian) heavy cavalry from the Hungarian plain to Hadrian's Wall. They took with them their horse culture and chivalry. Lucius Artorius Castus, prefect of the VI Legion Victrix, was the officer in charge.

A.D. 177 — Because of persecution of Christians in Gaul, some fled to Britain.

ca. A.D. 179 — In the reign of good King Lucius, Jesus Christ was acknowledged as the Messiah, this being the first nation to receive Christianity. (See ca. A.D. 156)

A.D. 185–254 — The life of Origen of Alexandria, an early Christian exegete and philosopher. He was later condemned as a heretic at the Fifth Ecumenical Council in A.D. 553.

A.D. ca. 187 — Legends of a church dedicated to St. Mary in Glastonbury, said to be repaired and raised out of the ruins of a former church.

A.D. 193–216 — Tertullian of Carthage's *An Answer to the Jews* notes that Britain was already "subjugated to Christ" in the late second century.

A.D. 196 — Clodius Albinus, Roman governor of Britain, declared himself emperor, crossed the Channel, and invaded Gaul. He was defeated by Severus in 197, allowing Hadrian's Wall to be breached by the Caledonii. Severus then had several campaigns in Britain in the early third century. Severus died in A.D. 211.

A.D. 208 (28 Jun.) — Nineteen thousand Christians from Lyon were put to death by Emperor Lucius Severus.

A.D. 235–238 — Reign of Roman emperor Maximinus; Christians suffered persecution.

A.D. 249–251 | Persecution of Christians during reign of emperor Decius.

A.D. 251–253 | Reign of Roman Emperor Gallus; Christians suffered persecution.

A.D. 253–260 | Persecution of Christians occurred during reign of Emperor Valerian.

A.D. 284–305 | Persecution of Christians during reign of Diocletian.

A.D. 303 | Severe persecution of Christians by Diocletian began.

A.D. 304 | St. Albans was martyred, one of the first Christians slain in Britain.

A.D. 305–311 | Persecution of Christians by Roman Emperor Galerius.

A.D. 313 | "Edict of Milan" issued by Constantine (I) the Great ended harassment of the Christian Church and gave toleration to all religious groups in the Roman Empire.

A.D. 314 | Conference at Arles, to which the Emperor Constantine summoned all bishops of western Europe; it included three British bishops, one each from York, London, and Lincoln (more probably Colchester).

A.D. 325 | The first ecumenical council of the "Church" was held at Nicea under the rule of the Emperor Constantine.

A.D. 326 | Helena, mother of Constantine the Great, journeyed to Israel and designated the major historical and sacred sites of Christianity.

A.D. 330 | Constantine the Great founded Constantinople as a new, wholly Christian capital of the empire.

A.D. 342–420 | Jerome translated Greek scriptures into Latin.

ca. A.D. 350 | Nag Hammadi Scrolls were translated from Greek to Coptic.

ca. A.D. 350 | Earliest extant copies appear of the Greek New Testament (Sinaiticus, Vaticanus).

ca. A.D. 350 | Gradual process of withdrawal of Roman legions from Britain began; it was completed in A.D. 410.

A.D. 354–430 | The life of Saint Augustine, bishop of Hippo.

A.D. 367 | New Testament collated by Bishop Athanasius of Alexandria.

ca. A.D. 370 | King Cunedda Wledig of North Wales lived.

ca. A.D. 376 | The Huns deployed the Alans in the vanguard of their army, leading the battles which gave them victory. The Alans were Samatrian warriors and described by the Roman historian Ammianus Marcellinus as "tall and handsome, with yellowish hair and frighteningly fierce eyes (blue or green)." They were led by *Dux Bellorum* (war lords, or battle leaders). (See A.D. 410.)

A.D. 381 | During the reign of Theodosius (379–395) Christianity was made the state religion at Council of Constantinople.

ca. A.D. 382	The Roman Church decreed that anyone convicted of heresy would not only be excommunicated but would also be liable for execution. This was the first time that capital punishment was applied by a Christian organization. It would be almost another two hundred years before the church had widespread civil authority to carry out this punishment.
ca. A.D. 383	The theologian St. Augustine of Hippo introduced the false doctrine of original sin and formulated justification for religious compulsion and rigorous investigation of heresy. The first person to be executed for heresy in the West was Priscillian of Avila in 383.
A.D. 383	Magnus Maximus, a Roman general serving in Britain, was proclaimed emperor by his legionaries. This may be the Roman Emperor Maxen Wledig of Arthurian legend.
A.D. 389	Destruction of the famous public library at Alexandria. It was rebuilt, only to be later destroyed by one of the Muslim generals who said, "If the books in the library did not agree with the Koran, they were blasphemous, and if they did, they were superfluous!"[6]
ca. A.D. 390	Jerome began translating the Gospels into Latin.
A.D. 391	Pagan worship was actually outlawed by Emperor Theodosius I called the Great.

A.D. 395	Upon the death of Theodosius I the Great, the Western and Eastern Roman Empires were officially divided. Christianity became the official religion of both empires.
A.D. 397	New Testament books ratified at the Council of Carthage.
ca. A.D. 400	St. Ninian arrived at Whithorn.
ca. A.D. 409	Welsh monk Pelagius visited Rome.
ca. A.D. 410	Some of the Jerusalem Temple treasure was supposedly sent to Britain for safekeeping just before the sack of Rome.
A.D. 410	Roman army left Britain.
A.D. 410	Rome sacked by the Visigoth King Alaric with a large contingent of Alans. Alans, rather than Goths, probably obtained some of the Jerusalem temple treasure booty, if it still existed as a whole. (See ca. A.D. 376)
ca. A.D. 417	Migration of Visigoths to Spain and the Languedoc, with headquarters in Toulouse, Carcassonne, Rhedae (Renne-le-Chateaux) and Toledo. Visigoths adhered to Arian heresy and were condemned by the Catholic Church.
A.D. 418	Visigoth Empire straddled the Pyrenees—northern Spain, southern France.
ca. A.D. 420	The Nephite prophet Moroni deposited a number of records

and relics into the Hill Cumorah in northwest New York state in America.

A.D. 425 Council of Arles decreed it was sacrilege to touch or worship Druidictrees, fountains of stones or "infidel lighted torches."

ca. A.D. 425 Accession of King Vortigern in Britain.

A.D. 428–751 The Merovingian dynasty ruled kingdom of the Franks (Gaul).

A.D. 429 Bishops Germanus of Auxerre and Lupus of Troyes sent to Britain regarding Pelagian "Heresy."

A.D. 430 Missionary Palladius was ordained by Pope Celestinus and sent to Scotia Ireland.

ca. A.D. 430 St. Patrick, at age forty, bishop to Ireland. (See below, A.D. 431.)

A.D. 431 St. Palladius arrived and became first bishop of Ireland.

A.D. 431 Council of Ephesus pronounced final condemnation of Pelagius.

ca. A.D. 433 St. Patrick and St. Brigit remodeled original church building in Glastonbury. Goodrich says Brigit was born in ca. 454 (1988), 333.

ca. A.D. 445 Attila the Hun found a magical and fearsome sword of a war-god stuck in the ground. It became famous throughout Europe and may have been the inspirational source of the Arthurian Caliburn or Excalibur story.

ca. A.D. 447 King Merovee ascended to throne of Merovingians, or "Long-Haired Kings."

A.D. 449 First Anglo-Saxon mercenaries arrived in Britain.

ca. A.D. 450 Supposed birth year of King Arthur and Merlin. Goodrich says this was birth year of Merlin and that Arthur was born ca. A.D. 475 (1988), 334.

ca. A.D. 452 St. Ninian of Whithorn died.

A.D. 468–69 King Riothamus led 12,000 British soldiers to help Romans fight the Visigoths in Loire Valley, was defeated, and retreated to a town called Aballo, now known as Avallon.

A.D. 476 The last Roman emperor, Romulus Augustulus, was deposed by Odoacer, a German warlord and mercenary. The Western Empire officially ended.

A.D. 481–511 King Clovis I converted the Franks to Roman Catholicism.

ca. A.D. 487 King Fergus More took the Stone of Destiny from Iona to Dunstaffnage Castle in Scotland. (See ca. A.D. 513)

ca. A.D. 489 St. Brendan born in Ireland (Scotia).

A.D. 494 The ordination of women to leadership roles was banned by decree of Pope Gelasius. (This would be restored with Joseph Smith Jr. in Nauvoo, Illinois.)

A.D. 496 — Merovingian king Clovis and three thousand Franks baptized into Roman Catholic faith on Christmas Eve.

A.D. 507 — Visigoths defeated by Clovis and forced from Toulouse to Carcassonne, then south in Corbières region of Languedoc. Their treasure was supposedly hidden in ancient mines and caves in the area.

ca. A.D. 513 — Stone of Destiny taken to Argyle. (See ca. A.D. 487)

ca. A.D. 516 — Battle of Mount Badon, where King Arthur (Ambrosius Aurelianus?) defeated the Saxons. Phillips says it was A.D. 493 (1997), 38; Goodrich says it was ca. A.D. 500 (1988), 334.

A.D. 517 — Severus, bishop of Antioch, claims he discovered tomb of Virgin Mary just east of Jerusalem in Valley of Jehosaphat. This subterranean shrine was located in a dream by the bishop and no evidence proves that it was her actual tomb.

ca. A.D. 521 — Saint Columbia of Iona (A.D. 521–597) was born in Ireland.

A.D. 500s — St. David remodeled original church in Glastonbury.

A.D. 536 — One of the dates ascribed to Merlin's death.

ca. A.D. 537–38 — Supposedly King Arthur died or was wounded at Battle of Camlann. (See A.D. 542.)

ca. A.D. 540 — A comet in shape of a dragon devastated western Britain and Ireland, creating "The Wasteland."

A.D. 542 — Date that Geoffrey of Monmouth gives for the death of King Arthur. Castleden (2000), 211; Blake and Lloyd (2000), 193, say he died in 512. (See ca. A.D. 537–38)

ca. A.D. 542–60 — British monk and chronicler Gildas Badonicus wrote *De Exidio et Conquestu Brittanniae, The Ruin and Fall of Britain.*

ca. A.D. 543 — The Yellow Plague struck Britain. (See ca. A.D. 547)

ca. A.D. 546 — According to Rodney Castleden (2000), 211, supposedly King Arthur recovered from wounds at Camlann and lived another six to eight years, dying in Avalon.

ca. A.D. 546 — David, Archbishop of Meneva in Wales, visited the Old Wooden Church in Glastonbury.

ca. A.D. 547 — The Yellow Plague in western Britain further deteriorated the environmental problem called "The Wasteland." (See ca. A.D. 543)

ca. A.D. 547–49 — The mighty Welsh king Maelgwyn Gwynedd died of the Yellow Plague.

ca. A.D. 562 — Death of St. Arthmael (Armel), perhaps Arthur of legend.

A.D. 563 — St. Columba crossed over from Scotia (Northern Ireland) to Iona in northern England to set up headquarters for preaching the Gospel in the pagan part of Britain. Accompanied by twelve monks.

A.D. 568–570 King Alboin of Lombards (Gothic barbarians of the Danube) struck into Rome and conquered the north of Italy. Without an important battle he was proclaimed king of Italy in A.D. 570. With this the last vestiges of the Roman Empire fell and the Dark Ages began (see Gibbon, 783). The Empire was divided into ten kingdoms (horns) with a "little" horn being the papacy. This removed the restraining of papal power by the empire.

ca. A.D. 570 The death of Gildas III (516–570).

A.D. 570 Legend has it that St. Brendan sailed to America about A.D. 570. We are not certain what Brendan was doing in the New World, but it might have had something to do with depositing sacred records and relics in the Hill Cumorah in the American "wilderness." With the apostasy of Celtic Christianity and co-opting by the Roman Catholic Church and the Saxons, the woman (Church) mentioned in Revelation 12:6 now flies away into the "wilderness" for 1,260 calendar years, to be restored in 1830.

A.D. 570 Pope Gregory the Great's career began with the defeat of the Lombards. It was with this man that the "warrior popes" of the future were patterned.

ca. A.D. 570 Birth of Mohammed, the "lawless one," was revealed or born (2 Thessalonians 2:3).

ca. A.D. 573 According to Chris Tolworthy, many scholars believe that the Grail seeker Perceval was based on Peredyr, King of Ebrauc. Peredyr's famous and last great victory was in A.D. 573. Godwin thinks that Perceval is based on Brendan because they were contemporaries.[7]

ca. A.D. 577 St. Brendan died.

A.D. 577 Final major defeat of the demoralized Celtic forces at the Battle of Dyrham. The Celtic church no longer had the spirit and precious little to offer; it gave up after the battle.

A.D. 584 End of the reign of Merovingian Chilperic I (539–584). He was called "The Nero and Herod of his age." He murdered his wife about A.D. 570.

A.D. 588 John the Patriarch of Constantinople assumed title of "Universal Bishop." This caused great jealousy from Pope Gregory, who said "that whosoever in his elation of spirit called himself or sought to be called universal bishop, that man was the likeness, the precursor and the preparer for Antichrist."[8]

A.D. 590 Gregory of Tours's opus, *History of the Franks,* was written.

A.D. 591 In a homily, Pope Gregory the Great declared Mary Magdalene to be identified with the sister of Lazarus who anointed Jesus and the "sinner" in Luke's Gospel.[9]

A.D. 594	Death of Gregory of Tours (540-594) who wrote *The History of the Franks*.
A.D. 597	Pope Gregory I the Great sent St. Augustine of Canterbury as his emissary to Saxon-held Kent with the mission of converting pagan and Celtic Christian England to Catholic "Canon" Christianity.
A.D. 597 (9 July)	St. Columba of Iona, the "Dove of the Church" died.
A.D. 601	St. Augustine established the Roman Church diocese at Canterbury and Gregory consecrated Augustine as archbishop of Canterbury.
A.D. 601	One of the Glastonbury land grants was recorded by the king of Dumnonia. This is the earliest known record of Glastonbury.
A.D. 603	Roman sovereignty over the native British church failed at the Conference of Aust on the Severn River.
A.D. 603 or 612	Death of St. Kentigern in Glasgow.
ca. A.D. 606–607	The assumption of the papacy by the Roman Catholic Church divided the Celtic and Catholic churches. The Emperor Phocas "confirmed the right of the Roman See and bishops to the *headship of all churches*."[10] After an apostasy of

1,260 lunar years the gospel would be restored in 1830 by Joseph Smith.

ca. A.D. 610	Mohammed began to have visions.
A.D. 618 (16 Apr.)	On the isle of Eigg in Scotland, St. Donnan and his community of monks were massacred by a Pictish queen. Earliest recorded martyrdom of Celtic saint.
A.D. 622	The *Heijra*, or flight from Mecca to Medina, began the Islamic calendar.
A.D. 623–711	Muslim armies swept through Arabian Peninsula and Palestine and across the Near East and Africa and conquered and occupied Spain and southern France.
ca. A.D. 625	Paulinus remodeled original church in Glastonbury.
A.D. 632	Death of Mohammed, founder of Islam.
ca. A.D. 635	Birth of St. Cuthbert in Scottish Borders.
ca. A.D. 633	A mysterious small boat sailed into Boulogne-sur-mer harbor in northern France. No one was aboard the three-foot vessel, but a statuette of a black madonna and child, together with a copy of the Gospels in Syriac. No one knew where it came from, but it became the insignia of the city.
A.D. 637	When Northumbrian King Oswald desired to establish Christianity in

his kingdom he did not apply to Kent for missionaries, but to Iona.

A.D. 658 In Gaul, the Council of Nantes ordered the destruction of all remaining Druidical monuments.

A.D. 664 Council of Whitby. The Celtic (Culdee) Church was dissolved and officially subsumed into Roman Catholic Church.

A.D. 679 Merovingian King Dagobert II died.

A.D. 681 Mysterious date on tombstone at Rennes-le-Château (turns out to be a twentieth-century hoax).

A.D. 687 Construction of Dome of the Rock on Mount Moriah for the Caliph Abd al-Malik and Caliph Umar begun by Byzantine architects.

ca. A.D. 704 King Ine built the first Saxon church in Glastonbury.

ca. A.D. 711 Islamic Berbers (Moors) entered southern Spain and rapidly expanded northwards over Pyrenees until forced back by the Franks.

A.D. 712 A Glastonbury Saxon charter first mentioned XII hides (a measure of land) in relation to seaward harbor of Bleadney.

ca. A.D. 717 A hermit living in a remote place had a vision of a small book written by Christ.[11]

ca. A.D. 717 With expulsion of the Celtic clergy by Canon churches, we get

the word "Culdee" for old, non-Augustinian Christian churches.

ca. A.D. 725 Saxon King Ine or Ini of Wessex rebuilt the complex in Glastonbury with the first stone church about A.D. 725.

ca. A.D. 725 Bede wrote his *Chronicle*.

A.D. 731 The Northumbrian monk the Venerable Bede completed his *Ecclesiastical History of the English People* documenting the Anglo-Saxon conquest of England. As a pro-Saxon propagandist, he does not mention Celtic King Arthur.

A.D. 732 Charles Martel (d. 741) defeated Moors' invasion at Battle of Tours and Poitiers, saving Christian Europe.

A.D. 745 The unknown "chronicler" Sigebert noted that the relics of Mary Magdalene were removed to Vézelay, France, to protect them from the Saracens (see A.D. 882–884).

A.D. 756 The Scots and Picts defeated the Angles in battle, "the day that Scotland was born."

793 Viking raiders sacked the monastery at Lindisfarne in Northumbria.

795 The Vikings devastated Iona.

800 The Carolingian monarch Charlemagne was crowned Holy Roman Emperor by Pope Leo III in Rome.

ca. A.D. 800s	In the ninth century, Nennius wrote *Historia Britonum*.	ca. A.D. 950	The Welsh collection stories known as the *Mabinogion* appeared.
ca. A.D. 840	Kenneth mac Alpin, king of Dalriada, removed the Stone of Destiny from Dunstaffnage Castle to the Palace of Scone, the seat of Scottish kings.	A.D. 954	Count Guido bestowed the castle, Saint Michael's Church in Ventimigila, and land, to the monks of Lerins of Seborga.
A.D. 844	Kenneth mac Alpin united the Picts and the Scots and became the first true king of all Scotland.	ca. A.D. 958	The priceless *Harleian MS. 3859* was written regarding the genealogy of Wales.
A.D. ca. 870	The Welsh *Annals* makes no mention of a King Arthur.	ca. A.D. 1000	Viking Lief Ericson reached Vinland (possibly Massachusetts).
A.D. 882–84	Supposedly the remains of Mary Magdalene were moved ("holy thief") from southern France to Vézelay (see A.D. 745).	A.D. 1000s	In the eleventh century the *Culhwch and Olwen* was written.
ca. A.D. 886	Greek tradition says that the bones of Mary Magdalene were removed from Ephesus and taken to Constantinople by the Emperor Leo.	ca. 1012	First Cathar heretics arrived in Limousine, France.
		1016	Danish King Canute was king of all England and part of Scotland.
A.D. 899	The Emperor Leo VI transferred Mary Magdalene's alleged relics to a monastery in Constantinople (see A.D. 882–84).	ca. 1020	*The Life of St. Goeznovius* mentioned King Arthur.
A.D. 911	The Treaty of St. Clair signed on the Epte River, between Rollo with King Charles the Simple. Thus began the Sinclair line.	ca. 1050	About this time the monks of Vézelay, an abbey recently reformed and affiliated to Cluny, began to claim the bones of Mary Magdalene (see A.D. 745, A.D. 882–884).
ca. A.D. 900s	In the tenth century the *Spoils of Annwn* was written.	1058	Reign of Malcolm III or Canmore (1058–1093) of Scotland began.
		1059	Church at Rennes-le-Château consecrated to Mary Magdalene.
A.D. 942	Dunstan became the Abbot of Glastonbury. He reformed the monastery.	1066	William the Conqueror and the Normans invaded and conquered Britain.

ca. 1068	The Doomsday survey for the Normans was conducted.	1094	Hugues de Payen succeeded his father as Lord of Payen.

ca. 1070 A group of monks from Calabria in southeastern Italy, led by Prince Ursus, founded the Abbey of Orval in France near Stenay in the Ardennes. This is said to have formed the basis for the Order de Sion (see A.D. 1090 below).

1070 Future head of the Knights Templars, Hugues de Payen, was born.

1071 Jerusalem was devastated by Seljuk Turks.

ca. 1075 The Welsh cleric Lifric of Llancarfan, wrote *Life of St. Cadoc* and mentioned Arthur.

1079 Seborga became a principality of the Holy Roman Empire.

1080 A mystical number; for years it was thought to have been a date but in fact represents the divine feminine.

1085 Pope Urban II was elected.

1086 *Domesday Book* was completed.

ca. 1090 According to faulty information by Baigent, Leigh, and Lincoln, the Order of Sion was founded by Godfroi de Bouillon, nine years *before* the conquest of Jerusalem. Most scholars think it was 1099 that the order was founded, just *after* the conquest.

ca. 1090 Bernard of Clairvaux was born.

1095 Pope Urban II decreed that hence-forth those seeking ordination could not be married. (See ca. A.D. 1139)

1095 (27 Nov.) Pope Urban II preached the Crusades.

1096 The First Crusade occurred.

1098 (15 Jun.) The Templars found the Spear of Longinus in the Church of St. Peter at Antioch.

1098 The Cistercian Order was founded by a group of Benedictine monks from the Abbey of Molesme. This, at its core, was possibly a front for the *Rex Deus* line at that time.

1099 (14 Jun.) Godfroi de Bouillon, the Duke of Lorraine, and the Crusaders captured the Holy City of Jerusalem from the Moslems.

1099 (15 Jul.) In Jerusalem, Crusaders massacred Jewish and Muslim men, women, and children, and many Cities in the name of God.

1099 Godfroi de Bouillon offered king-ship of Jerusalem but preferred instead to be called Advocate or Guardian of the Order of the Holy Sepulchre. Any relationship with the Order of Sion is unclear.

ca. 1099 Augustinian canons establish the Order of Notre Dame de Sion, headquartered in the Abbey of Orval in Belgium. This Ordre de Sion, based on Mt. Sion in Jerusalem, eventually had monasteries in Calabria, the Holy Land, Sicily, and Orleans. (See A.D. 1079 and A.D. 1090.)

1099   Pope Urban II died.

1100   Godfroi de Bouillon, first occupier of Jerusalem and William II of England died.

1100   Baldwin I was made first Christian king of Jerusalem.

ca. 1100   *The Life of St. Carannog* told of Arthur encountering a dragon.

ca. 1101   Supposedly the date that Hugues de Payen married Catherine de St. Clair and was given Blancradock as dowry. This was probably false because de Payen was already married and St. Clairs were not yet in Scotland.

ca. 1104   Count Hughes of Champagne met in secret conclave with members of noble *Rex Deus* families Brienne, de Joinville, Chaumont, and Anjou, probably to discuss the Kingdom of Jerusalem and the sacred treasure.

ca. 1104   Count Hughes of Champagne, soon after the concave, traveled to the Holy Land with Hugues de Payen. While on his way he probably went to Seborga. Then in Byzantium he encountered the Gnostic Order of the Brothers of the East.

ca. 1108   The Count of Champagne returned home to his estates from the Holy Land, supposedly with a "scroll" in hand.

1112   Friar Gerard de Martigues formed the Order of the Knights of Malta.

1112–13   St. Bernard of Clairvaux and Fontaine family joined the Cistercian Order.

1113   Hospitallers of Jerusalem recognized by the papacy as a separate order.

ca. 1113 (Jun.)   Cistercian monastery founded in Seborga, northern Italy, by St. Bernard. Two monks, Gondemar and Rossal, sent to ostensibly protect a "great secret" or "great work."

1114   Count Hugh of Champagne and Hugues de Payen again set out for Holy Land. The Count announced intention of joining *la Milice du Christ* (pre-Templars).

ca. 1115   Count of Champagne returned from Kingdom of Jerusalem; mysteriously began to make large donations of land to the Cistercian Order.

1115   Bernard became Abbot of Clairvaux.

ca. 1116   Chinese began to sew pages to make stitched books.

1117 (Feb.)   St. Bernard released monks Gondemar and Rosal of Seborga to join seven other companion knights.

1118	Moslem massacre of three-hundred Christian pilgrims prompted Templars to organize to protect them.		Its significantly pre-dates the first of French romances by several decades and points to his status as well-known and recognized figure at that time.[12]
ca. 1118 (11 Sept.)	Prince Abbot Edward ordained first nine Templars (Knights of Saint Bernard); Principality of Seborga became unique and first sovereign Cistercian state in history.	1124–25	The Count of Champagne took oath of membership in Knights Templar, raising their number to eleven.
1118 (Nov.)	Eight Knights left for Jerusalem and began to excavate ruined Temple.	ca. 1125	William of Malmesbury wrote *Acts of the Kings of the English* (*Gesta regum Anglorum*).
1118	First Christian king of Jerusalem, Baldwin I, died; succession went to his cousin Baldwin II.	ca. 1126	Hugh Payens and another Templar, Andrew of Montbard, traveled to Europe to solicit funds and recruits for the Order and to obtain papal approval and a rule to live by. (See A.D. 1128.)
1119 (May 14)	Eight of the Knights arrived in Jerusalem. Hugues de Champagne came exactly six years later.		
1119	Knights of Christ in Jerusalem renamed under reign of Baldwin II— "Order of the Poor Knights of Christ and the Temple of Solomon". Patriarch Warmund of Jerusalem commanded them, "in remission of their sins," to defend pilgrim routes from bandits.	1126	Henry of Blois appointed Abbot of Glastonbury. He was uncle of Henri de Sully, Abbot of Fécamp Normandy, when its relics of the Holy Blood were discovered in 1171. Henri de Sully was no known relation to Henry of Sully, Abbot of Glastonbury, in 1191.
1120	Count Fulk d'Anjou hurried to Jerusalem, took the oath of allegiance to new Order of Templars.	ca. 1127	Nine Templars arrived from Jerusalem to Seborga. St. Bernard and Friar Gerard de Martiques were waiting for them. Hugues de Payen returned to Seborga and was ordained by St. Bernard as first Grand Master of the Knights Templar in the presence of 23 Knights and over 100 militia. The consecration with the sword was made by Prince Abbot Edward.
1120	St. Denis Cathedral in Paris began to be rebuilt; the birth of Gothic architecture.		
1120–1140	Frieze above north doorway of Modena Cathedral in Italy depicts an Arthurian adventure.		

ca. 1127 (late Dec.)   Main Templar excavations completed on Temple Mount (Sion).

1128 (Jan.)   Hughes de Payen and Andre de Montbard traveled to France and Scotland to confer with St. Bernard and the St. Clairs (actually the Rosslyns). (see A.D. 1126).

1128 (21 Jun.)   Scottish King David I granted lands at Temple in Midlothian to Hughes de Payen.

1128   Princess Matilda married Geoffrey IV of Anjou, grandson of King Baldwin II of Jerusalem and son of Count Fulk V, who became next king of Jerusalem in 1131. Matilda also gave land for Oxford preceptory to Payen de Montdidier.

1128   Payen de Montdidier became Templar Grand Master of England; embarked on major preceptory building program.

1128–29 (Jan.)   Templar order officially recognized and granted rule at Council of Troyes.

1129   Henry of Huntingdon's *Historia Anglorum* based on Bede, Nennius, and *Anglo-Saxon Chronicle* was published.

ca. 1129–30   William of Malmesbury in residence at Glastonbury Abbey, where he wrote *The Antiquity of the Church at Glastonbury* (*De Antiquitate Glastoniensis Ecclesiae*). Purpose was to show Glastonbury's ancient foundation owed no duty to Canterbury.

1130–1150   Chartres, Rheims, Amiens, and other cathedrals of Our Lady built on pattern of constellation Virgo employing principles of sacred geometry.[13]

1131   Count Fulk V of Anjou who financially supported Templars for previous seven years, became king of Jerusalem.

1132–35   Geoffrey of Monmouth wrote *The History of the Kings of Britain* (*Historia Regum Britanniae*) or *Matter of Britain*, published in 1136. Geoffrey was seen as justifying Norman invasion of Britain, suggesting British and Normans share a common past and enemy in the Saxons.

1136   Knights Templar founder Hughes de Payen died.

1136   Melrose Abbey established by Cistercians or "White Monks".

1139   Pope Innocent II, protege of St. Bernard, issued a papal Bull, which declared Templars owed no allegiance to any secular or ecclesiastical power other than to the Pope himself (Hopkins [2000], 19).

ca. 1139   Pope Innocent II required married priests to abandon their wives and families and practice celibacy. (See A.D. 1095.)

1140   Templars took relics from Jerusalem Temple to Scotland.

1140   Abbey of Kilwinning built to store

documents discovered by Knights Templar in excavations under Temple Mount in Jerusalem.

1140 William of Malmesbury wrote story of Holy Grail and Joseph of Arimathea.

ca. 1140–50 Caradoc of llancarfan wrote, *Life of St. Gildas.*

1140 Lordship of Payen reverted to Count of Champagne.

1140s The term *Templars* began to be used.

1145 (Mar.) The Knights Templar, acting with the agreement of Bernard of Clairvaux, gave a "rule" to the Children of Solomon in the Compagnonage (Guild), which outlined their conditions for living and working.

ca. 1146 Introduction of the *croix pattée* to Templar clothing.

1148–50 Date given for bringing of important Holy Blood Relic to Bruges, Belgium, from Holy Land by Philip of Flanders' father, Thierry of Alsace. This was an invention, and it actually came about 1256.[14] Philip of Flanders was Chrétien de Troyes's patron.

1152 Geoffrey of Monmouth became Bishop of St. Asaph.

1153 Bernard of Clairvaux died.

1154 Henry II ascended to throne of England, first of Plantagenets, son of Geoffrey IV of Anjou and Princess Matilda. He was probably of the Grail lineage.

ca. 1155 Norman/Jersey poet Robert Wace produces *Roman de Brut* (*Romance of Brutus*) written in the vernacular, the first of the French Romances. Wace first to introduce concept of the Round Table. It was written to show that Norman kings were descendants of King Arthur and therefore the returning and rightful rulers of Britain.

1165 Letter from a mysterious Prester John appears with copies to Pope Alexander III, the King of France; the Emperor in Constantinople (Manuel Commenius); and the Holy Roman Emperor Frederick II. Its twenty pages mention his Christian kingdom in the East and exhorts these Western kings to kill the treacherous Templars and pagans (Muslims). The letter is a forgery.

1169 Chrétien de Troyes wrote *Erec and Enide.*

ca. 1170 The Templar Madoc ab Owain Gwyned supposedly left his lands in Wales and sailed to Mobile Bay in Alabama, America, on the Gulf of Mexico.

1174 Abbey at Glastonbury burned.

1174 Bernard of Clairvaux made a saint.

ca. 1175 French romancer Chrétien de Troyes wrote *Lancelot.*

1178	Pope Alexander issued papal bull proclaiming Order of Notre Dame de Sion monasteries in Calabria, the Holy Land, Sicily, France, and elsewhere.
ca. 1180	Chrétien de Troyes wrote *Ywain*.
1180–85	Chrétien de Troyes wrote *Perceval*. First of Grail romances to burst upon European scene, the unfinished epic, *Perceval* or *Le Conte del Graal*.
1184	A candle burned down old church at Glastonbury.
1185 (10 Feb.)	Heraclius, patriarch of Jerusalem, consecrated Temple Church in London.
1185	Templars established their English headquarters at Temple, south of Fleet Street in London.
1185 (11 Jun.)	Consecration of beautiful Romanesque Gothic building at Glastonbury. Construction begun.
1187 (2–4 Jul.)	Splinter of the True Cross is lost to the Moslems at Templar defeat in Battle of Hattin and Jerusalem fell to Muslim Saladin and his Saracens.
ca. 1188	Conjectured split between Knights Templar and Ordre de Sion at "cutting of the elm" at Gisors. Order of Sion supposedly became known as Priory de Sion and gave itself the Gnostic subtitle of "Ormus" and a second subtitle, "Ordre de la Rose-Croix Veritas" (the Order of the True Red Cross). This event probably never occurred because there was no connection between the Templars and the fictional Priory de Sion.
1188	Kilwinning Abbey built (others say 1140 A.D.) dedicated to the Virgin Mary.
1189	Richard I, "The Lion Hearted," ascended to the throne of England. He is the second Plantagenet king and son of Henry II. He led the third crusade.
1190	Formation of "Teutonic Knights of St. Mary's Hospital at Jerusalem" took place in Acre.
ca. 1190	First continuation of *Perceval*, by anonymous Templar, titled *Perlesvaus*. (See A.D. 1208.)
1191	Abbot Henry of Sully and monks at Glastonbury Abbey miraculously "discovered" grave of King Arthur and Guinevere. This is no relation to Henri de Sully, Abbot of Fécamp in Normandy.
1194	Chartres Cathedral destroyed by fire.
1195	Ralph of Coggeshall visited Glastonbury.
ca. 1200	Robert de Boron's book *Joseph d'Arimathie* published; it may have been written as early as 1191. Between 1200 and 1210 de Boron wrote *L'Estoire du Graal (Romance of the History of the Grail)*, *Merlin*, and *Perceval*.

| ca. 1200 | Valle Crucis Abbey built in Vale of Llangollen in Eglwyseg Valley on Dee River in North Wales. |

| 1206 | At a conference of Montreal, the *Albigenses* (Cathars) professed "that the Church of Rome was not the spouse of Christ, but the church of confusion, drunk with blood of martyrs. That the policy of the church of Rome was neither good, or holy, nor established by Jesus Christ."[15] |

| 1206 | Construction of Amiens Cathedral begun. |

| ca. 1208 | *Perlesvaus* was written anonymously. (See A.D. 1190.) |

| 1208 | At beginning of Albigensian Crusade, Pope Innocent III admonished Templars for un-Christian behavior and referred explicitly to necromancy.[16] |

| 1209 (24 Jun.) | Albigensian Crusade begun against Cathar heresy at Béziers by king of France. |

| 1210 | Prose (Didot) *Perceval* was published. |

| 1210 | Wolfram von Eschenbach published *Parzifal*. First author to make Knights Templar Grail guardians. (See A.D. 1218.) |

| ca. 1212 | Pierre Vaux-de-Cernay, a chronicler, recorded that Albigensian Crusade burned the church on Mary Magdalene's feast day with everyone inside because they said that "Mary Magdalene was the concubine of Jesus." |

| 1214–15 | Templar seal showed Dome of the Rock as Temple of Solomon. |

| 1215–1235 | *Vulgate Cycle* written, included *Queste del Saint Graal* written by group of Cistercian monks, also called *Prose Lancelot*. It led to Christianization of Grail vessel. Later Protestant denominations rejected the story, full of imagery from the mass, as too Catholic. |

| 1217 | Fifth Crusade sought to secure chief port on Nile delta nearest to Palestine. |

| ca.1218 | German poet Wolfram von Eschenbach visited Holy Land, was so impressed by Templars that he made them guardians of the Grail castle in his epic, *Parzival*. (see A.D. 1210.) |

| ca. 1220 | Second continuation of *Perceval* published. |

| ca. 1220 | Third continuation of *Perceval* published. |

| 1224 | Birth of Thomas Aquinas (1224–1274), who died while giving commentary on Song of Songs. |

| 1230 | Heinrich von dem Turlin published *Diu Crone*. |

| 1233–1237 | "Holy Office of the Inquisition" founded, largely staffed by Dominican and Franciscan Orders, to create climate of fear for those |

who would be considered heretics. In subtler mode, it is now (2006) called by rather innocuous name of "Congregation for the Doctrine of the Father."

ca. 1240   *Peredur* published.

1244   Albigensian Crusade against Cathars ended at Siege of Montségur, the citadel seminary, and massacre of 200 Cathars. Treasure was supposedly smuggled to safety before the fall of the castle.

1244   Birth of Jacques de Molay.

1252   Henry III of England accuses Templars of "excessive pride."

1252   Inquisition permitted to apply extreme torture to anyone suspected of heresy. Approved by Pope Innocent IV, his inquisitors were essentially Dominican Black Friars and Franciscan Grey Friars.

ca. 1255   Prose *Tristan* is published.

1256   Isma'ili Assassin's library burned at Alamut in Persian mountains by Mongols.

1256   Bringing of Holy Blood relic to Bruges from the Holy Land by Philip of Flanders's father, Thierry of Alsace. (See A.D. 1148–50.)

1274   Albrecht von Scharfenburg published *Der Jüngere Titurel.*

1274   Second Council of Lyons discussed combining Knights Hospitaller and Knights Templar into a single religio-military order. Both Orders were against the idea.

1277   Edward I defeated Welsh and forced Llywelyn ap Gruffydd, Prince of Wales, to submit to him.

1278   Edward I visited Glastonbury on Easter for "second" exhumation and reburial of King Arthur and Guinevere.

1279   Teutonic Knights conquered Slavs of Prussia.

1279   Charles II, king of Naples, Sicily, Count of Provence, disinterred Mary Magdalene's skull and humerus in order to have them set in the gold and silver display casings they are in today. He erected a convent at La Sainte-Baume for the Dominicans to house the remains of Mary Magdalene.

1284   Presentation of King Arthur's Welsh crown at high altar of Westminster Abbey by Edward I.

1285   At age seventeen, Philip IV (the Fair) succeeded his father as king of France.

1291   Loss of Latin kingdoms in Holy Land, Templar stronghold port at Acre in Palestine fell to Saracens and ended all hope of recapturing Jerusalem. Templars formed an alliance with James, king of Majorca, to establish sovereign independent state to include Languedoc and its hidden treasure deposits.

1292–93 Jacques de Molay elected last Grand Master of Knights Templar.

1294 Boniface VIII made pope of Roman Catholic Church.

1296 King Edward I of England took Stone of Scone to Westminster Abbey, London, England. Some say it was fake and real one was kept hidden by Scots.

1297 Dominicans initiated Feast of St. Mary Magdalene on 22 July.

1300 Templars defeated at Tortosa some carried as prisoners to Egypt. Molay returned to Cyprus and considered a retreat to Europe.

1302 Boniface VIII issued a papal bull, *Unam Sanctam*; it proclaimed supreme papal power over kings. Philip IV publicly burned bull and seized lands of prelates loyal to the pope. Boniface offered throne of France to Emperor Albert of Austria.

1302–03 Scots defeated English at Battle of Roslin.

1303 (Mar.) Philip IV of France convened counsel in Paris to judge charges brought against Pope Boniface VIII almost identical to those later brought against Templars. Pope died of fits brought on by an attacker.

1304 Pope Benedict XI poisoned by Philip's agents after ten months in office.

1305 Archbishop of Bourdeaux elected Pope Clement V; the papacy transferred to Avignon, "the Captivity," under control of French King Philip IV.

1305 Robert the Bruce excommunicated by pope.

1306 Pope called Masters of Templars and Hospitallers to France to discuss combining both orders. Molay against this proposal.

1306 Philip the Fair called for arrest of all Jews in France.

1307 (Fri., 13 Oct.) Repression of Knights Templar by King Philip IV "the Fair" of France. Philip issued arrest warrants against all Templars, alleging heretical practices but in reality to gain control of their wealth.

1307 (22 Nov.) Pope Clement V agreed to call for arrest of Templars outside France.

1312 (22 Mar.) Catholic Church officially dissolved Templar Order by papal bull *Vox in Excelso* (this date subsequently became significant in Nazi Germany.)

1312 Papal council established Templars outside France were innocent of charges put forth by King Philip.

1313 Second papal bull, *Ad providam* gave all Templar assets to their rivals Knights Hospitallers and king of France. Order was suppressed but not men in it.

1314 (18 Mar.) Templar Grand Master Jacques de Molay burned to death, Ile de la Cité, Paris. His tormentor, King

Philip le Bel (1268–1314),
also died.

1314 (24 Jun.) Battle of Bannockburn fought on
Feast Day of St. John the Baptist.
With help from Knights Templar,
Scots defeated English.

ca. 1314 "Rosy Cross" affirmed to have been
instituted by Robert the Bruce.
Later became part of Royal Order
of Scotland.

1317 Conference of Frankfurt allowed
former German Templars to join
Hospitallers.

1319 King Dinis of Portugal encouraged
lawsuits by his Courts, asserting
royal rights over Templar holdings
and had Templar name changed
to Order of Christ, which was
approved by the pope in 1319. In
Spain Templars became known as
Order of Mantessa.

1320 (6 Apr.) Scottish Declaration of
Independence signed at Arbroath
with defiant statement, "So long
as a hundred of us are left alive,
we will never in any degree be
subjected to the English." Letter
to Pope John XXII explained
why Scotland was a people and
a nation. It influenced writing of
U.S. Constitution.

ca.1325 *White Book of Rhydderch* mades its
appearance.

1328 Treaty of Northampton sealed
Scotland's independence. English
offered to return Stone of

Destiny, but Scots did not
take up offer.

ca. 1329 Teutonic Knights held entire
Baltic region from Gulf of Finland
in north to Poland in south as a
papal fief.

1330 Death of Robert the Bruce at Battle
of Kinghorm. William St. Clair
died trying to take the heart of
Robert I (the Bruce) to Jerusalem.

1331 (Dec.) Edward III visited Glastonbury to
reaffirm Arthurian connections.

1335 *Perceforest* was published.

1345 Birth of Henry St. Clair, lord of
Roslin and famous navigator to
American northeast coast.

1345 Edward III gave his license to
John Bloom of London to dig for
grave of Joseph of Arimathea at
Glastonbury.

1348–50 Black Death enters France via
Marseilles. Within two years, one
third of French population died
from plague.

1350 *Sone de Nansai* was published.

1357 First-known exhibition of Shroud
of Turin in small church in French
town of Lirey. Henry of Poitiers
bans any further exhibition of the
Shroud.

1361 Scottish rite of "Strict Observance"
recorded a visit from speculative
masons from operative lodges

of Compannonage in France to Aberdeem lodge.

1361–72 New outbreak of Black Death epidemic occurred.

1367 A Lincolnshire monk noted body of Joseph of Arimathea was supposedly found in Glastonbury, placed in a silver casket, and placed in the east end of Joseph's Chapel as a place of pilgrimage.

ca. 1376 Tarot cards forbidden in Florence.

ca. 1376 First use of the word *Freemason*.

1380 First English translation of Bible appears, translated from Latin Vulgate by John Wycliffe.

1382–88 Another outbreak of Black Death disease.

ca. 1390 Alliterative *Morte Arthur* published.

1393 Ferri de Vaudemont established Confraternity of Our Lady of Sion in Nancy, France, in Lorraine, near Sion. Its relationship with earlier Order of Sion is unknown.

1398 (Jun.) Supposedly Henry Sinclair, with Niccolo and Antonio Zeno, an Italian mariner and naval admiral, sailed to La Merika in 1397, landing in Nova Scotia in June of 1398. If true, he possibly made it as far as Newport, Rhode Island.

ca. 1400 Stanzaic *Le Morte Arthur* was published.

ca. 1400 *Red Book of Hergest* made its appearance.

1409 First (1409–10) of four reform councils (Constance and Basel), the Council of Pisa supported claim that England was first Christianized Western country.

1409 Teutonic Knights decisively lost Battle of Tannenberg, ending their imperial aspirations of expanding their power to Russia.

1410 Order of the Golden Fleece founded by Philip the Good, duke of Burgundy. Order restricted to 24 knights initiates from major *Rex Deus* families (one from each family?). Pope Eugenius IV once called them "Maccabeans resurrected."

1417 (3 Mar.) In 1414–18, Council at Constance was Catholic Church's sixteenth ecumenical council. In the twenty-eighth session controversy arose over whether English Church had right to form its own nation. It supported claim that England was first Christianized Western country against challenge of French and Spanish ambassadors.

ca. 1420 *Sir Gawain and the Green Knight* published.

1424 Council at Sienna supported claim that England was first Christianized Western country.

1434 The 1431–1449 Council at Basel supported claim that England was first Christianized Western country.

It noted, "The Churches of France and Spain must yield in points of antiquity and precedence to that of Britain as the latter Church was founded by Joseph of Arimathea immediately after the passion of Christ."

1441   James II, king of Scotland, appointed St. Clair "Patron and Protector of Scottish Masons."

1441   Fire gutted Rosslyn castle, prompting idea for building chapel.

1446–1450   The planning of Rosslyn chapel by William Sinclair published.

1450s   Printing press invented and translations of Bible printed in Mainz, Germany, by Gutenberg.

1450–1486   The construction of the Rosslyn Shrine/chapel built at Roslin by William Sinclair.

1453   Eastern Roman Empire, Byzantine Empire, fell to Ottoman Turks.

1456   Muslims conquered Constantinople, caused Greek Christians to flee to Western Europe, taking learning and culture to Italy and the West.

1471   Sir Thomas Malory died.

ca. 1485   William Caxton (first English printer) published Sir Thomas Malory's *Le Morte D'Arthur*, written in 1470.

1485   Conventional date for end of Middle Ages in England.

1485–1603   Welsh Tudors occupied throne of England, starting with Earl of Richmond (King Henry VII) and ending with Elizabeth the First.

1486   Heinrich Kramer and James Spenger, two German monks wrote *Malleus Maleficarum* (The Witch's Hammer).

1488   King James IV of Scotland confirmed union of Knights Templars with Hospitallers of St. John.

1492   Moors finally expelled from Iberian Peninsula.

1492   Christopher Columbus arrived in West Indies; discovered the Americas.

1516   Erasmus's Latin/Greek Bible printed with corrections to the Vulgate.

1517   Martin Luther nailed his 95 theses to door of church in Wittenberg, challenging Roman Catholic Church.

ca.   Anonymous poem published by Richard Pynson, royal printer, "The Lyfe of Joseph of Arimathia."

1522   Remnants of Teutonic Order of Knights supported Martin Luther in 1522.

1529   Martin Luther published his translation of German Bible.

1534   English split with Roman Catholic Church.

1539	Dissolution of Roman Catholic monasteries, abbeys, and cathedrals by Henry VIII. Abbot Richard Whiting of Glastonbury murdered by henchmen of King Henry.
1545–1563	Council of Trent made liturgical book binding upon entire Roman Catholic Church.
1551	Henry Sinclair, Bishop of Ross and Oliver's brother, appointed abbot of Kilwinning, a crucial name in Freemasonry.
1566	Death of prophetic mystic, Nostradamus (1503–1566).
1570	In first compulsory Roman missal, Mary Magdalene given epithet of "penitent."
1571 (30 Sept.)	Oldest known direct relative of Joseph Smith Jr., Edwarde Smithe was baptized (father of Robert Smythe).
1578	Shroud first taken to Turin Cathedral in Italy.
1588	England defeated Spanish Armada.
1595 (4 Mar.)	Robert Smythe, son of Edwarde Smithe, was baptized. (See 1851.)
1598 (27 Dec.)	First documented minutes of a Masonic lodge by William Schaw on feast day of St. John the Evangelist.
1600	Supposedly, relics of Mary Magdalene placed in a sarcophagus by Pope Clement VIII, the head being placed in a separate vessel.

1601	King James VI of Scotland was initiated as a speculative Freemason at the Lodge of Perth and Scone (Scoon).
1603	Protestant James VI of Scotland becomes James I of England, union of English and Scottish crowns.
1611	The King James Bible was published in English, translated from Greek *Textus Receptus*.
1614	Rosicrucianism began sweeping Europe, greatly influenced by the Kabbala. *Fama Fraternitatis* was published, supposedly written by Johann Valentin Andreae (1586–1654), German Protestant pastor from Tubingen.
1617	Roman Catholic monastic order founded in Jerusalem at monastery of Our Lady of Mt. Zion in about 1100, whose monks, known as *Ordre de Notre Dame de Sion*, ceased to exist in 1617 and absorbed into Jesuits.
1625	Charles I crowned king of England.
1626 (30 Apr.)	Robert Smith, son of Robert Smythe, baptized (ancestor of Joseph Smith Jr.).
1642	Sir Isaac Newton born (1642–1727), later member of Royal Society.
1650	Cromwell's troops under General Monk attacked Rosslyn Castle, and then stabled their horses in the Chapel.

1652	Thomas Vaughan, Welsh Rosicrucian published first English translation of the *Fama Fraternitatis*.
1658	Oliver Cromwell died.
1662	Joseph's Chapel at Glastonbury partially ruined by Puritan fanatics; supposedly body of Joseph of Arimathea was moved to Paris churchyard to conceal its identity.
1666	Paris meridian line fixed. (See 1718.)
ca. 1677	One Dr. Plot referred to thorn at Glastonbury, ascribed its planting to Joseph of Arimathea.
1684	Scottish Masonic lodges known to have weapons funds.
1688 (11 Dec.)	Protestant mob from Edinburgh and villagers from Roslin damage chapel, abandoned until 1736.
1689	Britain had parliamentary monarchy by virtue of Bill of Rights; throne held only by consent of Westminster government.
1693	John Slezer published *Theatrum Scotiae*.
1714	First recorded minutes of Grand Lodge of York.
1715	First Jacobite campaign to restore Stewart line failed; refugees sent to France.
1717	Grand Lodge of London established; this new organization promptly disowned its Scottish origins because of its Stewart ties; sought to live under Hanoverian rule.
1717	Major Druidic resurgence "Call to the Druids" by antiquarian John Toland of London.
1718	Paris meridian was first plotted. (See 1666.)
1725	Formation of Irish Grand Lodge and Lodge of St. Thomas in Paris.
1729 (20 Jan.)	Principality of Seborga remained a Cistercian state until this date, when sold to Vittorio Amedeo II of Savoldo Piedmont and King of Sardinia.
1736	Sir John Clerk of Penicuik renovated Rosslyn Chapel.
1736	Formation of Scottish Grand Lodge of Freemasonry.
1738	Papal bull issued by Pope Clement XII strongly condemned Freemasonry for deism and religious indifferentism. (See 1829.)
1744	Dr. Forbes, bishop of Caithness, wrote *An Account of the Chapel of Rosslyn*.
1745	Second Jacobite campaign begun to restore Stewart line.
1752	Grand Lodge of Ancients founded by Dermott.
1757	Birth of visionary poet and artist William Blake in London.

1761	Grand Lodge of France issued patent to spread Scottish Rite Freemasonry in America.	1799	Unlawful Societies Act brought in by William Pitt of England.
1776 (4 Jul.)	Declaration of Independence by the thirteen British colonies in America, signed by many Masons.	1801	Frenchman traveling in Turkey, C. S. Sonnini of Society of Agriculture in Paris, was presented a Greek by Sultan of Turkey in 1801. Document asserts that Apostle Paul, after visiting Spain, went to Britain to preach, met Druids who said their rites descended from Jews.
1782	Revived Templars of the Strict Observance and Canons of the Temple met at Convent of Wilhelmsbad, a Masonic conference that exposed foolishness of both enterprises.	1801	Supreme Council of Thirty-third degree for United States of America was formed.
1787	Formation of United States of America with Constitution.	1804–1810	William Blake wrote *Jerusalem* as introductory poem to *Milton*.
1788	Abbé Bigou, seeing the approaching French revolution, hid Hautpoul archives in crypt of his church at Rennes-le-Château.	1805 (23 Dec.)	Joseph Smith Jr. born in Sharon, Vermont. He is most important person born on earth in last one thousand years. He is the "desired knight," the "Latter-day Galahad," and the "Fisher-King" all in one.
1789	French Revolution and aftermath destroyed millions of sacred relics. Revolution resulted in overthrow of monarchy, dispossession of aristocracy, and suppression of Catholic Church.	1809	Napoleon dissolved Teutonic Knights.
1794	Captain Dagobert, having no heirs, confided his archives concerning mines and their contents to Masonic brothers of Grand Orient Freemasonry.	1809	Birth of great English poet, Alfred Lord Tennyson (1809–1892). Reluctant to write about Grail quest, he did so with encouragement of Queen Victoria. His *Idylls of the King* (1859–1885) was remarkable achievement of Grail literature in Victorian era.
1798	Napoleon embarked on Egyptian campaign accompanied by members of Hautpoul and Chefdebien families and others steeped in Scottish Rite Freemasonry. Tried to establish a homeland for Jews in Egypt.	1813	Formation of United Grand Lodge of England.
		1813	Birth of German composer and

music theorist Richard Wagner. *Tristan und Isolde* based upon Arthurian subject matter. His final opera, *Parsifal,* came from his reading in 1845 of Wolfram von Eschenback's work of same title. However, he changed Grail stone back to Grail vessel.

1814   After French Revolution, Church of La Sainte-Baume was restored. In 1822, grotto consecrated afresh.

1818   Josef von Hammer-Purgstall published *Mystery of Baphomet Revealed*, which turned Templars into duplicitous idolaters.

1819   Supreme Council for England established. Duke of Sussex initiated into 33d degree by Admiral Smyth. Rewriting of Masonic ritual started by Duke of Sussex.

1820 (Spring)   Joseph Smith in Palmyra, New York, had a visitation by God the Father and the Son in Sacred Grove that led to founding of Mormon Church.

1823   Joseph Smith revealed that Hill Cumorah near Palmyra, New York, had golden plates of ancient sacred writing.

1829   In London, act of parliament allowed Catholics to worship, follow their own faith.

1829   Pope Pius VIII issued an encyclical, condemned craft of Freemasonry. (See 1738.)

1830 (6 Apr.)   The Church of Jesus Christ of Latter-day Saints was founded. Not since 570 A.D. had authority of God been on earth.

1830   All Masonic Craft ritual rewritten.

1836 (3 Apr.)   D&C 110 records the restoration of the sealing keys by Moses, Elias, and Elijah of the fathers and sons.

1837   First preaching of Gospel in Britain, exactly 1,260 years after the death of St. Brendan (A.D. 577), the prophet who came to America with precious and sacred relics (for the Hill Cumorah?).

1838–1843   Lincolnshire diarist Lady Charlotte Guest published *Mabinogion* in three volumes, collection of twelve separate Welsh tales she had translated.

1839   While in Liberty Jail, Joseph ordained his son Joseph III to be his successor (according to Emma Smith). Others remember letter written from this jail saying that Quorum of Twelve, led by its longest-serving Apostle, was to lead Church.

1841 (24 Oct.)   Orson Hyde sent by Joseph Smith to dedicate land of Israel for return of the Jews. He did so on the Mt. of Olives and erected a pile of stones as a witness.

1843 (28 May)   Joseph Smith administered first ordinances of the Holy Order.

1844   Joseph Smith Jr. martyred at Carthage Jail in Illinois.

1845 — Mormon Orson Hyde traveled to Palestine and dedicated land for return of Jews.

1845 — (Masonic) Supreme Council for Scotland established.

1847 (24 Jul.) — The Latter-day Saints under Brigham Young entered Salt Lake Valley in Utah.

1848 — Pre-Raphaelite Brotherhood founded by Dante G. Rossetti, Wm. Holman Hunt, John E. Millais, etc., and established Grail myths as one of their central themes.

1848 (19 Nov.) — Arsonist set fire to Nauvoo Temple in Illinois. In 1850, a tornado struck what was left.

1849 (21 Nov.) — Isaac Morley headed a Mormon pioneer wagon train that entered Sanpete County, Utah.

1852 (11 Apr.) — Bérenger Saunière born.
1852 (Jun.) — Those who believed that right of succession should fall to Joseph Smith's son, Joseph III, formed Reorganized Church of Jesus Christ of Latter Day Saints.

1854 (9 Apr.) — Orson Hyde announced at general conference in Tabernacle that Jesus was married at Cana to Mary and Martha and had children.

1855 — Dante Gabriel Rossetti painted watercolor based upon Sir Thomas Malory's *Morte d'Arthur*. Titled *Arthur's Tomb*, depicts Guinevere's and Lancelot's final meeting in an apple orchard at Arthur's tomb.

1855 — Albert Pike joined in rewriting rituals of Scottish Rite.

1859 — Alfred Lord Tennyson wrote *Idylls of the King*, which directly stated that Joseph brought the Cup to Glastonbury. Rossetti was asked to do illustrations for Tennyson's poems.

1864 — Red Cross established by Geneva convention.

1867 — Excavation of Templar tunnels in Temple Mount in Jerusalem by Lieutenant Warren of Royal Engineers. (See 1894.)

ca. 1870 — First attempt by East European Jews to create Zionism, for promotion of national homeland, supported by Rothschild family.

1870 — First Vatican Council established doctrine of papal infallibility.

1875 — Birth of Swiss psychologist and philosopher Carl Jung (1875–1961), pioneered idea of "the collective unconscious" dealing with shared pool of symbolism expressed in form of religion, myths and legends. His wife, Emma, published *The Grail Legend,* which followed these lines.

1876 — England broke link with Supreme Council for Scotland.

1877 — Dedication of Latter-day Saint temple in St. George, Utah, and inauguration of "the full temple endowment."

1877	Death of Mormon Church President Brigham Young.	Beardsley began series of three hundred illustrations for Sir Thomas Malory's *Morte D'Arthur* for publisher J. M. Dent.
1882	Death of Pre-Raphaelite artist Dante Gabriel Rossetti.	
1885 (1 Jun.)	Abbé Bérenger Saunière became parish priest of Rennes-le-Château at Church of St. Marie Madeleine.	1892 J. R. R. Tolkien born in Bloemfontein, South Africa. His Grailesque *The Lord of the Rings* was published in three volumes 1954–55.

1885 (1 Jun.) — Abbé Bérenger Saunière became parish priest of Rennes-le-Château at Church of St. Marie Madeleine.

1892 — J. R. R. Tolkien born in Bloemfontein, South Africa. His Grailesque *The Lord of the Rings* was published in three volumes 1954–55.

1886 — Henri de Guadermaris's painting "Les Saintes Maries" depicting the three Marys' arrival in boat off coast of Provence, France, shown at Salon de Paris.

1894 — Eight hundred years after Templars dug under Temple of Jerusalem, British army contingent led by Lieutenant Charles Wilson of Royal Engineers, probed secret depths of Temple Mount and found artifacts from earlier excavation by Templars. (See 1867.)

1888 — Saunière began renovations on Rennes-le-Château.

1891 — Death of Theosophical Society founder from Russia, Helena Petrovna Blavatsky (1831–1891).

1896 — A second or third-century A.D. Coptic papyrus was discovered in upper Egypt, famous *Gospel of Mary (Magdalene)*. It has Peter exclaiming that Jesus and Mary were intimate: "Sister, we know that the Savior loved you [Mary] more than other women."[17] It may have come from the Cairo Genizah (a storage place for sacred records of Jews that were worn or damaged). The fourth-century *Berlin Codex* is a fragment of Gnostic "Gospel of Mary." (See 1867.)

1891 (21 Jun.) — Bérenger Saunière dedicated statue of Lourdes virgin on supposed Visigothic pillar. (This pillar, according to a hoax, contained old parchments recording an ancient and explosive secret.)

1891 (21 Sept.) — Saunière recorded "discovery of a tomb" in his diary. It was probably Marie de Nègre d'Ables' (d'Hautpoul) grave with a "nest egg" of gold coins.

1897 & 1903 — Oxyrhynchus religious papyrus texts came out of Egypt. These include the *Gospel of Mary (Magdalene)*. (See 1896.)

1891–1894 — Sir Edward Coley Burne-Jones produced series of tapestries, "The Quest for the Holy Grail," featured striking representation of "Achievement of Sir Galahad."

1899 (2 Jul.) — At a Solemn Assembly in Salt Lake Tabernacle, prophet Lorenzo Snow and apostle George Q. Cannon

1892 — British artist and illustrator Aubrey

noted that those present were descendants of old apostles and of Jesus Christ himself.

1901 Building work begun on Villa Béthanie, Tour Magdala, a belvedere and gardens by B. Saunière at Rennes-le-Château.

1902 Lady Charlotte Guest's translations (1838–1843) published by J. M. Dent, *The Mabinogion* (*Tales of Youth*) series of Welsh myths and legends in prose form.

1904 Birth of mythographer Joseph Campbell, who wrote *The Hero with a Thousand Faces* (1949), suggests that there is a universal "monomyth." His *The Masks of God: Creative Mythology*, published in 1968, pays close attention to roots of Grail legends. His popular TV series with Bill Moyers, "The Power of Myth" metaphorically describes all religion.

1905 *Protocols of the Elders of Sion* published at Russian Court. They were an anti-Semitic fraud.

1906 J. W. Taylor's popular book, *The Coming of the Saints* was published at height of British-Israelitism. Nothing about a sacred marriage appears at this early date, not until after Nag Hammadi scrolls are found.

1906 Finding of blue glass cup with green surround, decorated with tiny crosses [Grail] at Bride's Well in Glastonbury.

1906 Birth of author T. H. White (1906–1964), noted for his *The Sword in the Stone* in 1939, *The Witch in the Wood* (1939), *The Ill-Made Knight* (1940), *Candle in the Wind* (1958) and *The Once and Future King* (1958).

ca. 1906 Stephen Adam's stained-glass window created for Saint Mary's Church in Dervaig, Isle of Mull, had Holy Grail implications.

1909 A. E. Waite published *The Hidden Church of the Holy Grail* but does not mention Jesus and Mary Magdalene bloodline.

1909 (1 Feb.) Saunière resigned his commission in Catholic Church, but continued to perform sacraments.

1912 Order in Austria called secretive *Thjule Gesellschaft* (Thule Society) founded. This new ultra left-wing, nationalist, anti-Semite Templar order was organized by D. Lanz von Liebenfels, a former Cistercian monk.

1914 Outbreak of World War I.

1917 (22 Jan.) Death of Béreger Saunière. Marie Dénarnaud, his housekeeper and lifelong confidante continues to live in Saunière's residence.

1917 (Oct.) Communist Revolution occurred in Russia.

1918 (11 Nov.) End of World War I.

1919 Formation of anti-Semitic and anti-Communist German Workers

Party, dedicated to racial superiority, German nationalism.[18]

1920 Adolf Hitler played major role in German Workers Party, called National Socialist Party—NAZI.

1920 Anthropologist Jessie Weston's book *From Ritual to Romance* examined pre-Christian aspects of Grail, releasing avalanche of theories and speculations about it.

1922 English poet T. S. Eliot wrote his poetic masterpiece, *The Waste Land*, influenced by Jessie Weston's *From Ritual to Romance* and poet Ezra Pound. He sees twentieth century becoming more sterile, vacuous, culturally arid.

1924 Adolf Hitler imprisoned following Munich uprising, wrote vainglorious *Mein Kampf* (*My Struggle*), in which he revealed episode with dark spirit to whom he gave his "will."

1928 Founding of *Opus Dei*, deeply devout and ultra right-wing Catholic organization, with strong political agenda and a dangerous practice known as self "corporal mortification." They became known as the enemies of the message of Holy Grail in Dan Brown's *The Da Vinci Code*.

1928 Vicar of Glastonbury supposedly found the silver casket of Joseph of Arimathea half buried in ground, removed it to Church. Nothing known about this today, however.

1930 Dr. Karl Hans Fuchs of Thule Society and Rudolph Hess visited Rosslyn Chapel.

1933 Adolph Hitler became Chancellor of Germany.

1933 Nazi SS Major Otto Rahn sent to Corbières to search for legendary Cathar treasure.

1934 Heinrich Himmler rented Wewelsburg Castle as spiritual home of Schutzstaffel.

1937 German archaeologists and occultist Otto Rahn published *The Courtiers of Lucifer*, which claimed that Cathars were Aryans who venerated Holy Grail as symbol of Lucifer. Rahn argued that Christianity was Jewish religion designed to benefit Jews.[19]

1938 (12 Mar.) The Anschluss (unification) of Germany and Austria.

1938 German SS snatched supposed Grail Hallow, the "Spear of Longinus" from Hapsburg Treasure House in Vienna, Austria, and delivered it to Adolf Hitler at Bertesgarden.

1938 German archaeologist Albrecht found in Iran a Persian castle (Takti-Tactus) near Mount of Shiz, might be where Holy Grail was taken. It was a round castle near deep ("bottomless") lake.

1939 Mysterious accidental death of Otto Rahn.

1939	Outbreak of World War II following German invasion of Poland.
1940 (10 May)	Rudolph Hess's "peace mission" flies his personal Messerschmitt to Scotland. However, he might have been attempting to obtain Holy Grail from Rosslyn shrine. His plane crashed, and he was imprisoned for remainder of his life.
1944	Massacre and destruction of Oradour-sur-Glane by SS Division Das Reich under command of General Lammerding. Six hundred kilos of gold bullion apparently hijacked from Nazis by Resistance.[20]
1945 (30 Apr.)	"Spear of Longinus" retrieved by General George Patton's American army. Hitler supposedly died same hour and day.
1945	Discovery of *Nag Hammadi*, codices of Gnostic gospels, in middle Egypt by two Egyptian peasants. Forty-six different works, such as *Gospel of Philip* and *Gospel of Thomas*. They led to ideas of Jesus' sexual relationship, which began to come out in the 1960s.
1946 (4 Jan.)	General Dwight Eisenhower ordered Imperial regalia stolen by Nazis be returned to Austria, including Spear of Destiny.
1946 (26 Jul.)	Saunière estate bought by entrepreneur Noël Corbu from destitute Marie Dénarnaud, who was allowed to remain at villa with family. Perhaps as a selling ploy or *raisone d'etre* for allowing her to

stay, Marie frequently referred to a treasure at Rennes and promised to reveal details before her death. Unfortunately, she didn't or couldn't reveal the secret at her death.

1946	*King Jesus*, a novel by Robert Graves, twentieth-century mythographer, suggested Jesus' lineage and marriage were concealed to keep them safe. He suggested: "Jesus' lineage and marriage were concealed from all but a select circle of royalist leaders. To protect the royal bloodline, this marriage would have been kept secret from the Romans and the Herodian tetrarchs, and after the crucifixion of Jesus, the protection of his wife and family would have been a sacred trust for those few who knew their identity. All reference to the marriage of Jesus would have been deliberately obscured, edited, or eradicated."[21]
1947	Taamireh Bedouin, a goat-herder, discovered cache of scrolls in cave on northwestern shore of Dead Sea. Near Qumrân, probably Essene in origin, scrolls are the oldest religious texts in Middle East.
1948	Founding of Israel and return of Jews to Holy Land in fulfillment of prophecy.
1950	Pope Pius XII officially declared Virgin Mary was "Assumed" into heaven and not buried. "Assumption of the Virgin" idea was first broached by St. Augustine and Pope Gregory in sixth century.

This is contrary to idea she was buried in Ephesus, Jerusalem, southern France, or Wales.

1953 (29 Jan.) Marie Dénarnaud died without revealing secret of Saunière's supposed treasure. Many of Saunière's possessions had been sold or stolen by this time.

1955 (10 Apr.) Opening of *l'Hôtel de la Tour* at Rennes-le-Château by Noël Corbu.

1955 Copper Scroll (Qumrân) opened and deciphered as an inventory of hidden treasures.

1955 London's *Daily Express* published article demanding recognition of Merovingian rights.

1956 (12, 13, 14 Jan.) Sensationalist reporter Albert Salamon wrote first articles on exaggerated claim of 18,5000,00 gold francs of treasure of Blanche de Castile at Rennes-le-Château. Ran in local newspaper *La Dépâche du Midi* from fabricated account given by Noël Corbu, proprietor of Tower Hotel in Rennes.

1956 (7 May) *Le Prieuré de Sion* (Priory of Sion) officially registered with "Sous Préfecture" of Saint-Julien-en-Genevois (Haute Savoie) by Pierre Plantard (1920–2000). It was formed in 1954 just after death of Paul Le Cour, who believed in formation of Orders of Knighthood called *Prieurés*. Pierre Plantard did not so much "copy" ideas of Paul Le Cour as use them as basis for his own creations of 1960s to 1970s.[22]

1960 Pierre Plantard and Phillipe de Chérisey meet Gerard de Sède. Thus started sinister cabal of Priory of Sion.

1961 (May) *L'ORTF* filmed television *program* on Rennes-le-Château titled *La roue tourne,* highlighting spectacular claims of treasure.

1961 George F. Jowett's romantic British-Israelite publication, *The Drama of the Lost Disciples,* renewed interest in early legends of Joseph of Arimathea.

1962 Gérerd de Sède's *Les Templiers sont parmi nous* published, with appendix by Pierre Plantard.

1962 (14 Jun.) Noël Corbu's *L'Histoire de Rennes-le-Château* deposited in archives at Carcassonne.

1962–1965 Second Vatican Council commissioned revision of 1570 Roman Mission. When report came out in 1970, the epithet for Mary Magdalene is no longer "penitent." (See 1969.)

1962 (3 Dec.) Descadeillas's *Notice sur Rennes-le-Château* deposited in archives at Carcassone. Descadeillas was an historian-librarian who attempted to check out Corbu's claims for Saunière and Rennes-le-Château. He found most claims to be ludicrous.

1963 (22 Nov.)	Assassination of President John F. Kennedy, whose White House became known as Camelot. An increased interest in Grail may stem from this period.
1964	Henri Lobineau's *Genealogy of the Merovingian Kings* deposited in Bibliothèque Nationale. Lonbineau was a pseudonym for Pierre Plantard. Inspired by Louis Saurel's article, *"Les rois et les gouvernements de la France, des origins à nos jours,"* in French magazine *Les Cahiers de l'Histoire* (Num. 1, 1960). Plantard added fictitious "Merovingian ancestors."
1965	Julien Origas, a French ex-Nazi, joined Order of the Solar Temple. All excavations in and around Rennes-le-Château were formally prohibited.[23]
1966 (13 May)	*A Merovingian Treasure at Rennes-le-Château* deposited in Bibliothèque Nationale (again by Plantard under a pseudonym).
1966 (20 Jun.)	False extracts from Eugene Stüblein's book deposited in Bibliothèque Nationale (regarding Rennes-le-Château).
1967 (20 Mar.)	Phillip de Chérisey's forged documents, *Le Serpent Rouge,* planted in Bibliothèque Nationale.
1967 (27 Apr.)	Forged documents *Les Dossiers secrets d'Henri Lobineau* were surreptitiously deposited in Bibliothèque Nationale. It has never been explained why, if *Les Dossiers Secrets* were so secret, they were deposited in a national library where anyone could read them.[24]
1967	Raphael Patai's book, *The Hebrew Goddess,* outlined idea of need of the feminine, upon which later books on bloodline of Holy Grail depended.
1967 (Oct.)	Gérard de Sède's sensationalist book, *L'Or de Rennes,* was published. It was originally a Pierre Plantard manuscript that was constantly refused by various publishers until rewritten by de Sède, a professional author. Philippe de Chérisey was entitled to a share of book's profits for creating and providing manuscripts.
1968	William E. Phipps's article, "Did Jesus or Paul Marry?" *Journal of Ecumenical Studies* 5, (1968), 741–44.
1969	John W. Taylor's 1906 book, *The Coming of the Saints* was reprinted, becoming one of the last major British-Israel publications.
1969	Ogden Kraut published his controversial book, *Jesus Was Married,* quoting Mormon prophets, apostles, and other leaders saying that Jesus Christ was a polygamist and had a number of children. This small self-published book may have some influence on William E. Phipps.
1969	Roman Catholic Church revised liturgy for Mary Magdalene's feast.

It removed taint of prostitute or penitent from her canonization. Mention of both Lazarus and Bride (Psalm 45) were also deleted. The next year the revised Roman missal came out to that effect. (See 1962–65.)

1970 William E. Phipps's brilliant and scholarly book, *Was Jesus Married?* (New York: Harper & Row, 1970), set stage for most later publications with this as their thesis.

1970 (Dec.) Henry Lincoln first met Gerard de Sède.

1971 (Feb.) Lincoln first visited Rennes-le-Château.

1971 (Mar.) De Sède gave Lincoln solution and key to code for Parchment one.[25]

1971 John Michell's influential book *The City of Revelation* was published. It began to popularize *gematria* concepts.

1971 (Sept.) BBC filmed programs at Rennes-le-Château.

1972 (12 Feb.) BBC broadcast Lincoln's *The Lost Treasure of Jerusalem?*

1972 (Winter) William E. Phipps, "The Case for a Married Jesus," *Dialogue: A Journal of Mormon Thought* 7 (4) 1972. First scholarly treatise on Christ's marriage within LDS Church circles, written by a non-Mormon.

1973 William E. Phipps published *The Sexuality of Jesus*, continuing his ideas of a married Christ.

1973 Jean-Luc Chaumeil, journalist who had become deeply involved with Pierre Plantard, wrote story claiming that secret dossiers were a hoax.

1974 René Descadeillas's scholarly book *Mythologie du Trésor de Rennes* was published debunking many "facts" presented by Corbu, de Sède, and Lincoln. But myth had grown too strong for Descadeillas's fine research and more interest in hoax continued unabated.

1974 (30 Oct.) Lincoln's *The Priest, the Painter, and the Devil* was broadcast by BBC.

1975 Director Terry Gilliam's film and irreverent Grail spoof, *Monty Python and the Holy Grail,* was successfully released and remains popular.

1978 Eric Rohmer's film, *Perceval le Gallois,* stuck closely to story of Arthurian/Grail quest through work of Chrétian de Troyes.

1978 (Nov.) Dr. Vern G. Swanson began research on bloodline of Christ, Joseph Smith Jr., and Holy Grail.

1979 (Mar.) Henry Lincoln first met Pierre Plantard and de Chérisey.

1979 (27 Nov.) Lincoln's BBC broadcast, *The Shadow of the Templars,* was aired.

1981 (17 Jan.) Hoaxster Pierre Plantard claimed to have been made Grand Master of Priory of Sion, where up to that time he had been its General.

1981	John Boorman's film *Excalibur* explored some underlying pre-Christian themes of Holy Grail.	**1988**	Carbon dating of Shroud of Turin established its earliest possible origin to be A.D. 1260.
1982	Lincoln, Baigent, and Leigh published *Holy Blood, Holy Grail* and began frenzy for next two decades of books and research on Holy Grail. It claimed that Jesus and Mary Magdalene were married, Jesus survived crucifixion, they went to southern France, and the Merovingian dynasty was their posterity.	**1988**	Gérard de Sède published *Rennes-le-Château: Le dossier, les impostures, les pahtasmes, les hypothèses* admitting dossiers were forged and that the Merovingian line does not exist today.
1984	Plantard, supposedly because of "*maneouvres*" by his "Anglo-American" brethren that he could no longer put up with, retired in 1984. For all we know the Priory disintegrated, or went to Barcelona with an attorney as its current Grand Master.	**1989**	Director Steven Spielberg's action film *Indiana Jones and the Last Crusade* was based upon a story by George Lucas. Starring Harrison Ford, it was third film in Indiana Jones trilogy.
1985 (Jul.)	Death of Phillipe de Chérisey, forger of *Le Serpent Rouge* and *Les Dossiers Secrets d'Henri Lobineau*, and co-conspirator with Pierre Plantard.	**1990 (Apr.)**	In *Vaincre* (#1, 11 April 1990) Pierre Plant was quoted from his article "The Merovingian Myth": "I have never claimed to be a descendant in the male line of Dagobert II, nor a pretender to the French throne, anymore than I have ever claimed to be a descendant of Jesus. All that is a writer's hoax, the aim of which was and remains the generation of financial profit from the publishing of books or the making of films." He also said the Priory never had anything to do with the Knights Templars, being founded in 1681, but related to Compagnie du Saint Sacrament and to Les Enfants de Saint Vincent.
1986	Duke of Kent declared that ancient references to such extreme-sounding physical penalties as "having one's tongue cut out and his throat slit" if he broke his oaths would be removed from candidates' obligations in United Grand Lodge of England.		
1986	Baigent, Leigh, and Lincoln's *The Messianic Legacy* was published.	**1991**	First public access to full collection of Dead Sea Scrolls.
1988	Supposed Poussin tomb was demolished by landowner because of too many trespassers.	**1991**	Director Terry Gilliam's second film debunking the Grail myth. *The Fisher King* starred Robin Williams.

| 1992 | Barbara Thiering's on-the-edge research *Jesus the Man* was published, noting that Christ was human, married, then divorced, and survived the crucifixion (a theme that continues). |

| 1993 | Pierre Plantard was humiliated by Judge Thierry Jean-Pierre investigating the "Patrice Pelat Affair". When Plantard retired from Priory de Sion, supposedly Roger-Patrice Pelat was made Grand Master. This friend of François Mitterand was involved in a securities scandal and committed suicide. Plantard was detained and after 48 hours of questioning admitted that he had made it all up. |

| 1993 | Margaret Starbird's best-selling book, *The Woman with the Alabaster Jar: Mary Magdalene and the Holy Grail,* began to make marriage of Jesus and Magdalene more popular among Catholics. See also further books in 1998 and 2003. |

| 1996 | Laurence Gardner published *Bloodline of the Holy Grail: The Hidden Lineage of Jesus Revealed,* most complicated "Jesus and Mary Magdalene" were married book thus far. Faulty footnoting and exaggerated claims weaken this publication's acceptance among scholars. |

| 1996 | Andrew's and Schellenberger's *The Tomb of God* published. |

| 1996 (27 Sept.) | BBC's *Timewatch* program on Rennes-le-Château aired. Bill Cran |

of Invision Production applied basic rules of historical research confronting authors of *The Tomb of God* with questions for which they had no answers.

| 1996 | Robert Lomas and Christopher Knight publish their *Hiram Key* book, dealing with Templars, Freemasonry, Roslynn Chapel, and Holy Grail. |

| 1996 | The Stone of Destiny (Scone) was returned to Edinburgh Scotland from Westminister Abbey in London. |

| 1997 | Lynn Picknett and Clive Prince published their highly-controversial *The Templar Revelation: Secret Guardians of the True Identity of Christ.* |

| 1997 (Jun.) | Vern G., Amber C., and Angela R. Swanson traveled to Glastonbury to research the Holy Grail. |

| 1997 | Henry Lincoln's book *Key to the Sacred Pattern* published. |

| 1998 (Jun.) | Vern G. and Judy Swanson, with Jerald Jacobs, traveled to Scotland to study Rosslyn Chapel and research the Holy Grail. |

| 1998 (Jun.) | Mormon Tabernacle Choir under Craig Jessop sing in London (with encore) William Blake's *Jerusalem.* |

| 1999 (Jun.) | Vern G. and Angela Swanson, Jerald Jacobs, Cheryl Stewart traveled to England, Wales, and Scotland in search of Holy Grail. |

2000 (3 Feb.)	Death of Pierre Plantard (1920–2000).
2001 (Jun.)	Vern G. and Angela Swanson, Tony and Traci Fieldsted traveled to England, Wales, in search of Holy Grail.
2002 (Jun.)	Vern Swanson, Tony and Traci Fieldsted traveled to Italy, France, England to search for Holy Grail.
2002 TV's	*Discovery Channel* produced popular programs regarding Jesus and Mary Magdalene's possible marriage.
2003	TV's *History Channel* produced more programs regarding Christ's bloodline and marriage.
2003 (Jun.)	Vern and Amber Swanson, Fieldsteds traveled to England, Ireland, and Scotland in search of Holy Grail.
2003	Dan Brown's best-selling novel, *The Da Vinci Code* published, deals with most major "alternative" ideas of Christ's bloodline. LDS Church members and other Christians take great interest.
2003 (3 Nov.)	ABC "New" aired its sympathetic special "Jesus, Mary, and Da Vinci," dealt positively with *The Da Vinci Code,* hosted by Elizabeth Vargas.
2003 (Dec.)	Thoroughgoing debunking of Rennes and Priory hoax made by Bill Putnam and John Edwin Wood in *The Treasure of Rennes-le-Château: A Mystery Solved* book.

2004 (Jan.)	Mary Malouf wrote article for *Salt Lake Tribune* on interview with Vern G. Swanson about Holy Grail and bloodline of Jesus Christ to Joseph Smith.
2004 Feb.–Mar.	Brigham Young University Museum of Art hosted lecture series "Mystery, Metaphor and Meaning: LDS Perspectives on the Da Vinci Code." Discussion on *The Da Vinci Code* with religion professor Dr. Eric Huntsman "Mary Magdalene: Biblical Enigma," (25 February); art historians Dr. Steven Bule, "The Da Vinci Code: Separating Fact from Fiction" (11 March); Dr. Vern Swanson (25 March, 1 April) talking about its implications to Mormon theology. Huge audiences of 800–900 people crowded the Museum of Art to hear about Christ's marriage. Because Swanson dealt directly with topic, his lecture was removed from published account, which was agreeable to him.
2004 (Aug.)	Sunstone Symposium invited Margaret Starbird to speak and participate on panels regarding Holy Grail bloodline. Weakness of her arguments became apparent.
2004 (5–13 Sept.)	Vern Swanson, Angela and Jason Jones, Traci and Tony Fieldsted travel to Israel to study sacred sites.
2005 (Feb.)	Tony Robinson (presenter/editor), "The Real Da Vinci Code," Channel 4, United Kingdom Television Documentary, was very negative on the subject.

2005 (Spring)	TV's History Channel aired *Beyond The Da Vinci Code*.
2005 (28 Jun.)	NBC, "Secrets of the Code," *Dateline with Stone Phillips*.
2006 (24 Mar.)	The History Channel "Digging for the Truth," with Josh Bernstein examines DNA from Merovingian bones and discovers no genetic relationship between them and near eastern genetics.
2006 (May)	Columbia Pictures produced and Ron Howard directed movie version of Brown's *The Da Vinci Code* novel, further popularizing idea that Jesus and Mary Magdalene were married.
2006 (Sept.)	Vern Swanson's magnum opus, *The Dynasty of the Holy Grail: Mormonism's Sacred Bloodline*, published.
2007 (Autumn)	Dan Brown's novel, *The Solomon Key* released. It deals with Masons and Mormons, set in New England and Washington D. C.

Notes

1. Most of the dates given are from Cleon Skousen, not Floyd Jones, *The Chronology of the Old Testament*. There is a difference of about twenty-four years in most cases between the dates provided by these two different sources.
2. Laidler, *Head of God*, 58.
3. Blake and Blezard, *Arcadian Cipher*, 265.
4. Gardner, *Illustrated Bloodline of the Holy Grail*, 100.
5. Starbird, *Mary Magdalene*, 167.
6. Starbird, *Magdalen's Lost Legacy*, 38.
7. Godwin, *Holy Grail*, 115.
8. Elliott, *Apocryphal New Testament*, 1:402.
9. I am indebted to Starbird for this and other dates; *Magdalen's Lost Legacy*, 160.
10. Elliott, *Apocryphal New Testament*, 3:163.
11. Barber, *Holy Grail*, 65; Godwin, *Holy Grail*, 10.
12. Morgan, *Holy Grail*, 36.
13. Starbird, *Magdalen's Lost Legacy*, 160.
14. Barber, *Holy Grail*, 130.
15. Allix, *Ecclesiastic History of the Ancient Church of Albigenses*, 1.
16. Burstein, *Secrets of the Da Vinci Code*, 180.
17. Gospel of Mary Magdalene (Papyrus Berolinensis 10) as quoted in Seaich (1980), 41, and Craig L. Tholson, 4:242. See also Seaich (1980), 42, regarding the third century "Bridal Chamber" scene in Questions of Mary, recorded by Epiphanius in the Panarion. There, Jesus is shown having carnal intercourse with Mary Magdalene, saying, "We must so do in order to have eternal life."
18. Patton and Mackness, *Sacred Treasure, Secret Power*, 305.
19. Morgan, *Holy Grail*, 137.
20. Patton and Mackness, *Sacred Treasure, Secret Power*, 306. A number of exact quotations are borrowed in the chronology section of their book for my book, for which I am grateful.
21. Margaret Starbird, as quoted in Burstein, *Secrets of the Da Vinci Code*, 20.
22. Paul Smith, http://priory-of-sion.com/psp/id22.html (2003).
23. Ibid.
24. Newman, *Real History behind The Da Vinci Code*, 69.
25. Putnam and Wood, *Treasure of Rennes-le-Château*, 237.

BIBLIOGRAPHY

This extensive bibliography represents the literature cited in the bibliographies of books on the Holy Grail and related material. Those works cited with an asterisk represents literature that the author has read and purveyed. The author is interested in knowing from others, which books in this bibliography should be rearranged, added, deleted or read more thoroughly. The author's e-mail address is vern.swanson@nebo.edu for those who have suggestions.

TOPICS LISTED IN THE FOLLOWING ORDER

MORMON & LDS RELATED

Abbott, Scot. Review of *Mormonism's Temple of Doom*, William J. Schnoebelen and James R. Spencer, *Dialogue: A Journal of Mormon Thought* 22, 2 (1989): 151–53.

*Anderson, James H. *God's Covenant Race*. Salt Lake City: Deseret News Press, 1938, 1943.

Anderson, Mary Audentia Smith. *Ancestry and Posterity of Joseph Smith and Emma Hale*. Independence, Mo.: Herald Publishing House, 1929.

*Anderson, Richard L. *Joseph Smith's New England Heritage: Influences of Grandfathers Solomon Mack and Asael Smith*. Salt Lake City: Deseret Book, 1971, 2004.

*Andrew, Laurel B. *The Early Temples of the Mormons*. Albany: State University of New York Press, 1978. 119–32, 142–45.

*Andrus, Hyrum L. *Joseph Smith—The Man and the Seer*. Salt Lake City: Deseret Book, 1963.

*———. *Joseph Smith and World Government*. Salt Lake City: Hawkes, 1963.

*———. *Doctrinal Commentary on the Pearl of Great Price*. Salt Lake City: Deseret Book, 1969.

*———. *Doctrines of the Kingdom*. Salt Lake City: Bookcraft, 1973.

*Andrus, Hyrum, and Helen Mae. *They Knew the Prophet*. Salt Lake City: Bookcraft, 1974.

Arbaugh, George B. *Revelation in Mormonism: Its Character and Changing Forms*. Chicago: University of Chicago Press, 1932.

*Ashment, Edward H. "The LDS Temple Ceremony: Historical Origins and Religious Value." *Dialogue: A Journal of Mormon Thought* 27, 3 (1994): 289–98.

*Barker, James L. *Apostasy from the Divine Church*. Salt Lake City: Deseret News Press, 1960.

*Barrett, Ivan J. *Joseph Smith and the Restoration*. Provo, Utah: Young House, 1973.

Barron, Howard H. *Judah, Past and Future*. Bountiful, Utah: Horizon Publishers and Distributors, 1979.

*Bates, Irene M., and E. Gary Smith. *Lost Legacy: The Mormon Office of Presiding Patriarch*. Urbana: University of Illinois Press, 1996.

Beecher, Maureen Ursenbach, and Lavina Fielding Anderson, eds. *Sisters in Spirit*. Urbana: University of Illinois, 1987.

Belnap, H. "A Mysterious Preacher." *Juvenile Instructor* 21 (15 March 1886).

Bennett, Archibald F. "The Ancestry of Joseph Smith the Prophet." *Utah Genealogical and Historical Magazine*, 20 (April 1929): 66–69.

———. "The Children of Ephraim." *Genealogical and Historical Magazine* 21 (April 1930): 67–77.

———. "Did Joseph of Arimathea Come to Britain?" *Deseret News*, September 1932, 3.

———. *Saviors on Mount Zion*. Salt Lake City: Deseret Sunday School Union Board, 1950.

Benson, Ezra Taft. "A Message to Judah from Joseph."

Discourse given at Calgary, Alberta, 2 May 1976.

———. "In His Steps." Brigham Young University *Speeches of the Year.* Provo, Utah: Brigham Young University Press, 1979.

Boren, Kerry Ross, and Boren, Lisa Lee. *The Widow's Son: The Esoteric History of the Prophet Joseph Smith and the Origin of Mormonism.* Salt Lake City, 1997.

———. *The Gold of Carre-Shinob.* Springville, Utah: Bonneville Books, 1998.

*———. *Following the Ark of the Covenant: Solving the Mystery of Sanpete County.* Springville, Utah: Cedar Fort, 2000.

*Brooke, John L. *The Refiner's Fire: The Making of Mormon Cosmology, 1644–1844.* New York: Cambridge University Press, 1994.

*Brown, S. Kent. "James the Just and the Question of Peter's Leadership in the Light of New Sources." *Sidney B. Sperry Symposium.* Provo, Utah: Brigham Young University Press, 1973.

*Brown, S. Kent, and Griggs, C. Wilfred. "The 40 Day Ministry." *Ensign,* August 1975.

*Brown, Matthew B. *All Things Restored.* American Fork, Utah: Covenant Communications, 2000.

*———. "David John Buerger, The Mysteries of Godliness." *Farms Review of Books* 10, 1 (1998): 97–131.

*Brown, Matthew B., Smith, Paul T. *Symbols in Stone: Symbolism on the Early Temples of the Restoration.* American Fork, Utah: Covenant Communications, 1997.

*Buerger, David John. "The Development of the Mormon Temple Endowment Ceremony." *Dialogue: A Journal of Mormon Thought* 20 (Winter 1987): 33–76.

*———. *The Mysteries of Godliness: A History of Mormon Temple Worship.* San Francisco: Smith Research Associates, 1994.

*Bule, Steve. "Leonardo Da Vinci." Museum of Art lecture series *"Mystery, Metaphor, and Meaning: LDS Perspectives on The Da Vinci Code,"* Brigham Young University, Provo, Utah, 11 March 2004.

Burnstein, Rabbi E. M. "Faith and Ideals of the Jewish Race." *Utah Genealogical and Historical Magazine* 16 (July 1925): 104–10.

*Bushman, Richard L. *Joseph Smith and the Beginnings of Mormonism.* Urbana: University of Illinois Press, 1984.

Carpenter, J. Hatton. "Preservation of the Purity of Israel's Race." *Utah Genealogical and Historical Magazine* 21 (October 1930): 163–71.

Carr, Robin L. *Freemasonry in Nauvoo.* Bloomington: Masonic Book Club and Illinois Lodge Research, 1989.

*Carrigan, Cky J. "Did Jesus Christ Marry and Father Children? A Survey of Mormon Teachings on the Marital and Parental Status of the Son of God." Lecture presented at the annual meeting of the Evangelical Ministries to New Religions, New Orleans Baptist Theological Seminary, 30 January 2004.

*Church Educational System Manual. *Church History in the Fulness of Times.* Salt Lake City: The Church of Jesus Christ of Latter-day Saints, 2005.

Clawson, Rudger. *Journal.* LDS Church Archives, 1899. 374–75.

*Compton, Todd. *In Sacred Loneliness: The Plural Wives of Joseph Smith.* Salt Lake City: Signature Books, 1997.

*Collier, Fred C. *Unpublished Revelations of the Prophets and Presidents of the Church of Jesus Christ of Latter Day Saints.* Salt Lake City: Collier's Publishing, 1981.

*———. *The Teachings of President Brigham Young: Vol. 3, 1852–1854.* Salt Lake City: Colliers Publishing, 1987. Volumes 1 and 2 have not been published.

*Cook, Lyndon, and Ehat, Andrew. *Words of Joseph Smith.* Provo, Utah: Brigham Young University Press, 1980.

*Corbett, Pearson H. *Hyrum Smith, Patriarch.* Salt Lake City: Deseret Book, 1963.

Cowdery, Oliver. "To the Elders of the Church of the Latter Day Saints," *Latter Day Saint's Messenger and Advocate.* Kirtland, Ohio. December 1835.

Cowley, Matthias F. *Wilford Woodruff.* Salt Lake City: Bookcraft, 1964.

*Cox, John H. "The Influence of the English-Speaking People in Preparing the Way for the Restoration." Paper presented to Young Men General Board, The Church of Jesus Christ of Latter-day Saints, Salt Lake City, 18 May 1989; revised 25 August 1999.

*Cureton, Nancy. "Many LDS Have Common Ancestors." *Church News*, 23 December 1984.

*Darter, Francis M. "A Root of Jesse." In *Zion's Redemption: Jerusalem and Zion of America to Be Redeemed.* Salt Lake City: Deseret News Publishing, 1933.

*Durham, Reed C., Jr. "Is There No Help for the Widow's Son?" Unpublished typescript of lecture given to the Mormon History Association's annual meeting held at Nauvoo, Illinois, 20 April 1974.

Edmonds, John K. *Through Temple Doors.* Salt Lake City: Bookcraft, 1978.

*Ehat, Andrew. "'They Might Have Known That He Was Not a Fallen Prophet'—The Nauvoo Journal of Joseph Fielding," *BYU Studies 19, 2.*

*———. "Joseph Smith's Introduction of the Temple Ordinance and the 1844 Mormon Succession Question." Master's thesis, Brigham Young University, 1982.

*Ehat, Andrew, and Lyndon Cook. *Words of Joseph Smith.* Provo, Utah: Brigham Young University Press, 1980.

*Epperson, Steven. *Mormons and Jews: Early Mormon Theologies of Israel.* Salt Lake City: Signature Books, 1992.

Flanders, Robert. "Brother Brigham and Sister Emma: Causes and Consequences of an Historic Mormon Antagonism," Utah: USU Special Collections, 1975.

*Foster, Craig L. "Irene M. Bates and E. Gary Smith, Lost Legacy: The Mormon Office of Presiding Patriarch." Book review, *Journal of Mormon History* (Spring 1997): 181–86.

*Fraser, Gordon H. *Is Mormonism Christian?* Chicago: Moody Press, 1957.

Frawley, D. *Gods, Sages and Kings.* Utah: Passage Press, 1991.

*Galbraith, David B., and D. Kelly Ogden, and Andrew C. Skinner. *Jerusalem, the Eternal City.* Salt Lake City: Deseret Book, 1996.

Gileadi, Avraham. *The Last Days: Types and Shadows from the Bible and The Book of Mormon.* Salt Lake City: Deseret Book, 1991.

Godfrey, Kenneth W. "Freemasonry in Nauvoo" and "Freemasonry and the Temple." *Encyclopedia of Mormonism,* 2:527–29.

———. "The Road to Carthage Led West." BYU Studies 8, 2 (Winter 1968): 204.

———. "Joseph Smith and the Masons." *Journal of the Illinois State Historical Society* 64 (Spring 1971): 79–90.

Goodwin, Sam H. *Mormonism and Masonry: A Utah Point of View.* Salt Lake City: Sugarhouse Press, 1921.

*Grant, Jedediah. In *Journal of Discourses.* 26 vols. London: Latter-day Saints' Book Depot, 1854–86.

Gregg, Thomas. *The Prophet of Palmyra.* New York, 1890.

Griffith, Michael T. *A Ready Reply: Answering Challenging Questions about the Gospel.* Bountiful, Utah: Horizon, 1994.

Gunn, Rodger S. Mormonism: Challenge and Defense. Salt Lake City: Hawkes Publishers, 1973.

Gunnison, John W. *The Mormons; or, Latter-day Saints, in the Valley of the Great Salt Lake.* Philadelphia: Lippincott and Grambo, 1852.

Hallwas, John E. "Mormon Nauvoo from a Non-Mormon Perspective." *Journal of Mormon History* 16 (1990).

Hamblin, William J., Daniel C. Peterson, and George L. Mitton. "Mormon in the Fiery Furnace or, Loftes Tryk Goes to Cambridge." Review of the *Refiner's Fire: The Making of Mormon Cosmology,* by John L. Brooke. *Review of Books on the Book of Mormon,* 6, 2 (1994).

Hansen, Klaus T. "The Theory and Practice of the Political Kingdom of God in Mormon History, 1829–1890." Master's thesis, Brigham Young University, 1959.

*———. *Quest for Empire, the Political Kingdom of God and the Council of Fifty in Mormon History.* Lansing: Michigan State University Press, 1967.

*Hansen, Vaughn E. *Whence Came They? Israel, Britain, and the Restoration.* Springville, Utah: Cedar Fort, 1993.

Harmer, Earl W. *Joseph Smith and Our Destiny: A Brief Vital Story of God's Covenant Race from Patriarchal Times to the Present of the Mormon Church.* Salt Lake City, 1942.

Hinckley, Gordon B. *Faith, the Essence of True Religion.* Salt Lake City: Deseret Book, 1989.

*Hoekema, Anthony A. *Mormonism.* Grand Rapids, Mich.: Eerdmans, 1963.

*Hogan, Mervin B. "Mormonism and Freemasonry: The Illinois Episode." *The Little Masonic Library* 2 (1977).

———. "Founding Minutes of the Nauvoo Lodge, U.D." Des Moines, Iowa: Research Lodge No. 2, 1971.

———. "The Two Joseph Smiths' Masonic Experiences" (17 January 1987): 13.

———. "Freemasonry and Mormon Ritual." MS, 1991.

*Hollstein, Lynne. "Joseph Smith Has Famous Kin." *[LDS] Church News* (23 December 1978): 9–10.

*Holzapfel, Richard Neitzel, Thomas A. Wayment, Eric D. Huntsman, and Andrew C. Skinner. *What Da Vinci Didn't Know: LDS Perspectives on the Code.* Roundtable discussion on CD. Salt Lake City: Deseret Book, 2004.

*Homer, Michael W. "Similarity of Priesthood in Masonry: The Relationship between Freemasonry and Mormonism." *Dialogue: A Journal of Mormon Thought* 27, 3 (Fall 1994): 1–113.

Howe, Eber D. *Mormonism Unvailed; or, A Faithful Account of That Singular Imposition and Delusion, from Its Rise to the Present Time.* Painesville, Ohio: The Author, 1834.

Hullinger, Robert N. *Joseph Smith's Response to Skepticism.* Salt Lake City: Signature Books, 1992.

Humpherys, Blanche. *You and I, Who Are We? Our Humpherys Heritage.* Salt Lake City: Northwest Publishing, 1992.

Huntington, Oliver B. *Journal 1847–1900.* Special Collections, Brigham Young University.

*Huntsman, Eric D. "Mary Magdalene: Biblical Enigma." Original presentation part of Museum of Art lecture series "*Mystery, Metaphor, and Meaning: LDS Perspectives on The Da Vinci Code,*" *Brigham Young University, Provo, Utah, 25 February 2004.* Revised presentation, 26 May 2004, KBYU Studios.

*Hyde, Orson. In *Journal of Discourses.* 26 vols. London: Latter-day Saints' Book Depot, 1854–86.

Irving, Gordon. "The Law of Adoption: One Phase of the Development of the Mormon Concept of Salvation, 1830–1900." *BYU Studies* 14, 3 (Spring 1974).

Ivins, Anthony W. "Israel in History and Genealogy." *Utah Genealogical and Historical Magazine* 23 (January 1932): 1–9.

———. *Journal.* 21 vols. LDS Church Archives, Salt Lake City, Utah.

———. *Mormonism and Freemasonry.* Salt Lake City: Deseret Book, 1934.

Jackson, Kent P. *Lost Tribes and Last Days: What Modern Revelation Tells Us about the Old Testament.* Salt Lake City: Deseret Book, 2005.

———. "Revelations Concerning Isaiah (D&C 86 and 113)." In *The Doctrine and Covenants. Vol. 1 of Studies in Scripture series.* Salt Lake City: Deseret Book, 1989.

Jenson, Andrew, ed. *Historical Record.* 9 vols. Salt Lake City: 1882–90.

———. *Autobiography of Andrew Jenson.* Salt Lake City: Deseret News Press, 1938.

Jessee, Dean C. "The John Taylor Nauvoo Journal." *BYU Studies* 23, 3 (Summer 1983).

———. *Personal Writings of Joseph Smith.* Salt Lake City: Deseret Book, 1984.

Johansen, Jerald R. *After the Martyrdom: What Happened to the Family of Joseph Smith?* Bountiful, Utah: Horizon Publishers, 1997.

*Johnson, Benjamin F. *My Life's Review.* Independence, Mo.: Zion's Printing, 1947.

*Johnson, Frank J., and William J. Leffler. *Jews and Mormons: Two Houses of Israel.* Hoboken, N.J.: Ktav Publishing House, 2000.

Jospe, Raphael, Truman G. Madsen, and Seth Ward, eds. *Covenant and Chosenness in Judaism and*

Mormonism. Provo, Utah: FARMS, 2001.

Kelly, Charles, ed. *The Journals of John D. Lee, 1846–47 and 1859.* Salt Lake City: University of Utah, 1984.

*Kimball, Heber C. In *Journal of Discourses.* 26 vols. London: Latter-day Saints' Book Depot, 1854–86.

Kimball, Mary Ellen. Journal. LDS Church Archives, Salt Lake City, Utah.

Kimball, Stanley B. "Heber C. Kimball and Family, the Nauvoo Years." *BYU Studies* 15, 4 (1975): 458.

*———. *Heber C. Kimball: Mormon Patriarch and Pioneer.* Urbana: University of Illinois Press, 1986.

*———. *On the Potter's Wheel: The Diaries of Heber C. Kimball.* Salt Lake City: Signature Books, 1987.

*Kraut, Ogden. *Jesus Was Married.* Salt Lake City, 1969, 1970.

*———. *The Segregation of Israel.* Dugway, Utah: Pioneer Press, 1979.

*Larsen, Stan, ed. *A Ministry of Meetings: The Apostolic Diaries of Rudger Clawson.* Salt Lake City: Signature Books, 1993.

Lightner, Mary Elizabeth Rollins. *The Life and Testimony of Mary Lightner.* 1905. Reprint, Dugway, Utah: Pioneer, 1966.

Littke, Joseph C. "The Mission and Travels of the Israelitish Peoples." *Utah Genealogical and Historical Magazine* 25 (January 1934): 1–13.

*Ludlow, Victor L. *Isaiah: Prophet, Seer, and Poet.* Salt Lake City: Deseret Book, 1982.

*MacGregor, Daniel. *A Marvelous Work and a Wonder: The Gospel Restored.* Independence, Mo.: Board of Publications, Church of Christ Temple Lot, 1923.

*Madsen, Truman G., ed. *The Temple in Antiquity.* Provo, Utah: Brigham Young University Religious Studies Center, 1984.

———. *Joseph Smith the Prophet.* Salt Lake City: Bookcraft, 1989.

*Martin, Walter R. *Kingdom of the Cults.* Grand Rapids, Mich.: Zondervan Press, 1965.

Matthews, Robert. *"A Plainer Translation": Joseph Smith's Translation of the Bible.* Provo, Utah: Brigham Young University Press, 1975.

———. "Our Heritage from Joseph of Israel." *Thy People Shall Be My People and Thy God My God. Sidney B. Sperry Symposium on the Old Testament.* Salt Lake City: Deseret Book, 1994.

Mauss, Armand L. "Culture, Charisma and Change: Reflections on Mormon Temple Worship." *Dialogue: A Journal of Mormon Thought* 20 (Winter 1987): 79–80.

*———. "In Search of Ephraim: Traditional LDS Conceptions of Lineage and Race." *Sunstone Symposium* paper, 30 July 1998. Early LDS teachings about premortal life combined with British-Israelism and Anglo-Saxon triumphalism to produce before 1930 the traditional LDS understanding about race and lineage.

*McConkie, Bruce R. *Doctrinal New Testament Commentary.* 3 vols. Salt Lake City: Bookcraft, 1965–73.

———. *The Mortal Messiah.* 4 vols. Salt Lake City: Deseret Book, 1979–81.

———. *The Millennial Messiah.* Salt Lake City: Deseret Book, 1982.

*McConkie, Joseph Fielding. *His Name Shall Be Joseph: Ancient Prophecies of the Latter-day Seer.* Salt Lake City: Hawkes Publishing, 1980.

McDermott, Do J. "Joseph Smith and the Treasure of Hiram Abiff." *The Cryptic Scholar* (Winter/Spring 1991): 40–50.

*McGavin, E. Cecil. *Mormonism and Masonry.* Salt Lake City: Bookcraft, 1947, 1956.

———. *The Family of Joseph Smith.* Salt Lake City: Bookcraft, 1963.

*Millet, Robert L., and Joseph Fielding McConkie. *Our Destiny: The Call and Election of the House of Israel.* Salt Lake City: Bookcraft, 1993.

Morcombe, Joseph E. "Masonry and Mormonism." *Masonic Standard* 11 (1 September 1906).

Morley, Richard Henri. "The Life and Contributions of Isaac Morley." Master's thesis, Brigham Young University, 1965.

*Nelson, Dale W. *The Migrations, Alliances, and Power of Israel in Western Europe and Central Asia: A*

Latter-day Saint Perspective on the Lost Tribes. Orem, Utah: Sharpspear Press, 2001.

*Newell, Linda King, and Valeen Tippetts Avery. *Mormon Enigma: Emma Hale Smith.* New York: Doubleday, 1984.

*Nibley, Hugh W. *The Mythmakers.* Salt Lake City: Bookcraft, 1961.

*———. *The World and the Prophets.* Salt Lake City: Deseret Book, 1974.

*———. *The Message of the Joseph Smith Papyri: An Egyptian Endowment.* Salt Lake City: Deseret Book, 1975.

———. "The Facsimiles of the Book of Abraham." *Sunstone* 5–6 (December 1979): 49–51.

*———. *Nibley on the Timely and the Timeless.* Provo, Utah: Brigham Young University Religious Studies Center, 1978.

———. *Mormonism and Early Christianity.* Vol. 4 of *Collected Works of Hugh Nibley.* Salt Lake City: Deseret Book and FARMS, 1987.

———. *Lehi in the Desert; The World of the Jaredites; There Were Jaredites.* Vol. 5 of *Collected Works of Hugh Nibley.* Salt Lake City: Deseret Book and FARMS, 1988.

*———. *The Temple and Cosmos.* Salt Lake City: Deseret Book and FARMS, 1992.

———. "On the Sacred and the Symbolic." In Nibley's *Temples of the Ancient World: Ritual and Symbolism.* Edited by Donald W. Parry. Vol. 12 of *Collected Works of Hugh Nibley.* Salt Lake City: Deseret Book and FARMS, 1994.

*Nibley, Preston. ed, *History of Joseph Smith by His Mother, Lucy Mack Smith.* Salt Lake City: Bookcraft, 1958.

*Nielsen, Donna B. *Beloved Bridegroom: Finding Christ in Ancient Jewish Marriage and Family Customs.* Utah: Onyx Press, 1999.

*Norman, Keith. "Book Reviews of *Jesus Was Married* by Ogden Kraut and *Was Jesus Married?* by William E. Phipps." *Sunstone* 1–2 (Spring 1976): 87–92.

Nyman, Monte S. "The Second Gathering of the Literal Seed: Doctrines for Exaltation." *Sidney B. Sperry Symposium on the Doctrine and Covenants.* Salt Lake City: Deseret Book, 1989.

*Nyman, Monte S., and Charles D. Tate, eds. *Isaiah and the Prophets: Inspired Voices from the Old Testament.* Provo, Utah: Brigham Young University Religious Studies Center, 1984.

Ostling, Richard, and Joan Ostling. *Mormon America: The Power and the Promise.* San Francisco: Harper, 1999.

Owens, Lance S. "Joseph Smith and Kabbalah: The Occult Connection." *Dialogue: A Journal of Mormon Thought* 27, 3 (Fall 1994: 117–94).

*Packer, Boyd K. *The Holy Temple.* Salt Lake City: Bookcraft, 1980.

Parry, Donald W., Daniel C. Peterson, and John W. Welch, eds. *Echoes and Evidences of the Book of Mormon.* Provo, Utah: FARMS, 2002.

Paton, Chalmers I. "The Mormons and Masonic Symbols." *The Freemasons,* 3, 1871.

*Perego, Ugo. "Power of DNA—Discovering Lost and Hidden Relationships." Genealogy and Family History Conference, Brigham Young University, 28 July 2005.

*———. "Reconstructing Joseph Smith Y-Chromosome: Genealogical Application." *Journal of Mormon History,* August 2005.

Perkins, Keith W. "John Lothropp, Forebear of Prophets, Presidents, and Others." *British Isles.* A vol. in the Regional Studies series. Provo, Utah: Brigham Young University Department of Church History and Doctrine, 1990.

*Petersen, Mark E. *Joseph of Egypt.* Salt Lake City: Deseret Book, 1981.

*Petersen, Scott R. *Where Have All the Prophets Gone? Revelation and Rebellion in the Old Testament and the Christian World.* Springville, Utah: Cedar Fort, 2005.

*Petersen, Zina Nibley. "The Divine Feminine and the Goddess Movement: A Mormon Medievalist Looks at One Issue in Dan Brown's *The Da Vinci Code.*" Museum of Art lecture series "*Mystery, Metaphor, and Meaning: LDS Perspectives on The Da Vinci*

Code," Brigham Young University, Provo, Utah, March 2004. Typescript in author's possession.

Peterson, Daniel C., and Stephen D. Ricks. *Offenders for a Word: How Anti-Mormons Play Word Games to Attack the Latter-day Saints,* Salt Lake City: Deseret Book, 1998.

*Phipps, William E. "The Case for a Married Jesus." *Dialogue: A Journal of Mormon Thought* 7, 4 (Winter 1972).

Porter, Larry C. "A Study of the Origins of the Church of Jesus Christ of Latter-day Saints in the States of New York and Pennsylvania, 1816–1831." Ph.D. dissertation, Brigham Young University, 1971.

*Pratt, Orson. *The Seer.* Washington, D.C. 1 (1853): 169–72; November 1853: 135.

*———. In *Journal of Discourses.* 26 vols. London: Latter-day Saints' Book Depot, 1854–86.

Pratt, Parley P. *Autobiography of Parley P. Pratt.* Salt Lake City: Deseret Book, 1970.

*———. *Key to the Science of Theology.* Reprint, Salt Lake City: Deseret Book, 1978.

Prince, Gregory A. *Power from on High: The Development of Mormon Priesthood.* Salt Lake City: Signature Books, 1995.

Proctor, Scot Facer, and Maurine Jensen Proctor, eds. *The History of Joseph Smith by His Mother.* Salt Lake City: Bookcraft, 1996.

Quinn, D. Michael. "*Organizational Development and Social Origins of the Mormon Hierarchy, 1832–1932: A Prosopographical Study.*" Master's thesis, University of Utah, 1973.

———. "The Council of Fifty and Its Members, 1844–1945." *BYU Studies* 20, 2 (Winter 1980).

*———. *Early Mormonism and the Magic World View.* Salt Lake City: Signature Books, 1987, 1998.

*———. *The Mormon Hierarchy: Origins of Power.* Salt Lake City: Signature Books, 1994.

*———. *The Mormon Hierarchy: Extensions of Power.* Salt Lake City: Signature Books, 1997.

*Rees, Leslie Pearson. "*Finding the Lost Tribes of Israel in Scripture,* History, and Legend." Unpublished MS, 1905.

*Reynolds, George. *Are We of Israel?* Salt Lake City: Deseret Sunday School Union, 1916.

Richards, Franklin D. "Ephraim and Manasseh in America." *Utah Genealogical and Historical Magazine* 23 (April 1932): 66–71.

*Richards, LeGrand. *Israel! Do You Know?* Salt Lake City: Deseret Book, 1954.

*———. *The Mormons and the Jewish People.* Salt Lake City: The Church of Jesus Christ of Latter-day Saints, 1982. [Pamphlet.]

*Richards, Samuel W. *Millennial Star* 15 (17 December 1853): 825.

*Ricks, Stephen D., and John W. Welch. *The Allegory of the Olive Tree: The Olive, the Bible and Jacob.* Salt Lake City: Deseret Book and FARMS, 1994.

*Roberts, Allen D. "Where Are the All-Seeing Eyes? The Origin, Use, and Decline of Early Mormon Symbolism." *Sunstone* 4 (May–June 1979): 22–37.

Roberts, B. H. *Defense of the Faith and the Saints.* Salt Lake City: Deseret News, 1912.

———. "Masonry and Mormonism." *Improvement Era* 24, 10 (August 1921).

Robinson, Stephen E. "The Apocalypse of Adam." *BYU Studies* 17, 2 (Winter 1977).

Robison, Elwin C. *The First Mormon Temple: Design, Construction and Historic Context of the Kirtland Temple.* Provo, Utah: Brigham Young University Press, 1997.

Romney, Thomas C., *The Life of Lorenzo Snow,* Salt Lake City, 1955.

*Saunders, Marijo. "Rethinking the 'Code': BYU Sponsors lecture series on Dan Brown's popular thriller." *Provo Daily Herald,* 23 February 2004.

Scarlet, Peter. "Church's Lineage of Patriarchs Ties Mormonism to Old Testament Days." *Salt Lake Tribune,* 19 November 1994.

*Seaich, Eugene. *Mormonism, the Dead Sea Scrolls, and the Nag Hammadi Texts,* 1980.

*———. *Ancient Texts and Mormonism.* Murray, Utah: Sounds of Zion, 1983.

Shields, Stephen L. *Divergent Paths of the Restoration.* Los Angeles: Restoration Research, 1990.

Short, Dennis R. *Questions on Plural Marriage.* Salt Lake City: 1974.

*Shute, R. Wayne, Monte S. Nyman, and Randy L. Bott. *Ephraim Chosen of the Lord: What It Means to Be of the Tribe of Ephraim.* Orem, Utah: Millennial Press, 1999.

Skousen, Eric N. *Earth: In the Beginning.* Orem, Utah: Verity Publishing, 1997.

*Skousen, W. Cleon. *The Third Thousand Years.* Salt Lake City: Bookcraft, 1964.

*———. *Isaiah Speaks to Modern Times.* Salt Lake City: Ensign Publishing, 1984.

Smith, E. Gary. "The Patriarchal Crisis of 1845." *Dialogue: Journal of Mormon Thought* 16, 2 (Summer 1983).

Smith, George D., ed. *An Intimate Chronicle: The Journals of William Clayton.* Salt Lake City: Signature Books, 1991.

Smith, George Albert. "*Memoirs of George A. Smith.*" MS. LDS Church Archives, Salt Lake City, Utah.

———. *Sharing the Gospel with Others.* Salt Lake City: Deseret Book, 1948.

Smith, George D., Jr. "Review of *Evolution of the Mormon Temple Ceremony: 1920–1990,* by Jerald and Sandra Tanner." *Sunstone* (June 1991): 51.

Smith, John Corson. "Mormonism and Its Connection with Freemasonry 1842-3–4, Nauvoo, Illinois." *The American Tyler* 19 (1 February 1905): 323–26.

*Smith, Joseph, Jr. *History of The Church of Jesus Christ of Latter-day Saints.* Edited by B. H. Roberts. 7 vols. 2d ed. rev. Salt Lake City: The Church of Jesus Christ of Latter-day Saints, 1932–52.

*Smith, Joseph F. *Millennial Star* (19 May 1874): 312; 62 (1900): 97.

*———. *Gospel Doctrine: Sermons and Writings of President Joseph F. Smith.* Salt Lake City: Deseret Book, 1919.

*Smith, Joseph Fielding. *Essentials in Church History, Salt Lake City:* Deseret Book, 1922.

———. "The Mission of Ephraim." *Utah Genealogical and Historical Magazine* 31 (January 1930): 1–4.

———. *Life of Joseph F. Smith.* Salt Lake City: Deseret News Press, 1938.

*———. *Teachings of the Prophet Joseph Smith.* Selected by Joseph Fielding Smith. Salt Lake City: Deseret Book, 1938.

*———. *The Way to Perfection.* Salt Lake City: Deseret Book, 1940.

*———. *Doctrines of Salvation.* Compiled by Bruce R. McConkie. 3 vols. Salt Lake City: Bookcraft, 1954–56.

*———. *Answers to Gospel Questions.* Compiled by Joseph Fielding Smith, Jr. 5 vols. Salt Lake City: Deseret Book, 1957–1966.

*Smith, Lucy Mack. *History of Joseph Smith by His Mother.* Salt Lake City: Stevens and Wallis, 1945.

———. *Biographical Sketches of Joseph Smith, the Prophet, and His Progenitors for Many Generations.* London and Liverpool: S. W. Richards, 1853. Reprint, New York: Arno Press and the *New York Times,* 1969.

*Snow, Eliza R. *Biography and Family Record of Lorenzo Snow.* Salt Lake City: Deseret News Press, 1884.

———. "O My Father," *Hymns,* Salt Lake City: The Church of Jesus Christ of Latter-day Saints, 1985, 292.

*Snow, Erastus. In *Journal of Discourses.* 26 vols. London: Latter-day Saints' Book Depot, 1854–86.

Snow, Leroi C. "An Experience of My Father," *Improvement Era* (September 1933): 677–79.

Snowden, J. H. *The Truth about Mormonism.* New York: George H. Doran Co., 1926.

*Southerton, Simon G. *Losing a Lost Tribe: Native Americans, DNA, and the Mormon Church.* Salt Lake City: Signature Books, 2004.

*Sperry, Sidney B. *Doctrine and Covenants Compendium.* Salt Lake City: Bookcraft, 1960.

———. *Journal of Book of Mormon Studies* 4, 1 (Fall 1995).

Staker, Susan, ed. *Waiting for the World's End: The Diaries of Wilford Woodruff,* Salt Lake City: Deseret Book, 2006.

*Starbird, Margaret. "Mary Magdalene," presentation, Salt Lake *Sunstone Symposium,* August 2004.

———. "Mary Magdalene: Bride in Exile," presentation, Salt Lake *Sunstone Symposium,* 27 July 2005.

*Stephens, Trent D., and Meldrum, D. Jeffrey. *Evolution and Mormonism: A Quest for Understanding.* Salt Lake City: Signature Books, 2001.

*Stuy, Brian. ed. *Collected Discourses.* Sandy, Utah: B.H.S. Publishing, 1987.

*Swanson, Vern G. "On the Trail of the Holy Grail." Museum of Art lecture series *"Mystery, Metaphor, and Meaning: LDS Perspectives on The Da Vinci Code,"* Brigham Young University, Provo, Utah, 25 March 2004.

———. "Who is the Holy Ghost?" *Line Upon Line: Essays on Mormon Doctrine.* Typescript. Salt Lake City: Signature Books, 1989.

*Talmage, James E. *Deseret News,* 28 April 1902.

*———. *The House of the Lord.* Salt Lake City: *Deseret News,* 1912.

*———. *Jesus the Christ.* Salt Lake City: Deseret Book, 1915.

———. *"Mary Magdalene, Christ's Friend, Most Maligned Woman in History."* 11 pages dated 10 May 1917, LDS Church Historical Library, NFo/M221.09/T151m.

Tanner, Jerald, and Sandra Tanner. *Evolution of the Mormon Temple Ceremony: 1842–1990.* Salt Lake City: Utah Lighthouse Ministry, 1990.

*Taylor, John. *The Mediation and Atonement.* Salt Lake City: Deseret News Press, 1882.

Thomasson, Gordon C. "Foolsmate." *Dialogue: Journal of Mormon Thought* 6 (Autumn–Winter 1971).

Thompson, John E. *The Masons, the Mormons and the Morgan Incident.* Ames: Iowa Research Lodge, n.d.

*Tolworthy, Christ. "What was the Holy Grail?" http://www.bibleman.net/The_Holy_Grail.htm, regarding A.D. 570 and the Great Apostasy.

Toscano, Margaret M. "Beyond Matriarchy, Beyond Patriarchy," *Dialogue: A Journal of Mormon Thought* 21, 1 (Spring, 1988): 32–57.

*Toscano, Margaret, and Paul Toscano. *Strangers in Paradox: Explorations in Mormon Theology.* Salt Lake City: Signature Books, 1990.

Tucker, Pomeroy. *Origin, Rise and Progress of Mormonism.* New York: D. Appleton, 1867.

*Tullidge, Edward W. *Women of Mormondom.* New York: Tullidge and Crandall, 1877.

*Underwood, Grant. *The Millenarian World of Early Mormonism.* Urbana: University of Illinois Press, 1993.

*Vogel, Dan. *Religious Seekers and the Advent of Mormonism.* Salt Lake City: Signature Books, 1988.

———. "The Locations of Joseph Smith's Early Treasure Quests." *Dialogue: A Journal of Mormon Thought* 27, 3 (Fall 1994): 197–231.

Walgren, Kent L. "James Adams: Early Springfield Mormon and Freemason." *Journal of the Illinois State Historical Society* 75 (Summer 1982): 121–36.

———. "Fast and Loose Freemasonry." *Dialogue: A Journal of Mormon Thought* 18 (Fall 1985): 172–76.

*Welch, John W., and Stephen D. Ricks, ed. *The Allegory of the Olive Tree: The Olive, the Bible and Jacob* 5. Salt Lake City: Deseret Book and FARMS, 1994.

*Wellnitz, Marcus Von. *Christ and the Patriarchs: New Light from Apocryphal Literature and Tradition.* Bountiful, Utah: Horizon, 1981.

White, Thomas. *The Mormon Mysteries: Being and Exposition of the Ceremonies of 'The Endowment' and the Seven Degrees of the Temple.* New York: Edmund K. Knowlton, 1851.

*Whitehead, Ernest L. *The House of Israel: A Treatise on the Destiny, History and Identifications of Israel in All the Five Branches.* Independence, Mo.: Zion Printing and Publishing, 1947. Reprint, Salt Lake City, 1972.

*Whitney, Orson F. *Life of Heber C. Kimball.* 1888. Reprint, Salt Lake City: Bookcraft, 1973.

Widtsoe, John A. "Temple Worship." *The Utah Genealogical and Historical Magazine* 12 (April 1921): 49–66.

———. *Evidences and Reconciliations.* Salt Lake City: Bookcraft, 1960.

Wood, Wilford C. *Joseph Smith Begins His Work.* 2 vols. Salt Lake City: Deseret News Press, 1963.

*Woodruff, Wilford. *Wilford Woodruff Journal.* Salt Lake City: Signature Books, 1991.

Woodworth, Cherie Kartchner. "Genealogy and Mythmaking: Joseph Smith, Queen Elizabeth, and Ivan the Terrible." *Sunstone Symposium*, 5 July 1999.

Wyl, W. *Joseph Smith, the Prophet, His Family and His Friends.* Salt Lake City: Tribune Printing and Publishing, 1886.

Young (Denning), Ann Eliza Webb. *Wife No. 19.* Hartford, 1876.

*Young, Brigham. "A Family Meeting in Nauvoo: Minutes of a Meeting of the Richards and Young Family Held in Nauvoo," *Utah Genealogical and Historical Magazine,* 11 (8 January 1845): 104–8.

*———. In *Journal of Discourses.* 26 vols. London: Latter-day Saints' Book Depot, 1854–86.

*———. *Deseret News,* 10 February 1867.

AMERICA

Anderson, Rasmus B., ed. *The Norse Discovery of America.* London: Norroena Society, 1906.

*Armstrong, Herbert W. *The United States and Britain in Prophecy.* Pasadena: Worldwide Church of God, 1967.

Ashe, Geoffrey, et al. *The Quest for America.* New York: Praeger, 1971.

Beamish, N. Ludlow. *The Norse Discovery of America.* London, 1906.

Birmingham, Stephen. *America's Secret Aristocracy.* New York: Berkeley Books, 1987.

Boland, Charles Michael, *They All Discovered America.* Garden City, N.Y.: Doubleday, 1961.

Bradley, Michael Anderson, with Deanna Theilmann-Bean. *Holy Grail across the Atlantic: The Secret History of Canadian Discovery and Exploration.* Willowdale, Ontario, Canada: Hounslow Press, 1988.

Bradley, Michael Anderson, and Michael Bardley. *Grail Knights of North America: On the Trail of the Grail Legacy in Canada and the United States.* Willowdale, Ontario, Canada: Hounslow Press, 1998.

Crooker, William S. *The Oak Island Quest.* Hantsport, Nova Scotia: Lancelot Press, 1978.

*Fanthorpe, Lionel, and Patricia Fanthorpe. *The Oak Island Mystery.* Toronto: Hounslow Press, 1995.

Furneaux, R. *Money Pit—The Mystery of Oak Island.* Fontana/Collins, 1976.

Hall, Manly Palmer. *America's Assignment with Destiny.* Los Angeles: Philosophical Research Society, 1931, 1951, 1979.

———. *The Secret Destiny of America.* Los Angeles: Philosophical Research Society, 1944, 1972.

Holzer, Hans. *Long Before Columbus.* Sante Fe, N.M.: Bear and Co., 1992.

Hutson, James H. *Religion and the Founding of the American Republic.* Washington, D.C.: Library of Congress, 1998.

Huyghe, Patrick. *Columbus Was Last.* New York: Hyperion, 1992.

Pohl, Frederick J. *Atlantic Crossings before Columbus.* New York: W. W. Norton, 1961.

———. *Prince Henry Sinclair: His Expedition to the New World in 1398.* Halifax, Nova Scotia: Nimbus, 1969.

Pope, Robert G. *The Half-Way Covenant: Church Membership in Puritan New England.* Princeton, N.J.: Princeton University Press, 1969.

Price, Richard. *Biography of John Lothrop, 1584–1653.* Salt Lake City: R. W. Price and Associates, 1984.

Ritchie, Robert C. *Captain Kidd and the War against the Pirates.* Cambridge: Harvard University Press, 1986.

APOCRYPHA, PSEUDEPIGRAPHA, AND COPTIC DOCUMENTS

Barnstone, Willis, and Marvin Meyer. *The Gnostic Bible.* Boston and London: Shambhala, 2003.

Budge, Ernest A. Wallis. *Miscellaneous Coptic Texts in the Dialect of Upper Egypt.* 2 vols. London: British Museum, 1915.

Charlesworth, James H., ed. *Old Testament Pseudepigrapha.*

2 vols. New York: Doubleday, 1983.

———. *Authentic Apocrypha.* Richland Hills, Texas: Bible Press, D. and F. Scott Publishing, 1998.

———. *The Old Testament Pseudepigrapha and the New Testament.* Harrisburg, Pa.: Trinity Press International, 1998.

Davies, Stevan L. *The Gospel of Thomas and Christian Wisdom.* New York: Seabury, 1983.

*Doresse, Jean. *The Secret Books of the Egyptian Gnostics.* New York: Viking Press, 1960. First published as *Les Livres Secrets des Gnostiques d'Egypte,* Paris: Librarie Plon, 1953.

Ehrman, Bart D. *The New Testament: A Historical Introduction to the Early Christian Writings.* 3d ed. New York: Oxford University Press, 2003.

*———. *Lost Scriptures: Books That Did Not Make It into the New Testament.* New York: Oxford University Press, 2003.

*———. *Lost Christianities: The Battles for Scripture and the Faiths We Never Knew.* New York: Oxford University Press, 2004.

Elliott, J. K. *The Apocryphal New Testament (Horae Apocalypticae).* Oxford, 1993.

Forgotten Books of Eden, The. Alpha House, 1927.

Goodspeed, Edgar Johnson. *Famous Biblical Hoaxes: Originally Titled, Modern Apocrypha.* Twin Brooks Series. Grand Rapids, Mich.: Baker Book House, 1956.

Isenberg, Wesley W. "The Gospel of Philip." (See Robinson, James M.)

Izquierdo, Josep. "The Gospel of Nicodemus in Medieval Catalan and Occitan Literature." *Izydorczyk* (1997).

James, Montaque R. *Acts of Pilate and the Gospel of Nicodemus in the Aprocryphal New Testament.* Oxford: Oxford University Press, 1924.

*King, Karen L. *The Gospel of Mary of Magdala: Jesus and the First Woman Apostle.* Santa Rosa, Calif.: Polebridge, 2003.

Layton, Bentley, *The Gnostic Scriptures: Ancient Wisdom for the New Age.* London: SCM Press, 1987.

Lost Books of the Bible, The. Alpha House, 1926.

MacDermot, Violet. *The Fall of Sophia: A Gnostic Text on the Redemption of Universal Consciousness.* Great Barrington, Mass.: Lindisfarne Books, 2001.

Mead, George Robert Stowe. *Gnosis of the Mind.* London: Theosophical Publishing Society, 1906.

———. *Pistis Sophia.* Kila, Mont.: Kessinger Publishing, 1921.

*Pagels, Elaine. *The Gnostic Gospels.* New York: Vintage Books, 1989.

———. *Beyond Belief: The Secret Gospel of Thomas.* New York: Random House, 2003.

Pearson, Birger, ed. *Nag Hammadi Codex VII.* Leiden, Netherlands: Brill, 1996.

Platt, Rutherford H., ed. *The Lost Books of the Bible.* New York: World Publishing, 1963.

Puech, Henri-Charles. "Gnostic Gospels and Related Documents." *New Testament Apocrypha* 2 vols. Edited by E. Henneche and W. Schneemelcher. Philadelphia: Westminster Press, 1963.

*Robinson, James M., ed. *The Nag Hammadi Library in English.* San Francisco: Harper and Row, 1977, 1988.

Schmidt, Carl. *Pistis Sophia.* Edited and translated by Violet MacDermot. Leiden, Netherlands: E. J. Brill, 1978.

Schneemelcher, Wilhelm, ed., and R. McLain Wilson, trans. *New Testament Apocrypha.* 2 vols. Rev. ed. Cambridge: J. Clarke and Co., 1991–92).

Walker, Alexander. Trans. *The Gospel of Nicodemus.* Edinburgh, n.d.

Wilson, R. McLain, and MacRae, G. W. "The Gospel According to Mary." *Nag Hammadi Library in English.* Edited by James M. Robinson. San Francisco: Harper and Row, 1977, 1988.

———. "The Gospel According to Mary." *Nag-Hammadi Codices 5, 2–5 and 6 with Papyrus Berolinensis 8502, 1 and 4.* Edited by Douglas M. Parrott. Leiden: E. J. Brill, 1979.

Wilson, Robert M. *The Gospel of Philip.* New York: Harper and Row, 1962.

ARTHUR AND ARTHURIAN LITERATURE

Andere, Mary. *Arthurian Links with Herefordshire.* Great Britain: Logaston Press, 1995.

Ashe, Geoffrey. *From Caesar to Arthur.* London: Collins, 1960.

Ashe, Geoffrey. *King Arthur's Avalon: The Story of Glastonbury.* London: Collins, 1957.

————. *The Quest for Arthur's Britain.* London: Paladin, 1968. Reprint, New York: HarperCollins, 1993.

*————. *Avalonian Quest.* London, 1982.

————. *A Guidebook to Arthurian Britain.* Wellingborough, 1983.

————. *The Rediscovery of King Arthur.* London: Anchor Press, 1985.

*————. *Arthur: The Dream of a Golden Age.* London: Thames and Hudson, 1990.

*Baillie, Mike. *Exodus to Arthur: Catastrophic Encounters with Comets.* London: B.T. Batsford Ltd., 1999.

Baist, G. *Parzival und der Gral.* Freiburg im Breisgau, 1909.

Barber, Richard. *The Figure of Arthur.* London: Longman, 1972.

————. *King Arthur in Legend and History.* London: Sphere, 1973.

*————. *King Arthur: Hero and Legend.* Woodbridge, Suffolk: Boydell Press, 1961, 1992.

————. *The Arthurian Legends.* Edited by R. Barber. New York: Barnes and Noble, 1993.

*————. *The Holy Grail: Imagination and Belief.* Cambridge: Harvard University Press, 2004.

Barber, Chris, and Pykitt, David. *The Journey to Avalon.* Newburyport, Mass.: Red Wheel/Weiser, 1993.

Beare, B. *Discovering King Arthur.* London: Quantum, 1999.

Berthelot, Anne. *King Arthur: Chivalry and Legend.* London: Thames and Hudson, 1996.

Biddle, M. *King Arthur's Round Table.* Woodbridge, Suffolk: Boydell Press, 2000.

*Blake, Steve, and Scott Lloyd. *The Keys to Avalon: The True Location of Arthur's Kingdom Revealed.* Shaftesbury: Element, 2000.

Brengle, Richard L., ed. *Arthur King of Britain.* New Jersey: Prentice-Hall, 1964.

Bromwich, Rachel. *Triodd Yns Prydein* (The Welsh Triads). Cardiff: University of Wales Press, 1977.

Bromwich, Rachel, A. O. H. Jarman, and B. F. Roberts, eds. *The Arthur of the Welsh.* Cardiff: University of Wales Press, 1993.

Bruce, J. D. *The Evolution of Arthurian Romance from the Beginnings down to the Year 1300.* 2 vols. Göttingen, Germany, 1923–24.

*Bryant, Nigel. *The High Book of the Grail: A Translation of the 13th Century Romance of Perlesvaus.* Cambridge: D. S. Brewer, 1978.

Carman, J. N. "Relationship of the 'Perlesvaus' and the 'Queste del Saint Graal.'" *Bulletin of the University of Kansas* 37 (1936).

*Castleden, Rodney. *King Arthur: The Truth behind the Legend.* London and New York: Routledge, 2000.

Cavendish, Richard. *King Arthur and the Grail: The Arthurian Legends and Their Meaning.* London: Weidenfeld and Nicolson, 1978, 1987.

Cawein, Madison J. *Waste Land.* Camelot Project at the University of Rochester, 1913.

Chambers, E. K. *Arthur of Britain.* London: Sidgwith and Jackson, 1927.

Chrétien de Troyes. *Le Roman de Perceval ou Le Conte del Graal* or *Perceval.* Edited by W. Roach. Translated by Nigel Bryant. Cambridge, N.J.: Rowman and Littlefield, 1982.

Coe, Jon B. and Simon Young. *The Celtic Sources for the Arthurian Legend.* Felinfach, Wales: Llanerch Publishers, 1995.

*Coghlan, Ronan. *The Illustrated Encyclopaedia of Arthurian Legends.* Shaftesbury: Element Books, 1993.

Comfort, William Wistar, ed. *Arthurian Romances by Chrétien de Troyes.* J. M. Dent and Sons, 1913.

Continuation of the Old French 'Perceval.' Edited by W. Roach. Philadelphia, 1952.

Coughlan, Ronan. *The Illustrated Encyclopedia of the Arthurian Legends.* Shaftesbury: Element Books, 1993.

Cox, George, and Eustace Jones. *Arthurian Legends of the Middle Ages.* Senate, 1995.

Darrah, J. *Paganism in Arthurian Romance.* Woodbridge: Boydell Press, 1994.

Day, D. *The Quest for King Arthur.* London: De Agostini Editions and Michael O'Mara Books, 1995.

De Troyes, Chrétien. *Perceval ou le Roman du Graal.* Preface by Armond Hoog. Translation and notes by Jean-Pierre-Foucher and Andre Ortais. Paris, 1949, 1974.

Doel, F., G Doel, and T. Lloyd. *Worlds of Arthur: King Arthur in History, Legend, and Culture.* Stroud, Gloucestershire: Tempus, 1998.

Doulens, Gautier de. *First Continuation of the Conte du Graal.* 13th-century MS.

Dunning, Robert. *Arthur: King in the West.* London, 1988.

Eliot, T. S. *Selected Poems.* London: Faber and Baber, 1954.

Elucidation, The: A Prolouge to the Conte del Graal. Edited by A. Thompson. New York: Publications of the Institute of French Studies, 1931.

Fife, Graeme. *Arthur the King.* London: Abe Books, 1990.

Fortune, Dion. *Avalon of the Heart.* London: Aquarian Press, 1936; London: Collins, 1938, 1986.

Fowler Wright, Sydney, *The Song of Arthur (Part 4: Carbonac).*

*Gilbert, Adrian. *The Holy Kingdom.* Bantam, 1998.

Goetinck, Glenys. *Perceval: A Study of Welsh Tradition in the Grail Legend.* Cardiff: University of Wales Press, 1975.

Golther, Wolfgang. *Parzival unter der Gral in der Dichtung des Mittelalters und der Neuzeit.* Stuttgart, Germany, 1925.

*Goodrich, Norma Loree. *King Arthur.* New York: Franklin Watts, 1986.

Green, R. L. *King Arthur and His Knights of the Round Table.* 1953. New Quin, India: Puffin, 1972.

Hamilton, Claire. *Arthurian Tradition.* London: Hodder and Stoughton, 2000.

Hoyle, Fred, and Chandra Wickramasinghe. "Influenza from Space?" *Current Science, Weekly Journal of the Indian Academc of Sciences* (January 2000).

Hylton, John Dunbar. *Arteloise: A Romance of King Arthur and the Knights of the Round Table.* The Camelot Project at the University of Rochester, 1887.

Jenkins, Elizabeth. *The Mystery of King Arthur.* New York: Coward McCann and Geoghegan, 1975.

Karcewska, Kathryn. "Prophecy and the Quest for the Holy Grail: Critiquing Knowledge in the Vulgate Cycle." *Studies in the Humanities* 37 (1998).

Kibler, William W., and Carleton W. Carroll, eds. *Arthurian Romances. (Chrétien de Troyes)* Harmondsworth, England: Penquin Books, 1991.

Knight, Gareth. *The Secret Tradition of Arthurian Romance.* Wellingborough: Aquarian Press, 1983.

Knowles, Sir James. *The Legends of King Arthur and his Knights.* Senate, 1997.

Lacey, Norris J. ed. *The Arthurian Encyclopedia.* Woodbridge, Suffolk, England: Boydell Press, 1986.

———. *The Lancelot-Grail Reader.* New York and London, Garland, 2000.

Lacey, Norris J., and Geoffrey Ashe. *The Arthurian Handbook.* New York: Garland Press, 1988.

*Littleton, C. Scott and Malcor, Linda A. *From Scythia to Camelot: A Radical Reassessment of the Legends of King Arthur, the Knights of the Round Table, and the Holy Grail.* New York: Garland, 1994, 2000.

Locke, Frederick W. The *Quest for the Holy Grail: A Literary Study of a Thirteenth-Century French Romance.* New York: A. M. S. Press, 1960.

Lofmark, Carl. *The Romance of Parzival and the Holy Grail.* Newton, Powys, Wales: Gwasg Gregynog, 1990.

Loomis, Roger Sherman. *Celtic Myth and Arthurian Romance.* New York, 1927.

———. *Arthurian Tradition and Chrétien de Troyes.* New York: Columbia University Press, 1949.

———. *Chrétien's "Perceval, or the Story of the Grail."* Mediaeval Romances, Modern Library ed. New York: Columbia University Press, 1952.

———. *Wales and the Arthurian Legend.* Cardiff: University of Wales Press, 1956.

———, ed. *Arthurian Literature in the Middle Ages.* Oxford: Clarendon Press, 1959.

MacInnes, J. "The Arthurian Legend." *World Mythology.* Edited by R. Willis. London: Piatkus, 1997.

Malory, Sir Thomas, ed. *Le Morte d'Arthur.* Harmondsworth, England: Caxton, Penguin, 1969.

Markale, Jean. *King Arthur King of Kings.* London: Gordon and Cremonesi, 1977.

Marx, Jean. *La Légende Arthurienne et le Graal.* Paris: Presses Universitaires de France, 1952.

Matthews, Caitlin. *Arthur and the Sovereignty of Britain: King and Goddess in the Mabinogion.* London: Arkana, 1989.

Matthews, John. *Grail, Quest for the Eternal.* New York: Crossroad, 1981.

———. *King Arthur and The Grail Quest.* London: Brockhampton Press, 1998.

*———. *The Mystic Grail: The Challenge of the Arthurian Quest.* London: Thorsens, 1997.

McHardy, Stuart. *The Quest for Arthur.* Edinburgh: Luath Press.

*Moffat, A. *Arthur and the Lost Kingdoms.* London: Weidenfeld and Nicolson, 1999.

*Morris, John. *The Age of Arthur: A History of the British Isles from 350 to 650.* Vols. 1–3. London: Weidenfeld and Nicolson, 1973; Chichester, 1977; London: Phoenix/Orion, 1995.

Newcomen, George [pseud., De Beverley]. *The Achievement of the Sangraele and the Death of Sir Galahad.* 1925.

Newstead, Helaine. *Brân the Blessed in Arthurian Romance.* New York: Columbia University Press and A. M. S. Press, 1939, 1966.

Nitze, William Albert, trans. *Le Roman de l'estoire du Graal.* Paris: Librairie Ancienne, Honoré Champion Editeur, 1927.

———. *Perceval and the Holy Grail: An Essay on the Romance of Chrétien de Troyes.* Berkeley: University of California Press, 1949, 1952.

Owen, D.D.R, trans. Introduction and Bibliography to *Arthurian Romances.* London: Everyman Library, 1993.

Parsons, J. C. "The Second Exhumation of King Arthur's Remains at Glastonbury, 19 April 1278." *Arthurian Literature* 12 (1987).

Paterson, Helena, and Courtney Davis. *King Arthur's Return: Legends of the Round Table and Holy Grail Retraced.* Poole, Dorset, England: Blandford Press, 1996.

Perlesvaus: The High History of the Holy Grail. Translated by Sebastian Evans. 1902. Reprinted, Cambridge: James Clarke and Co., 1986.

Perlesvaus, The (written by a pious chaplain in northern France or Lowlands between 1192 and 1225 A.D.) A recent publication includes *Perlesvaus (The High Book of the Holy Grail.* Translated by N. Bryant. New Jersey: Brewer, Rowman and Littlefield, 1978.

*Phillips, Graham, and Martin Keatman. *King Arthur: The True Story.* London, Arrow, 1992.

———. *Robin Hood: The Man behind the Myth.* London: Michael O'Mara Books, 1995.

Pollard, Alfred W. *The Romance of King Arthur and His Knights of the Round Table.* London: Macmillan, 1979.

Ponsoye, Pierre. *L'Islam et le Graal: étude sur l'esotérisme du Parzival de Wolfram von Eschenback.* Paris, 1957, 1958.

*Reid, Howard. *Arthur the Dragon King: The Barbaric Roots of Britain's Greatest Legend.* 2001.

Ritchie, Robert L. *Chrétien de Troyes and Scotland.* Oxford: University Press, 1952.

Rhys, John, *Studies in the Arthurian Legend.* Oxford, 1891.

Roach, William, ed. *Continuation of the Old French "Perceval."* 2 vols. Philadelphia: University of Pennsylvania Press, 1950–52.

Romance of Perceval in Prose (Didot–Perceval). Translated by D. Skeeles. Seattle: University of Washington Press, 1966.

Sir Gawain and the Green Knight. Translated by J. R. R. Tolkein. New York: Allen and Unwin, 1975.

Sir Gawain at the Grail Castle. Translated by Jessie Laidlay. Weston: David Nutt, 1903.

Skene, W. F. *Arthur and the Britons in Wales and Scotland.* Originally published as The Four Ancient Books of Wales, 1868. Reprint, Lampeter: Llanerch, 1988.

Sommer, H. O. *Vulgate Version of the Arthurian Romances.* 8 vols. Washington, D.C.: Carnegie Institution, 1909–1916.

Spence, L. "The Arthurian Tradition in Scotland." *Scots Magazine,* April 1926.

Stoker, Robert B. *The Legacy of Arthur's Chester.* London: Covenant Books, 1965.

*Tennyson, Alfred, Lord. The Holy Grail. Eighth book of the verse cycle *The Idylls of the King.* 1869.

Tolkien, J. R. R., E. V. Gordon, and Norman Davis, eds. *Sir Gawain and the Green Knight.* Oxford: Oxford University Press, 1979.

Topsfield, L. T. *Chrétien de Troyes: A Study of the Arthurian Romances.* Cambridge, 1981.

Vulgate Cycle, The: Edited by J. E. Burns. Columbus: Ohio State University Press, 1985.

Waite, Arthur Edward. *The Holy Grail: The Galahad Quest in Arthurian Literature.* Kila, Mont.: Kessinger Publishing, 1961.

Weston, Jessie Laidlay. *Legend of Sir Lancelot.* London, 1901. Reprint, AMS Press, 1978.

Whitaker, M. *The Legends of King Arthur in Art.* Cambridge: D. S. Brewer, 1990.

*White, Richard, ed. *King Arthur in Legend and History.* London: J. M. Dent, 1997.

White, T. H. *The Once and Future King.* London: HarperCollins, 1959, 1996.

Williams, G. A. *Excalibur: The Search for Arthur.* London: BBC Books, 1994.

Wolfram von Eschenbach. *Parzival* (written between A.D. 1195–1216) Translated by A. T. Hatto. New York: Penguin, 1980.

AVALON AND GLASTONBURY

Adam of Domerham. *Historia de Rebus Gestis Glastoniensibus.* Edited by T. Hearne. Oxford, 1727.

Alford, Henry. *The Ballad of Glastonbury.* 1853.

Ashe, Geoffrey. *King Arthur's Avalon: The Story of Glastonbury.* London: HarperCollins, 1957.

———. *The Glastonbury Tor Maze: At the Foot of the Tree.* Glastonbury: Gothic Image Publications, 1979.

———. *Avalonian Quest* London, 1982.

Benham, Patrick. *The Avalonians.* Glastonbury: Gothic Image Publications, 1993.

Bond, Frederick Bligh. *An Architectural History of Glastonbury Abbey.* Glastonbury, 1909, 1981.

———. *The Gates of Remembrance.* Oxford, 1918, 1978.

———. *The Company of Avalon.* Oxford, 1924.

———. *The Glastonbury Scripts.* Glastonbury, 1924–25.

———. *The Mystery of Glaston and Her Immortal Traditions.* London, 1939.

Bouyer, Louis. *Les lieux magiques de la legende du Graal: de Broceliande en Avalon* Paris: O.E.I.L., 1986.

Bradley, Marion Zimmer. *The Mists of Avalon.* New York: Del Rey Publications, 1982.

Bullied, Arthur. *The Lake Villages of Somerset.* Glastonbury Antiquarian Society, 1924.

Caine, Mary. *The Glastonbury Zodiac.* Grael Communications, 1978.

Caldecott, Moyra. *The Green Lady and the King of Shadows: A Glastonbury Legend.* Glastonbury: Gothic Image Publications, 1989.

Capt, E. Raymond. *The Traditions of Glastonbury: Christ's Missing Years Answered.* Thousand Oaks, Calif.: Artisan Sales, 1983.

Carley, James P. "Melkin the Bard and Esoteric Tradition at Glastonbury Abbey." *Downside Review,* 9 January 1981.

———. *Glastonbury Abbey: The Holy House at the Head of the Moors Adventurous.* Glastonbury: Gothic Image Publications, 1996.

———, ed. *John of Glastonbury's "Cronica."* Latin text with notes. Woodbridge: Boydell Press, 1978.

———, ed. *Glastonbury Abbey and the Arthurian Tradition.* Cambridge, 2001.

Carley, James P. and Townsend, D. *The Chronicle of Glastonbury Abbey.* Woodbridge: Boydell and D. S. Brewer, 1985.

Coles, Bryony, and John Coles. *Sweet Tract to Glastonbury: The Somerset Levels in Prehistory.* London: Thames and Hudson, 1986.

Critlow, Keith. "Notes on the Geometry of Stonehenge with comments on the Ming T'ang." *In Britain: A Study in Patterns.* RILKO, 1969; London, 1971. Revised edition as *Glastonbury and Britain: A Study in Patterns,* 1990.

Ditmas, E. M. R. *Traditions and Legends of Glastonbury.* Guernsey, UK: Toucan Press, 1979.

———. *Glastonbury Tor: Fact and Legend.* Guernsey, UK: Toucan Press, 1981.

Dobson, C. C. *Did Our Lord Visit Britain As They Say in Cornwall and Somerset?* 1860. Reprint, Glastonbury: Avalon Press, 1936, 1947; London: Covenant Publishing Co., Ltd., 1974, 1986, 1989.

Dunning, Robert. *Glastonbury.* Alan Sutton, 1994.

Eschenbach, Wolfram von. *Parzival.* Translated by A. T. Hatto. London and New York, 1980. Another translation by Charles E. Passage. New York, 1961.

Evans, Sebastian, ed. and trans. *The High History of the Holy Grail.* London, n.d., translated from the old French, from the *Book of Josephes* in the Glastonbury Abbey Library. J. M. Dent, 1898. Reprint, London: James Clarke, 1969.

"Following the Grail" and "Did Jesus Go to High School in Britain?" *Heart: for the Coming Revolution* (Winter 1985): 4–22, 112–15.

Freeman, E. A. *Avalonian Quest.* London: Methuen, n.d.

Gasquet, Francis Aidan. *The Last Abbot of Glastonbury.* (1895). Reprint, Wales: Llanerch Press, 1908.

Gennaro, Gino. *The Phenomena of Avalon.* Glastonbury, 1979.

Gibbs, Ray. *The Legendary XII Hides of Glastonbury: Legends of Joseph of Arimathea, His XII Hides, and King Arthur.* Felinfach, Wales: Llanerch Publishers, 1988, 1995.

Glaston, John de. *The Chronicle of Glastonbury Abbey.* London: Joseph, 1975.

Glastonbury Reader, A: Selections from the Myths, Legends, and Stories of Ancient Avalon. Hammersmith, London: Aquarian Press, 1991.

Goodall, John A. "The Glastonbury Memorial Plate Reconsidered." *The Antiquaries Journal* 66 (1986).

Greswell, William H. P. *Chapters in the Early History of Glastonbury Abbey.* Taunton, 1909.

Hall, Manly Palmer. "Legends of Glastonbury Abbey." *Philosophical Research Society Journal,* 18, no. 2.

Hearne, Thomas. *The Antiquities of Glastonbury.* Trinity College Library at Cambridge, 1717.

———. *John of Glastonbury.* (See also Adam of Domerham)

———, ed. *Adami de Domerham, Historia de Rebur Gestis Glastoniensibus.* Oxford, 2 vols. 1727.

*Howard-Gordon, Frances. *Glastonbury: Maker of Myths.* Glastonbury: Gothic Image Publications, 1982, 1997.

Hurd, Michael. *Rutland Boughton and the Glastonbury Festivals.* Oxford University Press, 1993.

John of Glastonbury. *The Chronicle of Glastonbury Abbey: An Edition, Translation and Study of John of Glastonbury's.* Woodbridge and Dover, New Hampshire, 1985.

Johannes Glastoniensis [John of Glastonbury], comp. *Glastoniencis Chronica (Cronica sive Antiquitates Glastoniensis Ecclesie).* Translated by B. Carley. Woodbridge: Boydell and D. S. Brewer, 1985.

Kenawell, William W. *The Quest at Glastonbury: a Biographical Study of Frederick Bligh Bond.* New York, 1965.

Lagorio, Valerie M. "The Evolving Legend of St. Joseph of Glastonbury." *Speculum* 46 (1971): 209–31.

———. "The Glastonbury Legends and the English Grail Romances." *Neuphilologische Mitteilungen* 79 (1978): 359–66.

Lewis, Rev. H. A. *Christ in Cornwall and Glastonbury the Holy Land of Britain.* Falmouth, England: J. H. Lake and Co., Ltd., 1939.

Lewis, Rev. Lionel Smithett. (Vicar of Glastonbury) *Glastonbury, the Mother of Saints.* Bristol: St. Stephen's Press, 1925.

———. *St. Joseph of Arimathea at Glastonbury or the*

Apostolic Church of Britain. Wells: James Clarke, 1922. Reprint, Cambridge: James Clark and Co., Ltd., 1982.

Lomax, Frank. Trans. *The Antiquities of Glastonbury by William of Malmesbury.* Facsimile report, Felinfach, Wales: Llanerch Publishers, 1980, 1992.

Magna Glastoniensis Tabula. MS at Naworth Castle.

Maltwood, Katherine E. *A Guide to Glastonbury's Temple of the Stars: Their Giant Effigies Described from Airviews, Maps and from the "High History of the Holy Grail."* London, 1927. Reprint,1964.

———. *Air View Supplement to a Guide to Glastonbury's Temple of the Stars.* 1937.

Mann, Nicholas R. *The Cauldron and the Grail.* Glastonbury, 1985.

———. *Glastonbury Tor: A Guide to the History and Legends.* Glastonbury, 1986.

*———. *The Isle of Avalon: Sacred Mysteries of Arthur and Glastonbury Tor.* St. Paul: Llewellyn Publications, 1996.

Matthews, John. *A Glastonbury Reader.* London: Aquarian Press, 1991.

*Michell, John F. *New Light on the Ancient Mystery of Glastonbury.* Glastonbury: Gothic Image Publications, 1990.

Moon, Adrian. *The First Ground of God: A History of the Glastonbury Abbey Estates.* Glastonbury, 1978.

Powys, John Cowper. *A Glastonbury Romance.* London: Macdonald, 1955.

Price, G. Vernon. *Valle Crucis Abbey.* Brython Press, 1952.

Radford, C. A. Raleigh. "Glastonbury Abbey," in *The Quest for Arthur's Britain.* Edited by Geoffrey Ashe. Paladin Books, 1968.

Rahtz, Philip. *Excavations on Glastonbury Tor, Somerset 1964–1966.* And S. Hirst *Beckery Chapel, Glastonbury 1967–68.* Glastonbury, 1974. Report on excavation.

———. *Glastonbury.* London, 1993.

Rahtz, Philip, and S. Hirst. Beckery Chapel, Glastonbury, 1967–68. Glastonbury, 1974. Report on excavation.

Riddy, Felicity. "Glastonbury, Joseph of Arimathea and the Grail in John Hardyng's *Chronicle.*" *The Archaeology and History of Glastonbury Abbey.* Edited by Lesley Adams and James P. Carley. Woodbridge: Boydell and D. S. Brewer, 1991.

*Roberts, Anthony, ed. *Glastonbury: Ancient Avalon, New Jerusalem.* London: Rider, 1976, 1978, 1992.

Robinson, Joseph Armitage. (Dean of Wells) *Two Glastonbury Legends: King Arthur and St. Joseph of Arimathea.* Cambridge: University Press, 1926.

———. *Somerset Historical Essays.* London: Oxford University Press, 1921.

Scott, John. *The Early History of Glastonbury: An Edition, Translation and Study of William of Malmesbury's, "De Antiquitate Glastoniensis Ecclesiae."* London and Woodbridge: Boydell Press, 1981.

Stokes, H. F. Scott. *Glastonbury Abbey During the Crusades.* (extracts) Adam of Domerham: Felinfach, Wales: Folk Press Edition, 1934. Reprint, Felinfach, Wales: Llanerch Publishers, 2000.

Treharne, Reginald Francis. *The Glastonbury Legends: Joseph of Arimathea, the Holy Grail and King Arthur.* London: P. Cresset, 1967.

Webb, A. E. *Glastonbury.* Glastonbury: Avalon Press, 1929.

Warner, Rev. Richard. *An History of the Abbey of Glaston and of the Town of Glastonbury.* Bath, 1826.

William of Malmesbury. *De Antiquitate Glastonie Ecclesie* (A.D. 1125–30) contains the first account of Joseph of Arimathea. It includes a Charter of St. Patrick. Trans. as *The History of Glastonbury* by J. Scott, 1981.

Williams, Mary, and Janette Jackson, ed. *Glastonbury, A Study in Patterns.* London, 1970. Revised edition as *Glastonbury and Britain, A Study in Patterns,* 1990.

Willis, Rev. R. *The Architectural History of Glastonbury Abbey.* Cambridge, 1866.

BRITAIN, IRELAND, SCOTLAND, THE DRUIDS, AND THE CELTS

Albany, HRH Prince Michael Stewart of [pseud. Laurence Gardner]. *The Forgotten Monarchy of Scotland.* Shaftesbury: Element Books, 1998.

Alcock, Leslie. *Arthur's Britain: History and Archaeology A.D. 376–634.* London, 1971.

———. *By South Cadbury Is That Camelot?* Thames and Hudson, 1972.

———. *Was This Camelot? Excavations at Cadbury Castle 1966–70.* New York: Stein and Day, 1972.

Alexander, W. L. *The Ancient British Church.* Religious Tract Society, London, 1889.

Alford, Cardinal Michael. *Fides Regia Britannica.* Vol. 2. Louvain: Joannes Matthias Hovius, 1663.

Anderson, Joseph. *Scotland in Early Christian Times.* Edinburgh: David Doublas, 1881.

Anderson, William. *Green Men.* London: HarperCollins, 1991.

Anglo-Saxon Chronicle, The. Translated by G. N. Garmonsway. London: Everyman, 1967.

Annales Cambriae (The Welsh Annals). Translated by John Morris. Chichester: Phillimore, 1980.

Ashe, Geoffrey. *Mythology of the British Isles.* London: Methuen, 1990.

Baring-Gould, Rev. Sabine. *Curious Myths of the Middle Ages.* London, 1867. Reprint, London: Methuen, 1912.

———. *Book of Cornwall. London: Methuen, 1899.*

———. *Further Reminiscences, 1864–1894.* New York: E. P. Dutton, 1925.

Baring-Gould, Rev. Sabine, and John Fisher. *The Lives of the British Saints.* 4 vols. London: Cymmrodorion Society, 1907–1913.

Barnes, J. *The Celts and Christianity.* London, 1968.

Bartrum, Peter C. *Early Welsh Genealogical Tracts.* Cardiff: University of Wales Press, 1966.

———. *A Welsh Classical Dictionary, People in History and Legend up to about A.D. 1000.* National Library of Wales, 1993.

Baugh, G. C., and D. C. Cox. *Monastic Shropshire.* Shrewsbury, 1982.

Beaumont, W. C. *The Mysterious Comet.* London: Rider and Co., 1932.

———. *The Riddle of Prehistoric Britain.* London: Rider and Co., 1946.

Bede of Jarrow (The Venerable). *The Ecclesiastical History of the English Nation.* Harmondsworth: Penguin Classics, 1955. Also called *A History of the English Church and People.*

———. *A History of the English Church and People.* Translated by J. A. Giles. London: Everyman, 1970.

Bhreathnach, E. *Tara: A Select Bibliography.* Dublin: Discovery Programme Monographs, 1995.

Blair, Peter Hunter. *The Origins of Northumbria.* Gateshead: Northumberland Press, 1948.

Bonwick, James. *Irish Druids and Old Irish Religions.* Salem, N.H.: Ayer Co., 1984.

Bord, Janet and Colin Bord. *Mysterious Britain.* Herts: Paladin, 1974, 1976.

———. *The Enchanted Land.* London: Thorsons/Harper Collins, 1995.

Bowen, E. *The Settlements of the Celtic Saints in Wales.* Cardiff: University of Wales Press, 1956.

Brennan, Martin. *The Boyne Valley Vision.* Dublin: Dolmen Press, 1980.

Brou, Marcel, and Willy Brou. *Les Secrètes des Druides.* Brussels, 1970.

Budden, Charles W. *Rambles Round the Old Church of Wirral.* Liverpool: Edward Howell, 1922.

Burns, M. *The History of Shropshire.* London, 1958.

Chadwick, Hector Munro. *Early Scotland: The Picts, Scots and Welsh of Southern Scotland.* Cambridge: Cambridge University Press, 1949.

———. *Studies in Early British History.* Cambridge: Cambridge University Press, 1954.

Chadwick, Nora K. *Celtic Britain.* New York, 1963.

———. *The Druids.* Cardiff, 1966.

———. *The Celtic Realms.* Harmondsworth: Penguin Books, 1967.

———. *The Celts.* Harmondsworth: 1970.

———. *The Age of the Saints in the Early Celtic Church.* Oxford: Oxford University Press, 1961. Reprint, London, 1981.

Collingwood, R. G., and J. N. L. Myres. *Roman Britain and English Settlements.* Oxford University Press, 1936.

Cressy, Hugh Paulinus Serenus. *Church History of Brittany.* Roven, France, 1668.

Critlow, Keith. "Notes on the Geometry of Stonehenge with comments on the Ming T'ang," in *Britain: A Study in Patterns.* RILKO, 1969; London, 1971. Revised edition is *Glastonbury and Britain, A Study in Patterns,* 1990.

Crossley-Holland, K. *British Folk Tales.* London, 1987.

Curtin, Jeremiah. *Myths and Folk-Lore of Ireland.* London, 1890. Reprint, 1975.

Davis, Rev. David, *The Ancient Celtic Church and the See of Rome.* Cardiff, 1924.

Davies, W. S., ed. "Giraldus Cambrensis de Invectionibus," *Cymmrodor* 30 (1920).

de Paor, Màire, and Liam de Paor. *Early Christian Ireland.* New York: Praeger, 1958.

Deanesley, Margaret. *The Pre-Conquest Church in England.* London, 1961.

Delaney, F. *Legends of the Celts.* London: Grafton Books, 1989.

Delap, D. *Celtic Saints.* Pitking, Great Britain, 1998.

Devereaux, Paul. *The Dreamtime Earth and Avebury's Open Secrets.* Glastonbury: Gothic Image Publications, 1992.

Dillon, Miles. *The Cycles of the Kings.* London: J. M. Dent, 1946.

———. *Early Irish Literature.* Chicago, 1948.

———. *Early Irish History.* Dublin: Three Candles, 1954.

Dillon, Miles, and Nora K. Chadwick. *The Celtic Realms.* New York, 1967.

*Dunford, Barry. *The Holy Land of Scotland: Jesus in Scotland and the Gospel of the Grail.* Aberfeldy: Brigadoon Books, 1996, 1997; Glenlyon Perthshire, Scotland: Sacred Connections, April 2002.

*Elder, Isabel Hill. *Celt, Druid, and Culdee.* London, 1947.

Ellis, Peter Berresford. *A Dictionary of Irish Mythology.* Constable, 1987.

Elvan of Avalon. *De origine Ecclesiae Britannicae.* Now lost, but quoted by Pitsaeus and Cardinal Baronius.

Evans, John Gwenogvryn. *The Book of Taliesin.* Llanbedrog, Wales: 1910.

Ferguson, John. "In Defence of Pelagius." *Theology* 83 (March 1980).

Filmer, W. E. *Who Were the Scots?* Kent, n.d.

Fletcher, J. R., and J. D. Stephen. *Short History of St. Michael's Mount Cornwall.* 1951

Forbes-Leith, William. *The Scots Men-at-Arms and Life Guards in France.* 2 vols. Edinburgh: William Paterson, 1882.

Ford, Patrick K. *The Mabinogi and Other Medieval Welsh Tales.* University of California Press, 1977.

Frantzen, Allen J. *Desire for Origins: New Language, Old English, and Teaching the Tradition.* New Brunswick and London, 1990.

Geoffrey of Monmouth. *Historia Regum Britanniae* [History of the Kings of Britain]. 1147. Edited and translated by Lewis Thorpe. Harmondsworth: Penguin, 1966.

Gildas III (A.D. 516–570). *De Excidio et Conquestu Britanniae.* Translated by M. Winterbottom. Chichester: Phillimore, 1978.

Gildas, *Cottonian MS.*

———. *The Ruin of Britain.* Edited by Hugh Williams. London: David Nutt, 1899.

Giles, J. A. *Chronicle of the Kings of England.* Trans. William of Malmesbury. London: Henry Bohn, 1847.

Giraldus Camrensis (Gerald of Wales). *The Journey through Wales and the Description of Wales.* Translated by Lewis Thorpe. Harmondsworth:Penguin, 1978.

Gougaud, Dom Louis. *Christianity in Celtic Lands.* Translated by Maud Joynt. Dublin: Four Courts, 1932.

Green, Miranda J. *The Gods of the Celts.* Stroud, Gloucestershire: Sutten, 1986.

———. *The Legendary Past: Celtic Myths*. London: British Museum Press, 1993.

———. *The Celtic World*. London and New York: Routledge, 1995.

———. *Dictionary of Celtic Myth and Legend*. New York: Thames and Hudson, 1997.

———. *The World of the Druids*. New York: Thames and Hudson, 1997.

Grimaldi, Rev. A. B. *History of the Anglo-Saxons*. Vol. 1.

Guest, Lady Charlotte, trans. *The Mabinogion* [from 1838 texts]. London: J. M. Dent, 1902. Reprint, London: Everyman Library, 1932.

Heath, Rev. Alban. *The Painted Savages of England*. London: Covenant Publishing, 1934.

Herbert, Algernon. *Britannia after the Romans*. London, 1836.

Hodgkin, Robert Howard. *A History of the Anglo-Saxons*. Oxford, 1935. See Vol. 1 on King Arthur.

Hole, Christina. *English Folklore*. Batsford, 1940.

"Introduction of Christianity into Britain, The" at www.ensignmessage.com/archives/chrstianinto.html (April–June 2002).

Jamieson, J. A. *Historical Account of the Ancient Culdees of Iona*. 1811. Reprint, 1890.

Jones, Gwyn, and Thomas Jones. *The Mabinogion*. London: Everyman, 1993.

Jones, Thomas. *Brut y Tywysogyon, Red Book of Hergest Version*. Cardiff: University of Wales Press, 1955.

Keating, Geoffrey. *The History of Ireland*. 1640. Translated by David Comyn and Rev. P. S. Dinnen. London: Irish Texts Society, 1902–14.

Kendrick, Thomas Downing. *The Druids: A Study in Keltic Prehistory*. London: Methuen, 1927. Reprint, London: Studio Edition, 1974.

———. *British Antiquity*. London, 1950.

Kenney, James F. *The Sources for the Early History of Ireland*. Dublin: Four Courts Press, 1966.

Lehane, Brendan. *Early Celtic Christianity*. 1968. Reprint, London: Continuum, 2005.

Loth, J. *Les Mabinogion*. Paris, 1889.

Lynch, Prof. M. *Scotland: A New History*. London: Pimlico, 1991.

MacEwan, A. R. *A History of the Church in Scotland*. London, 1913.

Mackie, Euan. *Science and Society in Prehistoric Britain*. London: Paul Elek, 1977.

MacNeil, Eoin. *Celtic Ireland*. Dublin: Martin Lester, 1921. Reprint, Dublin: Academy Press, 1981.

MacQuarrie, A. *The Saints of Scotland*. Edinburgh: John Donald, 1997.

MacRitchie, D. *Scottish Gypsies under the Stewarts*. Edinburgh, 1894.

Magnusson, Magnus. *Scotland: The Story of a Nation*. London: HarperCollins, 2001.

Maltwood, K. E. . *The Enchantments of Britain*. London and Cambridge: James Clarke, 1982.

Markale, Jean. *The Celts: Uncovering the Mystic and Historic Origins of Western Culture*. Vermont: Inner Traditions International, 1993.

———. *The Druids: Celtic Priests of Nature*. Vermont: Inner Traditions International, 1999.

Matthews, Caitlin. *Mabon and the Mysteries of Britain: An Exploration of the Mabinogion*. London: Arkana, 1987.

McCone, K. *Pagan Past and Christian Present in Early Irish Literature*. Maynooth, 1991.

McHardy, S. *Scotland: Myth, Legend and Folklore*. Edinburgh: Luath Press, 1999.

McKerracher, A. *Perthshire in History and Legend*. Edinburgh: John Donald, 1988, 2000.

McNeill, John T. *The Celtic Churches A.D. 200–1200*. Chicago: University of Chicago, 1974.

Michell, John F. *The Traveller's Guide to Sacred England*. Glastonbury: Gothic Image Publications, 1996.

Milner, Rev. W. M. H. *The Royal House of Britain: An Enduring Dynasty*. London: British-Israel-World Federation, 1927.

———. *Chronicles of Eri*. Vol. 2. London, 1931.

———. *The Heritage of Anglo-Saxon Race*. London: Covenant, n.d.

Mould, Daphne, and D. C. Pochin. *The Irish Saints*. London: Burns and Oates, 1964.

Murphy, Gerald. *Saga and Myth in Ancient Ireland*. Dublin: Three Candles, 1961.

Murray, R. *The Gypsies of the Border.* Galashiels: T. F. Brockie, 1875.

Nash, D. W. *Taliesin; or, The Bards and Druids of Britain.* London, 1858.

Nennius the Bard. *Historia Brittonium British History and the Welsh Annals.* Edited by John Morris. London: Phillmore, 1980.

Nicholson, H. Forthomme. "Celtic Theology: Pelagius." In *An Introduction to Celtic Christianity.* Edited by James P. MacKay. Edinburgh: T&T Clark, 1989.

North, John. *Stonehenge: Neolithic Man and the Cosmos.* London: HarperCollins, 1996.

Nutt, Alfred Trubner. *The Influence of Celtic upon Medieval Romance: Popular Studies in Mythology Romance and Folklore.* London: David Nutt, 1899.

O'Hanlon, John. *Lives of the Irish Saints.* 10 vols. Dublin: Duffy, 1875.

O'Hart, "Lineal Descent of the Royal Family of England." *O'Hart's Irish Pedigrees.* 1887.

O'Hogain, Daithi. *Myth, Legend and Romance: An Encyclopedia of the Irish Folk Tradition.* New York: Prentice Hall, 1991.

O'Rahilly, Thomas F. *Early Irish History and Mythology.* 1946. Reprint, Dublin Institute for Advanced Studies, 1964.

Parsons, Rev. R. *Three Conversions of England.* England, 1570.

Phillips, W. Alison, ed. *History of the Church of Ireland.* New York: Oxford University Press, 1910.

Piggott, Stuart. *The Druids.* New York: Thames and Hudson, 1968. This book claims the Joseph of Arimathea legend is baseless.

———. *Scotland Before History.* Edinburgh: Polygon, 1982.

Plummer, C. ed. *Lives of the Irish Saints.* 2 vols. New York: Oxford University Press, 1922.

Rash, Rev. A. F. *This Sceptred Isle.* London: Covenant Publishing, n.d.

Reade, W. Winwood. *The Veil of Isis or the Mysteries of the Druids.* London: C. J. Skeet, 1861.

Rees, A., and Rees, B. R. *Celtic Heritage: Ancient Tradition in Ireland and Wales.* London: Thames and Hudson, 1961.

Rees, B. R. *Pelagius: A Reluctant Heretic.* Woodbridge, Suffolk: Boydell Press, 1988.

———. *The Letters of Pelagius and His Followers.* Woodbridge, Suffolk: Boydell Press, 1989.

Rhys, John. *Celtic Folklore,* 2 vols. Clarendon Press, 1901.

Ritchie, A. *Picts.* Edinburgh: HMSO, 1989.

Roberts, L. G. A. *Druidism in Britain.* 3d ed., 1928.

Ross, A. *Pagan Celtic Britain.* London: Routledge and Kegan Paul, 1967.

———. *The Druids.* Stroud: Tempus, 1999.

Ross, Anne. *Pagan Celtic Britain.* London and New York, 1967.

Salway, Peter. *Roman Britain.* Clarendon Press, 1991.

Scott, Archibald B. *The Pictish Nation.* Edinburgh: T. N. Foulis, 1918.

Shaw, R. Cunliff. *Post-Roman Carlisle and the Kingdoms of the Northwest.* Preston: Guardian Press, 1964.

Sherley-Price, Leo. *Bede: A History of the English Church and People.* Penguin, 1968.

Skene, William Forbes. *Chronicles of the Picts and Scots.* Edinburgh: HM General Register, 1867.

———. *Celtic Scotland: A History of Ancient Alba.* Vol. 2. Edinburgh: David Douglas, 1877.

Spelman, Henrici. *Concilia, Decreta, Leges, Constitutiones, in re Ecclesiarum orbis Britannici.* London, 1639.

Spence, Keith. *Brittany and the Bretons.* London: Victor Gollancz, 1978.

Spence, Lewis. *The History and Origins of Druidism.* London: Rider and Co., 1947.

———. *The Magic Arts in Celtic Britain.* London: Constable, 1995.

Spottiswoode, J. *The History of the Church of Scotland.* London: R. Norton, 1666.

Stein, Dr. Walter Johannes. *The British, Their Psychology and Destiny.* London: Temple Lodge Press, 1990.

Stewart, HRH M. J. [pseud. Laurence Gardner]. *The Forgotten Monarch of Scotland.* Shaftesbury: Element Books, 1998.

Stokes, George Thomas. *Ireland and the Celtic Church*. London, 1886.

———. *Lives of the Saints from the Book of Lismore*. New York: Oxford University Press, 1890.

Swanton, Michael. *The Anglo-Saxon Chronicle*. J. M. Dent, 1996.

Tatlock, J. S. P. *Legendary History of Britain*. Berkeley, 1950.

Taylor, Thomas. *Celtic Christianity in Cornwall*. London, 1916. Reprint, Felinfch, Llanenett, 1995.

Taylor, S. "The Coming of the Augustinians to St. Andrews and version B. the St. Andrews Foundation Legend." *Kings, Clerics and Chronicles in Scotland, 500–1297*. Edited by Simon Taylor. Dublin: Four Courts Press, 2000.

Taylor, Rev. T. *Saint Michael's Mount*. 1932.

Thom, Prof. Alexander and A. S. Thom. Collated by A. Burl. "Magalithic Rings." *BAR, British Series* 81 Oxford, 1981.

Thomas, Charles. *Britain and Ireland in Early Christian Times*. London, 1971.

———. *Christianity in Roman Britain*. Batsford, 1981.

Thompson, W. F. *The White Tribes of Israel: Racial Origins and Migrations*. London, 1995.

Turnbull, A. *St. Andrew: Scotland's Myth and Identity*. Edinburgh: St. Andrew Press, 1997.

Ussher, Bishop James. *Britannicarum Ecclesiarum Antiquitates*. 1639.

Wade-Evans, Arthur W. *Welsh Christian Origins*. Oxford: Alden Press, 1934.

———. *Nennius's History of the Britons*. SPCK, 1938.

———. *The Emergence of England and Wales*. 2d ed. Heffer, 1959.

Warren, F. E. *The Liturgy of the Celtic Church*. Oxford: Oxford University Press, 1881.

Watson, W. J. "The Legend of Crewkerne." *Somerset County Herald*, 1920.

———. *The History of the Celtic Place Names of Scotland*. Edinburgh: William Blackwood, 1926.

Weldon, B. W. *The Evolution of Israel: The Story of the English Race from 721 B.C. to the Present Day*. London: Harrison and Sons, 1910.

The Welsh Mabinogion. Edited and translated by J. Gantz. London: Penguin, 1988.

Westwood, J. *Albion: A Guide to Legendary Britain*. London: Paladin Crafton Books, 1985, 1987.

William of Malmesbury. *Chronicle of the Kings of England*. Translated by B. Marriot. London, 1866.

Williams, Charles. *Taliesin through Logres and the Region of the Summer Stars*. Cambridge, N.J.: D. S. Brewer, 1982.

Williams, Taliesin, with Iolo Morganwg, Thomas Price, Owen Jones and the Society for the Publication of Ancient Welsh Manuscripts. *Iolo Manuscripts*. London: W. Rees, Llandovey and Longman and Co., 1848.

Winterbotham, M. *Gildas: The Ruin of Britain and Other Works*. London: Phillimore, 1978.

Wood, Juliette. "The Celtic Tarot and the Secret Tradition: A Study of Modern Legend Making." *Folklore* 110 (1999).

Wright, Dudley. *Druidism: The Ancient Faith of Britain*. London: Ed J. Burrow and Co., 1924.

BRITISH-ISRAELITISM

*Allen, Rev. John H. *Judah's Sceptre and Joseph's Birthright: An Analysis of the Prophecies of Scripture in Regard to the Royal Family of Judah and the Many Nations of Israel*. Merrimac, Mass.: Destiny Publishers, 1902.

Ackroyd, Peter. *Blake*. London: Minerva, 1995.

Aitchison, N. *Scotland's Stone of Destiny*. Tempus, Stroud, 2000.

*Anderson, James H. *God's Covenant Race*. 2d ed. Salt Lake City: Deseret News Press, 1943.

Balacius, Robert Alan. *Uncovering the Mysteries of Your Hidden Inheritance*. Sacred Truth Ministries, 2001.

Balmer, T. C. *The Israelitish Origin of the Anglo-Saxons, Irish, Scotch, and Welsh: An Historical Proof*. Liverpool, 1877.

Barczewski, Stephanie L. *Myth and National Identity in Nineteenth-Century Britain*. Oxford, 2000.

Bennett, W. H. *Symbols of Our Celto-Saxon Heritage.* Covenant Press, 1985.

Betham, W. *The Gael and the Cymbri; or, An Enquiry into the Origin, Religion, Language, and Institutions of the Irish, Scoti, Britons and Gauls, and the Caledonians, Picts, Welsh and Bretons.* London, 1834.

*Carew, Mairéad. *Tara and the Ark of the Covenant: A Search for the Ark of the Covenant by British-Israelites on the Hill of Tara (1899–1902).* Dublin: Royal Irish Academy, 2003.

Cope, Julian. *The Modern Antiquarian.* London: Thorsons, 1998.

Dawson, A. *The Hill of Tara: a personal visit.* Portadown, 1887.

Ferguson, W. *The Identity of the Scottish Nation.* Edinburgh: University Press, 1998.

Gayer, M. H. *The Heritage of the Anglo-Saxon Race.* Haverhill, Mass.: Destiny Publishers, 1941.

Glover, Rev. F. R. A. *England, the Remnant of Judah and the Israel of Ephraim: The Two Families under One Head; A Hebrew Episode of British History.* 1861. 2d. ed. Rivingtons, Waterloo Place, London, 1881.

Goodchild, John Arthur. *The Book of Tephi.* London: Kegan Paul, Trench, Trubner and Co., 1897.

Goudge, H. L. *The British-Israel Theory.* 5th ed. London and Oxford, 1941.

Hanan, Denis, and Aldersmith, H. *British-Israel Truth: A Handbook for Enquirers.* 13th ed. London, 1926.

Hanan, Denis. "Ephraim's Birthright," *Covenant People* 5, 1899.

*Hansen, Vaughn E. *Whence Came They? Israel, Britain, and the Restoration.* Springville, Utah: Cedar Fort, 1993.

Harris, Richard Reader. *The Lost Tribes of Israel.* London, ca. 1908.

Hewins, Prof. W.A.S. *The Royal Saints of Britain.* London: Chiswick Press, 1929.

MaCalister, R. A. S. "Temair Breg: a study of the remains and traditions of Tara." *Proceedings of the Royal Irish Academy* 34 C (1917–19): 231–99.

———. *Tara: A Pagan Sanctuary of Ancient Ireland.* London, 1931.

MacDougall, H. *Racial Myth in English History.* London: University Press of New England, 1982.

Massey, J. D. *Tamar Tephi; or, The Maid of Destiny, the Great Romance of the Royal House of Britain.* London, 1924.

McDonald, R. H. "The Hill of Tara." *Journal of the British Archaeological Association.* 1 (1895): 271–79.

Morgan, Rev. R. W. *The Churches of England and Rome.*

———. *St. Paul in Britain; Or, the Origin of British as Opposed to Papal Christianity.* London, 1860. Reprint, Covenant Publishing, 1925.

———. *The Saints in Britain.* London, n.d.

Murphy, Reverend D., and T. J. Westropp. "Notes on the Antiquities of Tara." *Journal of the Royal Society of Antiquaries of Ireland* 24 (1894): 232–42.

Oliver, W. H. *Prophets and Millennialist: The Uses of Biblical Prophecy in England from the 1790s to the 1840s.* Aukland and Oxford, 1978.

O'Riordain, S. *Tara: The Monuments on the Hill.* Dundalk, 1954.

Petrie, G., "On the History and Antiquities of Tara Hill." *Transactions of the Royal Irish Academy (Antiquities)* 18 (1839): 25–232.

Rees, Rev. W. J. Rice. *An Essay on the Welsh Saints; or, The Primitive Christians Usually Considered to Have Been the Founders of Churches in Wales.* London, 1836.

———. *Lives of the Cambro-British Saints.* London: Welsh MSS Society/Longman, 1853.

Reeves, William. *The Culdees of the British Islands As They Appear in History.* Royal Irish Academy of Dublin: M. H. Gill, 1864. Reprint, Felinfach, Wales: Llarnerch Publishers, 1994.

Stephens, J. C. "Genealogical Chart" showing the connection between the House of David and the Royal Family of Britain (n.d.).

Taylor, Gladys. *Our Neglected Heritage.* 5 vols. London: Covenant Books, 1969–74.

Taylor, John W. *The Coming of the Saints: Imaginations and Studies in Early Church History and Traditions.* London: Methuen and Co., Ltd, 1906; Reprint, London: Covenant Publishing, 1969.

"The Throne of Destiny." BBC TV Scotland, 1997.

Totten, Charles Adelle Lewis. *Our Race: Its Origin and Destiny—A Series of Studies on the Saxon Riddle.* 30 vols. New Haven: Our Race Publishing Co., 1891–1908.

Warner, R. B. "The 'Prehistoric' Irish Annals: Fable or History." *Archaeology Ireland* 4, 1 (1990): 30–33.

*Whitehead, Ernest L. *The House of Israel: A Treatise on the Destiny, History and Identifications of Israel in All the Five Branches.* Independence, Mo.: Zion Printing and Publishing Co., 1947. Reprint, Salt Lake City, 1972.

Wilson, George N. *Coincidences? Pointers to Our Heritage.* Wigan: Committee of North West British Israel World Federation, n.d.

Wilson, J. *Lectures on Our Israelitish Origin.* London, 1840.

———. "British Israelism." *Sociological Review* 16 (1968): 41–57.

———. "The Relation between Ideology and Organization in a Small Religious Group: The British Israelites." *Review of Religious Research* 10 (1968): 51–60.

CATHARS, LANGUEDOC, RENNES-LE-CHÂTEAU, AND SAINTS MARIES

Allix, Peter. *The Ecclesiastic History of the Ancient Church of Albigenses.* 1692. Reprint, 1821.

Andrews, Richard, and Paul Schellenberger. *The Tomb of God: The Body of Jesus and the Solution to a 2,000-Year-Old Mystery.* London: Little Brown and Co., 1996.

Aué, Michèle. Translated by Alison Hebborn. *The Cathars.* MSM, 1995.

Barber, Malcolm. "The Albigensian Crusades: Wars like Any Other?" *Dei gesta per Francos: Etudes sur les croisades deditees a Jean Richard.* 2001.

Bedu, Jean-Jacques. *Rennes-le-Château, Autopsie d'un Mythe.* Atelier Empreinte, Rennes-le-Château, 1990.

Bély, Lucien. *Aimer La Camargue et les Saintes-Maries de la Mer.* Rennes: Editions Ouest- France, 1992.

Bihalji, O. M., and Benac, A. *The Bogomils.* London: Thames and Hudson, 1962.

Birks, Walter, and Gilbert, R. A. *The Treasure of Montségur.* Wellingborough: The Aquarian Press and Crucible, 1987, 1990.

Blum, Jean. *Rennes-le-Château, Visigoths, Cathares, Templiers.* Paris: Editions du Rocher, 1994.

Boudet, H. *La Vraie Langue Celtique et le Cromleck de Rennes-les Bains.* 1886. Reprint, facsimile edition, Nice: Bélisane, 1984.

Boumendil, Claude, and Gilbert Tappa, eds. *Les Cashiers de Rennes-le-Château.* Nice: Editions Bélisane, 1984.

Byrne, Patrick. *Templar Gold: Discovering the Ark of the Covenant.* Nevada City, Calif.: Blue Dolphin Publishing, 2001.

Captier, Antoine, et al. *Rennes-le-Château.* Nice: Bélisane, 1985.

Chapelle, M. le Chanoine A. *Les Saintes-Maries De-le-Mer: L'Église et le Pèlerinage.* Cazilhac: Bélisane, early 20th century. Reprint, 1997.

Colinon, Maurice. *Les Saintes Maries de la Mer: Les pèlerins du clair de lune.* Cazilhac: Belisane, 2001.

Corbu, Clair, and Antoine Captier. *L'Héritage de l'Abbé Saunière.* Nice: Belisane, 1995.

Corbu, Noël [pseud. Anonymous]. *Histoire de Rennes-le-Château.* Carcassonne, Archives Départmentales, 2j248, deposited 14 June 1962.

Costen, Michael. *The Cathars and the Albigensian Crusade.* Manchester University Press, 1997.

Deloux, J., and J. Brétigny. *Rennes-le-Château: Capitale Secrète et l'Historie de France.* Paris: Editions Atlas, 1982.

Descadeillas, René. *Mythologie de Trésor de Rennes-le-Château.* Carcassonne, 1974.

de Sède, Gérald. *Les Templiers sont parmi nous, ou l'Enigme de Gisors.* Editions Julliard, 1962.

———. *L'Or de Rennes, ou la Vie Insolite de Bérenger Saunière.* Editions Juillard, 1967. A version of this book was published as *Le Trésor Maudit de Rennes-le-Château.*

———. *The Accursed Treasure of Rennes-le-Château.* Translation of *L'Or de Rennes, ou la Vie Insolite de Bérenger Sauniére* by Bill Kersey. DEK Publishing, 2001.

de Sède, Gèrald, and Sophie de Sède. *Rennes-le-Château: le dossier, les impostures, les phantasmes, les Hypotheses.* Paris: Julliard, 1967. Reprint, Paris: Editions Robert Lafont, 1988.

Douzet, André. *Lumières Nouvelles sur Rennes-le-Château.* Geneva: Editions Aquarius, 1995.

———. *Sauniere's Model and the Secret of Rennes-le-Château: The Priest's Final Legacy That Unveils the Location of His Terrifying Discovery.*

Ermengaud de Béziers [attributed]. *An Exposure of the Albigensian Heresies.* Archive Nationale Bibliotheave, Paris, 13th-century manuscript.

Fanthorpe, P. A. *The Holy Grail Revealed: The Real Secret of Rennes-le-Château.* Calif.: Newcastle Press, 1982.

Fanthorpe, Lionel, and Patricia Fanthorpe. *Rennes-le-Château: Its Mysteries and Secrets.* Ashford: Bellevue Books, 1991.

———. *Secrets of Rennes-le-Château.* York Beach, Maine: Samuel Weiser, 1992.

Fanthorpe, Lionel, Patricia Fanthorpe, and Tim Wallace-Murphy. *Rennes-le-Château: Its Mysteries and Secrets.* Red Wheel/Weiser, 2004.

Gay, Roberts. *Mystery of Rennes-le-Château—A Concise Guide.* Llanidloes, Wales, self-published, 1995.

Guébin, Pascal, and Moisoineuve Guébin. *History Albigeoise de Pierre des Vaux-de-Cerny.* Paris, 1951.

Hamilton, B. *The Albigensian Crusade.* Historical Association, 1974.

Hinkle, William M. *The Fleurs De Lis of the Kings of France, 1285–1488,* Carbondale, Illinois: Southern Illinois University Press, 1991.

*Hopkins, Marilyn, Graham Simmans, and Tim Wallace-Murphy. *Rex Deus: The True Mystery of Rennes-le-Château and the Dynasty of Jesus.* Shaftesbury: Element Books, 2000.

James, Stanley. *The Treasure Maps of Rennes-le-Château.* Bow, UK: Maxbow, Seven Lights Publishing, 1984.

Kersey, Bill. *Still Spins the Spider of Rennes-le-Château?* 2004.

Kurpiewski, Christopher M. "Writing beneath the Shadow of Heresy: The Historia Albigensis of Brother Pierre des Vaux-de-Cernay." *Journal of Medieval History* 31 (March 1905).

Lambert, Malcolm. *The Cathars.* Oxford: Blackwell, 1998.

Lamoureux, J. M. *Les Saintes Maries de Provence: Leur Vie et Leur Culte.* Cazihac: Bélisane, 1908. Reprint, 1999.

Lee, Sonia. "The Struggle between Cistercian and Cathar, A.D. 1145–1220 and Its Possible Influence on Holy Grail Literature." *Dissertations Abstracts,* 36:6 (1975) 3656.

Lincoln, Henry. *Key to the Sacred Pattern: The Untold Story of Rennes-le-Château.* London: Cassell Paperbacks, Windrush Press, 1997.

*———. *The Holy Place: The Mystery of Rennes-le-Château.* London: Weidenfeld and Nicolson Illustrated, 2002.

Lobineau, Henri. *Généalogie des Rois Mérovingiens et origine de diverses familles françaises et étrangéres de souche Mérovingienne, d'aprés Pichon, le Docteur Hervé et les parchmins de l'Abbé Sauniére de Rennes-le Château. (Aude,* Geneva 1956, *Bibliothéque Nationale,* lm3 4122 deposited in 1964. These were forged documents.

Mackness, Robin. *Oradour: Massacre and Aftermath.* London, Bloomsbury, 1988.

Madaule, Jacques. *The Albigensian Crusade: An History Essay.* Translated by Barbara Wall. New York: Fordham University Press, 1967.

Maitland, S. R. Trans. of Raynaldus "Annales." *History of the Albigenses and Waldenses.* London: C. J. G. and F. Rivington, 1832.

Marie, F. *Rennes-le-Château: Étude Critique.* S.R.E.S. Bagneux, 1978.

Markale, Jean. *Rennes-le-Château et l'Enigme de l'Or Maudit.* Paris: Editions Pygmalion/Gérald Watelet, 1989.

———. *The Templar Treasure at Gisors.* Inner Traditions, 2003.

———. *The Church of Mary Magdalene: The Sacred Feminine of the Treasures of Rennes-le-Château.* Vermont: Inner Traditions International, 2004.

Mazières, Abbé Maurice-René. *Les templiers du Bézu: Haute Vallée d'Aude.* Carcassonne, France: Société des arts and Sciences de Carcassonne, 1984.

Millar, John. "Richard Wagner, Rosslyn and the Mystery of Rennes-les-Château." *Newsletter of the Saunière Society* 2, no. 5/11 (1 January 1999).

O'Shea, Stephen. *The Perfect Heresy: The Life and Death of the Cathars.* New York: Walker and Company, 2000.

Oblonesky, D. *The Bogomils: A Study in Balkan Neo-Manichaeism.* Cambridge University Press, 1960.

*Patton, Guy, and Robin Mackness. *Sacred Treasure, Secret Power: The True History of the Web of Gold.* London: Macmillan, Pan Books, 2001.

*Putnam, Bill, and John Edwin Wood. *The Treasure of Rennes-le-Château: A Mystery Solved.* Stroud: Sutton Publishing, 2003, 2005.

Reznikov, Raimonde. *Cathares et Templiers.* Portet-sur-Garonne: Editions Loubatieres, 1993.

Richardson, Robert. *The Unknown Treasure: The Priory of Sion Fraud and the Spiritual Treasure of Rennes-le-Château.* 1998.

Rivière, Jacques. *La Fabuleux Trésor de Rennes-le-Château.* Editions Bélisane, Cazilhac, 1995.

Robin, Jean. *Rennes-le-Château—La Colline Envoutée.* Paris, Cuy Tredaniel, 1982.

———. *Opération Orth—L'Incroyable Secret de Rennes-le-Château.* Paris, Editions de la Maisnie, 1989.

Roquebert, Michel. *Cathar Religion.* Editions Loubtieres, 1997.

Saul, John M., Janice A. Glaholm. *Rennes-le-Château: A Bibliography.* London: Mercurius Press, 1985.

Saunière, Bérenger. *Mon Enseignement à Antugnac.* Nice: Bélisane, 1984.

Saunière, Émile. *Bérenger Saunière.* 2 vols. Émile Saunière Espéraza, France, 1989.

Serrus, G. *Pays Cathares.* Toulouse: Éditions Loubatières, 1990.

Vaux-de-Cernay, Pierre, William A. Silby, and Michael

D. Silby, trans. *The History of the Albigensian Crusade. Trans.* William A. Silby and Michael D. Silby. Woodbridge, 1998.

Smith, Paul. "The 1989 Plantard Comeback," (priory-of-sion.com/ psp/id60.html)

———. "The Priory of Sion and Alice Keel [Grailromantic]." home.graffiti.net/prioryofsion/poslist.html

Strayer, Joseph R. *The Albigensian Crusades.* Ann Arbor: University of Michigan Press, 1971.

Sumption, Jonathan. *The Albigensian Crusade.* London: Faber and Faber, 1978, 1999.

Thierry, Augustin. *Récit du Temps Merovingiens.* Beligum, 1840.

Vaux-de-Cernay, Pierre des. *Hystoria Albigensis.* 3 vols. Edited by Pascal Guébin and Ernest Lyon. Paris, 1926–39.

———. *A Description of the Cathars and Waldenses.* This book is cited by Margaret Starbird.

Wakefield, Walter L. *Heresy, Crusade and Inquisition in Southern France, 1100–1250.* Allen and Unwin, 1974.

Wakefield, Walter L., and Austin P. Evans. *Heresies of the High Middle Ages.* New York: Columbia University Press, 1969.

Wallace-Hadrill, J. M. *The Long-Haired Kings.* 1962. Toronto: Toronto University Press, 1982.

Wallace-Murphy, Tim, Lionel Fanthorpe, and Patricia Fanthorpe. *Mysteries of Templar Treasure and the Holy Grail: The Secrets of Rennes-le-Château.* 1991, 2004.

Warner, H. J. *The Albigensian Heresy.* London: SPCK, 1922.

Wolff, Philippe, ed. *Documents du l'histoire du Languedoc.* Toulouse: Edouard Privat, 1969.

Wood, David. *Genesis, the First Book of Revelations.* Tunbridge Wells: Baton Press, 1985.

Wood, David, and Ian Campbell. *Geneset: Target Earth.* Bellevue Books, 1994.

———. *Poussin's Secret.* Tunbridge Wells, England: Genesis Trading Co., Ltd., 1995.

Young, John K. *Sacred Sites of the Knights Templar: Ancient Astronomers and Freemasons at Stonehenge, Rennes-le-Château and Santiago de Compostela.* 2003.

DA VINCI CODE AND DAN BROWN

*Abanes, Richard. *The Truth behind the Da Vinci Code: A Challenging Response to the Bestselling Novel.* Eugene, Oreg.: Harvest House Publishers, 2004. Negative.

*ABC. "Jesus, Mary, and Da Vinci." *ABC Special.* Television documentary, 3 November 2003. Hosted by Elizabeth Vargas.

Beverley, James A. *Counterfeit Code: Responding to the Da Vinci Heresies.* 2005.

Blomberg, Craig. "The Da Vinci Code." *Denver Seminary Journal* 7 (2004). Negative.

*Bock, Darrell L. *Breaking the Da Vinci Code: Answers to the Questions Everyone's Asking.* Thomas Nelson Publishing, 2004. Negative.

*Bozell, Brent. "ABC's Empty Assault on Jesus." Editorial of 5 November 2003. *Conservative Chronicle* (12 November 2003): 28.

*Brown, Dan. *The Da Vinci Code.* New York: Doubleday, 2003.

———. *The Solomon Key.* Doubleday, forthcoming.

*Burstein, Dan. *Secrets of the Code: The Unauthorized Guide to the Mysteries behind The Da Vinci Code.* CDS Books, 2004. Balanced.

Chandelle, Rene. *Beyond the Da Vinci Code—The Book That Solves the Mystery.* 2005. For uncritical true believers.

Clark, Steven. *Da Vinci Code on Trial.* 2005.

*Cox, Simon. *Cracking the Da Vinci Code: The Unauthorized Guide to the Facts behind Dan Brown's Bestselling Novel.* New York: Barnes and Noble Books, 2004.

———. *Cracking the Da Vinci Code: An A to Z Guide to the Facts behind the Fiction.* Sterling Publishing, 2004.

Eble, Betsy. *Depth and Details: A Reader's Guide to Dan Brown's The Da Vinci Code.* 2004.

Eclov, Lee, and Sarah Hinlicky Wilson. *The Da Vinci Code and Other Heresies: What Is the Allure of Secret Knowledge about God?* E-Book, 2005.

*Ehrman, Bart D. *The Truth behind The Da Vinci Code: A Historian Reveals What We Really Know about Jesus, Mary Magdalene, and Constantine.* Oxford University Press, 2004. Somewhat negative.

*Ferris, Stewart. *The Key to the Da Vinci Code.* Cheam, Surrey: Crombie Jardine Publishing, 2005. Positive.

*Gardner, Laurence. *The Magdalene Legacy: The Jesus and Mary Bloodline Conspiracy—Revelations beyond The Da Vinci Code.* London: Element, HarperCollins, 2005. Positive.

*Garlow, James L., and Peter Jones. *Cracking Da Vinci's Code: You've Read the Book, Now Hear the Truth.* Grand Haven, Mich.: Faith-Based Nonfiction, Brilliance Audio, Cook Communication Ministries International, 2004. Negative.

Gilvin, Brandon. *Solving the Da Vinci Code Mystery.* 2004.

Goldstein, Bill. "As a Novel Rises Quickly Book Industry Takes Note." *New York Times* (21 April 2003). see www.nytimes.com

Greeley, Andrew. "Da Vinci Is More Fantasy Than Fact." Book review, *National Catholic Reporter* (3 October 2003). Negative.

Green, Dan. *The Lincoln Da Vinci Code—A Must For All Readers of The Da Vinci Code.* 2005.

*Haag, Michael, and Veronica Haag. *The Rough Guide to The Da Vinci Code: An Unauthorised Guide.* London: Rough Guides Ltd., 2004. Neither positive nor negative.

*Hanegraaf, Hank, and Paul L. Maier. *The Da Vinci Code: Fact or Fiction, a Critique of the Novel by Dan Brown.* Wheaton, Ill.: Tyndale House Publishers, 2004. Negative.

*History Channel. "Beyond the *Da Vinci Code*." Television documentary, Summer 2005.

Jones, Greg. *Beyond Da Vinci.* Afterword by Deirdre Good. 2004.

Kauffman, Richard, with Darrel Bock. *Engaging the Da Vinci Code: How Should Christians Respond to Pop Culture That Contradicts Bibilical Teaching?* E-Books, 2004.

Kellmeyer, Steve. *Fact and Fiction in The Da Vinci Code.* 2004.

*Lunn, Martin. *Da Vinci Code Decoded: The Truth behind the New York Times #1 Bestseller.* New York: Disinformation Company, 2004.

*Lutzer, Erwin W. *The Da Vinci Deception: Credible Answers to the Questions People Are Asking about Jesus, the Bible, and The Da Vinci Code.* Wheaton, Ill.: Tyndale House Publishers, 2004. Negative.

Miesel, Sandra. "Dismantling the Da Vinci Code." *Crisis Magazine* (1 September 2003). Negative.

Morris, David. *The Art and Mythology of The Da Vinci Code.* 2004.

*Newman, Sharan. *The Real History behind The Da Vinci Code.* New York: Penguin Group, Berkeley Books, 2005. Neither positive or negative.

*NBC. "Secrets of the Code." *Dateline with Stone Phillips.* Television documentary, 28 June 2005.

Olson, Carl E. "Cracking Up 'The Da Vinci Code.'" *Envoy Magazine* (23 August 2003). Negative.

*Olson, Carl E., and Sandra Miesel. *The Da Vinci Hoax: Exposing the Errors in The Da Vinci Code.* San Francisco: Ignatius Press, July 2004. Negative.

*Perdue, Lewis. *The Da Vinci Legacy: The Da Vinci Code Is Missing . . .* Pinnacle Books, 1983. Reprint, New York: A Tor Book, 2004. This was the first "Da Vinci" novel.

Petersen, Zina Nibley. "The Divine Feminine and the Goddess Movement: A Mormon Medievalist Looks at One Issue in Dan Brown's *The Da Vinci Code.*" Museum of Art lecture series "*Mystery, Metaphor, and Meaning: LDS Perspectives on The Da Vinci Code,*" Brigham Young University, Provo, Utah, March 2004.

*Price, Robert M. *The Da Vinci Fraud: Why the Truth Is Stranger Than Fiction.* Amherst, N.Y. Prometheus Books, 2005.

Roberts, Roxanne. "The Mysteries of Mary Magdalene: 'The Da Vinci Code' Resurrects a Debate of Biblical Proportions." *Washington Post,* 20 July 2003. www.danbrown.com/media/magdalene.html

*Robinson, Tony, presenter/editor. "*The Real Da Vinci Code.*" Channel 4, United Kingdom television documentary, February 2005.

Rogak, Lisa. *Secrets of the Widow's Son: The Mysteries Surrounding the Sequel to The Da Vinci Code.* 2005.

*Sangeet, Duchane, and Priya Hemenway. *Beyond the Da Vinci Code: From the Rose Line to the Bloodline, The Unauthorized Guide to Dan Brown's Best-Selling Novel.* New York: Barnes and Noble Books, 2005.

Shugarts, David A. *Secrets of the Widow's Son: The Mysteries Surrounding the Sequel to the DaVinci Code.* Amazon Books, 2006.

Taylor, Greg. *The Guide to Dan Brown's The Solomon Key.* The Essential Primer, 2006.

Teisch, Jessica, and Tracy Bar. *Da Vinci for Dummies.* 2005.

Thompson, Mary R. *Mary of Magdala: Facts The Da Vinci Code Misses.* 2005.

Turner, Tracy, *The Da Vinci Code Quiz-105: Questions to Crack the Code.* 2005.

Tyson, J. S. *Before the Da Vinci Code: An Introduction to the Original Encoded Secret Concerning Jesus, Mary, and a Child.* 2005.

Ward, Alyson. "Decoding 'The Da Vinci Code.'" *Fort Worth Star-Telegram,* 24 January 2004.

Websites: http://www.danbrown.com/ http://witcombe.sbc.edu/davincicode/contents-schedule.html www.waynecoc.org/DaVinciCode.html

*Welborn, Amy. *De-Coding Da Vinci: The Facts behind the Fiction of The Da Vinci Code.* Huntington, Ind.: Our Sunday Visitor Publishing, 2004.

Welborn, Amy, *The Da Vinci Code: A Catholic Response.* 2004.

Witherington, Ben. *Gospel Code: Novel Claims about Jesus, Mary Magdalene, and Da Vinci.* 2004.

Zimmerman, W. Frederick. *The Solomon Key and Beyond.* Forthcoming.

DNA RESEARCH

Babich, Dr. Harvey. "The Jewish People under the Microscope." *Derech HaTeva.* Vol. 4. Stern

College, Yeshiva University, 2000.

Cann, R., M. Stoneking, and A. Wilson. "Mitochrondrial DNA and Human Evolution." *Nature* (1987).

Cochran, G. "How the Ashkenazim Got Their Smarts." *Gene Expression,* November 2003. *The Discovery Channel,* C-TV, 25 April 1997.

Diskin, A. Z. "Are Today's Jewish Priests Descended from the Old Ones?" *Journal of Comparative Human Biology,* 2000.

Epstein, Nadine. "Family Matters: Funny, We Don't Look Jewish." *Hadassah Magazine.* January 2001.

Fuma, Julia. "Bringing Science to the Search for Family Roots." *The Forward,* 17 August 2001.

Grady, D. "Finding Genetic Traces of Jewish Priesthood." *New York Times,* 7 January 1997.

Halkin, Hillel. "Wandering Jews and Their Genes." *Commentary Magazine,* 1 September 2000.

Hammer, M. F., et al. "Jewish and Middle Eastern Non-Jewish Populations Share a Common Pool of Y-Chromosome Biallelic Haplotypes." *Proceedings of the National Academy of Science,* 6 June 2000.

Hirschberg, P. "Decoding the Priesthood." *Jerusalem Report,* 10 May 1999.

Kleiman, Rabbi Yaakov. *DNA and Tradition: The Genetic Link to the Ancient Hebrews.* Israel: Devora Publishing Company, 2004.

Narby, Jeremy. *The Cosmic Serpent: DNA and the Origins of Knowledge.* New York: Jeremy Tarcher/Putnam, 1998.

Olsen, Steve. "Mapping Human History—Genes, Race, and Our Common Origins." New York: Houghton Mifflin, 2002.

Ostrer, Harry, Dr. Chairman of the New York University Human Genetics Project. "A Genetic Profile of Contemporary Jewish Populations." *Nature Review,* November, 2001.

———. "Genetic Analysis of Jewish Origins." 2000. www.med.nyu.edu/genetics/ga_jewishorigins

Ovchinnikov, Igor V., Anders Gotherstroms, Galina P. Romanove, Vitaliy Kharitonov, Kerstin Lidens, and William Goodwin. "Molecular Analysis of Neanderthal DNA from the Northern Caucasus."

Nature 404 (30 March 2000): 490–93.

Parfitt, Tudor. *Journey to the Vanished City: The Search for a Lost Tribe of Israel.* London: Hodder and Stroughton, 2002.

*Perego, Ugo. "Reconstructing Joseph Smith Y-Chromosome: Genealogical Application." *Journal of Mormon History,* August 2005.

*Sangeet, Duchane, and Priya Hemenway. *Beyond the Da Vinci Code: From the Rose Line to the Bloodline, The Unauthorized Guide to Dan Brown's Best-selling Novel.* New York: Barnes and Noble Books, 2005.

Skorecki, K., and N. Bradman, and M. Hammer. "Y Chromosomes of Jewish Priests." *Nature,* 2 January 1997.

Southerton, Simon G. *Losing a Lost Tribe: Native Americans, DNA and the Mormon Church.* Salt Lake City: Signature Books, 2004.

*Stephens, Trent D., and D. Jeffrey Meldrum. *Evolution and Mormonism: A Quest for Understanding.* Salt Lake City: Signature Books, 2001.

Thomas, M., and D. Goldstein. "Founding Mothers of Jewish Communities." *American Journal of Human Genetics* 70 (May 2002).

Thomas, M., K. Skorecki, and D. Goldstein. "Origins of Old Testament Priests." *Nature,* 9 July 1998.

Travis, J. "'The Priests'" Chromosome? DNA Analysis Supports the Biblical Story of the Jewish Priesthood." *Science News,* 3 October 1998.

Wade, Nicholas. "DNA Clues to Jewish Roots." *New York Times,* 14 May 2002.

———. "The Human Family Tree: 10 Adams and 18 Eves." *New York Times,* 2 May 2000.

Watson, J., and F. Crick. "A Structure for Deoxyribose Nucleic Acid." *Nature* 171 (1953): 737.

EVE, VIRGIN MARY, MARY MAGDALENE, AND THE BETHANY SISTERS

Adams, L. *The Tomb of the Virgin Mary.* New York, 1978.

Annales Ecclesiastici, Vol. 1. Quoting *Acts of Magdalen.*

Ashe, Geoffrey. *The Virgin: Mary's Cult and the Re-Emergence of the Goddess*. London: Arkana, 1988.

Atwood, Richard. *Mary Magdalene in the New Testament Gospels and Early Tradition*. European University Studies Series 22, vol. 457. New York: Peter Lang, 1993.

*Baigent, Michael, Richard Leigh, and Henry Lincoln. *Holy Blood, Holy Grail*. Rev. ed. London: Arrow, 1996.

Baker, James T. "The Red-Haired Saint: Is Mary Magdalene the Key to the Easter Narratives?" *Christian Century* 94 (6 April 1977): 328–32.

Bedouelle, Guy. "Mary Magdalene—The Apostle of the Apostles and the Order of Preachers." *Dominican Ashram* 18, 4 (1999): 157–71. See www.womenpriests.org/magdale/bedouell.htm

Begg, Ean C. M. *The Cult of the Black Virgin*. Rev. ed. London: Arkana, 1996.

Bellevie, Lesa. *The Complete Idiot's Guide to Mary Magdalene*. Penguin Australia, 2005.

*Biema, David Van, and Lisa McLaughlin. "Mary Magdalene: Saint or Sinner?" *Time Magazine*, 11 August 2003, 52–55.

Birch, W. Grayson. *Veritas and the Virgin, or Jesus, the Son of God and the Children of Joseph and Mary*. Berne, Ind.: Berne Witness, 1960.

*Bock, Darrell L. "Was Jesus Married to Mary Magdalene? All the Available Evidence Clearly Points to an Answer of 'No.'" ABCNews.com (12 November 2003).

Boslooper, Thomas. *The Virgin Birth*. Philadelphia, 1962.

Brock, Ann Graham. *Mary Magdalene, The First Apostle: The Struggle for Authority*. Harvard Theological Studies 51. Cambridge: Harvard University Press, 2002.

Burkitt, Francis C. "Mary Magdalene and Mary, Sister of Martha." *Expository Times* 42 (1931).

*Chilton, Bruce. *Mary Magdalene: A Biography*. New York: Doubleday, 2005.

*de Boer, Esther. *Mary Magdalene: Beyond the Myth*. Translated by John Bowden. Trinity Press International, 1996.

Devine, R. J. *Holy Virginity*. Rome, 1964.

Dunstan, Victor. *Did the Virgin Mary Live and Die in England?* Megiddo Press, 1985.

Ebertshäuser, Caroline, et al. *Mary: Art, Culture, and Religion through the Ages*. Translated by Peter Heinegg. New York: Crossroad, 1998.

Fallon, J. E. "Mary Magdalene," *New Catholic Dictionary*, Vol. 9

Filliette, Edith. *Saint Mary Magdalene, Her Life and Times*. Newton Lower Falls, Mass.: Society of Saint Mary Magdalene, 1983.

Fiorenza, Elisabeth Schüssler. *In Memory of Her: A Feminist Theological Reconstruction of Christian Origins*. New York: Crossroad, 1984.

*Gardner, Laurence. *The Magdalene Legacy: The Jesus and Mary Bloodline Conspiracy: Revelations beyond The Da Vinci Code*. London: Element, HarperCollins, 2005.

Gazay, J. "Etudes sur les légendes de Sainte Marie-Madeleine et de Joseph d'Arimathie." *Annales du Midi* LI (1939): 225–84, 337–89.

George, Margaret. *Mary, Called Magdalene*. 2002.

Getty-Sullivan, Mary Ann. *Women in the New Testament*. Liturgical Press, 2001.

Good, Deirdre. *Mariam, the Magdalen, and the Mother*. Indiana University Press, 2005.

Harris, Anthony. *The Sacred Virgin and the Holy Whore*. Sphere, 1988.

*Haskins, Susan. *Mary Magdalen: Myth and Metaphor*. New York: Riverhead Books, 1995.

Hawtrey, V. Trans. *The Life of Saint Mary Magdalen*. New York, 1904.

Housley, Kathleen. "Solid Citizen or Prostitute—Two Millennia of Misinformation" [Mary Magdalene]. *Dialog* 27 (Fall 1988): 295–97.

Jansen, Katherine Ludwig. "Mary Magdalena: *Apostolorum Apostola*." In *Women Preachers and Prophets through Two Millennia of Christianity*. Edited by Beverly Mayne Kienzle and Pamela J. Walker. Los Angeles: University of California Press, 1998.

———. *The Making of the Magdalen: Preaching and*

Popular Devotion in the Later Middle Ages. Princeton University Press, 2001.

Jensen, Lone. *Gifts of Grace.* San Francisco: Harper, 1989.

Jones, F. Stanley, ed. *Which Mary? The Marys of Early Christian Tradition.* Society of Biblical Literature Symposium Series 19. Edited by Christopher Matthews. Atlanta, Ga.: Society of Biblical Literature, 2002.

Jordan, Michael. *Mary, the Unauthorized Biography.* London: Weidenfeld and Nicolson, 2001.

*Jusino, Ramon K. *Mary Magdalene: Author of the Fourth Gospel?* 1998. Treatise posted at: www.BelovedDisciple.org, and http://members.tripod.com/~Ramon-K- Jusino/magdalene.html#brownl

*King, Karen L. *The Gospel of Mary of Magdala: Jesus and the First Woman Apostle.* Santa Rosa, Calif.: Polebridge Press, 2003.

Kinstler, Clysta. *The Moon under Her Feet: The Story of Mary Magdalene in the Service of the Great Mother.* San Francisco: HarperCollins, 1989.

Lacordaire, Rev. Père. *Saint Mary Magdalene.* Derby: Thomas Richardson, 1880.

Lebeuf, A. "Maria Magdalena: The Morning Star." *Vistas in Astronomy* 39, 4 (1995).

Ledwith, Stuart. *Mary Magdalene: The Disciple Jesus Loved.* Soul Works International, 1990.

Leloupe, Jean-Yves. *The Gospel of Mary Magdalene.* Translated by Joseph Rowe. Rochester, Vt.: Bear and Company, Inner Traditions, 2002.

———. *The Gospel of Philip.* Rochester, Vt.: Inner Traditions, 2004.

———. *The Gospel of Thomas.* Rochester, Vt.: Inner Traditions, 2005.

Leslie, R. C. "The Woman That Was a Sinner." *Expository Times* 27 (1915–16).

Longfellow, Ki. *The Secret Magdalene.* EIO Books, 2005.

Maar, Raban (Archbishop of Mainz/Mayence, A.D. 776–856). *Life of Mary Magdalene.* Magdalene College Library, Oxford University. MS almost certainly of mid-twelfth-century construction. See Rabanus, Maurus.

Maisch, Ingrid. *Mary Magdalene: The Image of a Woman through the Centuries.* Translated by Linda M. Maloney. Liturgical Press, 1998.

Malvern, Marjorie M. *Venus in Sackcloth: The Magdalen's Origins and Metamorphoses.* Carbondale, Ill.: Southern Illinois University Press, 1975.

Manns, Frederic. "Magdala dans les sources littéraires." *Studia Hierosolymitana* I Studi Archeologici, Studium Biblicum Franciscanum Collectio Maior 22 (1976).

Marjanen, Annti. *The Woman Jesus Loved: Mary Magdalene in the Nag Hammadi Library and Related Documents.* Leiden: E. J. Brill, 1996.

*Markale, Jean. *The Church of Mary Magdalene: The Sacred Feminine of the Treasures of Rennes-le-Château.* Rochester, Vt.: Inner Traditions International, 2004.

Mary Magdalene: A Woman Who Showed Her Gratitude. 1988.

Mascall, E. L., and H. S. Box. *The Blessed Virgin Mary.* London, 1963.

McGowan, Kathleen. *The Expected One.* UK: Simon & Schuster, 2006.

Meredith, Garth H. "Saint Mary Magdalene in Mediaeval Literature." *The John Hopkins University Studies in Historical and Political Science,* series 67, no. 3, 1950.

Metcalfe, W. M., ed. "Magdalene." *Legends of the Saints in the Scottish Dialect of the Fourteenth Century.* Edinburgh and London: Scottish Text Society, 1896.

Meyer, Marvin, and Esther A. de Boer. *The Gospels of Mary: The Secret Tradition of Mary Magdalene, the Companion of Jesus.* San Francisco: HarperSanFrancisco, 2004.

Miegge, G. *The Virgin Mary.* Lutterworth, 1955.

Mycoff, David, trans. and intro. *The Life of Saint Mary Magdalene and of Her Sister Saint Martha.* Kalamazoo, Mich.: Cistercian Publications, 1989.

Nagast, Karbra. *Magda.* 1908. Notes that the first Magdalene was Ethiopian, black, and wise in magic; married to Solomon and had a son named David.

Newman, Barbara. *From Virile Woman to Woman Christ.* Philadelphia: University of Pennsylvania Press, 1995.

Pagels, Elaine. *Adam, Eve and the Serpent.* London: Weidenfeld and Nicolson, 1998.

Palmer, P. *Mary in the Documents of the Church.* London, 1958.

Pelikan, Jaroslav. *Mary through the Centuries: Her Place in the History of Culture.* New Haven, Conn.: Yale University Press, 1996.

*Phillips, Dr. Graham. *The Marian Conspiracy: The Hidden Truth about the Holy Grail, the Real Father of Christ and the Tomb of the Virgin Mary.* London: Sidgwick and Jackson/Macmillan Publishers Ltd., 2000.

*Picknett, Lynn. *Mary Magdalene: Christianity's Hidden Goddess.* London: Robinson, 2003.

Pissier, Abbé Alexander. *Le Culte de Sainte Marie-Madeleine a Vézelay.* Saint-Père, 1923.

Rabanus, Maurus (Archbishop of Mainz, Germany A.D. 776–856). *Life of Mary Magdalene.* Magdalene College Library, Oxford University. MS probably of mid-twelfth-century construction.

Ricci, Carla. *Mary Magdalene and Many Others: Women Who Followed Jesus.* Tunbridge Wells: Burns and Oates, 1994. First published as *Maria di Magdala e le Molte Altre: Donne sul cammino di Gesu.* Naples: M. D'Auria, 1991.

Robinson, Thomas. *Life and Death of Mary Magdalene.* Edited by H. O. Sommer. Oxford: Oxford University Press, 1899.

Sanders, Joseph N. "Those Whom Jesus Loved." *New Testament Studies* 1 (1955).

*Schaberg, Jane. *The Resurrection of Mary Magdalene: Legends, Apocrypha, and the Christian Testament.* New York and London: The Continuum International Publishing Group, 2002.

*Starbird, Margaret. *Woman with the Alabaster Jar: Mary Magdalen and the Holy Grail.* Santa Fe, N.M.: Bear and Company, 1993.

*———. *The Goddess in the Gospels: Reclaiming the Sacred Feminine.* Bear and Company, 1998.

*———. *Magdalen's Lost Legacy: Symbolic Numbers and the Sacred Union in Christianity.* Rochester, Vt.: Bear and Company, 2003.

*———. *Mary Magdalene: Bride in Exile.* Rochester, Vt.: Inner Traditions, 2005.

Thompson, Mary. *Mary of Magdala: Apostle and Leader.* ISBN 0809135–736

Thurian, M. *Mary: Mother of the Lord, Figure of the Church.* London, 1963.

"Vita Apostolica Mariae Magdalenae." *Monuments inédits sur l'apostolat de sainte Marie-Madeleine en Provence.* Vol. 2. Paris, 1848.

Ward, Benedicta. *Harlots of the Desert.* Kalamazoo, Mich.: Cistercian Publications, 1987.

*Warner, Marina. *Alone of All Her Sex: The Myth and Cult of the Virgin Mary.* London: George Weidenfeld and Nicolson, 1976. Reprint, New York: Alfred A. Knopf, 1983.

FREEMASONS AND ROSICRUCIANS

*Baigent, Michael, and Richard Leigh. *The Temple and the Lodge.* New York: Arcade Publishing, 1989.

Bennett, John. *Origin of Freemasonry and Knights Templar.* Kila, Mont.: Kessinger Publishing, 1907.

Béresniak, Daniel. *Symbols of Freemasonry.* Translated by Ian Monk. New York: Barnes and Noble Books, 2003.

Brown, Robert Hewitt. *Stellar Theology and Masonic Astronomy.*

Burchardt, Titus. *Chartres and the Birth of a Cathedral.* Ipswich: Golgonooza Press, 1995.

Cahill, E. *Freemasonry and the Anti-Christian Movement.* 5th ed. Dublin, 1959.

*Cain, Tubal. [pseud.] *Secrets of the Lodge: Origins, Practices and Beliefs of Freemasonry.* Denbighhshire, Wales: Delphi Publishing, 1999.

Carlile, Richard. *A Manual of Freemasonry.* 1860.

———. *A Manual of the First Three Degrees, with an Introductory Keystone to the Royal Arch,* 1943.

Carr, Harry. *Three Distinct Knocks and Jachin and Boaz.* Bloomington, Ill.: Masonic Book Club, 1981.

Cartwright, E. H. *Masonic Ritual.* Shepperton: Lewis Masonic, 1985.

Castells, F. P. *English Freemasonry.* London: Ryder and Co., 1931.

Churton, Tobian. *The Golden Builders: Alchemists, Rosicrucians and the First Free Masons.* Lichfield: Signal Publishing, 2002.

Cooper-Oakley, Isabel. *Masonry and Medieval Mysticism: Traces of a Hidden Tradition.* London: Theosophical Publishing House, 1900. Reprint, 1977.

Crawford Smith, D. *History of the Ancient Lodge of Scoon and Perth.* No. 3. Edinburgh, 1898.

Crossle, P., and J. H. Lepper. *History of the Grand Lodge of Free and Accepted Masons of Ireland.* Dublin, 1925.

Daraul, Arkon. *A History of Secret Societies.* Citadel Press, 1984.

Darrah, Delmar D. *History and Evolution of Freemasonry.* Chicago: Powner, 1979.

Findel, J. G. *The History of Freemasonry from Its Origins Down to the Present Day.* London: George Kenning, 1869.

Gould, Robert Freke. *A Library of Freemasonry.* 1906.

———. *Gould's History of Freemasonry.* 5 vols. London, 1887. Reprint, London: Caxton, 1933.

Godwin, Joscelyn, trans. *The Chemical Wedding of Christian Rosenkreutz.* Phanes Press, 1994.

*Hall, Manly Palmer. *The Lost Keys of Freemasonry.* Los Angeles: Philosophical Research Society, 1923. Reprint, 1976.

*———. *The Secret Teachings of All Ages: An Encyclopedic Outline of Masonic, Hermetic, Cabalistic and Rosicrucian Symbolic Philosophy.* Los Angeles: Philosophical Research Society, 1928. Reprinted as *Rosicrucian Philosophy,* Los Angeles: Philosophical Research Society, 1979.

Hamill, John. *The Craft: A History of English Freemasonry.* Wellingborough, England: Crucible, 1986.

Heline, Corinne. *Mystic Masonry and the Bible.* Santa Monica, Calif.: 1989.

Horne, Bro. Alexander. "The Saints John in the Masonic Tradition." Transactions of the Quatuor Coronati Lodge No. 2076, London, 1962.

———. *King Solomon's Temple in the Masonic Tradition.* London, 1961. Reprint, Wellingborough: Aquarian Press, 1972.

Jacob, Margaret C. *Living the Enlightenment: Freemasonry and Politics in Eighteenth-Century Europe.* New York: Oxford University Press, 1991.

James, John. *Chartres, the Masons Who Built a Legend.* Thames and Hudson, 1982.

Jennings, Hargrave. *The Rosicrucians—Their Rites and Mysteries.* London: 1870. Reprint, Health Research California, 1966.

Jones, Bernard E. *Freemasons' Book of the Royal Arch.* London: George G. Harrap, 1957, 1969.

*Knight, Christopher, and Robert Lomas. *The Hiram Key: Pharaohs, Freemasons, and the Discovery of the Secret Scrolls of Jesus.* London: Century, 1996.

*———. *The Second Messiah: Templars, the Turin Shroud and the Great Secret of Freemasonry.* London: Century, 1997.

*———. "The Holy Grail." *Mysteries of the Ancient World.* Edited by Judith Flanders. New York: Barnes and Noble Books, 1998.

*———. *Uriel's Machine: The Ancient Origins of Science.* London: Arrow, 2000.

*———. *The Book of Hiram: Freemasonry, Venus and the Secret Key to the Life of Jesus.* London: Century, 2003.

Knight, Stephen. *The Brotherhood—The Secret World of Freemasons.* New York: Dorset Press, 1984.

Laughlan, Royal, MBE, JP. *The Kilwinning No. 0 Masonic Lodge in Old Picture Postcards.* European Library, Zaltbommel/Netherlands, 1994.

Lawrence, J. *Freemasonry, a Religion.* Eastbourne: Kingsway, 1987.

Lennhoff, E. *The Freemasons: The History, Nature, Development and Sacred of the Royal Art.* London, 1994.

Lomas, Robert. *The Invisible College. The Royal Society, Freemasonry and the Birth of Modern Science.* London: Headline, 2002.

*———. *Turning the Hiram Key.* 2005.

Mackenzie, Kenneth. *The Royal Masonic Cyclopaedia. 1877.* Reprint, Wellingborough Northants: Aquarium Press, 1987.

Mackey, Albert G. *History of Freemasonry.* New York: Masonic History, 1897.

———. *Encyclopaedia of Freemasonry.* Rev. ed. Philadelphia: Everts, 1887.

Macoy, Robert. *A Dictionary of Freemasonry.* New York: Gramercy Books, n.d.

McIntosh, Christopher. *The Rosy Cross Unveiled.* Northamptonshire: Aquarian Press Ltd., 1980.

———. *The Rosicrucians: The History and Mythology of an Occult Order.* Wellingborough, Northants: Crucible, 1987.

McKay, A. G. *An Encyclopedia of Freemasonry.* New York and London, 1920.

McNulty, W. K. *Freemasonry: A Journey through Ritual and Symbol.* London: 1991.

Naudon, Paul. *Freemasonry—a European Viewpoint.* Translated from the French by Joseph Tang. Great Britain: Freestone Press, 1993.

O'Brien, H. *The Round Towers of Ireland; or, The Mysteries of Freemasonry, of Sabaism and of Buddhism, for the First Time Unveiled.* London, 1834.

Parker, Arthur C. *American Indian Freemasonry.* New York, 1919.

Piatigorsky, Prof. A. *Freemasonry.* London: Harvill Press, 1999.

Pike, Albert. *Morals and Dogma of the Ancient and Accepted Scottish Rite of Freemasonry.* Southern Jurisdiction of the United States. Charleston, S.C.: A. M., 1871.

Richardson, Jabez. *Richardson's Monitor of Freemasonry.* 1860. Reprint, Kila, Mont.: Kessinger Publishing, 1942.

Ridley, Jasper. *The Freemasons: A History of the World's Most Powerful Secret Society.* New York: Arcade Books, 2002.

Robert, B. H. "Masonry and Mormonism." *Improvement Era* 24, 10 (August 1921).

Robinson, John J. *Born in Blood: The Lost Secrets of Freemasonry.* New York: M. Evans and Co., 1989. Reprint, London: Arrow, 1993.

Stevenson, Prof. David. *The Origins of Freemasonry, Scotland's Century, 1590–1710.* Cambridge: Cambridge University Press, 1988.

———. *The First Freemasons.* Aberdeen University Press, 1989.

Stewart, J. J. *Freemason's Manual.* Philadelphia: Butler, 1851.

Tailby, S. R. *A Brief History of Lodge Mother Kilwinning No. 0.* Kilwinning, 1944.

Van Buren, Elizabeth. *The Secret of the Illuminati.* Sudbury, Suffolk: Neville Spearman, 1982.

Waite, Arthur Edward. *A New Encyclopedia of Freemasonry (Ars Magna Latomorum).* New York: Wings Books, 1970,1994.

———. *The Brotherhood of the Rosy Cross.* Kila, Mont.: R. A. Kessinger, 1998.

Ward, J. S. M. *Who was Hiram Abiff?* London: Baskerville, 1925. Reprint, Plymouth: Lewis Masonic, 1992.

———. *Freemasonry and the Ancient Gods.* London: Baskerville, 1926.

Webster, Nesta H. *Secret Societies and Subversive Movements.* London: Bowell, 1924. Reprint, G. S. G. and Associates, 1972.

White, Ralph. *Rosicrucian Enlightenment Revisited.* 1998.

Wilmshurst, Walter. *The Meaning of Masonry.* Gramercy Books, 1995.

Yates, Frances A. *The Rosicrucian Enlightenment.* London: Routledge, 1972.

GNOSTICISM, PAGANISM, HERESY, AND MYSTICISM

Adler, Margot. *Drawing Down the Moon: Witches, Druids, Goddess-Worshippers, and Other Pagans in America Today.* New York: Penguin-Arkana, 1997.

Alfrod, Alan. *The Phoenix Solution: Secrets of a Lost Civilization.* London: Hodder and Stoughton, 1998.

Bauer, Walter. *Orthodoxy and Heresy in Earliest*

Christianity. Edited by Robert A. Kraft and Gerhard Krodel. Translated by Philadelphia Seminar on Christian Origins. Philadelphia: Fortress, 1971.

Bayley, Harold. *The Lost Language of Symbolism.* 1912. Reprint, Totowa, N.J.: Rowman and Littlefield, 1974.

Beor, R. *Philo's Use of the Categories Male and Female.* Leiden, Netherlands: Brill, 1970.

Besant, Annie. *Esoteric Christianity.* Theosophical Publishing House, 1901.

*Blake, Peter, and Paul S. Blezard. *The Arcadian Cipher: The Quest to Crack the Code of Christianity's Greatest Secret.* London: Sidgwick and Jackson, 2000.

Blavatsky, Madame H. P. *The Secret Doctrine.* Theosophical Publishing House, 1888.

———. *Theosophical Glossary.* London, 1892.

Burkert, Walter. *Ancient Mystery Cults.* Harvard University Press, 1987.

Campbell, Joseph. *The Hero with a Thousand Faces.* New York: Pantheon Books, 1949.

———. *The Masks of God: Creative Mythology.* London: Secker and Warburg, 1968.

———. *The Power of Myth. Videorecording.* New York: Mystic Fire Video, 2001.

Clauss, Manfred. *The Roman Cult of Mithraism: The God and His Mysteries* New York: Routledge, 2001.

Clifton, Chas S. *Encyclopedia of Heresies and Heretics.* ABC-Clio, 1992.

Clube, S. V. M., and B. Napier. *The Cosmic Winter.* Oxford: Blackwell, 1990.

Couliano, Ioan P. *The Tree of Gnosis: Gnostic Mythology from Early Christianity to Modern Nihilism.* San Francisco: HarperSanFrancisco, 1992.

Davidson, Gustav. *A Dictionary of Angels, Including Fallen Angels.* New York: The Free Press, 1967.

Decker, Ronald, Depaulis, Thierry and Dummett, Michael. *A Wicked Pack of Cards: The Origins of the Occult Tarot.* New York: St. Martin's Press, 1996.

Doherty, Earl. *The Jesus Puzzle: Did Christianity Begin with a Mythical Christ?* Ottawa: Canadian Humanist Publications, 1999.

Drower, E. S. *The Mandaeans of Iraq and Iran: Their Cults, Customs, Magic, Legends and Folklore.* Oxford: Clarendon Press, 1937.

Ehrman, Bart D. *Jesus: Apocalyptic Prophet of the New Millennium.* New York: Oxford University Press, 1999.

Ellis, R. *Thoth. Architect of the Universe.* Edfu Books, 1997.

Fenton, Edward. ed. *The Diaries of John Dee.* Oxfordshire: Day Books, 1998.

Fortune, Dion. *Esoteric Orders and Their Work.* Wellingborough: Aquarian Press, 1987.

———. *The Mystical Qabalah.* Weiser Books, 2000.

Frazier, Sir James George. *The Golden Bough: A Study in Magic and Religion.* New York: Macmillan, 1951.

French, P. *The World of an Elizabethan Magus.* London, 1972.

Gettings, Fred. *The Secret Zodiac.* London: Routledge, Kegan Paul, 1987.

Godwin, Joscelyn. *The Theosophical Enlightenment.* Albany, 1994.

Grant, Robert M., ed. *The Secret Sayings of Jesus.* Garden City, N.J. Doubleday, 1960.

———. *Gnosticism: A Source Book.* New York: Harper and Row, 1961.

Hall, Manly Palmer. *The Secret Teachings of All Ages.* Los Angeles: The Philosphical Reseach Society, 1928.

Halliday, William R. *The Pagan Background of Early Christianity.* New York: Cooper Square Publishers, 1970.

Hansen, Paul D. *Visionaries and Their Apocalypses.* Philadelphia: Fortress Press, 1983.

Harding, M. *A Little Book of the Green Man.* London: Aurum Press, 1998.

Heelas, Paul. *The New Age Movement: The Celebration of the Self and Sacralization of Modernity.* Oxford, 1996.

Herrick, James A. *The Making of the New Spirituality: The Eclipse of the Western Religious Tradition.* Downers Grove, Ill.: InterVarsity Press, 2003.

*History Channel. "Banned from the Bible." *History Channel Special.* 25 December 2003.

Howard, Michael. *The Occult Conspiracy.* Rochester, Vt.: Destiny Books, 1989.

Hunt, R., ed. *The Drolls, Traditions, and Supersitions of Old Cornwall.* 1865. 2d series. Lampeter: Llarnerch Publishers, 1993.

Jewett, Paul K. *Man as Male and Female.* Grand Rapids, Mich.: Eerdmans, 1976.

Jonas, Hans. *The Gnostic Religion: The Message of the Alien God and the Beginnings of Christianity.* 1958. Reprint, London: Routledge, 1992.

Kienzle, Beverly. *Cistercians, Heresy and Crusade.* Woodbridge and Rochester, New York, 2001.

*King, Karen L. *What Is Gnosticism?* Cambridge: Belknap Press of Harvard University Press, 2003.

———. *Images of the Feminine in Gnosticism.* 2d ed. Harrisburg, Pa.: Trinity Press International, 2000.

Kingsland, William. *The Gnosis or Ancient Wisdom in the Christian Scriptures.* London: Allen and Unwin, 1937.

Kirby, Richard. *The Mission of Mysticism.* Society for Promoting Christian Knowledge, 1979.

Knight, Gareth. *A Practical Guide to Qabalistic Symbolism.* Red Wheel/Weiser, 2002.

Kramer, Samuel N. *The Sacred Marriage Rite.* Bloomington: Indiana University Press, 1969.

Lacarriere, Jacques. *The Gnostics.* UK: Peter Owen, 1977.

Layton, Bentley. *The Gnostic Scriptures: Ancient Wisdom for the New Age.* London: SCM Press, 1987.

Lucas, Jerry, and Del Washburn. *Theomatics: God's Best Kept Secret Revealed.* New York: Stein and Day, 1977.

Luckert, K. W. *Egyptian Light and Hebrew Fire.* New York: State University of New York Press, 1991.

Mathers, S. *The Cabala.* London: Kegan Paul, Trench, 1909.

Mead, George Robert Stowe. *Simon Magus: An Essay.* London: Theosophic Publishing Society, 1892.

———. *Gnosis of the Mind.* 1906.

———. *The Gnostic John the Baptizer: Selections from the Mandaean John Book.* London: John M. Watkins, 1924.

———. *Thrice Great Hermes: Studies in Hellenistic Theosophy and Gnosis.* North Beach, Maine: Samuel Weiser, 1992.

Meller, Walter Clifford. *Old Times: Relics, Talismans, Forgotten Customs and Beliefs of the Past.* London: T. Werner Laurie Ltd., 1925. Reprint, 1968.

Metzger, Richard, ed. *Book of Lies: The Disinformation Guide to Magick and the Occult.* New York: Disinformation Company, 2003.

Nash, Ronald H. "Was the New Testament Influenced by Pagan Religions?" *Christian Research Journal* 16, 2 (Winter 1994). See www.equip.org/free/DB109.pdf.

———. *The Gospel and the Greeks: Did the New Testament Borrow from Pagan Thought?* 2d ed. Phillipsburg, N.J.: P and R Press, 2003.

Pagels, Elaine. "Visions, Appearances, and Apostolic Authority: Gnostic and Orthodox Traditions." *Gnosis: Festchrift für Hans Jonas.* Edited by B. Aland. Göttingen, Germany, 1978.

Perkins, Pheme. *The Gnostic Dialogue: The Early Church and the Crisis of Gnosticism.* New York: Paulist Press, 1980.

Prokofieff, Sergei O. *The Spiritual Origins of Eastern Europe and the Future Mysteries.* London: Temple Lodge, 1993.

Rahner, Hugo, and S. J. Rahner. *Greek Myths and Christian Mystery.* London: Burns and Oates, 1957.

Raschke, Carl A. *The Interruption of Eternity: Modern Gnosticism and the Origins of the New Religious Consciousness.* Chicago: Nelson-Hall Press, 1980.

Ringgren, Helmar. *Religions of the Ancient New East.* Translated by John Sturdy. Philadelphia: Westminster Press, 1973.

Roberts, J. M. *The Mythology of the Secret Societies.* St. Albans: Granada, 1974.

Rosenberg, Alfred. *The Myth of the Twentieth Century.* Munich, Germany, 1930.

Rudolph, Kurt. *Mandaeism.* Leiden, Netherlands: E. J. Brill, 1978.

———. *Gnosis: The Nature and History of Gnosticism.* Translated by R. McLain Wilson. San Francisco: Harper and Row, 1984.

Runciman, Steven. *The Medieval Manichee: A Study of the Christian Dualist Heresy.* New York: Viking Press, 1961.

Rylands, L. Gordon. *The Beginnings of Gnostic Christianity.* London: Watts, 1940.

Scholer, David M. "Why Such Current Interest in the Ancient Gnostic 'Heresy'?" *Faith and Thought* 1, 2 (Summer 1983).

Schonfield, Hugh J. *The Essene Odyssey.* Shaftesbury: Elements Books, 1984.

Segal, Robert A., ed. *The Allure of Gnosticism: The Gnostic Experience in Jungian Psychology and Contemporary Culture.* Chicago: Open Court, 1995.

Silberer, Hebert. *Hidden Symbolism of Alchemy and the Occult Art.* 1917. Reprint, New York: Dover Publications, 1971.

Smith, Morton. *Clement of Alexandria and a Secret Gospel of Mark.* Cambridge: Harvard University Press, 1973.

———. *The Secret Gospel: The Discovery and Interpretation of the Secret Gospel according to Mark.* London: Victor Gollancz, 1974.

Smith, Scot, and Samantha Smith. *The Trojan Horse: How the New Age Movement Infiltrates the Church.* Huntington, 1993.

*Stoyanov, Yuri. The Hidden Tradition in Europe. London: Arkana, 1994.

———. *The Other God: Dualist Religions from Antiquity to the Cathar Heresy.* New Haven, Conn.: Yale University Press, 2000.

Talbert, Charles H. *Luke and the Gnostics.* Nashville, Tenn.: Abingdon, 1966.

Tardieu, M. *Trois Mythes Gnostiques, Adam, Eros et les animaux d'Egypte dans un écrit de Nag-Hammadi.* Paris, 1974.

Twyman, Tracy, and Boyd Rice. *The Vessel of God.* York Beach, Maine: Weiser Books, 2004.

Ulansey, David. *The Origins of the Mithraic Mysteries.* New York: Oxford University Press, 1991.

Van den Broek, R., and W. J. Hanegraaff, eds. *Gnosis and Hermeticism: From Antiquity to Modern Times.* Albany: State University of New York, n.d

Vere, Nicholas de. *The Dragon Legacy.* San Diego: Book Tree, 2004.

Ulansey, David. *The Origins of the Mithraic Mysteries.*

Oxford: Oxford University Press, 1989.

Walker, Benjamin. *Gnosticism: Its History and Influence.* Wellingborough: Crucible, 1989.

Welburn, Andrew. Introduction and Commentary. *Gnosis: The Mysteries and Christianity: An Anthology of Essene, Gnostic and Christian Writings.* Edinburgh: Floris Books, 1994.

Wilson, R. McLellan. *Gnosis and the New Testament.* Oxford: Blackwell, 1968.

———. *Gospel of Philip.* New York: Harper & Row, 1962.

Yamauchi, Edwin M. *Pre-Christian Gnosticism: A Survey of the Proposed Evidences.* Grand Rapids, Mich.: Tyndale Press, 1973.

Yates, Frances A. *The Rosicrucian Enlightenment.* Boulder: Shambala, 1978.

GODDESS AND THE DIVINE FEMININE

Alford, Alan. *Gods of the New Millennium: Scientific Proof of Flesh and Blood Gods.* London: Hodder and Stoughton, 1996.

Allan, R. *Diana, Queen of Heaven.* Aptos, Calif.: Adventures Unlimited/Pigeon Point Publishing, 1999.

Ashe, Geoffrey. *The Virgin: Mary's Cult and the Re-Emergence of the Goddess.* London: Arkana, 1988.

Barker, B. *Symbols of Sovereignty.* Newton Abbot: Westbridge Books, 1979.

Begg, Ean C. M. *The Cult of the Black Virgin.* Rev. ed. London: Arkana, 1996.

Bernard de Clairvaux. *On the Song of Songs.* Translated by Kilian Walsh, Mich.: Cistercian Publishers, 1976.

Blavatsky, Madame H. P. *Isis Unveiled.* 1891. Reprint, Pasadena: Theosophical University Press, 1988.

Bolen, Jean. *The Grail and the Goddess.* New York City: HarperCollins, 1995.

*Butler, Alan. *The Goddess, the Grail, and the Lodge: Tracing the Origins of Religion.* New York: O Books, 2004.

Cantarella, Eva. *Pandora's Daughters: The Role and*

Status of Women in Greek and Roman Antiquity. Translated by Maureen B. Frant. Johns Hopkins University Press, 1987.

Cloke, Gillian. *This Female Man of God: Woman and Spiritual Power in the Patristic Age, A.D. 350–450.* London: Routledge, 1995.

Daly, Mary. *Beyond God the Father: Towards a Philosophy of Women's Liberation.* Boston: Beacon Press, 1973.

Davis, Philip G. *Goddess Unmasked: The Rise of Neopagan Feminist Spirituality.* Dallas: Spence Publishers, 1998.

Dennis, James Teackle, trans. *The Burden of Isis.* London: John Murray, 1920.

*Freke, Timothy, and Peter Gandy. *The Jesus Mysteries: Was the "Original Jesus" a Pagan God?* New York: Three Rivers Press, 1999.

———. *Jesus and the Lost Goddess: The Secret Teachings of the Original Christians.* New York: Harmony Books, 2001.

Frazer, Sir James G. *The Golden Bough.* New York: Macmillan, 1922, 1970.

Gadon, Elinor, ed. *The Once and Future Goddess.* San Francisco: Harper, 1989.

Gardner, Jane F. *Women in Roman Law and Society.* Bloomington: Indiana University Press, 1986.

Gibby, Sian. "Mrs. God." *Slate,* 3 November 1993.

Gimbutas, Marija. *The Goddesses and Gods of Old Europe.* Berkeley: University of California Press, 1982.

Graves, Robert. *The White Goddess.* New York: Farrar, Straus and Giroux, 1952, 1961.

Green, M. *Celtic Goddesses.* London: British Museum Press, 1995.

Hauke, Manfred. *Women in the Priesthood? A Systematic Analysis in the Light of the Order of Creation and Redemption.* San Francisco: Ignatius Press, 1988..

———. *God or Goddess? Feminist Theology: What Is It? Where Does It Lead?* San Francisco: Ignatius Press, 1995

Heyob, Sharon Kelly. *The Cult of Isis among Women in the Graeco-Roman World.* Leiden, Netherlands: E. J. Brill, 1975.

Hopkins, Keith. *A World Full of Gods.* New York: Plume, 1999.

Horner, George, trans. *Pistis Sophia.* Intro. F. Legge. SPCK, 1924.

James, E. O. *The Ancient Gods: The History and Diffusion of Religion in the Ancient New East and the Eastern Mediterranean.* New York: G. P. Putnam's Sons, 1960.

———. *The Cult of the Mother-Goddess.* New York: Barnes and Noble, 1994.

King, Karen L. *Images of the Feminine in Gnosticism.* 2d ed. Harrisburg, Pa.: Trinity Press International, 2000.

Kraemer, Ross. *Her Share of the Blessings: Women's Religions among the Pagans, Jews, and Christians in the Greco-Roman World.* New York: Oxford University Press, 1992.

Kraemer, Ross, and Mary Rose D'Angelo. *Women and Christian Origins.* New York: Oxford University Press, 1999.

Kramer, Samuel Noel. *The Sacred Marriage Rite.* Bloomington: Indiana University Press, 1969.

Lyle, Jane, and A. T. Mann. *Sacred Sexuality.* Shaftesbury: Element Books, 1996.

MacDermot, Violet. *The Fall of Sophia: A Gnostic Text on the Redemption of Universal Consciousness.* Great Barrington, Maine: Lindisfarne Books, 2001.

Malvern, Marjorie. *Venus in Sackcloth.* Carbondale: Southern Illinois University Press, 1975.

Markale, Jean. *Courtly Love: The Path of Sexual Initiation.* Inner Traditions, 2000.

Matthews, Caitlin. *Sophia: Goddess of Wisdom.* London: Aquarian Press, 1992.

Neumann, Erich. *The Great Mother: An Analysis of the Archetype.* 1955. Translated by Ralph Mannheim. Princeton: Princeton University Press, 1972.

Newman, Barbara. *God and the Goddesses: Vision, Poetry and Belief in the Middle Ages.* Philadelphia: University of Pennsylvania Press, 2003.

*Patai, Raphael. *The Hebrew Goddess.* Detroit: Wayne State University Press, 1967, 1990.

Pope, Marvin H. *Song of Songs: A New Translation with*

Introduction and Commentary. Anchor Bible Series. Garden City: Doubleday, 1977, 1983.

Qualls-Corbett, Nancy. *The Sacred Prostitute: Eternal Aspect of the Feminine.* Toronto: Inner City Books, 1988.

Querido, Rene. *The Golden Age of Chartres: The Teachings of a Mystery School and the Eternal Feminine.* Edinburgh: Floris Books, 1987.

Ranke-Heinemann, Uta. *Eunuchs for the Kingdom of Heaven: Women, Sexuality and the Catholic Church.* Translated by Peter Heinegg. New York: Doubleday, 1990.

Ruether, Rosemary Radford. *Sexism and God-Talk: Toward a Feminist Theology.* Boston: Beacon Press, 1983.

Sawyer, Deborah F. *Women and Religion in the First Christian Centuries.* London: Routledge, 1996.

Schaup, S. *Sophia: Aspects of the Divine Feminine.* Nicolas-Hays, 1997.

Shadwynn. *The Crafted Cup: Ritual Mysteries of the Goddess and the Grail.* St. Paul: Llewellyns Pub., 1994.

*Starbird, Margaret. *The Goddess in the Gospels: Reclaiming the Sacred Feminine.* Rochester, Vt.: Bear and Company, 1998.

———. *The Feminine Face of Christianity.* 2004.

*Stone, Merlin. *When God Was a Woman.* New York: Dial Press, 1976.

Swedenborg, Emanuel. *Marriage and the Sexes in Both Worlds.* Philadelphia, 1881.

Torjesen, Karen Jo. *When Women Were Priests.* San Francisco: HarperSanFrancisco, 1993.

Walker, Barbara G. *The Woman's Encyclopedia of Myths and Secrets.* San Franciscp: Harper and Row, 1983.

———. *The Woman's Dictionary of Symbols and Sacred Objects.* San Francisco: Harper and Row, 1988.

Whitmont, Edward C. *Return of the Goddess.* New York: Crossroad, 1982.

Wijngaards, John. *No Women in Holy Orders?* Norwich: Canterbury Press, 2002.

Wolkstein, D., S. N. Kramer. *Inanna: Queen of Heaven and Earth.* New York: Harper, 1983.

HOLY GRAIL

Abdruschin. *In the Light of Truth: Message from the Holy Grail.* Muenchen: Verlage "Der Fuf," 1933, 1948.

Achad, Frater. *The Chalice of Ecstasy: Being a Magical and Qabalistic Interpretation of the Drama of Parzival.* Chicago, 1923. Reprint, 1994.

Adams, Oscar Fay. *The Return from the Quest.* 1886.

Adolf, Helen. *Visio Pacis: Holy City and Grail: An Inner History of the Grail Legend.* Pennsylvania State University Press, 1960.

Anderson, Lady Flavia Giffard. *The Ancient Secret: In Search of the Holy Grail.* London: Victor Gollancz Ltd., 1953.

Anitchkof, E. "Le Saint Graal et les rites Eucharistique." *Romania,* 55 (1929): 174–94.

*Ashley, Mike. *Chronicles of the Holy Grail.* Carroll and Graf Publishers, 1996.

*Baigent, Michael, Richard Leigh, and Henry Lincoln. *The Messianic Legacy.* New York: Dell Publishing, 1986.

*———. *Holy Blood, Holy Grail.* Rev. ed. London: Arrow, 1996.

Barb, A. A. "Mensa Sacra: Round Table and Holy Grail." *Journal of the Warburg and Courtauld Institute* 19 (1956): 40–67.

*Barber, Richard. *The Holy Grail: Imagination and Belief.* Cambridge: Harvard University Press, 2004.

Baring-Gould, Rev. Sabine. *The Holy Grail.* 1878. Reprint, llanfynydd: Unicom Press, 1976.

Barnwell, John. *The Arcana of the Grail Angel: The Spiritual Science of the Holy Blood and of the Holy Grail.* Bloomfield Hills, Mich.: Verticordia Press, 1999.

Baudry, Robert. *Graal et Littératures d'aujourd'hui.* Rennes, 1998.

Baumgartner, Emmanuèle. *L'Arbre et le Poin: Essai sur la Queste del Saint Graal.* Paris, 1981.

*Begg, Ian, and Deike Begg. *In Search of the Holy Grail and the Precious Blood—A Travellers' Guide.* New York: HarperCollins, 1995.

Benham, Patrick. *The Avalonians.* Glastonbury, 1993.

Bennett, Janice. *St. Laurence and the Holy Grail: The Story of the Holy Chalice of Valencia.* Libri de Hispania, 2002.

Bernstein, Henrietta. *Ark of the Covenant, Holy Grail.* Marina del Rey: De Vorss and Co., 1998.

Bertin, Georges. *La Quête du Saint Graal et l'imaginaire.* Condé-sur-Noireau, 1997.

*Bogdanow, Fanni. *The Romance of the Grail.* Manchester, England: Manchester University Press, 1966.

Bolen, Jean. *The Grail and the Goddess.* New York: HarperCollins, 1995.

Boron, Robert de. *Le Roman de l'Estoire dou Graal.* Translated by H. L. Skynner. London: Early English Text Society, 1861. Henry Lovelich's edition for the Roxburghe Club, London, 1863–64.

Bourre, Jean-Paul. *La Quête du Graal.* Paris, 1993.

Brown, Arthur C. L. *The Origin of the Grail Legend.* Cambridge: Harvard University Press, 1943. Reprint, New York: Russel and Russel, 1966.

Bryant, Nigel, trans. *The High Book of the Grail: A Translation of the Thirteenth Century Romance of Perlesvaus.* Cambridge and Totowa, N.J., 1978.

Bulgakov, Sergei. *Holy Grail and the Eucharist.* Edinburgh: Floris Books, 1997.

Bullock-Davies, Constance. "Chrétien de Troyes and England." *Arthurian Literature* I (1981):1–61.

Bumke, Joachim. *Wolfram von Eschenbach.* 5th ed. Stuttgart, 1981.

Burdach, Konrad. *Der Gral.* Stuttgart, 1938.

Cackett, S. W. Gentle. *The Antioch Cup.* London: Palestine and Bible Lands Exhibition, 1935.

Campbell, David E. *The Tale of Balain from the Romance of the Grail.* Evanston, Ill.: Northwestern University Press, 1972.

Cazelles, Brigitte. *The Unholy Grail: A Social Reading of Chrétien de Troyes 'Conte du Graal.'* Standford, Calif.: 1996.

Cérisy, Colloque de. *Graal et Modernité, Cahiers de l'Hermétisme.* Paris, 1996.

Charvet, Louis. *Des Vaus d'Avaron à la Queste du Graal.* Paris, 1967.

*Church, J. R. *Guardians of the Grail—And the Men Who Plan to Rule the World!* Rev. ed. Oklahoma City: Prophecy Publications, 1991.

Clarke, Lindsay. *Parzival and the Stone from Heaven.* London, 2001.

*Collins, Andrew. *Twenty-First Century Grail: The Quest for a Legend.* Virgin Book, 2004.

Comfort, William Wistar. *The Quest of the Holy Grail (La queste del saint graal).* Translated from the old French. London and Toronto: J. H. Dent and Sons Ltd., 1926.

Cooke, Rose Terry. *The New Sangreal.* 1888.

Cooney, Ellen. *The Quest for the Holy Grail.* San Francisco: Duir Press, n.d.

Corley, Corin. "The Second Continuation of the Perceval." Modern Humanities Research Association Texts and Dissertations, 24. London, 1987.

Coyajee, Jehangir Cooverjee. *Iranian and Indian Analogues of the Legend of the Holy Grail.* Bombay: D. B. Taraporevala, 1950.

Chrétien de Troyes. *Le Conte del Graal.* Translated by Ruth Harwood Cline. Athens: University of Georgia Press, 1985.

*Currer-Briggs, Noel. *The Shroud and the Grail: A Modern Quest for the True Grail.* London and Widenfeld and Nicholson, 1987.

D'Arcy, Anne Marie. *Wisdom and the Grail: The Image of the Vessel in the Queste del Saint Graal and Malory's Tale of the Sankgreall.* Dublin, 2000.

Dawes, Christopher. *Rat Scabies and the Holy Grail.* London: Sceptre, 2005.

Dundes, Alan. "The Father, Son and Holy Grail." *Literature and Psychology* 12 (1962): 101–12.

*Eco, Umberto. *Foucault's Pendulum.* Translated by William Weaver. London, 1989.

*Eisler, Riane. *The Chalice and the Blade: Our History, Our Future.* San Francisco: Harper and Row, 1987.

Ellwood, Robert. *The Cross and the Grail: Esoteric Christianity for the 21st Century.* 1997.

Erskine, John. *Galahad: Enough of His Life to Explain His Reputation.* Indianapolis: Bobbs-Miller, 1926.

Evans, Sebastian. *In Quest of the Holy Grail.* London: Dent, 1898.

Evola, Guilio, C.A. *Il Mistero del Graal.* Rome, 1972.

Evola, Julius. *Il Mistero del Graal e la Tradizione ghibellina dell'Impero (The mystery of the Grail and the Ghibelline tradition of Empire).* Bari, 1937.

Evola, Julius, and Guido Stucco. *The Mystery of the Holy Grail: Initiations and Magic in the Quest for the Spirit.* 1996.

Fiedler, Leslie. "Why is the Grail Knight Jewish? A Passover Meditation." *Aspects of Jewish Culture in the Middle Ages.* Edited by Paul A. Szarmach. Albany, 1979.

Field, Eugene. *The Vision of the Holy Grail.* 1905. Reprint, The Camelot Project at the University of Rochester.

Ford, Mary Hanford Finney. *The Holy Grail, the Silent Teacher.* Chicago: A. B. Stockham and Co., 1897.

Francke, Sylvia, and Cawthorne, Thomas. *The Tree of Life and the Holy Grail.* London: Temple Lodge, 1996.

Frappier, Jean. *Chrétien de Troyes et le mythe du Graal.* Paris 1972.

———. *Chrétien de Troyes: The Man and His Work.* Translated by Raymond J. Cormier. Athens, Ohio, 1982.

Furnival, Frederick J. *The History of the Holy Grail.* Translated by H. L. Skynner from *Roman l'Estoire dou Saint Graal,* by Sir Robert de Boron. London: Early English Text Society, 1861. Henry Lovelich's edition for the Roxburghe Club, London, 1863–64.

Gadal, A. *Sur le Chemin de Saint-Graal.* Haarlem, 1960.

*Gardner, Laurence. *Bloodline of the Holy Grail: The Hidden Lineage of Jesus Revealed.* Rockport, Mass.: Element, 1996.

*———. *Genesis of the Grail Kings: The Pendragon Legacy of Adam and Eve.* London: Bantam Press, 1999.

*———. *The Illustrated Bloodline of the Holy Grail: The Hidden Lineage of Jesus Revealed.* New York: Barnes and Noble, 2000.

*Gilbert, A., A. Wilson, and B. Blackett. *The Holy Kingdom.* London: Bantam, 1998.

Gilliam, R., ed. *Grails: Quest of the Dawn.* New York, 1994.

*Godwin, Malcolm. *The Holy Grail: Its Origins, Secrets and Meaning Revealed.* New York: Viking Studio Books, 1994.

Girouard, Mark. *The Return to Camelot.* New Haven and London, 1981.

Goetinck, Glenys. *Peredur: A Study of Welsh Tradition in the Grail Legends.* Cardiff, 1975.

———. "The Quest for Origins." In *The Grail: A Casebook.* Edited by Dhira A. Mahoney. New York and London, 2000. 117–47.

*Goodrich, Norma Loree. *The Holy Grail.* New York: HarperCollins, 1992.

Gowans, Linda M. "What Did Robert de Boron Really Write?" Forthcoming.

Greenslet, Ferris. *The Quest of the Holy Grail: An Interpretation and Paraphrase of the Holy Legends.* 1902.

Groos, Arthur. *Romancing the Grail: Genre, Science and Quest in Wolfram's Parzifal.* Ithaca and London, 1995.

Guénon, René. *Le Roi du Monde (The King of the World).* Paris, 1925. Reprint, 1958.

———. "L'ésoterisme du Graal." *Lumière de Graal.* Edited by René Nelli. Paris, 1951. 37–49.

Guthrie, Kenneth Sylvan. *Perronik, the "Innocent"; or, The Quest of the Golden Basin and Diamond Lance, One of the Sources of Stories about the Holy Grail, a Breton Legend.* After Souvestre, 1915.

*Hall, Manly Palmer. *Orders of the Quest: The Holy Grail.* Los Angeles: Philosophical Research Society, 1949. Reprint, 1996.

———. "The Holy Grail." Lecture audio tape. Copyright, Philosophical Research Society.

Hardyng, John. *Chronicle of John Hardyng.* 1812.

Harrison, Hank. *The Cauldron and the Grail: Ritual Astronomy and the Stones of . . .* Los Altos, Calif.: Archives Press, 1991.

Hawker, Robert Stephen. *The Quest of the Sangraal.* 1864.

Helinandus. *Chronicle of Helinandus* (Monk of Froidmont at the turn of the twelfth century, recording a hermit's vision from 717 A.D.). See *Lancelot Grail.*

*Heline, Corinne. *Mysteries of the Holy Grail.* Oceanside, Calif.: New Age Press, 1963, 1977.

Hieatt, Constance B. *The Sword and the Grail.* New York: Cromwell, 1972.

High History of the Holy Graal. Translated by Sebastian Evans. 1898.

Hucher, E., ed. *Le Saint-Grail, ou Le Joseph d'Arimathie, première branche des romans de la Table Ronde.* Paris, 1875.

Iolo Manuscripts. Translated by T. Williams. 1848.

Iselin, L. E. *Der morgenländische Ursprung der Graalslegende.* Halle, 1909.

*Jowett, George F. *The Drama of the Lost Disciples.* London: Covenant, 1961, 1996.

Joynt, M. *Golden Legends of the Grael.* Dublin, n.d.

*Jung, Emma, and Marie-Louise von Franz. *The Grail Legends.* Translated by Andrea Dykes. 1960. Reprint, Princeton: Princeton University Press, 1998. First published as *Graalslegende in pyschologischer Sicht.*

Kahane, Henry Romanos. *The Krater and the Grail: the hermetic sources of the Parzival.* Illinois Studies in Language and Literature 56. Urbana: University of Illinois Press, 1965.

Karczewska, Kathryn. *Prophecy and the Quest for the Holy Grail: Critiquing Knowledge in the Vulgate Cycle.* Frankfurt, 1998.

Kempe, Dorothy. *The Legends of the Holy Grail, Its Sources, Character and Development.* London: K. Paul Trubner and Co., 1905. Reprint, 1934.

Kennedy, Edward Donald. "John Hardyng and the Holy Grail." *Arthurian Literature* 8 (1998): 185–206.

Kennedy, Elspeth. *Lancelot and the Grail.* Oxford, 1986.

Kibler, William W. *The Lancelot-Grail Cycle: Text and Transformation.* Austin: University of Texas Press, 1994.

*Knight, Christopher. *The Holy Grail.* London: Weidenfeld and Nicolson, 1997.

Kramer, Alfred Robert. *Malory's Grail Seekers and Fifteenth Century English Hagiography.* New York, 1999.

Lacy, Norris J., ed. *The New Arthurian Encyclopedia.* New York: Peter Bedrick Books, 1986.

———. *Translation.* New York and London, 1993–96.

Lampe, Bernd. *Anfortas.* Durnau: Verlag der Kooperativ Durnau, 1990.

Lavenu, Philippe. *L'éesoterisme de Graal: Secret du Mont Saint-Michel.* Paris, 1989.

Le Bossé, Michel. "Le Graal, fiction our réalité?" *La Légende Arthurienne et la Normandie (Hommage à Bansard).* Edited by Jean-Charles Payen. Conddé-sur-Noireau, 1983. 191–201.

*Loomis, Roger Sherman. *The Grail: From Celtic Myth to Christian Symbol.* Cardiff: University of Wales Press, 1959, 1963. Reprint, Princeton, N.J.: Princeton University Press, 1991.

Lovelich, Henry. *The History of the Holy Grail.* Millwood, N.Y.: Kraus Reprint, 1969.

Mann, William F. *Labyrinth of the Grail.* 1999.

Markale, Jean. *Le Graal.* Retz, Paris, 1982. English edition, *The Grail,* published at Rochester, Vt.: Inner Traditions, 1999.

———. *King of the Celts.* Rochester, Vt.: Inner Traditions, 1994.

Matarosso, Pauline M. Trans. *The Quest of the Holy Grail.* New York: Penguin, 1969.

———. *The Redemption of Chivalry: A Study of the Queste del Saint Graal.* Geneva, 1979.

Matthews, John, ed. *At the Table of the Grail: Magic and Use of Imagination.* New York City: Viking Penguin, 1987.

*———. *Elements of the Grail Tradition.* Rockport, Mass.: Element Book, 1990.

*———. *The Grail: Quest for the Eternal.* New York: Thames and Hudson, 1991.

*———. *Sources of the Grail: An Anthology.* 1997.

*———. *The Mystic Grail: The Challenge of the Arthurian Quest.* New York: Sterling Publishing, 1997.

*Matthews, John, and Marian Green. *The Grail Seeker's Companion: A Guide to the Grail Quest in the Aquarian Age.* Aquarian Press, 1986.

Meeks, John, and Doris Meeks. "The Temple of the Grail." *The Golden Blade.* Rudolf Steiner Press, 1981.

*Michell, John F. *The Flying Saucer Vision: The Holy Grail*

Restored. London: Sidgewich and Jackson, 1967.

*————. *The City of Revelation.* London: Garnstone Press, 1971.

————. *The Dimensions of Paradise: The Proportions and Symbolic Numbers of the Ancient Cosmology.* San Francisco: Harper and Row, 1990.

*Michell, John F., and Christine Rhone. *Twelve-Tribe Nations and the Science of Enchanting the Landscape.* London: Thames and Hudson, 1991.

*Morgan, Giles. *The Holy Grail.* Harpenden, England: Pocket Essentials, 2005.

Nederlander, Munin. *Kitezh: The Russian Grail Legends.* London: Aquarian, 1991.

Nitze, W. A., and T. A. Jenkins. *Perlesvaus.* 2 vols. Chicago, 1937.

Nutt, Alfred Trubner. *Studies on the Legend of the Holy Grail, with Special Reference to the Hypothesis of Its Celtic Origin.* London: Harrison and Sons, 1888. Reprint, New York: Cooper Square, 1965.

————. *The Legends of the Holy Grail.* London, 1902.

O'Gorman, Richard. "Ecclesiastical Tradition and the Holy Grail." *Australian Journal of French Studies* 6 (1969).

Olschki, Leonardo. Translated by J. A. Scott. *The Grail Castle and Its Mysteries.* Manchester University Press, 1965.

Owen, Douglas David Roy. *The Evolution of the Grail Legend.* Edinburgh: Oliver and Boyd, 1968.

Patterson, Paige. "Holy Blood, Holy Grail—Holy Mackerel." *Christianity Today* 26 (3 September 1982): 28–29.

Pauphilet, Albert. *Etudes sur la Queste del Saint Graal.* Paris, 1921.

Peebles, Rose Jeffries. *The Legend of Longius in Ecclesiastical Tradition and in English Literature and Its Connection with the Holy Grail.* Vol. 9. Baltimore, Md.: Bryn Mawr College Monographs, 1911.

Perry, Lee. *The Holy Grail, Cosmos of the Bible.* New York: Philosophical Library, 1991.

————. *The Holy Grail: Source of the Ancient Science and Spirituality of the Circling Cosmos.* New York: Philosophical Library, 1993.

*Phillips, Dr. Graham. *The Search for the Grail.* London: Arrow, 1996.

*————. *The Chalice of Magdalene: The Search for the Cup That Held the Blood of Christ.* Rev. ed. Rochester, Vt.: Bear and Company, 2004. Originally titled *The Search for the Grail.*

Picknett, Lynn, and Prince, Clive. *The Sion Revelation: The Truth about the Guardians of Christ's Sacred Bloodline.* New York: Touchstone, 2006.

Pokorny, Julius. *Der Graal in Irland und die mythischen Grundlage de Graalsage.* Vienna: Anthropologische Gesellshaft, 1918.

*Prophet, Elizabeth Clare. *Mysteries of the Holy Grail.* Summit University Press, 1984.

Puech, Henri-Charles. *La Queste du Graal.* Paris, 1965.

Querido, Rene. *The Mystery of the Holy Grail.* Rudolf Steiner College, 1991.

*Ralls-MacLeod, Karen, and Ian Robertson. *The Quest for the Celtic Key.* Edinburgh: Luath Press, 2002.

*Ravenscroft, Trevor. *The Cup of Destiny: The Quest for the Grail.* York Beach, Maine: Samuel Weiser, 1982.

*————. *The Spear of Destiny.* York Beach, Maine: Samuel Weiser, 1982.

Redway, Nicola. "The Quest of the Holy Grail." *Christie's International Magazine* (October–November 1994).

Rhy, Ernest. *The Quest of the Grail: On the Eve.* (1905).

Ringbom, Lars-Ivar. *Graltemple und Paradies.* Stockholm, 1951.

Rivière, Jacques, *Le fabuleux, trésor de Rennes-le-Château! Le Secret de L'Abbé Saunière.* Nice, Bélisane, 1983.

Rohr, Richard. *Guest for the Grail: Soul Work and the Sacred Journey.* New York: Crossroad, 1994.

Rolt-Wheeler, Francis. *Mystic Gleams from the Holy Grail.* London, 1940.

Rossetti, Dante Gabriel. *God's Grail.* Written 1858; published 1911.

Roszak, Theodore. *Where the Wasteland Ends.* Faber and Faber, 1978.

Scherer, James Augustin Brown. *The Holy Grail: Six Kindred Addresses and Essays.* Philadelphia: J. B. Lippincott, 1906.

Schmidt, K. O. *The Message of the Grail.* Lakemont, Ga.: C. S. A. Press, 1975.

Schmitt, Ernest. *The Holy Grail: Truth and Fiction.* Grail Acres Publishing Company and Grail Message Foundation, n.d.

Shadwynn. *The Crafted Cup: Ritual Mysteries of the Goddess and the Grail.* St. Paul, Minn.: Llewellyns, 1994.

*Sinclair, Andrew. *The Sword and the Grail.* London: Century, 1992.

*———. *The Discovery of the Grail.* London: Century, 1998.

*———. *The Secret Scroll.* London: Sinclair-Stevenson, 2001.

Staley, J. Edgcumbe. *Heroines of Genoa and the Rivieras.* New York: C. Scribner's Sons, 1912.

Starbird, Margaret. *The Tarot Trumps and the Holy Grail: Great Secrets of the Middle Ages.* (ISBN 0–96784280–8, 80 pages).

Stein, Dr. Walter Johannes. *The Ninth Century and the Holy Grail.* First English edition. London: Temple Lodge, 1988, 1991.

Steiner, Rudolf. *Christus und die geistige Welt: Von der suche nach dem Heiligen Gral.* Dornach, 1925. First English edition entitled *Christ and the Spiritual World and The Search for the Holy Grail.* R. Steiner Press, 1963.

Sutcliff, Rosemary. *The Light beyond the Forest: The Quest for the Holy Grail.* 1980. Reprint, Duffin, 1994.

Tarade, Guy. *Les derniers gardiens du Graal.* Paris, 1993.

*Taylor, John W. *The Coming of the Saints: Imaginations and Studies in Early Church History and Tradition.* London: Methuen, 1906. Rev. ed. London: Covenant Publishing, 1969.

Thiering, Barbara. "The Unholy Grail: Notes on Laurence Gardner's *The Bloodline of the Holy Grail.*" http://groups.yahoo.com/group/qumran_origin/

Turlin, Heinrich von der. *The Crown (Die Crone).* Translated by J. W. Thomas. Lincoln: University of Nebraska Press, 1989.

Voragine, Jacobus de (Archbishop of Genoa). *Legenda Aurea.* 1275. First English edition entitled *The Golden Legend.* Translated by William Caxton. London, 1483. New edition translated by William Grayner Ryan. 2 vols. Princeton, N.J.: Princeton University Press, 1993.

*Waite, Arthur Edward. *The Hidden Church of the Holy Grail: Its Legends and Symbolism Considered in Their Affinity with Certain Mysteries of Initiation and Other Traces of a Secret Tradition in Christian Times.* New York: Weathervane Books, 1909.

Weston, Jessie Laidlay. *The Quest of the Holy Grail.* 1903. Reprint, New York: Haskel House, 1965.

———. *From Ritual to Romance.* 1920. Reprint, Princeton: Princeton University Press, 1993.

Williams, Robert. *Y Seint Greal, Jones (Wales).* 1876. Facsimile reprint, 1987.

Wood, Juliette. "The Holy Grail: From Romance Motif to Modern Genre." *Folklore* 3, 2 (October 2000): 171.

Wyatt, Isabel. *From Round Table to Grail Castle.* Sussex: Lanthorn Press, 1979.

Young, Ella. *The San-Grail.* 1920.

JESUS CHRIST, JAMES THE JUST, ST. JAMES, AND JOHN THE BAPTIST

Alvey, Ada. *In Search of St. James.* Cornwall: Cornish, 1989.

Ambelain, Robert. *Jesus ou le Mortel Sécret des Templiers.* Paris: Editions Robert Lafont, 1970.

Bauckham, Richard J. *Jude, 2 Peter.* Waco, Texas: Word, 1983.

———. *Jude and the Relatives of Jesus in the Early Church.* Edinburgh: T&T Clark, 1990.

———. "For What Offense Was James Put to Death?" In *James the Just and Christian Origins.* Edited by Bruce Chilton and Craig A. Evans. Leiden, Netherlands: Brill, 1999.

———. *James.* London: Routledge, 1999.

———. "All in the Family—Identifying Jesus' Relatives." *Bible Review* (April 2000).

*Bernheim, Pierre-Antoine. *James, the Brother of Jesus.* London: SCM Press, 1997.

Birch, W. Grayson. *Veritas and the Virgin or Jesus, the Son of God and the Children of Joseph and Mary.* Berne, Indiana: Berne Witness, n.d.

*Boren, Karen. *Messiah of the Winepress: Christ and the Red Heifer.* Provo, Utah: Beit Parah Publishing, 2002.

Borg, Marcus J. *Meeting Jesus Again for the First Time.* San Francisco: HarperCollins, 1995.

Brandon, S.F.F. *Jesus and the Zealots.* New York: Charles Scribner's Sons, 1967.

Bruce, Alexander B. *The Humiliation of Christ.* New York, 1887.

Buchanan, George. *Wesley, Jesus, the King and His Kingdom.* Mercer University Press, 1984.

Bultmann, Rudolf. *Jesus and the Word.* New York, 1934.

Cassels, Louis. *The Real Jesus.* New York, 1968.

Chilton, Bruce. "James in Relation to Peter, Paul, and the Remembrance of Jesus." In *The Brother of Jesus.* Nashville: Westminster, John Knox, 2001.

Crossan, John Dominic. *Jesus—A Revolutionary Biography.* New York: HarperCollins, 1994.

———. *Who Killed Jesus?* New York: HarperCollins, 1995.

*———. "Why Jesus Didn't Marry." Beliefnet.com (fall 2003).

*Crossan, John Dominic, and Jonathan L. Reed. *Excavating Jesus: Beneath the Stones, behind the Texts.* San Francisco: HarperSanFrancisco, 2001.

Driver, Tom F. "Sexuality and Jesus." *Union Seminary Quarterly Review* 20 (1965): 235–46.

Dudden, F. Homes. "Asceticism." In *A Dictionary of Christ and the Gospels.* New York, 1908.

*Eisenman, Robert. *James the Brother of Jesus.* London: Faber and Faber, 1997.

Eisler, Robert. *The Messiah Jesus and John the Baptist.* London: Methuen, 1931.

Erskine, John. *The Human Life of Jesus.* New York, 1945.

Evans, Craig A. "Comparing Judaisms: Qumranic, Rabbinic, and Jacobean Judaisms Compared." *Brother of Jesus.* Nashville: Westminster, John Knox, 2001.

*Farrar, Federic W. *The Life of Christ.* 1874, 1880.

Fideler, David. *Jesus Christ, Sun of God.* Wheaton, Ill.: Quest Books, 1993.

Finegan, J. *Hidden Records of the Life of Jesus.* Philadelphia and Boston: Pilgrim Press, 1969.

Finkelstein-Mountford, Lydia von. *Jesus in His Homeland.*

Fiske, Edward B. "Jesus: Did He Ever Take a Wife?" *New York Times.* (15 November 1970).

Fleetwood, Rev. John. *The Life of Our Lord and Saviour Jesus Christ.* Glasgow: William MacKenzie, 1900.

*Freke, Timothy, and Gandy, Peter. *Jesus and the Lost Goddess: The Secret Teachings of the Original Christians.* New York: Harmony Books, 2001.

*Gardner, Laurence. *Bloodline of the Holy Grail: The Hidden Lineage of Jesus Revealed.* Rockport, Mass.: Element, 1996.

*———. *The Illustrated Bloodline of the Holy Grail: The Hidden Lineage of Jesus Revealed.* New York: Barnes and Noble, 2000.

Geyser, A. S. "Jesus, the Twelve and the Twelve Tribes in Matthew." In *Essays on Jewish and Christian Apocalyptic.* Vol. 12. 1981.

Graves, Robert Van Ranke. *King Jesus.* London: Cassell, 1946.

Greenstone, Julian H. *The Messiah Idea in Jewish History.* Philadelphia: Publishing Society of America, 1943.

Groothuis, Douglas. *Searching for the Real Jesus in an Age of Controversy.* Eugene, Oreg.: Harvest House, 1996.

Grubner, Elmer R., and Holger Kersten. *The Original Jesus.* Element Book, 1995.

Hall, Manly Palmer. "The Unrecorded Years in the Life of Christ." Lecture notes no. 273.

Habermas, Gary R. *The Historical Jesus: Ancient Evidence for the Life of Christ.* Joplin, Mo.: College Press Publishing Co., 1996.

Hammond, Jeremy R. "Was Jesus Married?" *Yirmeyahu Review* (16 April 2004). www.yirmeyahureview. com/scripture/was_jesus_-married.htm

Haselden, Kyle. "The Inferno of Dreams," *The Christian Century* 70 (October 1960).

Hassnain, Prof. Fida. *Search for the Historical Jesus—From Apocryphal, Buddhist, Islamic and Sanscrit Sources.* Bath, England: Gateway Books, 1994.

Hengel, Martin. *The Four Gospels and the One Gospel of Jesus Christ.* Harrisburg, Pa.: Trinity, 2000.

Hurtado, Larry. *Lord Jesus Christ: Devotion to Jesus in Earliest Christianity.* Grand Rapids, Mich.: Eerdmans, 2003.

*Jenkins, Philip. *Hidden Gospels: How the Search for Jesus Lost Its Way.* Oxford: Oxford University Press, 2001.

Johnson, Luke Timothy. *The Real Jesus: The Misguided Quest for the Historical Jesus and the Truth of the Traditional Gospels.* San Francisco: HarperSanFrancisco, 1996.

Kazantzakis, Nikos. *The Last Temptation of Christ.* New York, 1960.

Kennedy, William H. *The Orbis Enigma: Do the "Descendants" of Jesus Christ Seek to Rule the World?* 2003. See www.geocities.com/jesuskids2003.

Kersten, Holger. *Jesus Lived in India.* Shaftesbury: Element Books, 1991.

Kersten, Holger, and E. R. Gruber. *The Jesus Conspiracy.* Shaftesbury: Element Book, 1992.

Klausner, Joseph. *Jesus of Nazareth.* New York, 1925.

———. *The Messianic Idea in Israel.* 1956.

Kraeling, Karl H. *John the Baptist.* London: Charles Scribner's Sons, 1951.

Lewis, H. Spencer. *The Mystical Life of Jesus.* 1929. Reprint, San Jose, Calif.: Ancient and Mystical Order Rosae Crucis, 1982.

Luther, Martin. "Table Talks." In *Luther's Works.* American edition. See http://ic.net/~erasmus/RAZ29.HTM.

Mead, G. R. S. *Did Jesus Live 100 BC?* London: Theosophical Publishing Society, 1903.

———. *The Gnostic John the Baptizer: Selections from the Mandaean John Book.* London: John M. Watkins, 1924.

Millard, Alan. *Discoveries from the Time of Jesus.* Great Britain: Lion Publishing, 1990.

Nielson, Donna B. *Beloved Bridegroom.* Phoenix: Onyx Press, 1999.

Osman, Ahmed. *House of the Messiah.* New York: HarperCollins, 1992.

Painter, John. *Just James.* Columbia, S.C.: University of South Carolina Press, 1997.

Pappas, Paul C. *Jesus' Tomb in India.* Berkeley: Asian Humanities Press, 1991.

Patey, Richard. "Is Not This the Carpenter?" *New Testament Studies.* 1984.

Paulk, Earl. *To Whom Is God Betrothed.* Atlanta, Ga.: K-Dimension Publishers, 1985.

*Phipps, William E. "Did Jesus or Paul Marry?" *Journal of Ecumenical Studies* 5 (1968): 741–44.

*———. "The Case for a Married Jesus." *Dialogue: A Journal of Mormon Thought* 7, 4 (Winter 1972).

———. *Recovering Biblical Sensuousness.* Philadelphia: Westminster Press, 1975.

———. *Was Jesus Married? The Distortion of Sexuality in the Christian Tradition.* Rev. ed. Lanham, Maryland: University Press of America, 1986.

———. *Genesis and Gender.* New York: Praeger, 1989.

*———. *The Sexuality of Jesus: Theological and Literary Perspectives.* Rev. ed. Cleveland, Ohio: Pilgrim Press, 1996.

*Prophet, Elizabeth Clare. *The Lost Years of Jesus.* Summit University Press, 1984.

Rappoport, Angelo S. *Medieval Legends of Christ.* Rhys, 1934.

Sapp, Stephen. *Sexuality, the Bible, and Science.* Philadelphia: Fortress Press, 1977.

Schmidt, N. *The Prophet of Nazareth.* New York, 1905.

*Shanks, Hershel, and Ben Witherington III. *The Brother of Jesus: The Dramatic Story and Meaning of the First Archaeological Link to Jesus and His Family.* London: Continuum, 2003.

*Smith, Morton. *Jesus the Magician.* London: Victor Gollancz, 1978.

*Spong, John Shelby. *Born of Woman: A Bishop Rethinks the Birth of Christ.* San Francisco: Harper, 1992.

Steinberg, Lev. *Sexuality of Christ in Renaissance Art and in Modern Oblivion.* 2d ed. Chicago: University of Chicago Press, 1996.

*Strachan, Gordon. *Jesus the Master Builder: Druid*

Mysteries and the Dawn of Christianity. Edinburgh: Floris Books, 1998.

Tabor, James W. *The Jesus Dynasty: A New Historical Interpretation of Jesus, His Royal Family, and the Birth of Christianity*. 2006.

*Thiering, Barbara. *Jesus the Man*. London: Doubleday/Transworld, 1992.

———. *Jesus of the Apocalypse*. London: Transworld/Doubleday, 1996.

Thomson, Dr. J. E. H. *Books Which Influenced Our Lord and His Apostles*. 1891.

Twycross, Stephen. "Was Jesus Married?" *Expository Times* 107 (1996): 334.

Vermes, Geza. *Jesus the Jew*. London: SCM, 1983.

Walker, Dr. Thomas. *What Jesus Read*. Scribners, 1925.

Webb, Robert L. *John the Baptizer and Prophet*. Sheffield: Sheffield Academic Press, 1991.

Wells, G. A. *The Jesus of the Early Christians: A Study in Christian Origins*. London: Pemberton, 1971.

*Wilson, A. N. *Jesus*. London: HarperCollins, 1993.

Wilson, Ian. *The Turin Shroud*. London: Victor Gollancz, 1979.

———. *Jesus: The Evidence*. San Francisco: HarperCollins, 1988.

Wise, Michael O. *The First Messiah: Investigating the Savior before Jesus*. New York: Harper Collins, 1999.

Witherington III, Ben. *The Jesus Quest*. Downers Grove, Ill.: InterVarsity Press, 1995.

*———. *The Brother of Jesus*. London and New York: Continuum, 2003.

Wright, N. T. *Jesus and the Victory of God*. Minneapolis: Fortress Press, 1996.

Zindler, Frank R. "Where Jesus Never Walked." *American Atheist* (Winter 1996–97).

JOSEPH OF ARIMATHEA AND MERLIN

Boron, Robert de. *Josef d'Arimathie* (also called *Merlin*). Thirteenth-century poem published by Francisque Michel. 1841. Edited by W. A. Nitze. Paris, 1927.

Bryant, Nigel, trans. *Merlin and the Grail: Joseph of Arimathea, Merlin, Perceval: The Trilogy of Prose Romances Attributed to Robert de Boron*. Woodbridge, Suffolk: D. S. Brewer, 2001.

Cabaniss, Allen. "Joseph of Arimathea and a Chalice." *Mississippi Studies in English* 4 (1963).

Capgrave, John. *De Sancto Joseph ab Arimathea*. Capgrave was the Principal of the Augustinian Friars in England, 1393–1464, often quoted from a book found by the Emperor Theodosius (ruled 375–395) in the Pretorium in Jerusalem.

Clarke, Basil. *Life of Merlin*. Cardiff: University of Wales Press, 1973.

Crawford, Deborah K. E. "St. Joseph in Britain: Reconsidering the Legends." *Folklore* (part 2) 1993.

———. "St. Joseph and Britain: The Old French Origins." *Arthuriana* 11, 3 (2001): 1–20.

Dames, Michael. *Merlin and Wales*. London: Thames and Hudson, 2002.

Gaster, Moses. *Jewish Sources of and Parallels to the Early English Metrical Legends of King Arthur and Merlin*. New York, 1887.

*Elder, Isabel Hill. *Joseph of Arimathea*. Glastonbury, 1999.

Gazay, J. "Etudes sur les légendes de sainte Marie-Madeleine et de Joseph d'Arimathie." *Annales du Midi*, LI (1939): 225–84, 337–89.

Geoffrey of Monmouth. *The Life of Merlin*. Edited by J. Parry. Urbana: University of Illinois Press, 1925.

*Goodrich, Norma Loree. *Merlin*. New York: Harper Perennial, 1988.

*Goodrich, Peter. "The Story of Grisandol." *The Romance of Merlin*. 1990. *History of That Holy Disciple Joseph of Arimathea* (ca. 1770). The Camelot Project at the University of Rochester.

Holmes, T. Scott. *The Origin and Development of the Christian Church in Gaul during the First Six Centuries of the Christian Era*. London: Macmillan, 1911.

Jarman, A. O. H. *The Legend of Merlin*. Cardiff, 1960.

———. "The Merlin Legend and the Welsh Tradition

of Prophecy." In *The Arthur of the Welsh.* Edited by Rachel Bromwich, A. O. H. Jarman, and Brynley F. Roberts. Cardiff: University of Wales Press, 1991.

Jones, Robert C. "Joseph of Arimathea: Biblical and Legendary Accounts." 1997. robertcjones@ mindspring.com

Joseph of Arimathea. *Joseph of Arimathea: A Critical Edition.* New York: Garland Publishers, 1983.

*Jowett, George F. *The Drama of the Lost Disciples.* London: Covenant Publishing, 1961, 1996.

Lagorio, Valerie. "Joseph of Arimathea: Vita of a Grail Saint." *Zeitschrift für romanische Philologie* 91 (1975): 359–66.

Lewis, Rev. Lionel Smithett. St. *Joseph of Arimathea at Glastonbury.* London: A. R. Mobray, 1927.

———. *St. Joseph of Arimathea at Glastonbury.* Edited by James Clarke. Covenant Books, 1955.

Map, Walter [possible author]. *History of the Holy Grail or Joseph of Arimathea.* Le Mans. Map was the chaplain of King Henry II of England.

*Markale, Jean. *Merlin.* English translation from French original, *Merlin L'Enchanteur,* 1981. Rochester, Vt.: Inner Traditions, 1995.

O'Gorman, R. *The Prose Version of Robert de Boron's Joseph d'Arimathie.* Oxford, 1970.

Parry, J. J. *The Vita Merlini.* Urbana: University of Illinois, 1925.

Paton, Lucy Allen, ed. *Prophecies de Merlin.* From manuscript 593 in Bibliotheque Municipale of Rennes, France. New York: MLA, 1966.

*Phillips, Graham. *Merlin and the Discovery of Avalon in the New World.* Rochester, Vt.: Bear and Company, 2005.

Riddy, Felicity. "Glastonbury, Joseph of Arimathea and the Grail in John Hardyng's *Chronicle.*" *The Archaeology and History of Glastonbury Abbey.* Edited by Lesley Adams and James P. Carley. Suffolk, England: Boydell and Brewer, 1991.

Scavone, Daniel C. *Joseph of Arimathea, the Holy Grail and the Turin Shroud.* Bloomington, Ind.: University of Indiana Press, 1996.

Schlauch, Margaret, trans. "Joseph d'Arimathie." In *Medieval Narrative.* New York, 1928.

*Skeat, Walter William. *Joseph of Arimathie, Otherwise Called the Romance of the Seint Graal, or Holy Grail.* London: Early English Text Society, 1871. Reprint, Felinfach, Wales: Llanerch Publishers, 1992.

Stein, Dr. Walter Johannes. *The Death of Merlin.* Edinburgh: Floris Books, 1990.

Stewart, R. J. *The Mystic Life of Merlin.* London: Arkana, 1986.

Stewart, R. J., and J. Matthews. *Merlin through the Ages.* London: Blandford, 1995.

Thompson, M. Trans. *Joseph d'Arimathie.* London, 1951.

*Tolstoy, Nikolai. *The Quest for Merlin.* London: Hamish Hamilton, 1985.

Zumthor, Paul. *Merlin le Prophète.* Lausanne, Switzerland, 1943. Reprint, Geneva, 1973.

KNIGHTS TEMPLAR, CRUSADERS, AND PRIORY DE SION

Addison, Charles Greenstreet. *The History of the Knights Templar, the Temple Church and Temple.* London: Longman and Co., 1842. Reprint, London: Black Books, 1995.

———. *The Knights Templar.* London, 1842, 1874.

Ambelain, Robert. *Jesus ou le Mortel Sécrets des Templiers.* Paris: Editions Robert Lafont, 1970.

Andressohn, John C. *The Ancestry and Life of Godfrey of Bouillon.* Bloomington, Ind.: University of Indiana Press, 1947.

Arnold, B. . *German Knighthood: 1050–1300.* Oxford: Clarendon Press, 1985.

Barber, Malcolm. "Origins of the Order of the Temple." *Studia Monastica* 12. Barcelona, 1970.

*———. *The Trail of the Templars.* Cambridge: Cambridge University Press, 1978, 1994.

———. *History* 66 (1981).

———. *The New Knighthood: A History of the Order of the Temple.* Cambridge: Cambridge University Press, 1994.

Barber, Richard. *The Knights and Chivalry.* New York: 1982.

Bennett, John. *Origin of Freemasonry and Knights Templar.* Kila, Mont.: Kessinger Publishing, 1907.

Bennett, M. "Jerusalem's First Crusader King: Godfrey de Bouillon." *BBC History Magazine,* May 2001.

Bernard of Clairvaux. "De laude novae militiae ad milites Templi liber." In *Sancti Bernardi Opera.* Edited by J. Leclercq et. al. Vol. 3. Rome, 1963.

Best, Nicholas. *The Knights Templar.* London: Widenfeld and Nicolson, 1997.

Bothwell-Gosse. *The Knights Templar.* London, 1912.

Boulton, D'Arcy J. D. *Knights of the Crown.* Palgrave: Macmillan, 1987.

Bouyer, Louis. *Les liens magiques de la legende du Graal.* Paris, 1986.

Bredero, A. H. *Bernard of Clairvaux: Between Cult and History.* Edinburgh: T&T Clark, 1966.

Bryden, Chevalier Robert. "The Germanic Tradition, The Scottish Knights Templar and the Mystery of the Holy Grail." *Scottish Knights Templar Magazine* (Winter 1984–85).

Burman, Edward. *The Templars: Knights of God.* Rochester, Vt.: Inner Traditions, 1990.

———. *Supremely Abominable Crimes: The Trial of the Knights Templar.* London: Allison and Busby, 1994.

Butler, Alan, and Stephen Dafoe. *The Warriors and the Bankers: A History of the Knights Templar from 1307 to the Present.* Belleville, Ontario: Templar Books, Thevou Publishing Group, 1998.

———. *The Templar Continuum.* Belleville, Ontario: Templar Books, Thevou Publishing Group, 1999.

Byrne, Patrick. *Templar Gold: Discovering the Ark of the Covenant.* Nevada City, Calif.: Blue Dolphin Publishing, 2001.

Charpentier, Louis. *Les Mysteres Templiers.* Paris: Editions Robert Lafont, 1967.

Coppack, G. *The White Monks: The Cistercians in Britain, 1128–1540.* Stroud: Tempus, 1998.

Cross, J. *The Templar's Chart.* New Haven, Conn., 1821.

Dafoe, Stephen. *Unholy Worship: The Myth of the Baphomet, Templar, Freemason Connection.* 1998.

Daraul, Arkon. *A History of Secret Societies.* Citadel Press, 1984.

Delaforge, Gaetan. *The Templar Tradition in the Age of Aquarius.* Putney, Vt.: Threshold Books, 1987.

Desgris, Alain. *L'ordre des Templiers.* Paris, 1994.

Desgins, A. *L'ordre de Templiers and La Chevalerie MaConnique Templière.* Paris: Trédaniel, 1995.

Douzet, André. *The Treasure Trove of the Knights Templar.* Edited and translated by Filip Coppens. 1997.

Durman, E. *The Templars, Knights of God.* Wellingborough: Aquarian Press, 1988.

Forey, A. *The Military Orders from the Twelfth to the Early Fourteenth Centuries.* Basingstoke: Macmillan, 1992.

Furlong, D. *The Keys to the Temple.* Judy Piatkus, 1997.

Graffin, Robert. *L'Art Templier des Cathedrales.* Garnier, 1993.

Haagensen, E., and Henry Lincoln. *The Templars' Secret Island: The Knights, the Priest and the Treasure.* Moreton-in-Marsh, Gloustershire: Windruss Press, 2000.

Hammer-Purgstall, Joseph von. *The Mystery of Baphomet Revealed.* 1818.

———. *The Guilt of the Templars.* N.d.

Holmes, E. *The Holy Heretics.* London: Watts, 1948.

Horvath, G. G. *The Knights of the Holy Grail.* Minerva Press, n.d.

Howarth, Stephen. *The Knights Templar.* William Collins, 1982. Reprint, Dorset Press, 1991.

*Knight, Christopher, and Robert Lomas. *The Second Messiah: Templars, The Turin Shroud and the Great Secret of Freemasonry.* London: Century, 1997.

Krey, A. C. *The First Crusade: The Accounts of Eyewitnesses and Participants.* Princeton, N.J.: Princeton University Press, 1921.

Kurtz, Katherine. *Tales of the Knights Templar.* 1995.

*Laidler, Keith. *The Head of God: The Lost Treasure of the Templars.* London: Weidenfeld and Nicolson, 1998.

Lamy, Michel. *Les Templiers.* Bordeaux, 1997.

Lizerand. *Le Dossier de l'Affaire des Templiers.* 1923.

Lord, Evelyn. *The Knights Templar in Britain.* Harlow, Essex: Longman, Pearson Education, 2002.

Maalouf, A. *The Crusades through Arab Eyes.* London: Al Saqui Books, 1984.

Martin, E. J. *The Trail of the Knights Templar.* London, 1928. Reprint, 1978.

Martin, Sean. *The Knights Templar.* Harpenden: Pocket Essentials, 2004.

Napier, Gordon. *The Rise and Fall of the Knights Templar: The Order of the Temple, 1118–1314, True History of Faith, Glory, Betrayal and Tragedy.* Staplehurst, UK: Spellmount, 2003.

Nicolson, H. *The Knights Templar: A New History.* Stroud: Sutton Publishing, 2001.

Olsen, Oddvar. *The Templar Papers: Ancient Mysteries, Secret Society, and the Holy Grail.* Franklin Lakes, N.J.: New Pages Books, 2006.

Parker, T. W. *The Knights Templar in England.* Tucson: University of Arizona Press, 1965.

Partner, Peter. *The Murdered Magicians: The Templars and Their Myth.* Oxford: Oxford University Press, 1981, 1982. Republished as *The Knights Templar and Their Myth.* Rochester, Vt.: Destiny Books, 1990.

*Patton, G., and R. Mackness. *Web of Gold: The Secret History of a Sacred Treasure.* London: Sidgwick and Jackson, 2000.

*Picknett, Lynn, and Clive Prince. *The Templar Revelation: Secret Guardians of the True Identity of Christ.* London: Bantam Press, 1997.

*Pinkham, Mark Amaru. *Guardians of the Holy Grail: The Knights Templar, John the Baptist and the Water of Life.* Kempton, Ill.: Adventures Unlimited Press, 2004.

Prawer, J. *Crusader Institutions.* Oxford: Clarendon Press, 1980.

Priory of Sion Website: www.priory-of-sion.com

*Ralls, Karen. *The Templars and the Grail: Knights of the Quest.* Wheaton, Ill., and Chennai (Madras) India: Quest Books, Theosophical Publishing House, 2003.

Read, Piers Paul. *The Templars.* London: Widenfeld and Nicolson, 1999.

Richardson, Robert. "The Priory of Sion Hoax." *Gnosis: A Journal of the Western Inner Traditions* 51 (Spring 1999).

Riley-Smith, J. *The First Crusaders, 1095–1131.* Cambridge: Cambridge University Press, 1997.

Rivière, Patrick. *Les Templiers et leurs mystères.* Rev. ed. Paris, 1997.

Robinson, John J. *Dungeon, Fire and Sword: The Knights Templar in the Crusades.* New York: Michael O'Mara Books, 1994.

Runciman, Steven. *A History of the Crusades.* Vols. 1–3. Cambridge: Cambridge University Press, 1951. Reprint, London: Penguin, 1991.

SeBorga, Mille Anni di Storia. *Seborga Agosto,* booklet, 1963; third printing, 1995.

Sanello, Frank, and William Travis Hanes. *The Knights Templar: God's Warriors, the Devil's Bankers.* Lanham, Md.: Taylor, 2003.

Serbaneco, Gérard. *Histoire de l'Ordre des Templiers.* Paris, 1970.

Seward, Desmond. *The Monks of War.* St. Albans: Paladin/Granade, 1974. Reprint, London: Penguin, 1995.

Sinclair, Andrew. *Jerusalem: The Endless Crusade.* New York: Crown Publishers, 1995.

*Sora, Steven. *The Lost Treasure of the Knights Templar: Solving the Oak Island Mystery.* Rochester, Vt.: Destiny Books, 1999.

*Stewart, Desmond. *The Monks of War.* London: Eyre Metheun, 1972.

Tull, George F. . *Traces of the Templars.* Goldthorpe, Rotherham: King's England Press, 2000.

Upton-Ward, J. M. *The Rule of the Templars: The French Text of the Rule of the Order of the Knights Templar.* Suffolk, England: Boydell Press, 1992.

Walsh, Michael. *The Warriors of the Lord: The Military Orders of Christendom.* Grand Rapids, Mich.: Eerdmans, 2003.

Wasserman, J. *The Templars and the Assassins: The Militia of Heaven.* Rochester, Vt.: Inner Traditions, 2001.

Waters, C. *Of Days and Knights: A Chronological History of the Crusades, the Templars and Similar Orders.* Whitby, England: Published by author, 2002.

Watson, William. *The Last of the Templars*. London: Harvill Press, 1998.

Wilkinson, J., J. Hill, W. F. Ryan, eds. *Jerusalem Pilgrimage, 1099–1185*. London: Hakluyt Society, 1988.

William of Tyre. *A History of Deeds Done beyond the Sea*. Translated by Emily A. Babock and A. C. Krey. New York: Columbia University Press, 1943.

MEROVINGIANS

Fouracre, Paul, and Richard A. Gerberding, eds. *Late Merovingian France, History and Hagiography*. Manchester, England: Manchester University Press, 1996.

Geary, Patrick. *Before France and Germany: The Creation and Transformation of the Merovingian World*. Oxford: Oxford University Press, 1988.

*Gregory of Tours. *History of the Franks* (A.D. 590), *Decem Libri Historiarum*. Translated by Lewis Thorpe. London: Penguin Books, 1974.

Hen, Yitzhak. *Culture and Religion in Merovingian Gaul, A.D. 481–751*. Leiden, Netherlands: E. J. Brill, 1995.

James, Edward. *The Franks*. Oxford: Blackwell, 1988.

Lobineau, Henri. *Généalogie des Rois Mérovingiens et origine de diverses familles françaises et étrangéres de souche Mérovingienne, d'aprés Pichon, le Docteur Hervé et les parchmins de l'Abbé Sauniére de Rennes-le Château Aude*. Geneva 1956, Bibliothéque Nationale, lm3 4122 Deposited in 1964. These were forged documents.

Twyman, Tracy R. *The Merovingian Mythos and the Mystery of Rennes-le-Château*. 2004.

Wallace-Hadrill, J. M. *The Long-Haired Kings*. 1962. Reprint, Toronto: Medieval Academy Reprints, 1982.

Wood, Ian. *The Merovingian Kingdoms, 450–751*. London: Longman, 1993.

NAZIS AND ADOLPH HITLER

Angebert, Jean Michael. *The Occult and the Third Reich: The Mystical Origins of Nazism and the Search for the Holy Grail*. Translated by Lewis A. M. Sumberg. New York: Macmillan, 1974.

———. *Hitler y la Tradicion Catara*. Barcelona, Spain, 1976.

Baigent, Michael, and Richard Leigh. *Secret Germany: Claus von Stauffenberg and the Mystical Crusade against Hitler*. London: Jonathan Cape, 1994.

Bernadac, Christian. *Le Mystère Otto Rahn (1904–1939): le Graal et Montsegur: du Catharisme au Nazisme*. Paris: Editions France-Empire, 1978.

Bertrand, M., and J. Angelini. *The Quest and the Third Reich*. New York, 1974.

Brennan, J. H. *Occult Reich*. London, 1974.

Buechner, Col. Howard. *Emerald Cup—Ark of Gold: The Quest of SS Lt. Otto Rahn of the Third Reich*. Metairie, La.: Thunderbird Press, 1991, 1994.

Campbell, Mary Baine. "Finding the Grail: Fascist Aesthetics and Mysterious Objects." In *King Arthur's Modern Return*. Edited by Debra Mancoff. New York and London, 1998. 213–25.

Daim, Wilfried. *Der Mann der Hitler die Ideen gab*. Vienna: Institut für Politische Psychologie, 1958.

Goodrick-Clarke, Nicholas. *The Occult Roots of Nazism: Secret Aryan Cults and Their Influence on Nazi Ideology*. New York: New York University Press, 1992.

Graddon, Nigel. *Otto Rahn—Argonaut or Dupe?* Penarth, Wales: Self-published, 1998.

Harris, Robert. *Selling Hitler*. Faber and Faber, 1986.

Jurgen-Lange, Hans. *Otto Rahn—Leben und Werk*. Engerda, Germany: Arun-Verlag, 1997.

King, Francis. *The Secret Rituals of the O.T.O.* London: C. W. Daniels, 1973.

———. *Satan and the Swastika*. London, 1976.

Pennick, Nigel. *Hitler's Secret Sciences*. Sudbury: Neville Spearmen, 1981.

Rahn, Otto. *Kreuzzug Gegen den Graal* [The Crusade Against the Grail]. Stuttgart and Freiburg, Germany,

1933. A Nazi and occult attempt to prove an Arian source for the Grail. This book was followed by *The Heart [Court] of Lucifer* [*Luzifers hofgesind*]. Berlin and Leipzig, 1935, 1937 Also dealing with a Cathar chalice theory and researches near Montségur.

Roboz, Steven. *The Holy Grail: From the Works of Rudolf Steiner.* Hudson, N.Y.: Anthroposophic Press [518] 851–2054; Steiner Book Center, 1991, as The Holy Grail.

Rosio, Bob. *Hitler and The New Age.* Huntington House, 1993.

Sayer, Ian, and Douglas Botting. *Nazi Gold.* London: Granada, 1984.

Skorzeny, Otto. *Skorzeny's Special Mission—Memories of the Most Dangerous Man in Europe.* London: Greenhill Books, 1997.

ROSSLYN AND ROSLIN

Anderson, R. "Notice of Working Drawings Scratched on the Walls of the Crypt at Roslin Chapel." *Proceedings of the Society of Antiquities of Scotland* 10 (1872–74).

Brydon, Chevalier Robert. *Rosslyn—A History of the Guilds, the Masons and the Rosy Cross.* Edinburgh: Friends of Rosslyn Chapel Trust, 1984, 1994.

Clerk, Sir John. *Memoirs of Sir John Clerk of Penecuik.* Edinburgh, 1893.

*Coppens, Philip. *The Stone Puzzle of Rosslyn Chapel.* Enkhuizen, Netherlands: Frontier Publishing, 2002.

Cooper, Robert. "Rosslyn Chapel: The Faces of Robert the Bruce." *Ashlar* 11 (2000).

*Countess of Rosslyn. *Rosslyn Country of Painter and Poet.* Edinburgh: Trustees of the National Galleries of Scotland, 2002.

Crawford, Barbara E. "Lord William Sinclair and the Building of Roslin Collegiate Church." In John Higgitt, *Medieval Art and Architecture in the Diocese of St. Andrews.* British Archaeological Association, 1994.

*Earl of Rosslyn. *Rosslyn Chapel.* Rosslyn Chapel Trust, 1997.

Fawcett, Richard. *Scottish Medieval Church.* Stroud, Gloucestershire: Tempus, 2002.

Forbes, Dr. Robert (Episcopalian Bishop of Caithness). *An Account of the Chapel of Roslin 1778.* 1774. Reprint, Edinburgh: Grand Lodge of Scotland, 2000.

Gerber, Pat. *The Search for the Stone of Destiny.* Edinburgh: Cannongate Books, 1997, 2000.

Ginn, Ward L., Jr. *The 'Bleeding Angel' in the Crypt of Rosslyn Chapel.* Saunière Society Newsletter. N.d.

Grant, Will. *Rosslyn: Its Chapel, Castle, and Scenic Lore.* Edinburgh: F. S. A. Scott, Dysart and Rosslyn Estates Kirkcaldy, 1936.

*Green, James. *Rosslyn Chapel: The Enigma—The Myth.* Temple Arch Publishers, 2002.

Hey, Father R. A. *The Genealogie of the Saintclaires of Rosslyn.* Edinburgh: Maidment, 1835.

Jackson, James. *Historical Tales of Roslin Castle from the Invasion of Edward I of England to the Death of Mary.* Edinburgh, 1836.

Kerr, Andrew. *Proceedings of the Society of Antiquaries in Scotland* 12 (1877).

*Knight, Christopher and Lomas, Robert. *The Hiram Key: Pharaohs, Freemasons, and the Discovery of the Secret Scrolls of Jesus.* London: Century, 1996.

*———. *The Second Messiah: Templars, The Turin Shroud and the Great Secret of Freemasonry.* London: Century, 1997.

*———. *The Book of Hiram: Freemasonry, Venus and the Secret Key to the Life of Jesus.* London: Century, 2003.

Millar, John. "Richard Wagner. Rosslyn and the Mystery of Rennes-les-Château." *Newsletter of the Saunière Society* 2, 5/11 (1 January 1999).

Morrison, Leonard A. *A History of the Sinclair Family.* Boston: Damprell and Upman, 1896.

Munro, J. "Rosslyn Chapel: Part 4: Inside and Around." *Ashlar* 4 (1998).

*Nisbet, Jeff. "Secrets of Rosslyn Chapel." *Mythomorph: Myth, History and the Quest.* www.mythomorph.com (27 May 2004).

Orr Ewing, A. D. (Grand Master Mason). Preface to *An*

Account of the Chapel of Roslin 1778. Edited by R. L. D. Cooper. Edinburgh: Grand Lodge of Scotland, 2000.

Oxbrow, Mark, and Ian Robertson. Foreword by Simon Cox. *Rosslyn and the Grail.* 2005.

Pohl, Frederick J. *Prince Henry Sinclair.* New York: Clarkson N. Potter, 1974.

*Ritchie, John, and Alan Butler. *Rosslyn Revealed, a Library in Stone.* 2006.

Simpson, J. "The Conservation of Rosslyn: An Unfinished Story of Decline and Recovery." In *Rosslyn: Country of Painter and Poet.* Edinburgh: Trustees of the National Galleries of Scotland, 2002.

*Sinclair, Andrew. *Rosslyn—the Story of Rosslyn Chapel and the True Story behind the Da Vinci Code.* 2005.

Slezer, John. *Theatrum Scotiae.* London, 1693.

Spence, Lewis. "Mystical Roslin." *Scotland's SMT Magazine,* May 1952.

*Stevenson, Winnie, and Veronica Meickle. *Old Roslin.* Roslin Heritage Society, Stenlake Publishing, 2003.

*Thompson, Rev. John. *The Illustrated Guide to Rosslyn Chapel and Castle, Hawthronden, etc.* Edinburgh: St. Giles' Printing Company and London: J. Menzies and Co., 1892. 3d ed. Edinburgh: MacNiven and Wallace, 1897.

To Roslin from the Far West. Edinburgh, 1872.

*Wallace-Murphy, Tim. *An Illustrated Guide Book to Rosslyn Chapel.* Friends of Rosslyn, 1990, 1993.

*———. *The Templar Legacy and the Masonic Inheritance within Rosslyn Chapel.* Roslin: Friends of Rosslyn, 1994.

*Wallace-Murphy, Tim, and Marilyn Hopkins. *Rosslyn: Guardian of the Secrets of the Holy Grail.* Shaftsbury: Element, 1999, 2000.

SCRIPTURES, CHRISTIANITY, AND JUDAISM

Abegg, Martin G., ed. *The Dead Sea Bible: The Oldest Known Bible.* New York: Harper, 1999.

Abrahams, Israel. "Marriages Art Made in Heaven." *Jewish Quarterly Review* 2 (1890).

———. *Studies in Pharisaism and the Gospels.* Cambridge, 1917.

Achtemeier, Paul J. *Romans.* Westminster: John Knox Press, 1985.

*Allegro, John Marco. *The Treasure of the Copper Scroll.* Doubleday, 1960.

Allwood, Rev. Philip. *Revelation of Saint John.* Vol. 1. London, 1829.

*Baigent, Michael, and Richard Leigh. *The Dead Sea Deception.* London: Arrow, 1993.

Bailey, D. Sherman. *Sexual Relation in Christian Thought.* New York, 1959.

Bainton, Roland H. *What Christianity Says about Sex, Love and Marriage.* New York, 1957.

Bakan, David. *Sigmund Freud and the Jewish Mystical Tradition.* Princeton, 1958.

*Barker, James L. *Apostasy from the Divine Church.* Salt Lake City: Deseret Book, 1960.

*Barnum, Rev. Samuel W. *A Comprehensive Dictionary of the Bible.* New York, 1869.

*Baronius, Cardinal Caesar. *Ecclesiastical Annals.* Ends A.D. 1198.

Bercot, David W. *A Glimpse of Early Christian Life.* Tyler, Texas: Scroll Publishing, 1991.

Bertholet, Alfred. *History of Hebrew Civilization.* New York, n.d.

Bickmore, Robert Barry. *Restoring the Ancient Church.* Phoenix, Ariz.: Cornerstone Publishing, 1999.

Blenkinsopp, Joseph. *Celibacy, Ministry, Church.* New York, 1968.

Bolland, Jean. *Acta Sanctorum.* Hymn of the 600s republished by Jesuit Bolland in the seventeenth century.

Bouyer, Louis. *Rite and Man: Natural Sacredness and Christian Liturgy.* Notre Dame, Ind.: University of Notre Dame Press, 1963.

Brandon, S. G. F. *The Fall of the Jerusalem and the Christian Church.* London: SPCK, 1951.

Bright, John A. *A History of Israel.* 1974. Reprint, Westminster, John Knox Press, 2000.

Brooke, G. *Temple Scrolls Studies.* Sheffield: Sheffield Academic Press, 1989.

*Brown, Raymond E., Joseph A. Fitzmyer, and R. E. Murphy. *The New Jerome Biblical Commentary.* Englewood Cliffs, New Jersey: Prentice Itall, 1989.

———. *The Community of the Beloved Disciple.* New York: Paulist Press, 1979

Bruce, F. F. *Biblical Exegesis in the Qumran Texts.* London: Tyndale Press, 1960.

*———. *Jesus and Christian Origins outside the New Testament.* Grand Rapids, Mich.: Eerdmans, 1974.

———. *Peter, James, and John.* Grand Rapids, Mich.: Eerdmans, 1979.

———. *The Canon of Scripture.* Downers Grove, Ill.: InterVarsity Press, 1988.

———. *The New Testament Documents: Are They Reliable?* Downers Grove, Ill: InterVarsity Press, 1960. Reprint, Grand Rapids, Mich.: Eerdmans and N.T. Wright, 2003.

Brunner, Emil. *The Christian Doctrine of Creation and Redemption.* Philadelphia, 1952.

Bultmann, Rudolf. *Primitive Christianity in Its Contemporary Setting.* Translated by F. H. Fuller. Glasgow: Fontana/Collins, 1960.

Burrows, Millar. *More Light on the Dead Sea Scrolls.* New York: Viking Press, 1958.

Butler, Thomas W. *Gospel of John.* Tracy, California: Quantum Leap Publications, 1998.

Callahan, Sidney C. *Beyond Birth Control: The Christian Experience of Sex.* New York, 1968.

Campenhausen, Hans von. *Tradition and Life in the Church.* Philadelphia, 1968.

Carroll, Vincent, and David Shiflett. *Christianity on Trial.* San Francisco: Encounter Books, 2002.

Carson, D. A. *Exegetical Fallacies.* Grand Rapids, Mich.: Baker Book House, 1984.

Carson, D. A., R. T. France, J. A. Motyer, and G. J. Wenham, eds. *New Bible Commentary, Twenty-First Century Edition.* Downers Grove, Ill.: Intervarsity Press, 4th ed., 1994.

Case, Rev. Ira. *Light on Prophecy.* Providence, 1871.

Chadwick, Henry. *The Early Church.* Rev. ed. New York: Penguin Books, 1995.

Chadwick, Owen. *A History of Christianity.* New York: St. Martin's Press, 1995.

Cole, William G. *Sex in Christianity and Psychoanalysis.* New York, 1955.

Couchoud, P. L. *The Creation of Christ: An Outline of the Beginnings of Christianity.* Translated by C. Bradlaugh Bonner. London: Watts, 1939.

Daniélou, Jean. *The Dead Sea Scrolls and Primitive Christianity.* Translated by Salvator Attanasio. New York: New American Library, 1962.

Danker, F. W., and Walter Bauer. *Greek-English Lexicon of the New Testament.* Chicago: University of Chicago, 2000.

Davis, John D. *The Davis Dictionary of the Bible.* Grand Rapids, Mich.: Baker Book House, 1924, 1972.

Davis, John G. *The Early Christian Church.* Grand Rapids, Mich.: Baker Book House, 1965.

Dodds, E. R. *Pagan and Christian in an Age of Anxiety.* New York: Norton, 1970.

*Dummelow, Rev. J. R. *A Commentary on the Holy Bible by Various Writers.* New York: Macmillan, 1954.

*Durant, Will. *The Age of Faith.* New York: Simon and Schuster, 1950.

*Edersheim, Alfred. *History of the Jewish Nation: After the Destruction of Jerusalem under Titus.* New York: Longmans, Green, and Co., 1856.

*———. *The Life and Times of Jesus the Messiah.* 2 vols. New York: Longmans, Green and Co., 1898.

———. *Bible History Old Testament.* Grand Rapids, Mich.: Eerdmans, 1977.

———. *The Temple: Its Ministry and Services As They Were at the Time of Christ.* Peabody, Mass.: Hendrickson, 1994.

Edgren, J. A. *Epiphaneia: A Study in Prophecy.* Chicago, 1881.

Ehrman, Bart. "Lost Christianities" on tape. Chantilly, Virginia: The Teaching Co., 2002.

Epstein, Louis M. *Marriage Laws in the Bible and the Talmud.* Cambridge, 1942.

———. *Sex Laws and Customs in Judaism.* New York, 1948.

Eusebius of Caesarea. *An Ecclesiastical History.* Translated by Rev. C. F. Cruse. London: Samuel Bagster, 1838.

———. *The History of the Church from Christ to Constantine.* London: Penguin, 1989.

*———. *Ecclesiastical History and the Martyrs of Palestine (Historia Ecclesiastica).* Grand Rapids, Mich.: Baker Book House, 1995.

Ewing, W. "Shiloh." In *Dictionary of the Bible.* New York: Charles Scribner's Sons, 1952.

Farrar, F. W. *History of Interpretation.* New York, 1886.

———. *The Life and Work of St. Paul.* London: Cassell & Co., 2 Vols. 1902.

Finkelstein, L. *The Pharisees: The Sociological Background of Their Faith.* Philadelphia, 1938.

Fiorenze, Elisabeth Schüssler. *The Book of Revelation: Justice and Judgment.* Philadelphia: Fortress Press, 1984.

Fox, Robin Lane. *Pagans and Christians.* New York: Alfred A. Knopf, 1988.

Foxe, John. *The New Foxe's Book of Martyrs.* Rewritten by Harold J. Chadwick. North Brunswick, NJ: Bridge-Logos Publishers, 1997.

Frend, W. H. C. *The Rise of Christianity.* Philadelphia: Fortress Press, 1984.

Freudmann, Lillian C. *Antisemitism in the New Testament.* University of America Press, 1993.

Funk, Robert, ed. *The Five Gospels.* New York: Macmillan, 1993.

Garvie, Alfred E. *The Abingdon Bible Commentary.* NY: Abingdon-Cokesbury Press, 1929.

Gaster, Theodor H. *Myth, Legend, and Creation in the Old Testament.* New York, 1969.

*Ginzberg, Louis. *Legends of the Jews.* 7 vols. Philadelphia: Jewish Publication Society of America, 1911, 1937.

Goguel, Maurice. *The Birth of Christianity.* Translated by H. C. Snape. New York: Macmillan, 1954.

Goodenough, Erwin R. *By Light, Light.* New Haven, Conn., 1935.

———. *An Introduction to Philo Judaeus.* New Haven, Conn., 1940.

———. *Jewish Symbols in the Greco-Roman Period.* New York, 1952.

Gottstein, Alon Goshen. "The Body as Image of God in Rabbinic Literature." *Harvard Theological Review* 87 (1994).

*Graham, Lloyd M. *Deceptions and Myths of the Bible.* Secaucus, N.J.: University Books, 1975.

Granqvist, Hilma. *Marriage Conditions in a Palestinian Village.* Helsingfors, 1931.

Grant, Frederick C. *Ancient Judaism and the New Testament.* New York, 1959.

Grant, Frederick C., and H. H. Rowley, eds. *Dictionary of the Bible.* Rev. ed. New York: Charles Scribner and Sons, 1963.

Grant, Michael. *The Jews in the Roman World.* London: Widenfeld and Nicolson, 1973.

*Grimm, Carl Ludwig Wilibald. *Thayer's Greek-English Lexicon of the New Testament.* Translated by Joseph H. Thayer. Milford, Mich.: Mott Media, 1982.

Guerin, Paul. *Vies des Saints (Lives of the Saints).* Paris: Bloud et Barrel, 1882).

Guiness, H. Grattan. *Light for the Last Days.* Toronto, 1886.

*Hagee, John. *Final Dawn over Jerusalem: The World's Future Hangs in the Balance with the Battle for the Holy City.* Nashville: Thomas Nelson, 1998.

Halliday, William R. *The Pagan Background of Early Christianity.* New York: Cooper Square, 1970.

Harnach, Adolf Von. *Marcion: das Evangelium Vom Fremden Gott.* Leipzig, Germany: J. C. Hinrichs'sche Buchhandlung, 1924.

Hastings, James. *A Dictionary of the Bible.* Sussex, UK: Hastings Publishers, 1898.

Hatch, Edwin. *The Influence of Greek Ideas and Usages upon the Christian Church.* London: Williams and Norgate, 1914.

Hennecke, Edgar, and Wilhelm Schneemelcher, eds. *New Testament Apocrypha.* Philadelphia: Westminister Press, 1963.

*Henry, Matthew. *Commentary on the Whole Bible.* Grand Rapids, Mich.: Zondervan, 1974.

Hereford, R. Travers. *Christianity in Talmud and Midrash.* KTAV Publishing, 1975

Hertz, Joseph H. *Sayings of the Fathers*. Springfield, New Jersey: Behrman House Publishing, 1986.

Higginbotham, D. L. *Color in Scripture*. Lafayette, Ind.: Truth for Today Bible Fellowship, 1992.

Isaksson, Abel. *Marriage and Ministry in the New Temple*. Lund, 1965.

James, Vanderkam, and Peter Flint. *The Meaning of the Dead Sea Scrolls: Their Significance for Understanding the Bible, Judaism, Jesus, and Christianity*. San Francisco: HarperSanFrancisco, 2002.

Johnson, Luke Timothy. *The Creed: What Christians Believe and Why It Matters*. Doubleday, 2003.

Jones, A. H. M. *The Herods of Judaea*. Oxford: Clarendon Press, 1938.

Jones, Floyd Nolen. *The Chronology of the Old Testament*. Green Forest Arizona: Master Books, 2005.

Jones, Maurice. "II Thessalonians." *A New Commentary on Holy Scripture*. London: Society for Promoting Christian Knowledge, 1928.

Jones, V. R. . *Woman in Islam*. Lucknow, 1941.

*Josephus, Flavius. *Antiquities of the Jews* and *The Wars of the Jews* in *The Works of Flavius Joseph*. Translated by William Whiston. London: Milner and Sowerby, 1870.

*Keil, C. F., and F. Delitzsch. *Commentary on the Old Testament*. 10 vols. Grand Rapids, Mich.: Eerdmans, 1969.

Kelly, J. N. D. *Early Christian Creeds*. New York: David McKay, 1972.

Kern, H. Trans. *Saddharma-Pundarika* [Lotus of the True Law]. New York: Dover, 1963.

Kingsland, William. *The Gnosis or Ancient Wisdom in the Christian Scriptures*. London: Allen and Unwin, 1937.

Koester, Helmut. *Ancient Christian Gospels*. Philadelphia: Trinity Press International, 1990.

Köhler, Ludwig. *Hebrew Man*. London, 1956.

Kreeft, Peter, and Tacelli, Ronald K. *Handbook of Christian Apologetics*. Downers Grove, Ill.: InterVarsity Press, 1994.

Lane, Robin. *Pagans and Christians*. New York: Penguin, 1988.

Lea, Henry. *History of Sacerdotal Celibacy in the Christian Church*. New York: Macmillan, 1907.

*Lewis, C. S. *That Hideous Strength*. 1945. Reprint, New York City: Scribner, 2003.

Mace, David. *Hebrew Marriage: A Sociological Study*. London, 1953.

Malinine, M., ed. *Codex Jung—Epistula Ialobi Apocrypha*. Stuttgart, 1968.

Maraoka, T. *Emphatic Words and Structures in Biblical Hebrew*. Jerusalem: E. J. Brill, 1983.

Martin, Malachi. *The Decline and Fall of the Roman Church*. London: Secker and Warburg, 1982.

McBirnie, William Stuart. *The Search for the Twelve Apostles*. Wheaton, Ill.: Tyndale House, 1973.

McBrien, Richard D. *The Harper-Collins Encyclopedia of Catholicism*. San Francisco: Harper-Collins, 1995.

McGiffert, Arthur C. *A History of Christian Thought*. New York, 1932.

Metzger, Bruce M. *Historical and Literary Studies: Pagan, Jewish, and Christian*. Grand Rapids, Mich.: Eerdmans, 1968.

———. *The Canon of the New Testament: Its Origin, Development and Significance*. Oxford: Clarendon, 1987.

Miller, Robert J., ed. *The Complete Gospels: Annotated Scholars Version*. Sonoma, Calif.: Polebridge Press, 1992.

Milman, Henry Hart. *History of the Jews*. New York: Everyman, 1939.

Momigliano, Arnaldo. ed. *The Conflict between Paganism and Christianity in the Fourth Century*. Oxford: Clarendon, 1963.

Montefiore, Claude G. *Rabbinic Literature and Gospel Teaching*. London, 1930.

Moore, George. *Judaism in the First Centuries of the Christian Era*. 2 vols. New York: Schocken, 1971.

Mosheim, Johann Lorenz. *An Ecclesiastical History, Ancient and Modern, from the Birth of Christ to the Beginning of the Eighteenth Century*. West Jordan, Utah, 1980.

Murry, J. Middleton. *Adam and Eve*. London, 1944.

Nash, Ronald H. "Was the New Testament Influenced

by Pagan Religions?" *Christian Research Journal* 16, 2 (Winter) 1994. See www.equip.org/free/DB109.pdf.

———. *The Gospel and the Greeks: Did the New Testament Borrow from Pagan Thought?* 2d ed. Phillipsburg, N.J.: P and R Press, 2003.

Nemoy, J. *Al-Qirqisani's Account of the Jewish Sects and Christianity*. Vol. 7. Hebrew Union College Annual, 1930.

Neufeld, E. *Ancient Hebrew Marriage Laws*. London, 1944.

Neusner, Jacob. *Invitation to the Talmud*. New York: Harper and Row, 1975.

New Catholic Encyclopedia. Washington, D.C.: Catholic University of America and the Gale Group, September 2002 ed.

Newman, Albert Henry. *A Manual of Church History*. 2 vols. Philadelphia: American Baptist Publication Society, 1900–1903.

Oberman, Hieko A. *Luther*. New York: Doubleday Dell, 1992.

Odeberg, Hugo. *3 Enoch or the Hebrew Book of Enoch*. New York: KTAV, 1973.

*Orr, William W. *50 Most Frequently Asked Bible Questions*. Wheaton, Ill.: Scripture Press, 1974.

Oulton, J. E. L., and H. Chadwick, eds. *Alexandrian Christianity*. Philadelphia, 1954.

Perowne, Stewart. *The Life and Times of Herod the Great*. London: Hodder and Stoughton, 1956.

Parrot, André. *The Temple of Jerusalem*. London, 1957.

Patai, Raphael. *Sex and the Family in the Bible and the Middle East*. New York, 1959.

———. *The Messiah Texts*. New York: Avon Books, 1979.

Pfeiffer, Robert H. *Introduction to the Old Testament*. New York, 1941.

Phillips, J. B. *The Young Church in Action: A Translation of the Acts of the Apostles*. New York: Macmillan, 1955.

Pope, Marvin H. *Song of Songs: A New Translation with Introduction and Commentary*. Anchor Bible Series. Garden City: Doubleday, 1983.

Rahner, Hugo, and S. J. Rahner. *Church and State in Early Christianity*. San Francisco: Ignatius Press, 1992.

Rappoport, Angelo S. *Myths and Legends of Ancient Israel*. 3 vols. London: Gresham, 1928.

*Ravenscroft, Trevor, and Tim Wallace-Murphy. *The Mark of the Beast*. UK: Sphere Books, 1990.

Revel, Hirschel. "Celibacy." *Universal Jewish Encyclopedia*. New York, 1948.

Richardson, C. C. *Early Christian Fathers*. Philadelphia, 1953.

Richman, Rabbi Chaim. "The Order of Burning the Red Heifer," Jerusalem: Third Temple Institute, Grace Publishers, 2001.

*Ritmeyer, Leen, and Kathleen Ritmeyer. *Secrets of Jerusalem's Temple Mount*. Washington, D.C.: Biblical Archaelogical Society, 1998.

Roberts, Alexander, and James Donalson, eds. With notes from A. Cleveland Coxe. *The Ante-Nicene Fathers: Translations of the Writings of the Fathers Down to A.D. 325*. Grand Rapids, Mich.: Eerdmans, 1867–85.

Robinson, James M., and Helmut Koester. *Trajectories through Early Christianity*. Philadelphia: Fortress, 1971.

Robinson, Maurice. *Indexes to All Editions of Brown Driver Briggs Hebrew—English Lexicon*. Sovereign, 2003.

Rosenvall, E. Alan. "Twelve Tribes of Israel through History." MS, 1989.

Sandmel, Samuel. *Philo's Place in Judaism*. Cincinnati, Ohio, 1956.

Schaff, Philip. *History of the Christian Church*. 7 vols. New York: C. Scribner's Sons, 1916–23.

*Schonfield, Hugh J. *A Radical Translation and Reinterpretation: The Original New Testament*. New York: Harper and Row, 1985.

Schürer, Emil. *A History of the Jewish People in the Time of Jesus Christ*. New York, 1891.

Slight, Benjamin. *The Apocalypse Explained*. Montreal, Canada, 1855.

Smallwood, E. M. *The Jews under Roman Rule.*

Leiden, Netherlands: E. J. Brill, 1976.

Strong, James. *The New Strong's Exhaustive Concordance of the Bible*. Nashville: Thomas Nelson Publishers, 1984; 1990.

Swain, Joseph W. *The Hellenic Origins of Christian Asceticism*. New York, 1916.

Tacitus. *The Histories*. Translated by Kenneth Wellesley. London: Penguin, 1995.

———. *The Annals of Imperial Rome*. Translated by Michael Grant. London: Penguin, 1996.

Taylor, Vincent. *New Bible Dictionary*. Leicester: Intervarsity, 1997.

Thiede, C. P., and M. D'Ancona. *The Quest for the True Cross*. London: Orion Books, 2000.

Unterman, Alan. *Dictionary of Jewish Lore and Legend*. London: Thames and Hudson, 1997.

Van Dam, Cornelius. *The Urim and Thummim: A Means of Revelation in Ancient Israel*. Winona Lake, Ind.: Eisenbrauns, 1997.

Vaux, Roland de. *Ancient Israel: Its Life and Institutions*. New York, 1961.

Vilnay, Z. *Legends of Jerusalem: The Sacred Land*. Philadelphia: Jewish Publication Society of America, 1973.

Waite, Arthur Edward. *The Hermetic Museum*. Red Wheel/Weiser, 1991.

———. *The Holy Kabbalah*. Oracle, 1996.

Walzer, R. *Galen on Jews and Christians*. Oxford, 1949.

Ward, Rev. William. *Prophetic History*. 5 vols. London, 1819–20.

Weil, Simone. *Intimations of Christianity among the Ancient Greeks*. Ark Pub., 1987.

Werblowsky, R., J. Zwi, and Geoffrey Wigoder, et al. *The Oxford Dictionary of the Jewish Religion*. New York: Oxford University Press, 1997.

Whitehead, Kenneth D. *One, Holy, Catholic, and Apostolic: The Early Church Was the Catholic Church*. San Francisco: Ignatius Press, 2000.

Wigoder, Geoffrey, gen. ed. *Illustrated Dictionary and Concordance of the Bible*. Jerusalem: Jerusalem Publishing House, 1986.

Wilken, Robert L. *The Christians as the Romans Saw Them*. New Haven, Conn.: Yale University Press, 1984.

Williams, Charles. *War in Heaven*. London: Eerdmans, 1978.

Wilson, Marvin R. *Our Father Abraham: Jewish Roots of the Christian Faith*. Grand Rapids, Mich.: Eerdmans, 1989.

Wolfson, Harry Austryn. *Philo: Foundations of Religious Philosophy in Judaism, Christianity, and Islam*. 2 vols. Cambridge: Harvard University Press, 1948.

*Wuest, Kenneth S. *The New Testament: An Expanded Translation*. Grand Rapids, Mich.: Eerdmans, 1961.

Wylie, Rev. J. A. *Seventh Vial*. London, 1868.

Yadin, Yigael. *The Scroll of the War of the Sons of Light Against the Sons of Darkness*. London, 1962.

*———. *The Temple Scroll*. Jerusalem and London: Weidenfeld and Nicolson, 1985.

Zeitlin, Solomon. *The Jewish Quarterly Review* 45 (1955): 107.

Zuckerman, Arthur J. *A Jewish Princedom in Feudal France*. New York: Columbia University Press, 1972.

GENERAL

Adams, H. *Mont Saint Michel and Chartres*. Boston: Houghton Mifflin, 1913.

Ammianus Marcellinus. Translated by W. Hamilton. *The Later Roman Empire*. Harmondsworth: Penguin Classics, 1986.

*Appleby, Nigel. *Hall of the Gods: The Quest to Discover the Knowledge of the Ancients*. London: William Heinemann, 1998.

Armstrong, Zella. *The Amazing Story of Madoc*. Chattanooga, Tenn.: Lookout Publishers, 1950.

Augustine. Letter to Pope Gregory. *Epistolae ad Gregorium Papa*. Ancient text.

Bachrach, B. S. *A History of the Alans in the West*. Minneapolis: University of Minnesota Press, 1973.

*Baigent, Michael, and Richard Leigh, Richard *The Elixir and the Stone*. Viking, 1997.

Barker, M. *The Lost Prophet*. London: SPCK, 1989.

———. *The Gate of Heaven: The History and Symbolism of the Temple in Jerusalem*. London: SPCK, 1991.

Ben-Dov, M. *In the Shadow of the Temple*. Translated by Ina Friedman. Jerusalem: Keter Publishing House, 1985.

Bernard de Clairvaux. *Treatise in Praise of the New Order of Knighthood*. New Jersey: Cistercian Publishing, 1976.

———. *On the Song of Songs*. Translated by K. Walsh. Michigan: Cistercian Publishers, 1976.

Bourke, C., ed. *Studies in the Cult of St. Columba*. Four Courts Press, 1999.

Bousset, W. *The AntiChrist Legend*. London: Hutchinson and Co., 1896.

Brunés, Tons. *The Secrets of Ancient Geometry—and Its Use*. Translated by Charles M. Napier, Copenhagen: Rhodos, 1967.

Burckhardt, T. *Chartres and the Birth of the Cathedral*. Ipswich: Golgonooza Press, 1995.

*Campbell, Joseph. *The Masks of God: Occidental Mythology*. Baltimore: Penguin Books, 1976.

Campos, Jose Guerra, and Jesus Precedo Lafuente. *Guide to the Cathedral of Santiago of Compostela*. Spain: Aldeasa, 1996.

*Carpenter, Frederic. *Ralph Waldo Emerson*. American Book, 1934.

Carroll, James. *The Sword of Constantine*. New York: Houghton-Mifflin, 2001.

Catholic Encyclopedia, The. CD-Rom from the 1914 edition.

Chamberlain, Houston Stewart. *Die Grundlagen des neunzehnten Jahrhunderts* [*The Foundations of the Nineteenth Century*]. 1910. Influenced Hitler.

*Charpentier, Louis. *The Mysteries of Chartres Cathedral*. 1966. Reprint, London: RILKO, 1993.

Collins, John. "Essenes," *Anchor Bible Dictionary*. 6 vols., Freedman.

Cornford, F. M. *Origin of Attic Comedy*. London, 1914.

*Critchlow, Keith. *Time Stands Still*. London: Gordon Fraser, 1979.

Daftary, Farhad. *The Assassins Legends: Mythos of the Ismai'ilis*. London, 1994.

Daniel, Glyn Edmund. *Myth or Legend?* London: BBC, 1955.

*Davidovits, Dr. Joseph, and Margie Morris. *The Pyramids: An Enigma Solved*. New York: Dorset Press, 1988.

Deacon, Richard. *Modoc and the Discovery of America*. New York: George Baziller, 1966.

De Vogel, C. J. *Pythagoras and Early Pythagoreans*. Royal VanCorcum, Netherlands, 1966.

*Dix, G. H. "The Messiah Ben Joseph." *Journal of Theological Studies* 27 (1926): 130–43.

Dobson, Rev. C. C. *The Mystery of the Fate of the Ark of the Covenant*. New York and London: Century, 1928.

Dunlop, John C. *History of Prose Fiction*. 1896. Revised ed. G. Bell & Sons, 1970.

Duncan, David Ewing. *Calendar: Humanity's Epic Struggle to Determine a True and Accurate Year*. Avon Books, 1998.

Durrant, Will, and Ariel Durrant. *The Age of Faith*.

Eisenman, Robert. *Maccabees, Zadokites, Christians and Qumran*. Leiden, Netherlands, 1983.

*Eliade, M. *The Myth of the Eternal Return*. London: Arkana, 1954.

Ellis, R. *Thoth: Architect of the Universe*. Dorset, England: Edfu Books, 1997.

Enslin, Morton Scott. *The Encyclopedia of Religion*. 1945.

Evangelium ii. *The Gospel of Us: A Late Middle English Version*. Translated by B. Lindstrom. 1974.

*Fanthorpe, Lionel, and Patricia Fanthorpe. *The World's Greatest Unsolved Mysteries*. Toronto: Hounslow Press, 1997.

Fasken, W. H. *Israel's Racial Origin and Migrations*. London: Covenant Publishing, 1934.

Ferm, Vergilius, ed. *The Encyclopedia of Religion*. Secaucus, N.J.: Popular Books, 1945.

Foster, John. *They Converted Our Ancestors*. London: SCM Press, 1965

Fulcanelli. *The Mystery of the Cathedrals*. Paris: Pauvert, 1925. Reprint, Aims International Books, 1982.

Gawler, J. C. *Our Sycthian Ancestors*. 1875. Reprint, Utah: Commonwealth Publishing, 1994.

Geyser, A. S. "The Twelve Tribes in Revelation."

International Journal of Studiorum Novi Testamenti Societas 28 (July 1982).

Gibbon, Edward. *Decline and Fall of the Roman Empire.* Everyman's Library, 1993.

Gibran, Kahlil. *Thoughts and Meditations.* N.Y.: Citadel Press, 1960.

Ginzberg, Louis. *Legends of the Jews.* 7 vols. Philadelphia: Jewish Publication Society of America, 1911, 1937.

Goodman, Martin, with Jane Sherwood. *The Roman World 44 B.C.–A.D. 180.* London and New York: Routledge, 1997.

Graves, Robert. *The Greek Myths.* 2 vols., Penguin, 1993.

Greene, Liz. *The Dreamer of the Vine.* Bodley Head, 1980.

Greer, John Michael. *The New Encyclopedia of the Occult.* St. Paul, Minn.: Llewellyn Publications, 2003.

Gregory of Tours. *Glory of the Martyrs* and *De Miraculis.* Trans. Raymond Van Dam. Liverpool University Press, 1988.

*Hancock, Graham. *The Sign and the Seal: The Quest for the Lost Ark of the Covenant.* New York: Simon and Schuster, Touchstone, 1992.

*———. *Fingerprints of the Gods: A Quest for the Beginning and the End.* New York: Crown Publishers, 1995.

Hannay, Herbert Bruce. *European and Other Race Origins.* London: Sampson Low, 1987.

Hanson, R. P. C. *Saint Patrick: His Origins and Career.* Oxford: Oxford University Press, 1968.

Hodder, Edwin. *On Holy Ground.* William P. Nimmo, 1878.

Hoffmann, J., *Celsus on the True Doctrine.* Oxford: Oxford University Press, 1987.

Hone, William. *Ancient Mysteries Described, Especially the English Miracle Plays, Founded on Apocryphal New Testament Story, Etc.* London, 1823.

James, John. *Chartres: The Masons Who Built a Legend.* London: Routledge and Kegan Paul, 1982.

Jobes, Gertrude. *Dictionary of Mythology, Folklore and Symbols.* 3 vols. New York: Scarecrow Press, 1961–62.

Jones, Robert. "Jewish Religious Parties at the Time of Christ, Part One: Pharisees and Sadducees."

robertcjones@mindspring.com (2000).

Jones, Steve. *In the Blood—God, Genes and Destiny.* London: HarperCollins, 1996.

*Josephus, Flavius. *Works.* Includes *Antiquities of the Jews, Jewish War, and Against Apion.* Edited by H. St. J. Thackeray, et al. London: Heinemann, 1926.

Kay, Gary. *The New World Religion.* Noblesville, Ind.: Hope International Publishing, 1998.

*Kenyon, K. M. *Digging Up Jerusalem.* London: Ernest Benn Limited, 1974.

King, Edward G. *The Yalkut of Zechariah.* Cambridge: Deighton Bell and Co., 1882.

Lawlor, Robert. *Sacred Geometry: Philosophy and Practice.* London: Thames and Hudson, 1982.

Lines, M. *Sacred Stones, Sacred Places.* Edinburgh: St. Andrew Press, 1992.

Locke, John. *The works of John Locke.* 9 vols. London: Rivington, 1824.

Lowell, James Russell. *The Vision of Sir Launfal.* 1848.

*Michell, John, and Christine Rhone. *Twelve Tribe Nations and the Science of Enchanting the Landscape.* Grand Rapids, Mich.: Phanes Press, 1991.

Morris, John, gen. ed. *Domesday Book: 8, Somerset.* Chichester: Phillimoe, 1980.

Newton, J. F. *The Builders.* London: Unwin Brothers, 1934.

Ohff, Heinz. *Artus: Biographie einer Legende.* München/Zürich: R. Piper Gmbh and Co., 1993.

Patmore, Coventry. "Delicate Sapientine de A'More." Religious 19th-Century Love Poem.

Penhallurick, R. D. *Tin in Antiquity.* London: Institute of Metals, 1986.

Pennick, Nigel. *The Ancient Science of Geomancy: Living in Harmony with the Earth.* London: Thomas and Hudson Ltd., 1979.

———. *Sacred Geometry: Symbolism and Purpose in Religious Structures.* Wellingborough: Turnstone, 1980.

Philip, J. A. *Pythagoras and Early Pythagoreanism.* University of Toronto Press, 1966.

Pitsaeus. *Relationes Historicae de rebus Anglicis. 1619.* MS.

Plinval, G. de, *Pêlage, ses écrits, sa vie et sa réforme.* Lausanne, 1943. On the monk Pelagius.

Rhys, John. *Lectures on the Origin and Growth of Religion.* London, 1892.

Sallustius. *Concerning the Gods and the Universe.* Cambridge University Press, 1926.

Schonfield, H. *The Passover Plot.* Rockport, Mass.: Element, 1985.

———. *The Pentecost Revolution.* Rockport, Mass.: Element, 1985.

———. *The Essene Odyssey.* Rockport, Mass.: Element, 1993.

Schwaller de Lubicz, Rene. *The Temple of Man: Sacred Architecture and the Perfect Man.* Translated by Robert Lawlor and Deborah Lawlor. Rochester, Vt.: Inner Traditions International, 1998.

Silberman, N. A. *Digging for God and Country: Archaeology and the Secret Struggle for the Holy Land, 1799–1917.* New York: Knopf, 1982.

Sulimirski, T. *The Sarmatians.* New York: McGraw-Hill, 1970.

Swire, Otta. *Skye: The Island and Its Legends.* London: Berlin Publishers, 2006.

Thompson, David. *The End of Time.* Sinclair-Stevenson, 1996.

Torrey, Charles C. "The Messiah Son of Ephraim." *Journal of Biblical Literature* 66 (1947): 253–77.

Vanderhorst, K. *Utrecht Psalter in Medieval Art.* Graz, 1984; Utrech, 1996.

Watkins, Alfred. *The Old Straight Track: Its Mounds, Beacons, Moats, Sites and Mark Stones.* Great Britain: Methuen and Co., Ltd., 1925. Reprint, London: Abacus, 1974.

Wilson, Ian. *Holy Faces, Secret Places.* London: Victor Gollancz, 1990.

Subject Index

Yadin, Yigael, on Jesus as an anti-Essene, 96 n.151

Young, Brigham, as common ancestor to many in the bloodline, 366; on endowments, 287 n.36; on freemasonry, 264; on Grail Inheritance, 345; on Joseph's work of the last days, 399; on marriage relations, 81, 82; on Saviors upon Mount Zion, 404; on the birthright status of Joseph, 350; on the bloodline of Joseph, 342; on the burden of the Twelve Apostles, 374; on the Seed of Abraham, 3; on the succession of Joseph Smith III, 370; on the Virgin Mary and Mary Magdalene, 29, 32 n.37; on the wedding of Jesus at Cana, 83; on true Christianity through Joseph, 363; on Zerah and the royal lineage, 21–22

Zadokites (see Sadducees)

Zerhites (Scarlet Thread), 26

Zion, as the Lost Grail Kingdom, 155

Scripture Index